HISTORY

OF

NEW NETHERLAND;

OR,

NEW YORK UNDER THE DUTCH.

BY E. B. O'CALLAGHAN, M. D.,

CORRESPONDING MEMBER OF THE NEW YORK HISTORICAL SOCIETY, AND HONORARY MEMBER OF THE HISTORICAL SOCIETY OF CONNECTICUT.

VOL. I.

SECOND EDITION.

"PLERAQUE EARUM QUÆ REFERAM PARVA FORSITAN ET LEVIA MEMORATU VIDERI, NON NESCIUS SUM. NON TAMEN SINE USU FUERIT INTROSPICERE ILLA, PRIMO ADS ECTU LEVIA, EX QUIS MAGNARUM SÆPE RERUM MOTUS ORIUNTUR." TACITUS.

NEW-YORK:
D. APPLETON & COMPANY,
346 AND 348 BROADWAY.
M DCCC LV.

TO

THEODRIC ROMEYN BECK, ESQ., M. D.,

This Tribute of the Author's Regard,

IS,

IN RETURN FOR MANY KINDNESSES,

Respectfully Inscribed.

PREFACE.

Circumstances of a public nature induced the writer of the following pages to enter, several years ago, into a somewhat extensive course of reading, with a view to determine, for his own satisfaction, the nature, as well as the extent of the constitutional rights enjoyed by the American Colonies, previous to the Revolution of 1776. Such an inquiry necessarily led to the investigation, not only of the amount of civil liberty which the colonists possessed at that time, but to the examination of the grounds on which that liberty rested, so as to distinguish between what had been guarantied by charter and the common law, and that which the colonists won for themselves in the course of their struggles against the prerogatives claimed by the Crown, and the usurpations sanctioned by Parliament. To master this subject, the histories of the several Colonies, beginning with Virginia, and terminating with Georgia, were examined, in connection with the Colonial Charters, the Journals of the Colonial Assemblies, and the laws of the several Provinces, so far as these were accessible.

The history of the Province of New York happened, not from any design, but by accident, to have been one of the last taken up, and then the author discovered that he could not go farther back than the year 1664. Smith and others alluded to the existence of a regular government previous to that date, and CHALMERS admitted that the English, after the surrender, "prudently copied what had been already established by the Dutch," but what the institutions were which the conquerors, instead of changing, "prudently copied,"—what was the history of the country, or the character of its first settlers, he was unable to ascertain.

Such a termination to his inquiry was calculated to excite, not to satisfy, curiosity. Here was a country possessing all the evidences of having been settled for half a century before its submission to the Duke of York. Well built towns, with a goodly number of inhabitants;[1] richly cultivated farms, and a moral, peaceable, and religious community, whose history was to be gleaned almost entirely from writers, who, by their position, the circumstances in which they were placed, their habits of thought, associations, and sympathies, were calculated rather to prejudice the mind, than to direct the judgment to a correct conclusion.

The determination was at once taken to examine this apparently unexplored region, and though the writer had no pretensions to teach others, yet he was desirous to learn for himself, who those men were, who, leaving the comforts of home, and of civilized society, first plunged into the depths of the forests on these coasts, and battled against the repulsive circumstances by which they were surrounded; what were the steps which they adopted to gain the confidence, or overcome the enmity of the Aborigines; what their sufferings and their social condition; whether they were worthy the land which gave them birth, or whether, as the humor of some has caused many to believe, they merely vegetated this

[1] Chalmers states, in his Political Annals, that the number of houses in the City of New York, at the time of the surrender, was 343, and of inhabitants 3,430.

life through, leaving no impress on the times in which they lived, nor on the country they inhabited.

On the threshold of this inquiry he was met by the assertion, that "the Dutch Colonial Annals are of a tame and pacific character, and generally dry and uninteresting."[1] This assurance did not, however, deter him from proceeding. He patiently analyzed between twenty and thirty volumes of Manuscript Records in the Secretary of State's office at Albany, and became soon convinced, maugre the peculiarity of the translation, that the opinion so confidently enunciated, was hastily formed, and did not accord with the evidence furnished by the papers left us by our Dutch predecessors. Instead of being "tame, pacific, dry, and uninteresting," they were found teeming with every material which could render historical research a work of pleasure and improvement.

When the contents of those volumes had been examined, the propriety of arranging the notes for publication was suggested. The writer, by this time, had become himself interested in the subject, and he therefore willingly set about this task. He was thus employed when Mr. BRODHEAD, whose very valuable labors, as Historical Agent, cannot be too highly appreciated, sent home sixteen volumes of Dutch documents which he had collected in Holland. It became necessary to collate whatever new facts, or connecting links these contained, and to examine various private papers which had been placed in the hands of the author.

To render all these available, and to avoid what the sententious Benson calls "the indiscretion of attempting the history of this country not well versed in the Dutch,"

[1] Chancellor Kent's Anniversary Disc. before N. Y. Hist. Soc., 1828, p. 8.

a knowledge of that language became now indispensable. This difficulty having been surmounted, the present volume was at length completed, bringing the History of New Netherland down to 1647, or the end of Director Kieft's administration.

In the course of composition many temptations offered to enter into lengthy disquisitions on points of minor importance, regarding which some difference of opinion exists; and to clothe the narrative with additional, though not perfectly legitimate, interest, by embodying traditions which might flatter national pride, yet not accord altogether with historical strictness. These were avoided, for the one would only fatigue, and the other was foreign to the author's plan—to admit such facts only as were supported by unexceptionable evidence. The character of that evidence will be seen by the Notes and Appendix, which, though arranged in such a manner as not to interrupt the progress of the general reader, who may not, perhaps, have either leisure or disposition to look for authorities, will, it is hoped, prove useful to those who may follow in the same field of investigation. Like blazed trees, they will, at least, point out to the future traveller the path of those pioneers who have preceded him in the forest, affording the benefit, at one and the same time, of their errors and their experience.[1]

[1] As the titles of some of the authorities are abridged, it may be proper to observe that—

"Alb. Rec." refers to Van der Kemp's Translation of the Dutch Documents in the office of the Secretary of State.

"Hol. Doc.," to the Dutch MSS. brought from Holland by Mr. Brodhead, and deposited in the same department.

"Lond. Doc.," to the MSS. obtained by the same gentleman in England, and deposited also with the Secretary of State.

For translations of Van der Donck's Beschryv. van N. N.; Lambrechten's N. N.; De Vries' Korte Historiael; and Acrelius' History of New Sweden, the author is indebted to the Collections of the New York Historical Society.

In reviewing the difficulties which have been surmounted, it would be wrong to forget those whose courtesy has done much to facilitate the progress of this work. Though it may seem invidious to particularize where all have been equally kind, it is only justice to mention that the Honorable S. Young, and the Honorable N. S. Benton, Secretaries of State, and the several gentlemen connected with that department, have, in the most polite manner, afforded every facility for making extracts from the records in that office. The author is indebted to the Honorable Mr. Corning, one of the Trustees of the State Library, and to the Librarian of the Albany Institute, for the privilege of consulting, at his own residence, many rare historical works which would not have been, otherwise, easy of access. To General Stephen van Rensselaer he is beholden, likewise, in a special degree, for the very handsome and unreserved manner in which that gentleman placed in his hands, his extensive and valuable collection of MSS., from which the chapter on the early settlement of Rensselaerswyck has been almost exclusively compiled, and many interesting papers borrowed, which are now given, for the first time, to the public. From the account books and court records of that " Colonie" have, also, been arranged the prices of imported merchandise, stock, and country produce; the list of the settlers under the first Patroon, and other tables which will be found in the Appendix.

The Map of New Netherland, which accompanies this volume, is in every particular an exact fac-simile of one of a very ancient date, discovered at the Hague, by Mr. Brodhead, in 1841, and is now published for the first time. That of Rensselaerswyck is a copy, on a reduced scale, of one drawn in 1630, by Gillis van Schen-

2

del. The author is indebted for the draft of it to A. Douw Lansing, Esq.

Whether, with all these valuable accessories, the work be worthy of the subject, it is now for others to say. Should its reception be such as to warrant the continuance of the author's labors, the remainder of the History of New Netherland, comprising the administration of Director Stuyvesant, will follow, as soon as the materials which have accumulated can be arranged and prepared for the press. In the mean time, as truth and historical justice are his main objects, the author hopes that those families, who possess ancient papers, however insignificant, will assist so far as to place them, for a limited season, at his disposal, receiving his assurance, that they shall be safely returned whenever required.

CONTENTS.

BOOK I.

FROM THE DISCOVERY OF AMERICA TO THE INCORPORATION OF THE DUTCH WEST INDIA COMPANY.

1492—1621.

CHAPTER I.

Discovery of America by Columbus—Jean and Sebastian Cabot visit the coast and claim the country for the King of England—Verrazzano enters the Bay of New York—Revolt of the Seven United Provinces from Spain—Interruption of Dutch commerce in consequence—The Dutch determine to compete with the Spaniards in the trade with India—Successive attempts to carry out that project—Willem Barentszoon and Jacob Heemskirk try to find a northern passage to India and fail—Repeat the attempt, and are again unsuccessful—A third effort made—Heemskirk winters in Nova Zembla—Returns to Holland—Project of finding a passage to India by the North abandoned—Several Dutch merchants send expeditions to the West Indies—Vessels in the employ of the Greenland Company said to have visited New Netherland, and to have built forts on the North and South rivers there, for the purpose of shelter for the crew in winter—The Company of Foreign Countries formed in Holland—Send four ships to India by way of the Cape—Expedition successful—Other expeditions follow—Dutch East India Company incorporated—A Dutch West India Company proposed—Plan therefor drawn up and published—Favorably received—Project interrupted by the truce with Spain—Dutch visit the River of Canada in search of furs—A private association in London resolve to look for a north passage to India—Dispatch a ship under command of Henry Hudson; who makes two voyages to the north, but is unsuccessful—Hudson proceeds to Holland—Is patronised by the Dutch East India Company—Sails from Amsterdam, in the Half Moon, on a voyage in search of a northwest passage to China and India . . . . Page 25

CHAPTER II.

Hudson sails from the Texel—Arrives off Newfoundland—Reaches the coast of America in the lat. of 41°—Proceeds thence south to Cape Cod, which he calls New Holland—Arrives at the Chesapeake—Returns north and discovers a great bay in latitude 39°—Continues his northward course—Descries the Highlands of Navesinck—Rounds Sandy Hook, and enters the Great North River of New Netherland—Has communication with the Indians on the west side of the bay—Appearance of the country—Continues his course upward towards a narrow river—Sends his mate to sound the channel, who comes into collision with the natives and is killed—Hudson retains two Indians as hostages—Explores the river—Goes ashore in the neighborhood of Castleton on a visit to an Indian chief, by whom he is hospitably entertained—Concludes his exploration of the river, and turns back—Tries an experiment on some of the natives—Is the first European who introduces intoxicating liquors among the Indians—Continues his downward course—Gets again into collision with the savages, several of whom are killed—Leaves the mouth of the Great River, and arrives in England—Sends an account of his discovery to Holland—Proposes to undertake a new voyage—Is ordered to Holland, where he arrives in the following year—The Dutch decline his proposition, and he re-enters the service of the London Company . . . . . Page 33

CHAPTER III.

Boundaries of the Dutch discoveries—Rivers therein—Appearance and condition of the country—The trees—Fruits—Plants—Wild Animals—Birds—Aquatic fowls—Fish—Reptiles—Natives of the country—Enumeration of the various tribes—Their physical appearance—Mode of hunting—Agriculture—Food—Clothing—Ornaments—Dwellings—Furniture—Villages—Canoes—Indian Women—Marriage—Polygamy—Travail—Political arrangements among the Indians—Wars—Weapons—Treatment of prisoners—Treaties of peace—Circulating Medium—Burial of the dead—Religious opinions—Manittous—Immortality of the soul—Superstitions—Opinions of the creation—Medicine men—Method of treating disease—Amusements—Gambling—Feeble means of resistance against the superior powers of the white men 43

CHAPTER IV.

Truce between the Dutch and Spaniards—Crisis favorable for Hudson's discovery—Private adventurers resolve to send a ship to the Great River—Erect forts thereupon—Establishment on the island of Manhattan under Hendrick Corstiaensen—Visited by Captain Argal, and obliged to acknowledge its dependence on the crown of England—States General grant exclusive rights to all who discover new countries—Edict of 27th March, 1614—Dutch send Adriaen Block, Hendrick Corstiaensen, and Cornelis Jacobsen Mey, with five ships, in search of new lands—They proceed to the mouth of the Great River of the Manhattans—Block's vessel burnt—Builds the Restless—Explores the East River—Discovers the Freshwater River,

&c.—Passes through the Sound and meets Corstiaensen—Returns home—Progress of Mey—His discoveries—Captain Hendricksen continues to explore the country in the Restless—Reports of discoveries laid before the States General—The country acquires, for the first time, the name of New Netherland—Charter or grant of October, 1614, to United New Netherland Company—Rivier van den Vorst Mauritius —Forts erected at each extremity thereof—Dutch drive an active trade among the Indians—Captain Hendricksen returns to Holland—His report—Expiration of the charter of Oct., 1614—Fort removed from Castle Island to the Noordtman's Kill—Treaty of the Dutch with the Five Nations—Causes leading thereto, and importance thereof . . . . Page 67

CHAPTER V.

The New Netherland Company petition for renewal of their charter—The ship Scheld sent to Manhattes—That country becomes more generally known—Attention of the Puritans directed thither—Review of the causes which drove these people to Holland—Desire to remove to America—The Rev. Mr. Robinson, their minister, intimates their wish to emigrate to New Netherland—The managers of the Dutch Trading Company lay this application before the States General and the Prince of Orange—Memorial to his Royal Highness on this occasion—Termination of the twelve years' truce—Request of the New Netherland Company on behalf of the Puritans decidedly refused—Captain Mey returns to Holland—Petitions for exclusive right to new countries he had discovered—Opposed—Incorporation of the Dutch West India Company 81

BOOK II.

FROM THE INCORPORATION OF THE DUTCH WEST INDIA COMPANY, TO THE OPENING OF THE FUR, OR INDIAN, TRADE TO THE INHABITANTS OF NEW NETHERLAND.

1621—1638.

CHAPTER I.

Charter of West India Company—Its various provisions—Comparison between it and those granted to other Companies for making settlements in America—Company do not commence operations immediately—Various vessels licensed to proceed, meanwhile, to New Netherland—Excite considerable jealousy among the English interested in planting Virginia and New England, who remonstrate to King James against the Dutch—English Ambassador at the Hague urges the States General to stay the departure of the Dutch ships—Their High Mightinesses disclaim all knowledge of the enterprise—English Ambassador's explanation thereupon to the

King—Dutch vessels proceed, notwithstanding, on their voyage—Several families desire to move to New Netherland—States General refer the matter to the West India Company—They approve of the design, but suggest that its execution be postponed until a Director General be appointed . . . . Page 89

CHAPTER II.

The West India Company takes possession of New Netherland—Several settlers and servants sent out—Fort Nassau built on South River—Fort Orange on the river Mauritius—Peter Minuit, of Wesel, arrives in the country as Director-general, accompanied by a colony of Walloons—First settlement on Long Island—First white child born—Members of Minuit's council—Duties of schout-fiscaal—First schout-fiscaal—Colonial secretary—Imports and exports—Dutch purchase island of Manhattans and adjoining islands from the Indians—A blockhouse erected on Manhattan Island, and called Fort Amsterdam—Murder of an Indian by some of Minuit's servants—Trade opened with the English settlement at New Plymouth—Correspondence and intercourse with that colony—Dutch alarmed at threats thrown out by their English neighbors—Apply to directors in Holland for a military force—Charles I. extends to the ships of the West India Company the privileges conferred by the treaty of Southampton on the vessels of the States General—Progress of trade—Renewed efforts in Holland to promote the settlement of New Netherland—The Assembly of the XIX. determine to establish lordships or "colonies" there—Heyn's victory over the Spanish silver fleet—Charter to Patroons in New Netherland 99

CHAPTER III.

Several directors of the West India Company acquire patroonships, or "colonies," in New Netherland—Associations formed to settle Zwanendal and Rensselaerswyck—Patroons' colonies confirmed and "sealed with the seal of New Netherland"—Quarrels between Directors of the Company and Patroons—Privileges granted to Patroons called into doubt—Director Minuit recalled—English Companies grant patents for Massachusetts and Connecticut—Evince considerable jealousy of the Dutch—The vessel in which Minuit and other servants of the Company are returning to Holland, is seized at Plymouth by order of the British government, for having traded to, and obtained her cargo in, countries subject to the king of England—Audience of the Dutch ambassadors with Charles I. in consequence—They demand the release of the Company's ship—The king declines—The West India Company call the attention of the States General to the matter—Lay before their High Mightinesses a deduction of their title to New Netherland—The States General resolve to maintain the Company's right to that country—Lengthy reply of Charles I. and the Lords Commissioners of England to the Dutch remonstrance—Refuse to permit the Dutch to encroach on and usurp one of his Majesty's colonies unless they consent to submit to his Majesty's government—The Company's ship released, "saving his Majesty's rights"—Continued misunderstanding between the Directors of the West India Company and the Patroons—Commissaries sent to the several "colonies" belonging to Patroons, to prevent the latter interfering in the fur-trade—Colonie of Zwanendal destroyed by the savages—De Vries visits South River and makes peace with the Indians—Profitable state of trade with New Netherland 121

CHAPTER IV.

WOUTER VAN TWILLER appointed Director-general—Arrives in New Netherland—His council—Other officers of the company in that country—First clergyman and first schoolmaster in New Amsterdam—An English vessel visits the Manhattans for the purpose of trading with the Indians on the Hudson's River—Director and council refuse her permission to ascend the river—Sails to Fort Orange, notwithstanding—Opens a trade with the natives thereabout—Is opposed by the commissary at that post—Indians prefer trading with the English factor, who had been in the Dutch service, several years before, in that quarter—Three vessels arrive with troops from Fort Amsterdam, to prevent the English trading with the Indians—Pull down the English tent—Force their people and goods on board their ship, which they convoy out of the river—Damages inflicted on the English—Quarrel between two English skippers at the Manhattans—Van Twiller opposes De Vries, who wishes to visit the Sound—Contentions in consequence—De Vries's opinions of the functionaries at Fort Amsterdam—Notelman, schout-fiscaal, superseded—Is succeeded by Van Dinclage—Van Twiller determines to build a fort on the Fresh River—Sketch of the quarrels between the Indians there—Tract of country called Conneticock purchased—Deed of sale—Fort Good Hope built—New Plymouth people determine to build a trading-house on the Fresh River—Proceedings in consequence—Van Twiller protests—This protest disregarded—Writes to the XIX.—Attempts to dislodge the English by force; without success—Improvements in New Amsterdam—New fort—Church and other houses erected—Improvements at Fort Orange and Fort Nassau—Schuylkill purchased—Resources of the West India Company—Trade of New Netherland . . . . Page 141

CHAPTER V.

Continued misunderstanding between the Directors and the Patroons—Pretensions of the respective parties—Referred to the States General—Committee appointed to investigate the same—Articles submitted by the Patroons containing their demands—Replications of the Company—Rejoinder on the part of Patroons—Owners of the William apply to Dutch ambassadors at London for damages—Threaten to apply to the king in council—Application communicated to States General—Referred to the Assembly of the XIX.—Memorial of the latter in reply—Request that the matter be referred to the Dutch and English ambassadors—States General decline to interfere—Quarrel between Van Twiller and Minister Bogardus—Peace made with the Raritans—Imports and Exports—Superintendent over Pavonia arrives in New Netherland 158

CHAPTER VI.

Encroachments of the New England people on New Netherland—Tear down the arms of the States General at Kievitts Hoeck—Van Twiller protests against the intruders, and makes representations to the directors—The English send Governor Winslow to London to complain against the Dutch—He is imprisoned there—English attempt a settlement on the South River—Are taken prisoners and sent to the Manhattans—First English settlers in New Amsterdam—Fort Amsterdam finished—Irregularities there—Director-general and several members of his council appropriate to themselves large quantities of the public domain—Settlement of Flatlands, or New Amersfoort commenced—Van Dinclage, schout-fiscaal, opposes Van Twiller—Is dismissed from office—Returns to Holland—Ulrich Lupold appointed in his place—Van Dinclage brings the affairs of New Netherland before the States General—Assembly of the XIX. remove Van Twiller—Willem Kieft appointed director-general of New Netherland—Prices at New Amsterdam and on the Connecticut—Van Twiller adds a number of islands to his estates—States General call the attention of the company to the retrograding condition of New Netherland—Require report thereupon—Queries submitted to the directors—Their answers—Propose surrendering the Indian trade—Unfavorable state of the colony—Causes thereof—States General insist on the adoption of some plan to encourage emigration to and the settlement of the country, so that New Netherland may not be lost or given away . . . . Page 168

CHAPTER VII.

Arrival of Willem Kieft, third Director-general—His council—Colonial Secretary, and schout-fiscaal—Other public officers—Their salaries—Condition of New Amsterdam—Irregularities there—Proclamations of director and council—Organization of court of justice—Proclamation against drunkenness—Arrival of immigrants—Purchase of land on Long Island—State of public morals—Regulations for the inspection of New Netherland tobacco—Rights of the Dutch threatened in the south—Swedish West India Company formed—Pieter Minuit, former director of New Netherland, appointed director of New Sweden—Arrives at the Delaware with some Swedes—Is boarded by the Dutch Commissary—Opens a trade with the natives—Purchases land and erects Fort Christina—Kieft protests against him several times, but in vain—Minuit returns to Sweden, leaving a colony of twenty men behind—Swedish ship seized in Holland on her return from "the West Indies"—Is released—States General urge the permanent settlement of New Netherland—New articles and conditions proposed by the Amsterdam chamber—a "new project" also submitted by parties friendly to the Patroons—Patroons seek to enlarge their privileges, and to reserve the country for manors and lordships—States General disapprove of both these plans—Proclamation opening the trade in New Netherland, and abolishing the monopoly hitherto enjoyed by the West India Company 180

BOOK III.

FROM THE OPENING OF THE INDIAN TRADE TO THE END OF DIRECTOR KIEFT'S ADMINISTRATION.

1639—1647.

CHAPTER I.

Consequences of the opening of the trade—Encouragement to emigration—English settlers in New Netherland obliged to take an oath of allegiance—Further encroachments of the English—Settle New Haven—Hartford people oppose the Dutch at Fort Good Hope—Controversy between the parties—Grant of Long Island to the Earl of Stirling—An agent appointed by that nobleman to settle that island—Further purchases by the Dutch thereupon—English cross over and commence settlements on the east end of Long Island—Additional grants by the Dutch on the western extremity—Lupold removed from office—Cornelis van der Huygens appointed schout-fiscaal—Other appointments—Renewal of the differences between the English and the Dutch on the Connecticut—Change of commissary at Fort Hope—The Norwalk Islands purchased by the Dutch—Additional purchases on Long Island—Earl Stirling's agent arrives at New Amsterdam—His pretensions disregarded—A party of English attempt a settlement west of Oyster Bay—Dutch expedition sent to prevent them—Prisoners taken and dismissed—Southampton and Southold commenced—English commence a settlement at Greenwich—Protested against—Proceedings in Holland regarding New Netherland—A new charter agreed upon by Assembly of the XIX.—Provisions thereof—Laid before the States General—Effects of opening the fur-trade on the Indians—Director Kieft determines to impose a tribute on them—Indians discontented—Occurrences at Staten Island—Property belonging to the company stolen—Kieft enraged against the Raritans—Sends an expedition against them—Attack—Result—Prices of sundry commodities at New Amsterdam—Still erected on Staten Island—Brandy and other liquors manufactured . . . . Page 205

CHAPTER II.

Murder of one of the company's slaves by six other negroes—Lots drawn to determine which should be executed—Scene at the place of execution—Proclamations against Drunkenness, and regulating the currency—New Haven people intrude on the South River—Protested against—Renewal of the difficulties on the Connecticut—Collision between the Dutch and English there—Rev. Hugh Peters sent by Massachusetts to England; commissioned to proceed to Holland to settle the difficulties between Connecticut and New Netherland—Propositions submitted to the

West India Company by Governors Winthrop and Haynes—Several English families propose removing from Massachusetts to Long Island—Privileges granted to them—A new colonie planted behind Newark Bay—Staten Island granted to Melyn—Other settlements at Hoboken—Increased misunderstanding between the Indians and the Dutch—The latter set a price on the heads of the Raritans—Peace concluded between both parties—A Weckquaesqueeck Indian assassinates a Dutch settler to avenge the murder of his uncle, committed twenty years previously—Kieft demands the murderer—His surrender refused—The murder justified—Meeting of the commonalty in consequence—Election of "the Twelve Men"—Their proceedings—Kieft displeased—Sends expeditions against the offending tribe, but effects nothing—The Twelve Men seek reforms in the government—Absolute power of the Director-general—Exercises legislative and judicial functions—Demands of the Twelve Men—Answers of the Director-general thereupon—Meeting of the Twelve Men forbidden on pain of corporal punishment—Expedition against the Weckquaesqueecks—Fails in discovering the enemy—Peace with these Indians . . . . Page 229

CHAPTER III.

Continued disagreements between the people of Hartford and the Dutch at Fort Good Hope—Kieft forbids all intercourse with the former—Greenwich comes under the jurisdiction of the Dutch—Progress of the English at the South River—Kieft determines to break up their settlements—Measures adopted with that view—Excitement at New Haven in consequence—Delegates from Hartford arrive at Fort Amsterdam to negotiate for the purchase of Fort Hope—Terms proposed by the Dutch—Movement in England against New Netherland—Lord Say's representations to the Dutch ambassador at London—Several English families remove from Massachusetts to New Netherland—Westchester, or Vredeland, settled—Surveyor appointed—A fine stone tavern built in New Amsterdam—George Baxter appointed English secretary—Ruinous condition of the church at Manhattans—Measures taken for the erection of a new building—First consistory in New Amsterdam—Contract for the proposed building—Inscription in front of the church—Renewal of misunderstanding with the Indians—Miantonimo conspires against the whites—General alarm in consequence—Some Dutch traders rob an Indian, who murders two settlers in revenge—Endeavors of the Indian chiefs to make satisfaction for the murder—Fail—Mohawks make a descent on the River Indians—The latter fly for protection to the Dutch—Are hospitably entertained—Remove to Corlaers Hook and Pavonia—Kieft determines to attack them—Is opposed by the principal men at New Amsterdam—Kieft will not listen to their objections—The attack—Cruelties practised against the Indians—Settlers on Long Island attack the Indians in their neighborhood—Eleven tribes proclaim war against the Dutch—All the Dutch settlements destroyed—Public discontents—Kieft endeavors to propitiate the Long Island Indians—The latter reject his ambassadors—A day of General Fast and Prayer ordered—Proposals to depose the Director-general—An attack made on his life—Disorders consequent thereupon—Arrival of a flag of truce from the Indians on Long Island—Ambassadors sent to invite them to Fort Amsterdam—Speech of the Indian chief—Treaty of peace and cessation of hostilities 251

CHAPTER IV.

Union of the New England colonies—Congratulatory letters sent by Director and council of New Netherland—Reply of the governor of Massachusetts—Proceedings of the Commissioners of the United Colonies regarding the Dutch—Sir Edmund Ployden Earl-palatine of New Albion—Boundaries of the Palatinate—Continued dissatisfaction of the Indians—The Wappingers attack a Dutch boat and commence hostilities—Several other boats attacked and Christians killed—Meeting of the commonalty—Election of the Eight Men—Names of the citizens present on this occasion—Conclusions of the Eight Men—Expel one of the board, and nominate another in his place—Army raised against the Indians—The latter attack some settlers on Staten Island and in the colonie at Achter Cul—Murder several persons, and overrun the country—Mrs. Hutchinson and family killed—Attack on Lady Moody—Further deliberations of the Eight Men—Prices at New Amsterdam—Letters to the Assembly of the XIX. and to the States General—Rules for the soldiers on guard—State of affairs on the Island of Manhattans . Page 279

CHAPTER V.

Offensive measures against the Indians—Expedition to Staten Island—Mayn Mayano slain—His head brought into New Amsterdam—Expedition to Greenwich—Fails in finding the Indians—Returns to Stamford—Collision between a Dutch soldier and Captain Patrick—Latter killed—Attack on an Indian settlement—Detachment return to the Manhattans—Expedition against the Weckquaesqueecks—Arrive at the castles of that tribe, but find them abandoned—Pennawitz, chief of the Canarsee tribe, discovered assisting the enemy—Expedition to Schout's Bay on Long Island—Attacks on the Heemstede and Mespath Indians—Triumph of the Dutch—Consequent outrage on some prisoners—Underhill proceeds to Stamford—Expedition against the Indians of that quarter—Description of the Indian camp—General attack thereupon—Important victory gained by the Dutch—Over five hundred savages slaughtered—Public thanksgiving at New Amsterdam therefor—Savages sue for peace—Treaties concluded between several of the river, and Long Island tribes and the Dutch—Proceedings of the States General on the petitions of the Eight Men—The West India Company unable to render any assistance—Their letter to the States—Two Spanish vessels taken and brought to New Amsterdam—Low state of the colonial treasury—Kieft resolves to have recourse to taxation—Convokes the Eight Men—Submits his plan—The Eight Men object—Kieft becomes irritated—Claims unlimited power—The Eight Men succumb—Excise duties provisionally imposed—The Eight Men treated with disrespect by Director Kieft—The Dutch expelled from Maranham, a province of Brazil—Fly to Curaçoa—Destitute condition of that island—Are sent to New Netherland—Arrive opportunely at Fort Amsterdam—Council resolve to continue the excise—The burghers oppose this arbitrary taxation—Prosecutions of the brewers—Persist in their refusal to pay the excise—Execution issued against them in consequence—Public discontent becomes very high—Parties formed—Protests against the Director-general—Complaints against him sent to Holland, demanding his recall—Letter of the Eight Men—Sad condition of the country—Strictures on Kieft's maladministration . . . . Page 296

CHAPTER VI.

Colonie of Rensselaerswyck—First settlers sent out by the Patroon—His jurisdiction—System of law in the colonie—Local courts—First magistrates—Population—Tenures—Patroon's privileges—Settlement of the Fuyck commenced—Beverswyck—Arrival of Adriaen van der Donck in the colonie, as Schout-fiscaal—First clergyman sent out—Agreement with him—Arrives with several other respectable settlers—A church erected—Its dimensions—Regulations concerning the Indian trade—Infractions thereof—Further regulations—Intrigues of Van der Donck—Threatened mutiny of the settlers—Return of the Mohawks from Canada—Are visited by Van Curler—Particulars of the interview with these tribes—Efforts to procure the release of a Jesuit and other French prisoners—Continued misunderstanding between Van der Donck and other local authorities—Van der Donck proposes to erect a colonie in Katskill—Orders from the Patroon forbidding this—Directs the dismissal of Van der Donck should he persist—The "Arms of Rensselaerswyck" sent out with a valuable cargo of goods—Arrives at the Manhattans—Difficulties between the supercargo and the authorities at New Amsterdam—Vessel and cargo seized—Protests and replications—Occurrences at Rensselaer-stein—A vessel fired into while passing that place, because she refused to lower her colors and bring to—Excitement in consequence—Prosecutions entered into against the commander of the post—Further protests—Death of the first Patroon—Nicolaus Coorn appointed Schout-Fiscaal—Quarrel between Van der Donck and Van Curler—Departure of the former for the Manhattans—Severity of the winter—Destructive freshet, and visit of whales to Rensselaerswyck 319

CHAPTER VII.

States General order an inquiry into the condition of New Netherland—Proceedings of the XIX.—Kieft recalled—Van Dinclage appointed, provisionally, in his place—Interesting report on the state of New Netherland—Recommendations contained therein—Proposed civil list—Modifications in the government, trade, &c.—Some Indian tribes desire a cessation of hostilities—Several of the Long Island tribes come in—Kieft concludes a peace at Fort Orange with the Mohawks and Mohegans—General peace between the aborigines and the Dutch—Low condition of the colony—Thanksgiving ordered—Additional purchases on Long Island—Orders received to explore the country for minerals—Proceedings in consequence—The ship by which specimens were sent to Holland, founders at sea, and all on board perish—Petrus Stuyvesant, Director at Curaçoa, besieges the island of St. Martin—Is obliged to raise the siege—Receives a severe wound—Returns to Holland—Is appointed Director-general of New Netherland—Submits a plan for the better management of the company's transatlantic possessions—Further changes proposed regarding the colonial trade—Differences of opinion in the Assembly of the XIX.—Departure of Stuyvesant postponed—New Netherland continues under the mismanagement of Kieft 347

CHAPTER VIII.

Fruits of faction—Quarrel between the Rev. Mr. Bogardus and Director Kieft—Progress of affairs at the South River—Sufferings of the first Swedish colonists—Resolve to abandon the river and to remove to the Manhattans—Are prevented by the opportune arrival of additional supplies and settlers—Boundaries of New Sweden—Royal appropriations for its support—Printz appointed governor—His salary—Strength of the Swedish establishment on the Delaware—Its annual expense—Dutch force at Fort Nassau—Instructions to Printz—Swedish forts on the South River—Swedes seize the Indian trade—Loss accruing to the Dutch in consequence—Seizure of a Swedish vessel in Holland—Proceedings attendant thereupon—Hudde appointed commissary at Fort Nassau—Some Dutch merchants send a venture to the South River—Their vessels ordered off by the Swedes—Several Dutch freemen receive grants of land on the Delaware—Measures taken to extinguish Indian titles—Company's arms erected on the spot—Swedes tear them down, and protest against the Dutch, who reply—High-handed measures of the Swedish governor—The Dutch traders appeal to New Amsterdam—Renewal of the controversy between Kieft and New Haven—Continued misunderstanding on the Connecticut—Correspondence with the commissioners of the United Colonies—The Director-general refers the matters to Holland—Instructions from the West India Company—Patents for new colonies at Katskill and Yonckers—Breukelen obtains manorial rights and municipal privileges . . . . Page 362

CHAPTER IX.

Termination of Kieft's administration—General condition of the country—Slaves—Their lot under the Dutch—Population of New Netherland—Revenue—Causes of the backward state of the province—Advanced condition of New England—Reflections—Settlements enumerated—Their government—Transfer of the municipal institutions of Holland to New Netherland—Errors of contemporary writers—Character of Director Kieft—Denies the right of appeal from his judgments—Harsh and tyrannical proceedings against the Rev. Mr. Doughty and Mr. Van Hardenbergh—General discontent—State of morals, religion, and education—Conclusion 384

APPENDIX 399

CONTENTS

OF

THE APPENDIX.

Page.

A.—Charter to the Dutch West India Company, ... 399

B.—Agreement between the Managers and Principal Adventurers of the West India Company, ... 408

C.—Names of the Directors of the West India Company to the end of the year 1636, ... 411

D.—Capt. Mason's and Sir Ferdinando Gorges' Letters relative to the Dutch in New Netherland, ... 415

E.—Report, &c., on the Condition of New Netherland, anno 1644, . . . 418

F.—Patent of Mespath, or Newtown, L. I., ... 425

Ff.—Some Particulars of the Rev. Mr. Doughty, ... 427

G.—Account of Expenses incurred by Kiliaen van Rensselaer, as Patroon, anno 1630, 1631, ... 429

H.—Names of Settlers in Rensselaerswyck, from 1630 to 1646, . . . 433

I.—Legal Custom, &c., in the Colonie of Rensselaerswyck, . . . 442

J.—Contract between the Rev. Johannes Megapolensis, Jr. and the Patroon of Rensselaerswyck; Dismissal of the Rev. Mr. Megapolensis by the Classis of Amsterdam; Patroon's consent that the Directors of West India Company should approve said dismissal, ... 448

K.—Memorandum for Dominie Megapolensis, &c.; Catalogue of Books for the Colonie of Rensselaerswyck, ... 452

L.—Arendt van Curler's Letter to Patroon of Rensselaerswyck, anno 1643 . 456

M.—Insinuation, Protest, &c. on behalf of Patroon, anno 1643, ... 466

N.—Debit and Credit Account of the Estate belonging to the first Patroon in Holland, at his decease, ... 468

O.—Van Curler's Account of the Quarrel between himself and Van der Donck, and Minute referring the latter's claim to Holland, ... 469

P.—Tenths in Rensselaerswyck for 1642, 1643, 1644, 1645, ... 472

Q.—Two leases in Rensselaerswyck, 1646, 1647, ... 473

R.—Prices in Rensselaerswyck from 1630 to 1646, ... 477

S.—Godyn's Notice of his intention to occupy the Bay of the South River, dated 19th June, 1629; and an Agreement, dated 7th Feb., 1635, between the Directors of the West India Company and Samuel Bloemmaert and others, for the conveyance to the former of the colonie of Zwanendael, ... 479

BOOK I.

FROM THE DISCOVERY OF AMERICA TO THE INCORPORATION OF THE DUTCH WEST INDIA COMPANY.

1492—1621.

CHAPTER I.

Discovery of America by Columbus—Jean and Sebastian Cabot visit the coast and claim the country for the King of England—Verrazzano enters the Bay of New York—Revolt of the Seven United Provinces from Spain—interruption of Dutch commerce in consequence—The Dutch determine to compete with the Spaniards in the trade with India—Successive attempts to carry out that project—Willem Barentszoon and Jacob Heemskirk try to find a northern passage to India and fail—Repeat the attempt, and are again unsuccessful—A third effort made—Heemskirk winters in Nova Zembla—Returns to Holland—Project of finding a passage to India by the North abandoned—Several Dutch merchants send expeditions to the West Indies—Vessels in the employ of the Greenland Company said to have visited New Netherland, and to have built forts on the North and South rivers there, for the purpose of shelter for the crew in winter—The Company of Foreign Countries formed in Holland—Send four ships to India by way of the Cape—Expedition successful—Other expeditions follow—Dutch East India Company incorporated—A Dutch West India Company proposed—Plan therefor drawn up and published—Favorably received—Project interrupted by the truce with Spain—Dutch visit the River of Canada in search of furs—A private association in London resolve to look for a north passage to India—Dispatch a ship under command of Henry Hudson; who makes two voyages to the north, but is unsuccessful—Hudson proceeds to Holland—Is patronised by the Dutch East India Company—Sails from Amsterdam, in the Half Moon, on a voyage in search of a northwest passage to China and India.

THE annals of the century succeeding the discovery of Columbus are filled with accounts of voyages undertaken with a view to explore the New World; some in quest of adventure; some in search of mines of the precious metals; some in search of a northwest passage to India: all in the hope of

BOOK I. securing for the projectors sudden and boundless wealth, or imperishable fame.

1497. Jean and Sebastian Cabot were among the earliest followers of the celebrated Genoese. Under a commission from Henry the VII. of England, they sailed for the western continent,
1498. and sweeping along the extensive coasts of North America, claimed, on this pretence, for their sovereign, the entire territory which they occasionally saw at a distance.

Jean de Verrazzano, a Florentine, in the service of the
1524. French monarch, who succeeded Cabot in these seas, entered, as it is maintained, the bay of New York, in the spring of 1524, and gave, on his return, an account of his voyage to his royal master.[1]

The inhabitants of the Low Countries, whom the physical condition of the territory which they occupied had from the earliest ages designed to be a maritime nation, and whom nature, education, and the circumstances in which they were placed, had directed to commercial pursuits, gave evidence, long before the voyage of Columbus, of a bold spirit of discovery. Sixty-eight years previous to the sailing of that expedition from Palos, Betencour, a native of the French Netherlands, had discovered the Flemish Islands, since called the Azores, and thus pointed the way to the western world.[2]

But when the triumph of Columbus placed it in the power of European monarchs to bestow unlimited territory on such
1510. of their favorites as would take the trouble of seeking it, Charles the Fifth granted, it is said, an island in America to the Sieur Beveren, who dispatched two armed vessels in search of his new estate. His were the first Dutch ships that had ever
1512. ventured on these seas. Two years afterwards Anthony Mo-

[1] An account of Verrazzano's voyage will be found, at length, in N. Y. Hist. Soc. Trans., (new series) i. 37. Stuyvesant alludes to it in his Manifest to the Governor and Council of Maryland (N. Y. Hist. Soc. Trans., iii. 374) in these words: "The French were in the year of our Lord God Almighty, 1524, the second followers of the discovery in these northern parts of this America, by Johan de Verrazzano, a Florentine." See also Beschryv. van America, by Jan Huyghen van Linschotten, Amsterdam, 1635. Bancroft (Hist. United States, i. 17) admits that Verrazzano visited the bay of New York.

[2] Vaderlansche Hist., ix., 151; Thuanus, lib. i., 7.

lock sailed in a Dutch craft to the Cape de Verde islands, and when Charles had succeeded to the rich inheritance of the Spanish Crown, and became sovereign of the Low Countries, the Dutch, it is maintained, had already pushed their way to America, and become familiar with a part of its coasts. Contrary to the general opinion, these voyages had preceded the revolution which took place under Philip the Second, and were only interrupted by that exciting event.[1] CHAP. I.

Seven provinces of the Spanish Netherlands, borne down by the weight of oppression and tyranny to which they had been long subjected, had determined, a few years afterwards, to achieve 1566.
their independence. To accomplish this they had recourse to arms. A long and bloody war ensued against the Spanish king, who, irritated now to the extremest degree against his rebellious subjects, issued an edict prohibiting the inhabitants of Spain and Portugal from holding intercourse with the revolted provinces. The enterprising people of the latter country were, by this royal decree, deprived of the advantages which they had hitherto enjoyed of carrying, from the countries lying around the Baltic, to the different ports in Spain and Portugal, great quantities of corn and naval stores, in return for which they received wine and fruit, the products of the South, the gold and silver of America, and the spices and other luxuries which the Portuguese imported from India.

The energies of the young republic were not, however, to be crushed by such vexations. Having so long acted as carriers for the Portuguese, the Dutch well knew the demand which existed for the rich productions of the East, and that this demand was every year increasing. They forthwith turned their attention to secure, in some other way, the advantages which they had hitherto possessed, and with that view, determined to compete with their oppressors even in the Indian seas.[2]

It was whilst men's minds were thus excited, that one Beets, 1581.
an Englishman, who had already made five voyages to the West Indies, proposed to lead an expedition to that quarter for, and on account of, the States of Holland, provided their High

[1] Recherches sur le Commerce des Hollandais in Voy. en Holland, par Sir John Carr; traduit par Mme. Keralio Robert, t. ii., 233, 234.

[2] Watson's Life of Philip III., ii., 85, 86.

BOOK I. Mightinesses would place four ships-of-war at his disposal. Though this offer was not accepted, the desire for adventure
1584. continued, and several voyages were made, northward to Archangel, and westward to the Cape de Verde Islands.[1]

Stimulated now both by desire of gain, and by hatred of the Spaniards, it was resolved to make an effort to discover a passage to India by the Northern Ocean; and three ships, outfitted
1594. by some Amsterdam and Zealand merchants, sailed with that
June 5. view from the Texel, under command of Willem Barentszoon and Jacob Heemskirk, shaping their course by the Straits of Weygat, and around Nova Zembla.

These enterprising navigators proceeded as far as 77° 45′ north; and having held out hopes on their return of eventual success, the States of Holland, and Maurice, Prince of Or-
1595. ange, equipped several vessels, which they placed under the same commanders, who came home, after an absence of four months, without accomplishing their design. The city of Amsterdam, no way discouraged by these failures, ordered two vessels to be equipped the following year. These sailed
1596. on the 18th May, again under Heemskirk, who was accom-
May 18. panied by Jan Cornelissen Ryp. Having reached the latitude of 80° 11′, they discovered land, along which they coasted for some time, and at length turned back. The ships separated at Beeren Island; Cornelissen returned home, and Heemskirk proceeded to Nova Zembla, where, at the last of August, he became so embayed in ice that he could proceed no farther, and was obliged to pass the winter in those Arctic regions, exposed to all the perils arising from an inclement season, ferocious animals, and scanty provisions. He finally succeeded in
1597. extricating himself and companions in the course of the following summer, and arrived safely at home, where every hope was now abandoned of finding a passage to China by the North.[2]

In the mean time, the project of participating in the West India trade continued to engage the attention of adventurers in the Netherlands; Gerrit Bikker, alderman and councillor of the city of Amsterdam, and Jan Cornelissen

[1] Vaderlandsch. Hist. ix., 152. Wagenaar Beschryving van Amsterdam, i., 407.

[2] Van Meteren Nederlansche Geschiedenis, vi., 410, 411, 412.

Leyen of Enckhuyzen, dispatched, separately, some vessels to that quarter in the course of the last mentioned year, but with what result is not stated.[1] Several vessels were again sent to the West Indies from the city of Amsterdam in 1598,[2] in the course of which year, it is said, some Dutchmen in the employ of a Greenland company, resorted to New Netherland, without any design, however, to make a settlement there, but with a view of having a place of shelter during the winter months; for which purpose, it is added, they built two small forts, one on the North, and one on the South river, to protect them against the attacks of the Indians.[3]

CHAP. I.

1598.

Some Amsterdam merchants who had formed a private trading association, entitled "The Company of Foreign Countries," while occupied in considering the best course to pursue in order to reach India, received an application from one Cornelis Houtman, a native of Flanders, then in prison for debt at Lisbon, who represented that, having made several voyages with the Portuguese to India, he was not only well acquainted with the navigation thither, but likewise with the details of the India trade. He offered, in case they would furnish him with means to purchase his liberty, to communicate to them all necessary information, and to undertake in person the conduct of their ships. This proposal was gladly accepted. His release was immediately purchased, and so satisfied were the merchants with the information which he gave on his arrival at Amsterdam, that they equipped a squadron of four ships, which they put under his command. After an absence of two years and four months, this expedition returned, to the great joy of the country, completely successful in all its objects.

[1] Wagenaar Beschryv. i., 408; Vaderlandsch. Hist. ix., 152.

[2] Wagenaar Beschryv. i., 416.

[3] Nieuw Nederlandt, gelegen aen de landen van America, tusschen de Engelshe Virginies en N. Engelandt, streckende van Zuydt Revier, gelegen op 38½ graeden, tot Cabo Malubaer, op de hoogste van 41½ graeden, is eerst bevaren door de Ingesetenen van desen Staat in den jaer 1598, en insonderheyt by die van den Groenlantsche Compaine, doch sonder vaste habitatie te maaken, als alleen tot een verblyff in de winter. Tot welcken eynde, aldaer twee fortjeens aen de Zuydt en Noordt Revieren tegens den aenloopden Wilden hebben geworpen. Rapport en advys over de gelegentheyt van Nieuw Nederlandt getrokken uyt de stukken en papieren by Commissie der Vergaderinge der XIXe in dato 15 dec 1644. Hol. doc. ii., 368

BOOK I. The way having thus been at length opened, different companies sprang up to participate in the wealth of the East. But competition has its evils as well as its advantages. The Indian market was in danger of being glutted, and the trade consequently injured; to prevent which, the States General called a meeting of the directors of all these companies, and obliged them to unite in one body, as a measure of policy, and a means of mutual protection against the enemy. This was accordingly done, and these private adventurers were shortly after-
1602. wards incorporated under the style and title of "The East India Company," one of the most powerful commercial societies of which we read in history.[1]

The voyages to the East Indies having produced large returns to those in the United Provinces engaged in that commerce, some were now of opinion that similar results would follow the erection of a well-regulated West India company, established on the same basis as that chartered in 1602. WILLIAM USSELINCX, an Antwerp merchant who had been in the habit of resorting to Spain and her islands, and who was well acquainted with the West Indian trade, was the principal of these projectors. Having communicated his ideas to some of the most influential citizens of Amsterdam and Middleburgh, he, at their suggestion, drew up proposals for the establishment of a West India Company, to be circulated among the merchants generally, in order to ascertain how far these would co-operate in carrying out the design. Having
1604. prominently set forth the various complaints entertained against the Spaniards, on account of the efforts which they had made to exclude the Netherlanders from the seas, and from all foreign traffic, Usselincx proceeded to call public attention to the recent discovery of several fertile and temperate countries and islands inhabited by friendly people, who, he represented, were desirous of entering into alliance with the Dutch nation, then at war with the Spaniards, against whom they also entertained feelings of enmity. In this way, another opportunity was offered to attack the common enemy in his weakest quarter. The inhabitants of these countries, he said, were not na-

[1] Watson's Philip ii., 86, 87, 91. Van Meteren, lib. xvii., xviii.

ked savages, but well-favored, well-clad people; apt to learn, and among whom it would be advantageous to send colonists to teach them agriculture, as the land was found well adapted for the raising of sugar, ginger, oil, wine, indigo, cotton, hops, dye-woods, and other products, as well as for obtaining gold and silver, and other minerals, "which are the sinews of war." He further represented that salt was to be found, in great abundance, in these countries, which would afford, in return, a good outlet for Dutch manufactures and merchandise. Apart from these commercial advantages, it was, moreover, to be hoped that in course of time the saving faith and gospel of Jesus Christ might be planted there, whereby the heathen would be rescued from the darkness of actual idolatry. The circular concluded by an invitation to all those who were friendly to the project, to subscribe what amount they should invest for the purpose of fitting out a fleet, as it was intended to choose directors forthwith, and to apply to the States General for a charter. It was, however, stated, as a preliminary, that no person should have a vote in the election of directors, unless such as had shares to the amount of two hundred pounds Flemish.

The project met general approval. The States of Zealand sent delegates to consult with deputies from Amsterdam, Dordrecht, Delft, Rotterdam, Harlem, Leyden, Gouda, Schiedam, Hoorn, Enkhuysen, Alkmaar, Edam, and Monnikendam, by whom, finally, a draft of a charter was drawn up, and submitted to the States General, for the incorporation of a Dutch West India Company, to trade exclusively, for and during thirty six years, to the coast of Africa, from the tropic of Cancer to the Cape of Good Hope, and to America, from the Straits of Magellan to Terra Nova, the islands thereabout included.

This charter was duly considered by their High Mightinesses, and on the point of being completed, when proposals for a general peace, or a temporary truce, were received from the Archduke, which interrupted any farther progress in the project that Usselincx had thus brought well nigh to perfection.[1]

[1] Van Meteren, ix., 185, 186, 187, 188, 193, 194. Vaderlands. Hist. ix., 227, 228, 229, 230.

BOOK I. 1607. In the mean time, Dutch vessels continued their explorations into distant seas, and were to be found this year searching for furs among the Indians on the River of Canada, whither they had been conducted by a treacherous Frenchman.[1] But the hope of effecting a passage by the north to China, principally absorbed the attention of scientific men, who earnestly discussed new projects and suggested new routes, in the vain expectation of working out, successfully, this great problem. A private association was formed in London, to attempt a northwest passage, at whose expense an expedition was placed under the direction of HENRY HUDSON, an intrepid English mariner, whose name has been immortalized by his valuable discoveries.

Of the early life of this celebrated navigator little is known, further than that he was a native of England, had received a thorough maritime education, and was a distinguished seaman. Under the auspices of the above society, he made two voyages
1608. to the north in the course of 1607 and 1608; but having, like all those who preceded him, failed in attaining the object contemplated by his patrons, the latter suspended operations, and Hudson shaped his course to Holland;[2] encouraged, probably, by the efforts making in that quarter to form a new commercial association to trade to the West Indies.

1609. The celebrated truce between the Dutch and Spaniards having been nearly completed, about this time, the more prominent reasons for the incorporation of a West India Company were removed; and Hudson, on his arrival in Holland, made proposals to the East India Company to renew the search after the long-desired passage to India by the north. Discouraged, however, by former fruitless attempts, and persuaded by the representations of Balthazar Moucheron, who had already been on a similar expedition, the Directors of the Zealand de-

[1] Belknap Biog. i., 337. "The avarice of these Hollanders," says this author, "was so great that they had opened the graves of the dead, and taken the beaver skins in which the corpses had been buried. This outrage was so highly resented by the savages at Canseau, that they killed the person who had shown the places where the dead were laid."

[2] Van Meteren, ix., 185. Moulton's Hist. New York, 195, 198, 200. Sparks' Amer. Biog. x., 188, 209.

partment opposed the Englishman's proposition; but the Amsterdam Chamber encouraged the enterprise, and furnished, for this important voyage, a yacht, or fly boat, called "The Half-Moon," which they manned with a crew of from sixteen to twenty men, partly English and partly Dutch sailors.[1] CHAP. I.

CHAPTER II.

Hudson sails from the Texel—Arrives off Newfoundland—Reaches the coast of America in the lat. of 41°—Proceeds thence south to Cape Cod, which he calls New Holland—Arrives at the Chesapeake—Returns north and discovers a great bay in latitude 39°—Continues his northward course—Descries the Highlands of Navesinck—Rounds Sandy Hook and enters the Great North River of New Netherland—Has communication with the Indians on the west side of the bay—Appearance of the country—Continues his course upward towards a narrow river—Sends his mate to sound the channel, who comes into collision with the natives and is killed—Hudson retains two Indians as hostages—Explores the river—Goes ashore in the neighborhood of Castleton on a visit to an Indian chief, by whom he is hospitably entertained—Concludes his exploration of the river, and turns back—Tries an experiment on some of the natives—Is the first European who introduces intoxicating liquors among the Indians—Continues his downward course—Gets again into collision with the savages, several of whom are killed—Leaves the mouth of the Great River, and arrives in England—Sends an account of his discovery to Holland—Proposes to undertake a new voyage—Is ordered to Holland, where he arrives in the following year—The Dutch decline his proposition, and he re-enters the service of the London Company.

HENRY HUDSON took his departure from Amsterdam on the fourth, and sailed from the Texel on the sixth of April, 1609. He doubled the North Cape in the course of a month, but the ice and the fogs preventing him reaching Nova Zembla, he determined to abandon his original plan, and to endeavor to discover a passage by the Northwest. He accordingly directed 1609. April 4.

[1] Vaderlands. Hist. x., 7. Van Meteren, x., 203. Lambrechtsen Kort Beschryv. van N. Nederlant. Moulton, 203. Van der Donk Vertoogh van N. Nederl.; also Beschryv. van N. Nederl. "The only trace of this voyage that was discovered in the papers of the East India Company," says Mr. Brodhead, "consisted of a memorandum of a single line in one of the ships' books, stating the fact that the yaght Halve Maan of forty lasts burden had been sent toward the north in the year 1608." Report, Assembly's Docs. 1842, i., 150.

BOOK I. his course towards America, and after various vicissitudes
through storms and ice, loss of foremast and sails, arrived off
1609. July 2. the banks of Newfoundland, in the beginning of July, where
he refreshed his men by a heavy "catch" of cod. He continued his course westward for some days, when he first
July 12. obtained sight of the coast of North America. The fog was
so thick, however, that he did not venture to near the land
for several days. The weather at length cleared up, and he
July 17. ran into a bay at the mouth of a large river in the latitude of
forty-one degrees. This was Penobscot bay, on the coast of
Maine.

Having remained here for the space of a week, during which
he had frequent and friendly intercourse with the natives, and
succeeded in cutting and rigging a new foremast, he took his
July 26. departure, and continued his voyage southward, having formerly learned from his friend, Captain John Smith, that there
was a passage to the Western Pacific Ocean, south of Virginia. In a few days he saw land trending north, and ter
Aug. 4. minating in a headland, which was recognised to be Cape Cod;
but to which, under the supposition that it was an island,
Hudson gave the name of New Holland, in compliment to the
country of his employers, by whom it was afterwards distinguished as Staaten Hoeck, or States' Point. Here he
experienced further friendly reception from the Indians, some
of whom came on board, and were kindly treated. They were
observed to have green tobacco; pipes, the bowls of which
were made of clay, and the stems of red copper.

The Half-Moon hence pursued a course south and west for
the next ten days, and at length arrived, about the middle of
Aug. 18. August, at the entrance of the Chesapeake Bay, where the first
effectual attempt to plant an English colony had been commenced only two years before. Hudson now retraced his
Aug. 28. steps, and in a few days afterwards discovered, in latitude thirty-nine degrees five minutes, a great bay, which has since been
called Delaware. Here he anchored the Half-Moon in eight
fathom water, and took possession, it is said, of the country.[1]

[1] Vanderdonk, speaking, in his Beschryving van Nieuw Nederlandt, of the South River or Delaware, says:—"This is the place where the ship Half-Moon first took possession."

From this place he coasted northward, the shore appearing low, like sunken ground, dotted with islands, and at length descried the Highlands of Navesinck, which, the journalist remarks, is a very good land to fall in with, and a pleasant land to see. He found himself, on the following day, at the mouth of three great rivers, the northernmost of which he attempted to enter; but having been prevented by a shoal bar at its mouth, he cast about to the southward, and after due examination of the sounding, rounded a low "Sandy Hook," and moored the Half-Moon, on the following morning, in latitude forty degrees thirty minutes, at a short distance from the shore, in the waters of "The Great North River of New Netherland."

CHAP. II. 1609. Sept. 2. Sept. 4.

While the ship lay here at anchor, the natives from the western shore came on board, and seemed to be highly pleased at the arrival of the Europeans. They brought green tobacco, which they desired to exchange for knives and beads. They had divers ornaments, as well as pipes, made of copper; plenty of maize, or Indian corn; dresses of deerskins, well cured, hung loosely around them.

The next day some men were sent in the boat to explore the bay further up. They landed on the western bank, which was lined with men, women, and children, by whom they were very kindly received, and presented with tobacco and dried currants. They found the land covered with dried oaks. The natives continued to flock on board the ship, dressed in mantles of feathers and fine furs; their necks adorned with ornaments of copper, and some of the women had hemp.

Sept. 5.

Hudson, discovering now that the bay was the entrance to what appeared to be an extensive river, sent five of the crew forward to make a more particular examination of the channel. They passed through the Narrows, sounding as they went, and saw "a narrow river to the westward, between two islands," which are now supposed to be Staten Island and Bergen Neck. They described the land as covered with trees, grass, and flowers; and the air filled with delightful fragrance. After proceeding upward for six miles, they turned back; when, from some unaccountable cause, the boat was attacked by two canoes containing twenty-six Indians, by whom John

Sept. 6.

BOOK I. Colman, an Englishman who had accompanied Hudson in his polar voyages, was killed by an arrow shot into his throat.
1609. Two others of the crew were wounded at the same time.

This was the first European blood that was shed in these
Sept. 7. waters. Hudson's companion was interred at Sandy Hook, and the spot where his remains were deposited has since preserved, in memory of the event, the name of Colman's Point.

Additional precautions were now taken against any sudden attack; but though the ship was visited on the following day by numbers of Indians, they did not manifest any knowledge of the fatal affray which had taken place. The day after,
Sept. 9. however, two large canoes, one of which was filled with armed men, came off to the vessel; but Hudson, suspicious of their intentions, would allow only two of the savages to come on board. These he determined to detain, and dressed them in red coats, whereupon the remainder returned on shore. Presently another canoe with two men came to the vessel; one of these was also detained on board, probably as a hostage, but he contrived to jump overboard soon after, and swam on shore. Thereupon Hudson weighed anchor, stood
Sept. 11. up through the Narrows, and finally reached New York harbor, where he rode all night. He was here again visited by the natives, who made a great show of love, giving tobacco and Indian corn; but they could not be trusted.

Hudson having ascended thus far, prepared now to explore the magnificent river which rolled its waters into the sea from unknown regions, in the probable hope that it would lead him to the long-sought-for passage to the Indies. He accordingly
Sept. 12. weighed in the afternoon of the 12th September, and commenced his memorable voyage up that majestic stream, which has since handed his name down to posterity.

But the wind was so light that it permitted him to proceed only a few leagues. The moment he anchored, the natives again renewed their visits in increased numbers, bringing oysters and vegetables. None, however, were allowed on board. The wind sprang up the next day, and the ship succeeded in making nearly forty miles. The land now began to grow very high and mountainous, and she reached soon after the
Sept. 14. entrance of wild, but sublime, highlands.

When he awoke, next morning, Hudson found a heavy mist overhanging the river and its shores, and concealing the summits of the mountains. But it soon cleared up, and he was about to proceed on his course, when the two savages whom he held as hostages, made their escape through the port-holes of the vessel, and swam on shore. The moment he was under weigh, they hailed the crew and expressed their indignation at the treatment they had been subjected to, by uttering loud cries of scorn and anger. Towards night the Half-Moon came in view of other mountains, which lay from the river's side, and anchored, it is supposed, near the present site of Cattskill landing. Here were found "very loving people and very old men," by whom the Europeans were well used. CHAP. II. 1609. Sept. 15.

Next morning a large number of the inhabitants of the country came off to the ship, bringing Indian corn, pumpkins, and tobacco, in return for which they obtained some trinkets. Having been occupied most of the day in taking in a supply of water, the Half-Moon did not start again till towards night; but she made no more than five miles, when the river becoming shoal, she cast anchor. Being now in the neighborhood of the present town of Castleton, Hudson went on shore in an Indian canoe, at the invitation of an old man, "the governor of the country," who was chief over forty men and seventeen women, and who occupied a house made of the bark of trees, exceedingly smooth, and well finished within and without. Here he found large quantities of Indian corn and beans, sufficient to load three ships, besides what were still growing in the fields. Sept. 16. Sept. 18.

On arriving at the house, two mats were spread to sit on; eatables were immediately brought in well-made red wooden bowls, and men were dispatched with bows and arrows for game, who soon returned with pigeons. A fat dog was killed, and skinned with shells which were got out of the water, and every sort of good cheer furnished. The Indians invited Hudson to remain all night, and were much disappointed when they discovered his determination to return on board. Imagining that it proceeded from the fear of their bows and arrows, they broke these in pieces and threw them into the fire. The land here

BOOK I. 1609. was observed to be of the finest kind for tillage, bearing trees fit for shipbuilding; pumpkins, grapes, plums, and other fruit. The Indians still crowded on board, exchanging furs and other articles of native produce for beads, knives, hatchets, or whatever trifles the sailors could spare them. The weather continuing fair, anchor was again weighed, and the Half-Moon
Sept. 19. ran two leagues higher up. The navigation of the river now becoming considerably obstructed, a boat was sent forward for the purpose of exploring the channel. It ascended several miles. The channel was found narrow, and the depth of the water variable.

Sept. 21. Distrusting the savages all along, Hudson determined now to try an experiment, which, by throwing them off their guard, would elicit any treachery which might be latent in their dispositions. He accordingly invited several of their chiefs into the cabin, and gave them plenty of brandy to drink, so as to make them intoxicated. The result was that one got drunk, and fell sound asleep, to the great astonishment of his companions, who "could not tell how to take it." They all took suddenly to their canoes and hurried ashore, leaving their stupified countryman behind them. Their anxiety for his welfare soon induced them, however, to return with a quantity of beads which they gave him, to enable him, perhaps, to bribe or exorcise "the foul fiend" which had possession of him. The savage slept soundly all night, and was quite recovered from the effects of his debauch, when his friends came to see him next day. So rejoiced were these people at finding their chief restored, as it were, to life, that they returned on board in crowds again in the afternoon, bringing tobacco and more beads, which they presented to Hudson, to whom they made an oration, showing him the country round about. They then sent one of their company on land, who presently returned with a great platter of dressed venison, which they caused Hudson to eat with them; after which they made him profound reverence and departed, all, save the old man, who, having had a taste of the fatal beverage, preferred to remain on board.

Such was the introduction among the Indians, by the first European that came among them, of that poison, which, combined with other causes, has since operated to deprive

CHAP II. 1609.

their descendants of almost a foothold in their native land, and caused, within a few centuries, the almost entire extinction of the Red race.[1]

The Half-Moon had now evidently ascended as high as she could go. She had reached a little below the present city of Albany, and Hudson having satisfied himself, by dispatching a boat some seven or eight leagues higher up, that he had gained the head of the ship navigation, prepared to retrace his course. The downward was not more expeditious than the upward voyage. The prevalent winds were southerly, and the ship could therefore make but little headway. The time, however, passed agreeably in making excursions on shore, where good ground for corn and other garden herbs was found, with great store of goodly oaks, walnut, and chesnut trees, yew trees, and trees of sweet wood in great abundance ; great store of slate for houses, and other good stones. The crew amused themselves, at other times, in receiving visits from the natives, who continued to crowd the ship in numbers.

Sept. 23.

Hudson had thus made about thirty miles, occasionally interrupted by the shallowness of the channel, and was lying at anchor opposite the spot where a city bearing his own name now stands, when two canoes put off from the place where the intoxication scene had occurred, on board one of which was the old man who had been made the subject of the strange experiment. He brought another old man with him, who presented Hudson with a string of beads, and pointed to the surrounding country, as though it were at his command. Hudson entertained them at dinner, with four of their women, and in the afternoon dismissed them with presents. He thence con-

Sept 26.

[1] It is a remarkable fact, says Moulton, that a tradition prevails at this day among the Iroquois, that a scene of intoxication occurred with a party of the natives on the arrival of the first ship. As a singular coincidence, also, a similar tradition prevails among the descendants of the Delawares. While Hudson, unconscious of its ulterior effects, was thus introducing the Indians to an acquaintance with the pernicious " fire water," on the banks of the North River, Champlain was giving the same people, about the same time, on the banks of Lake Iroquois, their first knowledge of gunpowder, an agent equally active, perhaps, in causing their final ruin. Fatal first gifts of the civilized Christian to the untutored heathen !

BOOK I. 1609. Sept. 29. tinued his voyage down the river, occasionally trading with or entertaining the people, and at length having arrived at the northern entrance of the passage through the Highlands, anchored on the first of October at the mouth of the Haverstraw Bay, in the vicinity of Stony Point.

Oct. 1. The vessel was no sooner perceived from the shore to be stationary, than a party of the mountain Indians came off in their canoes to visit it, apparently filled with wonder at every thing it contained. While the attention of the crew was now taken up with their visitors on deck, one of the savages managed to run his canoe under the stern, and climbing up by the rudder, found his way, by the window, into the cabin, from which he abstracted a pillow and a few articles of wearing apparel, with which he made off. The mate detected him in his retreat, fired at, and killed him. Hereupon all the other savages departed with the utmost precipitation, some taking to their canoes, others to the water. The boat was manned and dispatched after the stolen goods, which were easily recovered; but as the men were returning to the vessel, one of the Indians in the water seized hold of the boat, with the intent, as was supposed, to upset it. The cook seized a sword, and lopped off the hand of the unfortunate wretch, who sunk to rise no more. The ship was then weighed, and dropped down about five miles.

Oct. 2. On the following day they descended about seven leagues farther, and came to anchor. Here they were visited by a canoe, on board of which was one of the savages who had made his escape from the vessel as she was going up. Fearing treachery, Hudson would not allow either him or his companions on board. Two other canoes, filled with armed warriors, now came under the stern, and commenced an attack with arrows. They were repulsed with a loss of three men. More than a hundred savages now pushed off from the nearest point of land, but one of the ship's cannon having been brought to bear on these, killed two of the party, and the rest fled, thereupon, to the woods. But the savages were not yet discouraged. Nine or ten of the boldest of the warriors, probably incited by the two who had made their escape from the Half-Moon on her way up, threw themselves into a canoe, and made for the vessel, but these fared no better than those who preceded them. A cannon shot drove a hole through their canoe, and killed one of the men. This was followed by a discharge of musketry, which killed three or four more, and put an end to the battle. The Half-Moon now descended some five miles farther down, probably near Hoboken, and thus got beyond the reach of all enemies. CHAP. II. 1609.

Hudson had now thoroughly explored the river, from its mouth to the head of navigation, and had secured for his employers possessions which would reward them beyond measure for the expense they had incurred. For himself he had won an immortality, which was destined to hand down his name to the latest age. Happy at the result, he left "the great mouth of the Great River," and put to sea, with all sails set, to communicate to those in Holland, in whose service he was, the tidings of his valuable discovery. "We continued our course towards England," concludes the journal of this voyage, written by the mate, "without seeing any land by the way all the rest of this October, and on the seventh of November, stilo novo, being Saturday, by the grace of God we safely arrived in the range of Dartmouth, in Devonshire, in the year 1609."[1] Oct. 4.

Hudson, immediately on his arrival here, forwarded information of his return, and an account of his discoveries, to the directors of the East India Company in Amsterdam, and offered, at the same time, to make another voyage to the Northwest in the month of March following, provided they furnished, besides the men's wages, the sum of fifteen hundred guilders, in cash, to purchase necessaries in addition to what were already on board. He proposed, further, that six or seven of the present crew should be changed, but that the number of hands should consist altogether of twenty. His plan was to sail from Dartmouth on the first of March; to spend the

[1] The journal of Hudson's voyage up the North River will be found in N. Y. Hist. Soc. Trans. i., 102. Moulton furnishes, in the first part of his Hist. of New York, a minute running commentary on this journal, marking, as he goes along, the progress from day to day of the famous "Half-Moon." From these, and from the interesting sketch which Mr. Sparks has given of the voyage in his valuable life of Hudson, [Americ. Biog. x., 187,] the above particulars have been compiled.

BOOK I. month of April and half of May killing whales and other sea animals near the island of Panar; thence to sail to the North-
1609. west, where he would remain till the middle of September, and finally to return to Holland by the northeast of Scotland. These proposals, owing to contrary winds, did not reach the directors, who were ignorant for a considerable time of Hudson's arrival in England. When the news at length reached them, they ordered him to return immediately with his vessel to Holland. These orders he would have instantly obeyed, had he, as well as the English portion of his crew, not been forbidden by the authorities in England, who were exceedingly jealous of the maritime enterprises of the Dutch, to leave his
1610. native country, or to enter into the service of any foreign
Jan. power. It was supposed that the English were desirous themselves to send him with some ships to Virginia, farther to explore that part of America.[1] The Half-Moon returned to Holland, after a detention in England of eight months; but Hudson's connection with the Dutch East India Company ceased shortly
July 15. after his arrival in England. He re-entered the service of the London Company, by whom he had been originally employed, and perished at sea, after having discovered the bay in the northwest seas which still bears his name.

[1] Van Meteren, X., 206.

CHAPTER III.

Boundaries of the Dutch discoveries—Rivers therein—Appearance and condition of the country—The trees—Fruits—Plants—Wild animals—Birds—Aquatic fowls—Fish—Reptiles—Natives of the country—Enumeration of the various tribes—Their physical appearance—Mode of hunting—Agriculture—Food—Clothing—Ornaments—Dwellings—Furniture—Villages—Canoes—Indian women—Marriage—Polygamy—Travail—Political arrangements among the Indians—Wars—Weapons—Treatment of prisoners—Treaties of peace—Circulating medium—Burial of the dead—Religious opinions—Manittous—Immortality of the soul—Superstitions—Opinions of the creation—Medicine men—Method of treating disease—Amusements—Gambling—Feeble means of resistance against the superior powers of the white men.

CHAP. III. 1609. Boundaries.

THE territory on the continent of North America, now thrown open to the enterprise of the Dutch nation, was embraced between the extreme points on the sea coast at which Hudson, in the progress of his voyage, had cast anchor. It was bounded on the south by the Great Bay, since known as the Delaware; and on the northeast by New Holland, otherwise Cape Cod; and thus stretched from the thirty-eighth to the forty-first or second degree of north latitude. The great River of Canada formed its northern frontier, while its western limits were both unexplored and unknown.[1] Four large or principal

[1] Vander Donck, writing in 1649 of New Netherland, says—"It is situate on the north side of America, in the latitude of 38, 39, 40, 41, and 42 degrees, or thereabouts, along the sea coast. It is bounded on the northeast by New England; on the southwest by Virginia. The coast tends mostly S.W. and N.E., and is sandy alongside the ocean. To the north stretches the River of Canada, a great distance behind. The northwest region is still partly unexplored. . . . . . In the beginning, before any mention was made of the English, after our people had first discovered and explored the most northerly parts of New Netherland, and had been some distance away on that side of Cape Cod, as we find it described, they erected an escutcheon on Cape Cod, and took possession. . . . . . The boundaries, according as we understand, extend hence to Cape Hindlopen, four miles south of Cape Cornelis, in the latitude of eight and thirty degrees. . . . . The South Bay and South River, called by many the second great river of New Netherland, lies in the latitude of 38° 53′. It has two heights or capes; the northern called Cape Mey, the southern Cape Cornelis; and the bay itself is called now Port May; now Godyn Bay. These names were given

BOOK I. 1609. Rivers

rivers flowed within these limits into the sea; namely, the Great South River, in the latitude of 38° 53′; the North River, called also Rio Montanjes, or the Great River of the Mountains, in latitude 40°; the Hellegat, or East River, by which name was distinguished an inlet or arm of the sea, to the east of the Island of Manhattans, and a river of fresh water, which flowed into the last-mentioned inlet, but of which farther mention will be hereafter made.

The first of these rivers derived its name from its geographical position, being the southern boundary of the Dutch territory. It opened for a considerable distance, before it reached its embouchure, into a capacious bay, twenty-six miles long, and twenty-four miles broad, which received the waters of fourteen navigable tributaries. This river was considered by many equal to the great River Amazon.

The North River, called by the Indians the Cohotatea, ran a considerable, but yet unexplored, distance in a northerly direction, into the interior, receiving in its course the Maquaas or Mohawk, and other valuable streams, and carrying a flood tide over one hundred and fifty miles from the sea. It was esteemed by its first discoverers, both in point of trade and for the fertility of its banks, the finest river in North America. The other rivers were of equal value and importance, affording a ready communication inland with the native tribes in all directions.

The country thus watered was, however, a wide and uncul-

to the places at the first discovery, before they had others. The discovery occurred at the same time that the North River was discovered, by the same ship and people, who entered the south bay before they made the north bay, as the whole hereof is to be read in its length and breadth in 'The New World' of John de Laet." Vertoogh van N. N., kap. i. v. vii. viii. Heylen in his Cosmography says N. N. extended from 38½° to 41° 15′. The principal materials of this chapter are taken from Vander Donck's work above named; from the Beschryvinge van Nieuw Nederlandt, by the same author, an able translation of which, by the Hon. Mr. Johnson, is published in the N. Y. Hist. Soc. Trans. vol. i. new series; from Colden's Hist. of the Five Nations; Gallatin's Synopsis of the Indian Tribes; Trumbull's Hist. of Connecticut; Murray's British America; Wood's Sketch of Long Island; Proud's Hist. of Pennsylvania; Jarvis' Discourse on the Religion of the Indian Tribes, in N. Y. Hist. Col. iii., and Memoir on Mohegan Indians, in Mass. Col. ix. 77.

tivated wilderness, where nature luxuriated in pristine wildness and wealth. The soil along the sea side was light and sandy, mixed with clay. In the interior fine level land, well watered, intersected with high hills and lofty mountains of reddish sandstone, was everywhere to be found. The surface of the low lands was generally a black loam, mixed in some places with a strong clay, about a foot and a half deep on an average; in others, with gravel and stones. Near the rivers, and in the valleys, were extensive bottoms, affording every encouragement for industrious settlers and planters. Throughout the whole country vegetation was rapid, and all the natural productions luxuriant, owing to the constant decomposition of vegetable matter—plants, wild grass, and the deciduous foliage—which annually dying, furnished an ever renewing supply of rich manure. A primeval forest covered the face of the earth. Oaks of all kinds, some from sixty to seventy feet high without a knot; hickory, walnut, butternut, chesnut, beech, buttonwood, birch, ash, elm, pine, (both yellow and white,) maple, cedar, willow, whitewood, poplar, hemlock, spruce, tamarack, sassafras, linden, alder, and thorn, were found growing all around. Wild fruit was equally abundant, consisting of acorns, (some of which were very sweet,) chesnuts, beechnuts, walnuts, butternuts, hazelnuts, mulberries, cherries, currants, plums, gooseberries, medlars, bilberries, blackberries, raspberries, cranberries, and strawberries, the latter in such abundance that people lay down in the fields and ate them to satiety. Pignuts, artichokes, wild leeks and onions, wild peas, and other wild fruit also abounded. The entire land, both forest and bottom land, was, moreover, covered with vines, climbing up the loftiest trees or creeping along the lowly valleys, and bearing loads of grapes; some white, some blue; some large, some small; some very juicy and others not so good, yet all promising, if properly cultivated, an ample return to the vine-dresser. Innumerable medicinal plants were also to be found. Maidens'-hair, hartstongue, angelica, polypodium, mullein, sweetflag, sassafras, bayberry, crowfoot, plantain, marshmallow, marjoram, cranesbill, wild indigo, mezereon, sarsaparilla, violet, dragonsblood, touch-me-not, blessed thistle, agremony, snakeroot, coriander, pleurisyroot, spikenard, Solomon's seal,

Appearance of the country.

Trees.

Fruits.

Plants.

BOOK I. 1609. ginseng, motherwort, consumption root, and pennyroyal; with the uses of which, as well as of various others, which the country furnished, the natives were perfectly familiar in the cure of diseases or of wounds, received either in battle from other tribes, or from the wild animals of the forest. Numer-

Animals. ous species of these, panthers, bears, buffaloes, elks, deer, wolves, wildcats, foxes, raccoons, beavers, otters, fishers, minks, hares, muskrats, rabbits, squirrels, skunks, groundhogs, drummers, &c., furnished the natives, whose principal support was derived from the chase, with clothing and food at one and

Birds. the same time. The wild birds were as numerous as the wild animals. Eagles, falcons, sparrowhawks, sailinghawks, kites, ravens, castrills, crows, catowls, turkyes, partridges, pheasants, woodcocks, snipes, quails, cranes, herons, pigeons, landrunners, woodpeckers, thrushes, blackbirds, and a small but curious bird, called the West India bee or humming-bird, are those mentioned by the earliest writers, while they admit that they do not enumerate all the species of the winged tribe which were to be found in the country in those days. The waters

Water fowls. were as prolific of game as the air. Here were swans, geese, pelicans, ducks, teal, widgeons, brant, coots, divers, and eel-

Fish. shovellers. Fish of the finest qualities filled the rivers, the bays, and the sea, also, with life. Those in the fresh water were salmon, sturgeon, striped bass, drums, shad, carp, perch, pike, trout, thickheads, suckers, sunfish, catfish, eel, lampreys, divers, mullets, or frost-fish; those of the sea, codfish, shell-fish, weekfish, halibut, herring, mackerel, thornback, flounders, plaice, bream, blackfish, seal, lobster, oysters, crabs, peri-

Reptiles. winkle, clams, turtles, and porpoises. Snakes were among "the creeping things of the earth," but all harmless, except the rattlesnake, many of which, however, were not to be met with.

The richness of the soil and the abundance of game, favored particularly the maintenance and increase of the savage race which occupied the country at the period of Hudson's visit.

Indians. These people, though belonging to the common stock of the Algonkin-Lenape family, were cut up and divided into a number of separate and independent tribes or nations. To the east dwelt the Pequods and the Wampanoags, while the North River was divided between the terrible Maquaas or Mohawks, who occupied its upper waters, and imposed tribute on the surrounding tribes,[1] the Mahicanders or River Indians, who lined its banks on either side to its mouth, and the Matouwacks or Montauks of Sewan-hacky or Long Island, who exercised jurisdiction over thirteen minor tribes thereabout.

Beginning then with the Mohawks; these occupied the country on the west bank of the Cohotatea or Hudson River, from the head of the navigation back, some seventy miles. Opposite to them, to the east, the wigwams of the Mohegans stretched beyond the mountains to the Connecticut. South of this nation were settled the Waraonckins on the east, and the Waranancongyns on the west, in the vicinity of Esopus, where they were afterwards known as the Wappingi or Wappingers.

The east side of Tappaans bay was inhabited by the Pachamis, the Tankitekes, and the Wicquaeskeeks; the last mentioned of whom occupied a tract of land between the North and East Rivers, on the banks of two smaller streams, called the Sintsinck and the Armonck, a few miles north of the fierce Manhattœ or Manhattans, "a cruel nation," who held their council fires on an extensive island immediately south, which, retaining their name, was afterwards called MANHATTANS.[2]

[1] I have been told by old men in New England, who remember the time when the Mohawks made war on their Indians, that as soon as a single Mohawk was discovered in the country, their Indians raised a cry from hill to hill, A Mohawk! a Mohawk! upon which they all fled, like sheep before wolves, without attempting to make the least resistance, whatever odds were on their side. The poor New England Indians immediately ran to the Christian houses, and the Mohawks often pursued them so closely, that they entered along with them, and knocked their brains out in the presence of the people of the house; but if the family had time to shut the door, they never attempted to force it, and on no occasion did any injury to the Christians. All the nations round them have, for many years, entirely submitted to them, and pay a yearly tribute to them in wampum. They dare neither make war nor peace without the consent of the Mohawks. Two old men commonly go about, every year or two, to receive this tribute; and I have often had opportunity to observe what anxiety the poor Indians were under, while these two old men remained in that part of the country where I was. An old Mohawk sachem, in a poor blanket and a dirty shirt, may be seen issuing his orders, with as arbitrary an authority as a Roman dictator.—Colden's Five Nations, 3, 4.

[2] Bedenckinge over het aenvaerden vander landeryen in N. Nederlandt by

BOOK I. 1609.

The Hackingsacks were the opposite nation to these, on the west, between whom and the sea, dwelt the Raritans. This tribe, the first of the River Indians with whom Hudson had communication, occupied a rich and fertile valley, situated between two high mountains some distance the one from the other, through which flowed a fresh water river that disembogued in the Neywesinck or Navesinck bay on the south side of the Great Bay of the North River, lying between Sandyhook and Aquehonga Manacknong, or Eghquaous, as Staten Island was called;[1] but from this country the Raritans, some thirty years after this, were forced to migrate by the spring freshets, which frequently destroyed their stock of maize and other provisions, stored in winter in pits under ground, joined to repeated incursions and attacks from the Minsi and Delaware, or Lenno Lenape Indians,[2] whom the Dutch distinguished by the name of Sankhicans. Generally speaking, the tribes on one side of the river were the deadly enemies of those on the other.

The Delawares and Minsi occupied the country bounded east and south by the Hudson river and the Atlantic; west by the height of land which separates the waters falling into the Delaware from those that empty into the Susquehanna and Chesapeake. On the north they were in possession of the country watered by the Schuylkill to its sources. East of the Delaware the Lenape tribes were separated by the Catskill

den Secretaris van Tienhoven Anno 1650. Modern writers on Indian Terminology have been at much trouble to explain the reason why the island of New York was first called Manhattans. Some aver that it was because it signifies "the place of the original intoxication;" others, that the name was derived from "a species of wood growing there, of which the Indians made their bows and arrows." These are mere surmises, founded only on fancy. The early Dutch inhabitants give an explanation more consonant to common sense. It was so called "from or after the tribe of savages among whom the Dutch made their first settlement." (Den naem van oudts het soo behouden hebbende vander natie vander Wilden daer de Duytsen haer eerst by hadden neergeslaen.) Alb. Rec. xviii. 348. The original Dutch MSS., in book marked PP.; N. Y. Hist. Coll. iii. 375. It was the Dutch, therefore, and not the Indians, who first called the island of New York "Manhattans."

[1] Book of Patents iv. 63; Alb. Rec. viii. 161. Eghquaous was the Indian name as recorded by the Dutch.

[2] Van Tienhoven ut supra.

mountains from the Mohawks, who in that quarter seem to have been called Minquas. Between these and the Minsi, the Wappings, already mentioned, intervened, but the division line between the two last tribes is not ascertained.[1]

1609.

Various tribes are mentioned as inhabiting different points of the lands west of the Hudson, as the Naraticongs on the north side of the Raritan, and the Capitannesses, the Gacheos, and the Pomptons. It is added, that the Delawares were subdivided into the Assunpinks or Stony Creek Indians, the Rankokas or Chichequaas, Mingoes, Andastakas, who were located on Christian creek, Wilmington; Neshaminies, in Bucks co.; Schaka Maxons about Kensington, Philadelphia; Mantas or Frog Indians, near Burlington; and the Mennesinks, above the forks of the Delaware.[2]

The tribes on Long Island are represented to have been of the Delaware stock, though some doubt this allegation. Their settlements were generally on the borders of the island, an arrangement induced, it is to be supposed, by the facilities afforded for obtaining fish, and those shells from which sewan, or wampum, was manufactured, this section of the country having been for years the quarter from which that substitute for a circulating medium was obtained.[3] The principal tribes that occupied this fertile region were the Canarse, or Canarisse, who claimed the chief part of the lands in what is now called Kings county, Jamaica, and some part of Newtown. The Rockaways were settled on that section which still retains their name; they owned also some parts of Newtown and Jamaica. The Merrikoke and Marsapeague nations stretched from Rockaway through what is now Queen's county, into Huntington, on the south side of the island. The territory of the Mattinecock tribe extended from Flushing, through Queen's

[1] Gallatin. [2] Proud's Penn. ii., 294, 295

[3] Van Tienhoven held out the facilities which this island afforded for the manufacture of wampum as an encouragement to the Dutch, in 1650, to emigrate to New Netherland. Speaking of the eastern extremity of the island, he says—This Hook is right well situated for carrying on the trade in sewan, (wampum;) it is the mine of New Netherland. Because around and in the abovementioned waters, and in the islands thereof, are found the cockles whereof sewan is manufactured, which would afford great profit to such as would establish colonies or plantations there.

BOOK I. 1609. county, to Cowharbor, in Suffolk, on the north side.[1] The Nissaquagues extended their claim from the last-mentioned point to Stony brook, and the Setaukets from this to Wading River. The Corchaug Indians claimed hence to Southold, on the north side, while the territory of the Manhassetts was Shelter Island. The lands of the Secataugs adjoined the Marsapeagues, and extended to Patchogue, which tribe reached to South Hampton. The Shinecock nation extended from Canoeplace to Montauk, whilst these owned the peninsula, the point of which still perpetuates the name of that tribe whose chief was styled the Sachem of Long Island. It is right to mention, however, that much confusion obtains when comparing the above names with those handed down by the Dutch authorities—a confusion which is owing, perhaps, to the difference in the language in which these authorities wrote, as well as to the names which they gave the places where the Indians were located.

Their physical appearance.

The most prominent peculiarity that struck Europeans on coming into contact with this new race of men, was the differ ence which existed in their physical appearance, when compared with that of the inhabitants of the Old World—a difference which has since led physiologists to class them as a particular variety of the human species. Though generally well made, broad of shoulder and slender in the waist, capable of enduring much fatigue and hunger, their skin was discovered at once to be of a different color to that with which they had been always most familiar. It was of a red copper, or rather an obscure orange hue, not unlike the bark of the cinnamon-tree. It was at first supposed that this was the effect of climate; but it is now believed to be artificially produced by the habitual and constant use of unctuous substances, in which the juice of some root is incorporated, and by which this peculiar tinge is communicated to the skin of the Indian tribes of North America.

The face was broad and flat; the cheek-bones high; the

[1] This tribe is represented by Van Tienhoven to consist, in 1650, of only thirty families. They formerly had a great number of settlements, he adds, in Martin Gerrittsen's bay, or Mattinehook; but, at the time he wrote, it was mostly abandoned and waste. Bedenckinge, &c.

forehead low; the eye sunken, and dark brown; the nose small, with wide nostrils; and the mouth large, with lips somewhat thick. The hair differed remarkably from that of the Caucasian race. Instead of being fine and soft, it was coarse, black, and strong; every vestige of this appendage of manhood being, however, carefully removed from the Indian face, these people regarding a beard with peculiar antipathy. To supply the loss, they indulged, on certain great occasions, in the luxury of bedaubing and painting the face in a most fantastic and grotesque manner.

Features.

In respect to physical strength, the Indian ranked below the European; but though particularly averse to labor, his powers of perseverance were found to be equal to a vast amount of continued exertion, when such was required. Such a property was providentially bestowed on a people who derived their chief support from the chase. Hunting, with the Indian, was not only a pastime, but a necessary avocation of his life, to qualify him for which, as well as for war, all his education in youth, and all the riper energies of his manhood were directed. A rigid course of fasting, accompanied by dreaming and various superstitions, were the usual preliminaries to setting forth on the great hunt. Arrived at the lairs of the wild animals, a circle was formed, by the gradual contraction of which, all the game was pressed within a narrower compass, till, driven into the very centre of the ring, they fell beneath showers of arrows or spears, or the multiplied blows of clubs. On other occasions, they were driven to the bank of the river, or lake, where canoes were ready to intercept them the moment they took the water. Other means which experience or ingenuity suggested, such as traps, nets, springs, were also used, according as the nature or habits of the prey to be pursued dictated; for the beaver and the bear were different in every respect. But whatever was the game, the success in the chase was sure to be followed by rejoicings, songs, and dances, in which the men of the whole tribe united.

Hunting.

A rude description of agriculture was combined with the chase for the purpose of raising food. Patches in the neighborhood of the villages were laid under maize, tobacco, pumpkins, and other such products; and from the interview which

Agriculture.

BOOK I. 1609. Hudson had with the old chief, it is evident they raised abundance of corn. The grain, after harvest, was lodged under ground in holes lined with bark, and afterwards broken

Food. between stones, from the meal of which they made coarse bread, or cakes, and a thick sort of porridge called sappaan, a favorite dish among them. They used, however, for ordinary food, though they had no stated hours for their meals, meat and fish of every kind, clean and unclean, which they cooked in the plainest manner, entrails and all, mixing in their coarse cakes, and adding, on extraordinary occasions, beavers' tails, parched corn-meal, or very fat meat stewed with chesnuts. Dogs' flesh seems to have been in high esteem among them.

Notwithstanding the heavy dishes of which they made use, and the gluttony in which, when occasion offered, they indulged, consuming almost incredible quantities of food, they were capable of extraordinary abstinence, and even took a pride in long fasts, in which they could persevere for successive days. With all descriptions of intoxicating liquors they were unacquainted until Hudson introduced them to a know ledge of the all-destroying beverage.

Clothing. The clothing which they used was in every respect as rude as their food. It consisted, in the winter, of the skins of wild animals sewed together and hanging loosely from the shoulders; in summer, of a piece of skin tied round the waist. The children went generally naked; the females wore round their bodies fastened by a girdle their rude robe which extended below the knee, with an under-garment of dressed deer-skin girt round the waist, the lower border of which was tastefully ornamented with wampum. After the settlement of Europeans among them subsequently, men and women added to their dress a piece of duffils or coarse cloth, obtained in exchange for furs, which they hung over the right shoulder, the ends extending below the knees. This served as a cloak by day and a blanket by night. Their stockings and shoes were made of dressed deer-skin. The men went usually bare-headed, some wearing their hair only on one side, some on both sides of the head; others carried on the top a strip of hair from the forehead to the neck, about three fingers' breadth, which they cut short till about three fingers long, when it stood erect like a cock's comb, on both sides of which the hair was cut very close. The whole of this was smeared thickly with bears' grease. The women, on the other hand, usually bound their hair behind in a club, about a hand long, in the form of a beaver's tail, over which was drawn a square cap, ornamented frequently with wampum. Other ornaments of similar manufacture were sometimes encircled around their arms and necks, or pendent from their ears, with a few streaks of paint on their faces, when they desired to be excessively engaging. Both sexes were particularly fond of ornamenting their persons, each using, indiscriminately, ornaments originally intended for the other sex.[1] Hudson found the river tribes ornamenting their persons with feathers, shells, and glittering plates of copper suspended from the ears and nose, which, however, were not bored, but slit to such an extent as to allow a stick of wax to be passed through, to which all the ornaments, intended for these parts of the body, were appended.

Ornaments.

Though fond of these baubles and finery, the Indians were a slovenly and dirty race. While the European studied to keep his skin clean, and free from extraneous substance, the Indian's aim was to make his shine, like that of a roasted pig, by means of accumulated oil, grease, and paint.[2] Soot scraped from the bottoms of kettles, the juices of herbs of various tints, rendered adhesive by combination with unctuous substances, were lavishly used to make his appearance particularly hideous or terrific.

Dwellings.

Their habitations, though those of the Five Nations were of a superior class, were on a par with their other social ideas.

[1] The Indians had some singular ideas of the presents which, at the first visit, the Europeans gave them. The axes and hoes which they received, they hung as ornaments around their necks; and the stockings they used as tobacco pouches.—Heckewelder. The early French writers relate an amusing anecdote to show the confusion of Indian ideas in matters of dress. The Ursuline nuns, having educated a Huron girl, presented her, on her marriage to one of her countrymen, with a complete and handsome suit of clothes in the Parisian style They were much surprised, some days after, to see the husband, who had taken possession of the whole of the bride's attire, arrayed in it, and parading backward and forward in front of the convent, betraying every symptom of the most extravagant exultation, which was farther increased on observing the nuns crowding to the window to see him, and smiling at his singular appearance.—Murray, from Creuxius.

[2] Creuxius, Hist. Nov. Franc.

BOOK I. 1609. They were of the rudest construction, consisting merely of hickory saplings stuck in the ground and bent at the top into an arch, like a bow. These were covered with the bark of trees, secured to the poles. Some of these huts are represented to have been a hundred and eighty yards long, but none more than twenty feet wide. In the middle was the fire, an opening in the roof permitting the egress of the smoke. The furniture of these dwellings consisted of a few pots, kettles, or other such simple necessaries, without chairs, table, knives, or napkins. Their knife at first was a sharpened shell; their axe a sharpened stone. In wooden mortars they pounded their corn with stone pestles, and ate their food out of wooden bowls. Their couches were of bulrushes or the skins of wild beasts. A number of such dwellings composed a village, which formed the distinct and separate residence of a tribe, each under its own chief. This village was usually located some fifteen or twenty miles distant from any other, on the side of a steep hill, on the bank of some deep stream, near the corn patch, and was carefully protected by a strong stockade from the attacks of other tribes, for much mutual animosity prevailed between the Indian nations of New Netherland. These villages were not, however, fixed or permanent. The inmates were migratory in their habits, and remained not long in one place. They shifted according as the season prompted. The summer and spring found them on the seacoast, or river or lake side, in search of fish. In the winter they ranged the forest and hunting-grounds in search of game; and, wherever their business called them, 'twas easy to erect a rude dwelling such as they were accustomed to.

Villages.

Canoes.

Their boats or canoes were as rude in construction as their dwellings. Some consisted of the trunks of trees hollowed out, after an incredible degree of labor, by means of fire, or such miserable tools as they could invent. Others again were made of bark, sewed together with thongs made from the dried entrails or sinews of animals. Some of these canoes were capable of holding from twelve to fourteen persons, or one hundred and fifty bushels of grain.

Women.

Among these people women were nothing better than domestic slaves, on whom devolved all sorts of labor; such as planting corn, cutting and hauling firewood, carrying burdens, cooking, attending children, and whatever other hard work was to be performed. With such a low estimate of the sex, it is not surprising to learn, that scarcely a trace of what constitutes marriage among civilized nations was found among them. The man presented the woman with some offering or gift, which, if she accepted, sealed their agreement to live together, and this they continued to do so long only as it pleased them. They separated the moment they could no longer agree, in which cases the issue followed the mother.[1] Polygamy did not prevail much among them; each man had commonly but one wife. A plurality of wives was, however, allowed to the chiefs. Both men and women were excessively unchaste; though the latter, if married, considered such unchasteness disgraceful. Otherwise they placed no restraint on their passions, and consented to any act of lewdness for a few shillings.

CHAP. III. 1609.

Marriage

Polygamy.

Travail.

The period of travail was one in which the woman or squaw, as the Indian female was called, exhibited proofs of the strongest patience and endurance of suffering. When her time was near, she retired alone to a secluded part of the woods, near a running stream, where, having prepared a shelter for herself, she brought forth her offspring without assistance and without a moan. Immediately after her confinement, she immersed herself and infant in the cold brook, whatever was the season of the year, and returned home, after having passed a few days in her retirement, to apply herself again without a murmur to her usual routine of drudgery. Sickness after childbirth was very rare among them, and the children were usually weaned when a year old.

Having thus passed in hasty review the physical and social condition of the Indian race, it remains now for us to examine their political arrangements. These were based upon the funda-

[1] Van der Donck and Colden agree on this point. "As all kinds of slavery is banished from the country of the Five Nations; so (says the latter writer) they keep themselves free from the bondage of wedlock, and when either of the parties become disgusted, they separate without formality or ignominy to either, unless 'tis occasioned by some scandalous offence in one of them. In case of divorce, the children, according to the natural course of animals, follow the mother."

BOOK I. 1609. mental principle, in perfect keeping with their savage state, of the complete exemption from control of each individual; which permitted him, of right, to do whatever he pleased, unchecked

Police and government. and unconstrained, save by his own interests or passions. Each tribe had a separate government, separate laws, separate regulations, and its own chief; but during peace this chief had little or no power or authority, and was scarce better than any other of the nation. He was chosen from among the bravest, when a vacancy occurred, without any respect to the claims of the descendants of those who had already held that high office; for among them the chieftainship was not hereditary. Public affairs were managed by a council of the wisest, most experienced, and most warlike, called sachems; who, in like manner, obtained their authority by the general opinion entertained of their courage and address, and lost it by a failure in these qualities. Both the sachems and chiefs were, however, generally the poorest of the community, for they were obliged to give away and distribute all the presents or plunder they received in their treaties or in war, so that they had nothing left to themselves. There was no salary nor fees to make office an object of ambition to these primitive people.

Laws. Law and justice, in our acceptation of the terms, were in a great measure unknown among them. For minor offences there seems to have been scarcely any punishment, and even infanticide passed uncensured. Though capital offences were not frequent, murders were sometimes committed, in which cases the next of kin was the avenger, provided he met the murderer within twenty-four hours after the act, when he was authorized to take his life. Otherwise the murder could be atoned for by the payment of a heavy fine of wampum, and by the relatives of the murderer giving way, or precedence, to the nearest relatives of the murdered person on meeting them. But the rights of man were considered to have been forfeited by those who were taken prisoners in war, towards whom no pity was entertained, nor, in most cases, mercy shown.

With passions uncontrolled, absolute freedom of action, and excessive thirst for excitement and display, long-continued peace was not to be expected, and a state of war became the common lot and condition of the people. The whole tendency of their education and habits led to that point, and to be a great warrior was every Indian's highest aim.

Wars.

When the resolution was one taken to attack a distant tribe, the chief to whom the command of the expedition was assigned, entered on a course of the most rigid training and preparation. He examined the condition of the arms at the disposal of his followers, and commenced a series of incantations to learn the will of the Great Spirit, who was considered to preside over war. Orations of the most inflammatory description were delivered; the wampum belt was thrown on the ground, and was lifted by him only who was judged worthy to fill the post of second in command. The leader then began his series of mystic observances. He was painted black all over, and fasted most rigidly, never eating, nor even sitting down, until after the sun had set. From time to time, however, he drank of a strong decoction of some consecrated herbs, with a view to give vivacity to his dreams, or hallucinations, which were carefully noted down and scrutinized by the sages and old men. He was next subjected to the powerful action of the vapor bath; afterwards carefully washed and painted anew in bright and varied colors, in which red was the most predominant. The great war-caldron was next brought out, and placed over a huge fire. Into that caldron every one present, as well as those allies who had consented to take part in the expedition, threw some offering. A grand feast was now prepared. The chief sang his war-song. Other noted warriors, with faces painted in a most frightful manner, followed his example, each rising in his turn from his seat, and describing the great actions which he and his ancestors had performed; all being accompanied by the war-dance, to the sound of a tom-tom, or kettledrum, the only instrument of music they used.

Having now worked their passions up to the fiercest pitch, and converted themselves from men into demons, by the force of song, revelry, and rivalry, they proceeded to arm, after having passed the night in these exciting orgies; and marched forth with their Manitous, or little gods, placed in a common box as guardian spirits, occasionally yelling, as they went along, their terrific warwhoop.

BOOK. I. 1609.

Weapons.

At the epoch of which we write, the only arms with which the savage was acquainted, were bows and arrows; the heads of the latter were pointed sharp stones, fastened with resin; the war-club, the wooden spear, and a square shield which he bore on the left arm. His bowstrings were the sinews of deer, or wild hemp, and with these he took the field, trusting to numbers, ambuscades, yells, and sudden surprises, for victory over the foe.

On entering the enemy's territory, the strictest silence was observed among those who composed the war party. They crawled, rather than marched forward; jumping on trunks of trees, or proceeding through swamps and streams, they used every effort to leave no trace of their footsteps. Immediately after the break of day, they made their sudden and unexpected onslaught on the devoted tribe or village which they had come to destroy. In a moment the air was rent with the most unearthly yells. The twang of the bowstring—the whirr of the deadly arrow, followed in quick succession. The war-club was clutched; and the contest raged with all the fury of revenge and agony of despair, as if hell were suddenly opened and all its inmates let loose upon the earth. But the duration of these contests was, fortunately, as short as they were desperate. The vanquished were either taken alive, or, if slain, the victor placed his foot on the neck of his fallen enemy, and twisting a hand in his hair, drew forth his rude-fashioned knife, and with one sweep detached the scalp from the skull, and lodged it in a bag, the receptacle of these bloody testimonials of his still more bloody triumphs.

Prisoners.

The campaign terminated, the conquerors turned their steps homeward, with their prisoners, sending forward a messenger to announce to their friends the intelligence of their approaching return. In the mean time they engraved on some tree, in the neighborhood, the result of their enterprise. After their prisoners were secured, they did not subject them immediately to ill-treatment, nor if a woman were among the captives, did they offer any violence to her chastity. Their male prisoners were reserved for more exquisite torture. They were led through all the villages of their allies, or subjects, which lay near the road, the inmates of which were drawn up in two lines, through which the captives were forced, stark naked, to run the gauntlet. On this occasion they were exposed to every indignity, contumely, and assault, the women exhibiting even more ferocity than the men. The same sad reception awaited the captives at their journey's end, at which they often arrived beaten, bruised, and bloody; more dead than alive. If they, or any among them, were accepted by those who had lost any of their relatives in that or any former campaign, well: their sorrows were terminated. From that moment they were as one of the tribe; their wounds dressed, the finest clothing furnished them, and they became absolutely free, enjoying all the privileges of the person in whose stead they were adopted, save that they could no more return to their own country. If a young man or boy were adopted, all the other young men called him father; so that often a man of thirty was heard calling a boy of fifteen by that venerable appellation.

Woe awaited the unfortunate wretch who was rejected by all—who had none to adopt him. He was often kept for weeks, fed on the coarsest fare, and subjected to every ill usage, until at length, the council having determined on his fate, all the furies of vengeance were let loose on him, and his life was taken amid the most appalling tortures; which, however, he usually met with unflinching firmness. Tied to the stake, he chanted forth his death-song in triumphant tones, and proclaimed the joy with which he went to the land of souls to meet the embraces of his brave ancestors, who had taught him the great lessons of courage in fight and endurance under suffering. He recounted the glorious exploits of his life, and taunted his torturers by recapitulating the numbers of their tribe whom he had slain with his own hand. He flung back in their teeth his unextinguishable hate; and while the brand, the hatchet, and every engine of torture were applied, while his nails were torn from his fingers, and his flesh lacerated with red-hot pincers, or gashed with other weapons, or his bowels torn from his mangled body, he laughed at the feeble fury of his executioners, and expired, at length, overpowered, but not conquered, mocking and defying still, even in death, his savage and cruel tormentors.

War had its term like every other calamity, and a desire for

BOOK I. 1609.

Peace.

tranquillity usually followed these ebullitions of phrensy, as the sunny calm succeeds the desolating storm. On these occasions, the nation which sought for peace usually sent some individuals or chiefs of note to make overtures. Before these was borne the great calumet of peace, which, like the modern flag of truce, had a sacred character, and ensured security to the ambassadors, who were bearers, also, on these occasions, of belts of wampum, as presents in expiation of wrongs inflicted, or expositions of proposals which were to be submitted. In the centre of a great council assembled to receive this embassy, the ambassador, in a set, yet eloquent speech, submitted and supported his proposals, speaking in the name of his tribe and all their allies. "Lend me your ear," was the language of one of the ambassadors from the Five Nations, on an occasion similar to the one we are now referring to, "for I am the mouth of all my country; you hear all the Iroquois when you hear my word." Each proposition of these discourses was followed by laying down a belt of wampum, and if the proffered presents were accepted, similar presents were returned in exchange; the calumet was smoked; the contract sealed, and peace ratified by a solemn burial of the hatchet.

Wampum.

No article discovered among the savage races has ever obtained so universal a use as wampum, as it was termed by the English, or "seewan," as it was called by the Dutch. On the banks of the Hudson, on the shores of the Mississippi, and even on the distant borders of the river Niger, in western Africa, the disposition or custom of using shells as a circulating medium is found to have been equally common. The Indian tribes of New Netherland were unacquainted with gold or silver. They took the great conques and mussel shells which were cast on shore by the sea. From the inside of the stem of the former they manufactured a small smooth white bead which they perforated; and from the inside purple face of the latter they made also beads, in shape like a straw, one third of an inch long, which they bored longitudinally. These they strung on hempen thread, or on the dried sinews of beasts, and wove them afterwards into strips as broad as one's hand and about two feet long, which were then called belts of wampum. The black or purple was twice the value of the white.

"They value these little bones," says the Rev. Dr. Megapoensis, "as highly as many Christians do gold, silver, or pearls; valuing our money no better than they do iron." This minister once showed an Indian chief a rix-dollar. The sachem asked how much it was worth among Christians; when told, he laughed heartily, and said, "we must be great fools to value a piece of iron so highly, for if he had such money he should throw it in the river." CHAP. III. 1609.

This wampum, or seewan, constituted not only the money of the Indians, it served likewise as an ornament to their persons, and distinguished the rich from the poor, the proud from the humble. It was a tribute from the conquered to the conqueror. It ratified treaties, confirmed alliances, sealed friendships, cemented peace, and satisfied for murders committed; for the wampum belt washed away the memories of all blood that had been shed, and of all injuries that had been inflicted.[1]

Burials.

The dead, among these primitive people, were highly honored. The body of the deceased, after having been watched and bewailed for several days, was conducted, dressed in all its finery, to the place of interment, where it was fixed in a sitting posture on a stone, or block of wood, near which they placed a pot, a kettle, spoon or plate, with a trifle of money, and some provisions, which were considered necessary for the journey to the land of souls. The body was then surrounded with wood, or bark, to keep the soil from caving in; a large pile of earth, stone, or wood, was laid over the tomb, around which a number of palisades were also erected to protect the ground from violence, as these burial-places were considered

[1] Wampum continued to constitute the common currency of this country long after it ceased to belong to the Dutch. In 1673, there was, according to Dr. Miller, little or no certain coin in the government. Wampum passed for current payment in all cases. Six white and three black beads for a penny; and three times so much was the value of silver. The schoolmaster in Flatbush was paid his salary, in 1683, in wheat, "wampum value;" he was bound to provide a basin of water for the purpose of baptism, for which he received from the parents or sponsors twelve styvers, "in wampum," for every baptism. Ten years afterwards, in 1693, the ferriage for each single person from New York to Brooklyn was eight styvers in wampum, or a silver two-pence. "Cowries," a species of Indian shell, are used as money, at the present day, in the interior of Western Africa.

BOOK I. 1609. objects of peculiar veneration. At stated times the nearest relatives of the deceased gave vent, in wild howlings, to their renewed grief. The women painted their faces of a black color, shaved their hair in token of their sorrow, and burnt it on the grave of the dead,—especially if he had been a relative, or had been slain in battle. Once departed, the name of the deceased disappeared forever from among his tribe, and had no longer a place among men. But the strongest attachment to the bones and ashes of their fathers still remained; and when calamity, or dire necessity, forced them to quit their native soil, they were sure to convey along with them, if possible, these mouldering relics of their sires.

Religion. The notions entertained by the Indians of a future state, and of a Supreme and Almighty Creator, were, notwithstanding, crude and thoroughly carnal. To all systems of religion they were entire strangers, worshipping no Supreme Being. They, however, acknowledged the existence of a God in heaven from all eternity; but who, they alleged, was so engaged with the society of a beautiful female, that he took no note of the occurrences of this world. The principal worship was that of the Evil One. Of him they entertained great dread; and to him, when sick, or unsuccessful in war or the chase, they offered sacrifices. But of the Supreme Creator of all things, of whom Europeans spoke to them, they had no conception. "We know not that God," said they, when reasoned with; "we have never seen him; we know not who he is. We regard the sun and the moon much more than all your Gods, for they warm the earth; they cause the fruits thereof to grow." Who it was that created the sun and the moon, they stopped not to inquire—they endeavored not to comprehend.

Manittous. Apart from the Supreme Being, they believed in a multitude of minor spirits or tutelary guardians, and supposed that all animated creatures—whether human beings or wild animals, the elements, and even the plants—had their good spirits to watch over them. This spirit was the Indian's Manittou, who protected him from his infancy to his death. It was represented by the head of a man carved in miniature on a stick. Every Indian had one or more of these, which he carried

CHAP. III. 1609.

around his neck in a bag, or suspended on a string, and to these they addressed themselves on all important occasions, on a voyage, on the approach of a storm, intrusting to them even the guardianship of their camp during the night preparatory to engaging in an attack on an enemy's quarters.[1]

Immortality of the soul.

Yet they acknowledged, with all this, a distinction between the body and soul, believing the latter to be immortal, and to go, if good in this life, when the body ceased to live, to a place towards the south, where the climate was so fine that it had no need of covering there, for the air would be temperate, and the heat not over troublesome; where abundance of every good thing would be to be had without the labor of production; while, on the other hand, the souls of the wicked would be driven to another place, where they never should enjoy rest, contentment, or peace. With these impressions, a belief in ghosts easily followed, and was so general, that the moanings of the winds at night through the trees of the surrounding forest, or the howlings of the wild animals in the wilderness, were believed to be the lamentations of the spirits of the wicked, condemned to wander thus abroad without shelter or repose.

Superstitions.

Superstition, twin sister of ignorance, held them, also, in strongest bondage, and one of their most common operations was to hunt or drive the devil from among them, when they were more than usually unfortunate in war or hunting, or when about to enter on a new expedition. For this purpose they assembled in the afternoon, towards sundown, to powow, as it was termed, when they strove, by all sorts of harlequinades, to charm his satanic majesty. They commenced by jumping, bellowing, and grinning, as if possessed. Large fires were kindled, around and over which they danced; rolling, tumbling, bending, and making the most violent contortions, until the perspiration burst from every pore. Their behavior on these occasions would appal a stranger, for at once, and suddenly, all the devil drivers would unite in rolling, howling, tumbling, and clanging all sorts of hideous noises, until, as they said, some beast would appear to them, whose shape the devil would assume "for the nonce." If this beast were a

[1] Charlevoix, Journal, 236.

BOOK I. 1609. ravenous animal, they considered it a bad omen; if a harmless one, the sign was propitious. They conceived next that this animal replied to their questions; the answers they interpreted according to their fancy. The presence of Christians, on these occasions, marred the plot, and the devil, they said, would not on that account be forthcoming.

Creation of the world. Their opinions of the creation of this world were in keeping with their ideas of a future state, and equally vague. They imagined that a pregnant woman fell from heaven, and having got on the back of a tortoise, scraped the earth together from the bottom of the waters, until finally this globe became formed. From this female sprung, according to them, all sorts of animals; after which, the creation having been completed, the woman again reascended into heaven. They believed in more worlds than one, and that the Europeans came from another and more distant world.

Medicine men. All these crude and confused opinions were considerably fostered and encouraged by a class of persons among them, called medicine-men, or sorcerers, who lived by, and throve upon, the ignorance and simplicity of their dupes, and whose influence was almost unbounded among their tribe. For they pretended not only to divine the future, to expound the troubled and undigested dreams of the hunter and warrior, but to heal the wounds and diseases which these wild men received in their expeditions in search of glory or of food. Their medical or surgical skill was, however, of the humblest sort. The gum of the pine-tree furnished them with a ready application for wounds of all descriptions. Rheumatic pains or inflammatory diseases were subjected to the relaxing power of the vapor bath, with which were combined scarifications of the painful parts. From the vapor bath, the Indian medicine-man, the original Presnitz and first hydropath of this continent, flung his patient, all teeming with perspiration, into the nearest pond or river, and by this practice succeeded in many cases in restoring health. But should the disease exceed his skill, he immediately ascribed it to the secret agency of malignant spirits. He then changed his character. No longer a physician, he became a magician. He sung and danced around his patient, invoking his god with loud cries. He felt all over the sick man's body for the enchanted spot; rushed upon it like a madman; tore it with his teeth, often pretending to show a small bone, or other object that he had extracted, and in which the evil one had been seated. The process was repeated the next day, with increased violence, or the unfortunate patient was surrounded with men of straw, wearing wooden masks, all of the most frightful shapes, in the hope of scaring away the mysterious tormentor; or a painted image was made, which the medicine-man pierced with an arrow, pretending to vanquish the foul fiend thereby. Various other mummeries, each more absurd than the other, were had recourse to, in the midst of which the sick man expired, leaving the confidence of the people in their mighty medicine-man equally strong and unshaken. It is not strange that in such a state of society thousands were swept away on the visitation of any epidemic, or plague, which communications with Europeans afterwards might have introduced among them, the ravages of which their own ignorance and superstition only augmented in a tenfold degree.

Amusements.

The Indian life was not, however, a ceaseless round of toil and suffering. These people had their hours of relaxation, their seasons of amusement, as well as our more civilized nations; and at these times they, no doubt, enjoyed themselves with as much zest as the most polished circles.

Their favorite enjoyments were smoking, singing, and dancing. The first, however, was of a serious occupation rather than a light amusement. With it they opened their great councils; with it they closed their most important deliberations, for on every matter of weight the pipe was introduced, the calumet went round. Their music was of the simplest kind; their songs generally were extemporaneous histories of their own exploits in hunting or in war; or sometimes the praises of some ferocious animal which they had overcome. Their dances were of various kinds. They had the war-dance, the calumet or peace dance, the marriage-dance, and the mystic dance carried on by their jugglers, accompanied by the most gross superstitions. In the last dance, the devil was said always to perform a part.

Games

Their games were many, but partook rather of a gambling,

BOOK I. 1609. than a light character, and were usually preceded, like their war and hunting expeditions, by a course of fasting, dreaming, and other propitiatory devotions. The game of the bone resembled that of throwing dice, with this distinction, that the "bones" were thrown in the air instead of on a table, as among modern gamblers. Considerable excitement accompanied this game, and men have been known, as in our day, to stake and lose all they were worth on this chance hazard. The grand festival of dreams was, like the carnival of the European continent, an unbridled license from all decorum and rule. It continued for fifteen days, during which they ran about, frightfully disguised, committing every extravagance. He who met another, demanded an explanation of his dream, and, if not satisfied, he threw cold water, hot ashes, or dirt on the guesser, or rushing into his hut, broke and destroyed his furniture. Sometimes occasion was taken to give vent in this way to an old grudge. The moment the term of the feast had expired, order was re-established by a general feast, when all damages were scrupulously indemnified.

Such was the race which had possession of the continent of North America when first visited by the Half-Moon; such were their manners, habits, and customs. On a close and calm review of these, we cannot be surprised to find that the Indians steadily lost ground, from the moment they came into contact with the more civilized European, until at length they, as it were, entirely disappeared from our sight. They carried within themselves the seeds of their own destruction. Either totally ignorant of the arts of peace, or addicted excessively to the destructive pursuits of war, they were without resources to fall back upon, to protect their race from the superior knowledge, address, and cunning of the white man, whose energy, ambition, and avarice were not to be contented nor controlled, until he became exclusive ruler of the New World.

CHAPTER IV.

Truce between the Dutch and Spaniards—Crisis favorable for Hudson's discovery—Private adventurers resolve to send a ship to the Great River—Erect forts thereupon—Establishment on the island of Manhattan under Hendrick Corstiaensen—Visited by Captain Argal, and obliged to acknowledge its dependence on the crown of England—States General grant exclusive rights to all who discover new countries—Edict of 27th March, 1614—Dutch send Adriaen Block, Hendrick Corstiaensen, and Cornelis Jacobsen Mey, with five ships, in search of new lands—They proceed to the mouth of the Great River of the Manhattans—Block's vessel burnt—builds the Restless—Explores the East River—Discovers the Freshwater River, &c.—Passes through the Sound and meets Corstiaensen—Returns home—Progress of Mey—His discoveries—Captain Hendrickson continues to explore the country in the Restless—Reports of discoveries laid before the States General—The country acquires, for the first time, the name of New Netherland—Charter or grant of October, 1614, to United New Netherland Company—Revier van den Vorst Mauritius—Forts erected at each extremity thereof—Dutch drive an active trade among the Indians—Captain Hendrickson returns to Holland—His report—Expiration of the charter of Oct. 1614—Fort removed from Castle Island to the Noordtman's Kill—Treaty of the Dutch with the Five Nations—Causes leading thereto, and importance thereof.

CHAP. IV. 1609.

THE gallant and enterprising people under whose auspices Hudson had achieved his brilliant discovery, had just emerged from a long, bloody, but glorious contest for freedom, which they had waged with dogged determination against Spain since 1566. Pursuing their tyrants into the remotest recesses of their extensive possessions, they soon made themselves felt wherever they appeared, and finally struck such a fearful blow at the maritime preponderance of the enemy, by the victory gained in the year 1608 over the Spanish fleet, by Jacob Heemskirk, (the bold navigator who had wintered, as we have already mentioned, at Nova Zembla,) that the Spaniards readily concluded a truce, in the course of the following year, with the Dutch, whereby the independence of the latter was virtually, if not formally acknowledged.

It was at this crisis, when peace had at length returned, after an absence of more than forty years, and when numbers of people must, by the transition, have found themselves de-

BOOK I. 1609. prived of their accustomed active employment, and habitual excitement, that the intelligence of Hudson's discovery broke on the public, affording to private adventure a new field for the exercise of those energies which had hitherto been absorbed by the war, and which now would naturally seek new fields for the employment of its capital.

The commodities which abounded among the natives of the newly discovered countries, were objects of great demand in Europe. The furs that the rigors of the northern climate rendered indispensable to the inhabitants of Holland, and which they had hitherto obtained through Russian and other traders, were to be had now from the Indians in exchange for
1610. the veriest baubles and coarsest goods. Stimulated by these considerations, and by the hope of profitable returns, a vessel was dispatched by some Amsterdam merchants, freighted with a variety of goods, to the Manhattans, in the course of the following year.[1]

1611. The success of this venture seems to have given increased stimulus to the spirit of enterprise. New discoveries were projected; licenses were granted by the States General, on
Feb. 21. recommendation of the Admiralty, to two ships, the Little Fox, and Little Crane, ostensibly to look again for a
Sept. 7. northerly passage to China; and the cities of Amsterdam, Rotterdam, Hoorn, and Enckhuyzen, as well as several private merchants and citizens, applied for information to the States of Holland and West Friesland, relative to a certain newly discovered navigable river, and the proper course to be
1612. steered in proceeding thither.[2] These ships proceeded, on procuring the requisite information, to that quarter early in the ensuing spring; and of so much importance was the
1613. country now considered, that the traders erected and garrisoned one or two small forts on the river, for the protection of the

[1] Alb. Rec. xxiv., 167; Hol. Doc. i., 211; De Laet; Lambrechtsen; Moulton, 337; Heckewelder. Mr. Gallatin states in his Synopsis of the Indian Tribes, p. 41, on the testimony of the Rev. Mr. Heckewelder, that the Dutch made their first settlement on the shore opposite New York island, about the year 1610. All this, however, rests on mere tradition, and may be confounded with the visit paid the Raritans in 1609.

[2] Hol. Doc. i., 12, 13, 14.

fur-trade, which the new-comers began to drive with the Indians.[1] CHAP. IV.

The favorable position of the island of Manhattan for commerce was easily perceived by the Europeans from the first, and it soon became the head-quarters of the traders. Their establishment in that locality consisted now of four houses, under the superintendence of Hendrick Corstiaensen, who, by means of his trading-boats, visited every creek, inlet, and bay in the neighborhood, where an Indian settlement was to be found, and thus secured for his employers the furs and other valuable produce of the country.

But the growing prosperity of the infant post was now fated to experience an unexpected check. Capt. Argal, of Virginia, returning in the month of November of this year from a seemingly predatory visit to a settlement which the French had made at Port Royal, in Acadia, touched at the island of Manhattans, with a view, it is said, of looking after a grant of land which he had obtained there from the Virginia Company, and forced Corstiaensen to submit himself and his plantation to the king of England, and to the governor of Virginia under him, and to agree to pay tribute in token of his dependence on the English crown.[2]

Whether the merchants in Holland, who had thus far traded to the Manhattans, were alarmed by the intelligence of this threatening visit of the English commander, or anxious to secure to themselves the monopoly of a commerce the value of which they could now, in some manner, calculate, cannot be well known; but active steps were taken, early in the next year, to obtain an exclusive right to the trade of those distant 1614.
countries. Petitions were accordingly presented to the States March
of Holland and West Friesland, praying that the States Gen- 20.

Oock mede onder het oppergebeit van Uwe Hooge Moogende, alvoor den jaar 1614, daar een ofte tweede fortieren syn geleght, en met volck versien tot beschermingе van denzelven handel. Memorial of West India Comp., Hol. doc. ii., 138.

[2] Heylen's Cosmography, anno 1669, b. iv., 96; London documents; Beauchamp Plantagenet's New Albion; Burke's Virginia, 173; Stith's Virg., 133; Belknap's America, 45. A very interesting and valuable paper, written by the Hon. Mr. Folsom, on Argal's incursion, will be found in N. Y. Hist. Soc. Coll., new series, i., 333.

BOOK I. 1614. March 27.

eral be recommended to pass an ordinance conferring on those who may discover new lands the exclusive privilege of making six voyages thither. In compliance with this request, the following Octroy was formally passed, a few days after:

"THE STATES GENERAL of the United Netherlands. To all those to whom these presents shall come, or who shall hear them read, Health! BE IT KNOWN, Whereas, We understand it would be honorable, serviceable, and profitable to this country, and for the promotion of its prosperity, as well as for the maintenance of seafaring people, that the good Inhabitants should be excited and encouraged to employ and occupy themselves in the seeking out and discovery of Courses, Havens, Countries, and Places which have not, before now, been discovered or frequented; and having been informed by some traders that they intend, through GOD's merciful help, by diligence, trouble, danger, and expense, to employ themselves thereat, as they should expect to derive handsome profit therefrom, if it pleased Us to privilege, octroy, and favor them, that they should alone resort and sail to, and frequent the Courses, Havens, Countries, and Places, by them newly found and discovered, for six voyages, in compensation for their outlays, troubles, and dangers: With interdiction to all, directly or indirectly to resort or sail to, or frequent the said Courses, Havens, Countries, or Places, before and sooner than the first discoverers and finders thereof shall have completed the aforesaid six voyages:—

"We, therefore, having duly weighed the aforesaid matter, and finding, as herebefore stated, the aforesaid undertaking to be laudable, honorable, and serviceable to the prosperity of the United Provinces, and wishing that the trial should be free and common for all and every of the Inhabitants of this country, have, and do hereby, invite all and every of the Inhabitants of the United Netherlands to the aforesaid search, and, therefore, have granted and consented, grant and consent hereby that those who any new Courses, Havens, Countries, or Places shall from now henceforward discover, they alone shall resort to the same or cause them to be frequented, for *four* voyages, without any other person having the power

to sail, resort to, or frequent, directly, or indirectly from the CHAP. IV.
United Provinces, the said newly found and discovered
Courses, Havens, Countries, or Places, before the first finder 1614.
and discoverer thereof shall himself have made, or cause to be made, *four* voyages, on pain of confiscation of the ships and goods with which he shall contrary hereto make the attempt, and a fine of Fifty Thousand Netherlands Ducats, to the profit of the aforesaid finder or discoverer. Well understanding that the finder, on completion of the first voyage, shall be holden, within fourteen days after his return from said voyage, to deliver to Us a pertinent report of the aforesaid discovery, that, his adventures thereupon being heard, it may be adjudged and declared by Us, according to circumstances and distance, within what time the aforesaid four voyages shall be fully completed.

"Provided that We, hereby, do not understand to prejudice or in any way diminish our former Grants and Concessions; And if within the same time, or in one year, one or more Companies find and discover such new Courses, Passages, Countries, Havens, or Places, the same shall enjoy together there Our Grant and Privileges; and in case any differences or questions should arise concerning these, or happen otherwise to spring, or proceed from these Our Concessions, such shall be decided by Us, according to which each shall be bound to regulate himself. And in order that these our Concessions shall be known equally by all, have We ordered that these be published and affixed at the accustomed places in the United Countries.

"Thus Given at the Assembly of the High and Mighty Lords States General, at Gravenhague, this 27th day of March, in the year 1614."[1]

Shortly after this, the attempt was again renewed to com- June 21.
plete and obtain the charter for the proposed West India Company; several references on the subject were made by the Aug. 25.
States General, but these eventuated in nothing decisive, and
the charter remained unsanctioned during the continuance of Sept.
the truce between the Spaniards and the Dutch.

[1] Groot Placaat Boek, i., 563; Aitzema, i., 154; Hol. Doc. i., 15, 17, 19; Vaderlandts. Hist. x., 69.

BOOK I. 1614.

In the mean time, the Ordinance of the 27th March excited considerable animation and activity among adventurers. A number of merchants belonging to Amsterdam and Hoorn fitted out and dispatched five ships: namely, the Little Fox, the Nightingale, the Tiger, and the Fortune, the two last under the command of Adriaen Block and Hendrick Corstiaensen, of Amsterdam. The fifth vessel was called the Fortune also; she belonged to Hoorn, and was commanded by Captain Cornelis Jacobsen Mey.

The three last-named and now well-known navigators proceeded immediately on an exploring expedition to the mouth of the Great River of the Manhattans, but Block had the misfortune, soon after his arrival there, of losing his vessel, which was accidentally burnt. The indomitable energy of the Dutch skipper, however, soon triumphed over a misfortune which would have arrested the further progress of many men of less perseverance. He forthwith set about constructing a yacht, thirty-eight feet keel, forty-four and a half feet long, and eleven and a half feet wide,[1] which, when completed, he called the "Restless," significant of his own untiring industry; or, as one would be justified in concluding, of that enterprising city which now pushes its vessels into every sea, and whose commerce is known in every land. In this craft, the first specimen of European naval architecture in these waters, Skipper Block proceeded to explore the coast east of Manhattan Island. He sailed along the East River, to which he gave the name of "The Hellegat," after a branch of the river Scheld, in East Flanders;[2] and leaving Long Island, then

[1] When his (Block's) ship was accidentally burnt in the year 1614, he constructed there a yacht with a keel 38 feet long, 44½ feet from stem to stern, and 11½ feet wide. In this vessel he sailed through Hellegat into the Great Bay, (Sound,) and explored all the places thereabout, continuing his course as far as Cape Cod, where he fell in with the ship of Hendrick Corstiaensen. He afterward returned home, and left the yacht on that coast for further use. De Laet.

[2] Though the name of Hellegat is now confined to that point where the waters of the Sound unite with those of the East River, it originally belonged to the whole of the latter, which was called by the first discoverers the Hellegat River, after the branch of the Scheld situated between the manors of Axel and Hulst, in Flanders. A description of the Dutch "Hellegat" will be found in Martinet's Beschryv. der Nederlanden, iv., 4.

called Metoac, or Sewan-hacky, "the land of shells," on the south, he discovered the Housatonick, or river of the Red Mountain, and gave to the Norwalk islands the name of the Archipelagoes. Somewhat east of these, he came to the mouth of a considerable body of water flowing from the north-west. He ascended this stream as high as 41° 48′, where he found an Indian village, or fort, belonging to the Nawaas. This body of water, which has since been known as the Connecticut, he named the Fresh River. After an intricate navigation of some leagues, he passed into what he considered a great bay, but which is now known as the Sound, and through this gained the main ocean, and thus determined, for the first time, the insular character of Long Island. Off the eastern extremity of this island, he found two smaller islands, to one of which he gave his own name; to the other, that of his brother navigator, Hendrick Corstiaensen. He next discovered the great Narragansett bay, which he called the Bay of Nassau. He thoroughly explored this sea, determined its length and breadth, and gave to its eastern entrance the name of "Anchor;" to its western, that of "Sloop" Bay. Here he had some intercourse with the natives, whom he called Nahicans, and whom he describes as shy of disposition. From this place, Block continued his course to Cape Cod, which Hudson, it will be recollected, had already called New Holland, and there fell in with Hendrick Corstiaensen's ship.

While these navigators were thus engaged at the east, Captain Cornelis Mey was actively employed in exploring the Atlantic coast farther south. After having examined the southern shore of Long Island, and determined its length, he followed the continent until he reached the great Delaware Bay, (where Hudson had anchored on his return from the Chesapeake,) two capes of which still commemorate his visit; one, the most northward, being called after him, Cape Mey; another, Cape Cornelis; while the great south cape was called Hindlopen, after one of the towns in the province of Friesland.

On the return of these expeditions to Holland, the farther and more minute examination of the coast was committed to one Captain Hendrickson, who proceeded, in the small yacht

BOOK I. 1614. which had been built by Adriaen Block, and which he had left on the coast for farther use, to the Delaware, to ascertain the nature of that country, and to open a trade with the natives there.

In the mean time, intelligence of the discoveries made by Block and his associates having been transmitted to Holland, was received there early in the autumn of this year. The united company by whom they had been employed, lost no time in taking the steps necessary to secure to themselves the exclusive trade of the countries thus explored, which was guarantied to them by the ordinance of the 27th of March. They sent deputies immediately to the Hague, who laid before the States General a report of their discoveries, as required by law, with a figurative map of the newly explored countries, which now, for the first time, obtained the name of "NEW NETHERLAND." A special grant in favor of
Oct. 11. the interested parties was forthwith accorded by their High Mightinesses, in the following terms :

"The States General of the United Netherlands to all to whom these presents shall come, greeting. WHEREAS Gerrit Jacob Witsen, former burgomaster of the city of Amsterdam, Jonas Witsen and Simon Morissen, owners of the ship called the Little Fox, (het vosje,) Captain Jan de Witt, master; Hans Hongers, Paul Pelgrom, and Lambrecht van Tweenhuysen, owners of the two ships called the Tiger and the Fortune, Captains Adriaen Block and Hendrick Corstiaensen, masters; Arnoudt van Lybergen, Wessel Schenck, Hans Claessen, and Barent Sweetsen, owners of the ship the Nightingale, (Nochtegael,) Capt. Thuys Volckertsen, merchant in the city of Amsterdam, master; and Pieter Clementsen Brouwer, Jan Clementsen Kies, and Cornelis Volkertsen, merchants in the city of Hoorn, owners of the ship the Fortune, Capt. Cornelis Jacobsen Mey, master, have united into one company, and have shown to Us, by their petition, that after great expenses and damages, by loss of ships and other perils, during the present year, they, with the abovenamed five ships, have discovered certain new lands, situated in America, between New France and Virginia, being the seacoasts between 40 and 45 degrees of latitude, and now called NEW NETHERLAND:—

"And whereas, they further represent that We did, in the month of March, publish, for the promotion and augmentation of commerce, a certain consent and grant, setting forth that whosoever should discover new havens, lands, places, or passages, should be permitted exclusively to visit and navigate the same for four voyages, without permitting any other person out of the United Netherlands to visit or frequent such newly discovered places, until the said discoverers shall have performed the four voyages, within the space of time prescribed to them for that purpose, under the penalties therein expressed, &c., and request that We should be pleased to accord to them due testimony of the aforesaid grant in the usually prescribed form: 1614.

"Wherefore, the premises having been considered, and We, in our Assembly, having communication of the pertinent report of the petitioners relative to the discoveries and finding of the said new countries between the abovenamed limits and degrees, and also of their adventures, have consented and granted, and by these presents do consent and grant, to the said petitioners, now united into one company, that they shall be permitted exclusively to visit and navigate the above described lands, situate in America, between New France and Virginia, the seacoasts of which lie between the 40th and 45th degrees of latitude, and which are now named New Netherland, as is to be seen on the figurative maps by them prepared; and to navigate, or cause to be navigated, the same for four voyages, within the period of three years, to commence from the first day of January, 1615, or sooner, without it being permitted, directly or indirectly, to any one else to sail, to frequent, or navigate, out of the United Netherlands, those newly discovered lands, havens, or places, within the space of three years, as above, on penalty of the confiscation of the vessel and cargo, besides a fine of fifty thousand Netherlands ducats, for the benefit of said discoverers. Provided, however, that by these presents We do not intend to prejudice or diminish any of our former grants and concessions; and it is also our intention that if any disputes or differences should arise from these our concessions, that they shall be decided by ourselves.

BOOK I. 1614. "WE, therefore, expressly command all governors, justices, officers, magistrates, and inhabitants, of the aforesaid United Netherlands, that they allow said company peacefully and quietly to enjoy the whole benefit of this our grant, and to interpose no difficulties or obstacles to the welfare of the same. Given at the Hague, under our seal, paraph, and the signature of our Secretary, on the 11th day of October, 1614."[1]

Having thus obtained for themselves the exclusive right to visit and trade with the countries in America, lying between the fortieth and forty-fifth degrees of north latitude, of which they strangely claimed to be the first discoverers, so shortly after Hudson's visit, the above named merchants, who now assumed the name and title of "The United NEW NETHERLAND Company," proceeded to make the arrangements necessary to draw from their new possessions the largest returns. On an island situated at the head of the navigation, near the west bank of the Manhattan River, now named De Riviere van den Vorst Mauritius, or Prince Maurice's River, and immediately below the present city of Albany, they caused a trading house to be erected, thirty-six feet long and twenty-six feet wide. Around this was raised a strong stockade, fifty feet square, which was next encircled by a moat eighteen feet wide, the whole being defended by two pieces of cannon and eleven stone guns, mounted on swivels, and garrisoned by ten or twelve men. This post was placed under the command of Jacob Jacobz Elkens, who continued here four years in the employ of this association,[2] during which time he was well liked by the natives, with whose language he was thoroughly conversant. Another fort was erected, under the superintendence of Corstiaensen, on an elevated spot on the southern ex-

[1] Hol. Doc. i., 39, 40, 42, 43, 44, 45, 46. Chalmers states, in his Political Annals, p. 569, that "the name of New Netherland" had not any existence at the time of the incorporation of the Dutch West India Company—that is, in 1621. The above charter shows into what an egregious error this author has fallen.

[2] Al de wereldt genoegh bekent is, en hy Jacob Elkens selffs ten besten wiste, als alvoor den jaar 1614 gebruyckt synde in den dienst vandegeene die doen ter tyt octroy van U. H. Mogende hadden, om deselve revier en circumjacenten alleen te bevaren. Memorial of the xix to States Gen'l. Hol. Doc. ii., 136. Alb. Rec. xxiv., 167. The dimensions of the fort on Castle Island are given in the figurative map of 1616

tremity of the island Manhattan,[1] where an insignificant establishment had already existed in 1613, as already stated. Possession was thus taken of the two most important points on the river, to which the powerful Mohawks, the fierce Manhattes, and the various other tribes in the neighborhood, brought their valuable furs to be exchanged for European trinkets and duffels. The post at the mouth of the river was, however, the traders' head-quarters. Hither annually came the ships of the New Netherland Company, and hence was annually exported whatever had been collected from the Indians, after their hunting season, at the neighboring coasts and rivers; from the distant castles of the Five Nations to the hunting-grounds of the Minquas. Considerable activity consequently prevailed among the agents and other servants of the company in pushing trade, and exploring the adjoining coasts. Runners scoured the woods, in order to become acquainted with the habits of the Indians, their manner of dealing, and to establish friendly relations with those tribes to which the Dutch were not already known. 1615.

The "Restless" having now thoroughly examined the coast as far as 38°, and penetrated up the Delaware as far as the Schuylkill, Capt. Hendricksen returned to Holland in the summer of 1616, from his second voyage, for the purpose of laying before the managers of the company the particulars of his explorations. On being presented to the States General, he made a verbal report of his adventures, on the part of his employers, who, at the same time, petitioned their High Mightinesses, setting forth that they had, at considerable expense, discovered and explored certain countries, bays, and three rivers, lying in latitude from 38° to 40°, with a small yacht called the Restless, of about eight lasts burden, commanded by Capt. Cornelis Hendricksen, Jr., of Monnichendam, which yacht the petitioners had built in the aforesaid country. They thereupon demanded, in conformity with the provisions of the ordinance of March, 1614, the exclusive privilege of trading thither. 1616. Aug. 18.

Skipper Hendricksen's report, it is to be regretted, is

[1] Moulton, 344. Heylen's Cosmography, B. iv.

BOOK I. both meager and brief. After the detail of the preceding discoveries, he described the country as well wooded with oak, pine, and hickory, which trees, he added, were in some places covered with vines. He stated that he found in those parts, male and female deer, turkeys, and partridges, and that the climate was as temperate as that of Holland; that he had traded for seal and sable skins, furs, and other peltries, with the Minquas, from whom he had ransomed three of the company's servants, who had left their employment among the Mohawks and Mohecans, having given, in exchange for them, beads, kettles, and other merchandise.[1]

Whether it was that the States General were dissatisfied with the small amount of information furnished in this report, or that other interests had by this time sprung up, which were anxious to participate in the advantages of the trade to America, or that paramount reasons of public policy influenced their deliberations, their High Mightinesses laid this application on the table, and the exclusive grant to the New Netherland Company expired, by its own limitation, on the 1st of January,
1618. 1618,[2] in the spring of which year, the breaking up of the ice, and the accompanying freshet on the River Mauritius, or North River, did so much injury to the company's fort on Castle Island, that their servants were obliged to abandon it, and to remove a few miles south, to the banks of the Tawalsontha Creek, now called the Norman's Kill. Here, on a hill, called by the Indians Tawassgunshee, they erected a new fortification, and concluded with the great Confederacy of the Five Nations a formal treaty of alliance and peace.[3]

[1] Dat hij oock met inwoonderen van Minquas gehandelt, ende haer afgekocht heeft drie seckere persoonen, wesende van den Compagnie volck, welcke drie persoonen haer hadden laaten gebruycken ten dienste van de Maquas ende Mahicans, daervoor gevende ketelen, coralen, ende coopmanschappen. Hol. Doc. i., 53, 55, 59, 60, 61.

[2] Hol. Doc., i., 62, 91.

[3] Alb. Rec., xxiv., 167. Moulton, 346. The Dutch who settled New Netherland, now New York, in 1609, entered into an alliance with the Five Nations, which continued without any breach on either side, till the English gained this country. Colden's Hist. of the Five Nations, 33. The Norman's Kill derives its present name from Andries Bratt, who was surnamed "De Noorman," or Northman, having been a native, it is said, of Denmark.

This celebrated Indian confederation was composed of five tribes, namely, the Mohawks, Oneidas, Onondagas, Cayugas, and Senecas, and generally known by the name of the Iroquois. They inhabited that country bounded on the east by the great River Manhattes and Lake Irocoisia, or Champlain; on the west by Lake Erie and the River Niagara; on the north by Lake Ontario and the Great River of Canada; and on the south by the country of the Lenni Lenape, or Delawares. When the Dutch arrived in America, the tribes composing the Five Nations were at war with the Algonquin, or Canada Indians. But the latter having formed an alliance with the French, who, some years previous to this date, had commenced the settlement of New France, as Canada was called, derived such powerful aid from the fire-arms of their European allies, that the Iroquois were defeated in almost every rencontre with their ancient enemy. Smarting under the disgrace of these unexpected repulses, the Iroquois hailed the establishment among them, now, of another European nation familiar with the use of those terrible instruments, which, almost without human intervention, scattered death wherever they were directed, and defied the war club and bow and arrow as weapons of attack or defence. Though jealous by nature, and given to suspicion, the Indians exhibited none of these feelings towards the new-comers, whose numbers were too few even to protect themselves or to inflict injury on others. On the contrary, they courted their friendship, for through them they shrewdly calculated on being placed in a condition to cope with the foe, or to obtain that bloody triumph for which they thirsted. Such were the circumstances which now led to that treaty of alliance, which, as the tradition goes, was concluded on the banks of the Norman's Kill, between the Five Nations and the Dutch.

Nothing could surpass the importance the warlike inhabitants of those ancient forests attached to the ratification of this solemn treaty. Each tribe sent its chief as its ambassador to represent it on this occasion. The neighboring tribes—the Lenni Lenape and Mohegans—were invited to attend; and there in the presence of the earth, their common mother—of the sun, which shed its genial heat on all alike—by the mur-

BOOK I. 1618. murs of that romantic stream, whose waters had been made to flow by their common Maker from all time, was the belt of peace held fast by the Dutch and their aboriginal allies, in token of their eternal union. There was the calumet smoked, and the hatchet buried, while the Dutch traders declared that they should forthwith erect a church over that weapon of war, so that it could no more be exhumed without overturning the sacred edifice, and whoever dared do that should incur the resentment of the white men. By this treaty the Dutch secured for themselves the quiet possession of the Indian trade, and the Five Nations obtained the means to assert that ascendency which they ever after maintained over the other native tribes, and to inspire terror far and near among the other savages of North America.[1]

[1] Moulton, 346, 347.

CHAPTER V.

The New Netherland Company petition for renewal of their charter—The ship Scheld sent to Manhattes—That country becomes more generally known—Attention of the Puritans directed thither—Review of the causes which drove these people to Holland—Desire to remove to America—The Rev. Mr. Robinson, their minister, intimates their wish to emigrate to New Netherland—The managers of the Dutch Trading Company lay this application before the States General and the Prince of Orange—Memorial to his Royal Highness on this occasion—Termination of the twelve years truce—Request of the New Netherland Company on behalf of the Puritans decidedly refused—Capt. Mey returns to Holland—Petitions for exclusive right to new countries he had discovered opposed—Incorporation of the Dutch West India Company.

CHAP. V. 1618.

The charter of October, 1614, having expired, the trade to the Manhattans was, in a manner, thrown open, and thus competition was again excited among all who were acquainted with its value. The New Netherland Company did not, however, abandon the advantages which their local experience and establishments gave them. They petitioned the States General (Oct. 4.) for a renewal of their charter for a few years more, or at least for permission to trade to the "Island" of New Netherland. Their High Mightinesses seemed unwilling to renew the grant. Hendrick Eelkins, Adriaen Jans Engel, and associates, "owners and partners in the New Netherland Company," sent in a memorial, therefore, a few days after, setting (Oct. 9.) forth that they had already fitted a ship named the Scheld, for a voyage to the Manhattes, and requested permission to prosecute that voyage without any opposition from any of their late partners ; this request was granted,[1] and the Scheld sailed accordingly.

Though the above company had lost, by the expiration of their charter, the exclusive privileges which they had before possessed, the original members of the association seemed still to have enjoyed, notwithstanding, exclusively the trade to New Netherland under special licenses obtained from year to year. Well acquainted now with the fertility of the soil,

[1] Hol. Doc. i. 92.

BOOK I. 1618. the mildness of the climate, and the other physical advantages of the country, many among them began to turn their attention to the colonization of those distant parts, in the hope that by the establishment of industrious settlers and well-regulated plantations, their resources might be developed; wealthy colonies founded, and a permanent market finally created for the manufactures of Fatherland. The constant resort of vessels to that quarter—the favorable reports with which they returned—had, at the same time, made the country more generally known, while causes which had been at work for half a century, brought the subject of colonizing those distant possessions so immediately before them, that those interested in New Netherland could no longer defer its consideration. These causes were the persecution of the Dissenters, or Nonconformists, by the hierarchy and government of England.

A number of these men, dissatisfied with the ritual and ceremonies of the Church of England, had renounced, in the reign of Elizabeth, all communion with the establishment, and formed themselves into a separate congregation, under the charge of one Richard Brown, an English preacher of an ancient and honorable family, from whom they derived the name of "Brownists." They were finally forced, by stringent measures enforced against them, to leave their native country, whence they proceeded to Holland, where they formed a church according to their own model. Though this church eventually disappeared, the seeds of separation which Brown had sowed in England took deep root; his followers increased, as well in numbers as in zeal, in the succeeding century and reign, and again became marks for the exercise both of kingly and episcopal oppression. Many learned ministers and their followers, professing generally the puritanical principles of Brown, were obliged to leave the kingdom and retire, some to Amsterdam, some to the Hague, and others to Leyden. The congregation at the last-mentioned place was under the superintendence of the Rev. JOHN ROBINSON, a divine who tempered the strictness of his religious principles with more liberality towards other denominations than many others of his brethren.[1]

[1] Neal's Hist. of the Puritans, (Harpers' Ed.) 149, 242, 244.

After residing here a number of years, many causes combined CHAP. V.
to render these people dissatisfied with the country as a permanent abode. The soil they considered too marshy, and the 1618.
climate unwholesome. They felt disinclined, also, to continue under a government, where, by difference of language and habits, and by intermarriages, they might finally lose all love for and connection with their native land, and be swallowed up by, and disappear among, the subjects of a foreign nation. To perpetuate their race, to enlarge the British dominions, and to spread the glad tidings of the gospel, the younger portion of Mr. Robinson's congregation determined to remove beyond the seas, unto some country not already inhabited, there to enjoy freedom of conscience and civil liberty, after their own peculiar opinions. Moved by these considerations, they had already made frequent applications to the authorities in England for permission to emigrate to some part of America bordering on Virginia, with the view of planting a new colony there. By the interference of powerful friends they obtained such a promise as encouraged them to proceed in their project.[1] But 1619.
after a lapse of some years, fresh obstacles arose, so disheartening, that Mr. Robinson now caused an intimation to be conveyed to the Dutch Company engaged in trading to New Netherland, of the disposition felt by several of his flock to proceed, under certain conditions, to the last-mentioned country.

The managers of that company were too shrewd not to per- 1620.
ceive at once that an opportunity for promoting the settlement of New Netherland here offered itself, which it would be unwise not to embrace. They, therefore, took the earliest occasion to call the attention of the authorities of the United Provinces to the subject; and with that view addressed a memo- Feb.
rial to their High Mightinesses the States General, and a most 12.
respectful letter to the Prince of Orange.

Having detailed, in the latter communication, the fact that they had previously traded for several years to New Netherland, under the charter of 1614, and that another free city proposed now to send two ships to that country for trading purposes

[1] Hubbard's Hist. New England, (Mass. Hist. Soc. Col. vii.) 42, 44, 45, 46, 47.

BOOK I. 1620. also, they advert, in favorable terms, to the proposition which they had received from the Rev. Mr. Robinson, and to the necessity of colonizing the island Manhattan. "It now happens," say they, "that there resides at Leyden an English clergyman, well versed in the Dutch language, who is favorably inclined to go and dwell there. Your petitioners are assured that he knows over four hundred families, who, provided they were defended and secured there by the authority of your Royal Highness, and that of the High and Mighty Lords States General, from all violence on the part of other potentates, would depart thither with him, from this country, and from England, to plant, forthwith, everywhere there the true and pure Christian religion; to instruct the Indians of those countries in the true doctrine; to bring them to the Christian belief; and, likewise, through the grace of the Lord, and for the greater honor of the rulers of this land, to people all that region under a new dispensation; all under the order and command of your Princely Highness, and of the High and Mighty Lords States General.

"Your petitioners have also learned that His Britannic Majesty is inclined to people the aforesaid lands with Englishmen; to destroy your petitioners' possessions and discoveries, and also to deprive this State of its right to these lands, while the ships belonging to this country which are there during the whole of the present year, will apparently and probably be surprised by the English."

The petitioners concluded by requesting a favorable consideration for their request; so that, for the preservation of these lands in righteousness, the aforesaid clergyman and families might be taken under the protection of the United Provinces, and two ships-of-war be provisionally furnished for the security of those transatlantic possessions, which will, they allege, be of considerable importance, on account of the vast quantity of timber fit for ship-building and other purposes which they could supply, "when the West India Company would be formed."[1]

The Prince of Orange and the States General were now,

[1] Hol. Doc. i. 94, 95, 96, 97, 98.

however, absorbed in the consideration of matters of much greater moment, and of vastly greater importance, than the colonization of a distant and uninhabited island, or the struggles for rights of conscience of a few obscure Englishmen, who, however favorably esteemed and spoken of by the magistracy and people, generally, who knew them, were looked upon in Holland with a jealous eye by the established clergy, who regarded them as a set of discontented, factious, and conceited men, with whom it would be safest to have no connection.[1]

CHAP. V. 1620.

The twelve years' truce which had been agreed upon between the Seven United Provinces and Spain, was now about to terminate. The Archdukes, laboring under a delusion common to those who have forever lost the affections of their subjects whose confidence they have abused, sent a proposition to the States General again to return to their allegiance and subjection under the Spanish crown, with an assurance that should that proposition be accepted, it would be ratified not only by the Archdukes, but, also, by the Spanish monarch. But this insulting offer was scornfully rejected, and both parties prepared for the renewal of hostilities.[2] To aid in carrying out that war, offensive and defensive, by which it was proposed to prostrate a proud enemy, and to secure at the same time the permanent independence of the nation, the States General determined to concentrate the energies and capital of the various merchants who were now engaged in the American and West Indian trade, by erecting an armed mercantile association, on the plan of the East India Company, which would be invested exclusively with the commerce and territory of the New World, with power to erect fortifications, plant settlements, prosecute trade, and assist in crushing piracy and the common enemy. They, therefore, decidedly refused to entertain the petition of the New Netherland Company, or to grant the ships of war as requested.[3]

April 11.

Thus was changed the destination of that small band of men, who, in the midst of the rigors of a northern winter, on

[1] Neal's Hist. of the Puritans, [Harpers' Ed.,] 242 ; note.
[2] Vaderlandsche Hist. x., 419, 420.
[3] Hol. Doc. i., 103.

BOOK I. 1620. the rocky and inhospitable shores of Cape Cod, laid the foundations, this year, of a Republic, which, in the Providence of Almighty God, was to serve, in after ages, as an asylum for the oppressed of every land, and to vindicate, practically and triumphantly, man's fitness for self-government, unembarrassed by privileged peers or hereditary monarchs.[1]

Dutch navigators were, in the mean time, actively engaged exploring the coasts and rivers of New Netherland. Among these none seem to have been more enterprising than Captain Cornelis Jacobsen Mey, of Hoorn, who returned this summer to Holland with his ship, the Glad-Tidings, [de Blyde Boodschap,] and sent in a memorial to the States General, setting forth that he had discovered new, populous, and fruitful countries, and demanding a special grant to trade exclusively thither for four voyages, in accordance with the charter of March, 1614. But against this Henry Eelkins, Adriaen Jansen Engel, and partners, made a strong remonstrance. They alleged that they had, already, discovered from latitude 35° to 50°; that the exclusive trade to those parts belonged, consequently, to them; and they concluded by urging the rejection of Mey's petition, and that they be authorized to continue the trade.

Aug. 29.

[1] Some historians represent that "the Pilgrims" were taken against their will to New Plymouth, by the treachery of the captain of the Mayflower, who, they assert, was bribed by the Dutch to land them at a distance from the Hudson River. This has been shown, over and over again, to have been a calumny, and if any farther evidence were requisite, it is now furnished, of a most conclusive nature, by the petition in behalf of the Rev. Mr. Robinson's congregation, of Feb., 1620, and the rejection of its prayer by their High Mightinesses. That the Dutch were anxious to secure the settlement of the Pilgrims under them, is freely admitted by the latter. Gov. Bradford, in his Hist. of the Plymouth Colony, acknowledges it, and adds, that the Dutch "for that end made them large offers." Winslow corroborates this in his "Brief Narrative," and adds, that the Dutch "would have freely transported us [to Hudson River], and furnished every family with cattle," &c. Young's Chron. of the Pilg., 42, 385. The whole of this evidence satisfactorily establishes the good-will of the Dutch people towards the English; while the determination of the States General proves that there was no encouragement held out by the Dutch government to them to induce them to settle in their American possessions. On the contrary, having formally rejected their petition, they thereby secured themselves against all suspicion of dealing unfairly by those who afterwards landed at Cape Cod. It is to be hoped, therefore, that, even for the credit of the Pilgrims, the idle tale will not be repeated.

CHAP. V. 1620.

The States General recommended both these parties to meet and to arrange amicably their conflicting pretensions, but, for reasons already detailed, their High Mightinesses refused eventually to grant the privileges which had been demanded, and afterwards supplanted all private adventurers to those parts by the incorporation, in the course of the next year, of that great armed commercial association, the DUTCH WEST INDIA COMPANY.[1] Nov. 6

[1] Hol. Doc., i., 104, 105, 106.

BOOK II.

FROM THE INCORPORATION OF THE DUTCH WEST INDIA COMPANY, TO THE OPENING OF THE FUR, OR INDIAN TRADE TO THE INHABITANTS OF NEW NETHERLAND.

1621—1638.

CHAPTER I.

Charter of West India Company—Its various provisions—Comparison between it and those granted to other Companies for making settlements in America —Company did not commence operations immediately—Various vessels licensed to proceed, meanwhile, to New Netherland—Excite considerable jealousy among the English interested in planting Virginia and New England, who remonstrate to King James against the Dutch—English Ambassador at the Hague urges the States General to stay the departure of the Dutch ships—Their High Mightinesses disclaim all knowledge of the enterprise—English Ambassador's explanation thereupon to King James—Dutch vessels proceed, notwithstanding, on their voyage—Several families desire to move to New Netherland—States General refer the matter to the West India Company—They approve of the design, but suggest that its execution be postponed until a Director-General be appointed.

BOOK II. 1621. June 3.

THE charter establishing the Dutch West India Company bears date the third of June, 1621. It was modelled after that granted in the beginning of the seventeenth century to the celebrated East India Company, with which body it was designed to co-operate in extending national commerce, in promoting colonization, in crushing piracy, but, above all, in humbling the pride and might of Spain.

The central power of this vast association was divided, for the more efficient exercise of its functions, among five branches or chambers, established in the different cities of the Netherlands, the managers of which were styled Lords Directors. Of these, that of Amsterdam was the principal, and to this

BOOK II. 1621. was intrusted the management of the affairs of New Netherland The general supervision and government of the company were, however, lodged in a board or assembly of NINETEEN delegates; eight (increased in 1629 to nine) of whom were from the chamber at Amsterdam; four from Zealand; two from Meuze; and one from each of the chambers at Friesland, the North Department, and Groeningen. The nineteenth was appointed by their High Mightinesses the States General.

Apart from the exclusive trade of the coast of Africa, from the tropic of Cancer to the Cape of Good Hope, and of the coast of America, from the Straits of Magellan to the extreme north, this company was authorized to form alliances with the chiefs of the native Indian tribes, and obligated to advance the settlement of their possessions, encourage population, and do every thing that might promote the interests of those fertile countries, and increase trade. To protect their commerce and dependencies, they were empowered to erect forts and fortifications; to administer justice and preserve order; maintain police and exercise the government generally of their transmarine affairs; declare war and make peace, with the consent of the States General; and with their approbation, appoint a governor, or director-general, and all other officers, civil, military, judicial, and executive, who were bound to swear allegiance to their High Mightinesses, as well as to the company. The director-general and his council were invested with all powers, judicial, legislative, and executive, subject, some supposed, to appeal to Holland; but the will of the company, expressed in their instructions, or declared in their marine or military ordinances, was to be the law in New Netherland, excepting in cases not especially provided for, when the Roman law, the imperial statutes of Charles V., the edicts, resolutions, and customs of Fatherland, were to be received as the paramount rule of action.[1]

[1] Droit Belgique, observé dans les dix-sept Provinces des Pays-Bas et Liége, est composé, 1, des édits, placards, ordonnances, et déclarations des souverains; 2, des coutumes particulières des villes et territoires; 3, des usages généraux de chaque province; 4, du droit Romain; 5, des statuts et réglemens politiques des villes et autres communautés séculières; 6, des arrêts des cours souverains;

CHAP. I. 1621.

The States General engaged, among other things, to secure to the company freedom of navigation and traffic within the prescribed limits, and to assist them with a million of guilders, equal to nearly half a million of dollars; and in case peace should be disturbed, with sixteen vessels of war and four yachts, fully armed and equipped; the former to be at least of three hundred, and the latter of eighty tons burden. But these vessels were to be maintained at the expense of the company, which was to furnish, unconditionally, sixteen ships and fourteen yachts, of like tonnage, for the defence of trade and purposes of war, which, with all merchant vessels, were to be commanded by an admiral appointed and instructed by their High Mightinesses.[1]

Though the provisions of this charter contained nothing favorable to freedom, nor to the colonists who might happen to settle at any future time in New Netherland, it must not be concluded that the authorities from which it was derived were more unfriendly to freedom than the other European powers, who were engaged at this period in establishing plantations in America. In truth, the project, as well as the company, was one purely commercial, set on foot with the view of bringing additional resources to bear against the common enemy, Spain, and no precedents existed for charters to colonial associations more favorable than the one before us. The only settlements on the North American continent by authority of any crown, were those of Florida, Canada, and Virginia; and neither of these affords any proofs of greater liberality than that to the Dutch West India Company.

The commissions issued by France previous to, and at this

7, des sentences des juges subalternes; 8, des avis et consultations d'avocats. Il y a plusieurs coutumes particulières dans les Pays-Bas; les unes qui sont homologuées, d'autres qui ne le sont pas. Les premières, avant leur homologation, ne consistoient que dans une simple usage sujet à être contesté. Les homologations ont commencé au tems de Charles Quint. Depuis leur homologation elles ont acquis force de lois.—Encyclopédie Raisonnée, verbo "DROIT."

[1] For this charter, see Appendix A; also, De Laet, Hist. ofte Jaerlyck verhael. Aitzema, Historie i., 62; Johan Thasseus' Zeepolitie; "een seer net ende curieus Boeck," says Aitzema; Hazard's State Papers, i., 121. Groot Placaat Boek i., 566

BOOK II. 1621. period, authorized those to whom they were addressed to discover and take possession of new countries; build forts and concede lands and carry settlers thither; and conferred on the principal adventurers, whether private individuals or companies, the exclusive trade of those parts.[1] Under commissions such as these, containing no principles or privileges favorable to colonists, were founded, by companies of speculators, the cities of Quebec and Montreal.

By reference to the patent granted by Queen Elizabeth, in 1578, to Sir Humphrey Gilbert, it will be found that he was "authorized and empowered, from time to time, to correct, punish, pardon, and govern, and rule, according to his own good discretion, and to such statutes and ordinances as shall by him be devised," "as well in causes capital or criminal as civil," all such people as may thereafter inhabit the countries he may discover; such laws to be, "as near as conveniently may, agreeable to the laws and policy of England." The same power was given to Sir Walter Raleigh.[2] By the first Virginia charter, granted in 1606, each of the colonies of Virginia and Plymouth was to be governed by a council appointed by the king, according to instructions under the sign manual, subject, at the same time, to the superior direction of the company's council in England. The second charter, granted in 1609, repeated the clause of Queen Elizabeth's patent of 1578, conferring unlimited powers on the governors of the colony, who were to be appointed and removed, not by the sovereign, nor by the colonists, but by the London Company, which was also authorized to make "all manner of laws" necessary for the government of the same, and to abrogate them at pleasure. In cases where such laws were defective, the colonies were to be ruled "according to the good discretion of the company's governors," who had, moreover, the power to use and exercise law martial in case of rebellion and mutiny, which law, the

[1] Vide Commissions to the Marquis de la Roche, 12 January, 1598; to Chauvin, anno 1600; to Desmonts, 8th Nov., 1603. They may be seen in Mém. sur l'Amérique, tome iii., pp. 47, 53. See, also, Act of Incorporation of the Hundred Associates, by Richelieu, May, 1628, in Charlevoix, vol i.

[2] Hazard, State Papers, i., 26, 36.

historian says, "continued to be the common law and custom of the country down to 1619."[1]

Even as far down as 1628, the provisions of English colonial charters were not much more liberal. The charter of Massachusetts, granted by Charles I., in March of that year, seven years subsequent to that granted by the States General to the West India Company, although it gave the company in England the privilege of electing their governor, deputy governor, and other officers, carefully excluded the colonists from all such privileges; for it provided, that all the officers employed in the plantations "may by the company be empowered," in the words of Queen Elizabeth's patent to Sir H. Gilbert, granted fifty years before, "to correct, punish, pardon, and govern, and rule all subjects as may venture to the colony," according to the laws made by the association in England; and the governor and company declare, in 1629, only one year before their departure for America, that they have thought fit to settle and establish "an absolute government" at their plantations in Massachusetts Bay,[2] consisting of a governor and council; the latter composed of thirteen persons, two of whom, only, were to be elected "by the planters generally." All must admit this to have been a mockery of free institutions, or representative government.

On a review, therefore, of the patents down to 1628, granted for trading to, or settling in, America, we cannot find any more favorable to colonial liberty than that granted by the Dutch in 1621.[3] If that of Massachusetts proved eventually more favorable to the colonists, it was because the powers of that charter were exercised in the colony, and not at a distance of thousands of miles from it. Had it been otherwise, we are warranted in believing that it would have been far from promoting freedom in the plantation.

Though the West India Company obtained its charter in 1621, various circumstances prevented the commencement of operations for two years after. In the interval, however, their

[1] Chalmers, p. 39.

[2] Hazard, State Papers, i. 239, 256.

[3] Representative government was not accorded to Virginia, in 1619, by charter, but by instructions from the London Company. Chalmers, 39.

BOOK II. 1621. privileges were considerably amplified, and various amend ments and explanations introduced, in the fundamental grant.[1]

The spirit of enterprise was not suffered to lie dormant in the mean time. Merchants, and other public-spirited individuals, belonging to various parts of the United Provinces, continued to send ventures to the New World. Among the most active of these we find Hendrick Eelkens, Adriaen Jansen Engel, and Hans Joris Houten, of Amsterdam, with whose names the reader is now familiar. These gentlemen obtained Sept. 13. permission, in the fall of this year, to send their ship the White Dove, of eighty tons burden, to New Virginia, under the command of Captain Jans Houten. Dirck Volckertsen, Doctor Verus, and Doctor Carbasius, of Hoorn, Pieter Nannincks of Medenblick, Cornelis Volkertsen, and Pieter Schoder, were al- Sept. 24. lowed to send a vessel with a cargo of merchandise also to the Virginias; and Claes Jacobsen Haringcarpsel, counsellor and ancient alderman of Amsterdam, Petrus Plancius, minister of the gospel,[2] Lambrecht van Tweenhuyzen, Hans Claessen,

[1] De Laet, Hist. ofte Jaerlyck verhael van de Verrechtingen van de Geoctroye erde W. I. Compe.

[2] The Rev. PETRUS PLANCIUS, of whom mention is here made, was born at Dremontre, in Flanders, in 1552. He was educated at Honskote, but spent the greater part of his life at Amsterdam. He rendered himself celebrated in more than one respect. Having been ordained in 1577, he preached in divers parts of Brabant, by which he was exposed to great danger, owing to the high state of religious animosity in those days. He escaped being taken prisoner only by swimming the river Lys, leaving every thing behind him, especially his books, which were publicly burnt at Ypres. He was next called to Brussels, where he preached six years; but this city falling into the enemy's hands, he passed into Holland disguised as a soldier. He came in 1585 to Amsterdam, where he immediately resumed the ministry. Here he opposed Arminius and the Lutherans, and some time afterwards came out against "the Remonstrants." In 1618 he assisted at the Synod of Dordrecht, where he was chosen, with others, to superintend the translation of the Old Testament. He contributed, in the mean while, to the elucidation of geography, astronomy, navigation, and other mathematical sciences, and was one of the principal projectors of the Dutch expeditions to the East Indies. The first Dutch ship sailed thither by the aid of charts which Plancius had constructed. He likewise advised the expeditions to Nova Zembla, in the hope of discovering a nearer way to China, in which project he was very much engaged in 1608. He may be truly said to have been in this manner accessory, in an especial degree, to the discovery of the Hudson's river and New Netherland, to which we now find him sending a ven-

CHAP. I. 1621.

and company, "traders to certain countries by them discovered between Virginia and New France, situated between the latitudes of 40° and 45°, and called New Netherland, and to the adjacent territories, together with a great river lying between 38° and 40°," were licensed to send two ships, also fully freighted, one to the New Netherland, and the other to the aforesaid new river, which must doubtless be the Delaware, and to the small streams thereunto adjoining, to truck and trade with the natives of those parts. But the States General, anticipating the commencement of business by the West India Company, inserted a special proviso, in each of the abovementioned licenses, obliging the several parties interested to return on or before the next first of July, with their respective vessels and goods.[1]

This activity on the part of the Dutch excited considerable jealousy in England among those who were interested in the plantations already established in Virginia, and in the charter recently granted for the colonization of New England. The English ever maintained the right to the whole American coast, from the Spanish possessions in the south to those of the French in the north, on the triple ground of first discovery, occupation, and possession, as well as by charters and letters patent obtained from their own sovereigns. When intelligence was received that preparations were thus making in the United Provinces to send a fleet of merchant vessels to Virginia and New Netherland, the Earl of Arundel, Sir Ferdinando Gorges, and Captain Mason, active members of the Plymouth Company,[2] and Sir Samuel Argall, governor of Virginia, who had already paid a

ture in company with others. PLANCIUS died at Amsterdam on the 25th May, (N. S.) 1622, aged 70 years. He gave it in charge, on his death-bed, that his remains should not be interred in any church. He was accordingly buried in the South church-yard. There is a sketch of his life in Wagenaar's Beschryving der Stad Amsterdam, iii., 219, from which most of these particulars are taken.

[1] Hol. Doc. i., 107, 109, 111, 112, 113, 114.

[2] "Of all the persons who were concerned in the business of New England, or whose names were inserted in the grand council thereof, Sir Ferdinando Gorges and Capt. John Mason were the most active, and probably had the greatest interest therein." Hubbard, 226.

BOOK II. 1621. hostile visit to Manhattan Island, presented a remonstrance immediately to James I., complaining of such proceedings. His majesty, in consequence, directed Sir Dudley Carleton, his ambassador at the Hague, to urge upon their Lordships the States General the necessity of preventing the departure of those vessels, and to forbid their subjects to settle in that plantation. As this document contains the earliest distinct assertion by the British government of the illegality of the Dutch settlement on this continent, it is worthy of particular note.

Dec.15, O. S. "Whereas," say the Lords of the Privy Council, "his Majesty's royal predecessors have, for many years since, taken possession of the whole precinct, and inhabited some parts of the north of Virginia, by us called New England, of all which countries his Majesty hath, in like manner, some years since, by Patent, granted the quiet and full possession unto particular persons; nevertheless, wee understand that the year past the Hollanders have entered upon some part thereof, and have left a Colonie, and given new names to the several ports appertaining to that part of the country, and are now in readinesse to send for their supplie six or eight shipps: whereof his Majesty being advertised, wee have received his Royall commandment to signifie his pleasure that you should represent these things unto the States Generall in his Majesty's name, (who, *jure primæ occupationis*, hath good and sufficient title to those parts,) and require of them that as well those shipps as their further prosecution of that plantation, may be presently stayed."

1622. Feb. 5. On receipt of this dispatch, Sir Dudley Carleton proceeded to make inquiries into the subject, before he brought the matter under the notice of the States General. All he could learn, either from such merchants as he was acquainted with in Amsterdam, or from the Prince of Orange, or such of their High Mightinesses as he made inquiries of, was, that about four or five years previously, two companies of Amsterdam merchants had begun a trade to America, between the latitudes of forty and forty-five degrees, to which parts they had given, "after their manner," their own names of New Netherland, North and South sea, Texel, Vlieland, &c.; that they had since continued to send thither vessels, of sixty to eighty tons at most, to fetch furs, which was all their trade; for which purpose they have factors resident continually there, who truck with the savages; but the ambassador could not learn that the Dutch had, as yet, planted any colony there, or intended to do so. CHAP. I 1622.

In obedience, however, to the orders which he had received, he demanded an audience of the States General, to whom he presented a written memorial on the whole subject,[1] which was referred, at their request, to the deputies from Holland, who expressed a desire to inform themselves of the affair, concerning which they pretended ignorance. No further notice having been taken of the matter, Sir Dudley called the attention of their High Mightinesses again to his memorial, and requested that some order be taken upon it. Burgomaster Paauw was, therefore, directed to write to the participants in the trade to New Netherland for information. No letter in March 16.

[1] "Messieurs—J'ay reçu charge expresse du Roy mon maistre de representer a VVSS un surcroist de doleance aux affaires maritimes causé par les sujets de ces Provinces Unies, particulierement par les Hollandois, et de vous prier de sa part par vostre authorité d'y donner remede. C'est que plusieurs de ses sujets d'Angleterre, seigneurs et autres gens d'honneur et qualité, ayants desja longtemps passé prins possession de tous les precincts de Virginia, et planté leur habitations en certains endroicts du Nord quartier du dit pays, qui en a tiré le nom, [Nova Anglia,] S. M. desirant l'heureuse issue d'une si saincte et utile entreprinse qui tend a l'avancement de la Religion Chrestienne et l'accroissement du Commerce, a donné (comme il est notoire a un chacun) quelques années passées par ses lettres patentes la tranquille et pleniere possession de tout le dit pays a plusieures personnes particulieres. Quoy nonobstant, il est informé que l'année passée aucuns Hollandois ont mis pied sur quelques quartiers du dit pays, et y ont planté une Colonie, changeants les noms des ports et havres et les baptisants de nouveau a leur mode, avec intention d'y envoyer d'autres navires pour la continuation de la dite plantation, et que de faict ils ont maintenant six ou huit navires tous prests pour y faire voile. Or, S. M. ayant (jure primæ occupationis) de tiltre au dit pays non subject a contredict, m'a commandé de vous representer l'etat du dit affaire et vous requirer, en son nom, que par vostre authorité non seulement les navires desja equippez pour le dit voyage soyent arrestez, mais aussi que l'ulterieure prosequution de la dite plantation soit expressement deffendue. Ce que vous prendrez (Messieurs) s'il vous plaist en prompte deliberation, me faisant scavoir au plustot la responce que de vostre part j'en feray a Sa Majesté. Exhibé par escrit en l'assemblée des Etats G'raulx le 9$^{e.}$ de Febvier, 1622, et signé DUDLEY CARLETON." Lond Doc., i., 22, 23.

BOOK II. 1622. reply to this order has been discovered, and it is at least doubtful if any was ever returned to the British government. It has been asserted that the Dutch ambassador at London disclaimed, on the part of the States General, any such proceedings in reference to New Netherland as the Privy Council had complained of, but no document has been produced to support such an assertion.[1]

The death of King James, shortly after this correspondence, put a temporary termination to these wrangles. Carleton's representations seem to have been made rather as a protest to save British rights, than with a view to enforce them by taking possession, just then, of the territory in dispute. The Dutch ships proceeded, according to the design of the owners, on their voyage, but when the time approached to which their commission limited their absence, some of them had not yet
June 18. returned. Their owners were obliged, therefore, to petition the States General for an extension of time, and six months more were granted to them.[2]

Publications descriptive of the various plantations in North America began to emanate now from the press in Amsterdam, and plans were submitted for the removal of families to this continent. The West India Company, which was specially enjoined to promote the settlement of its transmarine possessions, had its attention called to the fulfilment of this part
April 21. of its obligations. A proposition was referred to it in the early part of this year, by the States General, to send some families to its American colonies. The company viewed the project with a favorable eye. It declared that it would be very advantageous to its interests, and promised to furnish employment to such persons as should proceed thither; but suggested, at the same time, that the matter should be postponed until the appointment of a director-general, to superintend the affairs of the country; while their High Mightinesses recommended, on their part, that the magistrates should be consulted in whatsoever should be proposed.[3]

[1] Lond. Doc. i., 15, 16, 17, 18, 19, 20, 21, 48; Hol. Doc. i., 117. Brodhead's Address before the N. Y. Hist. Soc., 24, 25, 26.

[2] Hol. Doc. i., 120.

[3] Ibid., 118, 119.

CHAPTER II.

The West India Company takes possession of New Netherland—Several settlers and servants sent out—Fort Nassau built on South River—Fort Orange on the river Mauritius—Peter Minuit, of Wesel, arrives in the country as Director-General, accompanied by a colony of Walloons—First settlement on Long Island—First white child born—Members of Minuit's council—Duties of schout-fiscaal—first schout-fiscaal—Colonial secretary—Imports and exports—Dutch purchase island of Manhattans and adjoining islands from the Indians—A blockhouse erected on Manhattan Island, and called Fort Amsterdam—Murder of an Indian by some of Minuit's servants—Trade opened with the English settlement at New Plymouth—Correspondence and intercourse with that colony—Dutch alarmed at threats thrown out by their English neighbors—Apply to directors in Holland for a military force—Charles I. extends to the ships of the West India Company the privileges conferred by the treaty of Southampton on the vessels of the States General—Progress of trade—Renewed efforts in Holland to promote the settlement of New Netherland—The assembly of the XIX. determine to establish lordships or colonies there—Heyn's victory over the Spanish silver fleet—Charter to Patroons in New Netherland.

CHAP. II. 1623. June 20.

THE West India Company having finally concluded its preparatory arrangements, and completed, with the sanction of the States General, the articles of agreement between the managers and the other adventurers,[1] lost no time in commencing operations and forming establishments in New Netherland, which was erected into a province, having been invested by their High Mightinesses with the armorial bearings of an earl.[2] The chamber of Amsterdam, to whose superintendence that extensive country was committed, having already, in the course of the preceding year, sent out some of its servants to that quarter, dispatched a ship called the "New Netherland" this season thither also, with a number of people, most of whom, however, were persons in the company's service. Captain Cornelis Jacobsen Mey and Adriaen Jorisz. Tienpont having been appointed directors of this expedition, the first-named of

[1] This agreement, as well as the names of the first directors of the company, will be found in Appendix B.

[2] Het wert een provincie genaemt, omdat het van haer Hoog Moogende met een Graeffelyck wapen is vereert. Hol. Doc. iv., 39.

BOOK II. 1623. these officers proceeded to the South or Prince Hendrick's River, on the eastern bank of which, fifteen leagues from its mouth, at a spot called by the natives Techaacho, in the vicinity of the present town of Gloucester, he erected Fort Nassau. This was the first settlement of Europeans on the Delaware.[1]

Another fortified post, called Fort Orange, was commenced on the west bank of the river Mauritius, as the North River was called, a few miles north of the redoubt which had been erected in 1618 on Tawalsontha creek, and thirty-six (Dutch) miles from the island of Manhattans.

1624. PETER MINUIT, or Minnewit, of Wesel, in the kingdom of Westphalia, having been appointed director of New Netherland, arrived in that country in the course of this year. Several families of Walloons, inhabitants of the frontier between Belgium and France, having been desirous to emigrate to America, applied, in the early part of 1622, to Sir Dudley Carleton, for permission to settle in Virginia, with the privilege of erecting a town there, and of being governed by magistrates to be elected by themselves. This application was referred to the Virginia Company, but the conditions the latter attached to the permission which they granted, seem not to have been satisfactory, and many of these Walloons turned their

[1] The names of the ship, and of the directors above mentioned, will be found in the report of 1644-5 to the Assembly of the XIX. The description of persons which were sent out, is stated in Verbael van Beverninck, p. 606: "Strax na't geobtineerde octroy hebben de Ed. Heeren Bewinthebberen diversche schepen met volck ende beestialen naa N. Nederlandt gesonden, by welck volck, synde meest Dienaaren van de meergemelde Compagnie, syn gekoft veel en verscheyden landeryen." There is some contradiction as to the precise year in which Fort Nassau was erected. Van der Donck fixes it at 1623—Vertoogh van N. N. c. iii.; so does Stuyvesant in his declaration to the governor of Maryland. The report above referred to, has it 1624; while a paper entitled Deductie, ofte Naecht ende claer verhael over de gelegentheyt van de Zuyt Revier, fixes its date at 1626. That Mey was the first European who made a settlement on the Delaware, is put beyond doubt by the evidence of the Sachem Mattehoorn, who declared before Stuyvesant, subsequently, that a skipper named Cornelis, with one eye, or having a film on the eye, (ofte hebbende een vlies op't ooge,) was the first, who, coming there, established himself on the South River. Hol. Doc. viii., 73. Moulton, 366, says that Fort Nassau was erected in 1623. See also Barker's Sketches of principal Settlements on Del., in Haz. Reg. i., 179, and Acrelius' Hist. N. Sweden.

attention subsequently to New Netherland, where a small number of them now arrived with Director Minuit. Some settled at first on Staten Island, but afterwards removed to a bay on the northwestern extremity of Long Island, called the Wahle-Bocht, or "the bay of the foreigners," which has since received the corrupt appellation of Wallabout. Here Sarah de Rappelje, the first child of European parentage, was born on the 6th June, 1625.[1] This settlement subsequently extended itself towards the western extremity of the island, which was called "Breukelen," after an ancient Dutch village of that name, situate on the river Veght, in the province of Utrecht.

The government of the small community which now composed the population of New Netherland, was committed to the Director and his council, consisting of Pieter Bylvelt, Jacob Elbertsen Wissinck, Jan Janssen Brouwer, Symen Dercksen Pos, and Reynert Harmenssen. This council had supreme executive and legislative authority in the colony. It was also the tribunal for the trial of whatever civil and criminal cases might arise, and all prosecutions before it were instituted and conducted by an officer called a "Schout Fiscaal," whose duties were equivalent to those performed among us by a sheriff and an attorney-general.[2]

[1] The Walloons were inhabitants of the frontier between France and Flanders, extending from the Scheld to the river Lys. They spoke the old French or Gallic language, and professed the reformed religion. During the thirty years' war, they distinguished themselves for their valor and savage spirit. The name comes, it is said, either from Wall, (water or sea,) or more probably, from the old German word Wahle, signifying a foreigner. The application of the Walloons to settle in Virginia is in Lond. Doc. i., 24. The Hon. Jer. Johnson of Brooklyn is of opinion, in a letter with which he has had the politeness to favor me, that George Jansen de Rapelje and Sarah his wife arrived at Staten Island, from Holland, in 1624, and that he prepared a cabin, at what is now called the Wallabout, for his residence, to which he removed in the spring of 1625. He adds, that Sarah Rapelje was born at the latter place on the 6th (Moulton says on the 9th) of June, 1625. Meyer's Annals of Holland States, anno 1624, quoted by Rev. Dr. De Witt, Proc. N. Y. Hist. Soc., 1844, 55.

[2] In every tribunal there is a Schout or sheriff, who convenes the judges, and demands from them justice for the litigating parties; for the word "schout" is derived from schuld, debt, and he is so denominated because he is the person who recovers or demands common debts, according to Grotius. The right of the sovereign, in criminal cases, is sustained before the court by the advocate

BOOK II. 1624. He was charged specially with enforcing and maintaining the placards, laws, ordinances, resolutions, and military regulations, of their High Mightinesses the States General, and protecting the rights, domains, and jurisdiction of the company, and executing their orders, as well in as out of court, without favor or respect to individuals ; he was bound to superintend all prosecutions and suits, but could not undertake any actions on behalf of the company except by order of the council; nor arraign nor arrest any person on a criminal charge, except on information previously received, or unless he caught him *in flagrante delictu.* In taking informations, he was bound to note as well those points which made for the prisoner, as those which supported the charge against him, and, after trial, he was to see to the proper and faithful execution of the sentence pronounced by the judges, who, in indictments carrying with them loss of life and property, were not to be less than five in number. He was, moreover, specially obliged to attend to the commissaries arriving from the company's outposts, and to vessels arriving from, or leaving for, Holland, to inspect their papers, and superintend the loading and discharging of their cargoes, so that smuggling may be prevented, and all goods introduced, except in accordance to the company's regulations, were at once to be confiscated. He was to transmit to the directors in Holland copies of all informations taken by him, as well as of all sentences pronounced by the court; and no person was to be kept long in prison at the expense of the company, without special cause, but all were to be prosecuted as expeditiously as possible before the Director and council.

The schout-fiscaal of New Netherland had no voice in the council. He was privileged to sit in that body merely when questions arose relating to finance, justice, or police, and give his opinion when asked, but not to vote. He was strictly forbidden to accept presents, or gifts, from any person whatsoever; and had to content himself with the civil fines and penalties adjudged to him, and such part of the criminal fines and confiscated wages of the company's servants, as the

fiscal, or attorney general of Holland. Van Leeuwen's Commentaries on Roman Dutch Law.

director and council, after prosecution, might allow. He was not to have any part, however, of captured prizes or confiscated goods. CHAP. II. 1624.

This office, perhaps the most responsible in the colony, was filled, during the administration of Director Minuit, by JAN LAMPO of Cantelberg. Isaac de Razier acted as bookkeeper of monthly wages, and second to the Director, also as provincial secretary. In the last-mentioned capacity he was afterwards succeeded by Jan van Remund, under whom Lenaert Cole acted as assistant.[1]

Under the superintendence of these authorities, the infant trade of the colony prospered apace. The imports from Holland were estimated at twenty-five thousand, five hundred and sixty-nine guilders, equal to about $10,654 ; in return for which were exported four thousand, seven hundred beaver and otter skins, which were valued at twenty-seven thousand, one hundred and twenty-five guilders, or $11,302. "Several ships" followed in the course of the ensuing year; one of which, 1625.
called "The Orange-Tree," of 150 tons, having touched at Plymouth, England, was there detained, and her captain Jan.28.
ordered to London, to appear before the Lords of the Privy Council, inasmuch as the place in America for which Feb. 8.
he was bound, was claimed to be comprehended in the grant made by his Britannic Majesty to divers of his subjects. The imports, this year, were reduced to eight thousand, seven hundred and seventy-two guilders, or $3,655, which was a falling off of two-thirds ; but the exported furs amounted to five thousand, seven hundred and fifty-eight skins, valued at thirty-five thousand, eight hundred and twenty-five guilders,[2] equal to $14,927 of our currency ; a large increase on the exportations of the preceding year.

In the mean time the Dutch occupied Manhattan Island merely by sufferance. But as it was now their determination 1626.
to make a permanent settlement thereupon, the company having appropriated an armed ship, of about three hundred tons

[1] The names of all the above functionaries, except De Razier's, I find annexed to Indian deeds, dated 1630 and 1631, among the Rensselaerswyck MSS.

[2] Lond. Doc., i., 34 ; De Laet Kort Verhael, 26, 29.

BOOK II. 1626. burden, and a yacht, the value of both of which was 120,000 florins,[1] to the trade of the country, it became necessary, both in justice and policy, to obtain a title to the soil. The island of Manhattans, estimated then to contain twenty-two thousand acres of land, was therefore purchased from the Indians, who received for that splendid tract the trifling sum of sixty guilders, or twenty-four dollars.

Intelligence of this fortunate arrangement was transmitted to the Assembly of the XIX., by the ship "The Arms of Amsterdam," which sailed from the River Mauritius on the 23d Sept. 23. September, and arrived in Holland on the fourth of November following; with the additional information that the little colony was in a most prosperous state, and that the women and soil were both fruitful. As an evidence of the latter fact, samples of the recent harvest, consisting of wheat, rye, barley, oats, buckwheat, canary-seed, beans, and flax, were sent forward; together with eight thousand, one hundred and thirty beaver skins, valued at over forty-five thousand guilders, or nearly $19,000. The imports were estimated at twenty thousand, three hundred and eighty-four guilders, or $8,494.[2]

On or about the same time that the island of Manhattans was purchased, the Director General and Council bought Eghquaous, or Staten Island, and some other places in that vicinity; and as a greater security for their lives and property, as well as for the better accommodation of the Company's servants, a blockhouse, surrounded with red cedar palisades, was thrown up on the south point of Manhattan Island, which post having now received the appellation of Fort Amsterdam, became the head-quarters of the government, and the capital of New Netherland.[3]

An occurrence, we regret to say, took place while this work was progressing, which must have impressed the uncivilized natives with an unfavorable idea both of European honesty and of European justice. One of the neighboring tribe of

[1] Hol. Doc., i., 147.

[2] Hol. Doc., i., 155. De Laet.

[3] Hol. Doc., vii., 70, 71. Verbael van Beverninck, 606. Alb. Rec., viii., 161. Moulton, 367. Report to the Assembly of the XIX., in the Appendix, shows the date of the erection of this fort.

Wickwasqueeck Indians had come, with his nephew, and another of his nation, to the Dutch post, to sell some beaver-skins. He was met unfortunately by three of Minuit's farm servants, who not only rifled the Indian of his property, but murdered him in cold blood. The nephew of the unfortunate man, who was then a mere youth, was a witness to this outrage. He returned home brooding over the wrong, and vowed to take vengeance when he should arrive at the years of manhood[1]—a vow which he too faithfully fulfilled, years afterwards, the Dutch having neglected to expiate the crime by a suitable present of wampum, in conformity with the customs of the Redman, or to punish the murderers, as justice and good policy demanded.

CHAP. II. 1626.

The activity with which the authorities at the Manhattans prosecuted trade among the Indians, exploring every creek, bay, and river, with their sloops and other craft, soon spread the intelligence of their settlement all around. The English, now settled some six or seven years at New Plymouth, had already heard much of the Dutch from the natives. Through the same medium, it is to be presumed, the Dutch heard of their English neighbors;[2] but neither party had, as yet, heard from, or met with, the other. Desirous, now, of extending their commercial relations, the Director and council transmit-

1627. March 9.

[1] De Vries (Korte Historiael ende Journael, &c.) alludes to this murder, and the time it occurred is distinctly mentioned by him—"when the fort was built." Capt. Patrick, writing in 1641, says that it occurred "over one and twenty years ago." This would have carried it back to 1620; but as no fort was building then, it must be concluded that the Captain's memory, or rather the memory of the sachem who furnished him with that as the distance of time when the murder was committed, must have deceived him. In Hol. Doc. v. 314, the murder is alluded to, also, and it is there represented as having been committed by three of Minnewitz' men. "De welcke (Wilt) van drye bouwknechten van den Commandeur Minnewitz was omgebracht." This marks the time precisely, as no other fort was built on Manhattan Island by Minuit except in the above year.

[2] In the year 1623, a Dutch trading vessel from New Netherland was stranded in Narragansett bay, near the mouth of Taunton river. In the same year the Plymouth people went on a trading voyage to Narragansett bay, it being the first time they had ventured so far towards the west. In this expedition they were not successful, because the Dutch had been accustomed to supply the natives with goods better suited to their wants than the Plymouth people were able to furnish. N. A. Rev. viii., 82

BOOK II. 1627. ted letters to the governor of New Plymouth, "written in a very fair hand, the one in French and the other in Dutch," and signed by Isaac de Razier, expressive of good-will, congratulating him on the prosperity of his infant colony, and offering to accommodate him with any goods or merchandise which the Dutch had, and which the English might want, in exchange for beaver or otter skins, or other wares.

March 29. (N. S.) An answer to these neighborly and polite proposals was returned by Mr. Bradford, governor of New Plymouth, in due course, in which he expressed many thanks for their friendly disposition, and alluded in grateful terms to the kindness the "Pilgrims" had experienced during their sojourn in Holland. In regard to trade, he stated that for the current year they were fully supplied with all necessaries, but promised to trade thereafter, should the rates be reasonable; and with that view desired to know at what price they would take beaver and other skins and commodities, and what sort of barter they would accept in exchange, such as tobacco, fish, corn, &c., and on what terms. Governor Bradford requested the Dutch people, at the same time, to forbear trading with the natives of Cape Cod bay and of the Narragansetts, which they had already been in the habit of doing, and concluded by putting them on their guard against vessels belonging to the other English plantations, which were commissioned to capture and expel all strangers trading within the limits of forty degrees.

Aug 7. To this communication the authorities at Fort Amsterdam sent a friendly reply, by John Jacobsen of Wiring, in which, at the same time, they firmly maintained their right to trade to those parts from which the English had desired them to forbear, alleging that they had traded thither above six and twenty years, and that they had authority for so doing from the States General and the Prince of Orange. As a testimony of their good feeling towards the New Plymouth people, they accompanied this letter with a present to Gov. Bradford, of "a rundlet of sugar and two Holland cheeses," which were very thankfully received. Aug 24. The governor, in his answer, reiterated his desire for the continuance of good neighborhood; expressed a wish for an opportunity to confer personally touching mutual commerce, and added that he should have sent a person for that purpose, but that he had no mode of conveyance at hand. He, at the same time, invited the Dutch authorities to depute some one of themselves to New Plymouth, as they had proposed, to make some regulations relative to trade, who would be cordially received. In sending this invitation, Governor Bradford considered it his duty again to warn the Dutch against the danger to which they were exposed from the vessels of Virginia, and from the fishing ships coming to New England, as, if they were met, they should assuredly be captured in the same manner as a French colony, years before, which was seated within these bounds. He concluded by calling their attention to the fact, that the English had navigated and planted in those parts well-nigh forty years, under patents and royal grants from Queen Elizabeth, and suggested if it were not best that the States General should come to some arrangement with the British court about the matter.

CHAP II. 1627.

The government at Fort Amsterdam was not slow to accept the invitation conveyed in Governor Bradford's letter. Isaac de Razier was dispatched in the bark Nassau as ambassador to the New Plymouth colony; and, having arrived in the neighborhood of that settlement, forwarded a letter thus addressed:— Oct. 4.

"Monsieur Monseigneur William Bradford, Governor Nieu Plemeuen.

"After the wishing of all good unto you, this serves to let you understand that we have received your acceptable letters, dated the 14th of the last month, by John Jacobsen of Wiring, who, besides, by word of mouth hath reported unto us your kind and friendly entertainment of him. For which cause, (by the good liking and approbation of the Director and Council,) I am resolved to come myself in friendship to visit you, that we may, by word of mouth, friendly communicate of things together; as also to report unto you the good-will and favor that the Hon'ble Lords of the authorized West India Company bear towards you. And to show our willingness of your good accommodation, have brought with me some cloth of three sorts and colors, and a chest of white sugar, as also some seawan, &c., not doubting but, if any of them may be service-

BOOK II. 1627. able unto you, we shall agree well enough about the prices thereof. Also, John Jacobsen, aforesaid, hath told me that he came to you overland in six hours, but I have not gone so far this three or four years; wherefore I fear my feet will fail me, so I am constrained to entreat you to afford me the easiest means that I may, with least weariness, come to congratulate with you. So leaving other things to the report of the bearer, shall herewith end; remembering my hearty salutations to yourself and friends, &c. From aboard the barque Nassau, the 4th Oct., before Frenchman's Point, Anno 1627. Your affectionate friend,

"ISAAC DE RAZIER."

According to the request contained in the above, Governor Bradford sent a boat for Mr. de Razier, "who came honorably attended with a noise of trumpeters." This meeting, it may well be imagined, was a source of pleasure on both sides. "It was the first meeting in the solitude of the New World between friendly colonists of two allied European nations," who had much to say about a country towards which both had feelings of strong affection.

A quantity of Dutch commodities was purchased on this occasion by the New Plymouth people; especially seawan, or wampum, which the English found to be afterwards very beneficial in their trade with the natives. This was the commencement of the intercourse between the Dutch and English colonists on these shores, which continued for many years, to the mutual advantage of both parties.

Oct. 11. At the departure of Mr. de Razier from New Plymouth, Governor Bradford wrote again to the Director and Council at Fort Amsterdam, in reference to the proposition regarding trade which had been made by their agent, but which the New Plymouth authorities could not, at the moment, favorably entertain, as they had sent a person to England and Holland for supplies, whose return they should necessarily await. In this communication they were again urged to clear the title to their plantation in these parts, which, it was asserted, "the king had granted by patent to divers nobles and subjects of quality." This the Dutch were recommended to do, "lest it be a bone of contention in these stirring evil times; for," it was added, "it will be harder and with more difficulty obtained hereafter, and perhaps not without blows."[1] CHAP. II. 1627.

The earnestness with which Governor Bradford asserted the right of the English to the country claimed now, or possessed by the Dutch, and urged the latter to clear their title; and the closing hint, that possibly force might be resorted to hereafter to vindicate the British pretensions, alarmed somewhat the authorities at Fort Amsterdam. They wrote, immediately, to Nov. 16. the directors of the company in Holland, and represented that the English at New Plymouth had threatened, notwithstanding all the kindness they had received from the Dutch, to drive the latter away, or disturb them in their possessions and little colony; and then concluded by calling for a force of forty soldiers, to aid them in repelling any hostile attacks.[2]

The company had, however, anticipated, and in some degree removed, before the receipt of this letter, many of the causes which might have led at this time to an interruption of good feeling between the Dutch and their English neighbors. For, though they did not, as Governor Bradford suggested, "clear their title," they obtained from Charles I. an order in council, in the month of September preceding, by which the Sept. 5 (O. S.) privileges which were secured, in 1627, by the treaty of Southampton, to all the national vessels of the States General, were extended to the ships of the company. By this order all ports, whether in the kingdom or territories of the British king, were at once thrown open to the Dutch vessels trading to or from New Netherland, which were thus protected from

[1] Bradford's Correspondence, in N. Y. Hist. Soc. Coll. (N. S.,) i. 360, et seq. Baillie's Mem. of Plym. i., 146, 147. Prince's N. E. Chron. 249. Moulton, 378.

[2] This intelligence, which was addressed to the XIX., was reported to the States General in the following words: "Brengen tyding dat sy aldaer (in N. N.) gedreigd worden van de Engelschen van N. Pleymoudt: (niettegenstaende de onsen voor desen aen deselfde alle goede correspondentie en vruntschap gepresenteerd hadden :) van hen te willen verjaegen ofte turberen in haer besit en geringe colonie. Versoecken derhalve adsistentie van veertig soldaten tot hunne defensie." Hol. Doc. i., 159, 160.

BOOK II. seizure by any of the cruisers frequenting the English colonies.[1]

1627. In the mean while, the trade with the Indians and adjoining plantations continued to be actively carried on. The company sent out four ships this year, with cargoes valued at fifty-six thousand, one hundred and seventy guilders, ($23,404,) being an increase on last year's imports of fifteen thousand dollars. There was, however, a falling off in the value of the furs returned, which, though amounting to seven thousand, eight hundred and ninety skins, were estimated at only twelve thousand, seven hundred and thirty guilders.

1628. Seven years had now nearly elapsed since the incorporation of the West India Company, and five since that body had been in active operation, yet nothing had been done to carry out that part of the charter which obliged them to advance settlements and encourage population in those fertile countries in North America committed to their charge. A few servants of the company, connected with the trading posts which served as a rendezvous for the neighboring Indians, were the only inhabitants, it may be said, of the extensive country claimed as New Netherland. Not a particle of the soil was reclaimed, save what scantily supplied the wants of those attached to the three forts which were erected within the limits of this rich and vast territory; and the only exports were the spontaneous products of the forest. Experience had demonstrated, in the interim, that no benefits had accrued to the company from this plantation, under the present system of management, except what the peltries produced;[2] the mode of life pursued

[1] This order will be found at length in Hol. Doc. ix., 292, et seq.; also in Lond. Doc. i., 36, 37, 38, 39. The treaty of Southampton is in Aitzema, i., 469.

[2] "Now the part which we have named New Netherland, though as regards climate it ought to be as warm, and as well adapted for the cultivation of fruit at least, as France, where it borders on Spain, has, nevertheless, been found excessively cold, and as subject to frost and other inconveniences as these still more northerly provinces. The people whom we have conveyed thither up to this time, have, on that account, been able to procure but scanty means of living, and have been, not a profit, but a loss to the Company. The trade which is carried on in peltries is right advantageous, but can, at the utmost, return, one year with the other, only 50,000 guilders," ($20,000.) Remonstrance of the W. I. Co. against Peace with Spain, 1629. Hol. Doc., i., 165.

by the people was very irregular, the expenses of the estab- CHAP. II.
lishment excessively high, and the results not as flattering as
anticipated. These considerations having been frequently 1628.
brought before the XIX., it was finally determined that the resources of the country, under their jurisdiction, would be most efficiently developed by the planting of "colonies," or seignorial fiefs or manors, there.

A meeting of the Assembly of the XIX. accordingly took March 28.
place early this year. It was attended by commissioners from their High Mightinesses the States General, and directors and assessors on the part of the principal partners; and a draft of a "charter of privileges and exemptions," which was considered alike serviceable to the company and advantageous to the patroons, masters, and private individuals who should plant colonies in New Netherland under its provisions, having been submitted, was referred, forthwith, to a committee for examination, which was instructed to report to a future meeting.[1]

It was while these plans were under consideration, that the arms of the company achieved a splendid and most decisive victory over the enemy, which, while it threw uncounted wealth into the coffers of the various partners, gave a sudden, yet most efficient, impulse to the permanent colonization of New Netherland.

Admiral Pieter Pieterssen Heyn having been put in command of the company's ships, proceeded to the West Indies,
and in the autumn of this year, captured, in Matanzas bay, Sept. 9.
the Spanish "Plate fleet," consisting of twenty sail, laden with gold, silver, and other valuable freight, estimated to be worth five millions of dollars. From this and other preceding conquests, the company's dividends advanced at once to fifty per cent.[2] When the committee, appointed in the spring of the preceding year to examine the proposed charter for the
establishment of colonies in New Netherland, brought in their 1629.
report, it was evident that Heyn's victory had considerable Feb. 26.
influence on the minds of many of the directors. It was, however, considered wise to address the several chambers on

[1] Hol. Doc. ii., 95, 96, 97.

[2] Vaderlands. Hist. ix., 69, 70.

BOOK II. 1629. April 18. May 29. June 7.

the subject, with a view to elicit their views on a matter of such importance. A number of amendments were subsequently suggested and proposed, and, after a further adjournment was agreed upon, in order to afford time for the fullest consideration, the whole project was again discussed in the latter part of May, and then referred a second time to a committee, to report all the articles complete to the Assembly of the XIX., who, on the seventh day of June, 1629, agreed to these important concessions,[1] which were duly ratified by the States General, and published in the following terms:

"FREEDOMS AND EXEMPTIONS

GRANTED BY THE ASSEMBLY OF THE XIX. OF THE PRIVILEGED WEST INDIA COMPANY, TO ALL SUCH AS SHALL PLANT ANY COLONIES IN NEW NETHERLAND:

"I. Such members of the said company as may be inclined to settle any colonie in New Netherland, shall be permitted to send in the ships of this company going thither, three or four persons to inspect the situation of the country, provided that they, with the officers and ship's company, swear to the articles, so far as they relate to them, and pay for provisions and for passage, going and coming, six stuyvers per diem; and such as desire to eat in the cabin, twelve stuyvers, and to be subordinate and give assistance like others, in cases offensive and defensive; and if any ships be taken from the enemy, they shall receive, pro rata, their proportions with the ship's company, each according to his quality; that is to say, the colonists eating out of the cabin shall be rated with the sailors, and those who eat in the cabin with those of the company's men who eat at table and receive the lowest wages.

"II. Though, in this respect, shall be preferred such persons as have first appeared and desired the same from the company.

"III. All such shall be acknowledged Patroons of New Netherland who shall, within the space of four years next after they have given notice to any of the Chambers of the Company here, or to the Commander or Council there, undertake to plant a colonie there of fifty souls, upwards of fifteen years

[1] Hol. Doc. ii., 98, 99.

CHAP. II. 1629.

old; one fourth part within one year, and within three years after the sending of the first, making together four years, the remainder, to the full number of fifty persons, to be shipped from hence, on pain, in case of wilful neglect, of being deprived of the privileges obtained; but it is to be observed that the company reserve the island of the Manhattes to themselves.

"IV. They shall, from the time they make known the situation of the places where they propose to settle colonies, have the preference to all others of the absolute property of such lands as they have there chosen; but in case the situation should not afterwards please them, or that they should have been mistaken as to the quality of the land, they may, after remonstrating concerning the same to the Commander and Council there, be at liberty to choose another place.

"V. The Patroons, by virtue of their power, shall and may be permitted, at such places as they shall settle their colonies, to extend their limits four miles[1] along the shore, that is, on one side of a navigable river, or two miles[2] on each side of a river, and so far into the country as the situation of the occupiers will permit; provided and conditioned that the company keep to themselves the lands lying and remaining between the limits of colonies, to dispose thereof, when and at such time as they shall think proper, in such manner that no person shall be allowed to come within seven or eight miles[3] of them without their consent, unless the situation of the land thereabout were such, that the Commander and Council, for good reasons, should order otherwise; always observing that the first occupiers are not to be prejudiced in the right they have obtained, other than, unless the service of the Company should require it, for the building of fortifications, or something of that sort; remaining, moreover, the command of each bay, river, or island, of the first-settled colonie, under the supreme jurisdiction of their High Mightinesses the States General, and the company: but that on the next colonies being settled on the same river or island, they may, in conjunction with the first, appoint one or more council, in order to consider what may be neces-

[1] Equal to sixteen English miles. [2] Or eight English miles.
[3] Thirty-two English miles.

BOOK II. sary for the prosperity of the colonies on the said river and island.

1629. "VI. They shall forever possess and enjoy all the lands lying within the aforesaid limits, together with the fruits, rights, minerals, rivers, and fountains thereof; as also the chief command and lower jurisdictions, fishing, fowling, and grinding, to the exclusion of all others, to be holden from the company as a perpetual inheritance, without it ever devolving again to the company, and in case it should devolve, to be redeemed and repossessed with twenty guilders per colonie, to be paid to this company, at the chamber here, or to their commander there, within a year and six weeks after the same occurs, each at the chamber where he originally sailed from; and further, no person or persons whatsoever shall be privileged to fish and hunt but the Patroons and such as they shall permit; and in case any one should in time prosper so much as to found one or more cities, he shall have power and authority to establish officers and magistrates there, and to make use of the title of his colonie, according to his pleasure and to the quality of the persons.

"VII. There shall likewise be granted to all Patroons who shall desire the same, venia testandi, or liberty to dispose of their aforesaid heritage, by testament.

"VIII. The Patroons may, if they think proper, make use of all lands, rivers, and woods, lying contiguous to them, for and during so long a time as this company shall grant them to other patroons or particulars.

"IX. Those who shall send persons over to settle colonies shall furnish them with proper instructions, in order that they may be ruled and governed conformably to the rule of government made, or to be made, by the Assembly of the Nineteen, as well in the political as in the judicial government; which they shall be obliged first to lay before the directors of the respective colleges.

"X. The Patroons and Colonists shall be privileged to send their people and effects thither, in ships belonging to the company, provided they take the oath, and pay to the company for bringing over the people as mentioned in the first article; and for freight of the goods five per cent. ready money, to be reckoned on the prime cost of the goods here; in which is, how ever, not to be included such creatures and other implements as are necessary for the cultivation and improvement of the lands, which the company are to carry over without any reward, if there is room in their ships. But the Patroons shall, at their own expense, provide and make places for them, together with every thing necessary for the support of the creatures.

1629

"XI. In case it should not suit the company to send any ships, or in those going there should be no room; then the said Patroons, after having communicated their intentions, and after having obtained consent from the company in writing, may send their own ships or vessels thither: provided, that in going or coming they go not out of their ordinary course; giving security to the company for the same, and taking on board an assistant, to be victualled by the Patroons, and paid his monthly wages by the company; on pain, for doing the contrary, of forfeiting all the right and property they have obtained to the colonie.

"XII. Inasmuch as it is intended to people the island of the Manhattes first, all fruits and wares that are produced on the lands situate on the North River, and lying thereabout, shall, for the present, be brought there before they may be sent elsewhere: excepting such as are from their nature unnecessary there, or such as cannot, without great loss to the owner thereof, be brought there; in which case the owners thereof shall be obliged to give timely notice in writing of the difficulty attending the same to the company here, or the commander and council there, that the same may be remedied as the necessity thereof shall be found to require

"XIII. All the Patroons of colonies in New Netherland, and of colonies on the island of Manhattes, shall be at liberty to sail and traffic all along the coast from Florida to Terra Neuf, provided that they do again return with all such goods as they shall get in trade to the island of Manhattes, and pay five per cent. for recognition to the company, in order, if possible, that after the necessary inventory of the goods shipped be taken, the same may be sent hither. And if it should so happen that they could not return, by contrary streams or otherwise, they shall, in such case, not be permitted to bring such goods to any other place but to these dominions, in order that under the

BOOK II. 1629. inspection of the directors of the place where they may arrive they may be unladen, an inventory thereof made, and the aforesaid recognition of five per cent. paid to the company here, on pain, if they do the contrary, of the forfeiture of their goods so trafficked for, or the real value thereof.

"XIV. In case the ships of the Patroons, in going to, or coming from, or sailing on the coast from Florida to Terra Neuf, and no further, without our grant, should overpower any of the prizes of the enemy, they shall be obliged to bring, or cause to be brought, such prize to the college of the place from whence they sailed out, in order to be rewarded by them; the company shall keep the one third part thereof, and the remaining two thirds shall belong to them, in consideration of the cost and risk they have been at, all according to the orders of the company,

"XV. It shall be also free for the aforesaid Patroons to traffic and trade all along the coast of New Netherland and places circumjacent, with such goods as are consumed there, and receive in return for them, all sorts of merchandise that may be had there, except beavers, otters, minks, and all sorts of peltry, which trade the company reserve to themselves. But the same shall be permitted at such places where the company have no factories, conditioned that such traders shall be obliged to bring all the peltry they can procure to the island of Manhattes, in case it may be, at any rate, practicable, and there deliver to the Director, to be by him shipped hither with the ships and goods; or, if they should come here, without going there, then to give notice thereof to the company, that a proper account thereof may be taken, in order that they may pay to the company one guilder for each merchantable beaver and otter skin; the property, risk, and all other charges, remaining on account of the Patroons, or owners.

"XVI. All coarse wares that the colonists of the Patroons there shall consume, such as pitch, tar, weed-ashes, wood, grain, fish, salt, hearthstone, and such like things, shall be brought over in the company's ships, at the rate of eighteen guilders ($7.20) per last; four thousand weight to be accounted a last, and the company's ship's crew shall be obliged to wheel and bring the salt on board, whereof ten lasts make a hundred. And in case of the want of ships, or room in the ships, they may order it over at their own cost, in ships of their own, and enjoy in these dominions such liberties and benefits as the company have granted; but in either case they shall be obliged to pay, over and above the recognition of five per cent., eighteen guilders for each hundred of salt that is carried over in the company's ships.

CHAP. II.

1629

" XVII. For all wares which are not mentioned in the foregoing article, and which are not carried by the last, there shall be paid one dollar for each hundred pounds weight; and for wines, brandies, verjuice, and vinegar, there shall be paid eighteen guilders per cask

" XVIII. The company promises the colonists of the Patroons, that they shall be free from customs, taxes, excise, imposts, or any other contributions, for the space of ten years; and after the expiration of the said ten years at the highest, such customs as the goods are taxable with here for the present.

" XIX. They will not take from the service of the Patroons any of their colonists, either man or woman, son or daughter, man-servant or maid-servant; and though any of them should desire the same, they will not receive them, much less permit them to leave their Patroons, and enter into the service of another, unless on consent obtained from their Patroons in writing; and this for and during so many years as they are bound to their Patroons; after the expiration whereof, it shall be in the power of the Patroons to send hither all such colonists as will not continue in their service, and until then shall not enjoy their liberty. And all such colonists as shall leave the service of his Patroon, and enter into the service of another, or shall, contrary to his contract, leave his service; we promise to do every thing in our power to apprehend and deliver the same into the hands of his Patroon, or attorney, that he may be proceeded against, according to the customs of this country, as occasion may require.

" XX. From all judgments given by the courts of the Patroons for upwards of fifty guilders, ($20,) there may be an appeal to the company's commander and council in New Netherland.

BOOK II. 1629.

"XXI. In regard to such private persons as on their own account, or others in the service of their masters here, (not enjoying the same privileges as the Patroons,) shall be inclined to go thither and settle; they shall, with the approbation of the Director and council there, be at liberty to take up as much land, and take possession thereof, as they shall be able properly to improve, and shall enjoy the same in full property either for themselves or masters.

"XXII. They shall have free liberty of hunting and fowling, as well by water as by land, generally, and in public and private woods and rivers, about their colonies, according to the orders of the Director and council.

"XXIII. Whosoever, whether colonists of Patroons for their patroons, or free persons for themselves, or other particulars for their masters, shall discover any shores, bays, or other fit places for erecting fisheries, or the making of salt ponds, they may take possession thereof, and begin to work on them in their own absolute property, to the exclusion of all others. And it is consented to that the Patroons of colonists may send ships along the coast of New Netherland, on the cod fishery, and with the fish they catch to trade to Italy, or other neutral countries, paying in such cases to the company for recognition six guilders ($2.40) per last; and if they should come with their lading hither, they shall be at liberty to proceed to Italy, though they shall not, under pretext of this consent, or from the company, carry any goods there, on pain of arbitrary punishment; and it remaining in the breast of the company to put a supercargo on board each ship, as in the eleventh article.

"XXIV. In case any of the colonists should, by his industry and diligence, discover any minerals, precious stones, crystals, marbles, or such like, or any pearl fishery, the same shall be and remain the property of the Patroon or Patroons of such colony; giving and ordering the discoverer such premium as the Patroon shall beforehand have stipulated with such colonist by contract. And the Patroons shall be exempt from all recognition to the company for the term of eight years, and pay only for freight, to bring them over, two per cent., and after the expiration of the aforesaid eight years, for recognition and freight, the one eighth part of what the same may be worth. CHAP. II.  1629.

"XXV. The company will take all the colonists, as well free as those that are in service, under their protection, and the same against all outlandish and inlandish wars and powers, with the forces they have there, as much as lies in their power, defend.

"XXVI. Whosoever shall settle any colonie out of the limits of the Manhattes Island, shall be obliged to satisfy the Indians for the land they shall settle upon, and they may extend or enlarge the limits of their colonies if they settle a proportionate number of colonists thereon.

"XXVII. The Patroons and colonists shall in particular, and in the speediest manner, endeavor to find out ways and means whereby they may support a minister and schoolmaster, that thus the service of God and zeal for religion may not grow cool, and be neglected among them; and that they do, for the first, procure a comforter of the sick there.

"XXVIII. The colonies that shall happen to lie on the respective rivers or islands (that is to say, each river or island for itself) shall be at liberty to appoint a deputy, who shall give information to the commander and council of that Western quarter, of all things relating to his colonie, and who are to further matters relating thereto, of which deputies there shall be one altered, or changed, in every two years; and all colonies shall be obliged, at least once in every twelve months, to make exact report of their colonie and lands thereabout, to the commander and council there, in order to be transmitted hither.

"XXIX. The colonists shall not be permitted to make any woollen, linen, or cotton cloth, nor weave any other stuffs there, on pain of being banished, and as perjurers to be arbitrarily punished.

"XXX. The company will use their endeavors to supply the colonists with as many blacks as they conveniently can, on the conditions hereafter to be made; in such manner, however, that they shall not be bound to do it for a longer time than they shall think proper.

"XXXI. The company promises to finish the fort on the

BOOK II. island of the Manhattes, and to put it in a posture of defence without delay.[1]

1629. The preceding charter, which transplanted to the free soil of America the feudal tenure and feudal burdens of continental Europe, is remarkable principally as a characteristic of the era in which it was produced. It bears all the marks of the social system which prevailed at the time, not only among the Dutch, but among the other nations which had adopted the civil law. The "colonies" were but transcripts of the "lordships" and "seigneuries" so common at this period, and which the French were establishing, contemporaneously, in their possessions north of New Netherland,[2] where most of the feudal appendages of high and low jurisdiction, mutation fines, pre-emption rights, exclusive monopolies of mines, minerals, water-courses, hunting, fishing, fowling, and grinding, which we find enumerated in the charter to patroons, form part of the civil law of the country at the present day. But however favorable the feudal tenure may be to a young country, and to agriculturists of small capital, whose interest it might be to husband their scanty means, in order the quicker and more effectually to enable them to reclaim their wild land, it cannot be denied that the charter before us had many faults and many imperfections. "While it secured the right of the Indian to the soil," says Moulton, "and enjoined schools and churches, it scattered the seeds of servitude, slavery, and aristocracy. While it gave to freemen as much land as they could cultivate, and exempted colonists from taxation for ten years, it fettered agriculture by restricting commerce and prohibiting manufactures."[3]

[1] Moulton, 388; Dunlap's N. Y., ii., Append. H.; N. Y. Hist. Soc. Coll. (2d Ser.) i., 369.

[2] The following are the dates of some of the earliest patents for seigneuries in Canada. St. Joseph, 1626; Notre dame des Anges, 1626; Rivière du Loup, 1633; Lauzon, 1636; Beauport, 1635. These and numbers of others may be found (some as late as 1788) in Bouchette's Topog. of Can., App. ii. et seq. Forty years after the establishment of the privileged order of patroons in New Netherland, the proprietors of Carolina attempted to introduce a privileged order of feudal lords in that province, under the title of "Langraves" and "Caciques," the former to be endowed with 16,000, and the latter with 4,000 acres of land each. But this memorable monument of Locke's folly perished soon after birth.

[3] Hist. of N. Y., 387, 388.

CHAPTER III.

Several directors of the West India Company acquire patroonships, or "colonies," in New Netherland—Associations formed to settle Zwanendal and Rensselaerswyck—Patroons' colonies confirmed and "sealed with the seal of New Netherland"—Quarrels between Directors of the Company and Patroons—Privileges granted to Patroons called into doubt—Director Minuit recalled—English Companies grant patents for Massachusetts and Connecticut—Evince considerable jealousy of the Dutch—The vessel in which Minuit and other servants of the Company are returning to Holland, is seized at Plymouth by order of the British government, for having traded to, and obtained her cargo in, countries subject to the king of England—Audience of the Dutch ambassadors with Charles I. in consequence—They demand the release of the Company's ship—The king declines—The West India Company call the attention of the States General to the matter—Lay before their High Mightinesses a deduction of their title to New Netherland—The States General resolve to maintain the Company's right to that country—Lengthy reply of Charles I. and the Lords Commissioners of England to the Dutch remonstrance—Refuse to permit the Dutch to encroach on and usurp one of his Majesty's colonies unless they consent to submit to his Majesty's government—The Company's ship released, "saving his Majesty's rights"—Continued misunderstanding between Directors of the West India Company and the Patroons—Commissaries sent to the several "colonies" belonging to Patroons, to prevent the latter interfering in the fur trade—Colonie of Zwanendal destroyed by the savages—De Vries visits South River and makes peace with the Indians—Profitable state of trade with New Netherland.

CHAP. III. 1629.

The charter of 1629 had not yet received the sanction of the Assembly of the XIX., nor the ratification of the States General, when several of the directors of the Amsterdam chamber of the West India Company, to which department, as we have already observed, the management of the affairs of New Netherland was committed, had already taken measures to secure for themselves a share of those privileges and advantages which it held out to enterprising capitalists. Seven days before the passing of that charter, the agents of Samuel Godyn and Samuel Bloemmaert purchased, from the native proprietors of the soil, the tract of country lying on the southwest side of the South River bay, extending inland from Cape Hindlopen thirty-two miles, and two miles in breadth; (June 1.)

BOOK II. which purchase was duly ratified on the 15th July of the next year, by the Director-general and council, at Fort Amsterdam.[1]

1630. April 18. Other wealthy and influential directors of the company hastened now to become patroons also, and early in the following spring, Bastiaen Jansen Krol, commissary, and Dierck Cornelissen Duyster, under-commissary at Fort Orange, having learned that a tract of land called Sannahagog, lying on the west side of the North River, extending from Beeren Island, by the Indians called Passapenock, up to Smackx Island, and in breadth two days' journey, was for sale, purchased the same from Paep Sikenekomptas, Nancouttanshal, and Sickoussen, the native proprietors, for Kiliaen van Rensselaer, a pearl-merchant in Amsterdam, and one of the directors of the West India Company.[2] Three months after-

[1] Hol. Doc. i., 176—180. In the English translations of this Dutch patent (Liber GG.) in the secretary of state's office, the name of Blommaert is omitted as a party to the Cape Hindlopen purchase, and Moulton, following that translation, represents Godyn accordingly as sole purchaser of this tract. I follow the Dutch patent in the Holland documents, which contains Blommaert's name, as well as the signatures of the Director-general and the members of his council, and of Sheriff Lampo.

[2] Kiliaen van Rensselaer, merchant of Amsterdam, director of the West India Company, and one of the first patroons of New Netherland, was the thirteenth descendant in a direct line from Henry Wolters van Rensselaer. He married, firstly, Hellegonda van Bylet, by whom he had one son, Johannes, who afterwards married his cousin, Elizabeth van Twiller. Kiliaen van Rensselaer married, secondly, in 1627, Anna van Wely, daughter of Joannes van Wely, merchant of Amsterdam, by whom he had four daughters and four sons, namely: 1, Maria; 2, Jeremias, (who married Maria, daughter of Oloff Stevensen van Cortland;) 3, Hellegonda; 4, Jan Baptiste, (who married Susan van Wely;) 5, Eleonora; 6, Susan, (who married Jan de la Court;) 7, Nicolaus, (who married Alida Schuyler;) 8, Rickert, (who married Anna van Beaumont;) Kiliaen van Rensselaer's sister (Maria) married Rykert van Twiller, and thus, it is presumed, the relationship originated between Wouter van Twiller, second director-general of New Netherland, and the first patroon of Rensselaerswyck. Of the above children, Maria and Hellegonda died unmarried. Johannes succeeded his father as Patroon, and Jeremias, Jan Baptiste, and Ryckert were, in succession, directors of "the colonie." Nicolaus was a clergyman of the Dutch Reformed Church. On being introduced to Charles II., then in exile at Brussels, he prophesied the restoration of that monarch to the throne of England, which circumstance obtained for him afterwards a cordial reception at the Court of St. James, when he visited London as chaplain to

wards, Gillis Hoossett purchased, in the presence of Jan Jansen Meyndertsen, Wolfert Gerrittsen, and Jan Tyssen, trumpeter, for the same gentleman, from Cottomack, Nawanemit, Abantzene, Sagisguwa, and Kanamoack, the lands lying south and north of Fort Orange, and extending to within a short distance of Moenimines Castle, then situate on what is now called Haver Island, at the mouth of the Mohawk; and from Nawanemit, one of the last-named chiefs, his grounds, called Semesseeck, stretching on the east side of the river, from opposite Castle Island to a point facing Fort Orange, and thence from Pœtanoek, the Mill Creek, north to Negagonse. These conveyances were subsequently ratified by the respective parties, in the presence of the Director-general and council of New Netherland, who signed an instrument to that effect, "sealed with the seal of New Netherland in red wax,"

CHAP. III. 1630. July 27 or 28. Aug. 8. Aug. 13

the Dutch embassy. In acknowledgment of the truth of the prediction, the king presented him with a snuff-box, on the lid of which was set his Majesty's miniature. This royal relic is still in the possession of the Van Rensselaer family at Albany.

Mde. Anna van Rensselaer died in Amsterdam on the 12th June, 1670, after a sickness of seven weeks, having survived her husband twenty-four years. Intelligence of her death, communicated by the following letter, was received in this country by her sons, Jeremias and Ryckert, on the 18th Sept., 1670:

"AMSTERDAM, 12th June, 1670.

"Dear Brothers—On the 9th inst. I communicated to you, among other things, por ship Duke of York, Johannes Luyck, skipper, the low condition of our beloved mother, who accompanied me home, sick, from Cralo to Amsterdam, on the 1st of April. After lying so long, without any strong fever, or any great pain, troubled only with asthma, accompanied by considerable cough and phlegm, and the sprue, she took her departure with great piety from the Church Militant here, to the Church Triumphant above, on the 12th inst., being this day, about one hour after noon, in the presence of all our sisters and brothers who are in this country, and that with a full understanding and trust in the mercy of God, the merits of her and our Saviour Jesus Christ, which, through the grace of the Holy Ghost and the belief in the Triune God, so strengthened her, that all her wishes were to be set free and to be with Christ, who hath taken her so mercifully to himself, that we all, though afflicted children, cannot be sufficiently thankful to God for so gentle and holy a death. Her body will be committed to the earth in a Christian manner, as in duty bound, on Tuesday next, being the 17th inst. There is no doubt of a stately funeral. May the good God grant her, and us with her, a joyous resurrection at the last day. Amen."

BOOK II. 1630. on the same day that the charter of 1629 was proclaimed at Fort Amsterdam. Nearly seven years afterwards—namely, on the 13th April, 1637—an intervening district called Papsickenekas, or Papsskenea, as the name is now pronounced, lying also on the east bank of the river, and extending from opposite Castle Island south to the point opposite Smackx Island, and including the adjacent islands and all the lands back into the interior, belonging to the Indian owners, was purchased "for certain quantities of duffels, axes, knives, and wampum," also for Mr. Van Rensselaer, who thus became proprietor of a tract of country twenty-four miles long, and forty-eight miles broad, containing, as is estimated, over seven hundred thousand acres of land, which now compose the counties of Albany, Rensselaer, and part of the county of Columbia.[1]

[1] The names of Director Minuit, Bastiaen Jansen Krol, Dirck Cornelisz Duyster, Peter Bylvelt, Jan Lampo, (schout,) Reynert Harmenssen, Jan Janssen Myndertz, are signed to the first of these deeds, which is certified by Lenaert Cole, assistant-secretary, "in the absence of Jan van Remund, secretary." The other instrument is signed by Pieter Minuit, director; Pieter Bylvelt, Jacob Elbertzen Weissing, Jan Jansen Brouwer, Symen Dircksen Pos, Raynner Harmenz, Lenaert Cole, assistant-secretary, in the absence of the secretary, "with the seal of New Netherland in red wax." Copies of all these deeds are in the Book of Patents, secretary of state's office, GG, 13, 14, 15, 16, 23, 24, 25, 26, and also among the Rensselaerswyck MSS. See also Hol. Doc. i., 181—184. The deed of the purchase of 1637 is likewise among the Rensselaerswyck MSS. It is endorsed, "Opdracht brief van 't landt aende Oostwal en de eylanden van Papsickaen, 1637." This purchase was effected by Jacob Albertzsen Planck, officier, or sheriff, of the patroon, in the presence of Gerrit de Reus and Brandt Peelen, both schepens, or magistrates of the colonie, and of Dirck Corssen and Jan Tiebkins, the one commissioner, the other skipper of the yacht "the Rensselaerswyck." The papers were signed in the director's chamber [bestelder kamer] of the colonie.

Those who have not closely studied the deeds of 1630, will be somewhat confused in reconciling dates and distinguishing landmarks. The latter have been the source of various lawsuits in the early settlement of the adjoining tracts. When application was made to the Duke of York, in 1678, for a warrant to erect the colonie into a manor, the parties interested experienced a good deal of trouble in consequence of this confusion, as we learn by a letter from Jan Baptist to Nicolaus van Rensselaer, dated London, $\frac{10}{20}$ June, 1678, of which the following is an extract:

"I must further inform you of what was nigh doing us great injury here. The lord-chancellor required of me clearer proof that the land above and below Fort Orange, mentioned in the deed of 13th August, 1630, only as 'south and

Pieter Heyser, skipper of the Whale, and Gillien Coster, commissary, had, in the mean time, secured by purchase from the Indians, for directors Godyn and Bloemmaert, the land, situate at Cape Mey, on the shore opposite their former purchase, extending sixteen miles in length along the South bay, and sixteen in breadth, thus forming a square of sixty-four miles.

CHAP III. 1630. May 5.

The lands in the neighborhood of Fort Nassau and Fort Orange having been thus appropriated, and the island of Manhattans being reserved to the company, Michel Paauw, another of the company's directors, caused the district called Hobokan-Hacking, situate opposite New Amsterdam, on the east side of the river Mauritius, to be purchased for him by the Director-general and council, to which was added, in the course of the

July 12. Aug. 10

north of Fort Orange to a little south of Moenimines Castle,' extended itself down to that. So I just found among my papers two certificates, (attestatien,) one of the 11th March, 1633, given by Gerrit Willems Oosterum, and the other of the 15th March, 1633, by the former Director, Peter Minuit, which declare that the purchase of the land, on the west side, stretched down to the Mill Creek, including Castle Island and the small tongue of land at the other side of the Mill Creek, (over de Molekill;) which two certificates I was obliged to have translated, which I also send you, as I do not want them, having the original Dutch by me. But it serves for illustration that, in the certificates, 'tis stated, 'to the Mill Creek, that is, where Albert the Noorman dwells, which lies on the west side of the river;' and in the deed, dated 13th August, 1630, 'tis stated, 'from Petanoek, the Mill Creek, unto Megagonse, which is situate on the east bank.' So, sir, you must perceive that there are two mill creeks; namely, Petanoek, the Mill Creek—the creek where Evert Pels did live in Greenbush, (in 't greene bosch;) and, in the certificates, reference is made to Albert the Noorman's Kill, commonly called the Mill Creek.

"There is, also, an obscurity in the certificates, which must be remarked. It is stated therein that the land was purchased and paid for in May, 1630; and in another deed of conveyance, which mentions some circumstances about Bastiaen Jansen Krol, it is expressly stated that the aforesaid land, from Moenimines Castle down, was purchased and paid for by Gillis Hoosett, on the 27th July, 1630, which does not seem to agree very well with the certificates. But this is thus explained: In the certificates aforesaid, allusion is made to a later purchase of land on the east side, the date of which is not stated in the certificates, which must be of the 27th July, 1630; for in the deed where Bastiaen Jansen Krol is mentioned, the date of the last purchase is set down, and in the certificates the date of the first, both which purchases are included in the deed of the 13th August, 1630." The dates of all these purchases are given in the map of Rensselaerswyck.

BOOK II. 1630. Nov. 22. following month, Staten Island, west of Hamel's Hooftden,[1] or "the Narrows;" and, some time after, Ahasimus, on which Jersey City now stands, and the peninsula Aressick, having the North River on the east, Hobokan-Hacking on the north, and surrounded by marshes "which served sufficiently for distinct boundaries."[2] The compensation to the natives for all these purchases was "certain cargoes, or parcels of goods."

The "colonie" on the South River was called Zwanendal, or the Valley of Swans; that opposite Manhattan island, Pavonia; and that in the neighborhood of Fort Orange, Rensselaerswyck. In the colony of Zwanendal was "cradled" the present flourishing state of Delaware. In that of Pavonia were laid the first foundations of the fruitful state of New Jersey.

The possession or proprietorship of these vast tracts of wilderness would, it was at once seen, prove rather a burden than a source of profit, if means were not adopted to reclaim and improve them. To accomplish this the more successfully, it was considered the properest course to form associations with other wealthy persons, and thus, by giving these a direct pecuniary interest in the undertaking, obtain more ample means to reach the object in view, while such an arrangement would, at the same time, allay some portion of that jealousy and dissatisfaction which other directors might naturally feel who had not been sufficiently alert to seize, at a more early period, the advantages proffered by the charter of 1629.[3]

Oct. 1. A copartnership was accordingly entered into between Kiliaen van Rensselaer, Samuel Godyn, Johannes de Laet, and Samuel Bloemmaert, with whom were associated Adam Bissels and Toussaint Moussart, who, by the terms of the contract, were constituted co-directors of Rensselaerswyck. The common stock of this association was divided into five shares, of which Van Rensselaer held two; De Laet, one;

[1] These "Hooftden," or headlands, were called after Hamel, one of the directors of the company. Moulton.

[2] Book of Patents, GG. 7, 8, 9, 17, 18, 19, 20, 21, 22, 27, 28, 29, 30, &c. Hoboken is so called after a village of the same name situate on the Scheld, a few miles south of Antwerp. Modern map-makers have converted Ahasimus into "Horsimus;" for what reason they, perhaps, would find it difficult to determine.

[3] Moulton, 404.

Godyn, one; and Bloemmaert and his associates, one; and the management of the affairs of the colonie was committed to a board consisting of four persons or votes, of which Van Rensselaer represented, or held two; Bloemmaert, or Bissels, one; and De Laet, or Moussart, one. Van Rensselaer was, however, not to have any rank or authority in the colonie superior to his associates, except the title of Patroon, which, with all its feudal honors, was vested in him alone, the partners binding themselves to do fealty and homage for the fief on his demise, in the name, and on the behalf of his son and heirs.[1]

CHAP. III. 1630.

[1] This contract, and the articles of agreement, are referred to in the judgment of the Court of Holland, dated 14th June, 1650, in re Bloemmaert et al. vs. Van Twiller et al., which judgment was ratified by the States General on the same day. Hol. Doc. v., 298. Alb. Rec. viii., 72, 73. Rensselaerswyck MSS. It has been maintained, by some, that there was no partnership interest in the colonie of Rensselaerswyck, and that the claim of Bloemmaert, De Laet, and the other partners was not allowed. But the judgment here referred to shows that such an assertion is contrary to the fact. The suit was decided in favor of Bloemmaert and his associates, and the executors of the first Patroon were condemned to account for the rents and profits, and to pay to each of the partners, or their heirs, their just quota. The partnership is, moreover, plainly admitted in the account of the disbursements for the first venture to Rensselaerswyck, anno 1630, wherein the sums advanced by the other co-directors are admitted and acknowledged. [See Appendix G.] Ample evidence of the fact will be further found by reference to the Rensselaerswyck MSS., and to Hol. Doc. vi., 303, 304, 306. De Vries also mentions the circumstance. Subsequently, however, Johanna de Laet, widow of Johannes de Hulter, and who married, secondly, Jeremias Ebbing, sold to the Van Rensselaers, in the year 1674, all her right and claim, as heiress of Johannes de Laet, to the colonie of Rensselaerswyck, for the sum of fl. 5,762 10st. or $2,301, which debt was discharged by the transfer to her of certain bouweries and lands which were deemed an equivalent. This lady was proprietor, among other tracts, of the Weyland, or pasture, lying between the third and fourth kills, now called, in the map of the city of Albany, Rutten and Fox creeks. On the 20th of April, 1685, Gerrit Bissels and Nicolaus van Beeck, (nomine uxoris,) both representing the children and heirs of Adam Bissels and Margt. Reust, entitled to one tenth part; and as attorneys for Abraham Elsevier (husband of Catharina Bloemmaert) and Isbrand Schenk, Constantina Bloemmaert, (widow of Isaac Sweers, in his lifetime, Vice-Admiral in the service of Holland,) and Juffrouw Anna Bloemmaert, (widow of Francois Romayn,) children and heirs of Samuel Bloemmaert and Catharine Reust, conjointly entitled to one tenth part of the colonie of Rensselaerswyck, sold, in Amsterdam, to Richard and Kiliaen van Rensselaer, Patroon of said colonie, their respective shares, being two tenths, or one fifth of the whole, for gl. 3,600, payable in three equal yearly parts. Thus all claims on the part of the original part-

BOOK II. Another association was formed, a few days afterwards, between Godyn, Van Rensselaer, Bloemmaert, De Laet, Mathias
1630. Oct. 16. van Cuelen, Hendrick Hamel, Johan van Harinckhouck, and Nicolaus van Sitterich, also directors of the West India Company, and Capt. David Pieterssen de Vries, for planting a colonie on the South River. Equalizing all expected advantages, they equipped a ship and yacht for that quarter, where they designed raising tobacco and grain, and prosecuting the whale-fishery, oil bringing then a fair price in Holland.[1] Preparations were also made to expedite farmers and cattle to Rensselaerswyck; and everywhere, at home and abroad, things wore the aspect of prosperity, and "promised fairlie both to the state and undertakers."[2]

In the mean time such had been the activity of the agents employed by the patroons to purchase their colonies, that the titles obtained from the Indians were laid, duly authenticated by the Director-general and council at Fort Amsterdam, before
Nov. 28. the Assembly of the XIX, early in the fall, when the new patroons received the congratulations of the other directors of
Dec. 2. the company. The formal enregistration of these patents followed a few days afterwards, when they were sealed "with
Dec. 16. the seal of New Netherland." Fourteen days subsequently, complete lists of the several patroonships were delivered to the company's solicitor, and the whole transactions were unani-
1631. mously confirmed by the Assembly of the XIX, at the meeting
Jan. 8. of that body in Zealand, in the beginning of the following year.[3]

ners, to any portion of the colonie, became finally extinguished; and that estate vested altogether and exclusively in the Van Rensselaer family.

[1] De Vries, Korte Historiael.

[2] The condition of Dutch settlements on the North River, at this time, is thus alluded to by a contemporary English writer:—"This which they have settled in New England upon Hudson's River, with no extraordinary charge or multitude of people, is knowne to subsist in a comfortable manner, and to promise fairlie both to the state and undertakers. The cause is evident:—The men whom they carrie, though they be not many, are well chosen, and known to be useful and serviceable; and they second them with seasonable and fit supplies, cherishing them as carefully as their owne families, and employ them in profitable labors, that are knowne to be of speciall use to their comfortable subsisting." The Planters' Plea; London, 1630.

[3] Hol. Doc. i., 176, 180, 181, 184. Letter of Patroons Paauw, Bloemmaert et al. to States General, ii., 100, 101.

Two vessels were dispatched this year to New Netherland. CHAP. III.
The imports amounted to 57,499 guilders, or about $23,000.
The exports consisted of 7,126 peltries, valued at 68,012 gl., 1631.
being a little more than the value of the imports.

Meanwhile the expedition under De Vries had safely arrived at the South River. The settlers, thirty in number, were landed, with their implements of husbandry, on the western shore, about three leagues within Cape Cornelius, near the entrance of a fine navigable stream, called the Hoarkill. Here the party proceeded, without loss of time, to erect a house surrounded with palisadoes, without parapets or breastwork, which served as their fort, trading-house, and place of residence. In the spring and summer they prepared their fields, put in their crops, and were in a fair way of succeeding, when De Vries left "Zwanendal" on his return to Holland, to report his proceedings to the interested parties there.[1]

The object of the Patroons seemed at first, however, to be a participation in the Indian trade, rather than the colonization of the country. They assumed to be privileged, by the 15th article of their charter, to traffic with the natives, not only along the coast and adjoining places, from Florida to Newfoundland, but throughout the interior, on the rivers and in the bays "where the company had no commissaries at the time the charter of 1629 was granted." The prospects which that trade afforded led them easily to interfere with what the other directors considered to be the vested rights of the company. This interference created such competition, and affected so directly the company's interests, that a revision of the Articles of Freedoms soon followed. New articles were Oct. 30.
proposed, limiting essentially the privileges already granted to Patroons; "nay, the whole of the Exemptions were questioned and called into doubt."[2]

[1] De Vries; Moulton, 405, 406, 407. All the authorities which Moulton quotes fix the year 1630 as the date of the erection of the fort at Zwanendal. De Vries says he sailed from the Texel Dec. 12, 1630. It remains to be determined if he could cross the Atlantic at that early period, and build his house, all in eighteen days. Possibly Moulton's authorities reckoned according to Old Style.

[2] De Articulen van Exemptien anno 1628 gearresteerd; 1629 gerevideert en

BOOK II. 1632. These quarrels were soon brought before their High Mightinesses the States General, who immediately called for a return of the names of all those to whom colonies had been
March 19. granted. The mischievous effects of these disputes did not stop here. De Razier fell into disgrace with his employers, "by reason of their factions;" Minuit, the Director-general, under whose administration those vast alienations of the public domain had taken place, was recalled, and the immediate colonization and settlement of the country, of which there had been some prospect, was thus, once more, indefinitely postponed.

Director Minuit embarked for Holland in the spring, together with Sheriff Lampo, in the ship Union, (Eendracht,) carrying with him five thousand beaver skins, on account of the company.[1]

The British companies, who had obtained charters from the crown to settle plantations in Virginia and New England, were, all this time, not unaware of the activity with which the Dutch were pushing their trade along the whole North American coast, from the Chesapeake to Cape Cod. Governor Bradford had already transmitted accounts to Sir Ferdinando Gorges and the council of New England, of the commercial intercourse between the inhabitants of Manhattans and the settlers at New Plymouth, with copies of the correspondence which had passed between himself and the Dutch. The more active members of the New England Company considered it, therefore, incumbent on them to adopt stringent measures to secure their privileges, and to preserve the rights with which they were invested by their charters; and the occasion soon offered to put their determination, in this regard, into execution.

geampliceert; door de Patroonen geamplecteert; anno 1630 daarover gecongratuleert; anno 1631 ex suprabondante gejustifeceert, zyn bedecklelyck gemineert op den 30 Octob. 1631, als wanneer nieuwe articulen gesmeed zyn, daarby de voorige vryheden en exemptien niet langer impetrabile waren, de patroonen belast en preciesheyt te presteren; saacken, die de ervarentheyd leerde niet practicabel te wesen; ja, alle de Exemptien in dispute getrocken. Patroons' letter to States General, June, 1634. Hol. Doc. ii., 102, 103.

[1] Ibid. i., 185, 210.

CHAP. III. 1632.

The company's ship in which Director Minuit and Sheriff Lampo were returning, "with a number of persons with their wives and children," to Holland, was forced, by stress of weather, to put into the port of Plymouth. She was seized, immediately on her arrival there, at the suit of the New England company, on a charge of having traded to, and obtained her cargo in, countries subject to his Britannic Majesty. Captain Mason, who had caused this step to be taken, followed it up by addressing a complaint to the secretary of state against the Dutch, who, he represented, "fell as interlopers" into the middle betwixt the plantations of Virginia and New England, "giving the name of the Prince of Aurange to the countrie and river of Manahata," which they planted, besides imposing "other Dutch names on other places, to the eastward of the said Manahata, as farr as Cape Cod, all which had been formerly discovered and traded unto, diverse tymes, by several Englishmen, as may be proved." He further represented that, notwithstanding the alleged disclaimer of the States General and their ambassador in 1621, they had maintained their position, fortified themselves in two several places, "and built shipps there, whereof one was sent to Holland of six hundred tunnes, or thereabouts;"—and though they had been warned by the people of New Plymouth to abstain from trading and making settlements in those parts, as "they were the territories of the king of England, yet they, nevertheless, with proude and contumacious answers, (saying they had commission to fight against such as should disturbe their settlement,) did persist to plant and trade, vilefying our (the English) nation to the Indians, and extolling theire owne people and countrie of Holland, and have made sundry good returnes of commodities from thence into Holland; especially this yeare they have returned, as reported, fifteen thousand beaver skynnes, besides other articles."[1]

March

April 2. O. S.

Director Minuit, indignant at what he considered an aggression on the company's rights, as well as on the law of nations, hurried up to London, where he laid before Messrs.

April 3.

[1] Lond. Doc. i., 47, 48, 49. For this letter, as well as for one from Sir F Gorges to Captain Mason on this subject, see Appendix, D.

BOOK II. 1632. April 5. Joachimi and Brasser, the Dutch ambassadors, an account of the seizure of his ship. Their excellencies lost no time in proceeding to Newmarket, where the king then held his court, and at an audience to which they were admitted, laid before his majesty a long remonstrance against the proceedings of the authorities at Plymouth. In this representation they exposed the fact that the Dutch had traded for a number of years to the river Manhattans, "now called the Maurice;" that they had, moreover, enjoyed the free use of his majesty's harbors and ports, in coming and going; and concluded by demanding the release of the Eendracht, so that she and her passengers and crew might be enabled to proceed on their voyage.

His majesty received this remonstrance with the most gracious attention, but gave, at the same time, the ambassadors to understand, that he was informed by the governor of Plymouth, that the States General had, on complaint of his royal father, forbidden their subjects to trade to those countries. His majesty should, however, abstain from saying any thing on the matter then, but promised to inquire further into it. In the mean time he declined ordering the release of the Dutch ship, until the whole affair should be further investigated.

April 10. Messrs. Joachimi and Brasser, on receipt of this reply, wrote to the Hague, detailing these particulars, and recommended that all documentary evidence, in support of the Dutch right to trade to New Netherland, be forthwith forwarded to them, "as that right will undoubtedly be sharply disputed in England."

The directors of the West India Company were, on their side, not idle. Immediately on learning the seizure of their ship, they addressed a memorial to the States General, setting forth the fact, which they attributed to the intrigues of the
May 5. Spanish ambassador in London, and in the course of some days afterwards, laid before their High Mightinesses, at considerable length, a deduction of their title to the country. This paper, embodying, as it must be presumed, the grounds on which the Dutch rested, at this early date, their right to

their North American possessions, deserves a more than passing attention.

"After the North River," they proceed, "commonly called the Manhattoes, also Rio de Montaigne, and North River, was first discovered, in the year 1609, by subjects of their High Mightinesses, and visited by some of their citizens in 1610, and following years, a grant was made in the year 1615, [11th Oct. 1614,] to some of their subjects of the trade to that country, to the exclusion of all others. A small fort and garrison were also established there, which were maintained, until the charter granted to the West India Company included these, as well as other countries.

"In the year 1606, His Britannic Majesty granted, by special charter, to his subjects the country south and north of the aforesaid river, under the name of New England and Virginia, with express condition that the respective companies should remain one hundred miles the one from the other, and leave so much between them both.

"Whereupon the English began, about the year 1607, a plantation by the river Sagadahoc, which the settlers afterwards abandoned; and no new plantation was undertaken by the English, north of New Netherland, before the year 1620, when one which they named New Plymouth was commenced behind Cape Cod.

"The English, themselves, place New England along the coast between the forty-first and forty-fifth degrees. The English began, in 1606, to frequent Virginia, which lies south of our aforesaid New Netherland, the limits of which they fix, according to their charter, from the thirty-seventh to the thirty-ninth degree.

"So that our limits, according to their own statement, should be from the thirty-ninth degree inclusive to the forty-first, between which degrees it is not known to us that they ever had any designs.

"What limits your High Mightinesses have given your subjects can be seen by the Octroy granted in 1615, [1614,] which your H. M. will please to cause to be examined. We have no knowledge of what His Majesty alleges regarding the demand made by his father, nor of what followed."

BOOK II. 1632. The directors, therefore, urged on the States General the propriety of instructing their ambassadors at the British court to demand the release of the company's ships and goods; for, they reasoned, the natives of America were free; subjects neither of the king of Great Britain nor of their High Mightinesses, and at liberty to trade with whomsoever they pleased. His majesty, they admitted, might confer, by charter, this trade on any association composed of his subjects, to the exclusion of all others his subjects; but it was, they insisted, contrary to all law and reason for any power to prevent the subjects of others to traffic in a country of which it never took actual possession, and a title to which it never obtained from the right owners, either by contract or purchase, much less to set up a claim to lands, the property of which the subjects of their High Mightinesses have obtained, partly by treaty with the proprietors of the soil, and partly by purchase. The directors concluded this able chain of reasoning, by demanding particularly of the States General to maintain their own sovereignty, the freedom of the seas, as well as the validity of those contracts which were entered into with distant nations, who, by nature, were independent of all, and had not been subjected to any power by conquest.

Copies of this vindication of the company's rights, as well as of the octroy of 1614, were immediately ordered by the States General to be sent to England to Messrs. Joachimi and Brasser, who were informed, at the same time, that it was the determination of their High Mightinesses to maintain the right of the West India Company to trade to New Netherland.

The remonstrance which the Dutch ambassadors had presented to Charles I., at Newmarket, had, in the mean time, been duly considered by the king's council, and Mr. Secretary Cook waited, some weeks after, on their excellencies with a
May 22. long and formal reply, on the part of his majesty and the Lords Commissioners of England, in support of the British claim to those countries, of which the West India Company had now possession in North America.[1]

[1] Thomas Morton, of Cliffords Inn, gent., addressed, this year, to the Right Honorable the Lords Commissioners of the Plantations, a pamphlet entitled "New English Canaan," being "an abstract of New England," in which he

CHAP. III. 1632.

"The Dutch demand restitution," say their lordships, "of a certain ship, seized at Plymouth, on her return from a certain plantation by them usurped, north of Virginia, which, they allege, they acquired from the natives of those countries. It is denied, first, that the savages were possessors bonæ fidei, of those countries, so as to be able to dispose thereof either by sale or gift, their habitations being changeable, (mouvantes,) uncertain, and only in common. Secondly, it cannot be proved, de facto, that all the natives of said countries were parties to the said pretended sale. And as regards the allegation that the said natives have their abode around about them, the truth is, the English surround them on all sides, as they have already well discovered when they prosecuted the maintenance of their rights against them. But more than this :—the rights belonging to his majesty's subjects in that country are justified by first discovery, occupation, and possession which they have taken thereof, and by charters and letters patent obtained from our sovereigns, who, for these purposes, were the true and legitimate proprietors there where the Lords the States have not assumed to themselves [ne se sont attribués] such pretensions, and have not granted any charter to their subjects conveying in itself any title or power to them. Which was proved [se verifia] in the year 1621, when the late king, of happy memory, on the complaint and remonstrance of the Earl of Arundel, of the knights Fer. Horges, (Gorges,) and Samuel Argall, and of Captain Mason, directed his ambassador to urge on their Lordships, the States General, to prevent the departure of certain vessels which were preparing to proceed to the aforesaid country, and to forbid their subjects to settle in that plantation; for their answer was, that they knew nothing of said enterprise, which indeed appeared very probable, because the said ambassador, after having informed himself more particularly of the matter, assured his majesty, in those letters, that it was only

accused the Dutch of a design to seize on "the Great Lake of Erocoise," (Champlain,) which, he adds, they can accomplish "by means of the river Mohegan, which by the English is named Hudson's River, where the Dutch have settled two well-fortified plantations already." Possibly this and other such publications of that day, may account for the tone of this reply of the English privy council.

BOOK II. 1632. two companies of merchants of Amsterdam, who, without the knowledge or advice of the said Lords, the States General, had commenced a traffic between 40° and 50°, in the limits of his majesty's plantation, to the said countries of Virginia, and had given to those places there the names of New Netherland, [Nouveaux Pays-bas,] Texel, Vlieland, &c., and sent ships of thirty and forty lasts to these regions in search of peltries; but that they had not learned that they had yet commenced, or meditated to establish a plantation there; and, moreover, that a goodly number of families, inhabitants of the said United Provinces, had then been soliciting him to procure for them a spot in the said country where they could dwell among his majesty's subjects. That now if those who are returned from there, and the others who have remained behind, wish to make a similar petition, and to submit themselves to his majesty's government, as his majesty's subjects, they may know if it shall please him to admit them in that quality, and thus permit them to proceed thither with their ships and merchandise, or to sell them here at the highest price; provided that their Lordships the States shall prevent them from proceeding thither any more, or frequenting in any manner those regions. To which, if they do not consent, his majesty's interest will not permit him to allow them thus to usurp and encroach on one of his colonies of such importance, which he has great cause to cherish and maintain in its integrity.

"By these replies to the aforesaid complaints, their Lordships the States General will understand how little ground they have to enter on their neighbors' territory, in defiance of any alienation thereof by his majesty."

This positive assertion of the British title to New Netherland does not appear to have brought forth any rejoinder from the ambassadors of their High Mightinesses. They, however, continued to press for the release of the Union, and their
May 27. demand was finally conceded by the lord high treasurer, "saving and without any prejudice to his majesty's rights," as the detention of the vessel, thus far, had all the effect the government desired, which was to assert a title that uninterrupted possession might possibly impair or destroy.[1]

[1] Hol. Doc. i., 187, 188, 190, 200, 202, 205, 210, 211, 212, 213, 214, 216,

In the mean time the unfortunate misunderstanding between the directors of the company and the Patroons, arising out of opposite constructions of certain articles of the charter of 1629, interrupted the efforts then beginning to be made to settle this new country. The former were particularly jealous of all interference in the Indian trade, which the company had specially reserved to itself; while the Patroons, on the other hand, considered that trade to be open to them, on certain conditions. So serious now became these differences, that some of the principal partners drew up a series of charges against the directors for having altered the exemptions, who, on the other hand, issued a placard strictly excluding all "private persons" from dealing in "peltries, maize, and wampum." The Patroons persisted that this did not apply to them, as they were privileged, not private, individuals; but the company determined otherwise, and in order to shut the Patroons and their people everywhere and at once from all traffic in the above commodities, sent commissaries and assistant-commissaries to the different colonies, or patroon ships, with instructions to post up the aforesaid placard there; to prevent any person, whether Patroon or vassal, from interfering in the forbidden trade; and to oblige the inhabitants of the several patroonships, by an oath, to refrain from trading in any way in Indian corn, sewan, or furs.[1]

CHAP. III. 1632. May 28. June 8. Nov. 18.

While these disputes were raging, intelligence reached Holland, unexpectedly, that the savages had utterly destroyed the colonie of Zwanendal, which De Vries had planted, in the beginning of the last year, at the mouth of the Delaware.

It happened that the Dutch, in keeping with the practice prevalent in those days, had erected, on taking possession of this new plantation, a pillar on a prominent part of their territory, to which they affixed, in token of sovereignty, a piece

219, 236, 237, 238, 239, 240, 246, 252. Beauchamp Plantagenet, in his singular pamphlet entitled "A Description of the Province of New Albion," (p. 18,) mentions the seizure of Minuit's ship in these words: "The next pretended Dutch governor, in maps and printed charts calling this part New Netherland, failing in paying of customes at his return to Plymouth, in England, was there, with his bever goods and person, attached to his damage of £1500."

[1] Hol. Doc. ii., 103, 104, 113.

BOOK II. 1632. of tin, on which they traced the emblem, or arms of the United Provinces. An Indian chief, in want of a tobacco pipe, took a fancy to this glittering sheet, for the purpose of supplying his want, and carried it off, ignorant that there was any impropriety in the act.

Gillis Hoossett, one of the company's men, whom De Vries had left in charge of his fort, inconsiderately viewed the innocent act of the untutored savage as a national insult, and evinced so much dissatisfaction, that the Indians, to make amends for this unintentional offence, killed the chief who had taken the piece of tin away, and returned with a token of the bloody deed. This naturally shocked the Dutch commander, who explained to the Indians that they had done wrong; that they ought to have brought the chief to him, and he should have told him not to repeat the act. But the spirit of wild revenge had been roused, meanwhile, in the breasts of the friends and kinsmen of the murdered chief, and they de termined on wreaking dire and dreadful vengeance.

The colonie of Zwanendal consisted, at this time, of thirty four persons. Of these, thirty-two were one day at work in the fields, while commissary Hoossett remained in charge of the house, where another of the settlers lay sick abed. A large bull-dog was chained out of doors. On pretence of selling some furs, three savages entered the house, and murdered Hoossett[1] and the sick man. They found it not so easy to dispatch the mastiff. It was not until they had pierced him with at least twenty-five arrows that he was destroyed. The men in the fields were then set on, in an equally treacherous manner, under the guise of friendship, and every man of them slain. Thus terminated the colonie of the Valley of Swans, to the great loss of the projectors, as well as to the great injury of their characters as cautious and prudent men.

It was after the occurrence of this melancholy and unforeseen catastrophe, that De Vries reached the mouth of the South River, at the close of the year, "promising himself great things, plenty of whales, and good land for cultivation."

[1] This Hoossett was an active agent in purchasing the lands around Fort Orange for Van Rensselaer.

He found his house destroyed, the palisades, by which it was surrounded, burned, and the heads and bones of his murdered men bestrewing the earth. No hum of industry enlivened the gloomy solitude. Not a human being appeared to respond to the signal gun, which De Vries ordered to be fired to give notice of his arrival. CHAP. III. 1632. Dec. 6

Having succeeded, however, on the next day, in opening a communication with the Indians, De Vries invited them to "a talk," as he considered it to be his best policy not to take notice of the past, finding he had no means to punish the guilty aggressors. The Indians came with their chief; and sitting down in a circle, concluded a peace with the Dutch, who presented them, in ratification of the treaty, with some duffels, bullets, axes, and Nuremberg trinkets. The natives parted with their visitors, greatly pleased that these had taken no notice of their treacherous behavior. Dec. 9

These things being thus satisfactorily accomplished, De Vries proceeded up the South River with a view to obtain supplies. The country was a wilderness uninhabited by any Europeans. Fort Nassau, which the Dutch had erected on the east bank of the river some ten years before, was abandoned, and now in possession of the Indians, who evinced a hostile disposition as far up as Timmerkill, or Cooper's Creek. 1633. Jan. 1.

Finding this unfavorable state of feeling, De Vries dropped down again opposite Fort Nassau, where he was visited by nine chiefs of the neighboring tribes, with whom he also concluded a permanent peace. The Dutch were now told to banish all suspicion, for all evil thoughts were at an end. De Vries offered the Indians presents in return for their beavers, with which they had ratified this peace; but these they refused. They had not given their presents to obtain any in return, but as tokens of their having made a firm peace.[1] Jan. 8.

The trade to New Netherland was exceedingly profitable during the past year. The company sent out one ship with a cargo valued at a little over thirty-one thousand guilders, ($13,000.) The exports consisted of fifteen thousand, one hundred and seventy-four skins, the greater portion of which

[1] De Vries.

BOOK II. 1633. was beaver. These were valued at one hundred and forty three thousand, one hundred and twenty-five guilders, equal to $57,250 of our currency. It is not to be wondered at, therefore, that the company was desirous of retaining such a trade in their own hands.[1]

[1] De Laet. "It is well knowne to some of our English nation that have lived in the Dutch plantation, that the Dutch have gained by beaver 20,000 pound a yeare." Morton's N. Eng. Canaan, published 1632. Capt. Mason's letter, dated April 2, 1632, O. S., in Lond. Doc. i., 47.

CHAPTER IV.

Wouter van Twiller appointed Director-general—Arrives in New Netherland—His council—Other officers of the company in that country—First clergyman and first schoolmaster in New Amsterdam—An English vessel visits the Manhattans for the purpose of trading with the Indians on the Hudson's River—Director and council refuse permission to her to ascend the river—Sails to Fort Orange, notwithstanding—Opens a trade with the natives thereabout—Is opposed by the commissary at that post—Indians prefer trading with the English factor, who had been in the Dutch service, several years before, in that quarter—Three vessels arrive with troops from Fort Amsterdam, to prevent the English trading with these Indians—Pull down the English tent—Force their people and goods on board their ship, which they convoy out of the river—Damages inflicted on the English—Quarrel between two English skippers at the Manhattans—Van Twiller opposes De Vries, who wishes to visit the Sound—Contentions in consequence—De Vries' opinions of the functionaries at Fort Amsterdam—Notelman, schout-fiscaal, superseded—Is succeeded by Van Dinclage—Van Twiller determines to build a fort on the Fresh River—Sketch of the quarrels between the Indians there—Tract of country called Conneticock purchased—Deed of sale—Fort Good Hope built—New Plymouth people determine to build a trading-house on the Fresh River—Proceedings in consequence—Van Twiller protests—This protest disregarded—Writes to the XIX.—Attempts to dislodge the English by force; without success—Improvements in New Amsterdam—New fort—Church and other houses erected—Improvements at Fort Orange and Fort Nassau—Schuylkill purchased—Resources of the West India Company—Trade of New Netherland.

CHAP. IV. 1633

The return of Director Minuit having rendered necessary the appointment of another Director-general over New Netherland, Wouter van Twiller, of Nieuwkerke, one of the clerks in the employ of the West India Company, and a near relative of the Patroon van Rensselaer, received that high and responsible office. This appointment occasioned, at first, considerable surprise. It seems to have been owing to the above connection, rather than to any particular merit of the nominee, who arrived at Fort Amsterdam in the spring of this year, in the company's ship the Salt Mountain, (de Zoutberg,) of twenty guns,[1] manned with fifty-two men, and having on

April.

[1] De Laet rates the Zoutberg at 140 lasts burden, carrying six metal and twelve iron guns. Appendix to Jaerlyck Verhael, 5. De Vries settles the date

BOOK II. 1633. board, for the service of the province, one hundred and four soldiers, the first military force ever detailed for New Netherland.

The council of the Director-general was composed of Captain Jacob Jansen Hesse, Martin Gerrittsen, Andries Hudde, and Jacques Bentyn. Conraed Notelman succeeded Lampo as schout-fiscaal, and Jan van Remund continued to act as colonial secretary. Among the other officers in the service of the company in New Netherland, during this administration, in addition to those mentioned in preceding pages, were Cornelis van Tienhoven, book-keeper of monthly wages; Claes van Elslandt, Jacob Stoffelsen, of Ziericksee, Jacob van Curler, Maurits Jansen, commissaries; Hans Jorissen Houten, who traded here in 1621, was governor or commissary of Fort Orange; Michael Poulaz of Pavonia, and Arent Corssen of Fort Nassau. Claes Jacobsen van Schagen acted as overseer at Fort Amsterdam, at which place the Rev. Everardus Bogardus officiated as minister of the gospel.[1]

The new Director-general was accompanied to the Manhattans by the carvel St. Martyn, or the Hope, which was captured from the enemy in the course of the preceding year. This vessel was commanded by Juriaen Blanck, and on board of her came Govert Lookermans an apprentice, who, immediately on his arrival, was taken, together with Jacob van Kouwenhoven, into the company's employ. The latter was

of the new Director-general's arrival, and furnishes the names of the schout-fiscaal and secretary under him, which are also given in Hol. Doc. ii., 88. Van Twiller married his cousin, Maria Momma, niece of the Patroon of Rensselaerswyck

[1] Hol. Doc. ii., 88; ix., 187; Alb. Rec. ii., 328, GG, 31, 57. The earliest mention I find of Rev. E. Bogardus is in Alb. Rec. ii., where reference is made to a letter from him to Van Twiller, dated 17th June, 1634. It is to be presumed that he came out with that Director-general. He is the first clergyman of whom we have any mention in New Netherland. Where he came from, originally, I have not been able to ascertain, but his brother, Cornelis Willemsen Bogaerdt, resided at Leyden, in South Holland, in 1647–8. Possibly he, also, might have been from that place. He married, about 1637 or 1638, Annetje, relict of Roeloff Jansen, of Masterlandt, the daughter of Tryn Jansen, midwife at New Amsterdam, and a connection, by marriage, of Govert Lookermans, surgeon Hans Kierstede, and Pieter Hartgers. The Rev. Mr. Bogardus was proprietor of a tobacco plantation on the island of Manhattans, which he rented, in 1639, on shares, to Richard Brudnel.

accompanied by his father to New Netherland. Adam Roelandsen, "schoolmaster," arrived at New Amsterdam about the same time.[1] CHAP. IV. 1633.

Van Twiller had scarcely been installed in his new government when he began to experience the troubles of office.

Messrs. William Clobery, David Morehead, and John de la Barre, merchants at London, dispatched, in the course of the preceding December, a vessel called the William, commanded by one Capt. Trevor, with passengers and goods for Massachusetts Bay; with further orders to set up a fishing-post at a place called Scituate, near New Plymouth, and then to proceed to the Hudson's River to trade.[2]

In conformity with the latter part of these instructions, the William arrived, in due season, opposite Fort Amsterdam, freighted with goods for the Indian trade, and having on board, as factor or supercargo, Jacob Jacobs Eelkins, who had been formerly commissary of the fort on Castle Island, in the service of the United New Netherland Company, which association, it will be recollected, traded to these parts previous to the incorporation of the West India Company. Immediately on casting anchor, Eelkins sent Wm. Deepings, "chirurgeon of said ship," ashore to invite the Director-general on board, but instead of accepting the invitation, Van Twiller ordered the messenger to direct the master of the ship and his factor to come to the fort, as he wished to inquire if they knew the Prince of Orange.[3] Eelkins, with the surgeon and gunner of the ship, proceeded accordingly ashore, where they found the Director-general and his officers in council together, who immediately demanded by what authority they had come hither, and what April 12.

[1] Hol. Doc. v., 396, 399; Alb. Rec. i., 52, 107, 172.

[2] Winthrop's Journal, 48.

[3] De Vries gives a different version of this affair. He says, "The Englishman invited the commander to dine with him. I, with some others, was of the company. The people soon got intoxicated, and began to quarrel. The Englishman was astonished that such irregularities could take place among the officers of the company, and that the commander had no more control over them, such things not being customary among them." Eelkins' deposition on oath, which I follow, makes no mention of Van Twiller having been on board the William; the passage in De Vries refers to a subsequent transaction, the particulars of which will be found a few pages further on.

BOOK II. 1633. was their business? Eelkins replied, that he had come to trade with the natives for furs, as he had formerly done. His commission was then called for, but this he refused to produce; he said he was within the king's dominions, and a servant, then, of his majesty's subjects; telling the council, at the same time, to look to what sort of commission they themselves had to plant within the dominions of the king of England. Hereupon the Director-general replied, that he had conferred with his council, and that they did not find it fitting that he (Eelkins) should pass up the river, as the whole of that country belonged to the Prince of Orange, and not to the English king.

April 17. After an interval of five days, the factor of the William went again on shore to the fort, to inquire if the director-general would permit him, in a friendly way, to ascend the river, stating at the same time that, if he would not allow it, he (Eelkins) would proceed without his consent, if it should cost him his life. But Van Twiller was immoveable. Instead of consenting, he ordered the ship's crew on shore, and, in the presence of all, commanded the Prince of Orange's flag to be run up the fort, and three pieces of ordnance to be fired off in honor of his highness. Eelkins, not to be outdone, immediately ordered his gunner to go on board the William—to hoist the English flag, and fire a salute also of three guns in honor of the king of England, which was accordingly done.[1] Van Twiller now warned Eelkins to take heed that what he was about did not cost him his neck. Eelkins, however, no way daunted, returned on board with the ship's crew. The anchor was weighed, and the William shortly after sailed up the river, "near to a fort called Orange."[2]

April 24. Director Van Twiller, incensed at this audacity, collected all the servants of the company in the fort before his door—ordered a barrel of wine to be broached, and having taken a bumper, cried out, "Those who love the Prince of Orange and me, emulate me in this, and assist me in repelling the violence committed by that Englishman!" The cask of wine was soon emptied, but the people were no ways disposed at first to trouble the Englishman. Capt. De Vries urged on Van Twiller,

[1] William Forde, the gunner, corroborates this statement.

[2] Hol. Doc. ii., 81, 83, 84, 85.

however, the necessity of vindicating the rights of the company; represented that the English ship had no authority except a clearance from the custom-house, which entitled them to trade, not to New Netherland, but to New England, and maintained that he, the Director, ought to send the armed ship the Salt Mountain after her, to force her down, and to drive her out of the river.[1]

The William having, in the mean while, arrived in the neighborhood of Fort Orange, the factor and crew went ashore "about a mile below that fort," set up a tent, and, having landed all their goods, immediately opened an active trade with the natives. It was not long before the news of these proceedings came to the ears of Houten, the commissary at Fort Orange. He forthwith embarked, with a trumpeter, on board a shallop, over which waved some green bows, and proceeded to where Eelkins was. "By the way the trumpet was sounded, and the Dutchmen drank a bottle of strong waters of three or four pints, and were right merry." The Dutch set up a tent by the side of that of the English; did as much as they could to disparage their cloth and other goods, with a view to hinder the latter's trade; but the Indians, having been well acquainted with Eelkins, who had "heretofore lived four yeares among them," and could speak their language, were a great deal more willing to trade with him than with the others, and he consequently had every prospect of advantageously disposing of his merchandise, having been fourteen days there, when a Dutch officer arrived from below, in command of three vessels—a pinnace, a carvel, and a hoy, bearing two letters, protesting against Eelkins, and ordering him to depart forthwith.

To enforce these commands came soldiers "from both the Dutch forts, armed with muskets, half-pikes, swords, and other weapons," and after having beaten several of the Indians who had come to trade with Eelkins, ordered the latter to strike his tent. In vain he pleaded that he was on British soil, and that British subjects had a right to trade there; the Dutch would not listen to any remonstrances. They pulled the tent about his ears—sent the goods on board—"and as they were carry-

[1] De Vries.

BOOK II. ing them to the ship, sounded their trumpet in the boat in disgrace of the English!"

1633. The Dutch now went on board the William, weighed her anchors, and ordered her down to Fort Amsterdam, their three vessels keeping her company all the time, to prevent any intercourse with the natives. On the arrival of the vessel opposite Manhattan Island, the Director-general ordered Eelkins to bring whatever furs he had on board to the fort, but this the latter refused to do. A list of all the peltries was then demanded and furnished.

Finding the object of the voyage thus frustrated, Eelkins demanded from some of the residents of New Amsterdam a certificate to prove the treatment which he had received; but Van Twiller, anticipating such a demand, and clearly foreseeing its object, had already ordered a proclamation to be affixed to the gate of the fort, forbidding any of the people to give such a paper, "on pain of death and loss of all their wages." And the William of London, the first English ship that ascended the Hudson, was forced to put to sea shortly after this, convoyed out of the river by a Dutch yacht. Her owners estimated the damages which they experienced on this occasion at five thousand pounds sterling. Had their ship remained but a month longer, they expected the Maquaas from the interior with four thousand, and the Mohegans with three thousand skins; for the annual trade in furs, on the North River, was, at this period, estimated at from fifteen thousand to sixteen thousand beavers.[1]

A quarrel occurred at the Manhattans between two English skippers about this time. One of these, a Capt. Stone, from Virginia, who was proceeding to Massachusetts Bay with a cargo of cows and salt, touched at New Amsterdam, and met a New Plymouth pinnace riding at anchor before that place. A few evenings after, Stone invited the Director-general on

[1] Hol. Doc. ii., 51, 55, 57, 61, 62, 63, 66, 67, 68, 76, 77, 86, 87, 88. "The names of some of the Dutch who were principal in the wrongs and injuries aforesaid, are Walter Van Twil, governor of Amsterdam fort, John van Remont his secretary, Martin Garritson, Conrad Noteman, A. Huddus, and Captain Jacob Johnson Hesse, councillors of said governor; and Hans Jorissen Houten, governor of Fort Orange." Eelkins' deposition.

board his vessel, where, after drinking some time together, he acquainted Van Twiller of an old grudge he had against the New Plymouth captain, who, he alleged, had said something against the Virginians, to revenge himself for which, he now proposed to seize his vessel and carry her away. Elevated with wine, or looking on the matter as a mere innocent freak, Van Twiller, it is added, consented, and the New Plymouth vessel was accordingly taken possession of by the Virginian. But some Dutchmen afterwards interfered, and rescued the craft; and, at the request of the Director-general, the master of the pinnace, "who was one of the council of Plymouth, promised, under a solemn instrument under his hand, to pass it by." This quarrel, however, was nigh having a disagreeable issue, for the moment the Virginian arrived at Boston, he was arrested on a charge of piracy, and obliged to give bail to answer the complaint.[1]

CHAP. IV. 1633.

The peremptory orders which the directors in Holland had given to exclude the patroons from all participation in the fur trade, which was now the principal, if not the sole, staple of the country, soon caused fresh excitement at Fort Amsterdam. Captain De Vries, who acted as leader in the establishment of the colonie of Zwanendal, was desirous to send his vessel to the coast north of Hellegat, previous to his return to Holland. But the Director-general, cognizant of the determination of the company, not only refused permission to De Vries' ship to proceed to that quarter, but ordered the vessel to be unloaded, on suspicion that he had furs on board. Surprised at this proceeding, and ignorant, we presume, of the company's orders, De Vries remonstrated; declared his vessel contained nothing but ballast; pleaded his privileges as a co-patroon, and exhibited the exemptions granted by the XIX. and approved by the States General. But finding all these of no avail, he then threw himself "on his reserved rights," and refused obedience to the orders of the Director-general. But Van Twiller was determined to search the ship, and ordered the guns of the fort to bear on the craft, with the intention of sinking her if she did not submit. "Thereupon," says De Vries, who

May 20.

[1] Winthrop's Journal, 50; Winth. N. Eng. i., 104.

BOOK II. 1633.

tells the story, "I ran to the point, where he stood with the secretary and one or two of his council, and told them that it seemed the country was full of fools; that if they would fire at something, they ought to have fired at the Englishman who was violating the rights of the river. This made them desist," and De Vries sent his vessel towards the Sound, the Director-general ordering one of the company's yachts to keep her company, lest she should enter into any barter with the Indians.

Fresh difficulties broke out on the return of this craft. Van Twiller would not allow De Vries to go on board before the company's boat had searched the vessel. To this, however, the latter would not consent, and the Director-general forthwith ordered twelve armed men to follow him, and prevent his departure; but De Vries succeeded in getting beyond their reach. Sheriff Notelman and Secretary Van Remunt visited him on board his vessel the next day, when the latter seeing some beaver-skins on board, ordered them to be seized, as they had not been entered at the fort; but the sheriff interposed, and called for wine, "he being somewhat of a bouzer, which," adds our authority, "was the case with nearly all of them." The secretary, however, persisted, and threatened to send an armed vessel after De Vries; but Notelman would not listen to any such proceeding. He was "dry," and would not be kept from his wine.[1] Notelman's wine-bibbing propensities cost him, however, soon after this, his office. He was superseded in the course of this summer, and in his stead Lubbertus van Dinclage, "an honorable man and a doctor of laws," was appointed schout-fiscaal of New Netherland.[2]

Stimulated, now, by a desire to increase the company's

[1] De Vries expresses throughout this part of his Journal, a very unfavorable opinion of the officers who had charge, at this period, of the company's interests at Fort Amsterdam. "He was astonished that the West India Company should send such fools to the colony, who knew nothing but how to drink themselves drunk. They would in the East Indies not be fit for assistants. In this way the company would soon go to destruction."

[2] "We wrote you last year, (1636,) on two different occasions, to pay to Lubbert van Dinclage his three years' salary as fiscaal of New Netherland, with the charges thereupon." Letter of the States General to the Assembly of the XIX., dated 30th April, 1637. Hol. Doc. ii., 167, 178. Dinclage is styled, (Hol. Doc. v., 217,) "een eerlyck man ende een doctor in de rechte."

returns, and to secure, permanently, for his employers, the trade of the valuable and extensive territory intervening between the North River and New Plymouth, and which had hitherto proved so lucrative, Director Van Twiller took immediate steps to purchase a tract situated so centrally as to form a rendezvous for the eastern and northeastern Indians, at the same time that it would admit of a ready and direct water communication with head-quarters. An extensive and beautiful table-land, called the Connittekock, lying on the west bank of the Fresh River, some sixty miles from its mouth, offered all these advantages, and this tract Van Twiller determined to purchase.

The Fresh Water River had, it will be recollected, been originally discovered by the Dutch skipper Adriaen Block, in the year 1614. Since that time it had been periodically and, we may add, exclusively visited by Dutch traders, whose annual purchases in that district amounted to not less than ten thousand beaver-skins, besides various other commodities with which that country abounded.

In the course of the preceding year, the arms of the High and Mighty the States General had been erected by Hans Eencluys, one of the company's servants, at the mouth of the river, at a spot called Kievit's hoeck,[1] which he had purchased from the natives for the company,[2] in order to secure, for the latter, free access to that valuable district, the trade of which the present measures were calculated more effectually to preserve.

The tract in question, and the whole of the river and country thereabout, originally belonged to the Indian chief Sequeen;[3] but disputes as to jurisdiction and title having arisen between him and the chief of the neighboring Pequod tribe, who lived on the east side of the river, near the sea-coast, it

[1] So called from being frequented by a bird called the Pee-weet, which the Dutch named Kie-veet, from its cry. The above "Hoeok" has since been named Saybrook by the English.

[2] Vander Donck's Vertoogh van Nieuw Nederland wegens de gelegentheyd, &c. desselfs. Hol. Doc. iv., 110.

[3] Sequin, says Trumbull, Hist. Conn. i. 40, was Sagamore under Sowheag, the great sachem of Mattabesick.

BOOK II. 1633. was mutually agreed upon, by both chiefs, to decide the question by pitched battle between their respective warriors, and that the victor, and his successors, should be, ever after, lords and right owners of the Fresh River. Three different engagements were successively fought before this vexed question could be settled. At length Meautiany, the Pequod chief, obtained the victory and the land. Sequeen, utterly prostrated, became subject to the Pequod, with whose consent and approbation he afterwards placed himself, with the remnant of his tribe, under the protection of the Dutch.[1]

Such was the state of affairs when Director Van Twiller dispatched Jacob Van Curler, one of his commissaries, with a party of men to the Fresh River, or the Connecticuck, as it was called by the Indians, to purchase the tract, already selected, for and on behalf of the privileged West India Company, and with orders to erect a fort thereupon. This purchase was effected on the eighth day of June,[2] on the terms and conditions contained in the following deed :—

June 8. " The aforesaid Van Curler, and the sachem named Wapyquart or Tattoepan, chief of Sickenames River, and owner of the Fresh River of New Netherland, called, in their tongue, Connetticuck, have amicably agreed for the purchase and sale of the tract named Sicajoock, a flat extending about a (Dutch) mile down along the river to the next little stream, and upwards beyond the kill, being a third of a (Dutch) mile broad to the height of land, on condition that all tribes might freely, and without any fear or danger, resort to the purchased land for purposes of trade ; and whatever wars might arise between them and others, may be waged or carried on without any of

[1] Verbael van Beverninck, 607.

[2] In some English statements the date of this purchase is fixed at 8th January, 1633. This, however, is evidently a mistake. Van Twiller, under whom the purchase was made, was not in the country in January, 1633. Besides, if he were, it would be doubtful if communication could be had with that section of the country, in mid-winter, so easily as to induce him to send his commissary and a party of men thither, with a necessary supply of provisions, &c., for their journey, when all this could be more readily accomplished by water in the month of June. The date, however, is given in the Dutch document which I translate, in the next note, which accords with the statement made in the report by the Rekenkamer. Appendix E.

them entering on our said territory. It is further expressly conditioned by this contract, and assented to by the aforenamed chief, that Sequeen should dwell with us, all at the request, and to the great joy of the sachem Altarbaenhoet, and all interested tribes. This has taken place, on the part of the Sequeen, with the knowledge of Magaritinne, chief of Sloop's Bay. The chief of the Sickenames is paid for the said land by Jacob Curler one piece of duffels, twenty-seven ells long; six axes, six kettles, eighteen knives, one sword-blade, one shears, and some toys. All which was signed by Jacob Van Curler, Fredrik Lubbertsen, Gillis Pieters, Claes Jans Ruyter, Domingo Dios, Barent Jacobz. Cool, and Pieter Louwensen."[1]

Van Curler, having thus obtained an indisputable title to this valuable tract of country, represented by some as being sixty miles in extent,[2] proceeded without delay to erect a trading-post thereupon, which he fortified with two pieces of ordnance and called "The House of Good Hope."

By the arrival of the bark Blessing from Massachusetts Bay shortly after this, Director Van Twiller received letters from

[1] Hol. Doc., ix. 187, 188. We find at page 189 of the same volume another record of the above transaction, of which we subjoin a translation for the benefit of the English reader. "Anno 1633, on the 8th of June, by Jacob Corlaer, commis, (clerk,) in the service of the W. I. Company, was purchased, by orders of the Director and Council of New Netherlands, from the Chief of Sickenames, with free will and consent of the inhabitants there, all that flat land, about a (Dutch) mile long across through the wood on the river, and about one third part of a mile broad, and a musket-shot over the kill where the said Corlaer, by orders aforesaid, has commenced building the trading-house called the Hope, situate on the Fresh River of the New Netherlands. With express condition, on the part of the purchaser and the seller, that all tribes of Indians shall be permitted to come freely thither, to trade with us; and that the enemies of one or the other nation shall not molest each other on the purchased tract; which conditions were agreed upon and concluded to the great satisfaction of the savages, especially of the Sequeen, all which occurred in the presence of all the company's servants then there." Stuyvesant, writing in Aug. 1664, says:—"Of the eight [7] witnesses who were present at the purchase and transfer, [of the above lands,] five are yet alive, who can and are willing to attest on oath, that the purchase was made and possession taken of the land before any Englishman had ever been on the Fresh Water River; that these were purchased of the natives, who then possessed these lands, who lived on the river, and declared themselves the rightful owners of these lands." Alb. Rec. xviii., 289.

[2] Report and advice, Appendix E.

BOOK II. 1633. the English governor at Boston, by which he learned, for the first time, that the king of Great Britain had granted the whole of the country, from the Narragansetts nearly to the Manhattans, to sundry of his majesty's subjects, thus ousting the Dutch summarily from all their territory in that quarter.[1] By these letters Director Van Twiller was also warned not to make any establishment within the limits of this pretended grant. This intelligence could not fail to excite a good deal of surprise at Fort Amsterdam. After having hospitably entertained those belonging to the vessel, and given them beaver for such commodities as they had to dispose of, he addressed Governor Winthrop a friendly letter expressive of his surprise at the purport of his communication, and informing him of the steps he had already taken on the Fresh River. It was in these words :

Oct. 4. "SIR—What you allege concerning the use of the river which you instance the king of England hath granted to his subjects, and therefore it seems strange unto you that we have taken possession thereof. It seems very strange unto me, who, for mine own part, could wish that his Majesty of England and the Lords States General would agree concerning the limits and parting of their quarters, that as good neighbors we might live in these heathenish countries. And, therefore, I desire you to defer your pretence or claim to said river, so long until the king of England and our superior magistrates or governors be agreed concerning the same. I have, in the name of the Lords States General and the Privileged West India Company, taken possession of the forementioned river, and in testimony thereof, have set up a house on the north side of said river, with the intent to plant, &c. It is not the intent of the States to take the land from the poor natives, as the king of Spain hath done by the pope's donation, but rather to take

[1] In the year 1631, the Earl of Arundel, president of the Plymouth Company, granted to Robert, Earl of Warwick, the country from the Narragansetts along the coast forty leagues, and from the Western Ocean to the South Sea. This grant was conveyed the following year, (1632,) under a vague and imperfect description, to Lord Say and Seal, and his associates. Haz. i., 305, 318; N. A. Review viii., 79.

it from the said natives at some reasonable and convenient price, which, God be praised, we have done hitherto. In this part of the world are divers heathen lands that are empty of inhabitants, so that for a little part or portion thereof, there needs not [be] any question. I should be very sorry that we should be occasion that the King's Majesty of England and the Lords the States General should fall into any contention. Wherewith ending, I commit you, with your whole family, unto the protection of Almighty God, being and resting your true friend,

CHAP. IV. 1633.

"Wouter van Twiller.

"Written in Fort Amsterdam, in New
Netherland, 4th Oct. 1633, N. S."[1]

In the mean while, however, Governor Winslow and Mr. Bradford of New Plymouth, having been invited by some Indians to make a settlement on the Connecticut, had proceeded to Boston, and proposed to Governor Winthrop and his council to join in the scheme of erecting a trading-house on the above-named river, so as to prevent the Dutch getting possession of that fine country. This proposal, however, was declined by the Massachusetts authorities.[2] Whereupon the Plymouth people, stimulated by the prospect of gain, and regardless as well of the rights of others, as of the sage counsels of their Massachusetts neighbors, proceeded to take possession of a country to which they had not a shadow of title.

Having prepared the frame of a house, they put it on board a bark which proceeded, coastwise, to the river Connecticut, under the command of one Lieutenant Holmes, who was accompanied by some sachems belonging to that section of the country. Having arrived at the mouth of the river, Holmes ascended the stream with his vessel towards a spot since called Windsor, the site of the proposed English settlement.

When this expedition had reached the point where the Dutch had raised their fort, those on board the bark were Sept. 16.

[1] Lond. Doc. i., 53, 54; Winthrop's Journal, 54, 55; Winth. N. Eng. i., 112, 113; Hubbard's New Eng. 171, 172; Trumbull's Conn. i., 34.

[2] Winthrop's Journal, 51; Trumbull's Conn. i., 33, 34.

BOOK II. 1633. hailed, and questioned regarding their destination and intentions. Having replied that their object was to trade, they were ordered to stop and strike their flag, and threatened with an attack in case of disobedience. This threat was, however, disregarded. The Plymouth people answered that their governor had ordered them to proceed, and that they "would go on." They were, therefore, suffered to pass, and having ascended about a mile and a half higher up, disembarked, erected their house, which they fortified, landed their provisions, and sent their bark home.[1]

Intelligence of this intrusion having been transmitted to the Manhattans, caused no little excitement there. Van Twiller immediately ordered the Dutch commissary to serve on the English officer the following protest:

Oct. 25. "The Director and council of New Netherland hereby give notice to William Holmes, lieutenant and trader, acting on behalf of the English governor of Plymouth, at present in the service of that nation, that he depart forthwith, with all his people and houses, from the lands lying on the Fresh River, continually traded upon by our nation, and at present occupied by a fort, which lands have been purchased from the Indians and paid for. And in case of refusal, we hereby protest against all loss and interest which the Privileged West India Company may sustain.

"Given at Fort Amsterdam, in New Netherland, this xxvth Octob. 1633."

Van Curler served, according to orders, this protest on Holmes, in the presence of Fredrik Lubbertsen and Carel Franssen, and demanded, at the same time, a written answer thereto; but the English lieutenant refused to give any such reply. He was there, he said, by command of the governor and council of New Plymouth, and there he was determined

[1] Trumbull's Conn. i., 30, 35. "About that time, namely, on the 16th September, (1633,) the English came first from New Plymouth and Massachusetts Bay, before the said fort, (Hope,) and declared their intention to settle three miles above the same, which the commissary residing there opposed as long as he was able; but was obliged, according to instructions, to allow them to proceed under protest." Report, Appendix E.

to remain, in the name of the king of England, whose servant he was.[1] CHAP. IV. 1633.

The Director-general sent an account of these encroachments to the Assembly of the XIX., and dispatched an armed force of seventy men to dislodge the English, but as these stood upon their defence, the Dutch soldiers withdrew without offering any violence.[2]

In the mean while, the authorities at Fort Amsterdam were actively engaged planning various forts and buildings, suitable to the growing trade and wants of the country. Orders were issued for the thorough reconstruction of the principal fort at New Amsterdam, to which place was now attached the privilege of "staple right," whereby all masters of vessels trading along the coast were obliged to unload at this port, or pay, in lieu, certain fixed duties.[3] It was determined to build a guard-house and a small barrack for the soldiers within that fort, and near it, on the East River, a church for general worship,[4] with a dwelling and stable adjoining, for the use of the Rev. Mr. Bogardus; a residence for the Honorable Mr. Gerritsen; a new bake-house; and a small dwelling "for the midwife." An appropriate mansion was ordered to be raised, "on the

[1] Hol. Doc. ix., 189, 190.

[2] Winthrop's Journal, 78; Winthrop's N. Eng. i., 153.

[3] En vertu du droit d'étaple toutes les marchandises qui descendaient les rivières, et passaient devant la ville, devaient être exposées en vente, et payer les droits des douanes établi soit par le Comte soit par la Commune. Les vaisseaux qui remontaient la rivière étaient assujettis à des pareilles obligations. Ce privilege occasionnaient nécessairement une foule de réclamations et de guerres civiles. Institutions judiciaires iii., 55.

[4] The site of this ancient church, (the first ever erected in New Netherland,) is determined by an entry in Alb. Rec. x., 355, anno 1656, as follows: "The house, lot, and appurtenances called 'the old church,' standing and situate on the East River, next to the alley which lays betwixt the house of Attorney-general Van Tienhoven and this house, and opposite the house of Mr. Hendrick Kip, are ordered to be sold to the highest bidder." Hendrick Kip lived, in 1665, in Bridge-street. Paulding's New Amsterdam. Speaking of this church, Judge Benson says, (Hist. Mem. 34,) "The site of the first church is perhaps not to be now further ascertained than as a piece of ground once called the Oude Kerck, (old church,) and afterwards the house of Allard Anthony, lying between Customhouse-street (the portion of Pearl-street between Whitehall and Broad streets) and Bridge-street, and fronting on Broad-street."

BOOK II. 1633. plantation," for the Director-general; on farm No. 1,[1] a barn, dwelling, brewery, and boat-house, "to be covered with tiles;" a goats' stable "behind the five houses," besides dwellings for the smith, the cooper, and the corporal; and several mills, one of which was to be adapted for grinding corn. "An elegant large house with balustrades, and eight small dwellings for the people," were directed to be raised at Fort Orange; two houses at Pavonia; and one large house in Fort Nassau on the South River.[2]

The trade on the last-named river had by this time become so valuable, that the authorities at the Manhattans determined, now, to take proper measures for its extension. Arent Corssen, commissary at Fort Nassau, was accordingly ordered to purchase, from the natives, a tract of land on the Schuylkill, one of the tributaries to the South River, which had been discovered in 1616. In conformity to these instructions Mattehooren, Alibakkinno, Sinquees, and a number of other chiefs, to whom the land belonged, were called together, and, being promised sundry cargoes of goods, sold to the Dutch, in the presence of Augustin Heermans, Govert Loockermans, Skipper Juriaen Blanke, Cornelis Janssen Coele, and Sander Leendertsen, servants of the company, the district then called Armenveruis and the adjoining country, situate on and around the Schuylkill, where a trading-post was subsequently erected and called Fort "Beversreede," on account of the valuable trade in beavers which was carried on, in and about that quarter, with the Minqua Indians.[3]

Such was the impetus given to the affairs of the country

[1] Farm No. 1, says Moulton, ran directly north of the company's garden outside the fort, from what is at present Wall-street, to Hudson-street, along Broadway in the city of New York; and went, in the time of the English, successively by the name of Duke's farm, King's farm, Queen's farm.

[2] Alb. Rec. i., 85, 86. "Their lordships sent a considerable number of families thither in the beginning, and erected, at considerable expense, three sawmills, which never produced any profit of consequence." Hol. Doc. iii., 97.

[3] Deductie, ofte naechte ende claer verhael, over de gelegentheyt van de Zuyt Riviere, gelegen in Nieuw Nederlandt &c. overgelivert aen de Hoog Moogende Heeren Staten General der Verinichde Nederlanden. Hol. Doc. viii., 32, 33, 35, 55, 56. The purchase of this tract by Corssen is also mentioned by commissary Hudde, in his report to Director Stuyvesant. Alb. Rec. xvii.

by the arrival of Director Van Twiller. Forts, mansions, and dwelling-houses went up in all directions, for he had a large idea of the West India Company's resources. Appearances possibly justified his impressions. That powerful association maintained, at this period, a force which gave it the character rather of an independent sovereignty, than of a chartered mercantile society. It owned one hundred and twenty vessels, ranging from three hundred to eight hundred tons burden, all fully armed and equipped ; and employed between eight and nine thousand men. More than one hundred thousand guilders value in peltries were exported during the last year, and nearly the same quantity this year, from New Netherland.[1] It is not surprising, then, that Van Twiller's plans were on an extensive scale. The chief essential to the prosperity of the colony still lacked, nevertheless. Scarcely one solitary agricultural settler had been, as yet, sent over by the company, to fell the forest or reclaim the wilderness.

The Indians manifested considerable ill-feeling towards the Dutch this year. Immediately after the departure of Eelkins, some of the latter, on the upper part of the river, were killed, and their cattle destroyed. The Raritans, also, attacked several of the company's servants, and committed other excesses ; and open war broke out between those at Fort Good Hope and the Pequods. What the origin of the misunderstanding with the Raritans was, we have no means of determining. As respects the last, it seems that some Indians who came to trade to Fort Hope having been killed by the Pequods, the Dutch, in revenge, slew the old Pequod chief and several of his tribe, which so incensed the latter, that a war with the Dutch was the result. This, however, was not the only evil consequence of this bad state of things. It drove the Pequods, in an evil hour both for themselves and the Dutch, to invite the English of Massachusetts Bay to make a plantation on the Connecticut.[2]

[1] Hol. Doc. iii., 97. Aitzema, i. De Laet, Kort Verhael

[2] Winthrop's N. Eng. i., 143.

CHAPTER V.

Continued misunderstanding between the Directors and the Patroons—Pretensions of the respective parties—Referred to the States General—Committee appointed to investigate the same—Articles submitted by the Patroons containing their demands—Replications of the company—Rejoinder on the part of Patroons—Owners of the William apply to Dutch ambassadors at London for damages—Threaten to apply to the king in council—Application communicated to States General—Referred to the Assembly of the XIX.—Memorial of the latter in reply—Request that the matter be referred to the Dutch and English ambassadors—States General decline to interfere—Quarrel between Van Twiller and Minister Bogardus—Peace made with the Raritans—Imports and Exports—Superintendent over Pavonia arrives in New Netherland.

BOOK II. 1633. July 24.

WHILE the occurrences narrated in the preceding chapter were passing in New Netherland, the differences between the several directors of the West India Company and the patroons in Holland continued to such a degree, as to impede materially the advancement of the country.[1] Both parties were in a complete state of antagonism as to the interpretation to be attached to the privileges conferred by the charter of 1629. The company claimed the monopoly of the fur-trade, and would confine the Patroons strictly to the development, by themselves and people, of the agricultural resources of their colonies; while the latter, who had already expended, as they alleged, a ton of gold on their three colonies, the yearly expenses of which amounted to forty-five thousand guilders,[2]

[1] De Vries refers to these misunderstandings in the following entry in his journal: "July 24. Arrived at Amsterdam, where I found my associates at variance with one another, and with other directors of W. I. Company, because I had traded two or four beaver-skins; certainly a circumstance not worth the while to talk of, it being granted by the 15th Art. that a Patroon shall have the privilege to do so, when the company has an officer or commissioner. So that our colonie making was now suspended. The directors have done nothing but fight with their own shadows."

[2] Haerselven verder geinvolveert hebben met aenteykenen van verscheyden Patroonaatschappen, waervan de oncosten, tot heden aengeweent en geconsumeert, nog verre een tonne gouts incontant passeren; en daerenboven jaer-

aiming at a quasi independence, claimed unrestricted trade along the coast and in the rivers; and, as successors to the "Lords Sachems from whom they purchased," exclusive commerce and jurisdiction within their patroonships, which they were extending on all sides; and within which they denied to the company and its officers the exercise of any authority, even to the posting of a placard

CHAP. V. 1633.

It is easy to anticipate that views so opposite must terminate, as we have already seen, in bringing into question not only the nature and extent of the charter, but even its validity. The company admitted, at once, the legality of the charter, but the great difficulty was to determine the extent of the privileges derived under it. With a view to settle all differences, the directors of the chamber at Amsterdam appointed a committee of five persons to negotiate with the patroons, and in case no agreement could be had, empowered these deputies to refer the whole matter to a committee of the States General, or to the high court of Holland. No better understanding followed this reference. The questions at issue were, therefore, referred to their High Mightinesses, who deputed six of their body to investigate the grounds of the dispute, and decide thereupon by a majority of votes.[1]

Nov. 24.

Dec. 19.

1634.

March 27.

May 13.

On the 16th June, 1634, Michel Paauw, Samuel Bloemmaert, Killiaen van Rensselaer, and Hendrik Hamel, Patroons of New Netherland, appeared before this committee, and handed in a paper containing, in a series of articles, their several pretensions. A knowledge of the contents of this paper being necessary to a thorough understanding of the views which the Patroons entertained at this time, as well of their privileges under the charter as of their claims against the directors of the company, we insert them here without any apology.

lyck tot onderhout van drie haer patronaatschappen, ter minsten met 45 duyzend guilden belast blyven. Letter of the Patroons, June, 1634. Hol. Doc. ii., 99, 100. A ton of gold is equal to 100,000 guilders, or $40,000

[1] Alb. Rec. xiii., 42, 43; Hol. Doc. ii., 39, 40, 91, 94, 120. The Lords Arnhem, Herberts, De Knuyt, Weede, Lecklama, and Haersotte, were first appointed, but owing to the absence of some of these, others were named to fill vacancies which subsequently occurred. The resolution of the directors admitting the validity of the charter of 1629, is among the Rensselaerswyck MSS

BOOK II. 1634. June 16.

"PRETENSIONS AND DEMANDS OF THE PATROONS OF NEW NETHERLAND, DELIVERED TO THE LORDS COMMISSIONERS OF THEIR HIGH MIGHTINESSES, ON THE 16TH JUNE, 1634, AGAINST THE LORDS DIRECTORS OF THE PRIVILEGED WEST INDIA COMPANY.[1]

"ARTICLE I. That the Freedoms and Exemptions, granted to the Patroons and their people within the limits of New Netherland and the dependencies thereof, must be maintained and observed by the Privileged West India Company justly and according to their tenor and contents; and be holden as a mutual contract, binding on both sides, whereby the invited Patroons sent their people and goods thither; in consequence whereof the Patroons claim to enjoy inviolate the privileges contained therein.

"II. That the company having, up to the 19th December, 1633, repeatedly called in question the conceded Freedoms, are bound to make good the manifest damages caused thereby to the Patroons.

"III. That in the Exemptions and Freedoms mention was made of the property of those lands only of which the company could dispose by virtue of their charter; and such extension is considered as referring only to fertile and uninhabited lands, or lands inhabited by individual Indians, having no chief, whom the Patroons were bound to satisfy for their ground: In addition to these, within the limits and extensions of the Patroonships which have been purchased, there exist Lordships having their own rights and jurisdictions, which the chiefs of said nations have ceded to the Patroons together with the proprietorship of the soil, as can be seen by the deeds of concession and conveyance. The Patroons maintain that such prerogatives and advantages, in that country, are absolutely theirs; and that the company hath no more power over the Patroons, as purchasers of such lands, than it had over the Lords Sachems the sellers, inasmuch as the intention of their High Mightinesses by the Octroy notoriously

[1] "Sustenue en eisch van de Patronen van Nieuw Nederlandt ongeleveert aen Heeren Gecommitterende van haer H. M. den 16 Junii, 1634, contra de Heeren Bewinthebberen van de Geoctroyeerde W. I. Co." Hol. Doc. ii., 105—114.

was, not to abridge any person in what is his, and consequently cannot be burdened with the venia testandi, justice and police, which are repugnant to the right already acquired by the Patroons. CHAP. V. 1634.

"IV. That under the term goods, mentioned in Articles X., XIII., XVI., must be understood such merchandise without which the permitted trade along the coast of Florida and Newfoundland cannot be carried on, nor the soil of the Patroonships paid for,—Item, shoes and stockings, and other necessaries of the people, which the natives of those countries do not use, belong to implements of husbandry, all necessary to the country people of the Patroons, every description of which the company promised to convey for nothing.

"V. That the company, having no ships, nor berths in their ships, for the use of the Patroons, cannot, conformably to the XIth Art., refuse, or any longer withhold their written consent from the Patroons, officially demanding the same, whereby the latter would lose the season and voyage, from which the ruin of the colonies, or at least great loss, would accrue.

"VI. That all places in New Netherland, the island of Manhattan excepted, are, by the XII. Art., free for the plantation of colonies.

"VII. That the Patroons may sail from the coast of Florida to Newfoundland, paying 5 per cent. recognition; therefore, the Patroons cannot be prevented sending ships or yachts, with all sorts of goods to New Netherland, without which the aforesaid coasts cannot be frequented, nor prizes taken from the enemy—Art. XIII., XIV., XVI., XXIII.

"VIII. Inasmuch as the company (Art. XV.) first absolutely, and afterwards by restriction, reserved the fur-trade everywhere on the coast of New Netherland, and the places circumjacent thereto, the Patroons say, that the inland trade, together with the territories of the Patroonships, is not included therein; and therefore that the Patroons are not obliged to pay, within their limits, one guilder for every merchantable skin. Item—That the Patroons may trade for all sorts of furs, without their colonies, and everywhere about the coasts of New Netherland, and the places circumjacent thereto, where the company had, at the time of granting of the Freedoms, no

BOOK II. 1634. commissaries for procuring goods, on payment of one guilder for each merchantable beaver or other skin. ITEM—Seawan being, in a manner, the only money of the country, wherewith the produce of the interior is purchased, must be considered as permitted goods, being the representative thereof.

"IX. That the company, pursuant to the tenor of Arts. X. and XVI., is obliged here, and by its servants in New Netherlands, seasonably to inform the Patroons and their commissaries, on demand, what places remain in its ships, in order that they may regulate their people, in regard to their numbers, goods, cattle, and implements; and having accommodation in its ships, not to refuse the Patroons the authorized loading therein, nor charge more than the allowed freight.

"X. That the appeal reserved to the Director and council in New Netherlands in civil actions of fifty guilders and upwards, should not prejudice, in the least, the higher jurisdiction, and other privileges of the Patroons.

"XI. Inasmuch as the company (Art. XXV.) hath promised to take the colonists of New Netherlands into its safe-keeping; to aid and defend them as well as possible against all inland and foreign wars and forces, with whatever power it may then have; the company, or its servants, having failed to do this, are bound to make good the injuries which befell the Patroons, their people, cattle, and goods there, and which they still continue to suffer.

"XII. That the Freedoms and Exemptions are permanent for all the partners, without the company having the power to infringe or restrict these to the prejudice of the Patroons.

"XIII. That the expenses incurred by the Patroons by travelling, consultations, vacations, or otherwise, for the necessary maintenance and justification of the Freedoms and Exemptions, in the service of the company and for the advantage of all the principal partners, ought to be defrayed by the privileged West India Company.

"XIV. That the company hath not the power to affix placards in the Patroons' colonies, without their knowledge and against their will, excluding all from the fur-trade; nor to introduce commissaries there to pursue that commerce, nor to oblige the inhabitants belonging to the Patroons, by an oath formed for that purpose, to abstain from trading in any way in furs, seawan, or maize. CHAP. V. 1634.

"XV. That the officers and magistrates of the Patroons in New Netherland may oppose themselves thereto; and whenever the company enters, notwithstanding, by force of arms the just sanctuary of the Patroons, and affixes such proclamations, they may demolish such posted placards as being repugnant to their Freedoms; for whenever the high officers of the Patroons were arrested—protesting against the wrong—'twas perceived, that their Patroons were deprived of the conceded Freedoms. Such proceedings should be declared null and void—the company should be charged to abstain from such for the future, and to make good the damages caused thereby.

"XVI. Finally, in case the company sought by direct or indirect means to induce the Patroons to abandon their colonies, the former should be declared holden to indemnify for all present, future, and past expenses and interests in the above mentioned matter."

These demands, seriously infringing on what the company considered its sovereign rights, and, what perhaps was of more grave concern, deeply affecting its exclusive privileges in matters of trade and revenue, were met by the directors requiring the patroons to hand in separate statements, as they had heretofore been in the habit of doing, of their respective claims, as their pretensions varied and had different foundations, and could not be understood from a united representation. The directors added, at the same time, that if the Patroons declared that they had no claim against the company, nor intended to institute any action against them, but merely wished to have the decision of the States General on the several points of the charter affecting the Patroons, the company would remain neutral, so as to permit those points to be examined and decided. To this the Patroons replied at some length, charging the directors again with not having allowed the charter of 1629 to have had its full effect, in consequence of which they had suffered serious injury and damage, for which they looked for indemnity. A preliminary question, however, arose, and which they now submitted;—that was, whether the privileges which June 22.

BOOK II. 1634. they claimed under the above charter were valid or not. On the result of this depended whether they should continue or abandon the further planting of colonies; when that was settled, they promised to produce a statement of their respective losses, and to give what further information may be required.[1] Upon so small a thread, at this remote period, hung the colonization of New Netherland!

While this discussion was going on, the news reached the English capital of the interruption which the William had met in the Hudson's River from Director Van Twiller, and the Dutch there. The proprietors of the vessel, urged on, no doubt, by the New England Company, between whom and the Virginia Society the Spanish ambassador was busily intriguing,[2] immediately waited on Messrs. Joachimi and Brasser, the ambassadors from the Hague at the Court of St. James, with a statement of the affair, and a demand for damages, failing the payment of which, they threatened to apply for redress to the king
May 27. in council. The Dutch ambassadors lost no time in communicating all the particulars to their High Mightinesses, who
June 13. immediately referred them to a committee for investigation. On a subsequent recommendation of this committee, the whole
June 20. of the papers were referred to the deputies of the West India Company, for an explanation of this misunderstanding, who addressed to the States General the following memorial:—

Oct. 25. "High and Mighty Lords! The Deputies from the Assembly of the XIX. are directed to represent and complain to your High Mightinesses that one Jacob Jacobz. Eelkins, having repaired last year unto the service of Mr. William Klobery

[1] Hol. Doc. ii., 115–117; 119–123

[2] Joachimi writes as follows, at this date, touching this intrigue: "Disputes have arisen here some months since between those who have the king's charter for Virginia, and those who sail to and plant New England. A noble lord, who would be sorry that any misunderstanding should exist between the English and Netherlands nations, has told me that the above disputes were not agitated because the above parties were suffering loss the one from the other; but in order that men might have occasion to quarrel with the Dutch about the possession of New Netherland. The above mentioned lord was of opinion that the above disputes were fomented by the Spaniards"—literally, "were forged in the Spanish forge," (gesmeed syn in der Spagniaerden smesse.) Hol. Doc. ii., 51, 52, 53.

and Company, arrived with the ship William, commanded by Skipper William Trevor, in the month of April, 1633, at the North River in New Netherland, at the Manhattes, to trade his goods thereabout and up the river, for peltries, on the invented pretext that the said river, and surrounding country, were in, and a part of, the domain of his majesty the king of Great Britain, without, however, having, as far as we know, or being willing, as we are informed, to exhibit the instructions, or commission of his majesty, which he might have for that purpose.

"It is, notwithstanding, sufficiently known to all the world, and best of all by this Jacob Eelkins himself, as he was, before the year 1614, in the service of those who, then, had a charter from your High Mightinesses to trade exclusively to this river and neighborhood, that the said river and adjoining country were discovered, at the cost of the Privileged East India Company, in the year 1609, before any Christians had been there, as was testified by Hudson, who was then employed by the said company, to find a northwest passage to China; that your High Mightinesses afterwards granted a charter to divers merchants to trade exclusively for peltries there, where, under the supreme command of your High Mightinesses also, before the year 1614, one or more small forts were erected and garrisoned with people for the protection of said trade; that, further, after the Privileged West India Company began to rule this country, not only the aforementioned little forts were rebuilt and enlarged, but the said company purchased from the Indians, the indubitable owners thereof, the Island of the Manhattes, lying right before the mouth of the said river, and there laid the foundations of a city.

"Divers colonies have been planted also, with the knowledge of this company, not only on the said river, but likewise on the South River, and others lying eastward of the abovementioned North River, by several natives and inhabitants of this country, who, for that purpose, purchased the lands and grounds with the respective limits and jurisdictions of the Indian chiefs, as the same is to be seen by divers conveyances and concessions made to the Patroons of the colo-

BOOK II. 1634.

nies by the Sachems (Sagmoen) and chief lords of the Indians, and those who had any interest therein. So that the said company hath commanded, possessed, and cultivated this country from the beginning of their charter, and carried on trade there, without any person having, with reason, questioned them thereupon, or sought to destroy their trade by force, except only some prohibited traders, and especially Jacob Eelkins, who lately attempted nothing less than to persuade, by false representations, his Britannic Majesty, that this country of New Netherland was a part of his domain on the continent of North America.

"And although our governor and officers there endeavored, in a friendly manner, to dissuade the abovementioned Jacob Eelkins to refrain from trading within their limits, he, notwithstanding, proceeded up the river, and having pitched his tent ashore, commenced to truck with the Indians in alliance with the company. So that our officers were necessitated, after divers negotiations and protests, as may further be seen by the written and authentic acts thereof, to weigh the said Eelkins' anchor, and to cause him to return from the aforesaid river. The company, by all these occurrences, hath suffered special loss, and their trade thereby hath been particularly damaged, and the injurious seed of discord hath been sown between the Indians and our people, who have theretofore lived with each other in good friendship; and other serious mischiefs have followed by the killing of men and cattle, whereof we expect further information by the next ship, which must now arrive soon; so that we have cause to complain, and to set forth great damages and losses against the masters of this Jacob Eelkins, for which they, on the contrary, complain against us, and make very heavy claims."

The memorial concluded by suggesting, in order to get rid of present difficulties, and to prevent their recurrence, to refer the whole matter to Sir William Boswell, the British ambassador at the Hague, on the one side, and Mr. Joachimi on the other, for the purpose of settlement, and further recommended that some measures should be taken by their High Mightinesses to establish the boundary line between the English and the Dutch in North America.

CHAP. V. 1634.

The States General declined to interfere in the matter, but advised the company to confer, themselves, on the subject with the English ambassador, and thus the affair remained in abeyance for the present.[1]

The even course of events in New Netherland was now disturbed by an open, and what appears to be an unseemly quarrel between the Director-general and the clergyman at New Amsterdam. The cause of the misunderstanding between the parties is unknown; but the minister is represented (by no friend of his, however) as having demeaned himself towards the Director in a manner "unbecoming a heathen, much less a Christian, letting alone a preacher of the gospel." He wrote him a letter couched in very strong language, called for, perhaps, by the laxity of conduct of the Director-general, who, the minister alleged, was "a child of the devil; a consummate villain, whose bucks were better than he; and to whom he should give such a shake on the following sabbath, from the pulpit, as would make him shudder," with a great deal more such abuse.[2]

June 17.

Van Twiller succeeded this season in concluding an advantageous peace with the Raritans, which, in the weak state of the colony, was good policy. There were no exports this year from New Netherland. The company sent out the Eendracht, or Union, again, with a cargo valued at 29,562 guilders. Jan Evertsen Bout, heretofore one of the company's servants, came a passenger in this ship, having been appointed by Mr. Paauw superintendent of his colonie at Pavonia.[3]

[1] Hol. Doc. ii., 51, 90, 131, 132, 134, 136–143, 144.

[2] Alb. Rec. ii., 328.

[3] Ibid. i., 96; De Laet; Hol. Doc. v., 399. Jan Evertsen Bout, mentioned in the text, was a native of Barneveldt, and a man of some note in N. N. He obtained a deed for a farm in 1638, which was the first settlement in the present town of Bergen, N. J. His wife's name was Tryntje Simenz. de Witt.

CHAPTER VI.

Encroachments of the New England people on New Netherland—Tear down the arms of the States General at Kievitts Hoeck—Van Twiller protests against the intruders, and makes representations to the directors—The English send Governor Winslow to London to complain against the Dutch—He is imprisoned there—English attempt a settlement on the South River—Are taken prisoners and sent to the Manhattans—First English settlers in New Amsterdam—Fort Amsterdam finished—Irregularities there—Director-general and several members of his council appropriate to themselves large quantities of the public domain—Settlement of Flatlands, or New Amersfoort commenced—Van Dinclage, schout-fiscaal, opposes Van Twiller—Is dismissed from office—Returns to Holland—Ulrich Lupold appointed in his place—Van Dinclage brings the affairs of New Netherland before the States General—Assembly of the XIX. remove Van Twiller—William Kieft appointed director-general of New Netherland—Prices at New Amsterdam and on the Connecticut; Van Twiller adds a number of islands to his estates—States General call the attention of the company to the retrograding condition of New Netherland—Require report thereupon—Queries submitted to the directors—Their answers—Propose surrendering the Indian trade—Unfavorable state of the colony—Causes thereof—States General insist on the adoption of some plan to encourage emigration to and the settlement of the country, so that New Netherland may not be lost or given away.

BOOK II. 1635.

THE English at the eastward having at length obtained a foothold on the Connecticut, the towns of Massachusetts soon rang with the fame of the fertility and "excellent meadows" of that valley; and these, consequently, became an object of great desire and competition among the New England people. It might have been expected, that when they had settled in America, they would, in gratitude for the hospitality which they had experienced at the hands of the Dutch during their long sojourn at Leyden, Amsterdam, and other cities in Holland and Zealand, have left New Netherland unmolested, and forborne to intrude on territory to which they had no claim. But, acting on the principle that they were the saints to whom the earth belonged, pride and self-interest entirely eradicated sentiments of justice and gratitude from their hearts.[1] They

[1] Lambrechtsen's N. Netherl., in N. Y. Hist. Coll. i., 98. "It can scarcely be believed," adds the same author, "that men so conscientious that they considered themselves in duty bound not to make the least concession in any dispu-

CHAP. VI. 1635.

stopped not, then, to inquire whether they had any legal title to the country; nor were they at all discouraged by the fact, that by virtue of prior discovery, chartered conveyance from a recognised government, and possession, the Dutch had, for years, been the just proprietors of the district. They at once pronounced the latter "always mere intruders," and, without a shadow of title, commenced a system of encroachments on their neighbors' territory, which, from the first, had no plea for its justification, but such as was prompted by self-interest and covetousness.[1] Emigrants from Watertown, Dorchester, Cambridge, Newtown, and other places, crossed the mountains, and commenced plantations in several places on the banks of the river. Nearly at the same time, an expedition under Mr. John Winthrop, son of the governor of Massachusetts, repaired by water to Kievitts Hoeck, where he erected a fort, and refusing a Dutch party permission to land on their own purchased

ted point about religious rituals, men so highly revering the Holy Scriptures, that they considered themselves in duty bound to distinguish their cities and villages by Biblical names, should so little care about their Netherland neighbors of the same religious profession, should so little respect their anterior possession." . . . . . "Deplorable consequences of ignorance and intolerance, so much more pernicious, yea, so much more contemptible, in men who had tasted, by experience, their bitter fruits."

[1] "It is not easy to discover on what ground the Dutch were regarded by the first settlers of Connecticut, or by their historian at this day, as mere intruders. They had made the discovery of Hudson's river, and established themselves on its banks. They had obtained a patent from their government, who had as good a right to grant lands discovered by their subjects, as any other state. This patent included the lands on Connecticut River, and this river was discovered by them before it was known by the English to exist, and before the grant of the New England patent. After trading with the Indians for several years, they purchased of them a tract of land, and built upon it a fort and trading-house, before the country had been taken possession of by the English; and the people of Plymouth and Massachusetts colonies, when they attempted to drive them from it, came without a shadow of title from the Plymouth Company, under whom they professed to claim. . . . . . Through the influence of Lord Say and Seal, and other friends of the colony at the court of Charles II., the people of Connecticut obtained from that prince, [1662,] soon after the Restoration, a charter with very ample privileges, containing a grant of all the lands embraced in the original patent, including the New Haven colony. This gave them the first legal title to the lands on which they had settled." N. A. Review, viii., 81, 85. See chapter in Van der Donck's Vertoogh van N. N, entitled, "Of the Right which the Dutch have to the Fresh River."

BOOK II. 1635. soil, offensively tore the arms of the States General from a tree, to which they had been affixed some years before, and in their stead, engraved, in derision, a buffoon's face. On the upper waters of the Connecticut, at a spot then called Agawan, but now Springfield, some distance above Fort Hope, a Mr. Pyncheon established a trading-post and plantation; and though Director Van Twiller made representations to Holland relative to these proceedings, and also protested against the intruders, the English not only refused to desist, but dispatched Governor Winslow, of New Plymouth, to make representations against the Dutch, which might, possibly, have had some effect, had not Archbishop Laud opposed his proceedings, and caused him to be thrown into prison, on the ground that he was a dissenter from the established church.[1] The River Connecticut was not the only theatre of these encroachments at this early date. Experiencing no energetic resistance from the authorities at Fort Amsterdam, the English next determined to attempt an assault on the company's territory at the South River. With a view to make a settlement there, a party consisting of George Holmes, his hired man Thomas Hall, and twelve or thirteen others, proceeded to the Delaware; but on their arrival at that point, Hall deserted his master, and the others, failing in their attempt on Fort Nassau, were made prisoners by the Dutch, and forwarded to the Manhattans in one of the company's boats. Instead of being punished for their aggressive conduct, these people, who were the first English settlers among the Dutch on Manhattan Island, were treated leniently by the Director-general, under whose patronage they established themselves in various ways around Fort Amsterdam.[2]

[1] Mr. Winslow, the late governor of Plymouth, being this year in England, petitioned the council there for a commission to withstand the intrusions of the French and Dutch, which was likely to take effect; but the archbishop being incensed against him, informed the rest that he was a Separatist; that he did marry, and thereupon, got him committed. He was afterwards discharged on petition. Winthrop's Journal, 89; Winthrop's N. Eng. i., 172; Cotton Mather's Magnalia, b. ii., c. 2.

[2] Verbael van Beverninck, 606; Trumbull's Conn. i., 36, 58; De Vries; Vanderdonck's Vertoogh van N. N.; Hol. Doc. iv., 110; v., 399; Report and adv. on the condition of New Netherland, Appendix E.

Two years had now elapsed since Van Twiller had commenced the erection of this fort. Though its dimensions were not extensive, being about three hundred feet long, and about two hundred and fifty broad, it was not finished until this year, owing, we presume, to lack of hands and the number of other buildings which he had undertaken. It was completed, it is said, by the company's negroes, at an expense of four thousand one hundred and seventy-two guilders, or $1688, in which sum was comprised, it is to be supposed, the cost of the several buildings which the fort contained.[1]

CHAP. VI. 1635.

The administration of Wouter Van Twiller had been, hitherto, marked by any thing but good order in the colony, or economy in the government. De Vries, who paid periodical visits to New Amsterdam, gives by no means a favorable view of the state of things there. On one occasion he was accompanied to the fort by Cornelis van Vorst, superior officer at Pavonia, who was carrying a present of claret to the Director-general, "of which article he knew he was fond." Another of the company's servants happening to be present, an altercation arose between the latter, Van Twiller, and Van Vorst, relative to a manslaughter which had recently been committed in the colonie. Matters, however, were soon made up, and Van Vorst, thereupon, proceeded to fire a salute in honor of the Director-general, from a stone gun which stood near the house. A spark from the wadding lodged on the roof, which "being covered with reed" caught fire, "and the whole building was consumed in less than half an hour!"

1636. July 26.

This was not the only disorder to which De Vries was a witness, and which these potations produced. Some time after, the first gunner gave a jollification at one of the angles of the fort, where a tent was erected, and tables and benches set for the several guests. In the midst of the revelry, the trum-

Aug. 8.

[1] Alb. Rec. i., 88; Hazard i., 397. The calculation made above of the dimensions of the fort, is based or founded on a statement contained in Hol. Doc. v., 11. It is there stated, that the church built by Director Keift in 1642-3, "occupied nearly one fourth part of the fort." (De Kerck bykans het vierde part van het fort beslaet.) Now this church was, as appears by the contract, 72 feet long, and 52 broad. This multiplied by four, would make the dimensions of the fort about as above stated.

BOOK II. 1636. peter blew a blast upon his trumpet, which considerably alarmed those partaking of the frolic. The koopman of the stores, and the koopman of the cargoes, were highly incensed at this interruption, and called the bugle-blower some hard names, in return for which the trumpeter gave each of them "a drubbing." The koopmen forthwith ran home for their swords, and, full of pot-valiant swagger, followed the trumpeter even to the Director's, for the purpose of "eating him!" They did not, fortunately, find the delinquent, who thus escaped the demolition with which he was threatened.[1]

A disposition prevailed, in addition to all this, among almost all the company's servants, to enrich themselves at their employers' expense, and to accumulate wealth without much regard as to the means. The Director-general, and the members of his council, by appropriating to themselves large portions of the public domain, encouraged, rather than checked this propensity. Van Twiller, Wolfert Gerritsen, Andreas Hudde, and Jacob van Curler, obtained from the Indians, in the course of this summer, without the knowledge or approval of the directors in Holland, three flatts of land on Long Island, amounting, it was estimated, to between ten and fifteen thousand acres.[2] The Director-general established a tobacco plantation on one part of his section; Gerritsen and Hudde had a well-stocked farm, called Achterveldt, on theirs; and Jacob van Curler hired Thomas Hall to superintend another farm, or plantation, which he commenced on his part. Elbert Elbert-

[1] At the Dutch plantation this summer, a ship's long boat was overset with a gust. Five men in her got on the keel and were driven to sea four days. Only one of them was saved: he was cast ashore on Long Island. Winthrop's Jour. 187.

[2] 16th June, 1636. The Director-General and council of New Netherland, residing at Fort Amsterdam, on the island of Manhattans, certify, that before them appeared, this day, Tenkirauw, Ketamiau, Ararykau, Aswackhou, Suarinkekinkh, Wappettawackenis, Ehetyl, owners, who, by the advice and in the presence of Penhawis, Cakapeteyno, chiefs in that quarter, have, for certain goods delivered to them, sold, &c., to Jacobus van Curler, the middlemost of the three flatts to them belonging, called Castateeuw, lying on the island Sewanhacky, between the bay of the North River and the East River. Same day, same parties sell to Hudde and Gerrittsen, the westernmost of the above flatts; and on the 16th July, same year, same Indians sell to Van Twiller the easternmost of those flatts. Alb. Rec. GG, 31, 35, 39. Van Curler transferred his part, called Cashutey, to Van Twiller in July, 1638. Alb. Rec. i., 30.

sen, one of Van Twiller's farm-servants, and Thomas Spicer settled in the same neighborhood about the same time, but without any deed for their land.[1] CHAP. VI. 1636.

Such were the circumstances under which was commenced the first settlement of the present town of Flatlands, on Long Island, which was originally called New Amersfoordt, after the birthplace of the celebrated Dutch patriot and jurist, OLDENBARNEVELT.

The irregular conduct and proceedings of the Director-general encountered serious opposition from Lubbertus van Dinclage, the schout-fiscaal. But Van Twiller, however good a boon companion, was not a man to brook opposition in his government. He arraigned the fiscal for his contumacy; condemned him to lose his wages, which were now three years in arrears; ordered him to proceed forthwith to Fatherland, to justify his conduct, and thus virtually deprived him of the offices which he held direct from the chamber at Amsterdam. Van Dinclage returned to Holland in the summer of this year. He was succeeded in office by a Hanoverian named Ulrich Lupold of Staden, in the diocese of Bremen, and on the 30th Aug. 30. of August addressed a memorial to their High Mightinesses the States General, in which he not only demanded redress of his own individual grievances, but called attention, at length, to the course of maladministration pursued in New Netherland, including in his accusations even the Rev. Mr. Bogardus, the clergyman at Fort Amsterdam.[2]

[1] Alb. Rec. i., 19, 29, 34; ii., 10; iv., 45, 46, 66; ix. 44. Elbert Elbertsen and Thomas Spicer, from Amersfoort, (says Stuyvesant in 1653,) usurped their lands many years ago without any deed. . . . . . . They are occupying such lands in said village fifteen to twenty years. Hol. Doc. v., 398.

[2] Hol. Doc. ii., 167, 178–181. It is to be regretted that Dinclage's letter on this occasion is not to be found, as it would throw considerable light on the history of Van Twiller's administration. The States General, in referring it to the Assembly of XIX., glance cursorily at its contents. Vanderdonk, in his Vertoogh van Nieuw Nederland, refers to Dinclage as competent to give a full account of Van Twiller's government, for he adds, "He is known to have reported thereon." Reference is made in the Alb. Rec. ii., 50, iii., 231, to "the records kept in Director Van Twiller's time;" but these, as well as Dinclage's report, are, we fear, irreparably lost, and thus the historian of this period is deprived of materials in every respect invaluable. The complaint against Bogardus is thus mentioned in the Alb. Rec. ii., 17:—"The Rev. Ev. Bogardus petitions the

BOOK II. 1637. This representation obtained, at first, no consideration from the West India Company, with some of the directors of which body Van Twiller was connected, as already mentioned. But the States General, at the repeated solicitations of Din-
April 30. clage, urged matters so strongly, that the Assembly of the XIX. found it incumbent on them, at length, to make a change
Sept. 2. in the administration. On the second of September, 1637, the Honorable Elias de Raedt, one of the directors of the company, appeared before their High Mightinesses, and requested them to commission WILLIAM KIEFT as director-general of New Netherland, which was accordingly done.[1] But Van Twiller took care, before he was superseded, to enlarge his own private estate, by the purchase from the Indians
June 16. of the island of Pagganck, lying south of New Amsterdam, now known as Governor's Island, which contained one hun-
July 16. dred and sixty acres of land; also of two islands in the river Hellegat: the greater, containing about 200 acres, called Tenkenas; the smaller, some 120 acres in extent, lay west of the latter, and was named Minnahanock. Abraham Pietersen of Haarlem obtained possession this year, in the name of the company, of the island Quotenis, situate in the bay of Narragansetts and adjoining Roode Island, which he occupied as a trading-post for a long time; as well as another island lying near the Pequot's River, which afterwards went among the English by the name of the Dutchman's Island.[2]

Though the means of determining satisfactorily the progress of the colony, its condition or population, at the epoch to which we have now arrived, are but scanty and scattered, we are enabled to form some conclusions as to the prices of provisions, and of the rate of wages in New Amsterdam. Rye was worth two florins and a half per schepel of three pecks; maize, one and a half to two florins; peas, four to five florins; wheat, three florins; broken barley, four florins;

Director-general and council for permission to return to Fatherland to defend himself against the charges brought by Lubbert van Dinclage. The council resolve (18th July, 1638) to retain the minister here, so that the increase of God's word may in no manner be prevented."

[1] Hol. Doc. ii., 183.

[2] Alb. Rec. GG, 41, 46; i., 89; xviii., 291.

whale oil, three florins the gallon; vinegar, two florins; pepper, two florins and a half per pound; gunpowder, one florin and a half; candles, ten stivers; shot and balls, two florins; pork, seven stivers; meat, six stivers; tobacco, twelve stivers; a hog, six months old, brought fifteen florins; nine hundred bundles of reed cost thirteen florins and a half; five hundred nails, two florins and a half; bricks per thousand, ten florins; a scythe, six florins; a keg of butter, twenty-five florins. A laborer in harvest got about eighty cents a day, on other occasions, sixty; while the price of a negro was forty florins, or $16.[1] CHAP. VI. 1637.

There was, at this period, a great scarcity in the adjoining settlements on the Connecticut, in consequence of the war between the English and the Pequods. Corn rose there to the extraordinary high price of twelve shillings a bushel. A good cow brought thirty pounds; a pair of oxen, forty pounds; a mare, forty pounds; and labor and other articles bore a proportional high rate. Whether the prices in New Netherland were affected by the war in Connecticut, or by the small quantity of provisions raised by the Dutch, it is impossible to determine.[2]

1638. The critical condition of New Netherland, threatened from without by greedy and encroaching neighbors, surrounded on all sides by uncivilized tribes, who were at best not much to be depended on, and who might, without warning, fall on the few Europeans settled in their midst and cut them off, in the same manner as the Indians had already destroyed the English on James River, occupied the attention, early this spring, of the States General. Their High Mightinesses had learned, and now officially announced, that the colony was retrograding every day more and more; that its population had not only not advanced as much as it ought, but that, on the contrary, though encouraged, it had, owing to the neglect of the West India Company, absolutely decreased, and that to such a degree, that subjects of foreign powers and princes were attempting to seize and appropriate the country to themselves, April 26.

[1] Alb. Rec. i., 89; ii., 59. Two florins and a half make a dollar.

[2] Trumbull's Conn. i., 78, 94.

BOOK II. 1638. and that unless means were provided, the whole of New Netherland would be invaded at once.[1] Indignant at these proofs of maladministration, they had already instructed their deputies to the meeting of the XIX., to investigate thoroughly the state of affairs in the Dutch possessions in North America, and to report the result of their inquiries without delay.

These deputies lost no time in attending to the matter confided to them. They drew up a series of queries embodying the information which they wished to obtain, and submitted these to the delegates from the company, who annexed their replies, shortly after, to the questions, and returned the whole, which was duly transmitted to the States General. This paper, remarkable for its brevity, is the more interesting as it affords a bird's-eye view of the real situation of the country, when its only inhabitants, from the Chesapeake to the Connecticut, consisted of a few feeble and almost defenceless fur-traders. We therefore annex it:

April 30.

"I. *Question.* How far do the limits of New Netherland extend along the sea-coast? *Ans.* Their High Mightinesses granted, anno 1614, to Jonas Wittsen and Tweenhuyzen, by special charter, and on expiration thereof to the West India Company, from Virginia upward; to wit, from Ciçapoa along the sea coast to Terra Nova.

"II. *Q.* Are these limits still possessed, at the present time, by the West India Company and citizens of this country? *Ans.* We occupy Mauritius, or the North River. Thereon are two forts, Orange and Amsterdam; and there is one house built for the company, and that is the greatest number of people. (*En dat is de meeste populatie.*)

"III. *Q.* If not, what nations have seized them, and under what pretext? *Ans.* The right is that of the strongest! The English reach from the northeast of New England to the Fresh River.

[1] De populatie in Nieuw Nederlandt niet alleen naer behooren niet en wordt bevordert, nemaer oock de begonste populatie aldaer genoechsaam verachtert, ende by de Compagnie van W. I. schynt geneglegeert te worden, sulx dat de ingesetenen van uytheemsche princen ende potentatien Nieuw Nederlandt onderstaen 't incorporen, ende ten sy daerinne tydelyck werde versien gants ende t'eenemael sullen invaderen. Hol. Doc. ii., 188.

"IV. *Q.* Can the company hold the remaining territory, and by what means? *Ans.* We can retain the remainder in proportion as we have people. From the North River, men can go into the interior as far as they please. CHAP. VI. 1638.

"V. *Q.* What Christian nations are neighbors above and below? *Ans.* The English enclose us from Virginia to New England, and as far beyond as we have been.

"VI. *Q.* Have they [the W. I. Co.] realized profit or loss since the planting of New Netherland? *Ans.* They have suffered loss. But it should be able to afford a profit, especially from corn.

"VII. *Q.* And in case of loss, should their High Mightinesses consider it requisite to preserve the limits of New Netherland, and to place the population on a better and surer footing? *Ans.* The company cannot people it, because the directors cannot agree among themselves. But some plan of proceeding must be considered.

"VIII. *Q.* Would it not be expedient to place the district of New Netherland at the disposal of the Generaliteit, [that is, the body of the States General]? *Ans.* They have no such intention, unless they derive profit therefrom. But they hope, now that they have taken some order about Brazil, that it will prove profitable in time. It is proposed to surrender the trade with the Indians, or something else."[1]

Such was the unpromising condition of New Netherland, as acknowledged by the West India Company, after the administration of its affairs by that powerful body for a term of fifteen years. Removed scarcely a degree from its primitive state of wilderness, uninhabited except by a few traders and clerks in the employ of a distant corporation, its rich and luxuriant soil almost wholly uncultivated and unreclaimed, for the number of farms as yet amounted to not much more than half a dozen around Fort Amsterdam, and the same number around Fort Orange, it afforded evidence, everywhere, of mismanagement; and when its progress is compared with that of the settlements in New England, proofs only multiply of still more culpable neglect, and another instance is only afforded that foreign compa-

[1] **Hol. Doc.** ii., 188, 189, 190, 192, 193, 194, 195.

BOOK II. 1638. nies, though they may retard, have never advanced the settlement of America. In truth, the directors of the West India Company, or rather those who composed its Amsterdam chamber, seem to have ruled New Netherland hitherto only with a view to promote their own special interests. For the advancement of these, immense sums had been expended; but no effort, of any consequence by its permanency, had been made to introduce, on a large scale, a sound and industrious population into the country. They appear rather to desire that it should be inhabited merely by their own servants; a project, which, if entertained, was as visionary as it would be suicidal, for when these dependents had completed their term of service, they, for the most part, returned home dissipated and poor, leaving the country worse than they found it, for it obtained, through them, "a bad and hungry name."[1]

The charter to the Patroons tended also, in no small degree, to retard the settlement of the province. Losing sight, for the most part, of their first duties as planters, the patroons diverted their energies and means in competing with the company for a share of the Indian trade. Quarrels and mutual bickerings ensued; the one party accused the other of having encroached on its special privileges, and the consequence was fatal to the prosperity of the country. The spirit of monopoly, which breathed throughout that charter, discouraged private enterprise and industry, so that individuals who were inclined to emigrate abandoned their design, "and durst venture nothing." It is true that the company introduced a few settlers previous to this period; but, unfortunately, most of these did not remain, and the directors did not persevere in the good work.[2] Had they filled the land, as the English were doing,

[1] Het liet sich aensien met den eersten als off de compagnie dit landt met haer eygen dienaars souden hebben willen populeren, hetwelck groot misverstant moeste wesen; want als haer tydt uyt was, vertrocken die weer, niet medebrengende als wat voor haer beurs, en voor het landt een quaden naem van grooten honger en andersints geven. Vertoogh van Nieuw Nederlant.

[2] Hadde men de eerste exemptie rechtsinnich betracht gelyckse leggen, en niet met singulier insichten gepractiseert; gewis daer souden haer meer liefhebbers van N. Nederland benaersticht hebben, dat te bevolcken en in te nemen. De andere clausulen oock, die men heeft weten inteyoeren, hebben de particu-

with thousands of moral, hardy pioneers; had they transported cattle, and encouraged the planting of towns and villages in the wilderness, instead of building solitary forts to serve as a rendezvous for lazy Indians and a few isolated traders, rendered the more defenceless by their isolation, the tide of encroachment from New England would not, at this date, have threatened to wash the walls of Fort Amsterdam; possibly, that collision between the two races, which was now commencing, would have been stayed, and that contest avoided, which terminated, after a continuance of thirty years, in the loss to the Dutch of every rood of land, to which they now, of right, laid claim. CHAP. VI. 1638.

The States General saw the error, and endeavored, now, though late, to apply a remedy. They enjoined on their delegates to the Assembly of the XIX. to insist, before they adjourned, on the adoption of such a plan as would effectually promote the settlement of New Netherland, and encourage, by advantageous proposals, all good and moral citizens of the mother country to proceed thither, so that, concluded their High Mightinesses, "this state may not be deprived of the said New Netherland by the indirect intrigues of any inhabitants of this country, and the attacks and invasions of foreign princes and potentates."[1]

It was at this delicate juncture, that the new Director-general entered on the performance of his duties.

lieren altyt den moedbenomen en ondergehouden, soo dat sy van die der kennis van hadden, onderrecht synde, niet dorsten bestaen. 'Tis wel waer, dat de compagnie wel eenige persoonen heeft overgevoert, maer niet daerby gecontinueert; soodat het weynich voordeel gedaen heeft; het hadde oock geen rechten aengangh, want het geschiede offer geen meeninge by ware geweest. Vertoogh van N. N.

[1] Soo hebben haer Hoog Moogende nae voorgaende deliberatie goet gevonden en verstaen. . . . . . dat de gemelte Heeren derselver gedeputeerden, voor 't scheyden van de aenwesende gecommitteerden . . . . . soodanige effective ordre sullen helpen beramen en stellen op de populatie van Nieu Nederlandt, en daertoe inviteren alle goede ingesetenen deser Nederlanden op soodangie voordelen en preeminentien alse, op approbatie van haer Hoog Moogende, sullen goetvinden alle coloniers aentebieden, op dat desen staet door indirecte ondercruypinge van eenige ingesetenen deser landen, en opdringinge ende invasie van die van uytheemsche princen ende potentaten van het voors: Nieu Nederland niet en worden ontset. Instructions from the States General to the deputies. Hol. Doc. ii., 190.

CHAPTER VII.

Arrival of WILLEM KIEFT, third Director-general—His council—Colonial Secretary, and shout-fiscaal—Other public officers—Their salaries—Condition of New Amsterdam—Irregularities there—Proclamations of director and council—Organization of court of justice—Proclamation against drunkenness—Arrival of immigrants—Purchase of land on Long Island—State of public morals—Regulations for the inspection of New Netherland tobacco—Rights of the Dutch threatened in the south—Swedish West India Company formed—Pieter Minuit, former director of New Netherland, appointed director of New Sweden—Arrives at the Delaware with some Swedes—Is boarded by the Dutch Commissary—Opens a trade with the natives—Purchases land and erects Fort Christina—Kieft protests against him several times, but in vain—Minuit returns to Sweden, leaving a colony of twenty men behind—Swedish ship seized in Holland on her return from "the West Indies"—Is released—States General urge the permanent settlement of New Netherland—New articles and conditions proposed by the Amsterdam chamber—a "new project" also submitted by parties friendly to the Patroons—Patroons seek to enlarge their privileges, and to reserve the country for manors and lordships—States General disapprove of both these plans—Proclamation opening the trade with New Netherland, and abolishing the monopoly hitherto enjoyed by the West India Company

BOOK II. 1638. March 28. WILLEM KIEFT, the third Director-general, arrived at the Manhattans on the 28th of March, 1638, in the Herring, one of the West India Company's ships, of two hundred and eighty tons burden, carrying two metal, sixteen iron, and two stone guns. His first step, on his assumption of the reins of government, was to organize a council of which he should retain the entire control. With this view, he appointed to a seat in the board Doctor Johannes La Montagne, a learned Huguenot gentleman, who had arrived in the country in the course of the preceding spring or summer, to whom he gave one vote, while he reserved two to himself.[1] Cornelis van Tienhoven, a native of Utrecht, and one of the oldest residents in the

[1] The date of Kieft's arrival is in Alb. Rec. i., 89. De Laet gives the tonnage and rate of the Herring. Dr. La Montagne must have arrived in the spring of 1637. He had a daughter born to him January 26, 1637, at sea off the island of Madeira. He is styled, (Hol. Doc. v., 38,) "een wel gestudeerdt man." He derived his commission at first only from Kieft, but it was afterwards approved by the directors in Amsterdam. Vanderdonck states that he had but one, while Kieft had two votes in the council, Vertoogh van Nieuw Nederlandt.

province, who had hitherto acted as book-keeper of monthly wages, to the satisfaction of the company, was promoted to be colonial secretary, with a salary of about two hundred and fifty dollars per annum, and sundry fees; and Ulrich Lupold was continued as schout-fiscaal, or sheriff, and attorney-general.

Among the other officers and servants of the company, we find mention made of Claes van Elslant, David Provoost, commissaries of provisions; Andreas Hudde, first commissary of wares; Jacob van Curler, inspector of merchandise; Laurens Haen, assistant ditto; Jacob Stoffelsen, overseer; Michel Evertsen, clerk of the customs;[1] Wybrant Pietersen, superintendent of merchandise; William Breedenbent, under sheriff; Philip de Truy, court messenger; Gerrit Schult and Hans Kierstede, surgeons; Hans Steen, midshipman; Jan Jansen, gunner; Fredrick Lubbertsen, first boatswain; Nicolas Koorn, serjeant; Hendrick Pietersen, mason; Gillis van der Gouw and Tomas Walraven, house-carpenters; Tymen Jansen, ship-carpenter; Gysbert op Dyck, commissary at Fort Good Hope; Jan Jansen van Ilpendam, commissary at Fort Nassau, where Pieter Mey acted as assistant; Bastiaen Janssen Crol, who came out about the year 1624, was still commissary at Fort Orange, where Dirck Stipel acted as wacht-meister, or serjeant, and Adriaen Dircksen, assistant commissary, to which charge he was appointed because he spoke correctly the language of the Mohawks, and was "well-versed in the art of trading with them." The Rev. Everardus Bogardus continued to officiate as clergyman at Fort Amsterdam, where Adam Roelantsen was schoolmaster.[2]

[1] Four brothers of the Evertsen family, named Jacobus, Volckert, Myndert, and Arendt, (relatives of this Michel,) lived in prosperous circumstances, some in Pavonia, and some on Manhattan Island, anno 1638. They cultivated tobacco with great success; one of them also had a tannery. Arendt Evertsen was afterwards a celebrated Dutch captain on the Sound, where he captured several vessels belonging to the New England colonies, during the hostilities between the English and Dutch in the time of Cromwell. Many respectable families of the name are still in this state.

[2] Alb. Rec. i., 6, 12, 17, 18, 26, 52, 65, 68, 99, 100, 101, 115, 148, 185, 247; ii., 1, 2, 13, 14, 15, 126.

The following were the salaries of some of the above officers: La Montagne, as member of council, 35 guilders [$14] per month. The book-keeper of monthly wages, 36 gl. [$14.40] per month, and 200 gl. [$80] a year for board;

BOOK II. 1638.

The council managed the general affairs of the government, and constituted, as under the preceding administrations, the ordinary court of justice, as well as the court of appeal from inferior tribunals. But on extraordinary occasions it was usual to adjoin to that board a few of the other inhabitants, selected mostly from among the company's servants, (who still formed the principal part of the population,) when special questions were to be deliberated upon, or special cases tried, in which, perhaps, one or other of the ordinary members of the council might be interested.

The government having been thus far organized, Director Kieft proceeded, pursuant to his instructions, to introduce some order into the company's affairs, which, in truth, were in a ruinous condition. The fort, completed but three years before, at a heavy expense, was in an utter state of decay; open at every side, permitting everywhere free ingress and egress, "except at the stone point." All the guns were off their carriages; the house in the fort, and the other public buildings, as well as the church, were entirely out of repair; the place on which the magazine for wares and merchandise had been erected "could with difficulty be discovered," the building itself having disappeared; and every vessel, except one afloat, and another on the stocks, was falling in pieces. Of "the three windmills," only one was in operation; the five farms belonging to the company were unoccupied by tenants, and thrown into commons, without a single creature, "not even a goat," remaining thereupon, the property of the company, while the farms belonging to the late Director were well furnished with dwelling and farm houses, agricultural implements, and stocked with brood-mares, milch-cows, oxen, goats, calves, and every thing else in the greatest abundance.[1]

mason, 20 gl. [$8] per month; gunner, 16 gl. [6.40] per month; commissary of stores, 36 gl. per month; carpenter, 18 gl. [$7.20] and 100 gl. [$40] a year for board; overseer, 30 gl. [$12] per month; Indian interpreter, 12 gl. per month, and 100 gl. per ann. for board; house-carpenter, 36 gl. per month. Alb. Rec. ii., 14.

[1] By an inventory taken of Van Twiller's property, it appears that he had "on farm No. 1.," 4 mares, 1 stallion, 1 gelding, 10 milch-cows, 1 yearling, 1 heifer, 11 oxen, 1 bull, besides the necessary farming implements; on the

The right which the company had reserved to itself of trading with the Indians, had been openly disregarded, for every person, whether in the public service or not, trafficked in peltries, without hesitation. Practices more injurious to the company's interests, also prevailed. Private individuals purchased, or appropriated to themselves, the most valuable furs, leaving the refuse only to be shipped on account of the directors, by which means the character of the furs, offered by the latter for sale in Holland, was seriously injured, and the company's receipts diminished, for they were undersold by the Russian traders, who furnished a better article at a lower price. The competition did not stop here. Those in New Netherland, who were concerned in these clandestine proceedings, shipped return cargoes, and thus the trade with the interior became entirely deranged. CHAP. VII. 1638.

To put an end to these irregularities, the Director-general issued proclamations, shortly after his arrival, forbidding the company's servants trading for the future in peltries under a penalty of loss of their wages, as well as of all claims they might have against the company; and all disobeying this order subjected themselves to confiscation of their goods and an arbitrary correction. No articles were hereafter to be exported without the special knowledge and permission of the authorities, under pain of confiscation; nor was any person whatsoever to trade for themselves, or others, in any part of New Netherland, without a license, on pain of sequestration of their furs, arbitrary punishment, and loss of all moneys due them by the company. Sailors were warned not to remain on shore after sunset without leave from the Director-general, and all communication from the shore with vessels in the stream, or April 15.

islands in Hellegat, 1 dwelling-house, 3 milch-cows, 3 bull calves, 1 mare, 1 stallion; on Nut island, a frame of a house, 21 goats; on "farm No. 3," 3 milch cows, 3 bull calves; on tobacco plantation at Sapohanican, now Greenwich, on the North River, which was surrounded by palisades, 1 good dwelling-house, 1 tobacco-house. At Forts Hope and Nassau the company had "30 goats and three negroes," while from their five or six farms on Manhattan Island, "which were now destitute of a creature," 16 milch-cows, 10 mares, a number of sheep and other stock had been sold and otherwise disposed of. Alb. Rec. i., 89, 91, 101.

BOOK II. 1638. from the latter to the shore, was as strictly forbidden. All tradesmen in the company's service, of whatever grade, were directed to proceed to, and leave off work, at stated hours; to obey the orders of their superiors and not to waste their time; and such as refused to do any necessary work were to be punished as turbulent and seditious persons. Finally, all persons were seriously admonished "to abstain from fighting; from carnal intercourse with heathens, blacks, or other persons; from rebellion, theft, false swearing, calumny, and all other immoralities," as certain condign punishment would surely overtake the guilty, as a terror to all evil-doers

This proclamation terminated by establishing Thursday in each week for the sittings of the court for the hearing and adjudication of all civil and criminal processes, and for a redress of all grievances of which any person might have to complain. Defaulters at this court subjected themselves to the payment, for the first time, of one shilling; second time, double that sum, and for the third default, judgment was entered against them. In consequence of the great mischief which was daily caused by immoderate drinking, another proclamation was subsequently issued, by which all, "except those who sold wine at a decent price, and in moderate quantities," were forbidden to sell any liquor under a penalty of twenty-five guilders, or $10, and the loss of their stock; and any person who dared to provide lodgings, after sunset, for any sailor, or servant belonging to the company, without leave from the Director-general, subjected himself to a similar fine. All seafaring persons found on shore, after the above hour, were to forfeit two months' wages for the first offence; for the second, all their wages, and to be expelled the company's service; and whoever was guilty of selling powder or guns to the Indians was to be punished by death.[1]

A few immigrants arrived this summer in the Dolphin from Fatherland, some of whom proceeded to Rensselaerswyck, which still continued to be, however, "a place of trifling consequence." A number of horses were also imported; and in anticipation of a greater influx of settlers, next year, Kieft

[1] Alb. Rec. ii., 3. 4. 8, 10, 11, 12, 188.

sent to Curaçoa for negroes, cattle, and salt. Additional settlements were being made on the western extremity of Long Island. The Director-general purchased, in the early part of August, from the natives, for eight fathoms of duffels cloth, eight fathoms of wampum, twelve kettles, eight adzes, eight axes, some knives, corals, and awls, a tract of land two miles broad, and four miles long, extending from the East River to the swamps of Mespeachtes, composing, we believe, the present settlement of Newtown. On Manhattan Island, La Montagne, and other private individuals, were beginning to make improvements. Abraham Isaacsen Verplanck took up a tract of land at Paulus Hoeck, and there was every prospect that settlements would multiply were the company's monopoly removed, and the trade of the country opened.[1]

1638. Aug. 1. Oct.

The state of morals in New Amsterdam was, at this period, however, by no means healthy, owing as well to the description of persons which trade brought thither, as to the absence, in a great part, of an agricultural population. Prosecutions for lewdness and thievery were frequent; there were some public executions for manslaughter and mutiny; and the authorities complained that several persons were becoming rich by appropriating to themselves the company's property, and using it as if it was their own. This state of things called forth proclamations, ever and anon, threatening fines and confiscations to evil-doers of whatever rank. But though the inhabitants were strictly forbidden to leave the Manhattans

[1] Abraham Isaacsen Verplanck's name was sometimes written Planck. He was, probably, a near relative of Jacob Alberts. Planck, first sheriff of Rensselaerswyck. He is represented as having been a wealthy as well as an excellent farmer, and to have been the proprietor of a large dairy. Gulian, son of Abraham Jacobs. Verplanck, was a leading merchant in New York in 1683, and having an interest in the north part of the manor of Cortland, moved thither. The Verplancks of Dutchess, Orange, and Geneva, (Ontario county,) are the descendants of this Gulian. Isaac, third son of Abraham Jacobs., settled in the neighborhood of Albany, where David, of Beeren Island, cousin of Philip, of Westchester, married Ariantje, daughter of Barent Pieterse Coeymans. This lady died without issue. Thereupon David Verplanck married a lady named Brouwer, of an ancient Dutch stock, by whom he had David, Johannes, Ariantje, and Isaac, the father of Col. Abraham Verplanck of Haquatuck, Coeymans, whose sons, again, have moved west, and settled in Batavia, Genesee county.

BOOK II. 1638. without a passport, the lust of wealth was apparently more powerful than government placards.[1]

In the mean time, stimulated by the great demand which prevailed in Europe for tobacco, efforts had been making for some years to render that weed one of the staples of the province. The rich virgin soil around and in the vicinity of New Amsterdam, was at the time well adapted for the culture of the plant, and tobacco plantations consequently multiplied to such a degree, that the Director and council considered it their duty now to regulate, by statute, the mode of cultivating tobacco, and to subject it to inspection, with a view to guard against frauds, and to preserve its character abroad. The following ordinance was accordingly issued :

Aug. 19. " Whereas, the Honorable Director and Council of the New Netherlands have deemed it advisable to make some regula-

[1] Alb. Rec. GG, 57 ; i., 65 ; ii., 33 ; iii., 419 ; La Montagne's farm was called Vredendal, or the Valley of Peace. It belonged to Hendrick de Foreest, deceased, and cost 1800 gl., or $720. This farm was one hundred morgens, or two hundred acres in superficies. It is described as lying " between the hills and kills, and a point on the East River called Rechgawanes, situate between the two kills." Three brothers of these De Foreests originally emigrated to America during the early Huguenot troubles. Two of these, Hendrick and Isaac, settled at New Amsterdam, where we find the latter living in the Brouwer-straat, now Stone-street. He was taxed, in 1653, one hundred guilders towards putting the city in a state of defence ; and twenty guilders, in 1655, to aid in paying off the public debt. He was one of the city magistrates in 1658. The third brother, whose name I cannot ascertain, settled at New Haven. David C. de Forest, son of Benjamin, and grandson of Benjamin, one of the descendants of this third brother, bequeathed, I understand, a sum of $5000, in 1823, for the establishment of a " De Forest Fund" in Yale College. This bequest is to remain at an interest of six per cent. until 1852, after which $1000 a year are to be expended in the free education and support, at that institution, of the male descendants of the donor, as well as of Jno. H. de Forest, of Humphreysville ; of Benjamin C. de Forest, of Watertown ; and Ezra de Forest, of Huntington, all of Connecticut ; and of the sons of the female children of David C. and Julia, his wife. In default of descendants aforesaid, the above sum is to be applied to the education of others of the same family name, giving preference to the next of kin to the donor. Failing candidates of the name of De Forest, the above is then to be applied annually to the education of young men in indigent circumstances, of good morals and suitable talents, who will consent to assume the name of De Forest. In the selection of these young men, " no religious or political opinions of the candidates or their families are to operate against them."

CHAP. VII.  1638.

tions about the cultivation of tobacco, as the chief aim and employ of many planters is to obtain a large crop, and thereby the high name which our tobacco has gained in foreign countries is injured ; to obviate which every planter is seriously warned to pay due attention that the tobacco appear in good condition ; that the superfluous leaves are cut away ; and, further, that the tobacco which is sponged is not more wetted than is required ; that what is intended to be exported from New Netherland be first carried to the public storehouse, to be there inspected, weighed, and marked, and to be paid there the duties which are due to the company ;—to wit, five of every hundred pounds weight, in conformity to the grant from the company. Those who transgress this ordinance shall lose all their tobacco by confiscation, and besides be arbitrarily corrected and punished."

Claes van Elslandt and Wybrant Pietersen were appointed tobacco inspectors, to carry out the provisions of the above act. The fees of inspection were fixed at ten stivers (twenty cents) for every hundred weight, and none was to be exported unless it had been previously inspected and declared merchantable.[1]

An order was issued, at the same time that the inspection of tobacco was directed, that no contracts, engagements, bargains, sales, or public acts, should be deemed valid, except such as were written by the secretary of the province. This law gave room, after a while, to a good deal of cavil. It was surmised that it was issued for the purpose of preventing any complaints emanating from New Netherland against the local authorities, and of depriving those, who might feel oppressed, of the power of making their grievances known to the company, or to the States General. But such sinister motives were promptly disclaimed. The mass of the people resident at, or frequenting the Manhattans, were unable or ill-qualified either to read or to write ; in transacting commercial or other affairs, accounts and papers which passed between them, written sometimes by a seafaring or laboring man, were either drawn up imperfectly, or in total opposition to the intention of

[1] Alb. Rec. ii., 19, 21. The fee in Virginia was one per cent.

BOOK II. 1638.

one or other of the parties, and led to constant misunderstandings and law disputes, sometimes for mere trifles, in which it was difficult, if not impossible, to come at the truth. To obviate such ill consequences for the future, the above order was made, which, in the circumstances, was, it must be admitted, one of prudence, perhaps of necessity, though it may be possible that it might afterwards have led to abuse.[1]

Director Kieft had not, however, been long settled in his new government, nor had he well commenced his work of reform, when he was called to vindicate the rights of his superiors, which were now being menaced from an unexpected quarter, in the southern section of New Netherland.

William Usselinx, the projector of the Dutch West India Company, dissatisfied, we presume, at the impediments which he and his plans experienced in Holland, proceeded to the court of Sweden, and submitted a scheme to the monarch of that country, for the establishment of a commercial association, similar to that which he wished to have established by the States General, with exclusive privileges to trade beyond the Straits of Gibraltar, and to plant colonies in Africa, America, and other parts of the globe. His plan was so warmly appreciated by Gustavus Adolphus, that an act incorporating a Swedish company was passed in 1626. In consequence, however, of the breaking out of the German war, and the death of the king, Usselinx was doomed to see his hopes again blasted. The project was postponed, until Peter Minuit, on being dismissed by the Dutch West India Company, directed his steps to Stockholm, and by his representations, and the patronage of the celebrated Oxenstiern, induced Queen Christina to entertain a favorable opinion of the pro-

[1] Alsoo in Nieuw Nederlandt meest landt-en Zee-lieden wonen, en om cleyne saaken veeltyds malcanderen voor't gerechte doen roepen, en veele niet leesen noch schryven connen, en veele geene duydelycke schriften noch bewysen brochten, en of sommige yts voorbrochten, was somtyds by d'een matroos of boer geschreven, mennichmael heel ondistinctelyck, en gants tegens de meening van die geene die 't hadde laten schryven, of syn verclaringe gedaen, waeruyt quam, dat den Directeur en raaden de saaken naer behooren en vereysch van rechte niet conde naer waerheyt weten. Van Tienhoven's Answer to Vanderdonck's Remonstrance.

CHAP. VII. 1638.

posal, which he renewed, to open a trade with, and establish a Swedish settlement on, this continent.[1] A man-of-war called the Key of Calmar, and a tender called the Griffin, were placed at his disposal, freighted with provisions, ammunition, and a supply of goods suited to this new market. He set sail, in the early part of this year, for the South River, accompanied by a small number, not exceeding fifty Swedes, the greater portion of whom were convicts transported from their native country on account of their crimes,[2] and arrived at Jamestown, in Virginia, in the latter end of March. During his sojourn at this port, he endeavored to procure a cargo of tobacco for the Swedish market, but this was refused, as it was contrary to the king's instructions to allow foreigners any participation in that trade. After a stay of ten days, during which he took in a supply of wood and water, he continued his voyage, and reached the Delaware a few days afterwards.[3]

April. Immediately on his arrival here, his ship was boarded by some of the Dutch residents, to whom he represented that he was on his way to the West Indies, and that he had called at the South River only for supplies, having obtained which, it was his intention to depart. This was soon found to be merely

[1] Holm's New Sweden, in Hist. Soc. Mem. of Penn. iii., 63; Acrelius' New Sweden.

[2] "Synde meest banditen naer de gemelte Zuyt Reviere getransporteert." Hol. Doc. viii., 34. This is corroborated by Holm, who says: "The generality of people who went, or were sent over from Sweden, were of two kinds; the principal of these consisted of the company's servants, who were employed by them in various capacities; the others were those who went to that country to better their fortunes. . . . There was a third class, consisting of vagabonds and malefactors, who were to remain in slavery, and were employed in digging the earth, throwing up trenches, and erecting walls and other fortifications." Holm, 73. See Haz. Reg. iv., 374. The practice was general throughout Europe, in those days, to transport criminals to America. "Such was the demand for labor in America," says Bancroft, "that convicts and laborers were regularly purchased and shipped to the colonies, where they were sold as indented servants." "The history of our colonization is a history of the crimes of Europe." Hist. United States ii., 250, 251. This remark is fully corroborated by Adam Smith: "It was not the wisdom and policy, but the disorder and injustice of the European governments, which peopled and cultivated America." Wealth of Nations, (Hartford Ed. 1818,) ii., 77, 78.

[3] Letter from Jerome Hawley, treasurer of Virginia, to Mr. Secretary Windebanke, in Lond. Doc. i., 57.

BOOK II. 1638. a pretext, for the Swedes, before long, exhibited signs of making a settlement. Pieter Mey, the Dutch commissary at Fort Nassau, called on Minuit, then, to produce his commis-

May 6. sion. But this he refused, as he already had declined to do in Virginia. He asserted, now, that his queen had as much right there as the Dutch, and that he should, by virtue of that right, proceed, without delay, to erect a fort. He then sent a sloop to the country above Fort Nassau to trade with the natives, and when she returned with a load of furs, dispatched her again to the same quarter. But this time, however, she was not allowed to pass the Dutch fort.

Intelligence of these encroachments having been forwarded to Fort Amsterdam, excited, it may well be imagined, considerable surprise. The Dutch considered that they already had a double title, that of discovery and occupancy, to the South River;—a title which was also "sealed with their blood." Strong in this conviction, Director Kieft expedited Jan Jansen van Ilpendam, one of his commissaries, to the Delaware, with orders to keep a sharp eye on Minuit, and should he discover in his proceedings any thing prejudicial to the West India Company's rights, to serve on him a protest with which he was provided.

On Jansen's arrival he found that the Swedish commander had already driven a considerable trade in peltries, and had purchased a small tract of land, situated upon Paghaghacking creek, or the Minquaas kill, and "included between six trees." Here he had erected a trading-house, and commenced a plantation, having paid a trifle for the land; promising the Indians, at the same time, half the crop of tobacco to be raised thereon, which, however, the savage afterwards complained he never got.[1] On the north side of this creek, which lies on the west

[1] The following is the declaration of Mattehoorn, the Indian chief who sold the above tract to Minuit:—"Dat als Minuyt met een schip in 't lant quam, voor de Minquaskil bleeff leggen, waerop hy Sackema doenmaels een huys hadde en woonde:—dat Minuyt hem aenboot en gaff een ketel en andere cleynichaden, versocht soo veel lant van hem, als hy Minuyt een huys coude opsetten, en een plantagie tusschen ses boomen begrepen, 't welck hy Sackema, hem vercoft heeft; en beloofde Minuyt hem de helfde van de tabacq die op de plantagie soude wasschen, hoe wel hem noyt gegeven."

side of the South River, some five (Dutch) miles from Nassau, Minuit had erected his fort, which, in honor of the queen, his mistress, he called Christina, and moreover set posts out, here and there, on which he caused to be engraved the letters C. R. S., surmounted, in token of sovereignty, with a royal crown. Jansen, in pursuance of the orders which he received at Fort Amsterdam, served on Minuit, hereupon, the following protest :— CHAP. VII. 1638.

"I, Willem Kieft, Director-general of New Netherland, residing on the island Manhattan, in the Fort Amsterdam, under the government of the High and Mighty States General of the United Netherlands, and the West India Company, privileged by the Senate Chamber in Amsterdam, make known to thee, Peter Minuit, who stylest thyself commander in the service of her majesty the Queen of Sweden, that the whole South River of New Netherland, both upper and lower, has been our property for many years, occupied with our forts, and sealed by our blood, which also was done when thou wast in the service of New Netherland, and is therefore well known to thee. But as thou art come between our forts to erect a fort to our damage and injury, which we will never permit; as we also believe Her Swedish Majesty hath not empowered thee to erect fortifications on our coasts and rivers, or to settle people on the lands adjoining, or to undertake any other thing to our prejudice; now, therefore, We protest against all such encroachments, and all the evil consequences from the same, as bloodshed, sedition, and whatever injury our trading company may suffer, and declare that we shall protect our rights in every manner that may be advisable."

This protest had no other result than to elicit an unsatisfactory answer from the Swedish commander. Kieft, thereupon, transmitted a second protest, which was also served on Minuit, who, however, refused to notice it, but having completed his arrangements, returned homeward, leaving behind him at Fort Christina, a garrison of twenty-four men, abundantly supplied with provisions and all sorts of goods.[1] Kieft, on reflec- June.

[1] Extracten uyt verscheyde missiven geschreven door Willem Kieft gewesen Directeur in Nieuw Nederlant aen de Bewinthebberen van de Geoctroyeerde

BOOK II. 1638. tion, found the force at his disposal too slender, and his resources too scanty, to authorize him to disturb the new-comers, protected as they were by a flag so respected as that of Sweden. He contented himself, therefore, with communicating all the particulars of the above intrusions to the directors at Amsterdam. These authorities, however, received evidence themselves of the enterprise of the Swedish Company in America, in a more direct and palpable manner than any letters could convey. A Swedish vessel, loaded with tobacco, Oct. having put into the Zuyder Zee, on her return voyage from the "West Indies," was seized at Medenblick, by order of the branch chamber of the Dutch West India Company at Enckhuysen. It was not until the Swedish resident at the Hague called the attention of the States General to the circumstance, that the arrest was removed, and the ship allowed to proceed home. The skipper's papers, under the authority of the crown of Sweden, were then considered satisfactory.[1]

The interest exhibited by the States General for the advancement of New Netherland, and the earnestness with which they urged, in the course of the last spring, the adoption of some well-digested plan for the encouragement of a sound and moral emigration, which would secure the permanent settlement of that country, caused those intrusted with the superintendence of the company's affairs to perceive that if they did not desire seriously to compromise their influence, the time had at length arrived when something must be done to develop more actively the resources of the fine and fertile province committed to their charge.

In accordance with these considerations, a committee had been appointed which devoted a considerable part of the summer to the matters and interests referred to them, and at length Aug. 30. submitted, through Johannes De Laet, one of the directors of the company, to the States General, a paper, entitled, "Articles and conditions drawn up and concluded by the Amsterdam chamber, with the approbation of their High Mightinesses

West Ind. Comp. ter Kamer van Amsterdam. Hol. Doc. viii., 50, 51; Alb. Rec. ii., 7, 8; Hazard's Register iv., 82; Vanderdonck, Vertoogh van N. N. Andreas Hudde's Report, Alb. Rec. xvii.

[1] Hol. Doc. ii., 228.

the States General of the United Netherlands, in accordance with the authority of the XIX., whereby the respective countries and places in New Netherland, and circumjacent thereto, shall henceforward be resorted to, traded with, and inhabited, according to such form of government and police as may at present, or shall hereafter be established there by the company or their deputies." The contents of this paper were as follows :—

"I. The company hereby retain unto themselves, and to such ministers to whom they shall commit the execution thereof, all high and low jurisdictions, together with the exercise of this and other appendages of public affairs, to administer, regulate, manage, and execute the same, subject to their High Mightinesses, in conformity to the instructions to be given concerning them, from time to time, by their directors, officers, and all others holding office or authority, without it being permitted to any one, directly or indirectly, to oppose them, on pain of correction, according to circumstances, as breakers and disturbers of the common peace.

"II. And inasmuch as it is of the highest importance, that in the first commencement and planting of the population, proper order should be taken for public worship, according to the practice established by the government of this country, the same religion shall be taught and preached there, according to the confession and formularies of unity here publicly accepted in the respective churches, with which every one shall be satisfied and content; without, however, it being by this understood, that any person shall be hereby, in any wise, constrained or aggrieved in his conscience; but each shall be free to live in peace and all decorum, provided he take care not to frequent any forbidden assemblies or conventicles, much less collect or get up any such; abstain forthwith from all public scandals and offences, which the magistrate is charged to prevent by all fitting reproofs and admonitions; and advise, if necessary, the company, from time to time, of what may be passing there, so that confusions and misunderstandings may be timely obviated and prevented.

"III. The company shall give orders through their deputies, that all forts, strongholds, and public places, which have already been built, or shall hereafter be erected there, shall be

BOOK II. 1638. properly maintained, preserved, and improved, to the best advantage of the commonalty, and that the general tax to be paid for the erection or building thereof, shall be levied and collected with the least inconvenience to the respective inhabitants, without it being in the power of the Director or his council to collect any of these before they have informed the company thereof, and obtained their consent. Which taxes shall remain specially affected to such works and charges to the maintenance of which they, at the commencement, were voted and granted.

"IV. And inasmuch as improvement is more and more promoted by the cultivation and peopling of these lands, and in order that no person be prevented by private possession and occupation from the use of the public streams, creeks, bays, and rivers, or by the appropriation of any islands, sand-spits, or dry marshes lying therein, all these shall, first, belong to the company which promises to establish, by the Director and council, such order concerning the use of these, that all inhabitants of those regions shall derive therefrom the greatest possible profit and advantage, unless the company may by experience be hereafter advised to make other disposition therein; which conclusions and dispositions every one shall be bound to follow without any concernment or gainsay. And if, however, any person shall be found to oppose himself thereto, he shall be corrected, and brought to his duty by the public authority.

"V. Equal justice shall be administered to all inhabitants and others frequenting those countries, in all civil and criminal matters, according to the forms of procedure and the laws and customs already made, or to be enacted; Expressly charging every officer there to contribute to this, and actively and firmly, as far as need be; and that, without any regard to person or persons, even in such cases where the matter may principally affect the company itself; in which cases the judges shall be specially bound to declare on oath, to follow no other order or law, than such as is considered to apply to or affect all private individuals.

"VI. And whereas, all the population cannot be fixed on one spot, but must be disposed of according to the inclinations of those going thither, and in order that the management of affairs be carried on, every inhabitant is bound and holden, all public charges and offices, such as the magistracy and those of honor and authority, and those which appertain to pious affairs, such as churches, willingly, at his place of residence, to undertake, and honestly and trustworthily to fill, for the public advantage, according to his oath and troth, and the instructions given therewith, without claiming any recompense or reward for the same. But such charges and offices as are onerous, or require the whole of a person's time, shall be rewarded at the discretion of the Director and his council, provided notification thereof be given to the company, and their approbation therefor obtained.

"VII. All public servants,. director, councillors, military commanders, clerks, skippers, and also all others receiving ordinary wages from the company, shall not, unless by permission from the same, follow any trading for themselves, or as factors, or on commission for others; much less take any lands or farms; but peaceably support themselves on their ordinary wages. And in case it happen that they transgress herein, they shall forthwith be degraded from such offices or rank as they may be invested with, besides forfeit to the company their earned monthly wages, and purchased lands or goods which may be found in their possession contrary to this article, or the value thereof, should they have traded or conveyed them away; and the respective officers and justices are charged to promote the execution hereof, without any connivance.

"VIII. For the maintenance of preachers, comforters of the sick, schoolmasters, and similar necessary officers, each householder and inhabitant shall bear such contribution and public charge as shall hereafter be considered proper; and as regards the form thereof, the Director and council there shall be written to, to execute the same on receiving instructions, with the least trouble and vexation.

"IX. The inhabitants there may, for themselves, or such others as shall instruct or commission them, build all descriptions of craft, either large or small, and with the same and no others navigate all rivers, and prosecute their lawful trade and barter, besides trade therein along the whole coast, from Florida to Newfoundland; and in case they happen to make any

BOOK II. 1638. prizes of the enemy, they shall bring such to the place of residence of the director there, to be sent hither, or by him be divided there; one-third part for the company, and two-thirds for the captor, provided, that in case the prize be sent here, the due portion of the company shall be first deducted.

"X. And should any wares or merchandise from any neighboring place there, or from any other kingdom or country, in any foreign ships be landed on the coast of New Netherland, and places adjacent thereto, within the limits of our grants, and in possession of the company, they shall not be touched nor unladen before being duly entered, and the recognitions thereupon be paid, which, in consequence of the heavy expenses and burdens the company has to incur, shall be reckoned at fifteen per cent. on what the said goods shall be estimated to be worth there; and thirty per cent. on whatever shall be exported in said foreign ships.

"XI. The company shall take under its protection and safeguard all those who resort to, or inhabit the said countries subject to their High Mightinesses the Lords States General; defend them against all assaults or trouble coming either from within or without, with such force as may, at the moment, be there, or they may afterwards send; provided that every one, whether trader or inhabitant, who happens to be there, consent to be employed with others on such occasion, for self-defence, under command of the respective officers; and to this end shall every male emigrant take with him, at his own cost, a musket and side-arms, and be enrolled, in case of apparent danger, into proper companies or squads.

"XII. In case any person shall discover or find any minerals, whether gold, silver, or other base metals, precious stones, crystals, marble, or such like, they shall, if discovered on the land of the finder, remain his property, on returning, after five years, one fifth part of the proceeds, without deducting any of the expenses, and that before such minerals, or before-mentioned specie shall be his benefit, or be removed from the place where they may be found; but for such as may be discovered on another man's land, or on the domain of the company, or on unappropriated land, the finder shall be rewarded according to the discretion of the director and council, unless among themselves they agree in a friendly manner, which agreement thus made shall be maintained. CHAP. VII. 1638

"XIII. Besides these general articles, another shall be introduced, to obey and respect such instructions, manifestoes, and commands, as have already been made, or shall hereafter be established, with the approbation of their High Mightinesses, concerning the planting of the country, and the trade there."

The patroons, between whom and the directors considerable misunderstanding still continued, were unwilling, seemingly, to allow this occasion to pass without making an effort to enlarge their own privileges, or to establish them on such a footing as would render themselves more independent, and further beyond the control, of the company. Some parties, strong in their interest, drew up, therefore, a draft of a new charter of "Freedoms and Exemptions for Patroons," or a "New Project," as it was termed, modifying, and essentially altering the charter of 1629, which they caused to be laid, also, before the States General for its sanction.

By this "New Project," the Patroons were to be allowed to extend their colonies six (Dutch) miles along the coast, or on both sides of a navigable river, instead of four miles on one side, or two on both banks, as the original charter allowed. Instead of being obliged to send out, within four years, fifty persons over fifteen years, they now demanded that the number should be forty-eight, without any regard to age, and that the time limited for their transmission should be extended from four to six years, exclusive of the first year of admission. They further required that themselves, and not the States General and the company, should be invested with "the command of such bays, rivers, and islands, as they should have planted," and be invested with "high, middle, and low jurisdiction,"[1] and all other feudal rights; that they be discharged from the obligation which Article IX. of the original charter imposed on them, of submitting to the directors, for their approval, whatever instructions they may send out or give for the

[1] That is, civil as well as criminal jurisdiction—extending to deprivation of life. Such villages as were invested with these, were called "free," or manors with capital jurisdiction; those not possessing them were simply, manors. Van Leeuwen.

BOOK II. 1638 government of their colonies, and that they should, in lieu, have the right to send such instructions as they pleased, subject only to the loose provision of having these generally conformable to the system of police and judiciary obtaining in Holland. The company was, moreover, to be bound to reserve and appropriate the fourth part of all their ships, and other vessels proceeding to New Netherland, to the accommodation of the patroons, their freight, and people, while, once in every year, a vessel should be dispatched from Amsterdam to that country, for the special accommodation of the patroons and their settlers, the former of whom were to be always privileged to send ships thither, which, in their outward and homeward voyages, were to be invested, as far as the capturing of prizes was concerned, with all the rights of company's ships, and be permitted, also, to trade along the coasts and neighborhood of New Netherland, and to purchase there all sorts of produce without any exception—thus proposing to throw open to the Patroons, but to no others, the trade in furs, corn, and wampum, which the company had hitherto claimed as a monopoly, and which had already produced so much trouble between the parties.

It was next proposed, by the "New Project," that the Patroons should be absolutely and forever free from all contributions, imposts, and excise, an exemption which the original charter limited only to ten years; that they should share all such freedoms and exemptions as the company then possess, or hereafter enjoy, and that the right of appeal from the Patroons' courts to the higher tribunal of the Director and council should be abolished, as well as the clause prohibiting manufactures in the colonie, which was entirely omitted in the "New Project." It was, further, required that Art. XXVIII. of the charter of 1629, should be fundamentally altered, and that, in future, the resident-agent or deputy of the Patroon at the Manhattes, should be, ex-officio, a member of the Director's council, and have a seat and vote at all meetings and deliberations of that body, in order to be enabled, thereby, to protect and advance, as it was alleged, the interests of the Patroons' colonists.

Imitating the policy pursued in those days by other European powers, who made their American colonies receptacles for those who, by their crimes or misfortunes, forfeited their citizenship in their native land, and were, therefore, banished "beyond the seas"—a policy which, to their honor be it recorded, the Dutch never sanctioned—the Patroons demanded, next, that the States General should furnish, from among the deserters, outcasts, paupers, vagabonds, and convicts of the parent country, a supply of servile laborers to be bound to work for them for their clothing and food, a certain number of years, after which they should be entitled to their freedom and restoration to society; and further, that every colonie should be entitled to receive twelve black men and women from every prize having negroes on board.

After enumerating a few other privileges of more or less importance, this "New Project" closed by proposing that all private individuals, and such as had not means, should be excluded from all participation in these proposed freedoms and exemptions, and should not be allowed to purchase or acquire any land or ground from the Indians; but that all such should be forced to repair to the colonies of the respective Lords Patroons; thus dividing and converting into manors, for a privileged class, to the exclusion of the hardy and industrious pioneer and sturdy and independent yeoman, whose wealth consisted in his strong right arm and a virtuous progeny, the whole country, from the Connecticut to the Delaware, save and except the island of Manhattans and Fort Orange, the lands and islands adjoining the same; with the colonies of Zwanendal and Pavonia, the latter of which the directors had already purchased from Michel Paauw for the sum of twenty-six thousand guilders, or $10,400. These different points were to be reserved exclusively to the company for the purpose of more efficiently enforcing their revenue laws and commercial regulations.[1]

Neither of these plans proved satisfactory to the States General. That of the Amsterdam chamber was evidently too

[1] This "new project" will be found in Hol. Doc. ii., 144–166. Van Tienhoven gives the price paid for Pavonia, Hol. Doc. v., 400. Kieft leased a farm in that colonie, in the name of the company, in July, 1638, (Alb. Rec. i., 55.) Paauw must have, therefore, been bought out before this date.

BOOK II. 1638. diffuse in several of its clauses. It was not a declaration of principles, nor a system of government for the administration of the public affairs of the province that was required, but a simple plan whereby the settlement of the wild lands, the introduction of cattle, and of a healthy and moral population, could be advantageously, cheaply, and speedily effected, and the country permanently secured to the United Provinces. De Laet's plan failed in embracing these views, and was pronounced by their High Mightinesses "unworthy to be entertained." It was referred, together with the "New Project," back to the Amsterdam chamber, with instructions to appoint a committee from their body to meet deputies from the States General on the following Monday, to examine and revise the whole subject of New Netherland, in order that their High Mightinesses may come to some conclusion regarding the planting of colonies and the introduction of stock into that quarter.[1]

Sept. 2.

The result of this reference became soon manifest. The monopoly of the New Netherland trade which the West India Company had now enjoyed for fifteen or sixteen years, was abolished; the trade, as well as the cultivation of the soil, thrown open to every person, whether denizen or foreigner who chose to embark in it, subject only to the conditions, regulations, and restrictions contained in the following important proclamation:—

[1] "De voors: articulen door de voors: Camer van Amsterdam ingestelt, met dienst ende voortsettinge van de colonien in N. Nederlant, niet en syn aenne melyck, gelyck deselve leggen, ende vinden haer H. M. oversulx goet, dat deselve geconcipieerde articulen ende conditien weder uyt gegeven sullen worden aen Sieur Johannes de Laet, Bewinthebber van de W. I. Compagnie, ende daerby gevoucht het voors: Nieuw Project, om hetselve aen de voors: Camer van de W. I. Compagnie tot Amsterdam gecommuniceert te worden, ende hun van wegen haer H. M. aenteseggen, dat sy jegens Maendach naest comende, den vi. deses, herwaerts willen stuyren eenige Gecommitteerden om met voorgaende Heeren Gedeputeerden van haer H. M. het geheele stuck van Nieuw Nederlant nader gevisiteert, ende geexamineert, ende als dan derselver gesamentlyke consideratien op het voors: stuk ter vergaderinge van haer H. M. ingebracht te worden, ter einde by haer H. M. op de plantinge van colonien ende vee in Nieuw Nederlant soodanige resolutie genomen mach worden, als men ten meesten dienste van desen staet ende voordeel van de compagnie bevinden zal te behooren." Resolution of States General, Sept. 2. 1638. Hol. Doc. ii., 224, 225.

"WHEREAS, the Directors of the Privileged West India Company, of the chamber at Amsterdam, are authorized by resolution of the XIX. to promote and improve the population and trade of New Netherland, therefore do they, with the approbation of their High Mightinesses, hereby make known to all and several the inhabitants of these States, their allies and friends, who may be inclined to sail thither and cultivate any lands there, and with that view to make use of the harbors of those countries, that they may forthwith convey thither, in the company's ships, such cattle, merchandise, and goods as they may find advisable, and receive whatever returns they or their agents may be able to obtain in those quarters therefor; on condition that all the goods shall first be brought to the company's store, so as to be equally put on ship-board in the best manner, paying the following recognitions and freights, the directors taking care that they be dispatched thither by the earliest conveyance:—

CHAP. VII. 1638.

"For all merchandise going thither shall, as recognition, be paid to the company here ten per centum in money, according to their value; and those coming thence hither fifteen per centum there, in specie or money, according to the pleasure of the company or their authorized agent, thus leaving eighty-five per cent. for their proprietor.

"And if any person should happen to make a mistake in the valuation of his goods, it shall be free to the company to take such goods, paying one-sixth more than they are entered at; but all concealed and hidden goods, either here or there, which, by secret plans or other deceptions, may be discovered on board the company's ships, shall be forthwith forfeited and confiscated to the benefit of the said company, without affording thereby any legal cause of action.

"For the freight of cattle and goods which shall proceed hence thither, or from that country here, the owners or factors, at the respective ports, shall agree with the company, or their officers, according to the value and description thereof, until a final arrangement and regulation be made; and the freight shall be paid in money at the place of unloading, and no person shall be permitted to touch or remove the same before he make it appear that both the recognition and freight have been paid

BOOK II. 1638. in full; and further and above, one per centum for each month that they remain in the company's store over fourteen days after being discharged; for all which the foresaid cattle and goods shall be severally answerable, or the owners be spoken to in their proper persons according to the choice of the directors or their agents.

"And whereas, it is the intention of the company to people the lands there more and more, and to bring them into a proper state of cultivation, the Director and council there shall be instructed to accommodate every one, according to his condition and means, with as much land as he, by him and his family, can properly cultivate. Which lands thus conceded to any person in the name of the company shall remain the property of the same, his heirs and assigns, provided he shall pay to the company, after it shall have been four [afterwards altered to ten years] pastured or cultivated, the lawful tenths of all fruits, grain, seed, tobacco, cotton, and such like; also of the produce of all sorts of cattle; of which property a proper deed shall be granted to them, provided that they undertake, in fact, the cultivation and pasture thereof: and failing therein shall incur, over and above the loss of said lands, such penalty and fine as shall be mutually agreed upon at the time; for which penalties and fines their successors, heirs, or assigns, shall be conjointly holden. And in order to prevent all confusion of interests which may occur there, through former proceedings, and are hereafter to be expected, no person shall henceforward be allowed to have any possessions there, or to hold any lands or houses which have not previously been derived from the company.

"The company shall, under obedience to the High and Mighty Lords States General, take care that the places and lands there be maintained quietly and peaceably in proper police and justice under their ministers, or the deputies of the same, conformably to the regulations and instructions thereupon already established and furnished, or hereafter to be made and communicated, after a knowledge and understanding of the matter.

"All those who proceed thither to settle the country, or for purposes of trade, shall, one by one, declare, under their signature, that they will, voluntarily, submit to these regulations, and to the commands of the company, and allow all questions and differences there arising to be decided by the ordinary course of justice established in that country, and freely suffer the execution of the sentences and verdicts without any further provocation; and they shall pay for the conveyance of their persons and board, in the cabin one guilder; in the hutte [the room in the ship above the master's cabin] twelve stivers; and between decks eight stivers per diem."[1]

[1] Hol. Doc. ii., 146, 147, 148–164, 205, 206–223.

BOOK III.

FROM THE OPENING OF THE INDIAN TRADE TO THE END OF DIRECTOR KIEFT'S ADMINISTRATION.

1639—1647.

CHAPTER I.

Consequences of the opening of the trade—Encouragement to emigration—English settlers in New Netherland obliged to take an oath of allegiance—Further encroachments of the English—Settle New Haven—Hartford people oppose the Dutch at Fort Good Hope—Controversy between the parties—Grant of Long Island to the Earl of Stirling—An agent appointed by that nobleman to settle that island—Further purchases by the Dutch thereupon—English cross over and commence settlements on the east end of Long Island—Additional grants by the Dutch on the western extremity—Lupold removed from office—Cornelis van der Huygens appointed Schout-Fiscaal—Other appointments—Renewal of the differences between the English and the Dutch on the Connecticut—Change of commissary at Fort Hope—The Norwalk Islands purchased by the Dutch—Additional purchases on Long Island—Earl Stirling's agent arrives at New Amsterdam—His pretensions disregarded—A party of English attempt a settlement west of Oyster Bay—Dutch expedition sent to prevent them—Prisoners taken and dismissed—Southampton and Southold commenced—English commence a settlement at Greenwich—Protested against—Proceedings in Holland regarding New Netherland—A new charter agreed upon by Assembly of the XIX.—Provisions thereof—Laid before the States General—Effects of opening the fur trade on the Indians—Director Kieft determines to impose a tribute on them—Indians discontented—Occurrences at Staten Island—Property belonging to the company stolen—Kieft enraged against the Raritans—Sends an expedition against them—Attack—Result—Prices of sundry commodities at New Amsterdam—Still erected on Staten Island—Brandy and other liquors manufactured.

CHAP. I. 1639.

THE opening of the trade with New Netherland was the commencement of a new era in the history of that country, and communicated a decided impulse both to its settlement and the increase of its population. Hitherto few, if any, of the company's servants were engaged in agriculture, or indeed remained in the country after their term of service had ex-

BOOK III. 1639. pired. But now that free trade was in a manner established, several of these, who had enriched themselves in the employment of the directors, demanded their discharge; set about erecting houses, making plantations, and spread themselves abroad seeking out the best land, and the most favorable positions for trade with the natives. Others purchased or built vessels, to convey goods to the north or south, and all at once New Amsterdam rung with the sounds of the axe and the hammer, for industry became filled with life and activity.

The directors in Holland, on the other hand, encouraged emigration by all means in their power. Free passage for themselves and families was offered to such farmers as were desirous of proceeding to New Netherland, where, on their arrival, they were promised to be furnished for six years with a farm, fit for the plough, a dwelling-house, a barn, a suitable number of laborers, four horses, an equal number of cows, sheep and swine in proportion, with the necessary farming implements, for which they were, however, to be bound to pay a yearly rent of one hundred guilders, (equal to $40,) and eighty pounds of butter. On the expiration of his lease, the tenant was to restore the same number of cattle that he had received on entering into possession, retaining for himself whatever increase there might have been, in the mean time, from the original stock. To those who owned farms, but who had not the means of providing stock, the company loaned cattle for a certain number of years, "on halves;" that is, on expiration of the contract the number furnished were restored, with half the increase. In both cases, the risk of death was borne equally by the respective parties. In addition to these, free settlers were also assisted with clothing, provisions, and necessaries, on credit, at an advance of fifty per cent. on the prime cost, and in some instances, with loans of money, without interest.[1]

But the emigration, this year, was not confined to this class. Some wealthy individuals came out from Holland with settlers, and large quantities of stock. Prominent among these were Joachim Pietersen Kuyter, of Darmstadt, who had

[1] De maniere die de West Indische Compagnie gevolcht heeft in 't eerste planten van Bouweryen. Hol. Doc. v., 155, 156, 157, 364; Alb. Rec. ii., 189.

formerly been a commander in the East Indies in the Danish service; and Cornelis Melyn, of Antwerp, Patroon of Staten Island. These gentlemen were encouraged by the Assembly of the XIX. to settle in New Netherland, and were accompanied by their families.[1]

The population received accession, likewise, from New England and Virginia. In the former colony, the persecuted, forgetting the principles for which they had been obliged to remove to America, turned persecutors, and now withheld the privileges of citizenship from all who refused to square their belief according to prescribed rule, or who were not members of a peculiar church; and denying freedom of conscience, and political rights, to such as differed with them on abstruse points, which possibly neither party clearly understood, punished a minority for their "heresy" by incarceration or banishment. Such a course necessarily produced discontent; "to escape from the insupportable government of New England," numbers, nay, "whole towns" removed to New Netherland, to enjoy, among the Dutch, that religious liberty denied them by their own countrymen; while several persons, whose time of service had expired in Virginia, where they had become familiar with the process of raising and curing tobacco, repaired now to the Manhattans, with a view to continue there the cultivation of that plant, which was in such general demand, and from which such large returns were to be obtained.[2]

The number of English residents, now under Dutch jurisdiction, became sufficiently large to direct the attention of the government to the necessity of obtaining from them some guarantee for their allegiance. They were therefore called on to take

We find mention made this year of "Cherry trees and peaches on a farm near Fort Amsterdam." Alb. Rec. i., 109. De Vries saw the Peach tree for the first time in Virginia in 1633.

[1] Joachim Pieters Kuyter en Cornelis Melyn, met permissie en welgevallen van de Vergaderinge van de XIX. der Generael W. I. Comp., sich met vrouwen ende kinderen ende met burgerlyke middelen nevens een groote aental van beestialen in den jaere 1639 uyt dese landen naer N. Nederlandt getransporteert. Hol. Doc. iii., 365.

[2] "Het lant heeft nooyt begonnen gepeupeleert te werden voordat de Vryheid gegeven was dat yder met de Wilden mochte handelen; alsoo tot die tyt

BOOK III. 1639. and subscribe an oath of fidelity "to their High Mightinesses the Lords States General, his Highness of Orange, and the Noble Director and Council of New Netherland; to follow the Director, or any of his Council, wherever they shall lead; faithfully to give instant warning of any treason, or other detriment to this country that shall come to their knowledge; to assist to the utmost of their power in defending and protecting with their blood and treasure, the inhabitants thereof against all its enemies."[1]

To the eastward, in the mean time, the English continued their encroachments. They no longer looked on the Connecticut as their western boundary. They longed for the fertile lands between that and the North River, and accordingly had, already, established themselves on a spot called Roodeberg, or Red Hill, by the Dutch; but to which the English gave the name of New Haven.[2] They purchased, likewise, several tracts

toe niemant maeckten aldaer te verblyven tot dat zyn verbonden tyt uytsouden zyn, en daerover de culture van 't lant luttel achten; jae selffs de colonie van Rensselaerswyck was noch van cleyne consequentie; maer sooras als 't selve was toegelaten, veele dienaars die te goet hadden by de compagnie, sochten haer paspoort, boude huyzen, ende maeckten plantagies, verstrooide haer wyt ende breet, yder soeckende het beste lant, ende naest gelegen te zyn van de Wilden omme alsoo bequaemlyk met haer te connen handelen; andere koften barcken omme daermede om Zuydt ende Noordt te vaeren coopmanschappen; ende alsoo de Heeren Bewinthebberen vrye passagie gaven van Hollant herwaerts aen, heeft ter oock eenigen doen comen: D'Engelsche aen d' anderesyde quamen mede beyde van Virginia als Nieuw Engelant. Eerstelyck veel servaants, die haer tyt by haer meesters uytgedient hadden, omme goede gelegentheyt van alhier taback tecomen planten; daernaer de huysgesinnen, ende entelyck by heele colonie, selffs gedwongen van aldaer te vertrekken, soo omme vryheid van conscientie te genieten, also het insupportabel gouvernement van Nieuw Engelant te ontgaen." Journael van Nieuw Nederlant, 1647; Report and Advice, Appendix E.

[1] A complete list of those who subscribed this oath does not appear on the Record, owing to the ravages of time. The following are the only names appended to it:—John Hathaway, Richard Brudnell, Abraham Lowmay, Francis Leslie, Edward Willson, George Homes, William Williamson. The three last attached their marks. Alb. Rec., ii. Abm. Page, Tomas Belcher, Peter Buyley, "from Newheert, in Somersetshire," and Richard Pither, Irishman, are also mentioned as residents under the Dutch at this time. George Homes and Thos. Hall built a house this year, at a place which they called Hopton, near the Deutel Bay, two miles above Curler's Hoeck, now corrupted to "Turtle" Bay.

[2] "They desired that their friends at Connecticut would purchase of the na-

1639.

June 9.

from the Indians in the adjoining districts, north, east, south, and west, on which they planted numerous towns. So rapidly did their settlements fill up, that Hartford already contained, at this period, a fine church, and more than one hundred dwellings, and the infant city of New Haven, a handsome place of worship, and more than three hundred houses. Strong in their numbers, they now absolutely denied to the Dutch all right or title to any possessions on the Fresh River, and carried their pretensions to the length even of ploughing and sowing the company's lands around Fort Good Hope, where they violently assaulted, and severely wounded, some of the men in charge of that post, whom they found at work in the fields.

Gysbert op Dyck, who had command of some fourteen or fifteen soldiers here, promptly protested against this unwarrantable aggression; but the English governor attempted to justify the encroachments of his countrymen on Dutch territory by saying, that the lands lay uncultivated—that the Dutch had been there already several years, and had done nothing to improve the country; and that "it was a sin to leave such valuable lands uncultivated, when such fine crops could be raised from them;"[1] a course of reasoning which, however conclusive it may appear to the party using it, cannot very safely be received as a justification of the proceedings for which it was intended as an apology; since, if admitted, it would at once afford to every person, who may incline to covet his neighbor's goods, a satisfactory plea to appropriate them to his own use.

It became now evident, that the spirit which had overrun the main, would not allow itself to be stayed by the narrow channel which intervened between that and the opposite and tempting shore of Long Island. The plea which justified the seizure of the Connecticut would be equally valid here, for here, also, "the lands lay uncultivated." Even were it not sufficient, an additional pretext was afforded by the fact that the Plymouth Company had taken upon itself to grant, at the

tive proprietors for them all the land that lay between themselves and Hudson's River, which was in part effected." Magnalia, B. i., c. 6.

[1] De Vries.

BOOK III. 1639. request of Charles I., in 1635, the whole of Long Island to William Alexander, Earl of Stirling, who, in the early part of the following year, appointed an agent to dispose of the lands, thus conveyed to him, to all who were desirous to purchase and settle them.

Kieft clearly saw, soon after his assumption of the government, the necessity of securing, by additional purchases from the Indians, this island, which the Dutch esteemed "the crown of the province," and which lay so contiguous to Fort Amsterdam. He therefore purchased, in the beginning of this

Jan. 15. year, from the native proprietors, that portion of the island extending from Rockaway eastward to Sicktew-kacky on the south side, and thence across to Martin Gerritsen's, or Cow Bay, on the north shore; by which purchase, and that of the preceding year, he embraced within the company's jurisdiction nearly the whole of the present county of Queens.[1]

The first English settlers from the main land crossed the Sound, shortly after this, and began a plantation at the eastern extremity of Long Island, where Lyon Gardiner purchased, this year, from Lord Stirling's agent, for a trifle, the island of Monchonock, containing an area of over three thousand acres. This was the first English settlement within the present limits

[1] Mechoswodt, chief of Marossepinck, Sinksink, otherwise called Schout's Bay, [now Manhassett,] and the dependencies thereon, sells to the W. I. Co., with the consent of Piscamoc, his cousin Swatterwochkouw, Kackpohoc, Ketachquaswas, joint owners, all the lands to them belonging on Long Island, beginning on the south side of said island, from Reckouw-hacky to Sicketew-hacky, and the said Sicketew-hacky in its breadth to Martin Gerritsen's (or Cow) Bay, and from thence in its length for the most part on and along the East River to the Vlaeck's kill, the above Indians to have the privilege to plant maize, hunt and fish on said lands. 15th January, 1639. Alb. Rec. GG, 59, 60; xxii. 8. The Rockaway Indians (says Thompson) were scattered over the southern part of the town of Hempstead, which, with part of Jamaica and the whole of Newtown, were the bounds of their claim. The greater part of the population was at Near Rockaway, and as far west as the present site of the Marine Pavilion. Those Indians who resided at the head of Maspeth Creek in Newtown were a portion of this tribe. Hist. Long Island, i. 92. Martin Gerritsen's bay lies west of Oyster Bay. Three creeks empty themselves into it, two of which are navigable. On the smallest of the three was situated the Indian village of Mattinekoock, which consisted, in 1650, of thirty Indian families. Previous to that date there was a vast number of natives settled hereabout, but they gradually disappeared. VAN TIENHOVEN, Hol. Doc, v., 137; Alb. Rec. xx., 1.

of this state; and the place has ever since been called Gardiner's Island, after the original purchaser.[1] The Dutch, whose settlements on Long Island had preceded those of the English by many years, were equally active on the western extremity. Grants were made in the village of Breuckelen to sundry individuals; we find a farm in progress this year at Gowanus; and a commencement made in Gravesend, in which town Anthony Jansen of Sallee, a French Huguenot of respectability, who arrived in the country, with his brother, in 1630, obtained a grant of one hundred morgen, or two hundred acres of land.[2] CHAP. I. 1639.

Little else worthy of note occurred during the remainder of the year, if we except the execution of one of the soldiers for mutiny against the Director, and the removal of Ulrich Lupold, the Fiscaal, or Attorney-general, from office. He was succeeded by Cornelis van der Huygens, who came out from Holland with a commission from the directors of the company as Schout-Fiscaal of New Netherland, at a yearly salary of three hundred and sixty florins, and an additional sum of three hundred for board. Lupold continued, however, in the public service as commissary of wares and merchandise, and occasionally assisted as member of the council. Some additional regulations were made to enforce order and regularity among the mechanics and laborers in the company's employ, who were directed to proceed to and cease from work only "at the ringing of the bell." Gillis de Voocht was appointed superintendent over them. Claes van Elslant and Wybrant Pietersen were removed, in the course of the winter, from office as inspectors of tobacco, and commissaries Jacob van Curler and David Provoost appointed in their stead; but the latter subsequently lost his place as commissary, on charges of neglect of duty, and being incorrect in his accounts, and was succeeded by his assistant Mauritz Jansen. Oloff Stevensen, who had arrived in the colony in 1637, attached to the military service of the company, was transferred in the July 13. Aug. 11. July 1.

[1] A lineal descendant of this gentleman was married recently to Mr. Tyler, late President of the United States.

[2] Thompson's Long Island, i. 304; ii., 170, 218; Alb. Rec. i., 116; Wood's Long Island, 9.

BOOK III. 1639. course of this summer to the civil department, as commissary of cargoes, at a salary of thirty guilders, or $12, per month.[1]

[1] Alb. Rec. ii., 57, 61, 83, 99, 132. OLOFF STEVENSEN, or OLOFF STEVENS VAN CORTLANDT, as he subsequently signed his name, left the company's service in 1648. On becoming a freeman he embarked in trade, built a brewery in New Amsterdam, and became wealthy. He was Colonel of the Burghery, or city trained bands, in 1649, in which year he was also appointed one of the NINE MEN. He was one of the signers to the Remonstrance transmitted to Holland against the maladministration of Director Kieft, and the high-handed measures of Director Stuyvesant. In 1654 he was elected Schepen of the city of New Amsterdam, and in 1655 appointed Burgomeester, which office he filled almost uninterruptedly to the close of the Dutch government. His place of residence was in the Brouwer-straat, now Stone-street. He had the character of being a worthy citizen, and a man most liberal in his charities. He had seven children, viz.: Stephanus, who married Gertrude Schuyler; Maria, who married Jeremias van Rensselaer, twelfth of July, 1662; Catherine, who married, first, John Derval, and secondly, Frederick Phillips; Cornelia, who married Barent Schuyler; Jacob, who married Eva Phillips; Sophia, who married Andrew Teller; and John, who died unmarried. Oloff Stevens van Cortlandt died some time subsequent to 1683, leaving his son, Stephanus, then a highly respectable merchant in New York.

On the death of his brother-in-law, Jeremias van Rensselaer, in 1675, the affairs of the colonie of Rensselaerswyck were administered conjointly, during the minority of Kiliaen van Rensselaer, (then twelve years old,) by the Rev. Nicolaus van Rensselaer, Mde. Maria van Rensselaer, and Stephanus van Cortlandt. Nicolaus had the directorship of the colonie; Mde. van Rensselaer was the treasurer; and Stephanus van Cortlandt had the charge of the books. Four hundred schepels of wheat were appropriated to defray the yearly expenses of this administration, of which Dom. Nicolaus (who then officiated as second clergyman in Albany) received one half. The remainder was divided between Mde. van Rensselaer and her brother. Dom. Nicolaus dying in 1679, the chief management of the minor's affairs devolved on his mother and uncle.

Stephanus van Cortlandt purchased, in the year 1683, large tracts from the Indians, in what are now the counties of Westchester, Putnam, and Duchess, for which he obtained a patent from Gov. Dongan in 1685, whose fees for the north half alone are said to have amounted to three hundred pieces of eight. Those lands were erected into what has since been called the Manor of Cortlandt. He died leaving twelve children, who intermarried with the De Peysters, Beekmans, Skinners, Bayards, De Lanceys, and Van Rensselaers. Though the manor has, in consequence of alienations and sales, long since ceased to exist except on parchment, the Van Cortlandt family continues to be one of the most respectable, as it is one of the most ancient, in this state. At the breaking out of the Revolution, one of the branches of the family was resident in England, the descendants of which have since intermarried with many members of the British nobility.

The spring of 1640 opened with a renewal of the differences between the English and the Dutch on the Connecticut River, touching the title to the soil around Fort Hope. Commissary op Dyck being about to make preparations for sowing the ground in the rear of that post, advised Mr. Hopkins, governor of Hartford, of his intention, and warned him, at the same time, against permitting any of his people to interrupt him. Hopkins, however, pertinaciously denied the validity of the Dutch title to the land, and maintained that the English had acquired their title from the right owners—that he was prepared to prove, by a chief of the Morahtkans, residing near the Pequods, that the latter never owned the soil, and that the right owners had left for the purpose of obtaining assistance from their friends. Op Dyck, on the contrary, insisted on the superior right of the company—referred to their long possession, which dated many years before the English knew of the existence of the river, and to their purchase, which had been made with the approbation of the natives. Whereupon the English governor called on the Dutch commissary to exhibit his title. "Show your right," said he, "we are prepared to exhibit ours;" adding, at the same time, that he was desirous to live in peace with the Dutch. To all this op Dyck responded in suitable terms. He wished only to use the company's lands. But to this neither the governor, nor the English people, would in any wise consent. On the contrary, the constable was sent with a posse of some ten or eleven men, who attacked the Dutch on the following day, while engaged ploughing the field in dispute, beat the horses, and frightened them so that they broke loose. They then returned next morning, and sowed the ground which the Dutch had ploughed. Commissary op Dyck protested forthwith, but Governor Hopkins refused to make any reply to this protest, "as it was written in Low Dutch." He called again on the commissary to produce his title. "The king," he said, "would support the English in their right as firmly as the Prince of Orange would the Dutch." The commissary maintained that he was not bound to produce his title; and as for the king of England, he well knew that his majesty did not desire to do any thing that should injure another. Hereupon

CHAP. I. 1640.

April 23.

April 24.

April 25.

BOOK III. 1640. he took his departure, and sent a party to plant barley in the field. These were also driven off. Op Dyck then went himself to do the work, but the English remained on the watch, and would not suffer him to proceed. Evert Duyckingh, another of the company's servants, having, in the mean time, succeeded in getting into the field with a hat full of barley, commenced sowing the grain; but had not proceeded far when he was knocked down with an adze, from which he received a severe wound on the head. Op Dyck was, thereupon, obliged to withdraw his men, having previously warned the English of the injury and wrong which his masters had sustained at their hands. These criminations and recriminations did not terminate here. The English were, evidently, determined to hunt the Dutch from the river. They, therefore, continued their aggressions in every possible shape during the remainder of the year. They seized the horses and cows belonging to Fort Good Hope and impounded them for trespass. (May 30.) The clergyman of Hartford seized a load of hay, which a Dutch driver was conveying to the fort, and applied it to his own use without giving any thing in return; (June 21.) and when the crop became ready for the sickle, the English drove off the men sent by the Dutch commissary to cut it down, and harvested it themselves.[1] (Aug. 15.) It was in vain that op Dyck protested, or the Director-general remonstrated. They lacked either the will, or the means to vindicate their rights, and the people of Hartford treated them accordingly. Op Dyck proceeded, some time after this, to Fatherland; (Oct. 25.) and Jan Hendricksen Roesen was appointed commissary of Fort Hope, with a salary of thirty-six guilders per month, equal to $173 per annum, and his board.[2]

The Director and council were, in the mean time, actively engaged purchasing the claims of the Indians to the soil in the neighborhood of the island of Manhattans. In the hope of staying the incursions of the English, who continued to extend their settlements westward, and in order "to maintain the charter and privileges granted by their High Mightinesses to

[1] Hol. Doc. ix., 192, 193, 194, 195, 196, 197.

[2] Alb. Rec. ii., 104.

the Noble the West India Company, in New Netherland," CHAP. I. 1640. April 19.
Cornelis van Tienhoven, secretary of the province, was dispatched early in the spring to the "Archipelago," to purchase that group of islands, which lay at the mouth of the Norwalk River, "and all the adjoining lands, and to erect thereon the standard and arms of the High and Mighty Lords the States General; to take the savages under our protection, and to prevent effectually any other nation encroaching on our limits, or making incursions on our land and territory." In further obedience to instructions directing the purchase, in the names of the States General, of the Prince of Orange, and of the West India Company, of all lands deemed proper for tillage and pasture, Director Kieft bought, in the following month, from May 10.
"the great Chief Penhawitz," head of the Canarsee tribe, all the land left to him by his father on Long Island, with all his hereditary rights and titles thereto.[1] This purchase, together with that from the Rockaway Indians, before mentioned, completed the Dutch title to all the lands bounded on the west by the East River, and on the east by the present county of Suffolk, which two points embraced all the territory on Long Island, over which the Dutch ever exercised jurisdiction.[2]

While Director Kieft was fancying that he had thus secured himself against all further encroachments on the part of the English, a Scotchman, named Farrett, presented himself at Fort Amsterdam, and claimed Long Island, under a commission from the Earl of Stirling. But his pretensions were utterly disregarded and himself dismissed, and forced to withdraw, followed by the jeers of the mob.[3] He was, however, not well gone, when a party of emigrants from Lynn, in the

[1] Alb. Rec. ii., 78, 83. The Canarsee tribe claimed the whole of the lands now included within the limits of Kings County, and a part of the town of Jamaica. Thompson, i., 93.

[2] The Hon. Samuel Jones, in his Notes on De Witt Clinton's Discourse, says, "The possessions of the Dutch on Long Island never extended above thirty miles east of New York." N. Y. Hist. Soc. Trans. iii., 324.

[3] In den jaar 1640 is by den Directeur Kieft gecomen een Schotsman, met een Engelse commissie en pretendeerden dit Lange Eylandt; doch zyn pretens warde niet veel geacht; dus vertrock hy weder sonder yetwes uytterechten, als alleenlyck dat hy het slechte volck wat induceerden. Van der Donck, Vertoogh van N. N.

BOOK III. 1640. colony of Massachusetts, crossed the Sound, and landed at the west side of Cow Neck, on territory belonging to the Dutch, where they commenced a settlement. They were not far advanced in their operations, when Sachem Penhawitz gave information to the authorities at Fort Amsterdam, "that some foreign strollers had arrived at Schouts Bay, where they were actually engaged building houses, felling trees, and that the said vagrants had even hewn down the arms of their High Mightinesses." Doubtful of the correctness of this unexpected intelligence, Director Kieft immediately sent Commissary van Curler to inquire into, and report on the matter. This messenger corroborated, on his return, the information given by the sachem. The arms of the High and Mighty Lords the States General had been contumeliously torn down, and a fool's head carved, in derision, on the tree to which they had been affixed.

May 10.

This intelligence created considerable sensation at Fort Amsterdam. Secretary van Tienhoven was ordered to proceed, without delay, with an armed force to the ground, "to surprise and surround the English, but to avoid having recourse to arms: to inquire who pulled down the escutcheon of their High Mightinesses; by what authority it was done, and to bring the trespassers to the fort to defend their conduct, taking beforehand an inventory of their goods." If, however, there was no hope to conquer the English by force, the secretary was then to avoid bloodshed by all means, and to protest against the intruders.

May 14. At the break of day, Secretary van Tienhoven departed, accompanied by the under-sheriff, a sergeant and twenty soldiers, and arrived, at the same hour on the following morning, on the ground where the English had commenced their settlement. He found one house built, and a second in progress of being raised. Howe, the leader of the squatters, had, however, withdrawn from the threatened danger, with all his party, except "eight men, one woman, and a babe," whom he left to answer for the trespass and outrage which had been committed.

May 15.

On demanding the authority under which they had acted, this party answered that they were empowered to settle there by a Scotchman named Farrett, Lord Stirling's agent, who left for the Red Hill, after he had thrown down the Dutch arms. Thereupon six of the trespassers, viz. Job Cears, George Wells, John Farrington, Philip and Nathaniel Cartland, or Kertland, and William Archer, or Harcutt, were conveyed to Fort Amsterdam; two men, the woman and child having been left behind in charge of the property. Van Tienhoven and his prisoners arrived at the fort on the 15th May. CHAP. I. 1640.

On the following day, the prisoners were examined on interrogatories before the Director and council. It appeared that they came originally from Buckinghamshire in England, and that they had been afterwards induced by Howe and Farrett to remove from Lynn, in Massachusetts, to Long Island. Their innocence of any intentional trespass having become manifest, they were liberated by the Director-general a couple of days afterwards, "on condition that they should leave the territory of their High Mightinesses." This they engaged to do under their signatures. May 16. May 19.

Director Kieft forwarded a statement of these proceedings to Governor Dudley at Boston, and took occasion at the same time to complain of this invasion of the Dutch territory. But the English governor represented that he had no authority over those people. They had voluntarily departed from his jurisdiction.

Howe and his associates returned to Long Island again in the fall. Immediately after their ejection, Farrett granted them a tract of land "bounded between Peaconeck and the easternmost point of Long Island, with the whole breadth from sea to sea," "in consideration," as he acknowledges, "of barge-hire, and of having been driven by the Dutch from the place where they were by me planted, to their great damage, together with a competent sum, amounting to four hundred pounds sterling," for which he gave his receipt. Here they planted the flourishing town of Southampton, in the possession of which they remained undisturbed. The adjoining town of South Old, on the north side of the island, was settled about the same time by some people from New England, without any opposition from the Dutch, who seem to have paid no attention to that section of the country. This June 12, O. S.

BOOK III. 1640. indisposition did not extend, however, to the parties who had established themselves east of the Manhattans, on the main, in the spring of this year, at Petuquapaen, now called Greenwich. Director Kieft protested against them, and warned them that they should be driven from their holdings, if they did not submit to the authority of his government. Such were some of the salutary effects of the firmness exhibited by the States General in 1638, and of the determination which they then expressed, to protect New Netherland against the attacks and invasions of foreign princes and potentates.[1]

The interests of New Netherland were, meanwhile, occupying the attention of the authorities in Holland. The States
Jan. 31. General had already appointed, at the beginning of the year, several deputies to confer with the Assembly of the XIX. concerning the differences between the Patroons and the company. These were instructed, at the same time, to suggest some plan whereby the country itself might not only be preserved, but its settlement promoted, and its inhabitants obtain the best possible privileges. This subject of reference engaged the consideration both of the Assembly and of the
July 17. deputies from the States General until midsummer, when, with the approbation of their High Mightinesses, a new charter of "Freedoms and Exemptions, for all Patroons, Masters, and private persons, who should plant colonies in, or convey cattle to New Netherland," was agreed upon. A copy of this im-
July 19. portant paper was laid before the States General, a few days afterwards, by the Honorable Elias de Raedt, who was duly accredited by his co-directors for that purpose.

[1] Alb. Rec. ii., 84, et seq.; Winthrop's Journal, 204; Winthrop's N. Eng. ii., 4, 5, 6, 7; Leechford, 44; Hol. Doc. ix., 198; Lond. Doc. i., 60, 61, 62. The date of Farrett's deed of the Southampton grant is stated in the last-mentioned "document" to have been 12th June, 1639. There is evidently an error here in the year; all the Dutch and English authorities fix the date in 1640. Mr. Thompson represents Farrett (Hist. L. I. ii., 53) as protesting against the English for having entered on the above lands, of which proceeding, it is added, he disapproved. The protest Mr. Thompson has published must have reference to some other transaction, as it will be seen by the extract above given from Farrett's deed of sale, that he acknowledges the English had been planted by him. He could not, therefore, very properly have protested against them.

This charter essentially modified that already granted. In the first place, the privileges confined by the charter of 1629 to "members" of the West India Company, were now extended to "all good inhabitants of the Netherlands," who were permitted to send three or four agents in the company's ships to examine the country, cabin-passengers paying fifteen stivers a day; those who went in the "orloop," or 'tween decks, to have their conveyance and board gratis. In case the land selected by these should not turn out afterwards as good as was expected, they were privileged to change it for more suitable localities; but the period allowed Patroons for completing the number of fifty settlers, which they were obliged to convey to their colonies, was limited to three instead of four years; one-third of the quota to be sent over annually. The extent of future colonies was to be confined to one (Dutch) mile, calculated at 1600 Rhineland rods, instead of four, along a coast, bay, or navigable river, and to two only into the interior of the country. But no two Patroonships on different sides of a river or bay should be selected right opposite each other, the company reserving to itself, as before, the lands between colonies, to dispose thereof as it might think proper; and all Patroons and colonists were to allow free passage by land and water to each other at the nearest point, and with the least damage, submitting themselves, in case of dispute, to the decision of the Director-general for the time being. To these Patroons were to be continued the feudal privileges of erecting towns, appointing officers over the same, (saving the company's rights,) with "high, middle, and lower jurisdictions," exclusive hunting, fishing, fowling, and milling, (grinding,) within their manors, to be holden as an eternal heritance, to devolve as well to females as to males, and to be redeemed on each such occasion, on the renewal of fealty and homage to the company, by the payment, within a year, of one pair of iron gauntlets and twenty guilders,[1] with the understanding, that in case of division of the fief, or manor,

[1] Soo wel op vrouw-oor als man-oor, te versterven ende te verheergewaden telckens met een paar ysere handschoenen aen de Compagnie te redimeren met twintig gulden, &c.

BOOK III. 1640. the parts were to possess the same privileges as the whole, each part to pay a similar fee as the whole, in case it should devolve to the original grantors.

Whoever should hereafter convey himself, and five souls over the age of fifteen years, to New Netherland, was to be acknowledged "a master, or colonist," and entitled to claim one hundred morgen, or two hundred acres of land, with the privilege of hunting in the public forest, and fishing in the public streams. If, by these means, the settlement of masters, or free colonists, should so increase as to become towns, villages, or cities, the company was bound to confer subaltern or municipal governments on them, to consist of magistrates and ministers of justice; which were, however, "to be selected and chosen by the Director-general and council, from a triple nomination of the best-qualified in the said towns and villages, to whom all complaints and suits arising within their district shall be submitted;" but from these courts, as well as from those of the Patroons, an appeal was to lie to the Director-general and council, where the sum in dispute exceeded one hundred guilders, or forty dollars, or where infamy might attach to the sentence; as well as from all judgments in criminal proceedings, where the same was allowed by the custom of Fatherland. The protection of the company was guarantied, in case of war, to the colonists; but these were bound to take proper measures for self-defence, each male adult emigrant providing himself, in Holland, at his own expense, with a firelock, or musket, of the same calibre as those in use in the company's service, or a hanger (verjager) and side-arms.

"No other religion was to be publicly tolerated or allowed in New Netherland, save that then taught and exercised by authority in the Reformed Church in the United Provinces," for the inculcation of which the company promised to support and maintain good and fit preachers, schoolmasters, and comforters of the sick.

The commercial privileges, accorded by the charter of 1629, were not only continued unchanged as far as Patroons were concerned, but now extended to all free colonists and inhabitants of New Netherland, and to the several partners of the company, on the following conditions: That all goods to be sent from Holland to that country, and intended for sale, whether by the company, the colonists, or the partners, should be brought to the company's warehouses to be examined, and the duties thereon paid at the rate of ten per cent. on their prime cost ; the cargo not to be broken before the arrival of the vessel at New Amsterdam, or such other place as the company may designate ; and five per cent. on all return cargoes, the value of which was to be determined in Holland, beavers, otters, and other peltries excepted, which were to pay to the Director-general and council an export duty of ten per cent. in cash, before leaving New Netherland, for the payment of which a receipt was to be produced on pain of confiscation of the furs. But no person was to leave New Netherland, with any goods obtained in barter there, without first registering them and obtaining a permit from the Director and council, and binding themselves to return, with their vessel and cargo, to the United Provinces, where they were to discharge their freight into the company's magazines according to their manifest, under the penalty of losing both ship and cargo, in case they had broken bulk, or of having any goods on board not duly entered.

This charter having, next, abolished the clause prohibiting the manufacture of woollen, linen, and cotton cloth, and other stuffs, and repeated the pledge to supply the colonists " with as many blacks as possible," the company declared that they reserved unto themselves all great and small tithes ; waifs ; estrays ; forests ; the right of coining money ; making roads ; erecting forts, and using the same in peace and war ; founding cities, towns, and churches ; maintaining the supreme and sovereign authority, the interpretation of all differences arising out of these privileges, with the express understanding that nothing already granted to the Patroons, relating to " high, middle, and low jurisdiction," should be, hereby, changed or diminished.

The company, finally, pledged itself to appoint and support within the province a governor, competent counsellors, officers, and other ministers of justice, " for the protection of the good and the punishment of the wicked." To this governor and council were to be committed all questions touching the free-

BOOK III. 1640. doms, sovereignty, domain, finances, and rights of the General West India Company; complaints in cases of privilege, unusual innovations, whether by foreigners, neighbors of New Netherland, or by the inhabitants of the latter country; together with the supervision of all customs, usages, or laws, with power to declare the same corrupt, or to abolish them as bad, if found so to be; they were also invested with the care of minor children, widows, orphans, and other unprotected persons, regarding whom, or whose affairs, application was to be made to this court holding prerogative jurisdiction; as well as of all matters relating to possession of benefices, fiefs, cases of lesæ majestatis, religion, and all criminal affairs, and the administration of the laws and justice in all matters in which the interests of the company were concerned. Of such importance was this new charter considered, that the several provinces composing the States General demanded copies thereof, with a view of communicating to their respective constituents, and of making more generally known, the favorable conditions on which immigration was now invited to New Netherland.[1]

Though the opening of the trade with the interior was productive, in the first instance, on the island of Manhattans and its immediate neighborhood, of considerable benefit, by the increase of population—planting of bouweries—introduction of stock—cultivation of tobacco and corn, and clearing and preparation of new lands,[2] it must be acknowledged, at the same time, that the temptations of the fur-trade were, on the other hand, so great, owing to the quick and excessive profits which it promised or produced, and the free and careless habits it engendered, that it is a matter of great doubt whether it was not, eventually, a greater injury than service to the community, and an obstacle rather than an encouragement to

[1] Hol. Doc. ii., 234, 235, 239–262.

[2] In plaats van seven bouweryen ende twee a drie plantagies, die alhier waren, sagh men dartich bouweryen soo wel gebouwt ende met bestiael versien als in Europa; en hondert plantagies, die in twee a drie jaaren oock geformeerde bouweryen soude geweest hebben. Want naerdat den Tabak uyt de gront was, wort daer koren ingesmeten sonder ploegen. Des Winters was men besich omme nieuw landen te prepareren. Journal van Nieu Nederlant.

CHAP. I. 1640.

the prosperity and settlement of this infant province. For a great many, under the impression that now was the accepted time to make their fortunes, spread themselves abroad among the Indians, far from their own countrymen, whom they regarded with suspicion, as rivals in this alluring trade; and thus reduced to a dangerous degree the strength of the country, as well as jeoparded their own individual safety. Too great a familiarity with the Indians was also the consequence of this indiscreet course; for to secure the friendship and preferences of these uncivilized people, every sort of allurement was had recourse to by the trader. They were invited to their tables; helped to wine and other liquors, and otherwise treated on such an equality, that quarrels and misunderstandings ensued rather than esteem and respect. Add to this, the Indians, whom the Dutch were in the habit of employing as servants, indulged in their natural propensities; often stole more than their wages came to, and then running away, communicated to their tribes the domestic arrangements of the Europeans, and made them acquainted with their habits, strength, and usages, so that they were enabled to turn this knowledge afterwards to account, in their wars, or other attacks.[1]

The Indians, on their side, if they were slow to perceive the encroachments of the whites on their homesteads, were soon made to feel the pressure of their presence. The cattle of the new-comers, wandering abroad through the woods, untethered and without a herdsman, destroyed the Indians' corn-hills, which were unprotected and unfenced; while the Dutch authorities, with a fatuity not easily to be accounted for, embroiled as they were with their English neighbors, came to the determination to levy tribute off the savages in corn, furs, or wampum, in return for the heavy expenses which were incurred by the company in the construction of forts, and the payment of soldiers, and under the shallow pretence that the Indians were thereby defended from their enemies; threatening the savages, at the same time, that measures should be taken, in case of non-compliance with these unjustifiable demands, "to remove their reluctance."[2]

[1] Ibid. [2] Alb. Rec. ii., 65, 81.

BOOK III. 1640.

This combination of unfavorable circumstances required but a slight addition to convert into estrangement whatever good understanding or friendship hitherto existed between the natives and the new-comers; and this provocation was not long wanting.

The inhabitants of Rensselaerswyck, who numbered at the time as many traders as individuals, noting the avidity with which the Mohawk sought after fire-arms, willingly paying the English twenty beavers for a musket, and from ten to twelve guilders for a pound of gunpowder, were desirous to share so profitable a trade. They commenced, accordingly, to furnish fire-arms to these Indians. The profits which accrued became soon known, and traders from Holland soon introduced large quantities of guns and other munitions of war into the interior. The Mohawks, thus provided with arms for four hundred warriors, swept the country from Canada to the sea-coast, levying tribute on the surrounding terror-stricken tribes.[1]

The latter, especially such as dwelt along the North River, endeavored not the less to place themselves, as far as weapons went, on an equality with the Mohawks, and importuned the Dutch settlers for fire-arms. But as the Director-general had forbidden the furnishing guns or powder to the Indians, on pain of death, the solicitations of the river tribes were in vain, and they remained, comparatively speaking, as defenceless as before.

It was while the aborigines were thus indisposed and irritated, that Director Kieft had recourse, in conformity, as he alleged, to orders from Holland, to the highly impolitic measure of taxing the Indians, as before mentioned; a proceeding the more unwise, as it eventuated in a long and ruinous war.

[1] Dese extraordinaire winste wert niet lange secreet gehouden; de Coopluyden uyt Holland comende, hebben haest vernomen, ende van tyt tot tyt groote mennichte overgebracht, soodat men de Maquaas in corten tyt gesien heeft met vierroers, kruyt en loot naer advenant. Vier hondert gewapende mannen hebben haer voordeel weten te gebruycken, voornamentlyck tegen haer vyanden, woonende langs de Riviere van Canada, daer sy nú veel profytelyck toghten opgedaen hebben, ende vantevooren luttel voordeels hadden; dit doet haer oock ontsien syn van de omlegende wilden, tot aen de zeecust toe, die haer generalyck tribúyt moeten geven. Journael van N. N.

The Indians expressed their astonishment at this proceeding in loud murmurs against "the Sakema of the fort, for daring to make such exactions." Sneers and reproaches followed "The Sakema," they said, "must be a mean fellow: he had not invited them to come and live here, that he should now take away their corn." The Dutch they reviled and despised. "They were Materiotty, or men of blood; they had neither Great Sachem nor Chief," alluding to their country being a republic, "and though they may be something on water, they were good for nothing on land."[1]

CHAP. I. 1640.

The feelings of the Indians towards the Dutch assumed, from this date, a manifest change, and such an appearance of hostility, that the Director-general considered it necessary to call on every inhabitant to provide himself with a gun, and to keep the same in good order. Notice was issued at the same time to the people, that they should be warned, in case danger occurred through the night, by the discharge of three can

May 9

[1] Daerover de Wilden niet minder getracht hebben om roers te becomen ende door de gemeensaamheyd die sy met de onse hadden, begonden haer te soliciteeren omme, roers ende kruyt; maer alsoo sulx op de galge verboden was, ende 't selve niet sekreet soude connen blyven, door de groote conversatie, soo hebben sy niet connen obtineren. Dit heeft, beneffens de voorige cleynachtinge, de haet seer vermeerdeert, dat haer beweeght heeft tegen ons te conspireren, beginnende eerst door injurien die sy sonder discretie overal uytstrooyden, ons scheldende voor Materiotty: (dat is te seggen:) Bloode Menschen; dat wy wel yets te water mochten wesen, maer te lande niet en dochten; en dat wy sonder Groote Sackima, ofte oversten waren. Journael van N. N.: compare De Vries; also Report and Advice in Appendix E.; Van der Donck says expressly, that Kieft alleged that the tribute on the Indians was levied conformably to orders from the directors in Holland, and that this led to the war. His words are:—"Ja, het staet van den oorloch, volgens het seggen van den Dr. Kieft is in het Vaderlandt mede eerst gesaeyt. Want de Directeur seyde expres ordre te hebben, om de contributie van de Wilden te vorderen." And again:—"De oorsaake van desen oorloch oordeelen wy te wesen het vorderen van de contributie, daer de Directeur ordre van de Majores toe secht te hebben." Vertoogh van N. N. Van Tienhoven does not undertake, in his defence of the colonial administration, to deny the exaction of this tribute, but endeavors to palliate its injustice, by saying that no contribution in corn was ever received from the Indians without having been paid for twofold, "for these people," he adds, "are so stingy that they would not give a herring unless they got a codfish in return." The directors positively deny having ever authorized any such contribution, or been cognizant of its having been levied. Hol. Doc. v., 30. Kieft's order, however, is inserted at length in Alb. Rec. ii.

BOOK III. 1640. non shots, at which signal they were to appear, armed, at the fort, each person under his respective corporal.[1]

When parties are indisposed the one towards the other, little is required to produce collision. Some of the company's servants landed, about this time, on Staten Island to take in water, on their way to the South River. Before they re-embarked, they stole some hogs belonging to their employers and to Captain David De Vries, who then had an infant settlement on that island. The blame was thrown on the Indians who lived on the Raritan, some fifteen or twenty miles distant, and whose guilt seemed the more probable, as they were charged with having made an attempt, only a short time previous, to seize a yacht sent to that quarter for furs, and to kill its crew, who, however, escaped with the loss of their canoe.

Prudence, it might reasonably be supposed, would have prompted Kieft to pass over, in the present excited state of feeling among the Indians, these petty aggressions, and to have endeavored to calm irritation by inquiring into, and removing the causes of any discontent that might exist. But prudence formed no trait in Kieft's character. The stealing of a few swine, and an isolated attack on a boat, which eventuated in scarcely any loss of property, and no loss of life, was declared to be "a case of great consequence," affecting the dignity of the States General, the respect due to the company

July 16. and its interest, and Secretary van Tienhoven was dispatched with an armed force of fifty soldiers and twenty sailors, under the command of Hendrick Gerritsen, skipper of the ship the Neptune, to attack the Indians, destroy their corn, and to make as many prisoners as he could, unless the savages should sue for peace and pay damages.

Arrived on the ground, Van Tienhoven lost all control over his followers, who demanded permission to slaughter and plunder the Indians at once. The secretary, irritated at this insubordination, quitted the party, warning them that they should have to answer for whatever mischief might result from their disobedience. But all his monitions were disregarded. He had not retired three-quarters of a mile, when

[1] Alb. Rec. ii., 82.

one of the Indians was shot; the chief's brother, whom the party had taken prisoner, was barbarously butchered by Govert Loockermans, one of the party. Similar acts of cruelty were committed by others, after which the soldiers returned, having burnt the crops belonging to the Indians, leaving, however, one Ross, the supercargo of the Neptune, dead on the field.

CHAP. I. 1640.

The effects of this injudicious proceeding were soon perceptible. Cornelis Melyn, Patroon of Staten Island, brought out a number of farmers to settle his colonie, but in consequence of these hostilities, several of them were deterred from going on the island, as they originally intended, and the progress of this settlement was, for the moment, interrupted.[1]

The settlers in and around New Amsterdam were generally supplied at this period from the company's store with whatever goods they required, at fixed prices, being, as already stated, fifty per cent. advance on their prime cost. A list of these prices was posted in a conspicuous place for public inspection. The value of produce and imported goods was as follows:—Indian corn, 60 cents; barley, 2 dollars; peas, \$3.25; wheaten flour, 1 dollar, per schepel of three pecks; pork, 5 stivers; fresh meat, 5 stiv.; butter, 8 stiv.; tobacco, 7 stiv.; dried fish, 12 stiv. (or 2 York shillings) per lb.; hard bread, 15 stiv.; cabbages, \$12 per 100; staves, \$32 per 1000 of 1200; a hog, 8 dollars; rye bread, 5 stiv., wheaten bread, 7 stiv., corn bread, 4 stiv. per loaf; sour wine, \$31 per hhd.; Spanish wine, 4 stiv., French wine, 10 stiv. per quart; sugar, 17 and 24 stiv. per lb.; grogram, 1 dollar, kersey flannel, \$1.20, cloth, 2 dollars, white linen, 18 to 20 stiv., red flannel, \$1.20 per ell; children's shoes, 36 stiv., or six York shillings a pair; brass kettles, 40 cents apiece. The inhabitants complained, it is right to add, that the goods in the company's store were overvalued; a complaint which was subsequently admitted to have

[1] Alb. Rec. i., 263; ii., 95, 96; Hol. Doc. iii., 165; v., 314. De Vries says Van Tienhoven took one hundred armed men along with him, but that it was against his orders to kill and plunder. Another authority represents the party to have been composed of "eighty soldiers." I follow the text of the Alb. Rec. Kieft is accused of having given to the soldiers themselves, at the moment of embarkation, even harsher orders than those he gave to Van Tienhoven.

BOOK III. 1640. sufficient foundation in fact, for Ulrich Lupold, the storekeeper in charge, was found guilty of extortion and malversation, and sentenced by the Director and council, by and with the advice of the principal inhabitants, to removal from office; to pay, in addition, a fine of eighty dollars, and to be banished to Holland. His sentence was, however, afterwards remitted on Lupold's petition; but he was ordered to satisfy the company for his malversations.

The first ardent spirits ever made in America, were manufactured, it is said, at the close of this year in New Netherland, by Willem Hendricksen, a native of Wesepe in Holland, who
Dec. erected a private still on Staten Island, for Director Kieft, from which, during six or seven months that it was in operation, he ran a considerable quantity of brandy and other strong liquors. Hendricksen was allowed twenty-five guilders per month while thus employed.[1]

[1] Alb. Rec. i., 156, 231, 232, 240, 248; ii., 107, 116. Hol. Doc. v., 105, 108.

CHAPTER II.

Murder of one of the company's slaves by six other negroes—Lots drawn to determine which should be executed—Scene at the place of execution—Proclamations against drunkenness, and regulating the currency—New Haven people intrude on the South River—Protested against—Renewal of the difficulties on the Connecticut—Collision between the Dutch and English there—Rev. Hugh Peters sent by Massachusetts to England; commissioned to proceed to Holland to settle the difficulties between Connecticut and New Netherland—Propositions submitted to the West India Company by Governors Winthrop and Haynes—Several English families propose removing from Massachusetts to Long Island—Privileges granted to them—A new colonie planted behind Newark Bay—Staten Island granted to Melyn—Other settlements at Hoboken—Increased misunderstanding between the Indians and the Dutch—The latter set a price on the heads of the Raritans—Peace concluded between both parties—A Weckquaesqueeck Indian assassinates a Dutch settler to avenge the murder of his uncle, committed twenty years previously—Kieft demands the murderer—His surrender refused—The murder justified—Meeting of the commonalty in consequence—Election of "the Twelve Men"—Their proceedings—Kieft displeased—Sends out expeditions against the offending tribe, but effects nothing—The Twelve Men seek reforms in the government—Absolute power of the Director-general—Exercises legislative and judicial functions—Demands of the Twelve Men—Answers of the Director-general thereupon—Meeting of the Twelve Men forbidden on pain of corporal punishment—Expedition against the Weckquaesqueecks—Fails in discovering the enemy—Peace with these Indians.

CHAP. II. 1641

To those who were superstitiously disposed, and whose anticipations of the future received a coloring from passing events, the year 1641 opened, in New Amsterdam, with an ill omen. The first month of the new year had not counted many days, when that "village" was thrown into considerable excitement by intelligence that a murder had been committed behind the fort. Six of the company's slaves had perpetrated the horrid deed. A fellow-slave was their victim. As there was no evidence, however, against them, torture, the common expedient of the law in such cases, was resorted to for the purpose of extorting self-accusation from the prisoners. But to avoid this terrible engine, the latter confessed that they had all jointly committed the act. The court was in a dilemma.

BOOK III. 1641 Jan. 17. The company could not afford, in the scarcity of laborers, to lose six of its negroes. Justice could not be defrauded. The difficulty was solved by a resolution that lots should be drawn in order to determine which of the six should be executed. The lot fell on Manuel de Reus, "the giant," and he was accordingly sentenced to be hanged.

Jan. 24. On the appointed day, the village of New Amsterdam poured forth its scanty population to witness the execution of the murderer. He was placed on a ladder in the fort, with two strong halters around his neck. The fatal signal was given, and the unfortunate man was turned off, when, horrid to relate! both the ropes broke, and "the giant" fell prostrate to the ground. Forthwith the inhabitants and bystanders cried aloud for pardon with great ardor; and so strong were their appeals, that the Director-general granted the culprit his life, under a pledge of future good behavior.

April 11. Some municipal regulations were issued in the course of this spring for the better observance of the Sabbath, and to check the prevailing vice of drunkenness on that day. The tapping of beer during divine service, or after ten o'clock at night, was strictly forbidden, under a penalty of ten dollars for each offence. Measures were also taken to prevent the deterioration of the currency, which heretofore consisted, entirely, of "the good splendid seawan, usually called Manhattans' seawan," four beads of which were equal to one stiver. But now, "nasty, rough seawan," fifty per cent. cheaper, was surreptitiously introduced from foreign places. This drove, according to the laws of currency, the better sort out of circulation; nay, threatened "the ruin of the country." This inferior article was therefore condemned to pass at five for one
April 18. stiver during the following month, and afterwards at six, at which rate circulated, subsequently, the loose, unstringed wampum, which served the community as change.[1]

The progress of these municipal reforms was, however,

[1] Alb. Rec. ii., 108, 109, 110, 111, 118, 119. "Ter tyde van den Directeur Kieft ging de Seewan voor vier die goet was; ende losse lompen wierden op ses stucx in een stuyver gestelt; de redenen waerom de losse seewan niet is affgeset is, om datter geen gelt anders hebbende, veel verliesen souden." Van Tienhoven.

1641.

now interrupted by the further attempts of the English at New Haven to usurp another section of the Dutch territory. A number of families—some fifty in all—belonging to that quarter, had become dissatisfied with their settlement on account of the sickliness of the place, and concluded, in the fall of the past year, to seek a more favorable climate and to remove to the South River, which country they claimed as part of Virginia. This expedition sailing in the beginning of April, in a bark belonging to a Mr. Lamberton, a New Haven merchant, put into New Amsterdam in its progress south, and communicated its designs to the Dutch authorities.

With the encroachments of the New Haven people at the east, and of the Swedes on the Delaware, fresh in his recollection, Director Kieft could not but look with an unfavorable eye on this movement, which would, in the nature of things, only add to the competition the Dutch were already contending against on the South River, in their trade with the natives, as well as to the difficulties which their title to the soil was already encountering. He considered it, therefore, to be his duty to express his disapprobation of the proceeding on the threshold, and accordingly ordered the following protest to be served on the interested parties:

" I, WILLEM KIEFT, Director-general in behalf of the High April 8.
and Mighty Lords the States General of the United Provinces, of his Highness of Orange, and the Noble Lords Directors of the Privileged West India Company, residing in New Netherland, make known to you, Robert Cogswell, and your associates, not to build nor plant on the South River, lying within the limits of the New Netherlands, nor on the lands extending along there, as lawfully belonging to Us, by our possessing the same long years ago, before it was frequented by any Christians, as appears by our forts which we have thereon; and also the mouth of the rivers sealed with our blood, and the soil itself, most of which has been purchased and paid for by Us, unless you will settle under the Lords the States, and the Noble West India Company, and swear allegiance and become subject to them, as the other inhabitants have done. Failing whereof, we protest against all damages

BOOK III. 1641. and losses which may accrue therefrom, and desire to be holden innocent thereof."

To this protest, Cogswell, who lay in the stream opposite Fort Amsterdam, replied, that it was not his intention to settle under any government, but to select some spot over which the States General had no authority; and in case no such place was to be found, it was his determination to return; or, if he settled within the limits of their High Mightinesses, to become subject, and swear allegiance to them.[1] With this explanation the party was allowed to proceed. On their arrival at the place of their destination, they purchased from the Indians large tracts of land on both sides of the South River; began to plant and set up trading-houses on Varken's Kill, or Hog Creek, and a short time afterwards fortified a post on the Schuylkill.[2]

With the return of the season for putting in the crops, the difficulties were renewed between the Dutch and the English on the Connecticut. Pieter Colet, Evert Duyckingh, and

April 15. Sybrant Sybols, set about preparing the company's lands around Fort Good Hope, but had not progressed far when a number of Hartford people came along. "Ye are smart farmers to be abroad so early in the morning," was their first salute; "but the ground ye work on is ours!" Pieter Colet would not submit to any such pretension. "We plough our own ground," he replied, "and we are determined to maintain our right." "What!" retorted the Englishmen, "will ye three resist the whole English village?" And thereupon they fell on the Dutch servants, and beat both them and their horses off the ground. Colet and Duyckingh proceeded immediately to Governor Hopkins and Mr. Haines for redress. But the question of title was here mooted again, and the Dutchmen left, repeating their determination—"please the Almighty God!"—to plough their own soil. They kept their words.

April. 17. Two days afterwards they proceeded again to work, and were again driven off by the Hartford men, who not only threw their implements of husbandry into the river, but ran a strong

[1] Hol. Doc. ix., 205.

[2] Hazard, ii., 213. Acrelius, Hist. of New Sweden.

fence of palisades across the road leading from the fort to the woods, in order to cut off all communication between the former and the interior, so that the Dutch could procure neither fuel nor any other necessaries. In addition to this, they impounded the company's hogs and cows, and, though the Dutch broke down the fence and threw the palisades into the river, the English continued their annoyances in all possible ways. CHAP. II. 1641. May 24.

Hendrick Roesen, the recently appointed commissary of this post, having deceased shortly after his arrival on the Connecticut, his widow, Elsje Goosens, transmitted intelligence of these unneighborly and unjustifiable proceedings to Fort Amsterdam. The Director-general and council ordered Doctor Johannes La Montagne to repair, with fifty soldiers and a couple of yachts, to Fort Good Hope, to defend that post and prevent a recurrence of these hostilities; but this expedition was subsequently countermanded, owing to the continued misunderstandings with the Indians. The authorities at Hartford seem to have felt as much aggrieved by the resistance of the Dutch, as the latter felt injured by the attacks of the English. They took immediate steps to confer with the governor and council of Massachusetts on the subject, but the latter, without determining the case for either side, recommended the Hartford people to be more moderate in their proceedings, and to allow the Dutch more than thirty acres of land, which were the limits to which the English had restricted Fort Good Hope.[1] May 26. June 6. June 21.

The news of the fall of Strafford and of Laud had now reached the English colonies. "Upon the supposal that great revolutions were at hand," the general court concluded to send delegates to England, to congratulate the people of that country on their happy success; to assist them by their advice in

[1] Hol. Doc. ix., 199, 200, 201, 202, 203; Alb. Rec. ii., 123. Hazard's State Papers, ii. N. Y. Hist. Soc. Coll. i., 274, 275. Winthrop alludes (Hist. N. Eng. ii., 32) to this order of Kieft's to send troops to the Connecticut, and then adds, "but it pleased the Lord to disappoint their purpose at that time, for the Indians falling out with them, killed some of their men at the Fort of Orange," [this is an error, it was at Staten Island;] "whereby they were forced to keep their soldiers at home to defend themselves." Winthrop's Journ. 224, 225.

BOOK III. 1641. establishing a right form of church-government, and to explain to their creditors the reasons which prevented them sending remittances at that time. The individuals selected for this important mission were the Rev. Mr. Welde, pastor of Roxbury; Mr. Hibbins, of Boston; Mr. John Winthrop, a member of the Massachusetts council; and the Rev. Hugh Peters, pastor of Salem, since well known on account of the active part which he took against Charles the First, the unhappy monarch of England; the fiery zeal which he evinced in favor of the usurper Cromwell; and the great misfortunes which he suffered after the Restoration, and which terminated only by his death on the scaffold.[1]

[1] The Rev. HUGH PETERS, the descendant of a wealthy and ancient English family, was born in 1599, and graduated at Cambridge, England, in 1622. He received holy orders from Dr. Mountain, Bishop of London; but in consequence of the active part which he took against the bishops, he was forced to leave the country, and to retire to Holland, where he officiated as minister to an English congregation at Rotterdam. He proceeded to New England in 1634, and was there elected minister of the church at Salem, and officiated afterwards in the great meeting-house in Boston, at which place he enjoyed a high reputation and was much respected. After a residence in New England of seven years, he was sent by the colonies as their ambassador to the parliament of England, for the purposes mentioned in the text, and also to obtain some favorable commercial privileges. On his arrival, he found the civil war at its height, and attached himself to the Parliamentarians with a "zeal which overwhelmed his judgment." He visited Holland in 1643, in several cities of which country he preached so violently against Charles I., that the English ambassador, Boswell, was under the necessity of complaining of him to the States General. He delivered a series of discourses to the English congregation at Amsterdam, in which he accused the king of exciting the Catholics of Ireland against Cromwell and his partisans in that country; and such effect had these sermons, that crowds of women, it is said, gave their wedding-rings to supply the English malecontents with funds. The Dutch connived at the whole of these proceedings. Peters was subsequently appointed chaplain to Cromwell, of whom he was so thorough a partisan, that he gave God thanks for the Drogheda massacre, where between three and four thousand people were put to death in cold blood. In the part he took against Charles I., his opposition assumed the character of the bitterest passion, and he is represented as having uttered the most terrible denunciations against that unfortunate monarch in the sermon which he preached before his majesty previous to his execution. "Bind fast your king with chains, and your nobles with fetters of iron," were the words which he is said to have taken for his text, when he compared Charles to Barabbas, and the red-coats to saviours and saints, "not inferior to those who surround the throne of God." But it is to be hoped that in this particular the

CHAP. II. 1641.

As Mr. Peters had, by his previous residence in Holland, become well acquainted with many of the directors of the West India Company, the governors of Massachusetts and Connecticut considered this a favorable opportunity to endeavor to enter into such arrangements with that body, as might obviate the recurrence of those late collisions which had disturbed public harmony on the Connecticut River. In this hope, they furnished the Rev. Mr. Peters with the following letter of credence,[1] accompanied by a series of propositions, which, if concurred in by the directors, would, they expected, be productive of beneficial results.

"Whereas, the bearer, Mr. Hugh Peters, minister of Salem, is sent, at the public request, to England, to negotiate with the present parliament there about such matters as concern us, which we confide to his care and fidelity, this is to authorize him, if occasion permit him to go to the Netherlands, to treat with the West India Company there, concerning a peaceable neighborhood between us and those of New Netherland, and whatever he shall further think proper touching the West Indies; wherefore we have agreed and consulted with each other, in a matter of such great importance, God willing, to Oct. 10.

accusation is overcharged, for Dr. Lingard says, "it should be recorded to the honor of that fanatical preacher," that it was at the request of Hugh Peters, that Dr. Juxon, Bishop of London, had been permitted to attend on Charles preparatory to his death. After the Restoration, the Rev. Mr. Peters was accused as a regicide. His trial was a scene of flagrant injustice. He was allowed no counsel, and was sentenced to die, though even false witnesses did not substantiate the charges on which he was condemned. He was hanged on the 14th Oct. 1660, exhibiting, even at the gallows, the most indomitable courage. "You may do your worst," was his last address to his unfeeling executioner; and with these words "the first freeman of Massachusetts who lost his life for opposition to monarchy," was launched into eternity. His course and his character have been differently appreciated by friends and enemies. Those praise and these asperse, according as bias has swayed their judgment. Whoever wishes to arrive at a just conclusion, may consult Bancroft's U. S. i., 383; ii., 32; Aitzema, ii., 936; Von Reaumer's Pol. Hist. of Eng. ii., 399; and Lingard's Hist. Eng. x., 257.

[1] Winthrop's New Eng. ii., 25, 26, 31, 32; Journal, 225; Hubbard's New Eng. 371, 432, 433. Hubbard, copying Winthrop, says that Peters did not carry a commission with him to treat with the West India Company. But in this, it will be seen, all these New England authorities are in error.

BOOK III. 1641.

reduce the particulars to be treated of, to such propositions as shall be presented on coming together.

(Signed) "JOHN WINTHROP,
Gov. of Massachusetts.
"JOHN HAYNES,
Gov. of Connecticut.

"This 10th day of Oct. 1641, in the Bay
of Massachusetts, in New England."

The "propositions" referred to in the above letter, and submitted to the West India Company, were :—

"I. That the Honorable Company will be pleased to devise some expedient for the settlement of the limits between New England and New Netherland, or at least to define for us their limits.

"II. That their Honors will wholly abstain from molesting our people on the Fresh River, alias the Connecticut, since we are willing that indifferent persons, if any such can be found, may examine our title.

"III. That the said company will set a price on their plantation, if they have any intention to part with it.

"IV. That if any Englishmen should remove from our district to the continent of the West Indies, being provided therefor with all necessaries, except ships and ordnance, which the company should furnish, what conditions would they be willing to require?

"V. That the company, knowing that the English in America amount to about fifty thousand souls, may be pleased to inform us in what manner we can be employed in advancing the great work there, being of the same religion with themselves, and such as we hope may be trusted, and furnish us with an analysis of such government as they, in conjunction with us, would be willing to grant there.

"VI. That the company would be pleased in all things to see in the inhabitants of New England, who number about forty thousand souls, a people who covet peace in their ways, the planting of the gospel above all things, and not to cause trouble or injury in any manner whatever to the company."[1]

[1] Hol. Doc. ix., 224, 225. The above is a translation from the Dutch, and possibly may not accord in all expressions with the English original.

CHAP. II. 1641.

What issue followed these propositions we are unable to determine. The terrible crisis that had overtaken England and the English monarchy, absorbed exclusively all men's attention. New England and New Netherland were for the moment alike forgotten. It is evident, however, that a desire very generally prevailed among the English at the east, to remove to the territories of the West India Company. A considerable number of "respectable Englishmen" came in the course of this summer from Lynn and Ipswich, Massachusetts, to examine the Dutch lands on Long Island, and to treat with the Director-general for permission to settle, with their clergyman, there. This permission was readily accorded on the following very favorable terms, in conformity with the provisions of the charter of 1640, which formed the basis of all future grants from the Dutch to the English. June 6

They were to take the oath of allegiance to their High Mightinesses the States General and the West India Company, and in return, to enjoy free exercise of religion, and if they desired to have a magistracy from among themselves, they were to be allowed to nominate three or more persons from the most respectable among them, from which the Director-general would select one or more schepens, or magistrates, to be invested with power to decide definitively in all civil cases to the amount of forty guilders, or sixteen dollars, above which sum an appeal was to lie to the Director-general and council. In criminal cases, they might proceed to, but not inflict capital punishment. They were empowered to erect towns, but could not construct forts except by special leave. Lands were to be shown to them free of expense, and whatever ground they might select, they were to hold free of rent or taxes for ten years; at the expiration of which time, they should be holden to pay the tenths of the produce. They were, in addition, to enjoy free hunting and fishing, and unshackled commerce, conformably to the privileges granted to New Netherland, but they were bound, in return, to make use of the weights and measures of the country.[1]

[1] Alb. Rec. ii., 122, 123, 169. The above privileges were those of a simple manor. Schepens were town magistrates whose authority was confined to causes between private individuals; matters of municipal polity; management

BOOK III. 1641. The families above referred to did not follow up their intention of moving to Long Island. Though satisfied with the "very fair terms" which the Dutch authorities offered, and which, with few exceptions, were similar to the immunities which they enjoyed in Massachusetts; their court was offended at their "strengthening the Dutch, our doubtful neighbors," and at their accepting from them that which the king had already granted by patent to the Earl of Stirling. They viewed, also, with particular displeasure, the assent which the English had given to the "oath of fealty." The consequence, Oct. 6. therefore, was, that the proposed emigration was prevented, and the parties were persuaded to remain in New England.[1]

Respectable Dutch planters continued, however, to take an interest in the settlement of the country. A new "colonie," of which Meyndert Meyndertsen, the Heer Nederhorst, was Patroon, was established in the beginning of this year on the main behind Staten Island, and extended from Achter Cul, or Newark Bay, north to Tappaan. Cornelis Melyn, a Dutch 1640. merchant, who visited New Netherland in 1639, had obtained July 3. from the directors in Holland an order for Staten Island, authorizing him to erect the same into a "colonie." But 1641. having, on his voyage out, been taken prisoner by the "Dunkirkers," who had also captured his vessel, he was obliged to Feb. 18. apply to the company for a passage for himself and family, Aug. 20. which obtaining, he arrived in New Netherland in the middle of the following summer, with his wife, children, servants, and a small venture valued at about one thousand guilders, in the ship the Eyckenboom, or Oak Tree. On the 19th June,

of town revenues, and the welfare and security of their locality, so far as the same was permitted by the above-mentioned charter. The nomination by the people of a double or triple number, from which the executive was to choose the person or persons to be commissioned as magistrates, was in conformity to the custom prevalent in many parts of Holland, where the inhabitants of various localities, down to 1672, submitted a double list to the Stadtholder, from which he selected one half to be magistrates. A somewhat similar custom prevails in England and Ireland, where the circuit judges submit the names of three gentlemen as sheriffs, from which list the crown "pricks" one to be commissioned as high sheriff of the county. See Van Leeuwen's Com.; also Institutions Judiciaires, iii., 165, 166.

[1] Winthrop's N. Eng. ii., 34; Journal, 226, 227.

1642, letters patent were issued, constituting him patroon of the whole of Staten Island, the bouwerie of Capt. De Vries excepted, and investing him with all the powers, jurisdictions, and pre-eminences appertaining to that privileged order. CHAP. II. 1641.

Aert Teunissen van Patten took a lease, this year, of Hoboken, situate in Pavonia, which he stocked with all sorts of cattle, and on which he erected a respectable bouwerie, and planted a considerable number of fruit-trees. So favorable, indeed, became the prospects of the country, that the Director-general and council established two fairs at New Amsterdam; one to be holden annually on the fifteenth October, for cattle generally; the other on the first of November, for hogs.[1] Sept. 15.

The ill-feeling which had existed for some time between the Dutch and the Indians, led unfortunately, this summer, to increased misunderstanding, accompanied by the shedding of blood. Staten Island became again the theatre of these sad deeds. The Raritan tribe, smarting under the attacks of the Dutch in the preceding spring, which they considered the more unjustifiable, inasmuch as they were guiltless of the charges made against them, determined now that the "Swannekins," as they called the Europeans, should have dead men instead of dead hogs to fight for. They accordingly made a descent on the bouwerie belonging to Captain De Vries, on Staten Island, killed four of his planters, and burned his dwelling and tobacco house. This assault, which was the more unexpected as the Indians had been suing for peace, and had assured the Dutch that the "talk" of their chief would be forthcoming in a few days, excited considerable anger in the mind of the Director-general. He forthwith resolved—contrary, however, to the express commands of his superiors, who seriously and particularly enjoined on him to cultivate good understanding with the Indians—to wage a war of extermination against the Raritans, and with that view invited his savage allies, who resided in the neighborhood, to July 4.

[1] Alb. Rec. ii., 134; iii., 13; xix., 143, 144; GG, 102, 103; Hol. Doc. iv., 247; De Vries Voyag. in ii. N. Y. Hist. Soc. Col. i., 264. The prices of stock about this time were: for a mare 400 gl., or $160; a colt, 250 gl., [$100;] a milch cow, 150 gl., or $60; Alb. Rec. i., 266.

BOOK III. 1641. take up arms in favor of the Dutch. To stimulate their thirst for blood, he offered ten fathoms of wampum for every head of a Raritan, and twenty fathoms for each of the heads of the Indians who murdered the people on Staten Island. Sept. 12 As a further measure of precaution, he ordered a small redoubt to be erected on that island "at the lowest expense."[1]

These rewards did not fail to arouse the bad passions of some of the neighboring savages. Pacham, chief of the Tankitekes, or Haverstraw Indians, who resided in the rear of Sing Sing, soon made his appearance at the fort with the hand of a dead man dangling at the end of a stick. It belonged to the chief who had killed the planters on Staten Island; and the savage, in presenting it, boasted that he had thus avenged the wrongs of the Swannekins, "whose friend he was." Peace was fortunately concluded, some time subsequently, between the Dutch and the Raritans, which, to their honor be it said, the latter forever after faithfully preserved unbroken, even when the whole of the neighboring tribes raised the hatchet and the warwhoop against the inhabitants of New Netherland.

Peace had not been concluded, however, before another murder was to be recorded. The child, whose uncle had been assassinated by the servants of Director Minuit, in 1626, had now grown to manhood. His uncle's spirit was still unappeased—his murder was unavenged. His voice was heard in the roaring of the storm—in the rustle of the leaves—in the sighing of the winds; and full of the conviction that that spirit could not find rest until vengeance should be had, the young Weckquaeskeeck[2] sought for a victim to offer to the

[1] Alb. Rec. ii., 128, 129, 133. This disgraceful practice of offering rewards for the murder of Indians, was common for a long time after this in the American colonies. Gov. Hunter, of Pennsylvania, offered, in 1756, $150 for every male Indian enemy over twelve years of age; for his scalp, or for a female Indian or child under twelve, $130; or $50 for the scalp of an Indian woman. Dunlap's N. Y. ii., App. clxx., clxxxi.

[2] Opposite Tappaan [says De Vries] lies a place called Wechquaesqueeck. Van Tienhoven, describing this place, states: "Wechquaesqueek, on the North River, five (twenty) miles above New Amsterdam, is a right good and suitable land for cultivation; contains considerable mayze land, which the Indians planted, rising from the shore; in the interior the country is flat and mostly

manes of the dead. Shrouding his evil purpose under the cloak of a friendly, or business visit, he called at the house of one Claes Cornelisz. Smits, the "Raadmaker," an aged settler, resident on the west side of the river, under pretence of making some purchases. The old man suspecting no harm, (for the Indian had been in the habit of working for his son,) set some food before him, and then proceeded to get from a chest, in which it lay, the cloth which the other wished to purchase. The moment he stooped, the savage seized an axe, struck him dead, and then withdrew, having rifled the house of all its contents.

CHAP. II. 1641.

This aggression on an old and helpless man excited, when it became known, considerable feeling at Fort Amsterdam. Director Kieft promptly demanded satisfaction from the chief to whose tribe the murderer belonged. But the sachem refused to make any atonement. "He was sorry that twenty Christians had not been immolated; the Indian had but avenged, after the manner of his race, the murder of a relative whom the Dutch had slain nearly twenty years before." On receipt of this answer, armed parties were sent out to retaliate, but they returned, having effected nothing.[1]

Aug. 20.

In this state of affairs, Director Kieft, in order to obviate all public censure, concluded to submit matters now to the community at large. All the masters and heads of families, residents of New Amsterdam and its neighborhood, were, therefore, invited to assemble in the fort on the 28th day of August, then and there to determine on "something of the first importance." The people met. It was the first time that their existence as a component part of the body politic had been recognised, or their influence acknowledged. Three propositions were submitted to them by the Director-general and council— Firstly, Whether it was not just that the recent murder should be avenged, and the village destroyed to which the murderer

Aug 23.

Aug. 28.

even; very abundantly watered with small streams and running fountains. This land is situate between two rivulets called Sintsinck and Armonck, lying between the East and North rivers." Bedenkinge over het aenvaerden van de landeryen in N. Nederlant.

[1] Journael van Nieuw Nederlant; Capt. Patrix brief in dato den 21 Aug. 1641; also Hol. Doc. v. 314. De Vries corroborates the statements in the text.

BOOK III. 1641. belonged, if he were not surrendered or punished? Secondly, In what manner this object ought to be accomplished? and, Thirdly, By whom the project should be effected?

Aug. 29. On the day following, the commonalty of New Amsterdam, and the adjoining settlements, handed in their opinions on these propositions. The harvest was still unsaved; the cattle scattered through the woods; many of the inhabitants at a distance. It was therefore considered prudent to wait for a more fitting opportunity to prosecute this undertaking. "Meanwhile all the means were to be got ready, and the Director-general was requested to procure two hundred coats of mail (malj rocken) from the north, as well for the soldiers as for the freemen who may be willing to pay their share in these expenses." It was further recommended that kind intercourse, and the trade in corn, be continued as usual, in order to throw the savages off their guard; and that no person, of whatever rank he may be, should on any account adopt any hostile measures, except against the murderer, until the hunting season, when, it was suggested, two expeditions should be got up—one to land in the neighborhood of "the Archipelago," or Norwalk Island—the other, at Wechquaesqueck; on which occasions the Director-general (who it was significantly hinted should "lead the van") was advised to employ as many of the most active negroes as he could spare, to be armed each with a tomahawk and half-pike. In the mean time, it was strenuously urged, that a messenger should be sent once, twice, "yea, even a third time," to demand, in a friendly manner, the surrender of the murderer, in order that he be punished according to his deserts.

Twelve men were then chosen by the commonalty at large, to co-operate with the Director-general and council, in the execution of the foregoing conclusions. The names of these delegates—the first representative body of which we have any mention in the annals of this state—were, Jacques Bentyn, Jan Dam, Hendrik Jansen, David Pietersen De Vries, Jacob Stoffels, Maryn Adriaensen, Abram Molenaer, Fredrik Lubbertsen, Joachim Pietersen, Gerrit Dircksen, George Rapelje, and Abram Plank.[1] They were immediately sworn into office,

[1] Hol. Doc. v., 327, 328, 329. Alb. Rec. ii., 136, 137.

Capt. De Vries having been named their president; but, though in every sense of the word the representatives of the people, their influence over the councils or determinations of the Director-general does not appear to have been very great. Kieft made this concession to popular rights neither willingly nor in good faith. It was wrung from him rather by the necessities of the times, to serve as a cloak to protect him from responsibility or censure; to be cast aside when it ceased to serve this purpose.[1] CHAP. II. 1641.

He was not, it seems, altogether pleased with the conclusions to which the commonalty had come; he was impatient to attack the Indians, against whom he entertained strong prejudices and dislike, and, therefore, when the winter approached, he called the Twelve Men again into his presence—not in a body, however, but separately—to obtain their consent to an attack, "as the time and opportunity were presenting themselves to surprise the Indians on their hunting expeditions." But the majority still counselled patience. The savages were not sufficiently lulled—it were better, some added, to await the arrival of a vessel from Patria; and thus Director Kieft was obliged to defer, to a future time, his attack on the unsuspecting natives.[2] Nov. 1.

But his purpose against the Indians did not sleep, for all that. The moment the winter effectually set in, and the rivers 1642.

[1] Van der Donck says, very plainly, that Kieft allowed these representatives to be chosen merely "to serve him as a cloak, and as cats-paws"—that they had neither vote nor voice in the council, and were of no moment, when their opinions differed from that of the Director, who looked upon himself as sovereign in the country. "De 12 mannen" (he says) "en daernaer de acht, hadden in gerechtsaacken noch stem, noch advys; maar sy waeren ten opsien van den oorloch en eenige andere voorvallende saaken gekoren, om als deckmantel en cattepooten te dienen; anders quamen in geen consideratie, en werden weynich geacht, als sy tegens des Directeurs meyninge yetwes verstonden; die sich doch inbielde, ofte immers andere wilde doen geloove, als souverain te wesen; endat alles in zyn handt absoluyt stont te doen en te laten." Kieft himself repudiated, before three months were passed, the idea that the Twelve Men were to have any participation in the management of public affairs; though De Vries (who was one of the Twelve) alleges that they were elected to take the reins of the government with Kieft. Van der Donk's view is, no doubt, the correct one.

[2] Alb. Rec. ii., 140, 141.

BOOK III. 1642. and streams became frozen over, he again called on the Twelve Men, to take into their consideration the three propositions which he had already submitted to them, and to decide what was best to be done. They could no longer, now, refuse their concurrence in the wishes of the Director-general. The murderer of Claes Smits had neither been delivered up nor punished. They therefore consented that preparations should be made
Jan. 21. for an expedition, in which they promised their co-operation, provided, however, the Director himself accompanied them, to prevent all disorder; and on condition, also, that he should furnish, in addition to powder and ball, provisions necessary for the expedition, "such as bread and butter;" and appoint, moreover, a steward to take charge of the same, in order that all waste should be prevented. "If any person required any thing more than bread and butter, he was to provide himself therewith." "But if it happened that God Almighty were pleased to permit one or more of the freemen to be wounded in the expedition, or in the attack on the savages, the noble Director and council were to remain obliged to support such wounded persons, and their families, in a decent manner, and to have them cured at the expense of the provident company."[1]

Having made these concessions to the personal wishes of the Director-general, the Twelve Men turned their attention to the faulty composition of their local government; to the unlimited power of the executive; and to the absence of all municipal authority in the settlements and villages which were gradually rising up.

Though a servant himself of the West India Company, nominated by the Assembly of the XIX., and commissioned by the States General, the Director was in fact absolute in New Netherland, and beyond all control within the colony. As representative of the sovereign authority, he extinguished Indian titles to land, and sanctioned all purchases from the aborigines. No contracts, engagements, transfers, bargains, nor sales were valid, except such as were passed before and written by his secretary. He erected courts; appointed,

[1] Hol. Doc. v., 330, 331.

either directly or indirectly, all public officers, except such as came out with commissions from Holland; made laws; issued ordinances; incorporated towns; imposed taxes; levied fines; inflicted penalties; and could affect the value of any man's property at a moment, by raising or lowering the value of wampum, which constituted the chief currency, at this period, of the country. He not only acted in an executive and legislative, but also in a judicial capacity. He decided all civil and criminal questions, without the intervention of a jury, such an institution being unknown in the province; and before him were brought all appeals from inferior courts. When we add to this the fact, that all such municipal regulations as circumstances demanded, emanated from him and his council, we cannot be surprised to learn that many things were left undone which ought to be attended to; that many things were performed, which might better have been left undone; and that dissatisfaction necessarily prevailed among the sturdy sons of that republic, who ever evinced a lively and honorable jealousy of despotic power.

This, indeed, could not well be otherwise. The colonial council consisted, as we have already remarked, of the Director-general and Mr. La Montagne, and as the management of the various interests of the country, and the performance of the numerous duties which we have enumerated, devolved on these two, they were necessarily obliged to call in some of the common people, usually the servants of the company, dependents on the pleasure of the Director-general, to assist in the administration of justice,—a course which, from the nature of things, excited suspicion, distrust, and discontent.

This faulty composition of the council attracted, therefore, the early attention of the Twelve Men. To obtain a reform of that, and other grievances under which they labored, their principal exertions were now directed. With this view, they Jan 21. addressed a respectful memorial to the Director-general, at the same time that they offered their services against the Indians, in which they called his particular attention to the fact, that in their native country—their beloved "Fatherland"—the smallest village had a board of from five to seven schepens,

BOOK III. 1642. or magistrates, for the management of its local affairs.[1] They asked that the same privilege should be extended to them, and that the council of New Netherland should be increased, as the Director already proposed, by the addition of four more persons, so that the board should consist in future of at least five members. And as rotation in office was a good and wholesome practice, they further demanded that two of these should annually retire, to be succeeded by two others from among "the twelve men." They objected, in the next place, to so many of the "common people" having seats on the bench; and required that the Director and council should not, hereafter, sit in judgment on any accused persons, or evil doers, unless, as was laid down in the instructions to the schout-fiscaal, five members of the council preside in the court. They further proposed, with a view to render the defence of the country more perfect, that there should be an annual muster of all male persons capable of bearing arms, each man to attend with his gun, and to be furnished by the company, on that occasion, with half a pound of powder; that every freeman should be allowed to visit all vessels arriving from sea, "whether Dutch, English, or French," after the fiscaal had been on board, "as is the custom in Holland;" and that all the inhabitants, "be they who they may," have the right to repair to and return from all places round about, belonging to friends and allies, and to transport thither such goods as they may please, on receiving the necessary permit, and paying such duties as the company may demand. Having thus disposed of those general matters, they next represented that in consequence of the sale, in New Netherland, of

[1] Dan les lieux où les Communes avaient acquis plus d'autorité, on trouve des Echevins comme juges nommés par le souverain. Il paraît qu'anciennement les Echevins Communaux, de même que les Scabini des Francs, formaient une classe, ou un état de personnes désignées comme plus propres à se charger de rendre la justice sans que le nombre total fût déterminé, ou qu'ils constituassent un tribunal permanent. Plus tard le nombre des Echevins fut fixé; et ce nombre est si souvent tellement petit qu'on ne peut douter qu'ils n'aient été plutôt un tribunal stable que des juges appelés selon la convenance du Bailli. Ce n'est que vers le quinzième siècle qu'on trouve généralement les Echevins nommés pour un certain tems, et positivement désigné comme formant un tribunal qui jugeait à la semonce du Bailli. Institutions Judiciaires, 165, 166.

cows and other stock by the English, the cattle owned and introduced by the Dutch were held in small esteem, and were not so valuable as they had heretofore been. They therefore asked—and it was a demand as injudicious as it was near-sighted and destructive to the improvement of their own stock—that the English should not be permitted, hereafter, to sell either cows or goats within the Dutch jurisdiction, but that this privilege should be confined to oxen and poultry. The currency of the country was the last subject to which their memorial referred. They asked, that its value should be raised, on the fallacious plea that it would thereby be retained in the province and not be carried off by foreign nations.

Director Kieft lent a favorable ear, for the moment, to this representation. He informed the petitioners that he had already written to Holland on the subject referred to in the first part of the memorial, and that he expected by the first ship, the arrival of "some persons of quality," and to be also furnished with a complete council. The presence of "common people" on the bench was caused, he said, by the fewness of the council, but he doubted if any persons had grounds to complain of unrighteous judgments on that account. If they had, he should like to know who they were. He consented to select four persons to assist in the administration of justice, and to sit in the council at certain times, when summoned so to do; with the further privilege of assembling together on public affairs, and voting on such propositions as should be submitted to them; to which extent their authority and power should be confined; and that two of these should retire every year. But as for the Twelve Men, he told them that they were not invested by the commonalty with any greater power than to give their advice as to the proper course to be adopted to revenge the murder of Claes Smits.[1] He agreed that there

[1] III. Dat den Raed van Nieuw Nederlandt van nu af sal compleet gehouden worden van raden, temeer, alsoo in 't Vaderlant den raet op een cleyne dorp, by vyff a 7 schepens bestaet; meede dat van nu voortaen by den Directeur en Raed genige misdadigen en sullen veroordeelt worden, ten ware sy vyff raden in 't getal sterck waren, endat, omdat de gemeene man daer veel plaets van heeft.

Answer: Daer is in Hollandt om geschreeven, soo dat wy vertrouwen met d'eerste schepen eenige persoonen van qualiteyt te becomen, en alsoo een

BOOK III. 1642. should be an annual muster, but refused to furnish the half pound of powder, as the company was bound to provide settlers with ammunition, in cases of emergency, and furnish the Patroons, besides, with sufficient means to defend themselves and property from attack. It was contrary to his instructions to permit the freemen to visit arriving vessels. "Such a course would lead to disorder," as several of the company's ships were expected at the Manhattans with prizes. This part of the memorial was, therefore, refused. But the inhabitants were allowed to visit the neighboring country, and the ports of friendly governments, on payment of the proper dues, on condition that the goods should not be sold to any of the public enemy. The Director-general concluded by promising that the English should not be permitted to sell cows or goats, for the future, within New Netherland, and that the value of the currency should be raised, as requested.

Having thus disposed of these various demands, without, however, carrying out, afterwards, the reforms in the council which he had so solemnly promised, Director Kieft seems to

geheele geformeerde Raet te hebben. Dat de geemene man veel plaets heeft, van swaackheyd des raets, can wel wesen; dan wy wenschten wel te weten offer oock iemant is, die sich heeft te beclagen, over onrechte sententie, en wie de geene syn, die daer veel plaets van hebben.

IV. Van gelyck, indien U. E. 4 persoonen gelieft te verkiezen, die in den Raed alhier acces sullen hebben, gelyck voor desen by U. E. is voorgestelt, zyn wy supplianten wel te vreden, te meer alsoo het lant met beswaert mach worden, sonder de 12 te vergaderen.

Answer: Wy syn wel te vreden 4 persoonen te verkiesen die de Gemeenten in haer recht helpen mainteneren, die wy oock in onzen raed willen sullen roepen, als den noot vereischt, meede seekere tyden in 't jaer bestemmen, om gezamentlyck over des lants saken te vergaderen; oock eenige articulen te beraemen, hoe hooch haer auctoriteyt sal strecken; de 12 mannen belangende, is ons niet bekent dat zy wyder macht van de gemeente ontfangen hebben, als alleen haer advys te geven, over de moort aen de zaliger Claes Smitz begaen.

VI. Ingevalle U. E. vier de bequaemste quam te verkiezen, omme in U. E vergaderingh te compareren, gelyck geseyt is, staet te noteren datter alle jaren twee van den 4 sullen afgaen, en ander twee in plaets gecoren worden uyt de 12.

Answer: Zyn wel te vreeden dat alle jaren twee van de 4 verandert worden Hol. Doc. iii., 176.

have had enough of popular movements, and popular representations. He, shortly after, issued a proclamation extinguishing the "Twelve Men," whom he forbade, on pain of corporal punishment, to hold any further meetings, without his express permission; "as they tend to dangerous consequences, and to the serious injury both of the country and of his authority."[1]

CHAP. II. 1642. Feb. 18.

Being now untrammelled, and rid of those who were hitherto a check on his actions, Kieft proceeded forthwith to indulge his desire for war. He ordered Hendrick van Dyck, ensign in the company's service, who had been already over two years stationed at New Amsterdam, to proceed with a force of eighty men against the Wechquaesqueeks, to execute summary vengeance upon that tribe, with fire and sword. To ensure complete success, the expedition was placed under the direction of a trusty guide, who professed to be intimately acquainted with the homes and haunts of the savages.[2]

This party started in the forepart of March, and pushed actively forward towards the Indian village, but fortune favored the red-man. The night set in clouded and dark; and when the expedition reached Armenperal, Van Dyck called a halt, notwithstanding the entreaties of his men to push on, ere the savages should have warning of their approach. An hour and a half was thus lost; the guide then missed his way, where-

[1] Hol. Doc. iii., 175, 176, 177, 178, 179, 180. The following is a translation of this placard:—"Whereas the commonalty hath, at our request, commissioned and charged the Twelve Men to communicate their good council and advice concerning the murder of one Claes Cornelissen Smitz, committed by the Indians, which now being done, We thank them for the trouble they have taken, and shall make use of their written advice, with God's help and fitting time; and as we propose no more meetings, as such tend to dangerous consequences, and to the great injury both of the country and of our authority; We, therefore, do hereby forbid the calling of any assemblies or meetings, of whatsoever sort, without our express order, on pain of being punished for disobedience. Done in Fort Amsterdam, 18th Feb., 1642, in New Netherland."

[2] Op dien tyd hadde den oorlochsucht den Directeur alingenomen, toch dese byeenkomste van de voors: 12 mannen heeft niet langer als den 18 February daeraen mogen standgrypen, off men heeft dieselvige op lyffstraffe haer byeenkomste laten verbieden; een weynich tyts daeraen den oorloch met die van Wesqueeckqueeck naer zyn eygen zyndelyckhied aengevangen, als blyckt by request van de 12 mannen. Letter of the Eight Men, Hol. Doc. iii., 214, 215.

BOOK III. 1642.

upon Van Dyck lost temper, and made a retrograde movement to Fort Amsterdam, whither he returned without having accomplished the object for which he had been detailed. The expedition, however, was not without its effect. The Indians had observed, by the trail of the white men, how narrowly they had escaped destruction, and therefore immediately sued for peace, which Cornelis van Tienhoven concluded with them, in the course of the spring, at the house of a settler named Jonas Bronck, who resided on a river to which he gave his name, situate east of Yonkers, in the present county of Westchester. One of the conditions of this peace was, the surrender of the murderer of Claes Smits, dead or alive; a condition which, however, was never fulfilled, owing either to unwillingness or inability on the part of the Indians.[1]

[1] Journael van Nieu Nederlant; Hol. Doc. iii., 107, 146, 166. Alb. Rec. ii., 202; iii., 25. "The tract between the Harlem River and the large stream next eastward, was Bronck's land. Jonas Bronck was the first proprietor of it." Benson's Mem. 27. Armenperal was the Indian name for one of the streams in that vicinity.

CHAPTER III.

Continued disagreements between the people of Hartford and the Dutch at Fort Good Hope—Kieft forbids all intercourse with the former—Greenwich comes under the jurisdiction of the Dutch—Progress of the English at the South River—Kieft determines to break up their settlements—Measures adopted with that view—Excitement at New Haven in consequence—Delegates from Hartford arrive at Fort Amsterdam to negotiate for the purchase of Fort Hope—Terms proposed by the Dutch—Movement in England against New Netherland—Lord Say's representations to the Dutch ambassador at London—Several English families remove from Massachusetts to New Netherland—West Chester, or Vredeland, settled—Surveyor appointed—A fine stone tavern built in New Amsterdam—George Baxter appointed English secretary—Ruinous condition of the church at Manhattans—Measures taken for the erection of a new building—First consistory in New Amsterdam—Contract for the proposed building—Inscription in front of the church—Renewal of misunderstanding with the Indians—Miantonimo conspires against the whites—General alarm in consequence—Some Dutch traders rob an Indian, who murders two settlers in revenge—Endeavors of the Indian chiefs to make satisfaction for the murder—Fail—Mohawks make a descent on the River Indians—The latter fly for protection to the Dutch—Are hospitably entertained—Remove to Corlaers Hook and Pavonia—Kieft determines to attack them—Is opposed by the principal men at New Amsterdam—Kieft will not listen to their objections—The attack—Cruelties practised against the Indians—Settlers on Long Island attack the Indians in their neighborhood—Eleven tribes proclaim war against the Dutch—All the Dutch settlements destroyed—Public discontents—Kieft endeavors to propitiate the Long Island Indians—The latter reject his ambassadors—A day of General Fast and Prayer ordered—Proposals to depose the Director-general—An attack made on his life—Disorders consequent thereupon—Arrival of a flag of truce from the Indians on Long Island—Ambassadors sent to invite them to Fort Amsterdam—Speech of the Indian chief—Treaty of peace and cessation of hostilities.

CHAP. III. 1642.

THE proposals conveyed to the West India Company from the governors of Massachusetts and Connecticut having had no result, the disagreements between the settlers at Hartford and the inhabitants of Fort Good Hope continued without any abatement. Complaints, similar to those already enumerated, were daily repeated against the English, who, it is but justice to say, accused, on their side, the Dutch of having sold guns to the Indians; of having demeaned themselves insolently towards the people on the Connecticut; of having entertained

BOOK III. 1642.

fugitives guilty of violating their laws; helped prisoners, under confinement, to file their irons, and to break jail; persuaded servants to run away from their masters, and purchased goods stolen from the English, which they refused afterwards to restore.

Kieft finding himself unable, under these circumstances, to obtain any satisfaction for the injuries which his government and his people had, notwithstanding his repeated protests, sustained, resorted now to the extreme measure of forbidding all intercourse with the people of Connecticut, or the purchase, either directly or indirectly, of any produce raised in the neighborhood of Fort Good Hope, in the expectation that he should succeed in exacting from the necessities and self-interest of the English, what he had failed to obtain from their sense of justice and gratitude.[1]

With those established at Greenwich he was more successful. These people having become, at length, convinced that
April 9. they were on Dutch territory, gave in their adherence to the authorities at Fort Amsterdam, to whom they swore allegiance, on condition that they should be protected against the Indians, and enjoy, as a manor, the same privileges as Patroons.[2]

[1] Alb. Rec. ii., 158; Trumbull's Conn. i., 122.

[2] Hol. Doc. ix., 204. The following is a translation of the agreement passed on occasion of Greenwich coming under Dutch jurisdiction:—"Whereas, we, Captain Daniel Patrick and Elizabeth Feake, ([a]) duly authorized by her husband Robert Feake, now sick, have resided two years about five or six (Dutch) miles east of the Netherlanders, subjects of the Lords States General, who have protested against us, declaring that the said land lay within their limits, and that they should not suffer any person to usurp it against their lawful rights; and, whereas, we have equally persisted in our course, during these two years, having been well assured that his majesty of England had pretended some right to this soil; and, whereas, we understand nothing thereof, and cannot any longer presume to remain thus, on account both of the strifes of the English, the danger consequent thereon, and these treacherous and villanous Indians, of whom we have seen sorrowful examples enough; We, therefore, betake ourselves under the protection of the Noble Lords States General, His Highness the Prince of Orange, and the West India Company, or their Governor-general of New Netherland, promising, for the future, to be faithful to them, as all honest subjects are bound to be; whereunto we bind ourselves by solemn oath and signature, provided we be protected against our enemies as much as possible, and enjoy henceforth the same privileges that all Patroons of New Netherland have

([a]) This lady is said to have been a daughter-in-law of Gov. Winthrop.

The party of English who had proceeded from New Haven to the South River, were, in the mean time, in active progress with their infant settlements on Hog creek and the Schuylkill. Director Kieft, trusting to the assurances which they had given him, that it was not their intention to settle within the company's limits, was not prepared for the intelligence that they had forgotten that promise. He expressed himself, therefore, in strong terms when he heard that they had settled on the South River without his permission. With the encroachments on the Fresh River strong in his recollection, he determined that this young colony should not take root, and accordingly dispatched the sloops St. Real and St. Martin with a strong force to the Delaware, with orders to Jan Janssen van Ilpendam, the commissary in that quarter, to proceed with these vessels to the Schuylkill, and demand of the English settlers by what authority they had landed and traded there; to require, also, of them to withdraw, should they not be furnished with a royal commission. In case they should refuse to retire, he was further instructed to arrest them, and have them conveyed on board the sloops, taking a full inventory of their goods, and then to destroy their trading-posts.

CHAP. III. 1642.

May 15.

May 22.

These orders were executed so promptly, that the English had not two hours to prepare for their departure. The expedition next proceeded to Hog creek, and, with the aid of the Swedes, destroyed the English settlement there, and then conveyed these people, and their goods, first to New Amsterdam, and the settlers, and a part of their property, afterwards to New Haven. Mr. Lamberton, of the latter place, was considered the principal instigator of these encroachments, and gave particular offence; having, though protested against, continued injuring the trade which the Dutch carried on with the Indians on the South River. It was, therefore, determined to prevent him interfering with that trade for the future, unless he should submit to the authority of the company, and pay the regular duties. He was, accordingly, compelled, when passing the Manhattans, shortly after, to give an account of what

Aug. 28.

obtained, agreeably to the freedoms. ixth of April, 1642. In Fort Amsterdam, (Signed) DANIEL PATRICK; Everardus Bogardus and Johannes Winkelman, witnesses."

BOOK III. 1642. peltries he had obtained on the Delaware, and to pay duties on the whole. The English estimated their damages, on these occasions, at five thousand dollars.

The excitement at New Haven, when these things became known, was very great. Threats of retaliation were publicly uttered, and to so great a height did this angry feeling extend, that Kieft found himself obliged, by approving the conduct of his servants, to assume the responsibility of their acts. Such of the inhabitants of New Amsterdam as had business afterwards at the "Red Mount," were under the necessity of providing themselves with passports, in which this responsibility was fully avowed.[1]

The authorities at Hartford began at length to experience some inconvenience from the system of non-intercourse which Director Kieft ordered to be observed. With a view to arrange, in some way, the differences which existed, they commissioned Messrs. Whiting and Hill, the former a magistrate at Hartford, to proceed as delegates to Fort Amsterdam, to negotiate the purchase of the company's lands around Fort Good Hope. These gentlemen arrived at the Manhattans in the course of July, and received a detailed explanation of the grounds on which the Dutch title rested, as well as documentary proofs that the Dutch were in possession of that quarter before any Christians arrived on the Connecticut. As it was desirable, however, that some arrangement should be made for the termination of the existing misunderstanding, the Director-general and council proposed ceding to the English the land on the
July 9. Fresh River, on condition that they should annually pay, so long as they may occupy such land, agreeably to the ordinances of the United Netherlands, the tenth part of the produce of the land at Hartford, whether cultivated by the plough or other-

[1] Alb. Rec. ii., 162, 177, 185. Hazard's State Pap. ii., 214. Trumbull's Conn. i., 123. Acrelius' Hist. New Sweden. Van der Donck corroborates the statement that the Swedes assisted the Dutch against the English. "Another Kill," he says, "is situate on the east bank (of the South River) called Hog creek, within three (Dutch) miles of the mouth of the river. Some English established themselves here, but Director Kieft drove them away, and protested against them, having been somewhat assisted by the Swedes. They determined together to keep the English out of there." Vertoogh van N. N.

wise, orchards and kitchen gardens excepted, provided these did not exceed a Dutch acre each, or in lieu of such tithes, such rent as should be agreed upon. These conditions were provisionally accepted, and the delegates returned home to submit them to their government, but they were not productive of any better state of feeling. The English persisted in harassing the Dutch; impounding their cattle found grazing on the common, and even preventing the transport to New Netherland of cattle not belonging to them.[1]

CHAP. III. 1642.

These feelings of animosity were not confined to the Connecticut. The agents from New England, who happened to be, this summer, in London, were active in making their complaints known to those interested in the settlement of the English colonies in America; so that even persons of quality had their feelings strongly prejudiced against the Dutch.

Lord SAY, who had a personal interest in New England, and was one of the founders of Connecticut, was among the most prominent of these; and the representations which he had received, had so great an influence on his mind, that his lordship took the earliest opportunity to remonstrate with Joachimi, the Dutch ambassador, then at the English court, to whom he addressed a memorandum, couched in the following terms:—

"Many Englishmen, (his majesty's subjects,) incorporated," said his lordship, "by his majesty's letters patent, having, with a view to avoid all difficulties, purchased land from the natives, the acknowledged and lawful owners thereof, have established sundry factories on the river Connecticut, in New England, where they have experienced various molestations and animosities from the Netherlands nation, who, having formerly erected a small trading-post on the aforesaid river, set up, by virtue thereof, a right to the whole; and not only that, but to all the country, from Narragansett Bay to the Hudson River, which they designated by the name of New Netherland, although granted by his majesty to sundry of his subjects, and exclusively inhabited by English people. Many protests have they presented against the peaceable proceedings

July 23.

[1] Alb. Rec. ii., 171, 172. N. Y. Hist. Soc. Trans. i., 276.

BOOK III. 1642. of the English, and in various ways and forms have they transgressed against them, adding thereto sundry threats and haughty arguments. All these did the English read, and although there are, at the furthest, not more than five or six Netherlanders resident on the said river Connecticut, where there are more than two thousand English, yet these have had recourse to no violent proceedings against the others, but have treated them with all civility—yea, under God, have they been a means of preserving their lives.

" 'Tis true, the Netherlanders sometimes aver that they purchased a portion of land, situate on the aforesaid river, from the Pequod Indians, and pretend a right thereto by virtue of said purchase. But it is very well known, (if any such purchase has been made, which as yet has never appeared,) that the Pequods had no other than an usurped title. And herein the weakness of their pretensions becomes apparent; that the English having addressed sundry letters to their governor, Willem Kieft, residing on Hudson's River, to refer the settlement of the said question to impartial arbitrators, he would not accept the proposal.

"It were desirable that they might be ordered to demean themselves in the place where they are, in a peaceable, neighborly manner, and to be content with their own limits, or to leave the river, which would tend most to their master's profit, it being very manifest that the returns have, and will, never repay expenses. Moreover, they live there in an ungodly way; beseeming, in no wise, the Gospel of Christ. Their residence there will never produce any other effect, than expense to their masters, and trouble to the English."

July 31. Violent language having been used about the same time by others, who did not hesitate to threaten that if the difficulties on the Fresh River were not shortly arranged, the Dutch should be forcibly ejected from that quarter before the end of the year, M. Joachimi thought it his duty to communicate to
Aug. 8. the States General, not only Lord Say's letter, but some report also, of the irritable state of feeling which existed abroad on the subject, and to recommend that their High Mightinesses should write to King Charles, and request his majesty to command those of New England not to disturb the Dutch

in New Netherlands, of which country they had possession before the arrival of the English. "For," his excellency added, "such commands must proceed from his majesty, and it might be taken ill that redress should be sought from the House of Parliament, whose orders probably would not be received in those far distant quarters." He urged, again and again, the necessity of losing no time in this matter, and in a subsequent dispatch, reminded their High Mightinesses of the near approach of the winter, and how much it behooved them to make such arrangements as would obviate all chances of hostilities between the parties in America. These communications were duly referred to the directors of the West India Company, and the States General instructed their ambassador to endeavor to allay all irritation, by representing, that it was not to be presumed that the Dutch, who were too weak, could succeed in overpowering the English, who were much the stronger, in that country. As for the threats which were uttered in England, their High Mightinesses did not regard them as of any consequence. "The power of that nation was rent in twain; one part contending against the other; and therefore she was not to be dreaded by foreign states."[1] But, meanwhile, religious persecution caused numbers to remove from New England to New Netherland.

CHAP III. 1642.

Oct. 17

The Rev. Francis Doughty, a dissenting minister, had emigrated to Massachusetts, like many others, for conscience' sake. But here he discovered that he had plunged "out of the frying-pan into the fire." Being at Cohasset, on the northern bounds of New Plymouth, in 1642, he happened publicly to assert "that Abraham's children should have been baptized," which gave so much offence to his hearers, that he was dragged out of the assembly, and otherwise harshly used.[2] This unchristian treatment determined him to remove to Long Island, whither he was accompanied by Richard Smith and several other settlers, then residents of Cohannock and other places. On application to the Dutch authorities at New Amsterdam,

[1] Hol Doc. ii., 278, 279, 280, 281, 282, 283, 293, 294, 305, 306. Aitzema, ii., 932.

[2] Leechford's News from New England. Cohasset was originally settled in 1635, when it was called Hingham.

BOOK III. 1642. March 28. they immediately obtained a patent for thirteen thousand three hundred and thirty-two acres of land at Mespath, as Newtown, L. I., was originally called, which was endowed with the usual privileges of free manors, such as free exercise of religion, power to plant towns, build churches, nominate magistrates, administer civil and criminal justice, subject, however, to the conditions and reservations contained in the patent, which was in keeping with the charter of 1640, and similar to that already offered in the preceding month of June, to the people from Lynn.

Mr. Throgmorton, with a number of his friends, who had already been driven with Roger Williams from Massachusetts

Oct. 3. by "the fiery Hugh Peters," procured permission to settle thirty-five families, some twelve miles east of the Manhattans, at a place now called West Chester, but which the Dutch at this time named Vredeland, or Land of Peace, a meet appellation for the spot selected as a place of refuge by those who were bruised and broken down by religious persecution. And the Lady Moody, who had become "imbued with the erroneous doctrine that infant baptism was a sinful ordinance," and had, in consequence, been excommunicated by those of New England, "to avoid further trouble," took shelter also among the Dutch, with her son Sir Henry and their followers, in the course of the next year. Her ladyship located at the southwest corner of Long Island "by the express will and consent of the Director-general and council of New Netherland," who called the settlement "'s Gravenzande," after the picturesque village (originally a walled city) of that name at the embouchure of the river Maas, where the ancient counts of Holland held their courts previous to their removal to the Hague.[1]

[1] Alb. Rec. xx., 7. Gov. Winthrop notices these emigrations, Hist. N. Eng. i., 42; ii., 85. The original patent to the Rev. Mr. Doughty and his associates, is inserted in Latin, in the Dutch Rec. G. G., 49. The MS. is peculiarly difficult to be deciphered, being in the contracted chirography of the seventeenth century. A translation of the document will be found in Appendix F; Martinet's Beschryv. iii., 279. The supposition that the town of Gravesend, on Long Island, derived its name from the first settlers having sailed from Gravesend, in England, is altogether gratuitous. It was the fashion with all European powers who had possessions in the New World, to transfer the names of towns in the mother country, to their new settlements in America. The Dutch were as

In order that regularity should be observed in drawing boundaries and division lines, Andreas Hudde was this year appointed surveyor, at a salary of two hundred guilders, or $80, per annum, with an additional fee of ten shillings per diem, and two stivers per morgen of two acres, besides the payment of his travelling expenses and ferriage. CHAP. III. 1642.

Increased accommodation for the numerous strangers who touched at New Amsterdam, on their way from New England to Virginia, became now necessary, as they occasioned the Director-general much inconvenience. " A fine stone tavern" was therefore erected for their use on a lot fronting the East River; and, " as many questions of law processes, with their various consequences, arise on account of the number of English which daily come to reside among us, and which disturb harmony and social intercourse more or less," Director Kieft, " though roughly acquainted with the English language, and somewhat initiated in the law," found himself in need of some one to assist now and then with advice and to write his letters. George Baxter was accordingly appointed English secretary to the Director-general and council of New Netherland.[1] Dec 11.

The church erected by Director Van Twiller, had, by this time, shared the fate common to all the public buildings constructed during his administration, and was now in such a state of dilapidation, that it was considered nothing better than " a mean barn." The necessity of a new church was admitted by the Director and council so far back as 1640; when, with a view to supply the funds requisite to defray the expenses of a new building, a portion of the fines imposed by the court of justice was appropriated to that purpose. But nothing practical eventuated from this arrangement. The accommodation continued to be of the most wretched description, when Captain David De Vries urged the matter anew on the consideration of the Director-general. " It was a shame," he said, " that the English should see, when they passed, no-

observant of this custom as any other nation, of which fact any person can satisfy himself by looking over a map of Holland.

[1] De Vries; Alb. Rec. ii., 169, 187, 202; iii., 409. Hudde's commission as surveyor bears date 26th June, 1642.

BOOK III. 1642. thing but a mean barn in which public worship is performed. The first thing they did in New England, when they raised some dwellings, was, on the contrary, to build a fine church. We ought to do the same," he continued; "we had good materials, fine oak wood, fine building-stone, good lime made from oyster-shells, which was better than the lime in Holland." This reasoning, backed by the intelligence that the colonists of Rensselaerswyck had it in contemplation to raise a church also, had considerable weight with Director Kieft. He seemed desirous to leave behind him a monument to perpetuate the memory of his zeal for religion, and forthwith inquired who should superintend the good work. There were not wanting "friends of the reformed religion." Joachim Pietersen Kuyter, "who was a good Calvinist, and had a good sett of hands," was elected deacon, and with Jan Dam, Captain De Vries, and Director Kieft, "formed the first consistory to superintend the erection of the projected church."[1]

These points having been arranged, the next question to be decided was, the site of the building. It was ordered to be erected within the fort. But this was looked upon in the light of "a fifth wheel to a coach," and excited considerable opposition among the commonalty, who represented that the fort was already "very small," and that it stood on the point, or extremity of the island, whereas a more central position ought to be selected for the accommodation of the faithful generally. It was, moreover, particularly urged that the erection of a church within the fort, would prevent the southeast wind reaching the grist-mill which stood thereabout, and thus cause the people to suffer, especially in summer, through want of bread.[2]

These objections were, however, overruled. It was with

[1] De Vries.

[2] Men spraake, dan, van de plaatse waerse staende soude. De Directeur wilde en oordeelde datse in het fort staen moest, daerse oock tegens wil en dank van de andere geset is; en immers soo wel past als het vyffde wiel aen een wagen; want behalve dat het fort cleyn is, op een punct leyt, dat meer importeren soude in cas van populatie. De Kercke die de gemeente, diese becostight hebben, eygen behoort te wesen, soo breeckse en beneemt den zuytoosten wint aen de koren-molen, die daeromtrent staet; het welcke een mede oorsaek is, dat men des zomers dickwils by gebreek van maalen sonder broot is Van der Donk.

justice remarked that the building would be more safe from the attacks of the Indians, within than without the fort. As to its being an impediment to the working of the wind-mill, it was remarked that the walls of the fort then impeded the action of the southeast wind on the mill, and prevented its working even before the erection of the church.[1] Naught, therefore, now remained but to find ways and means to defray the necessary expenses. Director Kieft promised to advance a few thousand guilders from the public chest. The remainder was to be raised by private subscription.

It happened about this time that the daughter of the Rev. Mr. Bogardus was being married. This was considered a favorable opportunity for raising the required subscription. So when the wedding party was in the height of good-humor, and mellow with the host's good cheer, the Director-general called on the guests to subscribe. The disposition to be generous was not wanting at such a time. Each guest emulated his neighbor, and a handsome list was made out. When the morning came, a few were found desirous of reconsidering the transactions of the wedding-feast. But Director Kieft would allow no such second thought. They must all pay without exception.[2]

He entered, as churchwarden, into a contract, forthwith, for the mason-work, with John and Richard Ogden, of Stamford, May. who engaged to build a church of rock-stone, seventy-two feet long, fifty-two feet broad, and sixteen feet over the ground, in a good and workmanlike manner, for the sum of two thousand five hundred guilders, equal to one thousand dollars. The churchwardens were to furnish the lime; to transport the stone

[1] Eer de kercke gebouwt was, conde de coornmolen met een zuyt oosten wint niet malen, doordien de wint door de wallen van't fort gestut wiert. Van Tienhoven's Answer to Van der Donck.

[2] De Directeur hadde dan besloten een kerck te doen timmeren, en dat ter plaetse daer het hem goet docht. Het man queert hem aan de penningen; en waer die te becomen? Het gebeurde om desen tyt, dat den Predikant Everardus Bogardus eene vrouw-voordochter bestede. Dese gelegentheyd oordeelde de Directeur een bequame tyt tot zyn voornemen te wesen, dat hy, naer den vierden off vyffden dronck oock in 't werck stelde, en hy selffs met een goet exempel voorgaende, liet de bruy-looffsgasten teyckenen, watse tot de kerck-geven wilde. Ider, dan, met een licht hoofd, teyckende ryckelick wech, de eén tegen de ander; en hoewel het eenige wel beroude, doen de sinnenweder 't huys quamen, sy moesten even wel betalen, daer viel niet tegen. Van der Donck.

BOOK III. 1642. from the river-side to the spot where the building was to be erected; and to allow the use of the company's boat to the contractors, who were to receive also a douceur of one hundred guilders, equal to $40, should the work be finished to the satisfaction of the employers.[1]

With such energy now was the work pushed forward, that the walls soon rose to their proper height, and the shingle roof soon followed. To commemorate the zeal both of the Director-general and of the commonalty on this occasion, a marble slab was placed conspicuously in front of the building, with the following inscription engraved thereon:—

Anno 1642;

"Willem Kieft, Directeur-Generael;

"HEEFT DE GEMEENTE DESEN TEMPEL DOEN BOÚWEN."[2]

[1] The following is a copy of the contract:—"Appeared before me Cornelis van Tienhoven, secretary in behalf of the General Privileged West India Company, in New Netherlands, the Hon'ble Wm. Kieft, Churchwarden, at the request of his brethren, the Churchwardens of the Church in New Netherlands, to transact, and in their name to conclude the following business; So did he, as Churchwarden, agree with John Ogden, about a church in the following manner:—John Ogden of Stamford, and Richard Ogden, engage to build, in behalf of said Churchwardens, a church of rock-stone, seventy-two feet long, fifty feet broad, and sixteen feet high, above the soil, all in good order, and in a workmanlike manner. They shall be obliged to procure the stone and bring it on shore near the fort at their own expense, from whence the Churchwardens shall further convey the stone to the place where it is intended to build the church, at their own expense. The Churchwardens aforesaid will procure as much lime as shall be required for the building of the aforesaid church. John and Richard Ogden shall at their own charge pay for the masonry, &c., provided, that when the work shall be finished, the Churchwardens shall pay to them the sum of 2,500 gl., which payment shall be made in beaver, cash, or merchandise, to wit:—if the Churchwardens are satisfied with the work, so that in their judgment the 2,500 gl. shall have been earned, then the said Churchwardens shall reward them with 100 gl. more; and further promise to John and Richard Ogden to assist them whenever it is in their power. They further agree to facilitate the carrying the stone thither, and that John and Richard Ogden may use during a month or six weeks the company's boat; engaging themselves, and the aforesaid John and Richard Ogden, to finish the undertaken work in the manner they contracted. Done in Fort Amsterdam, in New Netherlands. (Signed) Willem Kieft, John Ogden, Richard Ogden, Gysbert op Dyck, Thomas Willett." Alb. Rec. iii., 31. These Ogdens are the ancestors of the present families of that name in New York, New Jersey, &c.

[2] "Anno 1642, William Kieft, Director-general; hath the Commonalty

The immediate completion of this church was, however, doomed to be interrupted by the spirit of faction, and continued misunderstanding with the aborigines, the progress and ruinous consequences of which it becomes our duty now to relate. CHAP. III. 1642.

Shortly after the conclusion of peace with the Wechquaesqueeks in the spring of this year, Miantonimo, chief of the Narragansett tribes, whose ambitious spirit aimed at sovereignty over all the eastern Indians, visited the neighborhood of the Dutch settlements with a band of one hundred warriors, with a view, as it was represented, to urge the Indians into a general conspiracy against the English and the Dutch. So full, throughout the land, were men's minds of fear at the report of the intended massacre, that the strangest alarms seized hold of all, and a man could not halloo in the night, but it was supposed that he had fallen into the hands of the Indians, and was tortured by them unto death. Even Director Kieft became affected by these wild reports to such degree that he suspected the Indians not only of endeavoring to poison him, but even of making him the object of their diabolical incantations.[1]

In this conjuncture of terror and distrust, some traders stole a dress of beaver-skins from a savage whom they had previously stupified with brandy. He was of the Hackingsack tribe, who inhabited the country opposite the Manhattans, on the western shore. Enraged at his loss, on coming to his senses, he vowed to shoot the first "Swannekin" he should meet. He more than kept his word. An Englishman, residing on Staten Island, in the service of De Vries, was killed shortly after; and in a few days following, Gerrit Jansen van Vorst was also slain, while engaged roofing a house "be-

caused this Temple to be built." Van der Donck. Judge Benson, writing in 1817, says that when the fort was taken down "a few years since," the marble slab, above alluded to, was found, with the Dutch inscription on it, buried in the earth, and then removed to the belfry of the church in Garden-street, N. Y., belonging to the Dutch Reformed Congregation. On the destruction of the latter building by the great fire of 1835, this slab totally disappeared.

[1] Sommige van de omleggende Wilden practiseerde ons kruyt in den brant te steken, ende den Directeur te vergeven, ofte met haer duyvelerye te betoveren, gelyck naderhandt haer quade wille gebleecken heeft, soo door effect als report. Journael van Nieuw Nederlant. Winthrop's N. Eng. ii., 78, 79.

BOOK III. 1642. hind the Cul," as Newark Bay was called, in the colonie of the Lord of Nederhorst.

A deputation of chiefs from Hackingsack and Reckawanck, foreseeing the evil consequences of these outrages, hastened to New Amsterdam to make reparation, after the fashion of the red-man, by paying one or two hundred fathoms of wampum, as an expiatory offering, to wipe away, as they said, all memory of the deed. But Kieft would not listen to any compromise. Nothing less than the murderer would be accepted. In vain did the chiefs plead that the Dutch were themselves the cause of the murder. "You ought not to sell brandy to the Indians to make them crazy, for they are not," they said, "accustomed to your liquors. Your own people, though used to them, fight with knives and commit fooleries when drunk. We wish you, so as to prevent all mischief, to sell no more fire-water to our braves." This reasoning was of no avail. "You must surrender the murderer," repeated Kieft. "We cannot do it," the sachems replied, "he is off to the Tankitekes;" and again they presented their expiatory offerings. But these would not be received; so they returned to their homes, hopeless of effecting any reconciliation, for the man whom Kieft required at their hands, "was also the son of a chief." Hereupon the Director-general sent a message to Pacham, chief of the Tankitekes, warning him that no reparation had as yet been made for the Christian blood shed by the savages, and advising him that the Dutch would not wait much longer.[1]

1643. Winter came, and while the earth was yet buried in snow, a party of armed Mohawks, some eighty or ninety in number, made a descent upon the Wechquaesqueeks and Tappaen Indians, for the purpose of levying tribute. Struck with terror, these, amounting to between four and five hundred, fled in despair to the island of Manhattans, leaving seventy of their men on the field, and numbers of their women and children in the hands of the enemy. Half dead with hunger and cold,
Feb 7. these poor creatures presented themselves at the houses of the Dutch, by whom they were hospitably received and hu-

[1] Journael van Nieuw Nederlant; De Vries; Alb. Rec. ii., 212.

manely treated for the space of fourteen days. Even Kieft's better feelings gained, for the moment, the ascendency, and he ordered corn to be furnished to the half-famished wretches. But terror had entered so deep into their souls that they did not think themselves safe even here. Once more they fled, scattering themselves abroad, like leaves before the winter's wind, in various directions; some to Pavonia, where the Hackingsacks bivouacked one thousand strong; and others to "Rechtanck," a point a short distance east of Fort Amsterdam, now called Corlaer's Hook.[1]

Feb 21

During the whole of these misunderstandings with the aborigines, the inhabitants of New Amsterdam were divided in opinion as to the proper policy to be pursued towards them. One portion, the more numerous, at the head of which was David Pietersen De Vries, counselled patience, humanity, and kindness, by which course they felt satisfied that the uncivilized heathen would eventually be won over; for "the Indians, though cunning enough, would do no harm unless harm were done to them." Another party, headed by Secretary Van Tienhoven, and made up of restless spirits and men of strong passions, clamored for the extermination of the savages, masking, however, the ferocity of their desires behind professions of great indignation at the shedding of innocent Christian blood, which they were anxious to revenge.

At this crisis, when wisdom might have taken advantage of the feelings of gratitude excited in the breasts of the Indians, in return for the hospitable shelter recently afforded them by the Dutch, and have thus converted them into lasting friends, Maryn Adriaensen, Jan Jansen Dam, and Abraham Planck, three members of the late board of the "Twelve Men," and the most violent of the exterminators, took upon themselves, while Kieft was participating, at one of their houses, in the amusements of Shrovetide, when wine and "mysterious toasts" were in free circulation, to present to the Director-general a request, in the name of the commonalty, for which, however, they had not a shadow of authority, in which they reminded

Feb 22.

[1] Report and Advice, &c., Appendix E; Journael van Nieuw Nederlandt. The Indian name for Corlaer's Hook is found in Alb. Rec.

34

BOOK III. 1643. His Excellency that the Indians had not as yet made any reparation for the blood they had shed, nor fulfilled the conditions of the peace concluded at Bronck's the preceding spring. The character of the Dutch nation was suffering, they alleged, in consequence, while innocent blood was crying aloud to heaven for revenge. "But GOD having now delivered the enemy evidently into our hands, we beseech you to permit us to attack them, for which purpose we offer our persons, and propose that one party composed of freemen, and another of soldiers, be dispatched to different places against them."[1]

Feb.24. The counsel of the violent prevailed. Kieft resolved "to make the savages wipe their chops." In vain did Bogardus warn him not to be too rash, and La Montagne point to the defenceless condition of the colony, and advise patience until a vessel should arrive from Patria, for by his proceedings the Director-general "was about to build a bridge, over which war would stalk, ere long, through the whole country;" in vain did De Vries represent that such an attack could not be made without the order of the Twelve Men, nor without his consent as chairman of the board; in vain did he describe the mischief which overwhelmed the colonie of Zwanendal in 1630, and Staten Island in 1640, in consequence of "jangling with the Indians;" in vain did he foreshadow the ruin that would light on the Dutch themselves, who were settled all around, and had received no warning to be on their guard, so that they might escape, or prepare themselves to resist, the assaults of those Indians who should survive the attack. "You go," said he to Kieft, "to break the Indians' heads; it is our own nation you are about to destroy. Nobody in the country knows any thing of this!" But these words "would take no hold" Every thing had been pre-arranged. Secretary Van Tienho-

[1] Hol. Doc. iii., 146; Van Tienhoven was accused of having originated this letter. "In de jaar 1643 den 24 Feb. [22d] met alle dese omleggende wilden in vreede-saten; op dien tyd seggen wy, als wanneer den Directeur met drie van zyn consultanten, het vastenavondspiel ten huyze van een derselfder heeft gehouden, en zyn E. Jan Dam een verborgen santé daer op heeft gedronc-ken en weynich daagen daer aen, heeft laten executeren die vervloeghte acte met de vermooden van zoo veel onschuldige wilden over op Pavonia en Manatans. Letter of the Eight Men. Hol. Doc. iii., 220.

ven and corporal Hans Stein had already been to Pavonia, to examine the ground and to mark the position of the Indians. Director Kieft was panting to perform a feat worthy of the heroes of ancient Rome, and he was determined not to listen to reason. To every remonstrance he only replied—"The order is gone forth; it shall not be recalled!"[1]

Feb. 25.

In the dead of a bleak winter's night, between the 25th and 26th of February, two armed parties went forth from Fort Amsterdam. One, composed of freemen, headed by Maryn Adriaensen, a noted freebooter, who had recently removed from Rensselaerswyck to the Manhattans, a man of violent temper and quarrelsome disposition, proceeded, accompanied by Govert Lookermans, against the Indians at Corlaer's Hook. The other, consisting of a troop of soldiers under the command of their sergeant, and guided by one well acquainted with the retreat of the red-men, crossed over to Jan de Lacher's hoeck in Pavonia, where the principal body of the Indians slept, behind the settlement of Egbert Wouterssen, and adjoining the bouwerie of Jan Evertsen Bout, unsuspicious of any attack from those who, but a few days before, had sheltered and fed them. To secure success, the blessing of Heaven was blasphemously invoked on the expedition.[2]

[1] "Het woordt isser uyt; het moet 'er uytblyven." Hol. Doc. iii., 161, 174. "Voordat dese tochten geschieden, ende den oorloch in den Raadkamer: (daermede present den Predikant Bogardus:) beslooten zynde, is Cornelis van Tienhoven en Hans Steen gecommandeert van den Directeur en Raden omme op Pavonia tegaen, ende de situatie van Indianse huysen te besichtigen; waervan sy rapport gedaen hebben." Hol. Doc. v., 51, 52; De Vries, Korte Historiael.

[2] The following are transcripts of the commissions issued to the leaders of these expeditions:—"Whereas, the inhabitants in our neighborhood continue to reside in the country under great alarm, and cultivate their land in anxiety, through fear of the savages, who now and then have murdered some of them in a most villanous manner, without any previous provocation, and we cannot obtain any satisfaction for these massacres; we must, therefore, appeal to our arms, so that we may live here in security. In the full confidence that God will crown our resolutions with success; moreover, as the commonalty solicit, on the 22d Feb., 1643, that we may execute the same; we, therefore, hereby authorize Maryn Adriaensen, at his request, with his associates, to attack a party of savages skulking behind Corlaer's Hook, or plantation, and act with them in every such manner as they shall deem proper, and the time and opportunity shall permit. Done this 25th February, 1643."

BOOK III. 1643.

"I remained that night at the Director's," says an eye-witness, "and took a seat in the kitchen near the fire. At midnight, I heard loud shrieks, and went out to the parapet of the fort, and looked towards Pavonia. I saw nothing but the flashing of the guns. I heard no more the cries of the Indians. They were butchered in their sleep!"

The horrors of this night cause the flesh to creep when we ponder over them, now, two hundred years after their occurrence. Eighty Indians were slaughtered at Pavonia, and thirty at Corlaer's Hook, while sunk in repose. Sucklings were torn from their mothers' breasts, butchered before their parents' eyes, and their mangled limbs thrown quivering into the river or the flames. Babes were hacked to pieces while "fastened to little boards"—their primitive cradles!—others were thrown alive into the river; and when their parents, impelled by nature, rushed in to save them, the soldiers prevented their landing; and, thus, both parents and offspring sunk into one watery grave. Children of half a dozen years; decrepit men of threescore and ten, shared the same fate. Those who escaped and begged for shelter next morning, were killed in cold blood, or thrown into the river. "Some came running to us from the country, having their hands cut off; some lost both arms and legs; some were supporting their entrails with their hands, while others were mangled in other horrid ways, too horrid to be conceived. And these miserable wretches, as well as many of the Dutch, were all the time under the impression that the attack had proceeded from the terrible Mohawks."[1]

"Sergeant Rodolf is commanded and authorized to take under his command a troop of soldiers, and lead them to Pavonia, and drive away and destroy the savages being behind Jan Evertsen's, but to spare, as much as is possible, their wives and children, and to take the savages prisoners. He may watch there for the proper opportunity to make his attack successful; for which end Hans Stein, who is well acquainted with every spot on which the savages were skulking, accompanies him. He, therefore, shall consult with the aforesaid Hans Stein and the corporals. The exploit to be executed at night, with the greatest caution and prudence. Our God may bless the expedition. Done, Feb 24th, 1643." Alb. Rec. ii., 210, 211. Hol. Doc. iii., 148, 204.

[1] De Vries; The Journael van Nieuw Nederland says, the number killed at both places was eighty, and that thirty were taken prisoners.

On the following day, a man, named Dirck Straatmaker, CHAP. III.
proceeded with his wife to Pavonia, in company with some
Englishmen, "to plunder maize or any thing else." They 1643. Feb.26
were warned by the soldiers to return home, but they refused. "There was no danger; if there were a hundred savages, not one of them would injure us." The soldiers, hereupon, withdrew, but had not gone far when they heard a shriek. Straatmaker lay mortally wounded, and his wife dead by his side. The unfortunate man could have escaped, but he "did not wish to leave his poor wife." The Englishmen, "who had but one gun among them," were fortunately rescued.[1]

Flushed with victory, the respective parties returned to Fort Amsterdam, bringing with them thirty prisoners, and the heads of several of the enemy. Kieft, notwithstanding several of the commonalty protested against his proceedings and those of his three friends, received his soldiers and freebooters with thanks, rewards, and congratulations; while Van Tienhoven's mother-in-law, forgetful of those finer feelings which do honor to her sex, amused herself, it is stated, in kicking about the heads of the dead men which had been brought in, as bloody trophies of that midnight slaughter. The spirit of animosity against the Indians soon became epidemic. Settlers on Long Island, not to be behind their countrymen at the Manhattes, presented
a petition, signed in their name by Gerritt Wolfertsen, Jacob Feb 27.
Wolfertsen, Dirck Wolfertsen, and Lambert Huybertsen Mol, requesting permission to attack the Marreckkawick Indians, residing between Breucklen and Amersfoort.[2] Kieft refused to sanction this step. These Indians had been always the friends and allies of the Dutch, and an attack on them, now, would not only lead to a destructive war, especially as this tribe was on its guard and "hard to conquer," but it would add to the number of the public enemy, and be productive of ruinous consequences to the petitioners themselves. If, however, these Indians should demean themselves in a hostile

[1] Alb. Rec. iii., 117. Journael van N. N

[2] Hol. Doc. v., 320. These Wolfertsens were sons, we presume, of Wolfert Gerrittsen, who, with Hudde, purchased the Flatts, near the town of Flattlands, in 1636.

BOOK III. 1643.

manner, every one was permitted to defend himself as best he could.[1]

The latitude allowed by the latter part of this reply, was construed by the petitioners, who were ready to construe any movement on the part of the Indians into a show of hostility, as authorizing the execution of their projects. They immediately got up a secret expedition, and plundered the Marreckkawicks of two wagon loads of corn. The latter endeavored to prevent the robbery. A rencontre ensued, and two Indians lost their lives.[2]

This unjustifiable outrage led to consequences almost fatal to the Dutch. It estranged the Long Island Indians, the warmest of their friends, who now formed an alliance with the river Indians, whose hate knew no bounds when they discovered that it was the Dutch, and not the Mohawks, who had attacked them at Pavonia and Corlaer's Hook. The tomahawk, the firebrand, and scalping knife, were clutched with all the ferocity of phrensy, and the warwhoop rang from the Raritan to the Connecticut, for eleven tribes of savages proclaimed open war against the Dutch.[3] Every settler on whom they laid hands was murdered—women and children dragged into captivity; and though the settlements around Fort Amsterdam extended, at this period, thirty English miles to the east, and twenty-one to the north and south, the enemy burned the dwellings, desolated the farms and farm-houses, killed the cattle, destroyed the crops of grain, hay, and tobacco, laid waste the country all around, and drove the settlers, panic-stricken, into Fort Amsterdam.[4] "Mine eyes saw the flames of their towns," says Roger Williams; "the

[1] Hol. Doc. v., 337, 338. The answer was drawn up in council, in the fort, in the presence of the Director-general, the Fiscal, the Rev. Bogardus, Ensign Van Dyck, Gysbert op Dyck, and Oloff Stevensen.

[2] Journael van N. N.

[3] Genootsaack geworden tegens elff natien van wilden (: ten deser oorsaecke opstaende :) den openbaar oorloch aentenemen. Report and advice, Appendix.

[4] Two thousand Indians by them armed . . . . fall into war with the Dutch, destroyed all their scattering farms and boors, in forcing them to retire to their up fort, forty leagues up that river, and to Manhatas. Description of New Albion, 19.

frights and hurries of men, women, and children, and the present removal of all that could to Holland."[1] The planters, despairing of effecting a settlement in the country, threatened now to abandon New Netherland, or to move to Rensselaerswyck. Dreading the removal of the people en masse, the Director-general found himself obliged to take all the settlers into the company's service for a period of two months, for he had not soldiers sufficient for the public defence.[2]

CHAP. III. 1643.

March 1.

Pent up in the fort with all who could escape the vengeance of the savages, Director Kieft experienced, and had to bear, the wrath of the men and women who beheld their bouweries in flames, and found themselves reduced in a moment, by his insane conduct, from the comforts of competency to beggary. Women asked him for their husbands; men for their wives and children; and all taunted him with the ruinous consequences which followed his obstinate rashness. He endeavored, for a moment, to stem the torrent of public discontent, by sending Adriaensen again forth at the head of an armed force; but no good resulted. Adriaensen, though backed by an English company, came back from his bootless expeditions with the additional chagrin of having witnessed, in the destruction of his own property, the misery he inflicted on others returning, with tenfold severity, on his own head. Kieft next sent a delegation to the Long Island Indians to inquire why they were discontented, and to make them a proffer of his friendship. But these were too simple-minded to be imposed upon; too indignant to listen to his professions. "Call ye yourselves our friends? Ye are nothing but corn-thieves," they shouted from a distance, while they refused to hold any communication with the Dutch messengers.[3]

Foiled in all his plans, and now smarting under the additional disgrace of having his advances for a peace rejected by the uncivilized savages, Kieft cowered; and deprived of all other resources, determined to humble himself before that

[1] Rhode Island Hist. Rec. iii., 156.

[2] Alb. Rec. ii., 213.

[3] Den Directeur . . . sont voort eenigh volck overomme de reden te weten. De Wilden haer van verre verthoonende, riepen: "Zyt gy onse vrienden? gy zyt maer cooren dieven." Journ. van N. N.

BOOK III. 1643. Heaven whose laws he had offended, in the hope of obtaining from the Most High that mercy which he had refused to his fellow-men. "We continue to suffer much trouble and loss from the heathen, and many of our inhabitants behold their lives and property in jeopardy, which is doubtless the consequence of our sins," was the humble confession which he publicly made on proclaiming a day of General Fast and Prayer, and soliciting every one to prepare, by true penitence and unremitted supplication, to invoke God's mercy, "so that His holy name may not be slandered by the heathen through our iniquities."[1]

March 4.

All this, however, had not the effect of allaying popular discontent, nor of diverting public censure. The Director-general was still held responsible for the massacre on the night of the 25th February, which was now held in such general detestation by the honest burghers, that some among them seriously proposed to imitate the precedent offered by the neighboring province of Virginia, by deposing the Director, and bundling him back to Holland in the Peacock, then in port.[2] From this responsibility Kieft endeavored to extricate himself, by throwing the fault on those who had presented him the petition in the name of the commonalty. "You must blame the freemen for what has occurred." "You forbade those freemen to meet on pain of corporal punishment," was the retort thrown back at him: "how came it then?" He could make no reply.[3]

Maryn Adriaensen, one of the three who had signed the letter, became soon aware of the direction which Kieft was giving to public opinion, for he found himself the object of public reproach, and heard himself assailed as a murderer, and stigmatized as the chief cause of all the sufferings which his fellow-citizens had to endure at the hands of the Indians. Goaded by the recollections of all that he had risked, and all that he had lost, the freebooter armed himself with a cutlass

[1] Alb. Rec. ii., 214, 215.

[2] "Hendrick Snyder Kip said, We ought to send the Kievit (meaning the Director) back to Holland in the Peacock." Alb. Rec. iii., 109.

[3] See affidavits of Evertsen Bout, Stoffelsen, Arentsen, Cornelissen, Dercksen Blaauw, in Hol. Doc. iii., 149, 150, 151, 152, 154.

and loaded pistol, and rushed into the presence of the Director-general, where, presenting the weapon at Kieft's breast, he exclaimed, "What devilish lies are these you've been telling of me?" The assault would of a certainty have been fatal to the Director, had not Counsellor La Montagne, who happened to be near, grasped, with becoming presence of mind, the pistol with such quickness as to cover the pan with his hand, and thus the weapon fortunately missed fire; while Robert Pennoyer drew the sword from the scabbard and flung it on one side. With the assistance of the attorney-general and others, the assassin was immediately overpowered and committed to prison.

CHAP. III. 1643. March 21.

The attack was, however, the signal for a general rising among Adriaensen's followers. In an hour, the prisoner's son, accompanied by another desperado, presented himself, armed with a pistol and a gun, at the fort where Kieft was walking. On perceiving their approach, the Director-general retired towards his room, but was, notwithstanding, fired at on his retreat by young Marynsen, who, in return, was shot down by the sentinel, his head being afterwards affixed to a gibbet. A crowd of some five and twenty of Adriaensen's accomplices now collected around the Director's door; but not well relishing a personal interview with all these lawless men at once, Kieft ordered four of their number to be admitted. These demanded the prisoner's pardon; but as this could not be acceded to, the Director-general expressed his willingness to submit the whole matter to the citizens at large, to adjudge in the case as their consciences should suggest, with permission to the prisoner's friends, to select some from among themselves to assist in the investigation.

Instead of communicating this proposal to the congregation, amounting now to over five hundred men, Maryn's friends selected twenty-five or thirty persons who reiterated the demand that the prisoner be released, "which of course was refused." They then elected eight from among themselves, "one of whom was already a convicted criminal," who, without hearing any of the parties, or taking cognizance of any complaints or papers, ordered Adriaensen's release on payment of a fine of five hundred guilders, ($200,) and on condi-

BOOK III. 1643. tion that he absent himself from the Manhattans for and during the space of three months. This proceeding being entirely irregular, was refused the sanction of the authorities. Desirous, however, of paying some deference to public opinion, Director Kieft determined, "in accordance with the invariable custom in affairs of consequence," to adjoin some of the most respectable of the commonalty to the council, which, notwithstanding the Director's solemn promise to the Twelve Men in January, 1642, still consisted of only two persons. But owing to either his own unpopularity, or to the fear of Maryn's associates, Kieft found "none so poor to do him reverence." "No one would or dared to assist us." The Director-general
March 28. thereupon resolved to send the prisoner, with all the documents appertaining to the case, to Holland, that he may be tried there, "lest it might be insinuated that we acted in a passion." Thither Adriaensen, it is said, was shipped in irons accordingly.[1]

Spring, the season for fishing, hunting, and planting, was

[1] Alb. Rec. ii., 216, 217, 218, 219; iii., 94. Winthrop, and after him Hubbard, Trumbull, and all the New England authorities who allude to this transaction, represent that Adriaensen, whom they call "Marine, the Dutch Captain," assaulted Kieft for having preferred Capt. Underhill to him as commander, about this time, of the Dutch forces against the Indians. But the Albany Records and the Journael van Nieuw Nederlandt, which embody Kieft's personal statement, make no mention of this motive. They ascribe Maryn's movement solely to irritation at being assailed as a murderer, and made thereby the scape-goat for public censure to centre on. "What devilish lies have you been telling of me?" is his complaint, and not, Why do you put another over me? Besides, Underhill did not enter into the Dutch service until the fall of this year, several months after the above assault. The latter's promotion could not, therefore, have been the cause of Maryn's attack on Director Kieft. In truth, the statements of New England writers, in general, on matters occurring in New Netherland, must be received, for obvious reasons, with extreme caution. They serve to embarrass rather than to facilitate the labor and progress of the historian.

The freebooter, it seems, returned to New Netherland some years after this, and, notwithstanding the above outrage on the Director-general's person, obtained a grant from Kieft, on the 11th May, 1647, of "a piece of land on the west side of the North River, known by the name of Awiehaken," which "is bounded on the south by the kill of Hoboken, and runs thence north to the next kill, and with the same breadth into the woods, until it contains 50 morgens of land." Alb. Rec. GG, 491.

now at hand. The Indians saw the necessity of intermitting their wars, to prepare food for themselves and families. They made advances, therefore, for the re-establishment of peace.[1] Three Indians, messengers from "the great chief Pennawitz," sachem of the Canarsee tribe, approached the fort, bearing a white flag. They were sent to inquire why the Dutch had murdered his people, who had never injured them? The opportunity was seized to obtain a cessation of hostilities, and Captain David P. De Vries and Jacob Olfertzsen volunteered to go to Rockaway, to have "a talk" with the Indians. They arrived in the evening at the wigwam of the "one-eyed" chief, by whom they were hospitably entertained. His residence was situated some miles from the shore, and he was surrounded by between two and three hundred warriors, the owners of some thirty horses.

CHAP. III. 1643. March 4.

The Dutch ambassadors were led forth next morning into the woods, where they found sixteen chiefs awaiting their arrival. Seated in a circle, these placed the delegates from the Manhattans in the centre, and then one of the chiefs, holding a bundle of little sticks in his hand, slowly arose and addressed the Dutchmen in the following words:

"When you first arrived on our shores, you were often in want of food. We gave you our beans and our corn. We let you eat our oysters and fish; and now, for a recompense, you murder our people."

Here the sachem paused It was the first count in the indictment. He laid down one of the little sticks, and then proceeded:

"The men whom you left here at your first trip, to barter your goods until your return, we cherished as we would our eyeballs. We gave them our daughters for wives, and by

[1] 't Saysoen om de beestialen uyttejagen comt: dit verobligeerden veele den pays te begeren. Van d'anderezyde de wilden oock sienden dat het tyt was mayz te planten, waren nietmin begerigh om te vreden, soo dat naer eenige communicatie de pays beslooten wert. Journael van N. Nederlandt. "In the spring and part of the summer, they (the Indians) follow fishing. When the wild herbage begins to sprout up in the woods, the first hunting season begins, and then many of their young men leave the fisheries for the purpose of hunting; but the old and thoughtful remain at the fisheries until the second and principal hunting season." Van der Donck's Descript. of N. Netherland.

BOOK III. 1643. these have they had children. There are now numbers of Indians who come from the mixed blood of the Indians and Swannekins. Your own blood have you spilt in this villanous manner." And here he laid down another stick. Many more remained untold in his hand. Many more were the complaints which the red-man had to record.

At the conclusion of the chieftain's speech, De Vries invited the sachems to accompany him to Fort Amsterdam. They consented, and gave each of the Dutch delegates, in token of their sincerity, ten fathoms of wampum, equal in value to sixteen dollars. But just at the moment of embarkation, another Indian, armed with bows and arrows, came running towards the shore, and endeavored to dissuade the chiefs from proceeding. "Are ye fools," he asked, "to go to the fort to those villains who have murdered your friends? When ye go, the governor will keep ye all, and the Indians will then be without chiefs." For a moment the sachems hesitated; but on De Vries pledging his word, they became reassured, and consented to proceed, "for the Indians had never heard a lie from him, which was not the case with many of the Swannekins."

March 25. This party, twenty in number, arrived at Fort Amsterdam about three o'clock in the afternoon, and concluded a treaty of peace with the Dutch, in ratification of which some presents were made to these Long Island chiefs, who were requested to bring in the river Indians, in order that peace might be concluded with them also.[1]

[1] De Vries; Alb. Rec. ii., 215. Winthrop, and all the New England writers since his time, who have referred to the above treaty, represent that it was mainly brought about by the influence and interference of Roger Williams. "The issue had been uncertain but for the presence of Roger Williams at Manhattan, on his way to England. His mediation gave a truce to Long Island." Bancroft's U. S. ii., 291. It was by the influence of Williams, says Gamell, copying Knowles, (art. Life of Williams, in Sparks's Am. Biog. xiv., 117,) that the fiery zeal of the Indians was appeased, and peace restored to the Dutch settlements. Historical truth, and no desire to detract from the high merits of the purely-minded Rhode Island philanthropist, requires us to doubt the correctness of these statements. De Vries, who was the principal actor in bringing about this peace, relates (N. Y. Hist. Soc. Coll. New Series, i., 270) the several steps which preceded its conclusion, with a minuteness and fidelity commanding convic-

Nearly a month elapsed before these could be persuaded to believe in the sincerity of the Dutch. Trusting at last to the representations of his brethren on Long Island, the chief of the Hackingsacks appeared at the fort, with authority to conclude a peace both for his own and the neighboring tribes, the record of which is in these words : CHAP. III. 1643.

"This day, the twenty-second of April, 1643, between WILLEM KIEFT, Director-general, and the council of the New Netherlands on the one side, and Oratatnin, Sachem of the savages residing at Ack-kin-kas-hacky, who declared that he was delegated by and for those of Tappaen, Reckgawawane, Kicktawanc, and Sintsinck, on the other side, is a PEACE concluded in the following manner, to wit : April 22.

"All injustices committed by said nations against the Netherlanders, or by the Netherlanders against said nations, shall be forgiven and forgotten forever; reciprocally promising, one the other, to cause no trouble, the one to the other; but whenever the savages understand that any nation, not mentioned in this treaty, may be plotting mischief against the

tion, but makes no mention or allusion to Mr. Williams. The Indians made the first overtures to the Dutch. "No one had the courage to go" to Long Island but De Vries and Olfertszen. It was with them alone that the Indians had the "talk," and when the latter hesitated to come to New Amsterdam—when "the issue" was truly "uncertain," it was on the representations of De Vries alone, that the chiefs ventured to place themselves in the power of Kieft, "for the Indians had never heard a lie from him." In the whole of this transaction, Mr. Williams's name is not once mentioned. That he did endeavor to mediate, at one time, we presume at some earlier date, is probable, from his letter to the general court of Massachusetts, (Rhode Island Hist. Coll. iii., 155.) But he used his influence with the Dutch, and not with the Indians, and his efforts then were unavailing. "The name of peace, which some offered to mediate, was foolish and odious to them. . . . . Before we weighed anchor their bouweries were in flames, &c." In no part of this letter does Mr. Williams encourage the idea that he used his influence with the Indians, or persuaded them to make peace. On the contrary, he endeavored to influence the Dutch —Director we suppose—but he failed. De Vries's minute testimony, and Mr. Williams's silence as to any participation of his in bringing about the treaty, afford conclusive evidence, in our opinion, of the incorrectness of the positions assumed by the New England historians on this point. The fact that Winthrop places the date of the treaty in June, while the actual record shows it to have been in March, is enough, we should think, to invalidate any statement of his in the matter.

BOOK III. 1643. Christians, then will they give to them a timely warning, and not admit such a nation within their own limits."

To secure this peace, presents were mutually exchanged, and the Almighty God was implored to direct the savages to observe its conditions; but the latter were not satisfied with what they had received, and—presage ominous of further evil—they went away grumbling.[1]

[1] Alb. Rec. ii., 220. De Vries. The original name of the Croton River was Kicktawanc, and of the lands adjacent to it on the south, Sintsinck.

CHAPTER IV.

Union of the New England colonies—Congratulatory letters sent by Director and council of New Netherland—Reply of the governor of Massachusetts —Proceedings of the Commissioners of the United Colonies regarding the Dutch—Sir Edmund Ployden Earl-palatine of New Albion—Boundaries of the Palatinate—Continued dissatisfaction of the Indians—The Wappingers attack a Dutch boat and commence hostilities—Several other boats attacked and Christians killed—Meeting of the commonalty—Election of the Eight Men—Names of the citizens present on this occasion—Conclusions of the Eight Men—Expel one of the board, and nominate another in his place—Army raised against the Indians—The latter attack some settlers on Staten Island and in the colonie at Achter Cul—Murder several persons, and overrun the country—Mrs. Hutchinson and family killed—Attack on Lady Moody—Further deliberations of the Eight Men—Prices at New Amsterdam—Letters to the Assembly of the XIX. and to the States General—Rules for the soldiers on guard—State of affairs on the Island of Manhattans.

CHAP. IV. 1643.

THE principal men in New England having taken into their serious consideration the troubles which were now prevailing in the mother country, and the unprotected state of the colonies in consequence; and duly weighed, in connection with these, the claims which the Dutch so pertinaciously put forward, together with the restless and hostile demonstrations of the surrounding Indians, considered their safety could be effectually secured only by forming a confederation, offensive and defensive, of the separate colonies of Massachusetts, Plymouth, New Haven, and Connecticut, which was accordingly completed on the nineteenth of May this year, under the style and title of "The United Colonies of New England." May 19.

Intelligence of this union having reached Fort Amsterdam shortly after, the Director-general and council considered such an occurrence to furnish a fitting opportunity to obtain a redress of grievances, and to establish a better understanding in that quarter. He therefore dispatched, in the course of July, a sloop to Boston, with letters written in Latin, and signed by Secretary Van Tienhoven, addressed to the governor and sen- July 20.

BOOK III. 1643. ate of the United Provinces of New England. After having, in the first place, congratulated his excellency on the confederation which had been entered into between himself and the other colonies, Kieft took occasion to repeat his complaints of the grievous wrongs and insufferable injuries committed by New Haven and Connecticut on the Dutch; he next directed attention to the misrepresentations made by Lord Say, Mr. Peters, and others, to the Dutch ambassador at London; and concluded by inquiring of Governor Winthrop whether he should aid or desert him, so that he might know his friends from his enemies.

July 27. The governor of Massachusetts submitted this communication to such of his council as were at Boston, after which he replied, expressive of his sorrow for the differences which had arisen between the Dutch and his brethren at Hartford He hoped that the good understanding which had existed between the people of Massachusetts and the Dutch ever since they had come to these parts might continue, and suggested that the present differences might be arranged by arbitration in England, Holland, or America. He added, however, by way of explanation, that according to the articles of confederation, each colony was obliged to study the welfare and interests of the other colonies as well as its own; that his letters should be duly weighed by those who were to give further answer; in the mean while, he trusted that their ancient friendship should not be interrupted, and that each party would carefully avoid all injuries until final arrangements should be made either here or in Europe; as the controversy at Hartford about a small piece of land, in so vast a continent as that of America, was, he wisely remarked, too trifling to cause a breach between Protestants so intimately related in feelings and religion as were the Dutch and the English.

Sept. 7 The question came up at the first meeting of the commissioners, held soon after at Boston, at which the New Haven delegates presented a statement of what they considered the hostile and oppressive conduct of the Dutch towards the English, at the South River, and other places. Connecticut also made various complaints. Hereupon the president was ordered to communicate these several charges to the Director-general at the Manhattans, and to demand satisfaction for the injuries of which they complained. Governor Winthrop was, also, directed to write respecting the Dutch title to the land at Hartford, which the commissioners could not acknowledge until they had more light; and to assure the Director that as they would not wrong others, so would they not desert their confederates in a just cause. These replies did not satisfy Kieft. He again wrote, reiterating his complaints, and re-urging the soundness of the Dutch title to Hartford.[1]

While the Director-general was thus engaged, vindicating the company's jurisdiction over the lands on the Connecticut River, a new claimant appeared at Fort Amsterdam, and asserted his right to all that part of New Netherland embraced between the North and South rivers, (now constituting the state of New Jersey,) together with a portion of Virginia. This personage was Sir Edmund Ployden, Earl-palatine of the province of New Albion.

Straitened in circumstances, and circumscribed in means, this worthy knight happened to be thrown into jail in England for debt, whereupon he solicited from King Charles the First a patent to settle the Delaware River. But having been unsuccessful at court, he addressed himself to the king's favorite, Strafford, then viceroy of Ireland, who took upon himself to grant to his friend, in 1634, a tract of land beginning at Cape Mey, whence it extended west forty leagues up the Delaware; thence north forty leagues; after which it inclined east for the same distance to the Hudson River to "Sand-heey," or, as we presume, Sandy Hook; from which place the line ran south along the coast to the cape from which it first started. This grant included, moreover, all the islands in the sea "within ten leagues of the shore of the said region, called by the names of Pamonk, (or Long Island,) Hudson's, or Hudson's River Isles, or by whatever other name, with all ports for shipping and creeks of the sea to the same adjoining." This territory was, at the same time, erected into a province, or "free county palatine," over which the patentee was cre-

[1] Winthrop's Journal 303, 304, 305; Winthrop's N. Eng. ii., 129, 130, 157; Hubbard's N. Eng. 433, 434, 435. Trumbull's Conn. i., 126, 134, 135

BOOK III. 1643. ated Earl-palatine, and for its settlement a company was formed, consisting of forty-four lords, barons, baronets, knights, gentlemen, and adventurers, under the style of "the Albion Knights for the conversion of the twenty-three kings" of Charles River, as they called the Delaware. It was not, however, by lords and baronets that colonies were to be planted in America. It was, rather, by the poor, the patient, and the daring. Either the means of this goodly company were too slender, or their plans too crude, or, what is more probable, their patent was utterly valueless, and this colony had no other but a pseudo-parchment existence. The company, the colony, and the Earl-palatine, have disappeared from the face of the earth, leaving scarcely a trace to mark either their whereabouts or their existence. Sir Edmund Ployden retired to Virginia shortly after his appearance at New Amsterdam, "for he would not quarrel with the Dutch," who now became, again, a prey to all the horrors of an Indian war.[1]

The peace, which had been concluded in the spring, was considered by the River Indians in every respect unsatisfactory. The presents they had received were looked upon as by no means commensurate to the enormous losses which they had experienced at the hands of the white men; and Kieft, when their complaints came to his ears, took, unfor-
July 20. tunately, no pains to remove their dissatisfaction by opportune presents, but rather aggravated the existing ill-feeling by abusing the Indians, and inducing, by a bribe of two hundred fathoms of wampum, their chief, who came to warn him of his danger, "to kill those boobies who desired to war with the Swannekins."[2]

In the mean while, Pacham, the crafty leader of the Tankitekes of Haverstraw, visited all the Indian villages, and stimulated the savages to rise and massacre the Dutch. The spirit of evil found minds too well-disposed to receive his counsel and to take up the tomahawk. The Wappinecks, or Wappingers, residing on the North River, about half way be-

[1] Hazard's State Papers i., 160, 161; Van der Donck's Vertoogh van N. N.; Barker's Sketches in Hazard's Reg. i., 180; Plantagenet's New Albion; Bancroft's United States ii., 296; Alb. Rec. iii., 224; xviii., 349.

[2] De Vries.

tween the Manhattans and Fort Orange, with whom the Dutch never had any dispute, were the first to commence hostilities. They attacked an open boat coming from the latter post, laden with four hundred beaver skins, and murdered Willem Cornelissen Coster, one of the crew.[1] The booty acquired on this occasion tempted others to make similar attacks on two other boats, which were also overpowered. But in an attempt to surprise a fourth, the savages were repulsed with a loss of six men. Nine Christians lost their lives in these rencontres, and one woman and two children were led away captives. Another party of Indians murdered an old couple, whom they visited under pretence of selling some beavers, and inflicted, at the same time, five wounds on an unfortunate settler, who succeeded, however, in making his escape to Fort Amsterdam in a boat; bearing along with him, in his arms, a little child, who had already lost both father and mother in the first attack, and now was deprived of its grandfather and grandmother, having been thus twice miraculously snatched, by the interposition of Providence, from the clutches of the savages ere it was yet two years of age. Numbers of others were also murdered about this time by the Indians, who came under the guise of friendship to warn the Christians of approaching danger.[2]

CHAP. IV. 1643. Aug. 7

The hour of peril brought with it again the necessity of consulting the people; and Kieft, who never respected either popular rights or popular representatives, found himself, after a lapse of six or seven months, compelled to call the commonalty together anew to take into consideration such propositions as he should submit for the general good. The people met accordingly in the fort. They were called on "to elect five or six persons from among themselves," to consider maturely the articles which the Director-general and council were prepared to propose. But they preferred leaving the responsibility of choosing the "select men" to the executive, reserving to themselves, however, the right to reject such person or persons as might not be pleasing to them, and against

[1] Alb. Rec. iii., 143.
[2] Journael van N. N.; Winthrop's N. Eng. ii., 130.

BOOK III. 1643. whom they might have any thing to object.[1] A board of EIGHT MEN was subsequently chosen, a certificate of whose election was recorded in the following terms :

Sept. 13. "WE, the undersigned, declare that we have elected Joachim Pietersen, Jan Damen, Barent Dircksen, Abraham Pietersen, Isaack Allerton, Thomas Hal, Gerrit Wolfertsen, and Cornelis Melyn, maturely to consider the propositions submitted to us here by the Director and Council of New Netherland, approving hereby what the aforesaid persons shall herein treat of and determine. (Signed,)

"Philip Grave, Cornelis × Swilwan, Jan × Haer, Albert

Hol. Doc. iii., 141. The following is a translation of this interesting record: "We, the undersigned, having appeared in the fort at the request of the Noble Director and Council, to express our opinions on their Honors' proposal, as they have required of us to elect five or six persons from among ourselves to weigh maturely the articles laid before us, so have we considered it wise to leave to the Director and Council the doing that; namely, the selection of those persons; provided that we may reject the person or persons against whom there might be any thing to object, and are not pleasing to us.

(Signed.)

"J. P. Kuyter,
Barent × Dircksen,
Cornelis Wittensen,
Cornelis Jacobs. × Hille,
Abm. Pietersen,
Govert Lookmans,
Gerrit × Wolpherts,
Barent Janssen,
Hans × Hansen,
Jan × Picces,
Richard × Colfex,
Cornelis × Souleman,
Pieter Linde,
Jan Snediker,
Isaak × de Forest,
Abraham × Jacobse,
Cornelis Volckers,
Claes × Caerlessen,
Willem Adriaensen,
Thomas Hall,
Thomas × Sandersen,
Benj'n. Pawley,
Heyndrick × Heyndricksen,
Wolfert × Gerrits,
Abraham Planck,
Louis × Crain,
Pieter Colet,
Heindrick Heindricksen Kype,
Claes × Montelaar,
Claes Jansen Ruter,
George × Homs,
Ambrosius × Losman,
Richard
Cornelis Twits,
John Pathaway,
Cornelis Melyn,
Sibert Claessen,
Cornelis Lambertsen × Cool,
Jan Jansen Damen,
Isaak Allerton,
Jacob Couwenhoven,
Jan Verbruge,
Cornelis Dircksen Hoochlant,
Wilheim Goulder,
Pieter Adriaensen,
Laurens × Pietersen,
P. R. Gichhous."

Such as have a × affixed to their names made their mark.

Jansen, Teunis × Cray, Jacob × Stoffelsen, Cornelis Willemsen, Claes × Corstersen, Richert × Gebbers, Reyner × Jansen, Joris × Bastelaar, Egbert Woutersen, Pieter Linde, Wolphert × Gerrits, Isaak × de Forest, Ab. × Jacobse, Pieter Colet, Govert Loockmans, Jacob Couwenhoven, Willem Adriaensen, Jan Verbrugge, Thoman × Sandersen, Ambrosius × Losman, Wilheim Goulder, Jan × Picces, Benj'n. Pawley, Laurens × Pietersen, John Pathaway." CHAP. IV. 1643.

The first meeting of the above representatives was held two days after their election, pursuant to a summons from the Director-general, "to consider the critical circumstances of the country." One of their earliest acts was to mark their disapprobation of those who had demanded permission to attack the Indians. With this view, they required the exclusion of Jan Jansen Dam from the board, as they refused to sit with him, he being one of the signers of the letter of the twenty-fourth of February last. Dam protested in strong terms against this proceeding, and especially against Kieft, by whose misrepresentations, he averred, he had been deceived into signing the letter. But these excuses availed him naught. He was excluded, and Jan Evertsen Bout selected by the other seven to fill the vacancy. It was then resolved to renew the war "either by force or stratagem," against the river Indians, but to preserve peace with the Long Island tribes, "if they commit no hostilities;" to encourage the latter, "if they could be persuaded," to bring in "some heads of the murderers;" and to engage and arm as large a body of men as the freemen could afford to pay. At this meeting, several good and wholesome regulations were passed forbidding tippling and taverns, in lieu of which a course of religious exercises, accompanied by preaching, was ordered for the space of a week. This order, we regret, however, to have to add, was entirely neglected by the minister charged with its execution. The Eight Men then adjourned, having previously agreed to meet on every Saturday evening to watch the progress of affairs.[1] Sept. 15.

[1] Hol. Doc. iii., 144, 145; v. 323; Alb. Rec. ii., 231. "Desen acht mannen hebben wel eenige goede en behoorlycke articulen beraemt, voorbiedende

BOOK III. 1643. The Director-general immediately proceeded to arm the settlers and company's servants, and to engage the English inhabitants, (who were now threatening to quit the country,) the commonalty having agreed to defray the third part of their expenses. This corps, consisting of between fifty and eighty men, shortly after swore "fidelity to the High and Mighty Lords the States General, the Prince of Orange, the West India Company, and the Director and Council of New Netherland;" to "sacrifice their lives in their and the country's service, and to obey the Director, as dutiful officers and soldiers are bound to do."[1]

The enemy did not allow Kieft, or his troops, much time for preparation. A small force, consisting of "five soldiers, five boys, and one man," detailed for the defence of the colonie "behind the Cul," (or Newark Bay, as it is now called,) belonging to the Lord of Nederhorst, was attacked by a strong Sept. 17. party of savages in the course of the night of the 17th September, and after a desperate resistance, were finally obliged to retreat; the house having been fired over their heads. They escaped with considerable difficulty in a canoe, saving nothing but their arms. Another small force, which had been dispatched to the same quarter for the protection of the farm Oct. 1. of Jacob Stoffelsen, was visited some ten or fifteen days afterwards, by a party of nine Indians, under a pretence of friendship, who finding the soldiers unarmed, murdered all in the house, except the farmer's step-son, whom they carried off to Tappaen, after having burned all the farm-houses and produce,

all tafernien en alle andere onhebbelyckheden. Stelden weder in plaetse een weeck predicatie, als by de ordre gesien can worden, toch 't is by den Officier tot executie niet gebracht." Letter of the Eight Men, 28th October, 1644. Hol. Doc. iii., 215.

[1] Soo wert 'er goetgevonden dat men soo veel Engelsche souden aennemen alsser in 't lant te becomen waren, die nu togh van meeningh waren te vertrecken; waervan de Gemeente een derde part soude betalen; dese beloften geschiet by de Gemeente, maer de betalinge volght niet. Journael van N. N. The number to be paid by the commonalty was, according to another authority, fifty men. Report and advice, Appendix E. Trumbull [Hist. Conn. i., 139] represents these "fifty Englishmen" to have been a bodyguard to Kieft's person, as "he could not trust himself" among the people. But this is an error

CHAP. IV. 1643.

while Aert Theunissen, a planter at Hoboken, was surprised, as he was trading at the Beargat, outside Sandyhook, and murdered by the savages, who afterwards destroyed both his cattle and plantation.[1]

The greatest terror prevailed everywhere. Pavonia, Achter Col, the greater part of Manhattan, and most of Long Island were in the hands of the enemy, now consisting of seven different tribes, amounting, it was estimated, to fifteen hundred warriors. While the work of destruction was going on in the above quarters, other parties of savages crossed over to the main, and cleared all before them as far east as Stamford. Thither the celebrated Mrs. Anne Hutchinson had retired from her persecutors in Massachusetts, but the Indians had discovered her retreat. They appeared at first friendly, as was their wont when making their visits. But on discovering the defenceless condition of the inmates, they killed her and her son-in-law, Mr. Collins, with her own son, Francis, and all the other members of her family, besides a number of other persons in the neighborhood, belonging to the families of Mr. Throgmorton and Mr. Cornhill. Eighteen persons, in all, fell victims here to these barbarians, who, putting the cattle into barns, burnt the whole. Passing, thence, over to Long Island, they attacked the plantation of the Lady Moody at Gravesend several times, who would have, doubtless, shared the fate of the unfortunate Mrs. Hutchinson, had not her ladyship had a guard of forty men to protect her. Indeed so bold now had the Indians become, that they hesitated not to attack isolated bodies of the Dutch in their visits to the outposts around Fort Amsterdam, on one of which occasions Ensign van Dyck had a narrow escape of being killed, having received a ball in his right arm, which passed across his body, grazing his chest.[2] Oct. 6.

[1] Alb. Rec. iii., 153; De Vries; Van der Donck's Vertoogh van N. N.; Hol. Doc. iv., 247. Beeregat, the first inlet without the cape on the New Jersey shore. Benson's Mem. 21. See also Van der Donck's Beschryving van N. N.

[2] Winthrop's Journal, 308; Winthrop's N. Eng. ii., 135, 136; Hubbard, 345, 346; Alb. Rec. ii., 238; Gorton's Simplicity Defended, in Rhode Isl. His. Soc. Rec. ii., 59. Wilde's Rise, Reign, and Ruin of the Antinomians contains this pious exultation at the destruction of Mrs. Hutchinson:—"The Indians set upon them and slew her and all her children; save one that escaped, (her own hus-

BOOK III. 1643. To oppose these wild hordes the Dutch force amounted to no more than two hundred and fifty or three hundred settlers, and between fifty and sixty soldiers, badly provided, however, with ammunition; while Fort Amsterdam, "open to the enemy day and night," was nothing better than a ruin, around whose crumbling walls helpless women and children lay huddled together in huts of straw!

Such was the condition of things in New Netherland at the close of September, and beginning of October, when Director Kieft again convoked the Eight Men, to deliberate on what was best to be done. Two vessels—the Seven Stars and Neptune—were at anchor in the harbor, laden with provisions destined for Curaçoa. It was at once proposed to unload these ships—turn their cargoes into the fort—retain the greater number of the crew and marines to aid against the savages; and
Oct. 6. next to apply to New Haven for an auxiliary force of one hundred and fifty men. To meet expenses, the Director-general was recommended to draw a bill of exchange on the company for twenty-five thousand guilders, ($10,000,) and to give the English a mortgage on New Netherland as collateral security for the payment of this debt.[1]

The greater portion of this plan was, however, rejected by Director Kieft. With a self-will for which he was characteristic, he sent away the ships; refused to retain the men belonging to these vessels, at the moment he was under the ne-

band being dead before)—a dreadful blow! Some write that Indians did burn her to death with fire, her house and all the rest that belonged unto her, but I am not able to affirm by what kind of death they slew her. . . . . . God's hand is more apparently seen herein to pick out this woful woman, to make her, and those belonging to her, an unheard of heavy example of their cruelty to others."

[1] De vreese meer over 't lant comende, de Aght Mannen vergaderen formeren een propositie by geschrift, waerinne sy versoecken dat men na de Noordt souden senden by onse gebeuren d' Engelsche om hondert vyftigh mannen tot hulp te versoeken; tot betalinge van deselve soude men een wisselbrief verleenen van vyffentwintigh duyzent gulden, ende tot versekeringe dat deselve voldaen worden, soude men N. Nederlant soo lange aen de Engelsche verpanden . . . . gelyck oock weynich dagen van te vooren hadde beslooten, dat men de victualie gedestineert naer Curaçoa, uyt de schepen soude lossen, ende 't meeste volck vandeselve behouden, ende de Schepen alsoo ledigh wegsenden. Det wert den Directeur nogh niet aengenomen nogh goetgevonden Journ. van N. N.

cessity of applying to New England for an auxiliary force, and exported provisions while the people around him were but scantily supplied; for peas sold at this period for three florins or $1.20 per schepel, (three pecks;) rye bread for eight cents, wheaten bread 14 cents per loaf; hard bread, 6 cents, pork, ten cents, dried fish, five cents, beef, nine cents, and tallow, for five cents per pound; Spanish wine for thirty-two cents, and blubber oil for twenty cents per pot.[1]

Agreeably to the preceding arrangement, Captain John Underhill, who now was engaged to lead the Dutch forces, proceeded to New Haven, with Mr. Isaac Allerton, in the hope of engaging the government of that colony to raise the auxiliary force which was required. But this application had no effect. New Haven was prohibited by the articles of confederation from joining separately in war, and Governor Eaton and the general court not being satisfied of the justice of the quarrel between the Dutch and the Indians, rejected the proposal which Kieft had made.[2] In this abandoned condition, the Eight Men were under the necessity of writing to Holland. They addressed letters both to the Assembly of the XIX. and to the States General; which memorials, the first ever sent to Europe from a popular body in this state, interesting for their truth, and affecting for their simplicity and pathos, were couched in the following touching terms:

Oct. 24.

"Honorable Lords—Rightly hath one of the ancients said, that there is no misery on earth, however great, that does not manifest itself in time of war. We, poor inhabitants of New Netherland, have now to complain, that having enjoyed for a long time an indifferent peace with the heathen, Almighty God hath finally, through his righteous judgment, kindled the fire of war around us during the current year with the Indians, in which not only numbers of innocent people, men, women, and children, have been murdered in their houses, and at their work, and swept captives away, (whereby this place with all its inhabitants is come to the greatest ruin;) but all the boweries and plantations at Pavonia, with twenty-five lasts [2700

[1] Alb. Rec. iii., 159.

[2] 3 Mass. Hist. Coll. vii., 244.

BOOK III. 1643.

bushels] of corn and other produce have been burnt, and the cattle destroyed.

"Long Island is destitute also of inhabitants and stock, except a few insignificant places over against the main, which are about to be abandoned. The English who have settled among us have not escaped. They too, except one place, are all murdered and burnt.

"Staten Island, where Cornelis Melyn established himself, is unattacked as yet, but stands expecting an assault every hour.

"On the island of Manachatas, [Manhattans,] from the north unto the Fresh Water,[1] there are no more, at this date, than five or six places inhabited; these are threatened by the Indians, every night, with fire, and by day, with the slaughter of both people and cattle.

"Achter Cul, where the Honorable Van der Horst founded a colonie, is altogether in ruins. Thus no other place remains for us, where we can lodge ourselves with women and children, than around and adjoining Fort Amsterdam, on the Manachatas.

"No resistance is offered the enemy for want of men, arms, and ammunition, with which this place is very slenderly supplied. The fort is defenceless and entirely out of order, and resembles (with submission) rather a molehill than a fort against the enemy. On the other hand, the enemy is strong and mighty. They have formed an alliance, one with another, with more than seven different tribes, well supplied with muskets, powder, and ball, which they have procured and daily receive from private traders, in exchange for beaver, and with which they murder our people. The woods and the thickets are now also useful to them, for they have removed all their women, children, and old men into the interior. The rest of the warriors daily menace our lives with fire and sword, and threaten to attack the fort with all their strength, now consisting of fifteen hundred men. We have to guard this post at

[1] There was formerly a "fresh water" pond where a part of Centre-street and its vicinity, in New York, are now situate. It is to this pond that allusion is made above.

all hours, for all the outside places are mostly in their hands. Thus it is through their good-will that any cattle remain alive in the whole country.

CHAP. IV. 1643.

"How wretched it fares with us afflicted people throughout the land, your Honors can easily conceive, for the country's welfare and prosperity are composed principally of people, cattle, and houses, in which we jointly and severally have expended all the means that we have been able to realize.

"Our population consists, for the most part, of women and children. The freemen (not counting the English) are about two hundred in number, who must protect, by force of arms, their families, which now lie concealed in straw huts, around outside the fort.

"The cattle are partly burnt and killed; the remainder conveyed to the fort on the Manhattes, where, for want of forage, they must starve through the coming winter, if not immediately slaughtered.

"The houses have been, for the most part, fired and destroyed. Those yet standing are in danger of being also burnt. It is much to be apprehended that this is but the beginning of our troubles, especially as these Indians kill off our people, one after the other, which they will continue to do, while we are burdened with our muskets, our wives and little ones.

"While the people are ruined, the corn and all other produce burnt, and little or nothing saved, not a plough can be put this fall into the ground, so that not a hundred schepels will be sown hereabouts, and much less in the spring. If any provisions should be obtained at the east from the English, we know not wherewith we poor men will pay for them; while private traders have, for the last three or four years, drained us by their extortions, and made this country wretchedly poor; for this must follow so long as the industry of the land is at a stand-still.

"The cattle being destroyed, the dwellings burnt, the mouths of the women and children must remain shut. We speak not now of other necessaries, such as clothes, shirts, shoes, and stockings. Matters, in fine, are in such a fix, that it will be with us according to the words of the prophet;—Who draws the sword, shall die of hunger and cold.

BOOK III. 1643. "We turn, then, to you, Honorable Lords General; we pray and beseech your Honors, with humble hearts, to be pleased to assist us in this sorrowful plight, and to extend, by the earliest opportunity, a helping hand, with such means as your Honors may, in your wisdom, consider best. We have sent herewith a remonstrance also to the High and Mighty Lords, wherein we have besought of them, that this place, and we all, with wives and children, may not be delivered over a prey to these cruel heathens. Relying on which, we remain your Lordships' faithful subjects, lawfully elected and authorized by the Honorable the Director and council, and the whole commonalty of New Netherland. (Signed,) Cornelis Melyn, Abm. Pietersen, Gerrit Wolphertsen, Isaack Allerton, Thomas Hall, Jan Evertse Boút, Barent Dircksen, Joachim Pietersen. Done at Fort Amsterdam, this 24th Oct., in New Netherland, anno 1643."[1]

The remonstrance to which the Eight Men refer at the close of the above letter, was to this effect:

Nov. 4. "To the Noble, High and Mighty Lords, the Noble Lords the States General of the United Netherland Provinces:—

"Noble, High and Mighty Lords! As no sacrifice is more acceptable to our God than an humble spirit and a contrite heart, so nothing should, in like manner, be more pleasing to all Christian princes and magistrates, than to lend an ear to their complaining, and to extend their hand to their distressed subjects.

"So is it, then, that we, poor inhabitants of New Netherland, were pursued in the spring by these wild heathens and barbarous savages, with fire and sword. Daily have they cruelly murdered men and women in our houses and fields; and with hatchets and tomahawks struck little children dead in their parents' arms, or before their doors; or taken them far away into captivity. Cattle of all descriptions are destroyed

[1] Hol. Doc. iii., 134, 135, 136, 137, 138, 139, 140. Isaac Allerton, whose name is signed to the above, was one of the memorable hundred and one "Pilgrims," who came out from Holland in the Mayflower. He was assistant to Governor Bradford for many years, and removed to New Netherland in 1641. He died in 1659.

and killed, and such as remain, must perish this approaching winter for want of fodder.

"Every place almost is abandoned: We, wretched people, must skulk, with wives and little ones, that still are left, in poverty together, by and around the fort on the Manhattes, where we are not one hour safe. While the Indians daily threaten to overwhelm us, little can be planted this autumn, and much less next spring; so that it must come to pass, that we all, who may survive, shall die, with women and children next year, of hunger and sorrow, unless our God take pity upon us.

"We are all, here, from the smallest to the greatest, without counsel or means; wholly powerless. The enemy meets with no resistance. The garrison consists of but fifty or sixty soldiers; without ammunition. Fort Amsterdam, utterly defenceless, stands open to the enemy day and night. The company hath, here, few or no effects, as the Director informs us. Were it not for this, there had still been time to receive, ere all were lost, some assistance from the English at the east; but we helpless inhabitants, while we must abandon all our property, are exceedingly poor.

"These heathens are strong in might. They have formed an alliance with seven other nations; are well provided with guns, powder, and ball, in exchange for beaver by the private traders, who have had for a long time free course here. The rest they take from our brethren whom they murder. In fine, we experience the greatest misery, which must astonish a Christian heart to see or to hear.

"We turn, then, in a body to you, High and Mighty Lords, acknowledging your High Mightinesses as our sovereigns, and the Fathers of Fatherland. We supplicate for God's sake, and for the love which their High Mightinesses bear towards their poor and desolate subjects here in New Netherland, that their High Mightinesses would take pity on us, their poor people, and urge upon and command the company, (to whom we also make known our necessities,) to forward to us by the earliest opportunity such assistance as their High Mightinesses should deem most proper, in order that we, poor and forlorn beings, may not be left, all at once, a prey, with women and children,

BOOK III. 1643. to these cruel heathens. For should suitable assistance not arrive very quickly, according to our expectations, we shall be forced, in order to preserve the lives of those who remain, to remove ourselves to the east among the English, who would like nothing better than to have possession of this place; especially on account of the superior convenience of the seacoast, bays, and large rivers, besides the great fertility of this soil—yea, this alone could provision and supply yearly twenty, twenty-five to thirty ships from Brazils or the West Indies, with all necessaries. Done at Manhattans in New Netherlands, this 3d Nov., 1643. Stil. Rom."[1]

Having dispatched these urgent petitions to Holland for assistance, Kieft set about introducing some sort of order and discipline into the heterogeneous force which circumstances enabled him to muster. With this view the following regulations were ordered to be enforced "when on guard:"—

Nov. 12. "I. Whoever abuses the name of God when on guard shall pay a fine for the first offence, of ten stivers; for the second, 20 stivers; for the third, 30 stivers.

"II. He who speaks scandal of a comrade during the time he is on guard, shall pay thirty stivers.

"III. He who arrives tipsy or intoxicated on the guard, shall pay twenty stivers.

"IV. He who neglects to be present without sufficient cause, fifty stivers.

"Lastly, He who, when the duty on the guard is well performed, and the sun is risen, and the reveillé beat, fires a musket without his corporal's orders, shall pay one guilder."

With all these rules and regulations, the state of affairs on the island Manhattans was by no means improving. The presence of even this small garrison seems to be productive rather of increased disorder. Complaints were daily made of the stealing and killing of hogs, goats, as well as of other irregularities, which increased so fast, that it "threatened to end in plunder and robbery," and it was feared that people would "at last murder one another," in consequence of the impunity

[1] Hol. Doc. ii., 323, 324, 325, 326, 327, 328. This memorial or remonstrance was signed by the Eight Men in the same manner as the petition to the XIX., which precedes it

of the delinquents. The incursions of the savages continued unnoticed and unopposed, so that, at length, the community began loudly to complain. Kieft, desirous to shake the blame off himself, cited Sheriff Van der Huygens before him, and entered a strong protest against that officer for his neglect of duty. "The fault alone is chargeable to you," said he, addressing the fiscal in terms of strongest censure, "and you dare to blame the Director that you are not duly supported! You are now commanded to execute your office, so that you may not skulk behind that pretext. The Director and council, and all the soldiers are at your service, besides your under-sheriff, jailer, and the negroes."[1]

CHAP. IV. 1643.

[1] Alb. Rec. ii., 236 ; iii., 169

CHAPTER V.

Offensive measures against the Indians—Expedition to Staten Island—Mayn Mayano slain—His head brought into New Amsterdam—Expedition to Greenwich—Fails in finding the Indians—Returns to Stamford—Collision between a Dutch soldier and Captain Patrick—Latter killed—Attack on an Indian settlement—Detachment return to the Manhattans—Expedition against the Weckquaesqueecks—Arrive at the castles of that tribe, but find them abandoned—Pennawitz, chief of the Canarsee tribe, discovered assisting the enemy—Expedition to Schout's Bay on Long Island—Attacks on the Heemstede and Mespath Indians—Triumph of the Dutch—Consequent outrage on some prisoners—Underhill proceeds to Stamford—Expedition against the Indians of that quarter—Description of the Indian camp—General attack thereupon—Important victory gained by the Dutch—Over five hundred savages slaughtered—Public Thanksgiving at New Amsterdam therefor—Savages sue for peace—Treaties concluded between several of the river and Long Island tribes and the Dutch—Proceedings of the States General on the petitions of the Eight Men—The West India Company unable to render any assistance—Their letter to the States—Two Spanish vessels taken and brought to New Amsterdam—Low state of the colonial treasury—Kieft resolves to have recourse to taxation—Convokes the Eight Men—Submits his plan—The Eight Men object—Kieft becomes irritated—Claims unlimited power—The Eight Men succumb—Excise duties provisionally imposed—The Eight Men treated with disrespect by Director Kieft—The Dutch expelled from Maranham, a province of Brazil—Fly to Curaçoa—Destitute condition of that island—Are sent to New Netherland—Arrive opportunely at Fort Amsterdam—Council resolve to continue the excise—The burghers oppose this arbitrary taxation—Prosecutions of the brewers—Persist in their refusal to pay the excise—Execution issued against them in consequence—Public discontent becomes very high—Parties formed—Protests against the Director-general—Complaints against him sent to Holland, demanding his recall—Letter of the Eight Men—Sad condition of the country—Strictures on Kieft's maladministration.

BOOK III. 1644.

PREPARATORY arrangements having at length been completed, offensive movements were commenced against the savages, and the Director-general considering that he might, at the same time, beneficially annoy the Spaniards, authorized the privateer La Garce to proceed on a cruise towards the West India Islands.[1]

[1] This privateer was owned by the following persons:—Capt. Blauvelt, commander, Jan Jansen Dam, Hendrick Jacobsen, Pater Vaer, Jacob van

One of the first expeditions from Fort Amsterdam, this year, was against the Indians on Staten Island, who had cut off all communication with the western bank of the river. A party, consisting of forty burghers, under Captain Joachim Pietersen Kuyter; thirty-five Englishmen, under Lieutenant Baxter; supported by several of the soldiers under their sergeant, Peter Cock, the whole being under the command of Counsellor La Montagne, crossed over from the Manhattans late in the evening, and having made a landing without opposition, proceeded to scour the island. They marched the whole of the night. On their arrival at the spot where they expected to meet the enemy, they found the place abandoned. They had the good fortune, however, to fall in with and secure five or six hundred schepels of corn, with which they returned, after having set fire to the village.

Mayn Mayano, a stout and fierce chief, who resided between Greenwich and Stamford, some twenty-five miles northeast of Fort Amsterdam, had dared to attack, about this time, with bow and arrows, three Christians whom he had met on their return home, and who were armed with muskets. The savage had already succeeded in killing one of the three, and was engaged in close combat with the second, when he was fortunately slain by the third, who brought the fellow's head into the fort, and communicated intelligence to the Director and council of the numerous injuries the settlers in that quarter had suffered at the hands of this chief and his tribe, though they and these savages had had no previous differences. A detachment of one hundred and twenty men was immediately detailed under the above-named officers, in three yachts to Greenwich, where they landed the same evening, and thence marched the whole night, to the place where they were informed the Indians were encamped; but they did not succeed in meeting the enemy. The latter had been advised of the approach of the Dutch, or these had been led astray. The detachment, thereupon, returned in no very good humor to Stamford, where a halt was called.[1]

Couwenhoven, Adriaen Dircksen Coe, Jan Labatie, and Adriaen van der Donck.

[1] Alb. Rec. ii., 250; Journael van N. N.

BOOK III. 1644. One of the party happened to fall in, at the house of Captain Underhill in this village, on a Sunday afternoon while the inhabitants were at church, with Captain Daniel Patrick of Greenwich, on whose representations the troops had been dispatched from Fort Amsterdam. Feeling naturally nettled that so many men had been deluded, at such a critical time, into what appeared an idle wild-goose 'chase, the Dutch sol
Jan. 2. dier charged Patrick with treachery. The latter retorted, spat in his accuser's face, and then turned to go away. Incensed at the insult, the Dutchman drew a pistol and shot Patrick in the back of the head. He fell dead, never uttering another word. The soldier was apprehended, but escaped afterwards from custody.[1]

In the mean time four of the Stamford people had volunteered to go as scouts, and endeavor to find where the savages had removed to. On the return of some of these, five and twenty of the boldest of the detachment were sent to an adjoining village, where a prospect was held out of success. By a forced march, they came undiscovered to a small Indian settlement, which they attacked, slaying eighteen or twenty of the savages, and taking one old man, two women and some children, prisoners, with a view to exchange them for Christians of a like age and sex. The Indian wigwams were otherwise all unoccupied. The detachment returned after this to Manhattans.

The old Indian thus taken prisoner, proposed now to the Dutch, in the hope of obtaining favor at their hands, to lead any of their troops against the Weckquaesqueecks, who were said to be intrenched in three castles at the north. Lieu-

[1] Winthrop's Journal, 320; Winthrop's N Eng. ii., 151. Hubbard, copying Winthrop, says of this Captain Patrick—"He was entertained in the Massachusetts, and brought out of Holland—having been one of the Prince's guard there—to teach the people military discipline. He was made a freeman, admitted a member of the church of Watertown, but being proud and otherwise vicious, he was left of God to a profligate life, which brought him at last to destruction by the hand of one of that people from whom he sought protection, after he had fled from the yoke of Christ in the Massachusetts, the strictness of whose discipline he could neither bear in the church nor yet in the country." Hist. N. Eng., 426. Patrick's wife's name was Annetje van Beyeren. She married subsequently Tobias Feeck, sheriff of Flushing.

tenant Baxter and Sergeant Cock were, thereupon, ordered to proceed under the guidance of this old man, with sixty-five men against this tribe. But this party was in no way more fortunate than those which had already gone on similar expeditions. They found the castles of the Indians formidable in construction, and well adapted for defence. They were built of five-inch plank, nine feet high, and bound around with thick beams, and studded with port-holes. Though it was calculated that thirty Indians could hold out, in one of these, against two hundred soldiers, strange to tell, the whole were found uninhabited. The Dutch, thereupon, burnt two of these strongholds, reserving the third as a point to retreat to, in case of necessity. From this place they next marched between thirty and forty miles further, but discovered nothing save a few huts. They now retraced their steps, having met with only one or two Indians, whom they killed, and a few women and children, of whom they made prisoners, burning whatever corn fell in their way.

Intelligence was now received at Fort Amsterdam, that Pennawitz, of Long Island, in whom the Dutch had generally so much confidence, was countenancing the enemy in an underhand way ; his people having been discovered secretly killing the Christians, and burning their houses. A body, one hundred and twenty strong, composed of burghers under Capt. Pietersen, of Englishmen under Sergeant-major Underhill, and the old soldiers under Peter Cock,—the whole expedition being under the command of Counsellor La Montagne,—were ordered to proceed in three yachts to Schouts or Sheriff's Bay, on Long Island. Having landed without molestation, they marched to Heemstede, and having succeeded in killing an Indian spy, whom they had discovered on the lookout, they divided themselves into two sections. Underhill proceeded, at the head of one of these, composed of about fourteen Englishmen, against the smaller Indian settlement. Eighty men were dispatched against the larger village, named Matsepe, (Mespath,) and such was the success with which both these excursions were crowned, that they left one hundred and twenty savages dead on the field ; while the loss on their own side was only one man killed, and three wounded The tri-

BOOK III. 1644. umph thus achieved was, however, afterwards tarnished, it is said, by brutal outrages openly committed by the soldiery on a couple of Indians who had been taken prisoners; one of whom was hacked to pieces with knives, while stripes of flesh were cut from the other's yet living body, which was otherwise shockingly mutilated; his head having been finally cut off in Beaver Lane. Director Kieft and Counsellor La Montagne are accused of having countenanced these tortures by their presence.[1]

On his return from Heemstede, Capt. Underhill was ordered to Stamford, to obtain particulars of the whereabouts of the savages. He brought word back, that they were encamped some five hundred strong in that direction, and that the old guide urged the forwarding a body of troops immediately thither, as he was desirous, on the one hand, to prove that the former ill success of the Dutch was not his fault; on the other hand, anxious for protection, as his life was in constant danger.

Feb. One hundred and thirty men embarked, accordingly, under Captain Underhill and Ensign Van Dyck, in three yachts, and landed the same evening at Greenwich. But a severe snowstorm having set in, detained them at that settlement the whole of that night. The weather, however, moderated towards morning, when the party set forward, and arrived, soon after, at the foot of a rocky mountain, over which some of the men had to crawl, with considerable difficulty, on their hands and feet. The evening, about eight o'clock, brought them to within a few miles of the enemy. Their further progress was, however, now impeded by two rivers, one of which was some two hundred feet wide, and three in depth. It was considered

[1] The particulars of the above expeditions are taken from the Journael van Nieuw Nederlandt. Allusion is made to the outrages committed against the Indians in the following query proposed to Van Tienhoven at the Hague, in 1650: Off niet seekere twee Wilden, op de cortegarde gevangen, waren van Heemstede gehaelt, door de Soldaten in 't gesichte van alle de wereldt, d'eene met messen, in coolenbloede, gesneden en doodgesteken; den anderen levendich riemen uyt het lyff gesneden; voorts syn mannelyckheyd, noch levende, affgesneden, in het beverspad, daer sy hem daernae het hooft affsloegen? Off Kieft en La Montagne daer niet mede present by waren, als de riem uyt der levenden lyff gesneden wierden? Hol. Doc. v., 320, 321.

best to remain here awhile, in order to refresh the men and to make arrangements for the coming attack. After a rest of a couple of hours, the party again set forward at ten o'clock. It was full moon, and the night so clear—" a winter's day could not be brighter"—that the Indian village was soon discovered at a distance. It consisted of three rows of houses, or huts, ranged in streets, each eighty paces long, and backed by a mountain which sheltered it from the northwest wind.

But the Indians were as much on the alert as their enemy. They soon discovered the Dutch troops, who charged forthwith, surrounding the camp, sword in hand. The Indians evinced, on this occasion, considerable boldness, and made a rush, once or twice, to break the Dutch line and open some way for escape. But in this they failed, leaving one dead, and twelve prisoners in the hands of the assailants, who now kept up such a brisk fire, that it was impossible for any of the besieged to escape. After a desperate conflict of an hour, one hundred and eighty Indians lay dead on the snow, outside their dwellings. Not one of the survivors durst now show his face. They remained under cover, discharging their arrows from behind, to the great annoyance of the Dutch troops. Underhill now seeing no other way to overcome the obstinate resistance of the foe, gave orders to fire their huts. This order was forthwith obeyed; the wretched inmates endeavoring, in every way, to escape from the horrid flames, but mostly without success. The moment they made their appearance, they rushed, or were driven, precipitately back into their burning hovels, " preferring to be consumed by fire, than to fall by our weapons."

In this merciless manner were butchered, as some of the Indians afterwards reported, five hundred human beings. Others carry the number to seven hundred; " the Lord having collected the most of our enemies there, to celebrate some peculiar festival." Of the whole party, no more than eight men escaped this terrible slaughter by fire and sword. Three of these were badly wounded. Throughout the entire carnage, not one of the sufferers—man, woman, or child was heard to utter shriek or moan.

This expedition having been thus crowned with complete

BOOK III. 1644. success, the wounded, fifteen in number, were attended to, and sentinels posted to prevent surprise. Large fires were then kindled, as the weather was still excessively cold, and the conquerors bivouacked, during the remainder of the night, on the field of battle. They set out next morning on their return, in good order, "marching with great courage over that harassing mountain, the Lord enduing the wounded with extraordinary strength," and arrived at Stamford at noon, after a march of two days and one night, during which they had little repose and less comfort. The English received the soldiers with friendly hospitality, proffering them every possible kindness. Two days afterwards the detachment arrived at Fort Amsterdam, where a public thanksgiving was ordered for the brilliant success which attended the New Netherland arms.[1]

Though the savages continued still to be troublesome to such a degree as to oblige the Dutch at Manhattans to erect a
March 31. solid fence "from the great bouwery across to the plantation of Emanuel," as a protection for the cattle when out at pasture, the few settlements that remained unscathed were about now to be relieved, for awhile, from the attacks of the Indians. The late punishment inflicted on these, and the approach of spring, made them desirous for peace, and they therefore solicited the intervention of Captain Underhill to procure a cessation of hostilities.

Mamaranack, chief of the Indians residing on the Kicktawanc, or Croton River; Mongockonone, Pappenoharrow, from the Weckquaesqueecks and Nochpeem; and the Wap-

[1] Journael van N. N. This, I presume, is the battle alluded to by Trumbull,—Hist. Conn. i., 161; Wood's Long Island, 34, note; Thompson's Long Island i., 106,—as "the great battle fought between the Dutch and Indians in that part of Horse Neck called Strickland's plain, now included in the town of Greenwich, Conn." Trumbull says that three hundred Indians were killed by the Dutch. But all the above writers, the one copying the error of the other, fix the date of the battle in 1646; but this evidently is a mistake, for a general peace was established between the Indians and Dutch in August, 1645. It is stated, in a pamphlet entitled "Second Amboyna Tragedy," that the Indians offered Underhill a hogshead of wampum if he would retreat with his forces, but that he refused, hazarded the above attack, and killed fourteen hundred of the enemy!

pings from Stamford, presented themselves, in a few days, at Fort Amsterdam, and having pledged themselves that they should not, henceforth, commit any injury whatever on the inhabitants of New Netherland, their cattle and houses, nor show themselves, except in a canoe, before Fort Amsterdam, should the Dutch be at war with any of the Manhattan tribes; and having further promised to deliver up Pacham, the chief of the Tankitekes, peace was concluded between them and the Dutch; who promised, on their part, not to molest them in any way, but to allow them to cultivate their fields in peace, and as a guarantee of their sincerity, surrendered several of their prisoners. CHAP. V. 1644. April 6.

Ten days after the conclusion of this treaty, Gonwarrowe, sachem of the Mattinecocks, on Long Island, who had suffered so much in the late attack at Heemstede and Mespath, appeared also at the fort, and went security for the adjoining villages of Matinnecock, Marospinck, as well as for Ack-kinkas-hacky, on whose behalf he solicited peace, which was granted, on the condition that neither of them should attempt to harm the Dutch, nor afford shelter to any of the tribes at Rocken-hacky, (Rockaway?) "the Bay," and Marechhawick; that they should separate from them, and communicate these articles to their sachem on "Mr. Fordham's plains." If, however, any should be slain by any of the hostile tribes, or among the latter, by the Dutch, these were to be held guiltless. To all these conditions the sachem assented, after which "he was favored with some presents."[1] April 15.

The urgent appeals for succor and relief, which the Eight Men had transmitted at the close of the last year to the States General and the West India Company, had already reached their destination. Their High Mightinesses, moved by the urgency of these representations, immediately had them re- April 5

[1] Alb. Rec. ii., 247, 248. As it may be interesting, at this distance of time, to understand the locality of those Long Island Indians, we would mention that the Matinnecocks owned Flushing, Newtown, Cow-harbor, and other neighboring places. The Marsapeagues (Marospinck?) extended from Rockaway to Huntington. "The Bay" adjoined Jamaica; and the Marechhawick Indians dwelt between that and Brooklyn. "The great plains" are those of Hempstead, L. I., which were granted to Mr. Fordham.

BOOK III. 1644. ferred to the Assembly of the XIX., with a strong injunction to adopt prompt measures for the protection of the petitioners. These representations were, notwithstanding, unproductive of any good effect. The West India Company was bankrupt; its directors without means and without credit; its different chambers torn with dissensions and filled with distrust, the one against the other, and unable to defend their colonial possessions, which the revolution progressing through England only saved at this moment from the gripe of Great Britain. To save themselves from utter ruin, the directors in Holland were endeavoring to form a union with the richer and more powerful East India Company. In this helpless condition they wrote to the States General:

April 23. "It has grieved us, collectively and individually, in our innermost hearts," said they, "to learn the desolate and miserable condition of the poor people there; the rather, finding ourselves so utterly unable not only to bring those precious colonies to such a state for the company, as would for once authorize us to expect, with time, the long looked-for profits from thence, but to send, at present, to the poor inhabitants who have left their Fatherland, in the hope of finding the means of honorably maintaining their wives and children there, those supplies so earnestly demanded for the maintenance and defence of their lives against the barbarous tribes of the country. And though we are of opinion that long delays will cause additional suffering, as well in New Netherland aforesaid, as in other distant places, whereby the company, and, consequently, this nation, must apprehend no less danger from the scarcity of divers required and necessary provisions, ammunition, merchandise, &c., it behooves us to represent, respectfully, to your High Mightinesses, that the company has fallen altogether into such impotency and discredit, that it cannot, without effectual assistance from the States, any longer either supply those distant places, or continue even the further necessary payments here. We, therefore, most humbly beseech your High Mightinesses to be pleased to take these embarrassments into such consideration as the constitution of the said company, for the welfare of the state, so urgently requires. The good and willing shareholders, who have contributed so largely to the advancement of this nation's prosperity, and have already, provisionally, passed a profitable resolution, authorizing a union with the East India Company; let their High Mightinesses not discourage, nor make them despond of contributing to so wholesome a work as the union of these two eminent companies should be for this state. The vigorous continuation of the said company and its foreign affairs, at least the payment of its daily expenditure, would, thereby, be not a little promoted, and placed, with a present subsidy of about one million, in good, prosperous, and profitable order." CHAP. V. 1644.

Urging these views in terms which evidently prove the derangement and embarrassed condition of their financial affairs, the directors concluded by stating, that the committee whom they had deputed to present their letter was authorized to receive their High Mightinesses' conclusions thereupon, which they earnestly hoped would be favorable to their prayers.

No immediate result, however, followed this application. The States General ordered copies of the directors' letter to be forwarded to the provincial chambers of the West India Company,[1] and consequently all action was postponed for the moment, as regarded the relief of the suffering colonists of New Netherland, whose condition, all this while, was by no means one to be envied, and to whom the Assembly of the XIX., in the mean time, dispatched letters expressive of their sympathy and desire to afford them every assistance in their power. April 27.

The peace, or rather the hollow truce, which had been entered into between the Dutch and the Indians was of little or no advantage. The principal tribes were still out, and as hostile as ever to the Hollanders, whose few remaining bouweries and dwellings they continued to harass in every possible way. The pay of the soldiers engaged by the commonalty went on, in the mean time, and no funds were available to provide for this portion of the public expense. The prospect of relief from home was, as we have shown, slender and cheerless in the extreme. A bill of exchange, drawn in

[1] Hol. Doc. ii., 329, 332, 333, 334, 335, 337.

BOOK III. 1644. the course of last November on the directors in Amsterdam, for the trifling sum of two thousand, six hundred, and twenty-two guilders, ($1045,) had been returned protested for non-acceptance,[1] and thus misfortune seemed to threaten this devoted country from every quarter. In the midst of these dis-
May 29. couragements, Captain Blauvelt entered the port with two Spanish prizes, laden with sugar, tobacco, ebony wood, and wine, which the privateer La Garce had captured in the Caribbean Sea, after a severe contest.[2] But though valuable, these prizes and their cargoes could not be made available at this precise time, since they could not be declared confiscate without due course of law. Under such deplorable circumstances, recourse was had, for the first time in the annals of the colony, to the unpopular expedient of imposing taxes on the impoverished commonalty to defray the public exigencies. To obviate objections which such a step would necessarily create at first, the Director-general and council determined to call again together the Eight Men.

This popular body had not been assembled since the fourth of November of the past year, though various measures of public importance had been adopted, and though it had been agreed upon at their first meeting that their sittings should be weekly. Now, however, that money was required, their meeting could no longer be deferred. The state of the public
June 18. treasury was, therefore, submitted to them, as well as the exigencies of the public service. To meet the latter, it was proposed that certain excise duties should be levied, without which it was impossible to retain the English soldiers. This course did not meet the approbation, at first, of the Eight Men. They represented the difficulty of raising funds in that way, in the present condition of the people, beggared as they were by the war; and gave it as their opinion that the imposition of taxes was the attribute of a higher authority than that possessed by the Director-general. It should emanate from and be first ordered by the Lords Majors.

Kieft was not prepared to allow his authority to be thus impugned. The refractory board was told, in sharp terms, that

[1] Alb. Rec. iii., 212.

[2] Alb. Rec. ii., 250, 251.

he had more power in the country than even the company, and that he could do as he pleased, for he derived his commission not from the Directors, but from the States General.[1] The Eight Men succumbed. But in yielding the point, they suggested, that the more proper and least burdensome course would be, to oblige the private traders, who by their commerce with the settlers and natives had realized such large gains, to contribute something to the treasury, and thus relieve the commonalty. A plan, embracing an excise, and an additional duty on certain exports, was concluded upon; and in a few days after the following proclamation was issued, establishing for the first time, in this country, an excise on wines, beer, and other liquors:

CHAP. V. 1644.

June 21.

"WHEREAS, the general war, which we have been forced to wage against the surrounding savages, hath obliged us, in order to retain the country, and to employ an extraordinary quota of soldiers, who must necessarily be paid, together with the other heavy expenses caused by the war; to accomplish which we have spared none of the available means of the Hon'ble the West India Company, but have, in addition, been obliged to raise as much money as we could obtain on bills of exchange drawn on the honorable the directors; and, whereas, we are now devoid of all means, and despair of suddenly receiving any assistance from Holland, in this our necessity; We, therefore, are constrained to find out some means to pay the soldiers, or else to dismiss them, which, according to all appearances, will tend to the utter ruin of the country, especially as the farming season is at hand, whereby the people must live, and fodder must be procured for the remaining cattle; for neither grain nor hay can be cut without soldiers. These things, then, being gravely considered, so is it, that by the advice of the Eight Men chosen by the commonalty, no better nor more suitable means can be agreed upon, after duly weigh-

[1] Hierover heeft hem den Directeur seer vergramt, en met een gealtreert gemoet tegens ons (: in presentie van den Fiscaal en Montaigne:) gesecht:—Ick hebbe hier meerder macht als de Compagnie; dierhalven mach ick hiertelanden doen en laten wat myn gelieft; voochde daer verder hy, want ick en hebbe myn Commissie niet van de Compagnie, maer van de Heeren Staten. Letter of the Eight Men.

BOOK III. 1644. ing all the premises, than to impose some duties on those wares from which the good inhabitants will experience the least inconvenience, as the scarcity of money is very general:—

"We have, therefore, enacted and ordained, and hereby do enact and ordain, that there shall be paid on each 'half vat' (or barrel) of beer tapt by the tavern-keeper, two guilders, half to be paid by the brewer, and half by the tapster—the burgher who does not retail it, to pay half as much; on each quart of Spanish wine and brandy four stuyvers; French wine two stuyvers, to be paid by the tapsters; on each beaver-hide brought to the port, and purchased within our limits, one guilder; triplets and halves in proportion. All on pain of forfeiting the goods; one third for the informer, one third for the officer, and the remainder for the company. All this provisionally, until the good God should grant us peace, or that we shall be sufficiently aided from Holland."

June 24. The duties on the beaver were, subsequently, reduced to fifteen stivers, but it was ordered that all then on hand should be brought in and marked, under the penalty of being confiscated. These imposts, however, continued to cause much dissatisfaction. The commonalty, especially the traders, looked on the whole proceeding with an unfavorable eye, and Kieft seems to have attributed much of the discontent to the Eight Men. He took an early opportunity to manifest his displeasure against some of the most prominent members of that body. Towards the end of the month he sent for Joachim Pietersen Kuyter, Cornelis Melyn, and Thomas Hall, for the purpose, ostensibly, to confer further with them on the subject of these duties. June 30. These gentlemen waited on him accordingly. But instead of giving them an audience, he left them to dance attendance in his ante-chamber, from eight o'clock in the morning until past midday, without condescending to see them, though, as they allege, they had frequently sent in word by his servant, that they were in waiting to hear what he had to propose. They were, finally, obliged to depart to their respective abodes, "as wise as when they came."[1]

[1] Dat men de acht mannen met cleyne reputatie heeft bejegeert, en weynich syn geacht, hetselve hebben wy, onderschreven, in compagnie met Thomas Hal, by experientie bevonden, sulx dat den Heer Kieft ons, ultimo Juny, 1644,

While these quarrels and misunderstandings were going on between the Director-general and the Eight Men in New Amsterdam, the Dutch authorities at the Island of Curaçoa were much perplexed by the inopportune addition to the population of that place, of between four and five hundred persons, in the West India Company's service, who arrived there from Maranham, one of the northern provinces of Brazil, whence the Dutch had been expelled with severe loss by the Portuguese.[1] Curaçoa had already been frequently visited by failure of the crops and actual famine, and was, at this time, suffering from want of provisions. As it was impossible to furnish, or indeed to procure food for so many people, it was determined to remove the greater part of them to New Netherland, the Director of that place having already sent word that he was in want of men to assist him against the savages, with whom he was then at war. One hundred and thirty soldiers under the command of Captain Jan de Fries, and a number of other persons, the whole amounting to about two hundred souls, were accord-

May 18.

liet beroepen, wegens het opsteleen van den geëysten toll, en van 8 uyren tot over 12 in de saele heeft laten sitten, sonder dat ons een wordt werde gevraecht, alhoewel wy syn E. door den boode meermalen lieten aendienen, dat wy waren gecomen en daer wachten om aentehoeren het geene syn E E. ons geliefde voorstellen; doch ons is niet een wort tot openinge van 't syn E E. toegesonden, en hebben derhalven onverrecht de saecke wederom moeten vertrekken, soo wys alswy gecomen waren. Joachim P. Kuyter and Cornelis Melyn to Director Stuyvesant. 1647. Hol. Doc. iii., 192.

[1] While Portugal was under the dominion of Spain, Brazil was attacked by the Dutch, who got possession of seven of the fourteen provinces into which it is divided. They expected soon to conquer the other seven, when Portugal recovered its independence by the elevation of the family of Braganza to the throne. The Dutch, then, as enemies to the Spaniards, became friends to the Portuguese, who were likewise the enemies of the Spaniards. They agreed, therefore, to leave that part of Brazil which they had not conquered to the king of Portugal, who agreed to leave that part which they had conquered, to them, as a matter not worth disputing about with such good allies. But the Dutch government soon began to oppress the Portuguese colonists, who, instead of amusing themselves with complaints, took arms against their new masters, and by their own valor and resolution, with the connivance, indeed, but without any avowed assistance from the mother country, drove them out of Brazil. Smith's Wealth of Nations, ii., 63. A full report on this revolt against the Dutch in Brazil is to be found in Aitzema iii., 30 ; in Vaderlant. Hist. xii., 11, 12 ; and in Southey's Hist. of Brazil, ii., c. xxix. The W. I. Company estimated its loss at the hands of the Portuguese at 280 tons of gold.

BOOK III. 1644. May 26. ingly embarked on board the Blue Cock, commanded by Captain Willem Cornelissen Oudemarkt, for New Amsterdam, where they unexpectedly, but providentially arrived in the beginning of the following month of July, to the great relief and joy of the inhabitants, who were already beginning to despair of all succor.[1]

Kieft was now considerably embarrassed as to the disposition of this force; whether he should retain them at Fort Amsterdam or distribute them through the interior; and, if retained, how they were to be supplied with clothing and provisions. A meeting of the council was called to consider these grave July 21. difficulties. It was attended by the Director-general, Bastiaen Janssen Crol, Mr. La Montagne, Attorney-general Van der Huygens, Capt. Jan de Fries, and Capt. Oudemarkt, who determined to retain Capt. de Fries at the Manhattes; to fill up the ranks under his command with old soldiers to the number of one hundred and fifty men; and to dismiss gradually, "in the most civil manner," the remaining English soldiers. It was further concluded to billet on each of the commonalty, according to his rank and circumstances, one or more of the above soldiers, for whom the company was to pay whenever it should have means.

But clothing remained yet to be provided for these troops. The Director-general avowed his inability to furnish these necessaries. The company's stores were empty. Winter was approaching. "Naked men were useless; nay more, they were a severe burden." The council was again convoked. The same members again assembled, and they resolved to con-Aug. 4. tinue the duties and excise which had already been "provisionally" imposed, with a view to supply means to clothe the troops. The duties on beaver remained unaltered, but every tun of beer which the brewers sold to the tavern-keepers for twenty-two florins, or $8 80, was to pay three guilders, or a dollar and a quarter, while every brewer was required to send in a return of the quantity manufactured by him before he could dispose of any part thereof. Willem de Key was ap-

[1] Alb. Rec. ii., 260; xii., 49, 50, 52, 55; Hol. Doc. iii., 187; Winthrop's Journal, 342; Winthrop's N. England, ii., 179.

CHAP. V. 1644.

pointed receiver of these imposts, with an allowance of five per cent. for his trouble and loss of time.

Nothing could surpass the excitement produced by this arbitrary taxation. The first duties were imposed with the explicit understanding that they should be continued only until relief should arrive. That relief had now been received, but instead of proposing to remove the burdens temporarily enacted, a decree was issued to continue them indefinitely. And for what? For the clothing of the company's soldiers, when it was one of the company's obligations to protect its subjects from all foreign and domestic wars. If the settlers could be obligated to furnish clothing for the troops, they might, with equal propriety, be required to furnish ammunition, cannon, or transports. The tax in question was, moreover, arbitrarily imposed. The commonalty had its chosen representatives, whose prerogative it was, and not that of the paid and dependent servants of the West India Company, to impose these taxes, if necessary. It was, therefore, determined to resist the payment of the excise. The attorney-general was, on the other hand, ordered to collect the tax with the utmost rigor of the Aug 18.
law. The contumacious brewers were summoned before the same council that imposed the tribute, and asked why they refused to obey the placard? "Were we voluntarily to pay the three florins," they replied, "we should offend the Eight Men and the whole commonalty." But Kieft had no idea of being Aug. 25.
thwarted by such constitutional scruples. Judgment was given against the brewers, and thus another victory was achieved in New Netherland over popular rights.[1]

This triumph was, however, purchased, like all such victories, at the price of the peace and harmony of the community. Factions and party rent the citizens in twain. One section sided with the Director, the other with the EIGHT MEN; and henceforward the impression became a conviction, that neither justice nor the government was impartially administered. "Those on the Director's side could do no ill, how badly soever they demeaned themselves; those who opposed him were always wrong, however well they acted."[2] In the

[1] Alb. Rec. ii., 260, 261, 264, 265, 267

[2] Van der Donck, Vertoogh van N. N.

BOOK III. 1644. bickerings and personalities which ensued, the attorney-general seems to have had his hands full of prosecutions against individuals, for attacks on Kieft's character. One of these trials alone consumed six weeks of the summer, and that at a time when the Indians were prowling actively around unmolested, committing whatever damage they pleased on the inhabitants and their property, or attending, undisturbed, to securing their crops or their catch of fish. This waste of a valuable season was the more to be regretted, if not censured, since, by the arrivals from Curaçoa, Kieft now could bring into the field a force of between three and four hundred men, allowing still a sufficient number for garrison duty.[1] So strong was the opinion that this inaction was highly detrimental to the public interests, for already the Indians had commenced killing the Dutch settlers, that Thomas Hall and Barent Dircksen protested against the Director-general in strong terms for

Aug. 6. adhering to it. Cornelis Melyn wrote to M. van Nederhorst, and addressed a remonstrance to the States General, calling their attention, in urgent terms, to the deranged condition of things in the colony. The Eight Men also sent home a complaint, in the fall of the year, to the directors of the company, in which they reviewed at length, and in highly condemnatory terms, the course and administration of Director Kieft, on whose recall they insisted in the strongest manner:

Oct. 28. "We have been greatly gladdened," they began, "by the miraculous arrival of the Blue Cock here, as we expected that the field would be taken with between three and four hundred men, (not counting the sailors and settlers,) divided into three companies, each one hundred and thirty strong; and that by this force, the neighboring savages, from fifteen to twenty miles around, would have had their produce destroyed, and

[1] The following was the estimated available force at this time:

Men arrived in the Blue Cock	130
Old soldiers numbering between 40 and 50	45
English in the pay of the Dutch	50
Mariners willing to serve	55
Freemen, not including the English nor the company's servants	200
Total available force	480

Hol. Doc. iii., 187.

their tribes stript of all the provisions which they have collected against the winter, whereby great injury would have been inflicted on the enemy, and their people brought to terms. But nothing in the least has been done. In all this time, scarce a foot has been moved on land, or an oar laid in the water.

"The Indian prisoners, who could have been of great service to us as trusty guides, have been given away to the soldiers, and allowed to go to Holland. Others of them have been sent to the Bermudas, as a present to the English governor.[1] The oldest and most experienced soldiers, who were acquainted for several years with all the paths here, have obtained their passports, and been permitted to return home. In the mean while have the savages conveyed away, according to their pleasure, the fish caught by their people this last summer on the river, of which they made use as they wished, and without hinderance.

"Our fields lie fallow and waste; our dwellings and other buildings are burnt; not a handful can be either planted or sown this fall on the deserted places; the crops which God the Lord permitted to come forth during the past summer, remain on the field standing and rotting in divers places, in the same way as the hay, for the preservation of which we, poor people, cannot obtain one man. We are burdened with heavy families; we have no means to provide necessaries for wife or children; and we sit here amidst thousands of Indians and barbarians, from whom we find neither peace nor mercy. We have left our beloved father-land, and unless the Lord our God had been our comfort, we must have perished in our misery.

"There are among us those who, by the sweat and labor of their hands for many long years, have endeavored, at great

[1] The practice of reducing Indians to slavery is as old as the discovery of America. It was continued for nearly two centuries by the English colonies. In 1637 the colony of Massachusetts sent fifteen boys and two women as slaves to Bermuda, but the skipper having missed that island, took the consignment to Providence, and sold them there. Governor Winthrop bequeathed several Indian slaves by will; and frequent mention of such "chattels" is met with in the annals of New York. For a very interesting and instructive chapter on ancient and modern slavery, see Bancroft's U. S. i., 159, (10th Ed.)

BOOK III. 1644. expense, to improve their lands and villages; others with their private capital have equipped, with all necessaries, their own ships, which have been captured by the enemy in coming hither, though they have continued the voyage with equal zeal, and at considerable cost. Some, again, have come hither with ships, independent of the company, freighted with a large quantity of cattle, and with a number of families, who have erected handsome buildings on the spots selected for their people; cleared away the trees and the forest; enclosed their plantations and brought them under the plough, so as to be an ornament to the country and a profit to the proprietors, after their long laborious toil.

"The whole of these now lie in ashes through a foolish hankering after war; for all right-thinking men here know that these Indians have lived as lambs among us, until a few years ago, injuring no man, affording every assistance to our nation, and in Director Van Twiller's time, (when no supplies were sent for several months,) had furnished provisions to several of the company's servants, until, as they state, they had received supplies. These hath the Director, by various uncalled-for proceedings, from time to time, so estranged from us, and so embittered against the Netherlands nation, that we do not believe that any thing will bring them and peace back, unless that the Lord God, who bends all men's hearts to his will, propitiate their people; so that the ancient hath very truly observed: Any man can create turmoil, and set the people one against the other; but to establish harmony again, is in the power of God alone.

"A semblance of peace was attempted to be patched up last spring with two or three tribes of savages towards the north, by a stranger[1] whom we, for cause, shall not now name without one of the company's servants having been present, while our principal enemies have been unmolested. This peace hath borne little fruit for the common advantage and reputation of our Lords; . . . . . for so soon as these savages had stowed away their maize into holes, they began again to murder our people in various directions. They rove

[1] Captain Underhill; vide ante p. 302.

in parties continually around, day and night, on the Island of Manhattans, slaying our folks not a thousand paces from the fort; and 'tis now arrived at such a pass, that no one dare move a foot to fetch a stick of fire-wood without a strong escort.

CHAP. V. 1644.

"The two bouweries in 'the Bay,' and the three on this island, one of which belongs to the Honorable Company, run great danger of being burnt this winter, for never have these savages shewn themselves so bold and insolent. The cause of this is that they have experienced no opposition this summer from us, nor have lost any of their crops; and thus have they circumvented us by a stratagem under pretence of peace. Had the season, as we requested, been employed diligently, (which is most necessary in time of war,) with the force of the Blue Cock, beyond a doubt the Indians would have made advances themselves, and there would be some hope of enjoying, against the arrival of a new governor, a general peace.

"But little heed has been taken of this. The wished-for time has been allowed to pass away, and people have been occupied with private quarrels and prosecutions, especially about sending pearls [to Holland] by Laurens Cornelissen, Skipper of the Maid of Enckhuyzen, whose trial continued six weeks, and who was, moreover, banished. . . . . .

"Two guides have been recently sent from the north, with whom Captain De Vries was dispatched with a party, on the 22d instant, on an expedition to that country, killing eight men; but it is as men say, 'For every new enemy we kill, another stands next morning in his place.' We shall now have to wade through rivers and creeks, in frost and snow, with these new and naked soldiers, who have resided in warm climates for so many years. . . . . .

"A want of powder is again beginning to be felt. Over 2500 pounds were taken from Pieter Wyncoop, of which, up to this time, not five hundred weight have been consumed against the enemy.

"Little or nothing of any account has been done here for the country. Every place is going to ruin. Neither counsel nor advice is taken. Men talk of nothing else but of princely power and sovereignty, about which La Montagne argued a

BOOK III. 1644. few days ago in the tavern; maintaining that the power of the Director here was greater, so far as his office and commission were concerned, than that of His Highness of Orange in the Netherlands."

The Eight Men next refer, at considerable length, to the expedition against the Indians at Pavonia and Corlaer's Hook, in the beginning of the last year, and to the efforts of the Twelve Men to check that outrage; to the election of the Eight Men; to the supercilious manner in which these were always treated by Kieft; to the imposition of direct taxes against their will, as they pretended this power belonged only to the authorities at home. They then explain the proposition they had made to oblige the private traders to contribute to the support of the soldiers, while the other and more obnoxious plan was adopted, which they still join in condemning, at the same time that they put the directors on their guard against a "Book" "ornamented with sundry water-colors," which Kieft had transmitted to them by the Blue Cock, in which his Excellency treated in a very prolix manner about the origin of the war.[1] "It contains," say they, "as many lies as lines, as we are informed by the minister, and by those who have read it." They will not dispute, they add, about the nature of the birds which are in the forests, nor what sort of fish are in the rivers, nor about the length and breadth of the land, which is merely a copy of what has been written long years ago. "It would be well to inquire," they hint, "how the Director-general can so aptly write about these distances and habits, since his Honor, during the six or seven years that he has been here, has constantly resided on the Manhattans, and has never been farther from his kitchen and bedroom, than the middle of the aforesaid island."

Reverting again to the attack on "the shelterless Indians," on the night of the 24th February, 1643, the Eight Men detail the secret proceedings of those who planned that unfortunate expedition, preparatory to setting it on foot; and, prom-

[1] The fragment of the "Journal of New Netherland" found in the Royal Library at the Hague, by Mr. Brodhead, looks very like a part of this "book," for it inclines strongly to Kieft's side, and contains statements somewhat highly colored.

ising to send the directors at some future time a full account of what occurred in the country for the preceding six or seven years, they conclude : CHAP. V. 1644.

"Honored Lords—This is what we have, in the sorrow of our hearts, to complain of; that one man, who has been sent out sworn and instructed by his lords and masters, to whom he is responsible, should dispose here of our lives and property, according to his will and pleasure, in a manner so arbitrary, that a king would not be suffered legally to do. We shall terminate here, and commit the matter wholly to our God, whom we pray, and heartily trust, will move your Lordships' minds, and bless your Lordships' deliberations, so that one of these two things may happen ; that a governor may be speedily sent with a beloved peace to us, or that their Honors will be pleased to permit us to return, with wives and children, to our dear fatherland. For it is impossible ever to settle this country until a different system be introduced here, and a new governor be sent out with more people, who shall settle themselves in suitable places, one near the other, in form of villages and hamlets, and elect from among themselves a bailiff, or schout, and schepens (magistrates) who shall be empowered to send deputies to vote on public affairs with the Director and council ; so that, hereafter, the country may not be again brought into similar danger."[1]

The settlement of New Netherland experienced, as may now readily be conceived, a severe check by the continuance of the war. Some English families had, however, crossed the Sound from Stamford, in the spring, and commenced a plantation on the north side of Long Island, east of Martin Gerritsen's, or Cow Bay, at a quarter which the Dutch had already called Heemstede, after a place of some respectability of the same name, in the island of Schouwen, and province of Zealand. In the fall of the year they obtained a liberal patent of Nov. 16. incorporation from the Director-general and council, similar to that already granted to other towns, by which they were empowered to manage their own local affairs ; establish courts of limited civil and criminal jurisdiction ; and nominate such

[1] Hol. Doc. iii., 206–222.

BOOK III. 1644. among them as possessed public confidence, to be afterwards commissioned as magistrates of their town by the Director-general.[1] Both the English and the Dutch settlers placed a high value on the privilege of electing, and of being governed by, their own freely chosen magistrates.

[1] Heemstede . . . is het fraaste en belangrykste dorp des eilands, (Schouwen.) Martinet Beschryv. iii., 318. The patent will be found at length in Thompson's Hist. Long Isl. ii., 4, 5. Robert Fordham, John Sticklan, John Ogden, John Lawrence, Jonas Wood, and John Carman, were the first Patentees of this town. Caleb Carman, son of John, was the first white child born in Heemstede. He was blind from his birth, which took place on the 9th Jan., 1645.

CHAPTER VI.

Colonie of Rensselaerswyck—First settlers sent out by the Patroon—His jurisdiction—System of law in the colonie—Local courts—First magistrates—Population—Tenures—Patroon's privileges—Settlement of the Fuyck commenced—Beverswyck—Arrival of Adriaen van der Donck in the colonie, as Schout-fiscaal—First clergyman sent out—Agreement with him—Arrives with several other respectable settlers—A church erected—Its dimensions—Regulations concerning the Indian trade—Infractions thereof—Further regulations—Intrigues of Van der Donck—Threatened mutiny of the settlers—Return of the Mohawks from Canada—Are visited by Van Curler—Particulars of the interview with these tribes—Efforts to procure the release of a Jesuit and other French prisoners—Continued misunderstanding between Van der Donck and other local authorities—Van der Donck proposes to erect a colonie in Katskill—Orders from the Patroon forbidding this—Directs the dismissal of Van der Donck should he persist—The "Arms of Rensselaerswyck" sent out with a valuable cargo of goods—Arrives at the Manhattans—Difficulties between the supercargo and the authorities at New Amsterdam—Vessel and cargo seized—Protests and replications—Occurrences at Rensselaerstein—A vessel fired into while passing that place because she refused to lower her colors and bring to—Excitement in consequence—Prosecutions entered into against the commander of the post—Further protests—Death of the first Patroon—Nicolaus Coorn appointed Schout-fiscaal—Quarrel between Van der Donck and Van Curler—Departure of the former for the Manhattans—Severity of the winter—Destructive freshet, and visit of whales to Rensselaerswyck.

THE charter of 1629 having provided that every colonie should contain, within four years after its establishment, at least fifty persons over fifteen years of age, one fourth of whom should be located within the first year, the parties interested in the settlement of Rensselaerswyck lost no time in complying with these conditions. Early in the spring of the following year, a number of colonists, with their families, and provided with farming implements, stock, and all other necessaries, sailed from the Texel, in the company's ship the Een dracht, Capt. Jan Brouwer, commander, and arrived in safety at the Manhattes, after a passage of sixty-four days. In a short time afterwards they landed at Fort Orange, in the vicinity of which they were furnished with comfortable farm-houses and other dwellings, at the expense of the Patroon and

CHAP. VI. 1630. March 21. May 24.

BOOK III. 1630. his associates. Other settlers followed, with additional stock, each succeeding season, and thus were laid the foundations of those moral, wealthy, and prosperous settlements which we now behold in and around the present city of Albany.[1]

Invested as well by the Roman law, as by the charter, with he chief command and lower jurisdiction, the Patroon became empowered to administer civil and criminal justice, in person, or by deputy, within his colonie; to appoint local officers and magistrates; to erect courts, and to take cognizance of all rimes committed within his limits; to keep a gallows, if such were required, for the execution of malefactors, subject, however, to the restriction that if such gallows happened, by any accident, to fall, pending an execution, a new one could not be erected, unless for the purpose of hanging another criminal.[2] The right to inflict punishments of minor severity was necessarily included in that which authorized capital convictions, and accordingly we find various instances, throughout the record of the local court, of persons who had, by breaking the law, rendered themselves dangerous to society, or obnoxious to the authorities, having been banished from the colonie,[3] or con-

[1] Utgeef ende betaelinge van 't gunt Kiliaen van Rensselaer als Patroon, &c. tot behout van de gemelte colonie by zyn leven uytgegeven ende betaelt heeft. A translation of this highly interesting record of the expenses incurred for the removal of settlers, &c., to Rensselaerswyck in 1630, 1631, as well as a table containing the names of the first settlers, will be found in Appendix G, H. Sir Edmond Andros' report to His Royal Highness the Duke of York, anno 1678, bears honorable testimony to the labor of the first Patroon in settling the colonie. The date of the sailing of the Eendracht is given in Alb. Rec. i., 199.

[2] The name of the "Scherprechter," or hangman to Rensselaerswyck, will be found in the list of the early inhabitants of the colonie. The following is an item at the credit side of his account. "For so much coming to him for executing the late Wolf Nysen, fl. 38." Groet Boek, No. F. 96.

[3] The following translation of a sentence of banishment pronounced on one of the colonists will serve to illustrate the text. "By the President and Council of the Colonie of Rensselaerswyck. Having heard the free confession of Adriaen Willemsen, at present in confinement, to wit:—That he on Saturday last, the 6th of Aug., at the house of the Patroon, where the Commissary-general, Arendt van Curler, resides, climbing in through the window of said house, stole seven beavers, and at noon of the following Monday, eight beavers and one "drieling," [third of a skin]; also, that on Saturday aforesaid he had stolen from the cellar of the said house a half [skin] which remained. And having,

demned to corporal chastisement, fine, or imprisonment, according to the grade of their offences. CHAP. VI. 1630.

In civil cases, all disputes between man and man; whether relating to contracts, titles, possessions, or boundaries; injuries to property, person, or character; claims for rents, and all other demands between the Patroon and his tenants, were also investigated and decided by these courts; from the judgment of which, in matters affecting life and limb, and in suits where the sum in litigation exceeded twenty dollars, appeals lay to the Director-general and council at Fort Amsterdam. But the local authorities, it must be added, were so jealous of this privilege that they obliged the colonists, on settling within their jurisdiction, to promise not to appeal from any sentence of the local tribunal.

The laws in force here were, as in other sections of New Netherland, the civil code, the enactments of the States General, the ordinances of the West India Company, and of the Director-general and council, when properly published within the colonie, and such rules and regulations as the Patroon and his co-directors, or the local authorities might establish and enact.

The government was vested in a general court, which exercised executive, legislative or municipal, and judicial functions, and which was composed of two commissaries, ("Gecommitteerden;") two councillors, styled indiscriminately "Raets-persoonen," "Gerechts-persoonen," or "Raedts-vrienden," or "Schepenen," and who answered to modern justices of the peace. Adjoined to this court were a colonial secretary, a

moreover, examined the demand of the prosecutor against the aforesaid delinquent, observing what appertains thereto; We have hereby ordered and adjudged, and do order and adjudge, that the said delinquent shall be taken to the public place where justice is executed, and there be ignominiously tied to a post for the space of two hours, with some of the stolen property on his head; after which he shall prostrate himself at the feet of the Worshipful Magistrates, (de Edele Heeren van den Gerechte,) and beg of God and justice for forgiveness; that he, moreover, shall be henceforward, and forever, banished out of this colonie, and never more return thereto. Done in Collegio, this 13th day of August, anno 1644. By order of their worships the President and Council of this Colonie of Rensselaerswick. ARENDT VAN CURLER."

See also Van Tienhoven's Cort Bericht. Hol. Doc. v., 380.

BOOK III. 1630. sheriff, or "schout-fiscaal," and a "Gerechts-bode," court messenger, or constable. Each of these received a small compensation, either in the shape of a fixed salary or fees; the commissaries and magistrates, fifty, one hundred, or two hundred guilders annually, according to their standing; the secretary one hundred guilders; and the court messenger one hundred and fifty, with the addition of trifling fees for the transcript and service of papers. The magistrates of the colonie held office for a year, the court appointing their successors from among the other settlers, or continuing those already in office, at the expiration of their term of service, as it deemed proper.

The most important functionary attached to this government was, as throughout the other parts of the country, the "Schout-fiscaal," who, in discharge of his public functions, was bound by instructions received from the Patroon and co-directors, similar in tenor to those given to the same officer at the Manhattans. No man in the colonie was to be subject to loss of life or property unless by the sentence of a court composed of five persons, and all who were under accusation were entitled to a speedy and impartial trial. The public prosecutor was particularly enjoined not to receive presents or bribes, nor to be interested in trade or commerce, either directly or indirectly; and in order that he might be attentive to the performance of his duties, and thoroughly independent, he was secured a fixed salary, a free house, and all fines amounting to ten guilders, [$4,] or under, besides the third part of all forfeitures and amendes over that sum, were his perquisites.

Jacob Albertsen Planck was the first sheriff of Rensselaerswyck. Arendt van Curler, who originally came out as assistant commissary, was appointed, soon after his arrival, commissary-general, or superintendent of the colonie, and acted as colonial secretary until 1642, when he was succeeded by Anthony de Hooges. Brant Peelen, Gerrit de Reus, Cornelis Teunissen van Breuckelen, Pieter Cornelissen van Munickendam, and Dirck Janssen were, if not the first, at least among the earliest magistrates of the settlement.[1]

[1] Arendt van Curler was one of those characters who deserve to live in history. His influence among the Indians was unlimited, and in honor of his

The population of the colonie consisted at this remote period of three classes. Freemen, who emigrated from Holland at their own expense; farmers and farm-servants, who were sent out by the Patroon, who judiciously applied his large resources in promoting the early settlement of the country, and in assisting the struggling industry of his people. To accomplish this laudable object, a number of farms were set off, on both sides of the river and adjoining islands, on which he caused dwelling-houses, barns, and stables to be erected. CHAP. VI. 1630.

memory, these tribes addressed all succeeding governors of New York by the name of "Corlaer." He possessed feelings of the purest humanity, and actively exerted his influence in rescuing from the savages such Christians as had the misfortune to fall into their hands, of whose danger he might receive timely notice. On his marriage with Antonia Slaghboom, the widow of Jonas Bronck, he visited Holland, and on his return moved to the Flatts above Albany, where he had a farm. He was proprietor of a brewery in Beverwyck, in 1661. Being a cousin of the Van Rensselaers, he had considerable influence in the colonie, where he was a magistrate to the time of his decease. He was one of the leaders in the settlement of Schenectady in 1661–2; and on the surrender of New Netherland, was specially sent for by Governor Nicoll, to be consulted on Indian affairs and the interests of the country generally. He was highly respected by the governors of Canada, and the regard entertained for him by M. de Tracy, Viceroy of that country, will be best judged of by the following extract of a letter which that high personage addressed him, dated Quebec, 30th April, 1667:—

"If you find it agreeable to come hither this summer, as you have caused me to hope, you will be most welcome, and entertained to the utmost of my ability, as I have great esteem for you, though I have not a personal acquaintance with you. Believe this truth, and that I am, Sir, your affectionate and assured servant, TRACY."

Having accepted this invitation, Mr. Van Curler prepared for his journey. Gov. Nicoll furnished him with a letter to the Viceroy. It bears date May 20th, 1667, and states that "Mons'r Curler hath been importuned by divers of his friends at Quebec to give them a visit, and being ambitious to kiss your hands, he hath entreated my pass and liberty to conduct a young gentleman, M. Fontaine, who unfortunately fell into the barbarous hands of his enemies, and by means of Mons'r Curler obtained his liberty." On the 4th July following, Jeremias van Rensselaer, writing to Holland, announces, that "our cousin Arendt van Curler proceeds overland to Canada, having obtained leave from our General, and been invited thither by the Viceroy, M. de Tracy." In an evil hour he embarked on board a frail canoe to cross Lake Champlain, and having been overtaken by a storm, was drowned, I believe, near Split-Rock. In his death this country experienced a public loss, and the French of Canada a warm and efficient friend.

BOOK III. 1630. These farms were suitably stocked with cows, horses, or oxen, and, occasionally, sheep; and furnished with ploughs, wagons, and other necessary agricultural implements, all which preliminary expenses were defrayed by the proprietor, so that the farmer entered on the property unembarrassed by the want of capital, which often tends to impede the progress of settlers in new countries. Some of those farms were then valued, and an annual rent was fixed, equivalent in some sort to the interest of the capital expended on their improvement, and payable semi-annually in grain, beavers, and wampum. Other farms were let out on halves, or for the third of their produce; the Patroon was entitled, at the same time, to half the increase from the stock, and reserved to himself one-tenth of the produce of each farm, and in various instances stipulated for a yearly "erkentenis," or acknowledgment, of a few pounds of butter. The tenant was privileged, however, to compound, by the payment of a fixed annual sum, for the tenths of the farm, or for his halves or thirds. He was bound, at the same time, to keep the fences, buildings, or farming implements, in repair, and to deliver them up in the same good order in which he had received them, subject in all cases to ordinary wear and tear, but the Patroon bore all risks of destruction of the buildings, cattle, and other property which might accrue from war, or misunderstanding with the Indians. Wild or unimproved land was usually leased for a term of ten years free of rent or tenths, subject, however, to be improved by the lessee, all improvements falling to the Patroon on the expiration of the lease. In addition to the facilities above enumerated, each of the settlers, on leaving Holland, were, like those sent by the West India Company to the Manhattans, generally furnished with clothing and a small sum in cash, the latter to be repaid, at some future occasion, in produce or wampum, with an advance on the principal of fifty per cent. This, however disproportionate it may now seem, cannot be considered unreasonable or extravagant, when it is understood that the difference, at the time, between colonial and Holland currency was nearly forty per cent., while between the latter and the value of wampum it was vastly larger. The Patroon was bound, at the same time, to supply his colonists with a sufficient number of laborers to assist them in the work of their farms. As a compensation for his trouble in engaging these, and for his advances in conveying them to America, he was entitled to the sum of sixteen guilders, or six dollars, per annum for each laborer, over and above the yearly wages which the farmer was to allow such servants, and which ranged from forty to one hundred and fifty guilders, and board. This sum provided these servants with necessary clothing, and in the course of time placed at their disposal wherewith to enter on a farm on their own account. It is to be remarked, however, that the first Patroon seriously complained that his settlers not only threw altogether on him the payment of these wages, but took large quantities of goods from his store, for which they made no returns whatever, though they were bound to settle at the end of each year, and to hand in an account of the produce of the farm, distinguishing the Patroon's tenths, halves, or thirds, the amount paid for wages, and their own expenses, so as to allow him to ascertain what his own profits and losses were at the close of each annual term.

In return for his outlay and trouble, the civil code, which, it must be always borne in mind, was the fundamental law of this colonie, vested in the Patroon several privileges common to the feudal system. At the close of the harvest, the farmer was bound to hand in a return of the amount of grain which he had for sale, after deducting what was due to the landlord by the lease, and offer to him or his commissary the preëmption of such produce. In case he refused to buy it, then the farmer was at liberty to sell the same elsewhere. The like rule obtained in regard to cattle. When these were to be sold, the first offer was also to be made to the Patroon, in order, we presume, that he should have an opportunity of retaining the stock within the colonie. Every settler was, likewise, obligated to grind his corn at the Patroon's mill, and the latter was equally obligated to erect, and keep such mill in repair, at his own expense, for the accommodation of his colonists. No person could hunt or fish within the limits of the colonie, without license from the Patroon, who, on the exchange, sale, and purchase of real estate within his jurisdiction, was entitled to the first offer of such property; or if he

BOOK III. 1630. declined to resume it, to a certain portion of the purchase money, except such mutation occurred in the natural line of descent. Finally, it was his right, as "lord of the manor," to succeed to the estate and property of all persons who might die intestate within his colonie.[1]

Under the fostering care of its first Patroon, and the prudent management of its local magistracy, the colonie of Rensselaerswyck progressively, though slowly, advanced. Portions of its inhabitants occasionally returned to Fatherland, to spread the tidings of their prosperity, and to invite their friends and relatives to join them in their new homes, which, from the abundance and cheapness of provisions, deserved truly to be called "a land flowing with milk and honey."[2] A hamlet gradually arose. On account, it is said, of the crescent form of the bank of the river at this point, this hamlet was first
1634. called the "Fuyck," or "Beversfuyck," and afterwards "Beverswyck," by which name the present city of Albany was legally known until 1664, though it was familiarly called "the Fuyck," by the Dutch, for many years after the entire country had passed into the hands of other masters.[3]

[1] Charter to Patroons; Van Tienhoven's Korte Bericht; Jus Patronatus in Corpus Juris Civilis, t. iii.; Domat's Civil Law, t. ii., Van Leeuwen, 43, 44; Reght Gebruyck tegen het Misbruyck vande Openstaende reckeninge. [For a translation of this edict, in which the Patroon recapitulates many of the obligations of the colonists, see Appendix I.] Several of the above arrangements are common to all new countries, and still exist in the seignories of Canada, and in many manors in England.

[2] The creeks running through the settlement, as well as the river in front, abounded with fish; the woods with deer and other game. Pike and sturgeon were caught in the Fourth, or Fox, Creek, and one of the latter could be bought for a knife. "The year before I came here," (1641,) writes the Rev. Mr. Megapolensis, "there were so many turkeys and deer that they came to the houses and hogpens to feed, and were taken by the Indians with so little trouble, that a deer was sold to the Dutch for a loaf of bread, or a knife, or even a tobacco pipe." Short account of the Maquaa Indians.

[3] The names of the first hamlet, or village, are taken from the Rensselaerswyck MSS. The earliest mention I have met of "Beverswyck," or "Beverwyck," as the name is indifferently written, was in a minute, dated 1634, the original of which was on a small, almost illegible scrap of paper which I found accidentally among the above MSS. That the Dutch continued to call Albany "the Fuyck," long after the surrender of the country to the English, is evident from letters among the Rensselaerswyck MSS. "De huysen in de Fuyck" is

In order to give greater stability to his settlement, and to become better acquainted with its condition, Mr. Van Rensselaer, it is alleged, visited the colonie in person in 1637. His stay in the country, if he ever did come, was, however, not very long. The demise or resignation of Sheriff Planck now required the appointment of a new officer, and the peculiar position of the settlers, surrounded on all sides by rude and unconverted savages, demanded the guardian supervision and solacing comforts of religion, for as yet neither church nor clergyman existed in Rensselaerswyck. To secure an efficient administration of justice, and to provide a properly qualified clergyman for his people, consequently became a paramount duty.

CHAP. VI. 1637. 1640.

Adriaen van der Donck, "a free citizen of Breda,"—a lineal descendant of Adriaen van Bergen, part owner of the famous turf-sloop in which a party of Dutch troops were clandestinely introduced, in the year 1590, into the castle commanding that city, then in the hands of the Spanish, by which stratagem that stronghold fell into the hands of their High Mightinesses the States General,—and a graduate of the University of Leyden, was selected as the successor of Sheriff Planck. He entered on the performance of his duties, as schout-fiscaal of Rensselaerswyck, in the course of a month or two after his appointment, having, previous to his departure from Holland, taken a lease from the Patroon of the west half of Castle Island, called "Welysburg."[1]

1641. July.

an expression in one of S. van Cortlandt's letters, dated N. Yorck, 20th April, 1681, as well as in several others of an anterior date.

[1] De Laet makes mention, in his Hist. of the West Indies, p. 200, of one Adriaen Ver Donck, who was in the employ of the West India Company as commissary on the coast of Brazil, in 1630, and who was placed under arrest on suspicion of holding correspondence with the enemy, but liberated afterwards, as nothing tangible could be brought against him. Whether this individual and the sheriff of Rensselaerswyck were one and the same person, I have no means of determining. The following instructions from the Patroon to Van der Donck are among the Rensselaerswyck MSS.:

"Memorandum for the officer Adriaen Van der Donck, this 18th July, 1641, in Amsterdam. Whereas divers farmers pass by the carpenters and other of the Patroon's laborers, who not only must go idle, but, moreover, employ others and strangers out of the service of the Patroon, whom they must pay at a higher rate than his people, which tends greatly to the injury of the Patroon,

BOOK III. 1642. March 6. The Rev. Johannes Megapolensis, "the pious and well-learned minister of the congregation of Schoorel and Berge," under the classis of Alkmaer, was duly called to disseminate the light of the gospel among the Christians and heathen in the colonie, and regularly commissioned "to preach God's word there; to administer the holy sacraments of baptism and the Lord's Supper; to set an example, in a Christian-like manner, by public precept; to ordain elders and deacons; to keep and govern, by and with the advice and assistance of the same, God's congregation in good discipline and order, all according to God's Holy Word, and in conformity with the government, confession, and catechism of the Netherland churches, and the synodal acts of Dordrecht."[1]

March 22. The allowance guarantied to this clergyman was free passage

to the downfall of the colonie, to the transgression of his ordinances, and is directly contrary to their promises and concluded contracts: The officer is, therefore, charged to prosecute all such before the commissioners of the Noble Patroon, and to bring the matter also before the council of the colonie, (excluding those who may have been accessories to such proceedings,) in order to provide therefor by stricter statutes or ordinances, and to punish the delinquents by penalties and fines, agreeably to law. And in testimony of the truth, have these been signed on the date above written.

"Kiliaen van Rensselaer,

"Patroon of the Colonie of Rensselaerswyck.

"He shall also inquire touching the person who had charge of De Laetsburg, and was left there by Gerrit de Reus. The said bouwerie had, in May, 1638, among other things, thirty-one morgens of winter grain [winter coorn] taxed on the field, by four farmers, at five and seventy guilders [$30] the morgen [of two acres;] where the said corn has been left, and now is; if he hath fulfilled his engagements or not; if he hath been a defaulter; in fine, how it happened that from so great a number of acres, so little is forthcoming; and on discovery of the guilty, to punish them as an example to others, as more fully is mentioned in the letter to Arendt van Curler.

"Kiliaen van Rensselaer.

"In case the individual whom Gerrit de Reus left on the bouwerie, should refer (which I do not expect) to the heir of his master, let him be advised that the heir hath given me a procuration which I have sent to Director Kieft."

In the "Maentgelt Boeck van den 1638 tot 1649," kept in the colonie, Van der Donck's account opens on 9th Sept., 1641.

[1] This gentleman was the son of the Rev. Joannes Megapolensis, minister of Coedyck in Holland, and of Hellegond Jansen. He married his cousin Machteld Willemsen, daughter of Willem Steengs, or Heengs, who was his senior by three years. See Appendix J; also Alb. Rec. v., 323, 339.

CHAP. VI. 1642.

and board for himself, his wife and four children, who accompanied him to New Netherland; an outfit of three hundred guilders, or one hundred and twenty dollars, and an annual stipend, for the first three years, of eleven hundred guilders, ($440,) thirty schepels of wheat, and two firkins of butter, or in place thereof, should he prefer it, sixty guilders in cash. This salary was to be further increased by an addition of two hundred guilders a year, for the second term of three years, if the Patroon were satisfied with his services. A pension of one hundred guilders per annum was secured to his wife, in case of his demise within the above term, for and during whatever time might remain unexpired of his engagement.

These preliminaries having been thus arranged, an obstacle was unexpectedly thrown in the way of Mr. Megapolensis' departure by the directors of the West India Company, who claimed the exclusive right to approve of his appointment. To this, however, the feudal lord of Rensselaerswyck demurred; and it was not until after a lapse of several months that a compromise was agreed to, the directors approving of the appointment under protest on the part of Mr. Van Rensselaer, saving his rights as Patroon.

June 6. The Rev. Mr. Megapolensis and family embarked, together with Abraham Staes, surgeon, Evert Pels, brewer, and a number of other freemen, farmers, and farm-servants, shortly after this, in the ship the Houttuyn, or Woodyard, which was freighted with a quantity of goods for the colonie—between two and three hundred bushels of malt for Mr. Pels—four thousand tiles, and thirty thousand stone for building—besides some vines and madder, the cultivation of which the Patroon was desirous of introducing among his people.[1] On the arrival of Mr. Megapolensis at Rensselaerswyck, a contract was concluded for the erection of a dwelling for himself and family, Aug. 11.

[1] Mr. Pels erected a brewery in the colonie; Dr. Staes became one of the council in 1643, and was appointed president of the board in 1644, at a salary of 100 florins ($40) per annum. He obtained license to trade in furs, and had also a considerable bouwerie, besides pursuing the practice of his profession. He was the ancestor of the Staats of the present day, the original name having assumed shortly afterwards the termination it now bears.

BOOK III. 1642. but the contractor having failed in fulfilling his agreement, a house belonging to Maryn Adriaensen, constructed entirely of oak, was subsequently purchased for his use, for the sum of three hundred guilders, or one hundred and twenty dollars. For the convenience of the settlers at Tuscameatick, (as Greenbush, at the opposite side of the river, was called by the Indians,) a ferry was next established near the foot of the Beaver's Kill, (where it still continues to ply;) and as it was the Patroon's intention that the church, the minister's dwelling, the attorney-general's residence, and the houses for the tradespeople and mechanics, should be erected in one vicinity, so as to constitute a "Kerckbuurte," or settlement around the church, orders were transmitted that no persons (farmers and tobacco planters excepted) should, for the future, establish themselves, after the expiration of their term of service, elsewhere than in the vicinity of the church, and according to the plan now sent out by the Houttuyn; "for," it was justly observed, "if every one resides where he thinks fit, separated far from other settlers, they, should trouble occur, would be unfortunately in danger of their lives, as sorrowful experience hath demonstrated around the Manhattans."[1] A church, thirty-four feet long, and nineteen feet wide—the first in this quarter—was erected in the course of the following year. Though humble in its dimensions, when compared with modern edifices of a similar sacred character, it was considered, at this time, sufficiently ample for the accommodation of the faithful, "for the next three or four years, after which it might be converted into a school-house, or a dwelling for the sexton." A pulpit, ornamented with a canopy, was soon added for the preacher, as well as pews for the magistrates and for the deacons, and "nine benches" for the congregation. The expense of all this necessary furniture amounted to the sum of thirty-two dollars. While providing accommodation for the living, the dead were not forgotten. The "church-yard" lay in the rear, or to the west, of the Patroon's trading-house—in what is now very correctly called "Church" street: and in order "to be safe from

[1] Patroon's Memorandum for Dom. Megapolensis, 3d June, 1642. A translation of this interesting paper will be found in Appendix K.

the ravages of the Indians," the infant hamlet, living and dead, nestled close under the guns of Fort Orange.[1] CHAP. VI. 1643.

One of the principal aims of the first founders of Rensselaerswyck seems to have been to secure for themselves the valuable trade in furs, the chief mart for which centred at the point where they made their purchase and commenced their settlement. To engross this the more effectually, all foreign and unlicensed traders were rigidly excluded from the colonie. The Patroon and his partners were the only privileged importers of European merchandise, the company having, in con-

[1] The date of the erection of the above church is taken from Van Curler's letter to the Patroon, dated June, 1643, which will be found translated in the Appendix L ; Kieft, when proposing, in 1642, to erect a church in New Amsterdam, referred to the then contemplated erection of this church in Rensselaerswyck. That it was erected in 1643, is evident from Megapolensis' tract on the Maquaas, published in 1644, in which allusion is made to it. The expense of the pulpit, pews, &c., is taken from the " Groet Boek der Colonie Rensselaerswyck," anno 1645–6, p. 56, in which we find to the credit of " Willem Fredericksz" the following entry :—"Voor dat hy in de kerck heeft gemaakt een Predickstool, het verwulf, een stoel voor de overicheyt, een ditto voor de Diaconie, een cosyn met 2 lichten, een kruys cosyn dicht gemaackt, en daerin een kusje, een hoeckje nevens de stool, met een banck in een winckelhaeck, en 9 bancken, te saemen voor, 80 fl." This church was sufficiently wealthy in 1647, (May 29,) to loan 200 guilders to the Patroon, for which the Diaconie, or deacons, received the obligation of the colonial court, payable in one year after date, at 10 per cent. See account-book F. Rensselaerswyck MSS. ; also the obligation itself in the Gerechtsrolle. A new " stoop," or steps, was added in 1651, to the front of the above building, which accommodated the faithful until 1656, when a second church was erected at the junction of what are now State and Market streets. In 1715, a new church was erected on the latter site, including within its walls that of 1656. The church of 1715 was finally pulled down in 1806. Fort Orange stood at the lower part of what is now Market-street, nearly midway between Denisson and Lydius streets. The Patroon's trading-house was on the north side of the fort, on the verge of the moat by which the latter was surrounded. This trading-house disappeared some time previous to 1649, when the ground on which it stood was leased for " a garden" to Pieter Hertgers and Anthony de Hooges, at a rent of one guilder, or 40 cents, a year. In the lease was reserved the right to run a street through this " garden" " to the churchyard," [tot kerckhof,] which lay west of this lot, on what is now Church-street. The hof, or yard, of the Patroon's house lay north of the trading-house. The first location of Beverswyck, " near the bend of the river,"—" close by the fort"—" to be safe from the ravages of the Indians,"—is mentioned with minute precision in Alb. Rec. iv.

BOOK III. 1643. sequence of the war and other causes, ceased to keep Fort Orange supplied with foreign goods. All settlers were bound under oath not to purchase any peltries from the Indians, on pain of forfeiting their goods and wages, unless duly licensed to carry on such trade, for such a privilege was exclusively vested in the Patroon by the sixth article of the charter. The majority of the settlers subsequently obtained such permission; received goods on credit from the Patroon's store, and every farmer, as De Vries observes, became a trader. They were, however, obliged to bring in all the furs which they purchased to the Patroon's magazine, to be sent over to Holland to him, he retaining, as his share, half the profits. This condition was afterwards modified so far as to allow him to retain only the sixth beaver, and one guilder recognition, or duty, on each of the remaining five-sixths.[1] This system soon produced results which were naturally to be expected. Competition raised the price of peltries nearly one hundred per cent. Prior to 1642 the price of a merchantable beaver, which averaged about an ell square, was six hands, or fathoms, of wampum. In the course of that year the article commanded from seven to seven and a half; but when the traders found that the agents of the Patroon, as well as the officers at Fort Orange, did not refuse paying that price, they immediately offered nine; and in the following year advanced the rate to ten fathoms of white wampum for each skin. A joint proclamation was hereupon issued by the authorities of Rensselaerswyck, and those of the Fort, fixing the price of furs at nine fathoms of white, or four and a half of black wampum, and forbidding all persons whatsoever, whether servants of the company or residents in the colonie, from going into the woods to trade in advance with the Indians, on pain of seizure of all their goods. Another proclamation

[1] Rensselaerswyck MSS., Appendix I. Master Abraham (Staes,) Henrick Albertzen, Reyer Stoffelsen, Sander Leendertsen en anderen die met de Heer Patroon gecontracteert hebben om te moogen handelen waren gehouden alle de selve pelteryen, telcke reyse in specie het getal aentebrengen, ende aen de Patroon, en nymant vreemts overtesenden, ende daerenboven van yder beever een gulden en dan noch het seste part aenden Hr. Patroon, ofte zyn gecommitteerden te betaelen, op confiscatie van alle de pelteryen en voorts van al des effecten, volgens de voors. persoonen haer contracten. Gerechtsrolle ady den 3 December, 1648, in re Claes Gerrittsen.

was also issued, prohibiting all traders to come with their sloops within the limits of the colonie under the penalty of forfeiting the same. And on the following court-day a third proclamation followed, for the better securing the monopoly of the import trade to the Patroon, by which the inhabitants of the colonie were absolutely forbidden purchasing any goods from the local traders. Orders were given at the same time to Sheriff Van der Donck to enforce these regulations with strictness and severity. 1643

This functionary, between whom and Van Curler, and the other officers of the colonie, considerable jealousy and ill-feeling already existed, had no desire to render himself unpopular with the colonists. "He should not," he said, "make himself the worst man in the colonie, nor be suspected by the colonists, for his term as officer was but short." He therefore not only refused to enforce these regulations, but when, a few days afterwards, the colonists, contrary to the prohibitions of the court, did purchase duffels and sundry other goods which had been surreptitiously introduced, he connived at their proceedings, and either told the suspected parties to put their goods out of his sight, or neglected entirely to execute his duty, or to make any seizures. Not content with this disobedience of orders, he proceeded, next, secretly to foment feelings of discontent and mutiny among the people, before whom he placed the abovementioned placards in a most odious light, and whom he persuaded into the belief that Van Curler was endeavoring "to steal the bread out of their mouths." His representations had eventually such an effect on the public mind, that a conspiracy was formed against the commissary-general among several of the colonists, who drew up a strong protest against that officer, which, in order that they might remain undiscovered, the ringleaders signed in the form of a "round robin," by affixing to the paper their signatures in "a circle." This done, they next denounced Van Curler in the most vehement terms. Some proposed driving him from the colonie as a rogue; others, more vindictive and turbulent, insisted on taking his life. These threats, fortunately for the character of the settlers, were not followed up by any overt act. Van der Donck professed, all the while, an honest

BOOK III. 1642. desire to second the wishes of the constituted authorities. But when the time for testing his sincerity arrived, he was found wanting in the fulfilment of his promise.[1]

While these contentions and altercations were distracting the little hamlet of Beverswyck, intelligence was received Aug 15. that war-parties of the neighboring Mohawks had returned victorious from one of their wild forays against their hereditary enemies, the Hurons and the French, and had brought with them several Christians whom they had taken prisoners. Arendt van Curler, weighing well the necessity of maintaining, in the feebleness of the colonie, a good understanding with these wild tribes, and full of hope that he could rescue the French captives from their danger, proceeded, in company with Jan Labadie and Jacob Jansen van Amsterdam, to the country of the Mohawks, with suitable presents, in order to confirm the ancient friendship which had hitherto continued uninterrupted between them and the Dutch, and to obtain new guarantees for the security of the inhabitants and property in Rensselaerswyck. This visit was highly pleasing to the Indians, who detained, at each of their three castles, the Dutch ambassadors a quarter of an hour, until a salute was fired in honor of their visit, "for my arrival," writes Van Curler, "diffused great joy among them." Parties were sent out in quest of game, who returned with some "excellent turkeys," and feasting and good cheer gave substantial proofs of a sincere and hearty welcome.

Van Curler's benevolent mind was, however, ill at ease in the midst of these rejoicings. The Christian captives might be doomed to undergo, in a few days, at the stake, all the tortures which savage cruelty and ingenuity combined could invent to render death more terrific and appalling. Among the prisoners was the mild and disinterested Father Jogues, a learned Jesuit missionary—"one of the first to carry the cross into Michigan, and now the first to bear it through the villages of the Mohawks." Despising ease, comfort, life, and every attachment which nature renders dear to man, he preferred captivity, suffering, and mutilation, to an abandonment of his

[1] Van Curler's letter to the Patroon, Appendix L.

tender converts; and now awaited, in resignation and prayer, the crown of martyrdom for which his soul had so long panted. CHAP. VI. 1642.

To save these unfortunate men, Van Curler called together the chiefs of the different Mohawk castles. He recalled to their minds the friendship and alliance which had so long existed between them—and demanded the release of their captives, offering, at the same time, for their ransom, presents to the amount of six hundred guilders, which, to their honor be it recorded, the Dutch settlers of the colonie, forgetful of all differences of creed, and actuated by the holy impulses of the Gospel, had generously subscribed to purchase the freedom of their Christian brethren. The savages, however, were not to be moved, either by appeals to ancient friendship, or by the Dutchmen's presents. They were willing to grant to their allies whatever was in their power, but on the point under discussion they would remain silent. Curler well knew how the French treated those who fell into their hands. Had the chief not been successful in his attack, the Iroquois would have been burnt. For the liberation of the French prisoners he could not treat. In a few months the warriors of the several nations would assemble, and then the matter would be finally disposed of. All Van Curler could effect was to persuade the savages to spare the lives of their prisoners, and to promise to restore them to their country. Escorted by a party of ten or twelve armed Indians, the Dutch ambassadors now returned to Beverswyck, their minds filled with admiration of the lovely country through which they travelled.[1]

The disinterested missionary continued now to solace his captivity by spreading the light of Christianity through the benighted region into which Providence had cast his lot. Though his labors were most signally blest, and numbers of converts were brought into the fold, the hearts of the principal savages continued hardened against him. In one of his visits with some Indians to Fort Orange, he learned that intelligence had been received that the Mohawks were defeated by the 1643. July. 29.

[1] Daer leyt qualyck een halven daegh van den colonie, op de Maquaas Kill, 'dat schoonste landt dat men met oogen bezien mach. Van Curler's letter.

BOOK III. 1643. French at Fort Richelieu, and that he, on his return, would assuredly be burnt. The commander of the fort counselled him, thereupon, to escape. A vessel was about to proceed to Virginia. There he would be safe. Father Jogues demanded until the morrow to consider this proposal, "which greatly surprised the Dutch." The offer was finally accepted, but it was not so easy to evade the vigilance of his savage companions. Innumerable difficulties followed. He at length succeeded in secreting himself in the hold of a sloop in the river, where close air and a horrid stench made him almost regret that he had not remained among the cruel Iroquois, who now, enraged at the escape of their victim, crowded to Beverswyck, and demanded, with violent gestures and angry words, the surrender of their prisoner. The Dutch were much embarrassed. They could not consent to deliver over a Christian brother to the tortures and barbarities of the heathen. The States General had sent out orders that every means should be used to rescue from the savages those Frenchmen who might fall into their power. On the other hand, the colonie was too feeble to make any resistance. In this dilemma the offer was again renewed to ransom the fugitive; after considerable wrangling, the Indians accepted this offer, and presents to the amount of about one hundred pieces of gold were accordingly delivered them. Father Jogues was sent to New Amsterdam, where he was most kindly received and clothed by Director Kieft, who
Nov. 5. gave him a passage to Holland in a vessel which sailed shortly after. But misfortune was not yet weary of persecuting the Christian missionary. The vessel was driven in a storm on the coast of Falmouth, where it was seized by wreckers, who, as merciless as the savages, stripped Father Jogues and his companions of every article of their wearing apparel, and left them bruised and naked to pursue their journey as best they could.

1644. In the course of the following year Father Bressani, another Jesuit missionary, fell into the hands of the Iroquois. "Beaten, mangled, mutilated; driven barefoot over rough paths, through briers and thickets; burnt, tortured, wounded, and scarred, he was eye-witness to the fate of one of his companions who was boiled and eaten. Yet some mysterious awe protected his life, and he too was at last humanely rescued by the Dutch," who purchased his freedom at a large sum, and, with true Samaritan kindness, dressed his wounds and nursed him until he was perfectly convalescent, when they supplied him with clothing, "of which he stood in much need," and sent him to the Manhattans. Here he was received in the most hospitable manner by the public authorities, who furnished him, at his departure for Europe, with the following letter of safe-conduct:— CHAP VI. 1644.

"We, Willem Kieft, Director-general, and the Council of New Netherland, to all those who shall see these presents, greeting: Francis Joseph Bressani, of the Society of Jesus, for some time a prisoner among the Iroquois savages, commonly called Maquaas, and daily persecuted by these, was, when about to be burnt, snatched out of their hands, and ransomed by us for a large sum, after considerable difficulty. As he now proceeds with our permission to Holland, thence to return to France, Christian charity requires that he be humanely treated by those into whose hands he may happen to fall. Wherefore we request all governors, viceroys, or their lieutenants and captains, that they would afford him their favor in going and returning, promising to do the same, on like occasion. Dated in Fort Amsterdam, in New Netherland, this xxth September, anno Salutis, 1644, Stylo Novo." Sept. 20.

These and many other acts of similar kindness secured ever afterwards, for both the inhabitants and authorities, as well of Rensselaerswyck as of New Netherland generally, the warm attachment and regard of the Jesuit missionaries, who at the risk of health and life were disseminating the truths of the Gospel among the Indian tribes in the valley of the Mohawk, and along the shores of the great lakes, and who, it may be safely said, allowed no occasion to pass without giving expression to their gratitude and respect.[1]

[1] Van Curler's letter; Megapolensis' Short Account of the Maquaas; Charlevoix, Hist. de la Nouv. France, i., 240; Creuxius, Hist. Canadensis, 352, 386, 389, 391, 403; Bancroft's Hist. of the United States, iii., 132, 133, 134. The Rev. Father Jean Pierron writes to Mr. Van Rensselaer from "Tinniontogen," 6th Nov. 1667: "Je me tiens tellement obligé de l'honneur que j'ay reçu de vous à Schenecté qu'éternellement j'auray de l'affection pour votre

BOOK III. 1643. It became apparent now from the ill-feeling which existed between Sheriff Van der Donck and the other functionaries in the colonie, and which had already caused in two instances an exchange of blows, that the former could not comfortably prolong his stay in Rensselaerswyck, or hold his office, very agreeably, much longer. He determined, indeed, to return to Holland in the course of the next year, as he was desirous to become a Patroon himself, with which view he proceeded, with several colonists, to Katskill, to purchase the lands there from the Indians, for the erection of an independent colonie. But the moment the Patroon of Rensselaerswyck received intelligence of this "dishonest" move on the part of "his sworn officer," he immediately forwarded instructions to Van Curler, couched in the following stringent terms:—

"The Patroon of the Colonie of Rensselaerswyck having, on the sixth of this month, given a commission to Pieter Wyn-
Sept. 10. coop, commis. on board his ship, to purchase for a reasonable price from the natural owners and inhabitants, and from their chiefs, their lands lying about Katskill, in consequence of certain information which he had that Adriaen van der Donck, his sworn officer, dishonestly designed to purchase for him and his, to the prejudice of him, the Patroon, his lord and master, the said lands, lying under the shadow of his colonie. Therefore he, by virtue of the sixth and twenty-sixth articles of his Freedoms and Exemptions, doth claim that no person shall, against his will, approach within seven or eight miles of him; also,

compagnie, et de l'inclination à l'obliger, si jamais j'en ay l'occasion. Le noir et le blanc, ni la diversité de la réligion n'empêcheront pas cette amitié." And Father Joannes de Lamberville, who was a missionary at Onontague (Onondaga) in 1685, addresses Jeremias van Rensselaer in terms testifying equal respect for his character, though he never saw him—"Illustrissime Domine, Etsi de facie nec ego tibi, nec tu mihi cognitus sis, tuum tamen mihi nomen, tuaque mihi probe nota sunt merita, dignusque es cui quacunque datâ obsequy tibi deferendi occasione, pronœ voluntatis specimen exhibeatur." Viceroy Tracy, writing to Gov. Nicolls in 1667, also bears testimony to the humane conduct of the Dutch in these words:—"The French nation is too much inclined to acknowledge courtesies, not to confess that the Dutch have had very much charity for the French who have been prisoners with the Maquaas, and that they have redeemed divers, who had been burnt without their succor. They ought also to be assured of our gratitude towards them, and to any others who shall exercise such Christian deeds as they have done."

that he hath power to enlarge his colonie, on condition of planting a proportionate number of colonists there, which number was, even by this vessel, so increased that he hath already included the same, from Ransselaers-Stein down to Katskill, remaining on the same side, within his resort. And, further, having obtained certain information that such is, indeed, also true, the commissary-general, Arendt van Curler, together with the aforesaid Pieter Wyncoop, are charged not to inquire of the above-named Van der Donck if it be true, (inasmuch as the Patroon hath by him sufficient proof thereof,) but him to constrain, should he have done so, to desist, de facto, therefrom, and to cede and to make over to him, the Patroon, all whatsoever he hath acquired, conformably to his oath, having sworn to be true and faithful specially to him, his injury to prevent and his advantage to promote, both which in this matter have not happened; and in case the said purchase be not yet effected, that he, in presence of the commissaries and council of the colonie, do promise, under oath, not to proceed therewith, but to respect him the Patroon, and to afford to his (agents) all favor and help, that they may be allowed to make the aforesaid purchase to the best advantage; and should he refuse the one, or the other, to secure his person, inasmuch as he also endeavored, per fas et nefas, (met minne ofte onminne,) to return home in case the Patroon should not consent to discharge him; and inasmuch as the lease of his bouwerie, which he hath taken and agreed for in person with the Patroon, hath still long to run, which he cannot set aside without consent, but shall be bound to keep during that time. And in witness of the truth hath the Patroon subscribed these with his hand, and sealed them with his and the colonie's seal, in Amsterdam, this 10th September, 1643.

"KILIAEN VAN RENSSELAER,

[SEAL] "Patroon of the Colonie of Rensselaerswyck.

"In case Van der Donck should prove obstinate, he shall be degraded from his office, and left on his bouwerie to complete his contracted lease, without allowing him to depart, and his office shall be conferred, provisionally, on Nicolaus Coorn,

BOOK III. 1643. till further orders, divesting him of all papers appertaining to his charge. But if he will desist, then his office, and his bouwerie, shall he be allowed to hold. Actum as above.

"KILIAEN VAN RENSSELAER,

"in quality as herein above stated."[1]

This order, which had the effect of arresting Van der Donck's intended colonie at Katskill, was conveyed to New Netherland by the Patroon's ship, "The Arms of Rensselaerswyck," which was dispatched with an assorted invoice of merchandise, consisting of woollen, linen, and cotton goods, ready-made clothing, silks, glass, crockery, leather, fruit, cheese, spices, brandy, gin, wines, cordials, tobacco-pipes, nets, looking-glasses, beads, axes, adzes, razors, knives, scissors, bells, nails, spoons, kettles, thimbles, pins, needles, threads, rings, shoes, stockings, gloves, combs, buttons, muskets, pistols, swords, shot, lead, canvass, pitch and tar, candles, stationery, and various other commodities, valued at twelve thousand eight hundred and seventy guilders, to be bartered with the Indians and other inhabitants of the country for tobacco, furs, and other produce. To ensure entire success for this venture, the skipper, supercargo, and pilot of the ship were allowed a direct pecuniary interest in the proceeds of the voyage.

Sept. 12.

The system of licenses introduced by the Patroon, and the profits which resulted, had already incited a number of private individuals to embark in the fur-trade. As a consequence, this staple was altogether taken out of the hands both of the Patroon's and the company's servants, who could purchase scarcely a skin, while private traders exported thousands of peltries. A number of unlicensed traders now resorted to the colonie, who drew the Indians away into "secret trading-places," where, by means of higher prices, they got possession of the most valuable furs, "not caring whether or not the trade was so injured as to render the Patroon unable to meet the expenses of his colonie." Having thus "debauched" the

[1] Naerder ordre aen Arendt van Curler en Pieter Wyncoop wegen Katskill. Rensselaerswyck MSS.

savages, these interlopers succeeded next, by means of "wine and strong drink, which they sold at an usurious rate," in "perverting" many of the colonists, from whom they got, not only peltries, but even large quantities of grain, which the farmers disposed of without either respecting the Patroon's pre-emption right, or paying the tenths, or accounting for the halves or thirds which they were bound by lease to pay.[1]

To arrest these illicit proceedings, the Patroon adopted two measures which would, he expected, put a stop to the injuries which his interests were sustaining from the competition that was then exhausting and impoverishing his colonie. One of these was the erection of a fortified post and trading-house at Beeren, or Bear's Island, the southern boundary of his estate, which, by commanding the channel of the river, would exclude all vessels, but his own and those of the West India Company, from the upper waters of the Hudson. The other was, to send out a stock of goods sufficient to supply, through his establishments at Beverswyck and Beeren Island, the Mohawks and river Indians, and all the neighboring settlers, with whatever they may require in barter for their produce, whether furs or corn.[2] It was with a view to carry out the latter part of this project, that "the Arms of Rensselaerswyck" now sailed with the above-mentioned valuable cargo.

She arrived at the Manhattans while the war with the In-

[1] Insinuatie, Protestatie ende Presentatie van weghen den Patroon 8th Sept., 1643. Appendix M.

[2] The twofold character of the Patroon's establishment at Beeren Island—fort and trading-house—as all such posts in those days were—is clearly established by the following entry in the account current with Coorn, who had charge of the establishment:—Groet Boek, No. F., 23:

For merchandise according to invoice for Rensselearstein, on which is charged cent. per cent. advance	fl. 913.10
For materials for the armory ['t waepen huys]	671. 8
For carpenters' tools [timmergreetschap]	71. 7
For ammunition	1094.10
For paper, pens, and a flag besides	44.19
For necessaries for the boat	171.15

Beeren island is a small precipitous island, containing eight or ten acres, situate immediately south of Coeyman's landing. It was recently sold by Mr. Van Rensselaer for $500.

BOOK III. 1644. dians was at its height, and at the moment when Kieft was sorely distressed for clothing for the troops which he had enlisted. A requisition was immediately made on Pieter Wyncoop, the supercargo of the ship, for a supply of fifty pairs of shoes to be distributed among the soldiers, payment for which was offered "in silver, beavers, or wampum," at such price as the supercargo might demand. But Wyncoop, perceiving that he could sell these goods to more advantage to the inhabitants than to the Director, injudiciously refused to comply with this requisition. A forced levy was the result, and as many soldiers were equipped with shoes from the ship, as "killed five hundred of the enemy." The evil consequences of Wyncoop's refusal did not stop here. The ship was immediately overhauled by authority of the Director and council, and a considerable quantity of powder and a number of guns found on board, which were not enumerated in the manifest, and which Wyncoop was charged with intending to sell to the savages. These articles having been made contraband by law, and their introduction forbidden on pain of death, were, together with
March 8. the ship, forthwith confiscated.

Wyncoop now, too late, perceived the error into which either his instructions or his covetousness had plunged him.
March 17. In the hope, however, of retrieving his loss, he instituted an action against Cornelis Van der Huygens, the Fiscaal
March 18. at Fort Amsterdam, against whom he protested, in strong terms, for having unloaded his ship, which proceeding he pronounced an insult, a reproach, and a wrong inflicted on the Honorable Patroon, "the first and oldest patriot of the land," and for which aggression he now demanded redress from the Director-general and council. It was much fitter for the fiscal, he added, to discharge and to confiscate such ships as came and traded hither without any commission, and thereby brought contempt on the country and its government, than to affront a Patroon who hazarded so much for his colonists and New Netherland. He finally maintained that the powder which he had on board was for the ship's use, and for the defence of "Rensselaers-Stein," or Castle Rensselaer, as the
March 19. fortification on Beeren Island was called. This plea profited nothing. The powder was not mentioned in the manifest, and

the explanation which was offered was merely used as "a cloak" to cover the real design. "It is far from us," concluded the attorney-general, "to insult the Patroon. On the contrary, we are willing to aid him in promoting the welfare of his colonie. But it is you who are endeavoring to frustrate his noble plans, by associating exclusively with private traders, and striving to take them with you to the colonie in direct opposition to the commands of the Patroon, who hath sent out this ship to keep free traders from that place. If your conduct is just, free merchants cannot be prevented trading thither, and they will be justified in so doing. I deny that any damage whatever has been done. Are you of a contrary opinion? Cite me before any court of justice, whenever you please." CHAP. VI. 1644. March 22.

Arendt van Curler, finding that no satisfactory issue was to be expected from this litigation, finally proposed that the ship should be released, and the whole case referred to the Directors in Holland for their decision. As the vessel was suffering considerable injury from detention, this proposal was acceded to, "so that the Patroon should have no reason to complain;" on the express condition, however, that no goods should be landed from the vessel until permission was obtained from the company, and that such articles as were already seized by the attorney-general should remain confiscated, as they had not been included in the invoice. The vessel sailed soon after for Holland, whither Van Curler also proceeded to give an account of his stewardship.[1] Oct. 26.

In the mean time Nicolaus Coorn, "Wacht Meester," or commander in the service of the Patroon, had completed his fort on Beeren Island, on which he mounted a number of cannon, sufficient not only for its defence, but for the complete command of the river. A claim to "staple right" was then boldly set up; a toll of five guilders, or two dollars, imposed on every trading-craft passing up or down, which were also obliged to lower their colors in honor of Rensselaers-Stein. And thus a sovereign jurisdiction was asserted over this navigable highway against all persons, save and except the servants of the West India Company.

[1] Alb. Rec. ii., 244, 246, 277; iii., 192, 193, 194, 195, 277. Rensselaerswyck MSS.

BOOK III. 1644. It was in the summer of 1644, that the yacht the Good Hope, of which Govert Lookermans was master, sailed from Fort Orange for New Amsterdam. Passing Beeren Island, the craft was hailed, and peremptorily ordered "to lower his colors." On being asked for whom, the commander replied, "For the staple right of Rensselaerswyck." But the skipper refused, with an oath, to strike his flag "for any individual save the Prince of Orange and the Lords his masters;" where-
July 5. upon Coorn fired several shots at the vessel, one of which, says the record, "perforated our princely flag," about a foot above the head of the skipper, "who kept the colors constantly in his hand."

Such an outrage as this could not fail to create excitement at New Amsterdam, when the particulars became known. Philip de Truy, "marshal of New Netherland," summon-
Aug. 2. ed Coorn to appear immediately at the Fort to answer for
Oct. 8. his conduct. The latter pleaded the authority of his Patroon. But this was considered no justification. He was condemned in damages, and forbidden to repeat the offence on pain of corporal punishment. He was further required to obtain Van Rensselaer's approval of the sentence, which should be executed on him without fail, if that approval were not forthcoming. This proceeding was followed soon after by a strong protest from Attorney-general Van der Huygens, against the establishment on Beeren Island, which was declared to be inconsistent with the privileges granted to Patroons and lords of manors. No Patroon, it was maintained, could extend his colony, by the fifth article of the charter, more than four miles along one bank, or two miles on both sides of the river, while Beeren Island was more than two miles from the limits of the colonie. The bold attempt to construct a fort there, to command the river, and to debar Fort Orange from free navigation, would, it was added, be ruinous to the company; it was therefore peremptorily ordered that no building whatsoever, much less a fortification, should be constructed beyond the limits of Rensselaerswyck, and Coorn was formally threatened with further prosecution should he persist in his lawless transactions.

But Nicolaus Coorn, commander of Rensselaers-Stein,

was not to be intimidated by the paper bullets of Director Kieft's attorney-general. "As the vice-commander of the Honorable Van Rensselaer," he replied, "I call on you, Cornelis van der Huygens, attorney-general of New Netherland, not to presume to oppose and frustrate my designs on Bear's Island; to defraud me in any manner, or to cause me any trouble, as it has been the will of their High Mightinesses the States General, and the Privileged West India Company, to invest my Patroon and his heir with the right to extend and fortify his colonie, and make it powerful in every respect. . . If you persist in so doing. . . . . I protest against the act of violence and assault committed by the Honorable Lords Majors, which I leave them to settle, while this undertaking has nothing else in view than to prevent the canker of free traders entering his colonie."[1]

CHAP. VI. 1644. Nov. 18.

In the spirit in which this protest was drafted, were the feudal pretensions of the Lord of Rensselaerswyck asserted and maintained, notwithstanding the conviction of Coorn and the warning of Van der Huygens, during the remainder of the Patroon's life. The same policy was steadily continued by his executors for several years after his death, which event took place in Amsterdam, in the year 1646.[2]

1646.

With the demise of the first Patroon terminated, also, Van der Donck's connection with the colonie. He was succeeded in his office of "fiscaal" by Nicolaus Coorn. He did not, however, quit Rensselaerswyck before experiencing a heavy loss in the destruction of his house on Castle Island by fire, in consequence of which he and his wife temporarily removed to Van Curler's residence, the hospitalities of which were generously offered to him by its proprietor. Differences of opinion now arose between him and Van Curler, as to the party on whom the loss of the house should fall; one maintaining that the property was at the risk of the Patroon; the other, of the lessee. A quarrel ensued. Van der Donck gave Van Curler the lie, whereupon the latter ordered him out

Jan 17. Feb. 23.

[1] Alb. Rec. i., 90; ii., 2, 35, 192, 234, 235, 263, 273, 275; iii., 187, 188, 219. Van Tienhoven, Corte berichte. Hol. Doc. v., 364.

[2] A debit and credit account of Kiliaen van Rensselaer's estate in Holland, at the time of his decease, will be found in Appendix N.

BOOK III. 1647. of his house. Van der Donck removed immediately to Fort Orange, where he remained until the opening of the navigation, when he proceeded to the Manhattans. In the mean
April 28. time, his claims were referred for adjustment to the proprietors in Holland.[1]

The winter which had just terminated, was remarkably long and severe. The North River closed at Rensselaerswyck on the 25th November, and remained frozen some four months. A very high freshet, unequalled since 1639, followed, which destroyed a number of horses in their stables; nearly carried away the fort, and inflicted considerable other damage in the colonie. "A certain fish of considerable size, snow-white in color, round in the body, and blowing water out of its head," made at the same time his appearance,
March 29. stemming the impetuous flood. What it portended, "God the Lord only knew." All the inhabitants were lost in wonder, for "at the same instant that this fish appeared to us, we had the first thunder and lightning this year." The public astonishment had scarcely subsided, when another monster of
April 19. the deep, estimated at forty feet in length, was seen, of a brown color, having fins on his back, and ejecting water in like manner, high in the air. Some seafaring people, "who had been to Greenland," now pronounced the strange visiter a whale. Intelligence was shortly after received that it had grounded on an island at the mouth of the Mohawk, and the people turned out in numbers to secure the prize, which was, forthwith, subjected to the process of roasting, in order to extract its oil. Though large quantities were obtained, yet so great was the mass of blubber, the river was covered with grease for three weeks afterwards, and the air infected to such a degree with the stench, as the fish lay rotting on the strand, that the smell was perceptibly offensive for two (Dutch) miles to leeward. The whale, which had first ascended the river, stranded, on its return to sea, on an island some forty miles from the mouth of the river, near which place four others grounded, also, this year.[2]

[1] The minute of the quarrel between Van Curler and Van der Donck, together with the minute of reference of the latter's claims, will be found in Appendix O.

[2] These particulars are taken from an old book kept by Antonie de Hooges,

CHAPTER VII.

States General order an inquiry into the condition of New Netherland—Proceedings of the XIX.—Kieft recalled—Van Dinclage appointed, provisionally, in his place—Interesting report on the state of New Netherland—Recommendations contained therein—Proposed civil list—Modifications in the government, trade, &c.—Some Indian tribes desire a cessation of hostilities—Several of the Long Island tribes come in—Kieft concludes a peace at Fort Orange with the Mohawks and Mohegans—General peace between the aborigines and the Dutch—Low condition of the colony—Thanksgiving ordered—additional purchases on Long Island—Orders received to explore the country for minerals—Proceedings in consequence—The ship by which specimens were sent to Holland, founders at sea, and all on board perish—Petrus Stuyvesant, Director at Curaçoa, besieges the island of St. Martin—Is obliged to raise the siege—Receives a severe wound—Returns to Holland—Is appointed Director-general of New Netherland—Submits a plan for the better management of the company's transatlantic possessions—Further changes proposed regarding the colonial trade—Differences of opinion in the Assembly of the XIX.—Departure of Stuyvesant postponed—New Netherland continues under the mismanagement of Kieft.

CHAP. VII. 1644.

THE affairs of New Netherland had now reached a crisis which necessitated again the intervention of the States General. Complaint had followed complaint from that country—mismanagement had accumulated on mismanagement in the administration of its affairs, and an inquiry could no longer be postponed. The country was a source of no profit to the West India Company; the opening of the trade had not advanced its settlement, for those whom commerce attracted thither, remained not in the province. They deranged the trade, but did not add to the population. Their High Mightinesses, in appointing deputies this year to the Assembly of the XIX., instructed them, particularly, to inquire whether it would not be better to confine the trade with the interior of

Secretary of Rensselaerswyck, endorsed, "Copye van eenige acten ende andere aenmerckelycke notitien," and from Van der Donck's Beschryv. van N. N. The island at the mouth of the Mohawk goes since by the name of Walvisch, or Whale Island. De Hooges refers to the visit of a similar large fish "many years ago," which caused great wonder at the time, but he does not mention the year, nor furnish any further particulars of the circumstance.

BOOK III. 1644. New Netherland to the resident inhabitants of that quarter, and to grant these the additional privilege of trading to Brazil, and thence back to the Manhattes; and enjoined, at the same time, on those delegates, to report fully on the condition of the country, as well as to state what, in their opinion, was required to promote its welfare and prosperity.

The whole subject of the war between the Indians and the Dutch, its origin, progress, and unfortunate consequences, were discussed, accordingly, at this meeting of the various branches of the company, and the complaints of the colonists fully considered. Dec. 10. The immediate result was, the recall of Director Kieft, in order that he should justify the various acts of his administration, and the appointment, provisionally, in his place, as Director, of Lubbertus van Dinclage, who had previously served in New Netherland as schout-fiscaal, and was "well liked by the Indians."[1] It was further resolved, to refer all the letters and papers from the colonists, as well as those relating to the affairs of the colony, to the company's Rekenkamer, or chamber of accounts, to examine the same, and to report to the next Assembly of the XIX. in what manner the injuries which the colony had sustained could be repaired, its population advanced, and itself rendered profitable to the company.[2]

[1] Mr. Van Dinclage had been dismissed from office, it will be recollected, by Van Twiller, in 1636. He had been since that time a yearly applicant to the XIX. and to the States General for redress, his salary during three years that he had been in office having been withheld. He had, in the interim, sued the company for his wages; without any success, however, for we find him, even now, eight years after his dismissal, still petitioning for his pay. A compromise seems to have been, at last, effected with him, though the Amsterdam chamber of the company does not appear to relish his appointment as Kieft's successor, even provisionally. Full details of his struggles against the company will be found in Hol. Doc. ii., 167, 169, 171, 173, 177, 178, 179, 180, 181, 182, 232, 275, 313, 316, 318, 321, 322.

[2] In order to remedy various disorders which had crept into the affairs of the West India Company, a bureau, or board of accounts, was established in 1643, consisting of six accountants; two from the Amsterdam chamber, and one from each of the other departments. It was the duty of these to consider what should be prepared for the meeting of the XIX., and to assist that Assembly with their advice; to keep accounts with all the chambers in the United Provinces, and the foreign conquests, and therefrom to form a general book, which should at

CHAP. VII. 1645. March.

A copious and most interesting report followed this reference. Tracing the growth and progress of New Netherland from its discovery to the incorporation of the West India Company; thence to the passing of the charter to the Patroons; after that, to the breaking out of the war, and then detailing the ruin which this involved on that fertile country, it proceeded to pass in review the various propositions which Director Kieft and the Eight Men had submitted, to correct, as well as to prevent the recurrence of the existing unfortunate state of things. The former, estimating the Indians only at three hundred strong, advised their extermination, and demanded, for that purpose, a force of one hundred and fifty soldiers. The others, calculating the enemy at some thousands, were of opinion that their destruction was impossible, and that the tranquillity of the country would be better secured by a general peace, of which, however, they entertained but slender hope, so long as Kieft remained at the head of affairs, as the Indians entertained a particular aversion against him. They recommended that colonists, in order to obviate future wars, should be obliged to settle nearer each other in towns and villages, so as to be better able to assist one another in time of danger; that Fort Amsterdam should be repaired, as it was now in such a ruinous condition that men strode over the walls instead of going through the gate; and that it should be built of stone, the expense attending which, was estimated at from twenty to twenty-five thousand guilders, or $10,000. The settlement of the bounds between the English and Dutch possessions was particularly urged, as well as the promotion of the population of the country, by crediting emigrants with the cost of their passage, and by the introduction of a large number of field-laborers and negroes. New Netherland, it was next advised, should be made a rendezvous for ships of war, being better adapted for that purpose than Curaçoa, by its abundance of provisions and building-timber, and the

all times exhibit the condition of the company; to make a repartition of the expenditure and income, and decide all disputes arising therefrom; also, to maintain good correspondence between all the chambers, and to cause the resolutions of the XIX. to be immediately and diligently executed. Hol. Doc. iii., 321.

BOOK III. 1645. readiness with which vessels can thence reach the West Indies, and there discover the designs of the enemy. It was further demanded that the company should maintain a well-furnished store and cellar at New Amsterdam, for the supply of necessaries, at certain reasonable prices, for cash or barter, to the inhabitants, who otherwise would be seriously imposed upon by private traders. Should these private traders be, however, allowed to remain, it was urged that they should be bound to dispose of their goods at a certain fixed price. Finally, the colonists demanded that the Director's council be composed of four or five members, in order that justice and the authority of the company may be efficiently maintained, and the respect of the neighboring provinces properly secured.

It will be seen from the preceding review, continues this report, into what ruin and confusion New Netherland has fallen, in consequence of foolishly waging an unnecessary war without either the knowledge or the authority of the XIX. here, and in opposition to the will of the commonalty there; and what excessive advances are now required to repair existing misfortunes. No returns have been made for several years. That country, on the contrary, has cost the company, as it appears from their books, over half a million of guilders, [$220,000,] from the year 1626 to the year 1644 inclusive, over and above the returns received from thence; so that it is very questionable if the company would not be more benefited by the loss altogether of New Netherland, than by the continuance of these heavy expenses. As it was impossible for the directors, however, to disembarrass themselves of this charge consistently with their obligations, and as there was still a prospect that matters were not irremediable, it was recommended that some effort should be made to improve the country, by settling such questions as were still undecided, and by introducing such reforms as prudence and experience might suggest.

With this view, it was advised that the differences between the Dutch and their English neighbors at the east should be settled as early as possible, and then that such of the latter as were found to be on Dutch soil, should be obliged to submit to Dutch jurisdiction and government, and be considered as original subjects. Immediate peace with the Indians was, above all things, advised, as it would be "not only impossible but unchristian" to adopt the exterminating advice of the Director-general, whose recall, as well as that of his council, is particularly insisted upon, in order that they may show cause for, and justify to the Assembly of the XIX., the manner in which they administered the public affairs, especially "the bloody exploit of which they were guilty on the 28th February, 1643;" and that a person be sent out, as Director, duly qualified, on the one hand, to advance the interests of the company, and the welfare of the commonalty; on the other, to maintain a good understanding with the English, and more particularly with the Indians.

CHAP. VII. 1645.

The plan of forming hamlets and villages in New Netherland, after the manner of New England, was highly approved of; it was advised that Fort Amsterdam should be repaired "with good clay and firm sods" by the soldiers, at the smallest possible expense, and a schedule was submitted with the report, of the establishment which it was considered advisable to maintain in the colony for the administration of its affairs as well as for the garrisoning of the above fort, the total annual expense of their support being estimated at twenty thousand and forty-six guilders, or eight thousand and sixteen dollars of our currency.[1] This force amounted in all to sixty-nine

[1] Estimate of the expenses to be defrayed by the West India Company, according to the above plan:—

1 Director,	Yearly,	fl.	3,000
1 Second, to act as koopman and receiver,	"		1,440
1 Fiscaal,	"		720
1 Secretary and bookkeeper,	"		720
1 Clerk of Merchandise,	"		720
1 Assistant,	"		300
1 Clergyman,	"		1 440
1 Schoolmaster, reader, and sexton,	"		360
1 Constable,	"		240
1 Provost,	"		180
1 Corporal, to act as gunsmith,	"		180
1 Commander,	"		720
Carried forward,			10,040

BOOK III. 1645. persons, fifty three of whom were military; but to make up for the small number of the latter, the colonists were to be bound to provide themselves and servants, under certain penalties, with fire-arms and other weapons, to act, in case of need, as a reinforcement to the garrison, for, hereafter, the Director, colonists, and all others, were to be expressly forbidden to engage any soldiers, whether few or many, at the expense of the company.

It was next advised that the Council of the New Netherlands should consist of three persons; namely, the Director-general, as president; the Second, or Vice-director; and the Fiscaal, as adjoined counsellor, by and before whom all matters touching police, justice, the sovereignty and rights of the company should be treated and decided; with the understanding, however, that in criminal affairs the commander take the place of the fiscaal; two capable persons being adjoined to the court from among the commonalty. As the respective colonies were allowed, by the 28th clause of the charter of 1629, to depute one or two persons, at least every twelve months, to acquaint the Director and council of the state and condition of their colonies, it was now suggested that those deputies should, at the summons of the Director-general, hold an Assembly every six months, for mutual intercommunication, and the general advancement of the welfare of the people, with power, moreover, to deliberate on all questions which might concern the prosperity of their colonies, the propitiation of the Indians, and the neighboring provinces, the mainte-

	Brought forward,		10,040
1	Ensign,	Yearly,	540
2	Sergeants,	"	600
2	Corporals,	"	432
1	Drummer,	"	156
4	Cadets,	"	720
40	Soldiers,	"	6,240
1	Surgeon,	"	300
1	Skipper,	"	300
4	Sailors,	"	624
1	Boy,	"	108
			fl. 20,040
			$8,016

nance of free privileges, the correction of abuses, and the upholding of the statutes and the laws. The Amsterdam standard of weight and measure only, was, however, to be used throughout the whole country. CHAP. VII. 1645.

Emigration from Holland was recommended to be facilitated by every means, in order to promote the peopling and settlement of the New Netherland, especially of the island of Manhattans, where settlers, it was suggested, should obtain as much land as they could cultivate, either by planting tobacco, "for which the soil was considered well adapted," or grain, or other produce, as they might find most profitable. And it was further added, that it would be wise to permit the Patroons, colonists, and other farmers, to import as many negroes from the Brazils as they could purchase for cash, to assist them on their farms; as (it was maintained) these slaves could do more work for their masters, and were less expensive, than the hired laborers engaged in Holland, and conveyed to New Netherland, "by means of much money and large promises."

The Patroons, colonists, and freemen inhabiting the country, should, it was further recommended, have the exclusive right to trade with the natives, from which all commission-merchants should be rigidly excluded, contenting themselves with the privilege of being allowed to exchange their cargoes with the inhabitants for peltries, tobacco, wheat, and other produce of the country. But on no account were munitions of war to be sold by the freemen to the Indians, nor by the importers to the freemen. The latter, however, were, as already suggested, to provide themselves for self-defence with one good musket and a set of side-arms, which were to be inspected every six months by the Director-general.

The Assembly of the XIX. were strongly advised to consider, if it would not be for the advantage of the colonists to permit them to trade directly with the Brazils, as they could export thither meal, groats, peas, beans, pipe-staves, plank, and other timber useful for ship and house-building; and to encourage the fisheries by allowing them, and none other, to sell the fish and caviary caught, salted down and pickled there; with the privilege of taking salt on the coast of Brazil, about Siara, or the West Indies; to use the same for the preserving

BOOK III. 1645. of green and dry fish; also to erect salt-pans in New Netherland to refine the above, in order to furnish fine salt for the cure of fish and meat; on the condition, however, of delivering all such exports into the company's stores at the Brazils, and on paying, in specie or coin, the proper duties, to sell their cargoes, without, however, being allowed to take away any money or specie in return, but only slaves, sugars, confectionary, ginger, tobacco, cotton, and other produce of the country, after having duly entered the same; to sail therewith to New Netherland direct, and neither to sell or exchange any part thereof on any pretext whatsoever, receiving a supercargo from the company to furnish a correct report of the voyage, and binding themselves to touch at Paraiba, to be there visited by the company again, so that all chance of smuggling may be obviated, and the payment of the proper duties secured, which now, the report concluded, should be strictly enforced on all imports and exports, in order that the increased expenses may be met and defrayed, and that some profit may accrue afterwards to the company on account of the increase of population.[1]

Spring, in the mean time, brought with it, as usual, a desire on the part of the Indians for a cessation of hostilities. Some tribes presented themselves at Fort Amsterdam with whom a
April 22. peace was concluded, in honor of which "a grand salute of three guns" was fired by Jacob Jacobsen Roy, who, however, unfortunately received a severe injury in the discharge of this duty, by the explosion of one of these pieces, which caused him to be a long time under the care of Surgeon Kierstede, and ultimately deprived him of the use of his arm. A large number of the enemy still continued the war, and it was therefore resolved, at a meeting of the council, at which the Director-general, M. La Montagne, the attorney-general, Captains Underhill and De Vries, Ensign de Leeuw, Oloff Stevensen, and Gysbert Op Dyck, commissaries, and Jan Evertsen Bout, and Jacob Stoffellsen, delegates, attended, to take some of the friendly Indians into the public service, and employ

[1] Hol. Doc. ii., 368–395. A translation of the above report will be found, at length, in Appendix E.

them against the enemy. Whiteneywen, sachem of the Mockgonecocks, from Long Island, was therefore engaged, with forty-seven of his warriors, and dispatched by water, with a commission to do all in his power "to beat and destroy the hostile tribes." He returned in a few days, empowered by Rockow, surnamed the Greatest, chief of the Cotsjewanninck's; Mamawicktow, chief of Cotsteyick; Weyrinteninck, chief of Meranta-hacky, to declare that he and they had taken under their protection the villages of Ouheew-hacky, Suchtahacky, Sichetany-hacky, Nisingqueeg-hacky, (at which place the Matinecocks were then residing,)[1] and Rechou-hacky, all which desired to make peace with the Dutch, for whom he pledged himself, that neither they nor any of their tribes should in any way injure the Christians; but, on the contrary, treat them with respect, and as a proof of his sincerity, he now proffered "the head and hand of one of our enemies." A treaty of peace was accordingly entered into with the foregoing tribes, in ratification of which a present was made to the Sachem Whiteneywen, and pledges exchanged of eternal amity.[2]

CHAP. VII. 1645. May 24. May 29.

Having thus succeeded in creating division among his enemies, Kieft turned his attention to the propriety of securing the friendship of the dreaded Mohawks residing around Fort Orange, whose name alone inspired terror among all the tribes west of the Connecticut, over whom they claimed to be sovereign, and from whom they exacted tribute. With this view, he repaired, with Counsellor La Montagne, to that post. Here, assisted by the officers and authorities of Rensselaerswyck, he succeeded in negotiating a treaty not only with that powerful nation—the strongest and fiercest of the country—but with the Mohegans, or Mahicanders, and the other neighboring tribes. To make suitable presents to the savages, in token of the ratification of this peace, Kieft was, however,

[1] The Matinecock Indians claimed jurisdiction over the lands east of Newtown as far as the west line of Smithtown, and probably to the west side of Nissaguag River, which falls into Smithtown Bay in the Sound. They had large settlements at Flushing, Glen Cove, Cold Spring, Huntington, and Cow Harbor, and were considered a wealthy tribe.

[2] Alb. Rec. ii., 298, 300, 301.

BOOK III. 1645. obliged to borrow money, so low were his funds at this period, among others, from Adriaen Van der Donck, sheriff of Rensselaerswyck.[1]

July 21. These precautions had the effect of persuading the remaining outstanding tribes of the utter hopelessness of any further opposition. Philip de Truy, the court-messenger, was shortly after ordered to invite the citizens to assemble in the fort on the next day, at the hoisting of the colors and the ringing of the bell, to hear the articles of the proposed treaty of peace read, when, they were assured, "if any one could give good advice, he might then declare his opinions freely." All the citizens answered kindly "except one Hendrick Kip, a tailor." He had already suggested the propriety of deposing Director Kieft, and the sturdy burgher was not now willing to do him any honor.

Aug. 29.

Aug. 30. At the hour appointed, the sachems of the surrounding tribes; Oratany, chief of the Hackingsacks, Sessekennick and Willem, chiefs of the Tappaans and of Rechgawawank, Pacham and Pennekeck, who answered for Onany, Majanwettenemin, Marechhawick, Nyack, and their neighbors on Long Island, and Aepjen, chief of the Mohegans, who spoke for the Wappinecks, the Wechquaesqueecks, the Sintsings, and the Kichtawancks, seated themselves, silent and grave, in front of Fort Amsterdam before the Director-general and his council and the whole commonalty; and there, having religiously smoked the great calumet, concluded, "in the presence of the sun and of the ocean," a solemn and durable peace with the Dutch, which both the contracting parties reciprocally bound themselves honorably and firmly to maintain and observe.

By this treaty, the Indians pledged themselves to apply, in case of difficulty or difference with the Christians, to the authorities at New Amsterdam for satisfaction, while the latter promised to complain to the proper sachem, should any Indian be guilty of aggression, so that justice may be directly administered on the guilty. No Indian should for the future approach, armed, the dwellings of the Christians on Manhat-

[1] Van der Donck's New Neth. N. Y. Hist. Soc. Trans. (2d Ser.) i., 127, 161; Alb. Rec. viii., 80.

tan Island; and the Dutch, on their part, engaged not to visit the Indian villages with their guns, except conducted thither by one of the aborigines. Finally, the latter promised to conduct the English girl, the daughter of the late Mrs. Hutchinson, whom they retained in captivity, to Stamford, to be surrendered to the inhabitants of that place, or else to convey her in safety to Fort Amsterdam, where the Dutch guarantied to pay the ransom which the English had promised for the maiden. 1645.

The ratification of this important treaty terminated, to the great joy of high and low, the disastrous and unrighteous war which had been waged, with but a short interval of five months, between the Indians and the Dutch, from July, 1640, to August, 1645, to the incalculable injury of the colony, to the manifest displeasure of the authorities in Holland, and in violation of the received laws of nations. At its conclusion, there were found around the Manhattans, besides private traders, no more than one hundred men, so desolating were its effects on the population; while the Indians were several thousands strong, and the New England colonies contained between fifty and sixty thousand souls. In celebration of the happy event, and in order "to proclaim the good tidings throughout New Netherland," the sixth of September was ordered to be observed, in the several English and Dutch churches, as a day of general thanksgiving, that God Almighty might be praised for the numerous blessings which he had been pleased, by his grace and mercy, to bestow on the country.[1] Aug. 31.

Advantage was taken of the re-establishment of good understanding with the natives, to purchase from the Long Island Indians the lands extending along the North River from Conynen, or Rabbits Island, to Gowanus, and to Weymit Spritten which were now added to the public domain. And Thomas Ffarrington, John Townsend, William Lawrence, Robert Ffirman, and others, who were forced to remove from Massachusetts in the spring of this year, obtained a patent, shortly after the peace, for sixteen thousand acres of land Sept. 10. Oct. 19.

[1] Alb. Rec. ii., 312, 314, 315, 316, 317; iv., 11; Hol. Doc. iii., 365; iv., 41.

BOOK III. 1645. Dec. 19. to the east of Mespath, which was duly incorporated by the title of Vlissingen, after the ancient trading-city of that name situated on the island of Walcheren. A patent, conveying equally liberal municipal privileges, was granted two months afterwards to the town of Gravenzande.[1]

While Kieft was engaged concluding these various treaties, he received instructions from Holland to turn his attention to the mineral wealth of the province. Ores of copper, iron, and lead had been already discovered in various parts, specimens of some of which had been conveyed to Europe by private individuals. The Director-general was therefore ordered to forward specimens of the various metals to the company, for the purpose of being tested. The first opportunity which offered for complying with these instructions, was during the negotiation of the peace at Fort Orange with the Mohawks. The Indian interpreter was observed to paint his face, after the fashion of his nation. The Director-general obtained a specimen of the substance which was used on that occasion. It was remarkably heavy, and of a greasy, shining appearance. Suspecting it to be some valuable mineral, he caused it to be subjected, in a crucible, to the action of a strong heat. The result of the experiment was encouraging. It yielded, in appearance, "two pieces of gold, worth about three guilders."
July 21. An officer, with a few men, was sent to the mountain where the sample was obtained, for a quantity of the metal, which, having been procured, was tested in the same manner as the first, and pronounced equally good; and so it was. For though not exactly gold, it was, equally, iron pyrites. Some time afterwards, samples of other minerals, found in one of the
Aug. 31. Nevesink mountains, near the Raritain, were brought by some

[1] Thompson's Long Island ii., 67, 68, 178; a volume of "Letters in Gov. Stuyvesant's time," in the Secretary of State's office, Albany, contains "several orders agreed upon by the inhabitants of Gravesende att several times," from which it appears that the first patentees of that town held a meeting about this time att Amersforte, at which they determined to fence in a certain quantitie of land to containe 8 and 20 shares. The said 8 and 20 shares were divided by lott, and every one was enjoyned, on penalty of forfeiture of the land, to build and inhabit in the towne by a day agreed uppon, for the mutual strengthening of one another, "for the peace with the Indians being new and rawe, their was still feares of theyr vprising to warre."

Indians, which having been deemed valuable, a party were sent out to explore the locality, and Kieft expressed the resolution to build a fort in the neighborhood, to secure the treasure, should the mines prove advantageous. "A few samples of a certain mineral which yielded" (what was represented to be) "gold and quicksilver," was the result of this exploring expedition; and so sanguine now became the Director-general of realizing a rich harvest in this new field, that an officer and thirty men were dispatched to continue the search, with orders to send as large a quantity as possible of the minerals to Fort Amsterdam. Samples of the whole were sent to Holland by way of New Haven. The vessel sailed at Christmas or New Year's, but the treasure never reached its destination. The ship foundered at sea. Arent Corssen, Kieft's messenger, was drowned, and "misfortune attended all on board." This accident did not, however, discourage the Dutch authorities. The directors at Amsterdam promised to send out a properly qualified person to examine and report on the iron mine discovered at Staten Island and near the Raritan, for they still entertained the hope that the prosecution of the search would prove of advantage to the company.[1]

CHAP. VII. 1645. Oct. 12. Dec. 25.

But while these authorities were thus engaged, circumstances had unexpectedly occurred in other portions of the company's possessions, which influenced considerably future arrangements regarding New Netherland.

Petrus Stuyvesant, Director of Curaçoa, determined, in the beginning of 1644, to make an attack on the island of St. Martin, then in the possession of the Portuguese, with a view to reduce that place. He accordingly laid siege to the capital, which he continued closely to invest for the space of twenty-eight days. But he was eventually obliged to abandon his object, succor having been thrown into the town by the enemy. In the course of these operations, he happened to receive a severe wound in the knee, which obliged him to return the following autumn to Holland, to obtain surgical aid, the hot climate of Curaçoa having been found unfavorable to the recovery of his health. He embarked accordingly in the

1644. April 4. Sept.

[1] Van der Donck's Descript. of N. N. Hol. Doc. ii., 362, 363; Alb. Rec. ii., 262, 312, 318, 323; xii., 397. Magnalia, B. i. c. 6.

BOOK III. 1645. Milkmaid, but a violent storm overtook the vessel in the British Channel. The supply of fresh water was then found to be reduced to about two hogsheads for sixty-one persons, the number on board at the time, many of whom were laboring under scurvy. The vessel was therefore forced to put into the first harbor in Ireland, whence Stuyvesant passed over in safety to Holland. His health was so far improved in the course of the next summer, that the company concluded to appoint him, instead of Mr. Van Dinclage, Director-general of New Netherland, the expenses of which government, as well as of Stuyvesant's outfit, the Assembly of the XIX. had now
July 6. agreed to divide, in common, among all the Chambers, instead of confining it to that of Amsterdam, which last department, however, charged itself to equip two vessels to convey the new Director-general and his suite to the Manhattans.

Sept. 21. General Stuyvesant submitted, some time after, to the Assembly of the XIX., then in session at Middleburg, a memorial containing various suggestions for the better management of the company's interests in their transatlantic territories. This, together with the instructions drawn up, in conformity with the suggestions contained in the report already referred to, for the guidance of the Director-general, and for the future government of New Netherland, was submitted to a special committee, which, after a laborious and protracted sitting, reported
Oct. 12. resolutions that revolutionized, in a manner, the whole trade of the colony.

From the first incorporation of the West India Company to the commencement of Kieft's administration, this trade, both internally with the Indians, and externally with the mother country, was a close monopoly, exclusively carried on by the company and its servants. A change took place in 1639, when a modification was introduced so far as to open the internal trade to all subjects of the States General, and of foreign powers at peace with the Dutch Republic. The carrying trade between Holland and America was still retained by the West India Company, or permitted only to vessels belonging to Patroons or other privileged persons. It was now deter-
Oct. 14. mined to throw this open to the ships of private merchants, and to permit these, in future, to carry merchandise and other freight

to New Netherland and the other Dutch American colonies, under certain regulations. The principal object of these seems to have been the concentration of all colonial commerce at New Amsterdam, for it was ruled that all merchandise sent to New Netherland, or to countries there adjoining, should first of all be conveyed to the above port, before being carried elsewhere, in order that the ships' papers should be there examined and registered, the vessels visited, and all contraband trade prevented. All return cargoes were likewise to be brought to the Manhattans, from whence the homeward-bound vessels were to clear, giving notice, at the time, of the port in Holland to which they were destined, and binding themselves to pay the duties on their return cargoes into that chamber from which they originally received a permit or license to make the voyage; they were not to break bulk, from the time they should leave New Amsterdam until their arrival at their port of destination in Fatherland, to which they were to proceed in as direct a course as possible, without touching at any other place, on pain of forfeiting ship and cargo. It was further determined to place Curaçoa, Aruba, and the other adjoining islands under the superintendence of the Director-general of New Netherland, and to reduce the company's establishment at the first-named place to a Vice-director and one hundred and fifteen persons. The committee stated, at the same time, that it would be much more advantageous to the company to abandon that island altogether, if such could possibly be done, with the consent of the States General.

Difference of opinion now ensued among the directors. Eventually, the arrangements agreed upon in July were reconsidered. Some of the chambers objected to pay their share of the expenses attendant on the change of management, and the consequence was, the department of Amsterdam retained, illegally and contrary to the wishes of the other chambers, (as it was alleged,) the exclusive administration of the affairs of New Netherland. General Stuyvesant's departure was indefinitely postponed, and the colony continued for over twelve months more under the mismanagement of Willem Kieft.[1]

[1] Hol. Doc. iii., 33, 40, 42, 46, 58, 59, 60, 61, 62, 63; v., 124; viii., 153; Alb. Rec. viii., 39, 40; xii., 45, 46, 47, 48, 63, 70.

CHAPTER VIII.

Fruits of faction—Quarrel between the Rev. Mr. Bogardus and Director Kieft —Progress of affairs at the South River—Sufferings of the first Swedish colonists—Resolve to abandon the river and to remove to Manhattans—Are prevented by the opportune arrival of additional supplies and settlers—Boundaries of New Sweden—Royal appropriations for its support—Printz appointed governor—His salary—Strength of the Swedish establishment on the Delaware—Its annual expense—Dutch force at Fort Nassau—Instructions to Printz—Swedish forts on the South River—Swedes seize the Indian trade—Loss accruing to the Dutch in consequence—Seizure of a Swedish vessel in Holland—Proceedings attendant thereupon—Hudde appointed commissary at Fort Nassau—Some Dutch merchants send a venture to the South River—Their vessels ordered off by the Swedes—Several Dutch freemen receive grants of land on the Delaware—Measures taken to extinguish Indian titles—Company's arms erected on the spot—Swedes tear them down, and protest against the Dutch, who reply—High-handed measures of the Swedish governor—The Dutch traders appeal to New Amsterdam—Renewal of the controversy between Kieft and New Haven—Continued misunderstanding on the Connecticut—Correspondence with the commissioners of the United Colonies—The Director-general refers the matters to Holland—Instructions from the West India Company—Patents for new colonies at Kattskill and Yonckers—Breukelen obtains manorial rights and municipal privileges.

BOOK III. 1646.

THE spirit of faction, which the war engendered, had, among other bad consequences, the effect of destroying the harmony and good understanding which had previously existed among the small number of citizens who resided in New Amsterdam. The Rev. Everardus Bogardus had, from the beginning, been suspected of siding with the commonalty and their representatives, in their differences with the Director-general. A rupture between the latter and the minister was the result, which eventuated now in a public quarrel, to the great scandal and affliction of the staid and religious portion of the community.

The habits of the Rev. Mr. Bogardus had been, unfortunately, far from temperate; his passions were consequently violent, and oftentimes his language coarse and unbridled. He had already had a personal quarrel with Director Van Twiller, towards whom he had behaved in an indecorous manner, attacking him even from the pulpit, which he is accused of having ascended in a state of inebriety.

Director Kieft, as much, perhaps, to vent an old spleen as to check this disorderly conduct, had already taken Bogardus to task, at the house of the attorney-general, in the early part of the past year, for having gone into the pulpit "drunk." He took occasion, also, to accuse him of uniting with the greatest criminals in the country; of taking their part; of defending them; of embracing the cause of Maryn Adriaensen, who had attempted to assassinate the Director-general, and of writing in favor of malecontents. The minister ill-brooked this reprimand. He attacked Kieft on the following Sabbath from the pulpit "in the most brutal manner." "What," he asked, "are the great men of the country but receptacles of wrath—fountains of wo and trouble? Nothing is thought of but to plunder other people's property—to dismiss—to banish—to transport to Holland." These hard hits at Kieft's public acts told. "To avoid giving greater scandal, the Director-general no longer assisted in the congregation." But his absence from church did not save him. At weddings, at christenings, in church and out of church, Bogardus spared him not. In vain Kieft admonished him by letter. Bogardus refused to receive his letters, and persisted in his attacks. "When you preached on the 22d of last December," writes the Director-general to him, "you publicly stated that you had often administered the Lord's Supper without partaking of it, and that you wished those who were the cause of this separation were cut off, for when the customary house-visiting is performed, they cannot give reasons for their continued absence. Your bad tongue is, in our opinion, the only cause, and your obstinacy that of its continuance, with those who encourage you to proceed in that road. On the 24th December, you informed your congregation how in Africa, 'owing to the intense heat, different animals copulate there together, by which various monsters are generated. But you knew not,' you added, 'from whence, in such temperate climates as ours, such monsters of men are produced. They are the mighty ones,' you said, 'but it was desirable that they were weak.' Children might tell to whom you here alluded. Similar ser-

BOOK III. 1646. mons, in which you have frequently indulged, have occasioned our absence from church."

Having thus, and in a number of other articles, enumerated the various misdeeds which he charged against the minister Director Kieft thus concluded his "New Year's offering:"

Jan. 2. "Inasmuch as your duty and oath imperiously demand the maintenance of the magistracy; and whereas your conduct stirs the people to mutiny and rebellion, when they are already too much divided—causes schisms and abuses in the church and makes us a scorn and a laughing-stock to our neighbors, all which cannot be tolerated in a country where justice is maintained, therefore our sacred duty imperiously requires of us to prosecute you in a court of justice, and we have accordingly ordered a copy of these, our deliberations, to be delivered to you, to answer in fourteen days."

A controversy, opened by a bill of indictment, could not well be passed unnoticed. Bogardus, who had hitherto returned Kieft's missals unopened, was now forced to reply;
Jan. 3. but his answers were declared useless and absurd; filled with
Jan. 15. idle subterfuge, calumnies, and injuries; a profanation of God's holy word, to vilify justice and the magistrate, and he was ordered to send in a more explicit answer. But finding that his answers were already considered unsatisfactory and "insolent," Bogardus, after repeated replies, wisely declined proceeding any further in "a deep discussion of this affair;"
March 22. and Kieft found himself embarrassed in a prosecution in which the charges were matter rather for investigation by the church, than by the state. In order to obviate all pretext of slander, he now invested the Rev. Mr. Megapolensis and the Rev. Mr. Doughty, both ministers of the Gospel, and two or three other impartial persons, with power to decide the matter in issue, provided Bogardus consented, previously, to abide by their judgment, (which the Director-general, on his part, promised to do,) and not to offend the latter, directly or indirectly, in public or in private. This proposal Bogardus rejected, and
April 12. appealed to the new Director and council, whose appointment, it seems, had already become known in the colony. Kieft, however, would not allow of this appeal, as it was not certain when the new Director should arrive, and ordered the prose-

cution to proceed, "to put a stop to the scandal and disorder which were prevailing more and more." But friends interfered in the mean time. The Director-general made a last appeal to the minister to be reconciled, and requested him to permit the Rev. Mr. Megapolensis to preach in the church on the following Sabbath, "as was his usual custom when in New Amsterdam," so that Kieft might hear him. This request was granted, and the quarrel terminated, like all such misunderstandings, to the apparent satisfaction of all the parties concerned, and seemingly for want of food to nourish it.[1]

CHAP. VIII. 1646.

The interests of the Dutch on the South River had, all this time, been subjected to serious damage at the hands of the Swedes. Though the West India Company had obtained complete control of the mouth of the Delaware, by the purchase, from the Patroons and their associates, in the year 1635, of the colonie of Zwanendal, for the sum of fifteen thousand six hundred guilders, or $6240,[2] the Swedish settlers continued undisturbed in their possessions in that quarter, ever since Kieft had protested against Minuit, and had managed, by underselling the Dutch with the Indians, to export no less than thirty thousand skins in the course of the year succeeding their first arrival in that country.

1639.

This competition, however, proved well nigh the ruin of that infant colony. For, having received no support either from the Swedish government or the Swedish West India Company, the first emigrants were so reduced that they found themselves, in the course of the second spring, necessitated to choose one of two alternatives: to remain and perish, or to abandon their settlement. Like prudent men, they made the latter choice, and resolved to move in a body to the Manhattans, the authorities at that place having given them every assurance of the most hospitable reception and entertainment. But just on the eve of their departure, a Swedish ship hove in sight, having on board Peter Holland, or Hollandaer, as deputy-governor, together with a considerable number of set-

1640. Sept.

Alb. Rec. ii., 334, 336, 338, 340, 342, 343, 346, 347.

[2] For a translation of the deed passed between the Company and the Patroons of Zwanendal on this occasion, and other papers, see Appendix S.

BOOK III. tlers, and a fresh supply of goods. The Swedes, much to the chagrin of Director Kieft, now abandoned all idea of leaving the South River, and purchased, it is said, from the Indians an additional quantity of land, extending as far as "a cannon bullet shot" from Fort Christina, "over against Mekaquatshoe, eight miles above the present town of Burlington." They shortly after added also, by purchase, all the land from the above fort to Duck Creek, where they erected, in token of sovereignty, "the arms of the crown of Sweedland." Mounce Kling, who had acted as deputy to Peter Minuit, followed with two vessels, some time afterwards, and purchased Upland, Tinnecum, and several other places, and from this time may be dated the permanent colonization of New Sweden.[1]

1641. The limits of that province, as claimed by its government, extended "from the borders of the Sea to Cape Henlopen in returning southwest towards Godyn's Bay; thence towards the Great South River, as far as the Minquaaskil, where Fort Christina is constructed; and thence again towards South River, and the whole to a place which the savages call Sankikan," now Trenton Falls. This district was about thirty German miles in length. In width, "as much of the country as they chose to take."

The Swedish authorities were not as indisposed as we might, a priori, be led to infer, to the settlement of natives of Holland within their jurisdiction. Mr. Henry Hochhammer obtained,
Jan. 24. O. S. in the early part of this year, a charter for the planting a colonie on the east side of the Delaware, four or five miles distant from Fort Christina, the provisions of which were, in most respects, similar to that granted to Patroons in New Netherland.
Jan. 30. Joost de Bogaerdt was commissioned by Queen Christina commander of this colonie, with a yearly salary of five hundred florins, or two hundred dollars, payable to his banker by the Swedish resident at the Hague. For the more efficient sup-

[1] Extracten uyt versheyde missiven geschreven door Wm. Kieft; MS certificate and deposition of certain ancient Swedes living on the west side of the Delaware, 25th June, 1684. The said "ancient Swedes" declared, in another deposition dated 11th January, 1683, that "the first of their nation that came and planted in this river and the creeks thereunto belonging, did find the Dutch possessed of said river."

port of the province of New Sweden generally, Her Majesty appropriated two millions, six hundred and nineteen dollars, to be collected annually from the excise on tobacco, and the fines imposed on those importing that weed into the kingdom without license, and, in the summer of 1642, appointed John Printz, (a lieutenant-colonel of cavalry in her service,) as governor of New Sweden for three years, at a yearly allowance of twelve hundred silver dollars, placing at the same time at his disposal, a force sufficient to support the rights of her crown on the South River.[1]

CHAP. VIII. 1642.

Aug. 16. O. S.

Governor Printz arrived in the Delaware in the fall of this year, accompanied by two vessels, the Swan and the Fame, and a number of settlers. He was instructed to observe a friendly demeanor towards the Dutch at Fort Nassau, "now occupied by about twenty men;" to explain to them the intentions of the crown of Sweden in planting the South River, and if the Dutch would respect the title of the latter, then to leave them undisturbed in their possessions at Fort Nassau, and at New Amsterdam, on the North River. But, on the contrary, should any hostile disposition be evinced, then force should be employed to repel it. He was likewise directed to claim that part of the east coast from Cape Mey to the Narraticon, or Raccoon Creek, (a few miles below the present city of Philadelphia,) including Hog Creek, where sixty English settlers had commenced a plantation, but to respect the Dutch colonie under the command of De Bogaerdt, and the privileges conceded to them, obliging these, however, should he think proper, to remove their settlement to a greater distance from Fort Christina, as they were but three German or twenty English miles from that post. In his trade with the natives he was to treat them "with much humanity and kindness," and "see that

[1] Appropriation for the government of New Sweden, anno 1642. 1 Governor, 800 Rix dollars; 1 Lieu. Governor, 192 ditto; 1 Sergeant Major, 120 ditto; 1 corporal, 72 ditto; 1 gunner, 96 ditto; 1 trumpeter, 72 ditto; 1 drummer, 60 ditto; 24 soldiers, 1,152 ditto; 1 paymaster, 120 ditto; 1 secretary, 96 ditto; 1 barber, 120 ditto; 1 provost, 72 ditto; and one man, 48 ditto; being an annual total of 3,020 Rix dollars. Beauchamp Plantagenet, in his Description of New Albion, and Acrelius, in his Hist. of New Sweden, allude to the above named Bogaerdt. In the translation of the latter work in the New Series of N. Y. Hist. Soc. Trans. p. 411, the name, however, is misspelled.

BOOK III. 1642. neither violence nor injustice be done them." On the contrary, he was to take care that they be instructed in the Christian religion, and furnished with whatever they required "at lower prices than those they received from the Dutch or the English their neighbors, so that they may by this means be disengaged from these people, and accustomed more" to the Swedes. He was particularly enjoined to turn his attention to the culture of tobacco; to inquire if silk-worms and silk could be raised there; to encourage the propagation of flocks of sheep and cattle, so that "a considerable portion of good wool may be sent here," and for the better securing of the trade in furs, to establish com missaries, and take especial care "that no person whomsoevei be permitted to trade in peltries with the Indians, but that this be done in the name and on the account of the Swedish Company, by the agents appointed for that purpose." The culture of the vine, the manufacture of salt, by evaporation, were also enjoined, as well as the exploration of the mineral wealth of the country. "A good quantity of oak and nut wood" was to be sent to Sweden as ballast, as "we must also try if the nuts by pressure may not furnish oil." The fisheries were also to be attended to, the country cultivated, and the colony governed "according to the laws, customs, and usages of Sweden," punishing by death or otherwise all offenders, "but not otherwise than according to the ordinances and legal forms, and after having sufficiently considered and examined the affair with the most noted persons, such as the most prudent assessors of justice that he can find and consult in the country." Before all, he was enjoined to "labor and watch that he render in all things to Almighty God the true worship which is his due, the glory, the praise, and the homage which belong to him, and to take good measures that the Divine service is performed according to the true confession of Augsburg, the Council of Upsal, and the ceremonies of the Swedish church, having care that all men, and especially the youth, be well instructed in all the parts of Christianity, and that a good ecclesiastical discipline be observed and maintained." The Dutch colonie established within her majesty's limits must not, however, be disturbed in the rights guarantied to it in religious matters.[1]

[1] Hazard's Register of Penn. iv., 177, 178, 200, 219, 220, 221, 314, 373

Immediately on the arrival of this Swedish governor, he established his residence at Tinnicum, or New Gottenburg, situate some ten or twelve miles below Philadelphia, where he erected a pretty strong fort, by laying heavy hemlock logs the one on the other. To secure still more effectually the country and its trade, he built at Hog or Salem Creek, on the east bank of the river Delaware, near its mouth, a fort, which he called Elsinburg, or Elsborg, and which he garrisoned with a lieutenant and twelve men, and strengthened with six or eight twelve-pounders. By means of this fort, he effectually secured the mouth of the river; and all vessels, no matter of what nation, entering the Delaware, were obliged to lower their colors and bring to here, to be visited until they obtained from Tinnicum Printz's permit to proceed.

CHAP. VIII. 1643.

Fort Christina, which Minuit had erected in 1638, and which was situate on the west side, about half a mile up the Minquaas Creek, commanded the passage to the country of the Minquaas. It was the principal Swedish trading-post, and contained a magazine well supplied with every description of merchandise. The avenue to the Indian country was still further secured by a third fort on an island at the mouth of the Schuylkill, right in front of fort Beversrede, erected by the Dutch in 1633, and thus every valuable point was seized on and garrisoned, so that finally no access to the Minquaas was left open to the Dutch. The trade with the savages fell, consequently, altogether under the control of the Swedes, and the Delaware became of little or no value to their rivals, who maintained at Fort Nassau, on the east bank of that river, a miserable trading-post, scantily supplied with goods or merchandise.

The loss experienced by the Dutch in consequence of being thus, in a manner, driven from this valuable district, will be more correctly estimated by reference to the opinions of writers on the spot. "We acknowledge freely," says Van der Donck, "that we are unable fully to describe the value and the advantages which this river possesses; for in addition to the navigation and trade, which are great, there are fourteen navigable rivers, creeks, and streams which fall into this river. Some of these are large, and boatable to a great distance, and may be well named rivers, as the ordi-

BOOK III. 1643. nary tides flow several miles up the same, where the waters meet and are fresh, and still remain wide and are tolerably deep. There are also many streams, presenting rich and extensive valleys, which afford good situations for villages and towns. The river itself is roomy, wide, clean, clear, deep, not foul nor stony, with good settings and anchorage. The tides are strong, and flow up near to the falls. The land is fine and level on both sides, not too high, but above floods and freshets, except some reed land and marshes. Above the falls the river divides into two large boatable streams, which run far inland to places unknown to us. There are several fine islands in this river, with many other delightful advantages and conditions, which are estimated by those who have examined the river, and who have seen much of the world, not to be surpassed by any other river that is known. Equalling in many respects the celebrated river of the Amazons, although not in greatness, yet in advantages with which this river and the neighboring land are favored, we would regret to lose such a jewel by the devices and hands of a few strangers,"—meaning the Swedes.

1644. The Dutch had, in truth, sufficient cause for such regret. In the active prosecution of the advantages they had secured, the Swedes freighted, this year, the Key of Calmar and the Fame with two valuable cargoes, consisting of 2,127 packages of beaver, and 70,421 lbs. of tobacco. In consequence, however, of the breaking out of war between Denmark and Sweden, and owing to stress of weather and other causes, these ships were obliged to put into Harlingen, a seaport in the province of Friesland, to revictual and repair. Immediately
Oct. 6. on their arrival, the West India Company, claiming the sovereignty of the country in which the cargo was obtained, placed officers on board, and demanded, by virtue of their charter and of other privileges granted them by the States General, the payment of import duties on the cargoes, and eight per cent. additional accruing to them, as recognitions, on all goods purchased and brought to Holland from their transatlantic possessions. This demand gave rise to a lengthy
Oct. 29. and rather warm correspondence between the Swedish ambassador at the Hague and the States General, in which the for-

CHAP. VIII. 1644

mer laid claim to the country around the South River, by right of purchase, preoccupation, and lawful possession, and maintained that no other power had any just pretension there. He protested, also, against the detention of these vessels belonging to the King his Master, on the ground that it was a violation of existing treaties between both countries, which guarantied to the ships of either power, freedom of commerce to the east and north seas; and qualified it as an unjustifiable piece of insolence, affecting in a serious degree the respect due to his Swedish Majesty, who never visited nor searched any of their High Mightinesses' ships touching at his ports, whether prizes or not, whatever were the goods or cargoes with which they were freighted; and concluded by demanding the removal of the company's officers, and that no part of the ships' cargoes should be disposed of for payment of the recognitions, as he categorically refused to pay any such exaction.

This representation had, eventually, such effect, that their High Mightinesses ordered the discharge of the cargoes, on payment simply of the customary import duties, but without the exaction of the eight per cent. recognitions by the West India Company.[1]

The question of the right of sovereignty over the South River and the land thereabout was not discussed, and matters continued, in that quarter, in an unsettled and in quite an unsatisfactory position.

The authorities at Fort Amsterdam were not, however, dis- 1646.
posed to sit quietly down and allow the valuable trade of that rich section of the country to be wrested entirely out of their hands, without making some effort to save, at least, a portion thereof. Jan Jansen van Ilpendam, the commissary in that
quarter, had been found guilty of fraud, and manifested other- Feb.
wise an unfitness for his situation, "having paid the Indians too high a price for furs." He was therefore removed, and Andreas Hudde was ordered to the South River, to superintend the company's commercial interests in that quarter.

[1] Alb. Rec. xvii., 321; Acrelius, Hist. New Sweden; Hol. Doc. ii., 340, 341, 342–345, 350–361; iv., 1, 2, 13, 14, 15, 18.

BOOK III. 1646. This functionary had not been long at his new post, when he became embroiled with the Swedish governor, who now, claiming supreme authority over the whole of that country, would not allow any Dutch merchants to trade, nor, indeed, any Dutch farmers to settle on or about that river.

A number of enterprising residents of New Amsterdam had dispatched a vessel to the Delaware, with a cargo to be exchanged with the Indians for furs, corn, and other barter. On
June 23. its arrival, Hudde ordered it to the Schuylkill, there to await the Minquaas. But Skipper Blanck, who commanded the sloop, had scarcely cast anchor, when he was ordered off by a Swedish officer. In vain did Hudde represent that the place had been always a rendezvous for traders; in vain did he counsel discretion—inquire by what authority the company was forbidden to trade there; and, finally, plead the alliance which existed between their High Mightinesses the States General and the Swedish Crown. Printz peremptorily order-
July 1. ed the skipper to quit the place, and threatened to confiscate his ship and cargo if he disobeyed. As the Dutch commissary could not afford any protection in the premises, and as the Swedish commander manifested every disposition to execute his threat, Skipper Blanck withdrew, and nothing was
July 12. left to Hudde but to report the matter to his superiors at Fort Amsterdam.

Governor Printz manifested his jealousy of the Dutch in every possible way, and as he was instructed to preserve the monopoly of the Indian trade, which commerce was the great bone of contention in those days, he endeavored to instil the same feeling into the minds of the natives. To effect this purpose the more certainly, he spread a rumor among the Indians that the Dutch intended to build a fort near "the great falls" (of Trenton,) to be garrisoned by two hundred and fifty men; that they would slaughter all the Indians on the lower part of the river, and, by means of the proposed post, prevent those above coming to the assistance of their brethren situated below. So effectually did he succeed in spreading alarm throughout the villages of the Indians, that the latter opposed every attempt which Hudde made to penetrate into the interior, when he attempted, in pursuance to orders received from the Director-general, to proceed to the upper part of the country to explore that section for minerals. CHAP. VIII.

1646. Aug. 10. It was in this state of things that Abraham Verplanck, Simon Root, Jan Andriessen, and Pieter Harmanse, obtained a grant of land on the west side of the South River, "lying almost over against the little island called 'Vogelsang' or singing bird (now Egg) island," for the purpose of making four plantations there, conditionally that the grant should be void if they did not settle on it within a year. Commissary Hudde received orders to extinguish by purchase the Indian title to the soil. Sept. 7. Hudde concluded the purchase, and erected, with the consent of the natives, and as was the custom on such occasions, the arms of the company, on the spot on which the Dutch freemen were making preparations to build. This proceeding excited fresh opposition on the part of the Swedes. They tore down Oct. 8. the company's ensign, declaring, at the same time, that they should have pulled down the colors of their High Mightinesses, had even these been raised on Swedish soil.[1] Governor Printz followed up this aggression by this emphatic protest:—

"Andreas Hudde! I remind you again, by this written Oct. 10. warning, to discontinue the injuries of which you have been guilty against the Royal Majesty of Sweden, my most gracious Queen; against Her Royal Majesty's rights, pretensions, soil, and land, without showing the least respect to Her Royal

[1] In corroboration of the above insult offered to the Dutch flag, we meet with the following passage in Van der Donck:—"The arms of their High Mightinesses were erected over Machchachansio, among the Sankikans, by order of Director Kieft, in token that the river, with all the adjoining country, and surrounding lands and soil, remained under the power and possession of their High Mightinesses. But what fruit did this bear, save lasting reproach to the country and lessening of respect? For the Swedes, with an insolence intolerable, tore them down; and now that they are allowed to remain so, it is considered, especially by their governor, to have been a Roman achievement. It is very true that several protests have been made as well against this, as against other occurrences, but they have had as much effect as the flight of a crow overhead. And it is supposed that if this governor had a supply of men, we should have as much trouble with him as we have had with the English, or any of their governors. This, in fine, is what appertains to the Swedes, about whom the company's officers can make pertinent declaration, for we further refer to all the papers, documents, and journals which remain in their hands." Vertoogh van N. N.

BOOK III. 1646. Majesty's magnificence, reputation, and dignity; and to do so no more, considering how little it would be becoming Her Royal Majesty to bear such gross violence, and what great disasters might originate from it; yea, might be expected. Secondly, with what reluctance, as I think, your nation, or your masters would, for such a trifle, come into collision with Her Royal Majesty, as you have no shadow of right for this your gross conduct; particularly, for your secret and unlawful purchase of land from the savages, by which you evidently betrayed your conviction of the justice, equity, and antiquity of your pretended claims, of which you so loudly boasted, and which, by this purchase, have been brought to light; showing clearly that you had no shadow of right to that place, of which you have taken possession, no more than to others on this river which you now claim, in which, however, you were never molested by her Royal Majesty or her plenipotentiaries. All this I can freely bring forward in my own defence, to exculpate me from all future calamities, of which we give you a warning, and place it at your account. Dated New Gothenburg, 30th Sept. stil. veteri. 1646."

Printz followed up his protest, by forbidding the Swedes to transact any business with the Dutch. Hudde, on the other
Oct. 22. hand, disclaimed all intention of encroaching on the rights of the Swedes, or to act in an unjust and clandestine manner. "The place we possess we hold in just deed," he replied, "perhaps before the name of the South River was heard of in Sweden." He complained of the insolent and hostile manner with which the arms of the company had been torn down, and of the insulting declaration that, had they been the colors of the Prince of Orange, they should have been trampled under foot. He warned Printz that these proceedings would eventually cause great calamities; protested his innocence of all disasters that might follow, and concluded by impressing on his attention that, as Christians, they should not, by their disagreements, render themselves a stumbling-block or laughing-stock to the savage heathens.

This paper obtained a very cavalier reception from the Swedish commander. He flung it on the ground, ordering one of his attendants to take charge of it, and when Hudde's messenger requested an answer to the letter of which he had been the bearer, Printz (whom De Vries describes as a man who weighed upwards of four hundred pounds, and drank three drinks at every meal) threw the Dutchman out of doors, and having taken a gun from the wall, threatened to shoot him, which, however, was fortunately prevented by the timely interference of the bystanders.

CHAP. VIII. 1646.

In this wise was the general behavior of the Swedes towards the Dutch on the South River at this period. Whenever any of the latter visited Printz's head-quarters, they were sure to be abused in an unwarrantable manner, and frequently returned "bloody and bruised." Commissary Hudde urged, in vain, rights acquired by prior possession. The Swedish Governor answered him with a profane jeer:—"The devil was the oldest possessor in hell, yet he, notwithstanding, would sometimes admit a younger one,"—with other language equally coarse, expressing, at the same time, the greatest contempt for the States General, as well as for the commissions issued by the company, under the authority derived from their High Mightinesses. To such a pitch did this insolence proceed at last, that the Dutch traders who resorted to the Delaware, complained to the commissary in the strongest terms, and obliged him to forward to the Director-general and council at New Amsterdam, a remonstrance on their part against the annoyances to which they were subjected, together with their claims for the redress of the various grievances which they suffered.[1]

In the mean time another controversy had sprung up with the people of New Haven, which diverted the attention of the Dutch, for the moment, from the encroachments of the Swedes. Some of the inhabitants of that colony had pur chased land from the Indians, between twenty and thirty (Dutch) miles up the country, towards the northwest, some twenty miles east of the North River, and about sixty miles from Fort Orange, and built a trading-house there.[2] Director

[1] Alb. Rec. xvii., 321, 322, et seq; Hazard's Reg. iv., 119; Acrelius, New Sweden.

[2] Van der Donck, in allusion to this post, has the following statement:— "The English of New Haven have a trading-post on the east or southeast side

BOOK III. 1646. Aug. 3. Kieft, who was jealous of every movement of his English neighbors, wrote in strong terms to Governor Eaton, claiming this place as a part of New Netherland, and protesting against such a settlement. He accused the New Haven people with entertaining an insatiable desire to possess that which belonged to the Dutch; with having, contrary to his protests, against the law of nations, and in contravention of ancient leagues between the kings of England and the States General, indirectly entered the limits of New Netherland, and usurped divers places therein. And, he continued, "because you and yours have of late determined to fasten your foot near the Mauritius River, in this province, and there not only to disturb our trade, of no man hitherto questioned, and to draw it to yourselves, but utterly to destroy it, we are compelled again to protest; and by these presents do protest against you, as against public breakers of the peace and disturbers of the public quiet." He concluded by threatening that if the New Haven people did not restore the places they had usurped, and repair the losses which the Dutch had experienced, the latter would manfully recover them by such means as God should afford, holding the English responsible for all the evils that might ensue.

Aug 22. To this letter Governor Eaton replied by the return of Lieut. Baxter, Kieft's messenger. He utterly disclaimed all knowledge of such a river as the Mauritius, and denied having, at any time, formerly or latterly, entered upon any place to which the Dutch had any known title, or, in any other respect, injured them. He admitted that they had recently built a small house within their own limits on "Paugussett River,[1] which falls into the sea in the midst of the English plantations, many miles, nay, leagues, from the Manhattoes,

of Magdalen Island, not more than six (Dutch) miles from the North River; for this island lies towards the upper part of the North River, twenty-three (Dutch) miles and a half higher up than Fort Amsterdam, on the east bank. It is erected with no other view than to encroach on the whole trade of the North River, or to destroy it altogether, for it is now free for all to resort to." Magdalen Island is on the east side of the Hudson's River, a little below Redhook, upper landing, Dutchess county.

[1] The ancient Indian name of Derby, Conn., and of the river Naugattuck, which empties into the Housatonic. Am. Hist. Mag. i. 203, note.

from the Dutch trading-house, or from any port on Hudson's River," but that they had not built, even there, until they had first purchased a title from the true proprietors. Governor Eaton next alluded to the injuries and outrages which the people of New Haven had received, both at the Manhattans and on the Delaware, at the hands of the Dutch; he declared that, notwithstanding all these injuries and the very unsatisfactory answers Kieft had hitherto given to their various complaints, the New Haven colony had, as he conceived, done nothing repugnant to the law of God, the law of nations, nor to the ancient confederation and friendship between their superiors at home; and concluded by assuring the Director, that he was ready to refer all differences between his people and the Dutch, for due examination and adjudication, to any authorities, either in this country or in Europe, feeling satisfied that his majesty, King Charles, and the English parliament, then assembled, would maintain their own rights against all unjust encroachments, and that even Kieft's superiors would, on due and mature consideration, approve the righteousness of the course pursued by the New Haven people. 1646.

The commissioners of the New England colonies met at New Haven shortly after this, when the above correspondence was duly laid before them. The people of Hartford embraced the occasion of bringing forward, at the same time, several accusations against the Dutch, who had "now grown to an insufferable boldness" on the Connecticut, where they still maintained a distinct establishment and an independent government at Fort Good Hope; while the Hartford colony, on the other hand, claimed obedience to its laws from the inhabitants of that post, which, they averred, was established within English territory. The Dutch were likewise charged with having inveigled an Indian slave, who, having become liable to public punishment, had fled from her master to the Dutch fort, where she was protected, notwithstanding she had been demanded by her master as his servant, and by the magistrates as a criminal. It was insinuated that she was retained for purposes of wantonness, and as "such a servant was part of her master's estate, and a more considerable part than a beast," they insisted that she be restored, for their children Sept. 9.

BOOK III. 1646. would not long be secure if this were suffered. With this conviction, the Hartford authorities had already dispatched a guard to recover the woman, even by force if necessary. David Provost, the Dutch commissary, had, however, resisted the guard, drew his rapier against them, and broke it on their arms; after which he withdrew into the fort, where he defended himself, successfully, against these invaders, of what he considered, his just jurisdiction.

These complaints having been duly heard, the commissioners considered it their duty to address Director Kieft concerning them, which they did at some length, expressing, at the same time, their great desire to examine carefully into the various differences so long existing between their confederates and the Dutch, in order that peace may be preserved. They reminded him that the governor of Massachusetts had written to him, some three years before, regarding the difficulties on the Fresh River, to all which he had returned an ignoramus, with an offensive addition which would be left to his better consideration. They next recapitulated the recent occurrences at Fort Hope, and declared that if the commissary had been slain in the proud affront which he had given, his blood would have been on his own head. Governor Eaton's answer to Kieft's protest they considered fair and just, and then expressed a hope that it would give satisfaction, and that they should receive such a reply to their own dispatch, by the return of their special messenger, as would testify to them his agreement with them "to embrace and pursue righteousness and peace."

Sept. 15.

In the course of the following week, the messenger returned with the answer of the Director-general and council, "To the most noble and worthy Commissioners of the Federated English met together at the Red Mounte, or New Haven, in New Netherland," couched in strong and indignant terms. The inhabitants of Hartford, they asserted, had deceived the commissioners with false accusations, as could easily be proved, as well by English as by Dutch testimony, and other authentic documents, if it were proper now to do so. A few particulars out of such a mass would, however, suffice, "as by the claw they may judge of the talons of the lion."

Sept. 22.

CHAP. VIII. 1646.

The Director-general then proceeded to rebut the several charges contained in the commissioners' letter. He maintained that the shedding the blood of the Dutch, of which the inhabitants of Hartford had been guilty, and the selling the company's cattle, proved sufficiently the equity of their proceedings. "And therefore your prejudgment, supported by this oath, Credo coxtius, as if you would say, Amen, Amen, seems wonderful to us, and contrary to the modesty requisite in such an assembly, which should always keep one ear for the other party." He denied that the woman who had been detained at Fort Hope was a slave. "She was neither taken in war, nor bought with a price." She was placed with the Director-general by her parents, to be educated. Notwithstanding all this, he promised that she should not be wrongfully detained; but whether her master should be indemnified, or she restored, he insisted that she should be baptized before she be allowed to marry. As for the attack of the Dutch commissary on the watch at Hartford, he considered that as watches were for the defence of towns against enemies, and not for the purpose of preventing friends returning to their own houses, the most prudent policy would be, to commit such a trust to men of experience, and not to ignorant boys, who, when they once find arms placed in their hands, think they may also lawfully cry out:—etiam nos poma natamus. "Certainly," continues the Director-general, "when we hear the inhabitants of Hartford complaining of us, we seem to hear Æsop's wolf complaining of the lamb, or the admonition of the young man who cried out to his mother, chiding one of her neighbors, 'Oh, mother, mother! revile her, lest she first commence attacking you.'" As for the answer of those of New Haven, it was such, he said, as he expected. "The eagle always despiseth the beetle-fly." He continued, notwithstanding, determined undauntedly to pursue his own right "by just arms and righteous means," and wound up with these emphatic words:

"We protest against all you Commissioners met at the Red Mount, as against breakers of the common league, and also as infringers of the special rights of the Lords the States, our superiors, in that ye have dared, without express commission,

BOOK III. 1646. to hold your general meeting within the limits of New Netherland."

With this missile, the commissioners, as they well might, expressed themselves much dissatisfied. Director Kieft had, they insisted, left many of their charges untouched, while on others he was misinformed. The Indian girl, they maintained, had been taken in war, and for her misconduct had been handed over to the civil authorities; she had fled from these and taken refuge in the Dutch fort, where, as the Dutch commissary had admitted, she was defiled. Such a practice, the commissioners add, "we would condemn in one of ours with any unmarried, much more with an unbaptized Indian. What order you have taken that she be returned—what satisfaction you have given for this wrong, we hear not. We conceive watches are in all places set to prevent inconveniences and mischiefs which may be done by enemies, or disorderly persons, and in all places a soberly and comely answer is expected. He that draws and breaks his rapier on a watch, neither attends his duty nor his safety." The commissioners next refer to the points in their last letter, which Director Kieft had passed unnoticed, and expressed their doubts that he could, either by witnesses or otherwise, prove that they had been deceived. "Your other expressions—your proverbs or allusions," they continue, "we leave to your calmer consideration." As for the protest with which the Director-general had closed his dispatch, they observed that though it was harsh, it agreed with the general strain of his letter, and concluded by stating that they had more reason to be offended with his protest, than he had with their meeting at New Haven; as, for aught they knew, they could show as good a commission for the one as he could for the other.[1]

Thus terminated Director Kieft's correspondence with the English colonies at the east. On a review of the whole, it will be admitted that, however good his case, the commissioners had the best of the argument on paper. By lack of tem-

[1] Winthrop's N. Eng. ii., 268, 276; Hazard's State Papers, ii., 55, 56, et seq.; N. Y. Hist. Soc. Trans. i., 189–199; Trumbull's Conn. i., 155, 156, 157, 158; Alb. Rec. xii., 398

CHAP. VIII. 1646.

per, and by an undignified style, the Director-general leaves an impression on the mind, at this distance, unfavorable to his ability as a diplomatist, as well as to his capacity for filling the high and delicate position which he was then occupying. It cannot, at the same time, be denied that the English afforded provocation sufficient to chafe a temper less irritable than that of Director Kieft, who, to his other troubles, had now the additional misery of feeling that his government was overwhelmed with debts to a large amount, which it was out of his power to meet, and for the means to liquidate which, he should be obliged to draw on the company in Holland, who were already too much dissatisfied with the manner in which he had administered the affairs of New Netherland, to honor any more of his drafts.

Nov. 22.

He took, however, the earliest opportunity to communicate the intelligence of the progress of the English encroachments at the northeast to the directors at Amsterdam, who contented them selves with instructing him to collect the most correct information, particularly as to the pretended right which the Indians had to sell to the English the soil situated within the Dutch limits in the direction of Fort Orange. He was further instructed to prevent the erection by the former of any trading-post in that quarter, by all possible means short of such dangerous proceedings as might provoke a war, of which the directors seem to have already had more than enough; to watch, in the mean time, the actions of his neighbors, who seemed now intent on appropriating to themselves the whole of the Dutch possessions in North America, and to oppose all further encroachments on their part.[1]

The annals of this year are marked by two extensive grants on the North River, for the purpose of establishing additional colonies. Regardless of the claims of the Patroon of Rensselaerswyck, the rich and fertile lands of Katskill were patented to Cornelis Antonissen van Slyck, of Breuckelen, in return for the eminent services he had rendered in bringing about a general peace, and in ransoming prisoners in the hands of the Indians, "which well-known services should

Aug. 22.

[1] Alb. Rec. xii., 398.

BOOK III. 1646. of right be duly acknowledged ;"[1] and Adriaen van der Donck, now disappointed in his attempt to plant a colonie in the neighborhood of Rensselaerswyck, obtained, in consideration of the assistance he afforded in negotiating the treaty between the Director-general and the Mohawks, and in return for the advances he then made to enable the government to purchase presents for those Indians, the tract of land called Nepper-

[1] The following is a translation of this patent. "We, Willem Kieft, Director-general, and council, on behalf of the High and Mighty Lords States General of the United Netherlands, His Highness of Orange, and the Noble Lords Directors of the Privileged West India Company, residing in New Netherland: To all who shall see or hear these presents read, Health. Whereas Cornelis Antonissen, [Van Slyck,] of Breuckelen, hath appeared before Us, and with his associates requested permission to settle in free possession the land of Katskill lying on the River Mauritius, there to plant with his associates a Colonie, which he hath promised to do, according to the freedoms and exemptions of New Netherland: We, therefore, considering the great service which the aforesaid Cornelis Antonissen hath conferred on this country, as well in the making of peace as in the ransoming of prisoners, and it being proper that such notorious services should not remain unacknowledged, We have, as Director and Council, conceded and granted to the aforesaid Cornelis Antonissen, the above-mentioned land of the Katskill, to plant there a Colonie, within the time therefor enacted, and in the order appointed, or to be appointed, by the Noble Lords Majors. Wherefore We, in the quality aforesaid, deed and transport in a true, free, and perpetual possession, to the said Cornelis Antonissen, the aforesaid lands of the Katskill, giving him full power, authority, and special command, to enter on, cultivate, and make use of the said lands in the same manner as he should conclude to do with his other patrimonial estate, without our in any manner, in quality aforesaid, having, reserving, or retaining thereon any part, action, or authority in the least, but as regards the same, desisting from all henceforth and forever; promising to maintain this transport firmly, inviolably, and irrevocably; to perform and to fulfil every part thereof under the penalty of answering therefor according to law, without art or guile. This is subscribed, and with our Seal in red wax, fully and perfectly confirmed. Done in Fort Amsterdam, in New Netherland, this 22d of August, of the year of our Lord and Saviour one thousand six hundred six and forty.

[Signed,] "Willem Kieft.

"By order of the noble Director-general and council of N. N.

"Cornelis van Tienhoven,
"Secretary."

Book of Dutch Patents, GG 157, translation 363. The original of the above patent, on a small piece of parchment, and written in fine old Dutch text, is among the Rensselaerswyck MSS. in a high state of preservation. It is from this last-mentioned document that the above translation was made, as I had not discovered the record in the Secretary of state's office at the time.

haem, but now known as Yonkers. This valuable property was situate on the east side of the Hudson River, about sixteen miles above New Amsterdam. It was bounded on the north by the Saw-kill, which the Indians called Maccakassin, and ran south to Nepperhaem ; thence to the Shorakapkock kill and to Papirinimen Creek, called by the Dutch " Spuytenduyvel," whence it stretched eastward to the river Bronx. The title of this colonie was " Colen Donck," and the proprietor thereof was invested with all the rights and privileges contained in the charter of 1629.[1]

CHAP. VIII. 1646.

The village of Breuckelen was also incorporated this year, in consequence, possibly, of the serious and urgent complaints made by the Eight Men in the fall of 1644. The inhabitants of that village were authorized to elect two schepens, or magistrates, with power to decide all cases within their jurisdiction, according to their charter; and to adjoin others to their number, should the duties of their office become too onerous. Any persons obstinately opposing these were to be deprived of their share in the land around the village. These privileges were subsequently further enlarged, on the representation of the schepens that they were unable to provide against cases of violence and trespass. A Schout was appointed to assist them. Jan Teunissen was commissioned to fill this office, dependent, however, on the company's schout-fiscaal at New Amsterdam.[2]

Nov. 26.

[1] Alb. Rec. viii., 79, 80; Hol. Doc. vi., 118; Book of Patents, i., 56.

[2] Alb. Rec. ii., 357, 358, 385; iii., 362, 363.

CHAPTER IX.

Termination of Kieft's administration—General condition of the country—Slaves—Their lot under the Dutch—Population of New Netherland—Revenue—Causes of the backward state of the province—Advanced condition of New England—Reflections—Settlements enumerated—Their government—Transfer of the municipal institutions of Holland to New Netherland—Errors of contemporary writers—Character of Director Kieft—Denies the right of appeal from his judgments—Harsh and tyrannical proceedings against the Rev. Mr. Doughty and Mr. Van Hardenbergh—General discontent—State of morals, religion, and education—Conclusion.

BOOK III. 1646.

THE administration of Director Kieft, though he was not superseded in fact until 1647, may now be said to have virtually terminated. Serious complaints, charging him with nothing less than tyranny, extortion, murder, theft, and other heinous crimes, had, as we have already seen, been transmitted to the directors of the West India Company, and produced his recall. But though his successor was appointed, the States General did not issue his commission immediately on its having been demanded. They were desirous of understanding what disposition had been made of the complaints from New Netherland, and it was not until the application had been iterated more than once, that their High Mightinesses ordered a new commission to be expedited.

What the actual condition of the country was at this remote period, may, in the absence of all materials of a statistical nature, be easily gleaned from the remonstrances of the commonalty, and the proceedings of the home authorities consequent thereupon.

Slaves constituted, as far back as 1628, a portion of the population. The introduction of this class was facilitated by the establishments which the Dutch possessed in Brazil and on the coast of Guinea, as well as by the periodical capture of Spanish and Portuguese prizes, and the circumstances attendant on the early settlement of the country. The expense of obtaining labor from Europe was great, and the supply by no means equal to the demand. To add to these embarrassments, the temptations held out by the fur-trade were so irresistible, that the servants, or "boere-knechts," who were brought over from Holland, were soon seduced from the pursuits of agriculture. Farmers were consequently obliged to employ negroes, and slave-labor thus became, by its cheapness and the necessity of the case, one of the staples of the country.

The lot of the African under the Dutch, was not as hopeless as his situation might lead us to expect. He was "a chattel," it is true; but he could still look forward to the hour when he too might become a freeman. In the years 1644 and 1646, several negroes and their wives, who had originally been captured from the Spaniards, had been manumitted, in consequence of their long and faithful services. To enable them to provide for their support, they obtained a grant of land; but as the price of their manumission, they were bound to pay yearly twenty-two bushels and a half of corn, wheat, peas, or beans, and one fat hog valued at eight dollars, failing which, they were to lose their liberty and return again to their former state of servitude. The emancipation of the parents did not, however, carry with it that of their offspring. "All their children already born, or yet to be born, remained obligated to serve the company as slaves." The fathers were moreover obligated to serve "by water or by land" when called upon so to do. The price of a negro averaged between one hundred and one hundred and fifty dollars. The detention of the children in slavery, after the emancipation of the parents, was highly disapproved of by the commonalty, who considered it a violation of the law of nature. "How any one born of a free Christian mother, could, notwithstanding, be a slave, and be obliged to remain such, passed their comprehension. It was impossible for them to explain it." The authorities attempted to palliate the act. "They were treated just like Christians." But this was considered alike unsatisfactory.[1]

The population, comprising all who came under the title

[1] Van Tienhoven; Alb. Rec. ii., 243, 378; xx., 296; xxi., 416, 417; Hol. Doc. iii., 351; Van der Donck's Vertoogh, van N. N.

BOOK III. 1646.

of the "Gemeente," or commonalty of New Amsterdam, amounted, in 1643, to five hundred men. This would give a total of twenty-five hundred souls. Allowing that Rensselaerswyck and the few towns on Long Island contained four hundred more, we should then be justified in estimating the whole population of New Netherland at that date, at about three thousand.

The public revenue was computed to amount to sixteen thousand guilders, or six thousand four hundred dollars per annum.

The population was seriously affected by the difficulties with the Indians. Many had removed to the neighborhood of Fort Orange; others returned to Holland; and numbers had been slain by the savages. The consequence was, that in and around Fort Amsterdam, the male adult population was reduced to one hundred at the close of the war.[1] By the removal of the first portion of the inhabitants, the population of the country was not, however, actually decreased. The only diminution it experienced, was by emigration and loss of life, and, these considered, we doubt much if, at the close of Kieft's administration, the population exceeded a thousand souls. This figure is, we admit, low, and after a lapse of so many years, creditable neither to the founders nor managers of the province, especially when contrasted with the progress and flourishing condition of the adjoining English colonies. But it could not well be otherwise. It was one of the natural consequences of the imperfect system and mismanagement of which the country was the victim. For the first thirteen years after its discovery, it was abandoned to the casual and rare visits of a few private trading-ships, which came for the mere purpose of taking away the furs that their servants or agents might have collected at Fort Orange or the Manhattans. When the West India Company became incorporated, this system was not altered. Those in the employ of that association merely took the place of their predecessors. The visits

[1] In Hol. Doc. iii., 369, it is asserted, that in 1648 not much more than one hundred males could be found besides the free traders. The population of New England then was 50 to 60,000.

of the company's ships were still made for the sole purpose of carrying back to Holland the collected peltries; and during Minuit's and Van Twiller's administrations, so exclusively was everybody absorbed in the Indian trade, so few were the agricultural settlers, and so little was agriculture attended to, that the colonists depended, we may say wholly, on the parent country for their supplies. These unfortunately failed one season under Van Twiller, and the consequence was, that the settlers around Fort Amsterdam were thrown for food on the charity of the Indians.

The evil consequences of the policy pursued by the directors in Holland towards New Netherland became apparent shortly after the removal of the Massachusetts Company to America. This association adopting a wiser system, encouraged immigration by every means compatible with the peculiar principles of their municipal government. The country became soon inhabited by industrious settlers, full of energy, who, stimulated by the freedom of trade which they enjoyed, and unfettered by those special privileges which followed wherever the civil law was established, spread themselves abroad in every direction, and soon seized on the richest portion of the Dutch possessions. Entertaining, as the West India Company did, no feeling for the prosperity of the country, except so far as the returns of the fur-trade were concerned; reduced to a state of bankruptcy by its vast undertakings elsewhere; distracted by internal dissensions, each chamber striving to secure for itself the largest share of profit at the expense of the smallest amount of disbursements,[1] it is not surprising that the encroachments of the people of New England resulted in success. Numbers effected what unprotected feebleness could not prevent; self-interest overpowered what national law alone supported, and the Dutch were forced, though unwillingly, to yield.

The reflections of the historian can neither recall the past, nor alter the course of human events. But the review of those

[1] Alle de inwoonders in Nieu Nederlandt gelooven dat de Bewinthebbers gants geen acht off regard op Nieu Nederlandt nemen, dan alsser wat te ontvangen is; hetwelcke, nochtans, maeckt dat sy te minder ontfangen. Van der Donck.

BOOK III. 1646. transactions will teach nations this abiding lesson:—that it is in vain to have either right or justice at their side, if they have not, at the same time, the means to maintain the one, and enforce the other; and to statesmen this wholesome truth, that as the government of an exclusive mercantile company is the worst of all governments for any country, so colonies can never be fostered or promoted by the commercial monopolies of such privileged associations.[1]

With the exception of the few individuals who possessed means sufficient to found Patroonships, or to establish plantations, the mass of the inhabitants of New Netherland, as is the case in all new countries, were far from wealthy. Van der Donck represents that the greater portion of them "brought nothing" to the country; a statement which is amply borne out by the fact that the government was called on, occasionally, to assist immigrants by advances, or loans of money, without interest, to enable them to make a beginning.

The greater number of the houses around forts Amsterdam and Orange were, in those days, low-sized wooden buildings, with roofs of reed or straw, and chimneys of wood. Wind or water mills were erected, here and there, to grind corn, or to saw lumber. One of the latter, situate on Nut or Governor's Island, was leased in 1639 for five hundred merchantable boards yearly, half oak and half pine.[2] Saw and grist mills were built on several of the creeks in the colonie of Rensselaerswyck, where "a horse mill" was also erected in 1646.[3] A brewery

[1] Smith's Wealth of Nations ii., 64.

[2] Alb. Rec. i., 155, 185; vii., 105, 114.

[3] 31 January, 1646: Contract for a Horse-mill. The mill situate on the fifth kill being, to the great damage of the Patroon, and inhabitants of the colonie, [Rensselaerswyck,] for a considerable time out of repair, or unfit to be worked, either by the breaking of the dam, the severity of the winter, or the high water, or otherwise; besides being out of the way, to the prejudice of the inhabitants in going and returning, a contract, after being duly proposed to the court, is, therefore, made with Pieter Cornelissen to build a horse-mill in the Pine grove, whereby not only the colonie, but also, if so be, the navigators who come hither, may be encouraged to provide themselves with other things. Pieter Cornelisz. shall complete the work for fl. 300, ($120.) I furnishing him fl. 200 in stones, two good horses, the expense of which is to be divided between us, half and half. The standing work, plank, labor, and other expenses, we

had been constructed previous to 1637, in the same quarter, by the Patroon, with the exclusive right of supplying retail-dealers with beer. But private individuals were allowed the privilege, notwithstanding, to brew whatever quantity of beer they might require for consumption within their own families.[1]

CHAP. IX. 1646.

The settlement of the country beyond the precincts of New Amsterdam received, as we have seen, a serious check by the Indian war. On the eastern extremity of Long Island, the English had established the towns of South Hampton and South Old. The plantations at the west end, under the jurisdiction of the Dutch, were, however, far more numerous, and now comprised Breukelen, Amersfoort, (Flatlands,) Gravenzande, Vlissingen, (Flushing,) Heemstede, Mespath, (Newtown,) and Gowanus. There was a small hamlet called Bergen, besides a number of valuable bouweries on what is now the Jersey side of the river, but this section suffered, comparatively speaking, more than any other from the savages, who laid

shall defray in common, bearing, each, equal profit and loss. On the completion of the mill, and on its being ready to go, Pieter Cornelissen shall work one day for himself and the other day for the Patroon, and so forth; the Patroon paying him one Rix dollar for his day. Should it happen, as we expect, that so great a demand shall arise, so that the mill will not supply all the colonie or strangers, (buytenwoonders,) then P. Cornelisz. is alone authorized and privileged to erect, in company with the Patroon, another such mill, on these or such other conditions as are now, or shall hereafter be agreed on. Signed, Anthony de Hooges, Pieter Cornelissen. Rensselaerswyck MSS. A mill worked by horses stood, in the course of the last century, as I am informed by an aged citizen, on the lot forming the northeast corner of Hudson and Grand streets, Albany. There was a mill also on the 3d or Rutten kill, in 1646.

[1] 26 Dec. 1646. Whereas their Honors of the Court of this Colonie find that Cornelis Segersz. notwithstanding former placards and prohibitions, has still presumed to meddle with what is not his business—with beer brewing—directly contrary to the grant and authorization given to the brewery of this colonie; Therefore their honors expressly forbid the said Cornelis Segersz. to brew, or cause to be brewed, or otherwise to manufacture any beer, except so much as shall be required by him for his own housekeeping, on pain of forfeiting twenty-five Carolus guilders, besides the brewed beer. The said Cornelis Segersz. is further warned that no cloak, or idle excuse shall hereafter avail, but that this ordinance shall be maintained and executed on the spot, without court process, if he shall make any mistake. Let him, therefore, prevent his loss. Actum Rensselaerswyck, 26th October, 1646. Pursuant to the resolution of their honors the magistrates of this colonie. A. De Hooges.

BOOK III. 1646. waste every cultivated spot from the Nevesinck to Tappaan. Rensselaerswyck was the only "colonie" which remained uninjured by the war. As a consequence its population generally prospered, and sundry farms were taken up. Beverswyck continued, however, in swaddling clothes, for the city which in 1845 holds over forty thousand inhabitants, contained in 1646 no more than ten houses. Several farmers had at an early date begun another settlement south of Beverswyck, to which they gave the name of Bethlehem. A few bouweries were also cultivated on the east side of the river, opposite Fort Orange. Katskill and its fertile bottoms had engaged at an early date the attention of the settlers at Rensselaerswyck, but the pretensions of opposite parties prevented any planting of consequence in that quarter, and Van Slyck, who had received a patent for lands there, had as yet made no commencement. The country between Rensselaerswyck and the Manhattans, on both sides of the river, still remained a wilderness. It is true that the Dutch had built a fort at Esopus, in the year 1614, contemporaneously with the erection of their post on Castle island.[1] This possibly might have been followed by the clearing of some small portions of land in that vicinity, but it is very doubtful whether any such settlements survived the destructive war of 1644–5. Van der Donck had also received a grant of Yonkers, but many years elapsed before he commenced a settlement there. These remarks apply in like manner to the Delaware, which, at this date, was, with the exception of Bogaerdt's colonie, destitute of any Dutch settlers, and entirely under the control of the Swedes.

In the municipal government of these settlements, two systems, essentially different in principle, obtained. In the "colonies" the superintending power was lodged in one individual, who, though the immediate vassal of the sovereign

[1] Moulton alludes to the settlement of some Hollanders among the Esopus Indians in 1617. But the following passage in the answer of the States General, dated Feb. 1665, to Sir George Downing, fixes the date earlier. Their High Mightinesses say: "Il y a plus de quarante ans qu'elle possede la ville de Nouveau Amsterdam avec ses forts; et plus de cinquante qu'elle est en possession des forts Orange et Esope; les uns et les autres avec les terres et pais qui en dependent." Hol. Doc., xi., 86.

authority from which he derived his lands, was himself lord paramount in his manor, where he not only represented the sovereign, but exercised feudal jurisdiction over his colonists, who stood, towards him, in the same relation that he occupied towards the supreme head of the state. For as he was bound to acknowledge, by fealty and homage, his dependence on the latter; so were they vassals of their Patroon, to whom they swore allegiance, at whose summons they were bound, if occasion required, to take up arms; to whose special courts, edicts, ordinances, and laws they owed obedience, being subject at the same time to the discharge of all the minor obligations due to him by virtue of the Roman law. In return for this obedience, the Patroon was bound to protect his colonists, who had the additional right to address themselves by appeal to the supreme authority at New Amsterdam, in case they were either aggrieved or oppressed.

In the transition of society, towards the close of the middle ages, from this state of servitude to a more enlarged liberty, some communes, or towns in our acceptation of the word, acquired for themselves, either by special favor or their own right hands, all independence of these feudal nobles, and held their privileges and immunities immediately from the crown. But as the feudal system acknowledged no other relation than that of vassal and sovereign, it became necessary to imagine, or invent, some bond, or link, whereby these semi-independent commonalties should be connected to the head of the state. By a fiction of law, each of them became to be considered, abstractly, a moral and responsible body, capable of the same duties, obligations, and constraints as an individual. They were incorporated, and in this corporate capacity, holding immediately from the state, they were considered as vassals; as such held land in fee, tendered fealty and homage, military service, and possessed, in fine, all the rights of Patroons.

One arrangement still remained to render the connection between this body and the supreme authority complete. It became necessary that it have a representative, through whom all communications should pass, from the commune, or town, to the sovereign, and from the latter to the district. For

BOOK III. 1646. this purpose the inhabitants were authorized, in the course of the fifteenth century, to elect from among themselves a certain number, double or triple, that required; from which the head of the government selected and appointed such as it considered best qualified to act as "schepens" or magistrates. These constituted a board, or council, by which all such communications were made: they constituted, at the same time, a local court to administer justice within their respective limits, to the extent and according to the provisions of their patent or charter; and to enable them to perform more effectually their duties, a schout, or sheriff, secretary, and marshal were adjoined. But in order to prevent the magistrates becoming too powerful, and with a view to equalize their functions, and to allow all to enjoy, in turn, the dignities which municipal honors conferred, their duration in office was limited, in conformity to sound principle, to one year, at the end of which a new election took place; a new set of names was sent in to the chief magistrate, who again made his selection from that list, and from the actual "schepens" in commission, who "were always con sidered as nominated."[1]

For more than a century previous to the period of which we now write, three hundred manors in the province of Holland alone, enjoyed all the rights of free municipalities, and exercised civil and criminal jurisdiction, to a limited extent. In removing to another hemisphere, the Dutch lost not their affection for their native country and its institutions. They brought with them the names of those places to which they were most attached, and in the course of time transferred also to their new homes the municipal system which we have described above, and with which they were most conversant.

"Those colonists who shall form within their limits such a settlement of people, as to constitute hamlets, villages, or even cities, shall obtain in such case middle and low jurisdiction, and the same rights as manors in the province of Holland; and

[1] **Institutions Judiciaires, iii., 47, 48, 49, 165, 166, 170, 171; Alb. Rec. x., 221. "It is customary in our Fatherland, and other well-regulated governments, that annually some change takes place in the magistracy, so that some new ones are appointed, and some are continued to inform the newly appointed." Alb. Rec. xix., 131.**

shall, in like manner, be capacitated also, to bear and use the names and titles thereof. And the qualified persons of such cities, villages, and hamlets, shall, in such case, be authorized to nominate for the office of magistrates, a double number of persons wherefrom a selection shall seasonably be made by the Director and council, the appointment of a schout, secretary, and court messenger, remaining to the company; with the understanding that the jurisdiction shall be holden in fief by the respective colonists and founders of cities and villages, to be disposed of and renewed, in case of the demise of those who shall be named, in manner hereinbefore stated. And justice shall be administered therein according to the style and order of the province of Holland, and the cities and manors thereof, to which end the courts there shall follow, as far as the same is possible, the ordinances received here in Amsterdam." CHAP. IX. 1646.

It was then to that Republican State—to the wise and beneficent modifications of the feudal code which obtained there, and not to "the puritan idea of popular freedom" introduced by emigrants from Connecticut—as some incorrectly claim—that New Netherland and the several towns within its confines were indebted for whatever municipal privileges they enjoyed.[1] The charters under which they were planted, the immunities which they obtained, were essentially of Dutch, and not of Connecticut origin, and those who look to New England as the source of popular privileges in New Netherland, fall, therefore, into an error, sanctioned neither by law, nor by history. Strange as it may seem, while every colonie, and almost every hamlet, had its local magistracy, the citizens of New Amsterdam, the capital of the whole province, continued, greatly to their discontent, without a voice in the management of their municipal affairs. The government of that city still remained in the hands of the Director-general and his council.

The high-handed and dictatorial manner in which Kieft

[1] Mr. Bancroft, in Hist. U. S. ii., 304, represents that "the large emigrations from Connecticut engrafted on New Netherlands the Puritan idea of popular freedom." In this he did injustice to the Dutch—inadvertently, no doubt—as every one must acknowledge who has examined the subject.

BOOK III. 1646. wielded his power, brought him into collision, at an early period, with the democratic spirit inherent in the breast of the Dutch republicans. He was a man of unpliant temper; inflated with the idea of his own importance; ill-disposed to brook contradiction, and construing all objections to his will, even though emanating from the pulpit, as attacks on his prerogative. "Had we been under a king we could not be worse treated," was the complaint of the people. One check to all this remained, to which the colonists looked for protection. This was the right to appeal from the Director-general's judgments to the court of Holland, or the States General. But this privilege Kieft cut off as early as 1643. The island of Manhattans was the capital of New Netherland, and to it was reserved the exclusive right, as the chief court of that country, to hear appeals from all surrounding colonies; and, on this pretence, it was maintained that no appeal could lie from the decisions of the Director-general and council at New Amsterdam.[1]

The Rev. Mr. Doughty, the English clergyman at Mespath, and Mr. Van Hardenbergh, merchant at New Amsterdam, were among the first to dissent from this conclusion. The former had complained against what he considered an unjust decision of the court at Manhattans, in regard to claims which he set forth to lands embraced within the Newtown patent. The other had been appointed curator to the estate of one Aert Teunissen, who, as we have already related, had been murdered by the Indians at Beeregat. Some property belonging to this estate had been seized on board a vessel, and in consequence of not having been entered, was confiscated. Appeals were lodged, in both these cases, from Kieft's judgments, Doughty was immediately fined ten dollars, and imprisoned twenty-four hours for his presumption.[2] Against the other appellant was pronounced the following sentence:

[1] Wat belanght 't weygeren van appel naer 't Vaderlandt, 't selve is geschiet, omdat in de exemptien 't eylandt van de Manhattans voor de hooft-plaats van N. N. wort gereserveert, en dat alle omleggende colonien haer appel daer hebben soude als 't hof van dat quartier. Van Tienhoven.

[2] The reader will find in the Appendix Ff. the statements in favor of and against Doughty in the above case.

"Having seen the written demand of the Honorable Fiscaal Van der Huygens against Arnoldus van Hardenbergh, in the case of appeal from our sentence dated 28th April ult., as appears by the signature of the aforesaid A. van Hardenbergh, from which sentence no appeal can lie, as is evident to him from the commission of their High Mightinesses the Lords States General and His Highness of Orange; therefore, the noble Director-general and council of New Netherland, observing the dangerous consequences which tend to the injury of the supreme authority of the magistracy of this land, as an example to others, condemn the aforesaid Arnoldus van Hardenbergh to pay forthwith a fine of twenty-five guilders, or to go to jail until the said fine be paid."

CHAP. IX. 1646.

Owing to these and various other harsh measures, the public mind became inflamed to a high degree. "Traitor," "villain," "liar," were epithets flung at the Director-general with unsparing hand; and, notwithstanding that banishments and heavy fines were imposed on the libellers, many threatened him with rougher usage when he should "take off the coat with which he was decorated by the Lords his masters."

"Where the shepherd errs the sheep go astray." Drunkenness and broils were of common occurrence. The people were "without discipline, and approaching to a savage state." "A fourth part of the city of New Amsterdam consisted of grog-shops and houses where nothing is to be got but tobacco and beer." Religion and education felt the baneful effects of these evil influences. The church which had been commenced in 1642, remained still unfinished, as if the country were without timber or a sawmill. The Director-general being distressed for money, applied to his own use the fines and forfeitures which had been appropriated to aid the completion of this sacred edifice.[1] In the mean while no efforts were made to convert the heathen, between whom and the settlers an un-

[1] Alb. Rec. ii., 160, 190, 262, 369; iv., 1; vii., 28, 29, 38, 300. Van der Donck's Vertoogh, c. xi. Wel is waer dat den Directeur Kieft, verlegen synde om gelt, in syn huys hadde hangen een bos, daer de Diakenen een sleutel van hadden, daerin alle cleyne breuken en boeten, die op de rechtdagen voor vielen gesteken waren; met kennisse van de diaconen heeft geopent, en 't gelt dat een moye somme was, op intrest genomen. Van Tienhoven Cort Bericht.

BOOK III. 1646.

licensed intercourse generally prevailed. And, though a college had been founded in Massachusetts some nine years before, the authorities of New Netherland made little or no effort, up to this time, to establish a common primary school in any part of this country. Some subscriptions had been entered into by the commonalty for the purpose of erecting a school-house in New Amsterdam, but these funds were also misappropriated, and this laudable undertaking failed in consequence.

Such was the state of disorganization into which the public affairs had fallen, when General PETRUS STUYVESANT assumed the government of New Netherland.

APPENDIX.

APPENDIX.

A.

A Charter given by the High and Mighty Lords, the States General, to the West India Company, dated the 3d *of June*, 1621.

The States General of the United Netherlands, to all who shall see these presents or hear them read, greeting: Be it known, that We, knowing that the prosperity of these countries, and the welfare of their inhabitants, depend principally on navigation and trade, which in all former times by the said countries were carried on happily, and with a great blessing to all countries and kingdoms; and desiring that the aforesaid inhabitants should not only be preserved in their former navigation, traffic, and trade, but also that their trade may be increased as much as possible in special conformity to the treaties, alliances, leagues, and covenants, for traffic and navigation formerly made with other princes, republics, and people, which We give them to understand must be in all parts punctually kept and adhered to: And We find by experience, that without the common help, assistance, and interposition of a General Company, the people designed from hence for those parts cannot be properly protected and maintained in their great risk from pirates, extortion, and otherwise, which will happen in so very long a voyage. We have, therefore, and for several other important reasons and considerations us thereunto moving, with mature deliberation of counsel, and for highly necessary causes, found it good, that the navigation, trade, and commerce, in the parts of the West Indies, and Africa, and other places hereafter described, should not henceforth be carried on any otherwise than by the common united strength of the merchants and inhabitants of these countries, and that for that end there shall be erected one General Company, which We, out of special regard to their common well-being, and to keep and preserve the inhabitants of those places in good trade and welfare, will maintain and strengthen with Our help, favor, and assistance, as far as the present state and condition of this country will admit: and, moreover, furnish them with a proper charter, and with the following privileges and exemptions, to wit: That for the term of four and twenty years, none of the natives or inhabitants of these countries shall be permitted to sail to or from the said lands, or to traffic on the coast and countries of Africa, from the Tropic of Cancer to the Cape of Good Hope, nor in the countries of America, or the West Indies, beginning at the fourth end of Terra Nova, by the Straits of Magellan, La Maire, or any other straits and passages situated thereabouts to the Straits of Anian, as well on the North Sea as the South Sea, nor on any islands situated on the one side or the other, or between both: nor in the western or southern countries, reaching, lying, and between both the meridians, from the Cape of Good Hope, in the east, to the east end of New Guinea, in the west, inclusive, but in the name of this United Company of these United Netherlands. And whoever shall presume, without the consent of this company, to sail or to traffic in any of the places within the aforesaid limits granted to this company, he shall forfeit the ships and the goods which shall be found for sale upon the aforesaid coasts and lands; the which being actually seized by the aforesaid company, shall be by them kept for their own benefit and behoof. And in case such ships or goods shall be sold either in other countries or havens they may touch at, the owners and partners must be fined for the value of those ships and goods: Except only, that they who before the date of this charter, shall have sailed or been sent out of these or any other countries to any of the aforesaid coasts, shall be able to continue their trade for the sale of their goods, and come back again, or otherwise, until the expiration of this charter, if they have had any before, and not longer: Provided, that after the first of July, sixteen hundred and twenty-one, the day and time of this charter's commencing, no person shall be able to send any ships or goods to the places comprehended in this charter, although that before the date hereof, this company was not finally incorporated: but shall provide therein, as is becoming, against those who knowingly by fraud endeavor to frustrate our intention herein for the public good: Provided that the salt trade at Ponte del Re may be continued according to the conditions and instructions by Us already given, or that may be given respecting it, any thing in this charter to the contrary notwithstanding.

II. That moreover, the aforesaid company may, in Our name and authority, within the limits herein before prescribed, make contracts, engagements, and alliances, with the princes and natives of the countries comprehended therein, and also build any forts and fortifications there, to appoint and discharge governors, people for war, and officers of justice, and other public officers, for the preservation of the places, keeping good order, police, and justice, and in like manner for the promoting of trade; and again, others in their place to put, as they, from the situation of their affairs, shall see fit: moreover, they must advance the peopling of those fruitful and unsettled parts, and do all that the service of those countries and the profit and increase of trade shall require: and the company shall successively communicate and transmit to Us such contracts and alliances as they shall have made with the aforesaid princes and nations; and likewise the situations of the fortresses, fortifications, and settlements by them taken.

III. Saving, that they having chosen a governor-in-chief, and prepared instructions for him, they shall be approved, and a commission given by Us: And that further, such governor-in-chief, as well as other deputy governors, commanders, and officers, shall be held to take an oath of allegiance to Us and also to the company.

IV. And if the aforesaid company in any of the aforesaid places shall be cheated under the appearance of friendship, or badly treated, or shall suffer loss in trusting their money or goods, without having restitution or receiving payment for them, they may use the best methods in their power, according to the situation of their affairs, to obtain satisfaction.

V. And if it should be necessary, for the establishment, security, and defence of this trade, to take any troops with them, We will, according to the constitution of this country, and the situation of affairs, furnish the said company with such troops, provided they be paid and supported by the company.

VI. Which troops, besides the oath already taken to Us and to his Excellency, shall swear to obey the commands of the said company, and to endeavor to promote their interest to the utmost of their ability.

VII. That the provosts of the company on shore may apprehend any of the military that have enlisted in the service of the aforesaid company, and may confine them on board the ships in whatever city, place, or jurisdiction they may be found; provided, the provosts first inform the officers and magistrates of the cities and places where this happens.

VIII. That We will not take any ships, ordnance, or ammunition belonging to the company, for the use of this country, without the consent of the said company.

IX. We having moreover incorporated this company, and favored them with privileges, We give them a charter besides this, that they may pass freely with all their ships and goods without paying any toll to the United Provinces; and that they themselves may use their liberty in the same manner as the free inhabitants of the cities of this country enjoy their freedom, notwithstanding any person who is not free may be a member of this company.

X. That all the goods of this company during the eight next ensuing years, may be carried out of this country to the parts of the West Indies and Africa, and other places comprehended within the aforesaid limits, and those which they shall bring into this country from thence shall be exempt from outward and home convoys; provided, that if at the expiration of the aforesaid eight years, the state and condition of these countries will not admit of this freedom's continuing for a longer time, the said goods, and the merchandises coming from the places mentioned in this charter, and exported again out of these countries, and the outward convoys and licenses, during the whole time of this charter, shall not be rated higher by Us than they have formerly been rated, unless We should be again engaged in a war, in which case all the aforesaid goods and merchandises shall not be rated higher by Us than they were in the last list in time of war.

XI. And that this company may be strengthened by a good government, to the general profit and satisfaction of all concerned, We have ordained that the said government shall be vested in five chambers of managers; one at Amsterdam,—this shall have the management of four-ninth parts; one chamber in Zealand, for two-ninth parts; one chamber at Maeze, for one-ninth part; one chamber in North Holland, for one-ninth part; and the fifth chamber in Friesland, with the city and country, for one-ninth part, upon the condition entered in the record of Our resolutions, and the act passed respecting it. And the provinces in which there are no chambers shall be accommodated with so many managers, divided among the respective chambers, as their hundred thousand guilders in this company shall entitle them to.

XII. That the Chamber of Amsterdam shall consist of twenty managers; the Chamber of Zealand of twelve; the Chamber of Maeze and of the North part, each of fourteen; and the Chamber of Friesland, with the city and country, also of fourteen managers. If it shall hereafter appear that this work cannot be carried on without a greater number of persons; in that case, more may be added, with the knowledge of the Nineteen, and our approbation, but not otherwise.

XIII. And the States of the United Provinces are authorized to lay before their High Mightinesses' ordinary deputies, or before the magistrates of the cities of these

51

Provinces, any order for registering the members, together with the election of managers, if they find they can do it according to the constitution of their Provinces. Moreover, that no person in the Chamber of Amsterdam shall be chosen a manager who has not of his own in the funds of the company, the sum of six thousand guilders; and the chamber of Zealand four thousand guilders; and the chamber of Maeze, of the north part, and of Friesland, with the city and country, the like sum of four thousand guilders.

XIV. That the first managers shall serve for the term of six years, and then one-third part of the number of managers shall be changed by lot; and two years after a like third part; and the two next following years, the last third part; and so on successively, the oldest in the service shall be dismissed: and in the place of those who go off, or of any that shall die, or for any other reason be dismissed, three others shall be nominated by the managers, both remaining and going off, together with the principal adventurers in person, and at their cost, from which the aforesaid provinces, the deputies, or the magistrates, shall make a new election of a manager, and successively supply the vacant places; and it shall be held before the principal adventurers, who have as great a concern as the respective managers.

XV. That the accounts of the furniture and outfit of the vessels, with their dependencies, shall be made up three months after the departure of the vessels, and one month after, copies shall be sent to Us, and to the respective chambers: and the state of the returns, and their sales, shall the chambers (as often as We see good, or they are required thereto by the chambers) send to Us and to one another.

XVI. That every six years they shall make a general account of all outfits and returns, together with all the gains and losses of the company; to wit, one of their business, and one of the war, each separate: which accounts shall be made public by an advertisement, to the end that every one who is interested may, upon hearing of it, attend; and if by the expiration of the seventh year, the accounts are not made out in manner aforesaid, the managers shall forfeit their commissions, which shall be appropriated to the use of the poor, and they themselves be held to render their account as before, till such time and under such penalty as shall be fixed by us respecting offenders. And notwithstanding, there shall be a dividend made of the profits of the business, so long as We find that ten per cent. shall have been gained.

XVII. No one shall, during the continuance of this charter, withdraw his capital or sum advanced from this company; nor shall any new members be admitted. If at the expiration of four and twenty years it shall be found good to continue this company, or to erect a new one, a final account and estimate shall be made by the Nineteen, with Our knowledge, of all that belongs to the company, and also of all their expenses, and any one after the aforesaid settlement and estimate may withdraw his money or continue it in the new company in whole or in part, in the same proportion as in this; and the new company shall in such case take the remainder, and pay the members which do not think fit to continue in the company their share, at such times as the Nineteen, with Our knowledge and approbation, shall think proper.

XVIII. That so often as it shall be necessary to have a general meeting of the aforesaid chambers, it shall be by Nineteen persons, of whom eight shall come from the chamber of Amsterdam; from Zealand, four; from the Maeze, two; from North Holland, two; from Friesland and the city and country, two; provided, that the nineteen persons, or so many more as We shall at any time think fit, shall be deputed by Us for the purpose of helping to direct the aforesaid meeting of the company.

XIX. By which general meeting of the aforesaid chambers, all the business of this company which shall come before them shall be managed and finally settled; provided, that in case of resolving upon a war, Our approbation shall be asked.

XX. The aforesaid general meeting being summoned, it shall meet to resolve when they shall fit out, and how many vessels they will send to each place, the company in general observing that no particular chamber shall undertake any thing in opposition to the foregoing resolution, but shall be held to carry the same effectually into execution. And if any chamber shall be found not following the common resolution, or contravening it, We have authorized, and by these presents do authorize, the said meeting immediately to cause reparation to be made of every defect or contravention; wherein We, being desired, will assist them.

XXI. The said general meeting shall be held the first six years in the city of Amsterdam, and two years thereafter in Zealand; and so on from time to time in the aforesaid two places.

XXII. The managers to whom the affairs of the company shall be committed, who shall go from home to attend the aforesaid meeting or otherwise, shall have for their expenses and wages, four guilders a day, besides boat and carriage hire: Provided, that those who go from one city to another, to the chambers, as managers and governors, shall receive no wages or travelling charges, at the cost of the company.

XXIII. And if it should happen that in the aforesaid general meeting, any weighty matter should come before them, wherein they cannot agree, or in case the votes are equally divided, the same shall be left to Our decision; and whatever shall be determined upon shall be carried into execution.

XXIV. And all the inhabitants of these countries, and also of other countries, shall be notified by public advertisements, within one month after the date hereof, that they may be admitted into this company, during five months from the first of July, this year, sixteen hundred and twenty-one, and that they must pay the money they put into the stock in three payments; to wit, one-third part at the expiration of the aforesaid five months, and the other two-thirds within three next succeeding years. In case the aforesaid general meeting shall find it necessary to prolong the time, the members shall be notified by an advertisement.

XXV. The ships returning from a voyage shall come to the place they sailed from; and if, by stress of weather, the vessels which sailed out from one part shall arrive in another,—as those from Amsterdam or North Holland, in Zealand or in the Maeze, or from Zealand in Holland—or those from Friesland, with the city and country, in another part,—each chamber shall nevertheless have the direction and management of the vessels and goods it sent out, and shall send and transport the goods to the places from whence the vessels sailed, either in the same or other vessels: Provided that the managers of that chamber shall be held in person to find the place where the vessels and goods are arrived, and not appoint factors to do this business; but in case they shall not be in a situation for travelling, they shall commit this business to the chamber of the place where the vessels arrived.

XXVI. If any chamber has got any goods or returns from the places included within the limits of this charter, with which another is not provided, it shall be held to send such goods to the chamber which is unprovided, on its request, according to the situation of the case; and if they have sold them, to send to another chamber for more. And in like manner, if the managers of the respective chambers have need of any persons for fitting out the vessels, or otherwise, from the cities where there are chambers or managers, they shall require and employ the managers of this company, without making use of a factor.

XXVII. And if any of the provinces think fit to appoint an agent to collect the money from the inhabitants, and to make a fund in any chamber, and for paying dividends, the chamber shall be obliged to give such agent access, that he may obtain information of the state of the disbursements and receipts, and of the debts; provided that the money brought in by such agents amount to fifty thousand guilders or upwards.

XXVIII. The managers shall have for commissions one per cent. on the outfits and returns, besides the prizes, and a half per cent. on gold and silver; which commission shall be divided—to the chamber of Amsterdam, four-ninth parts; the chamber of Zealand, two-ninth parts; the Maeze, one-ninth part; North Holland, one-ninth part; and Friesland, with the city and country, a like ninth part.

XXIX. Provided that they shall not receive commissions on the ordnance and the ships more than once. They shall, moreover, have no commission on the ships, ordnance, and other things with which We shall strengthen the company, nor on the money which they shall collect for the company, nor on the profits they receive from the goods, nor shall they charge the company with any expenses of travelling, or provisions for those to whom they shall commit the providing a cargo and purchasing goods necessary for it.

XXX. The book-keepers and cashiers shall have a salary paid them out of their commissions.

XXXI. The managers shall not deliver or sell to the company, in whole or in part, any of their own ships, merchandise, or goods; nor buy, or cause to be bought of the said company, directly or indirectly, any goods or merchandise, nor have any portion or part therein, on forfeiture of one year's commissions for the use of the poor, and the loss of office.

XXXII. The managers shall give notice by advertisement, as often as they have a fresh importation of goods and merchandise, to the end that every one may have seasonable knowledge of it before they proceed to a final sale.

XXXIII. And if it happens that in either chamber any of the managers shall get into such a situation, that he cannot make good what was intrusted to him during his administration, and in consequence thereof any loss shall happen, such chamber shall be liable for the damage, and shall also be specially bound for their administration, which shall also be the case with all the members who, on account of goods purchased, or otherwise, shall become debtors to the company, and so shall be reckoned all cases relating to their stock and what may be due to the company.

XXXIV. The managers of the respective chambers shall be responsible for their respective cashiers and book-keepers.

XXXV. That all the goods of this company which shall be sold by weight, shall be sold by one weight, to wit, that of Amsterdam; and that all such goods shall be put on board ship, or in store, without paying any excise, impost, or weigh-money: Provided that they, being sold, shall not be delivered in any other way than by weight; and provided that the impost and weigh-money shall be paid as often as they are alienated, in the same manner as other goods subject to weigh-money.

XXXVI. That the persons or goods of the managers shall not be arrested, attached, or incumbered, in order to obtain from them an account of the administration of the company, nor for the payment of the wages of those who are in the service of the company; but those who shall pretend to take the same upon them, shall be bound to refer the matter to their ordinary judges.

XXXVII. So when any ship shall return from a voyage, the generals or commanders of the fleets shall be obliged to come and report to Us the success of the voyage of such ship or ships, within ten days after their arrival, and shall deliver and leave with Us a report in writing, if the case requires it.

XXXVIII. And if it happens (which We by no means expect) that any person will in any manner hurt or hinder the navigation, business, trade, or traffic of this company, contrary to the common right and the contents of the aforesaid treaties, leagues, and covenants, they shall defend it against them, and regulate it by the instructions We have given concerning it.

XXXIX. We have, moreover, promised, and do promise, that We will defend this company against every person in free navigation and traffic, and assist them with a million of guilders, to be paid in five years, whereof the first two hundred thousand guilders shall be paid them when the first payment shall be made by the members: Provided that we, with half the aforesaid million of guilders, shall receive and bear profit and risk in the same manner as the other members of this company.

XL. And if by a violent and continued interruption of the aforesaid navigation and traffic, the business within the limits of their company shall be brought to an open war, We will, if the situation of this country will in any wise admit of it, give them for their assistance sixteen ships of war, the least one hundred and fifty lasts burden,—with four good, well-sailing yachts, the least forty lasts burden,—which shall be properly mounted and provided in all respects, both with brass and other cannon, and a proper quantity of ammunition, together with double suits of running and standing rigging, sails, cables, anchors, and other things thereto belonging, such as are proper to be provided and used in all great expeditions; upon condition that they shall be manned, victualled, and supported at the expense of the company, and that the company shall be obliged to add thereto sixteen like ships of war, and four yachts, mounted and provided as above, to be used in like manner for the defence of trade and all exploits of war: Provided that all the ships of war and merchantmen (that shall be with those provided and manned as aforesaid) shall be under an admiral appointed by Us, according to the previous advice of the aforesaid general company, and shall obey Our commands, together with the resolutions of the company, if it shall be necessary, in the same manner as in time of war; so, notwithstanding, that the merchantmen shall not unnecessarily hazard their lading.

XLI. And if it should happen that this country should be remarkably eased of its burdens, and that this company should be laid under the grievous burden of a war, We have further promised, and do promise, to increase the aforesaid subsidy in such a manner as the situation of these countries will admit, and the affairs of the country will require.

XLII. We have moreover ordained that, in case of a war, all the prizes which shall be taken from enemies and pirates within the aforesaid limits, by the company or their assistants; also, the goods which shall be seized by virtue of Our proclamation,—after deducting all expenses and the damage which the company shall suffer in taking each prize, together with the just part of his excellency the admiral, agreeable to our resolution of the first of April, sixteen hundred and two—and the tenth part for the officers, sailors, and soldiers, who have taken the prize,—shall await the disposal of the managers of the aforesaid company: Provided that the account of them shall be kept separate and apart from the account of trade and commerce; and that the net proceeds of the said prizes shall be employed in fitting out ships, paying the troops, fortifications, garrisons, and like matters of war and defence, by sea and land; but there shall be no distribution unless the said net proceeds shall amount to so much, that a notable share may be distributed without weakening the said defence, and after paying the expenses of the war, which shall be done separate and apart from the distribution on account of trade: and the distribution shall be made, one-tenth part for the use of the United Netherlands, and the remainder for the members of this company, in exact proportion to the capital they have advanced.

XLIII. Provided, nevertheless, that all the prizes and goods taken by virtue of Our proclamation shall be brought in, and the right laid before the judicature of the counsellors of the admiralty for the part to which they are brought, that they may take cognizance of them, and determine the legality or illegality of the said prizes: the process of the administration of the goods brought in by the company remaining, nevertheless, pending, and that under a proper inventory; and saving a revision of what may be done by the sentence of the admiralty, agreeable to the instruction given the admiralty in that behalf: Provided that the vendue-masters and other officers of the admiralty shall not have or pretend to any right to the prizes taken by this company, and shall not be employed respecting them.

XLIV. The managers of this company shall solemnly promise and swear, that they will act well and faithfully in their administration, and make good and just accounts of their trade: That they in all things will consult the greatest profit of the company, and, as much as possible, prevent their meeting with losses: That they will not give the principal members any greater advantage in the payments or distribution of money than the least: That they, in getting in and receiving outstanding debts, will not favor one more than another: That they, for their own account, will take, and during the continuance of their administration will continue to take, such sum of money as by their charter is allotted to them; and moreover, that they will, as far as concerns them, to the utmost of their power, observe and keep, and cause to be observed and kept, all and every the particulars and articles herein contained.

XLV. All which privileges, freedoms, and exemptions, together with the assistance herein before mentioned, in all their particulars and articles, We have, with full knowledge of the business, given, granted, promised, and agreed to the aforesaid company; giving, granting, agreeing, and promising, moreover, that they shall enjoy them peaceably and freely; ordaining that the same shall be observed and kept by all the magistrates, officers, and subjects of the United Netherlands, without doing any thing contrary thereto, directly or indirectly, either within or out of these Netherlands, on penalty of being punished both in life and goods as obstacles to the common welfare of this country, and transgressors of Our ordinance; promising, moreover, that We will maintain and establish the company in the things contained in this charter, in all treaties of peace, alliances, and agreements with the neighboring princes, kingdoms, and countries, without doing any thing, or suffering any thing to be done which will weaken their establishment; charging and expressly commanding all governors, justices, officers, magistrates, and inhabitants of the aforesaid United Netherlands, that they permit the aforesaid company and managers peaceably and freely to enjoy the full effect of this charter, agreement, and privilege, without any contradiction or impeachment to the contrary. And that none may pretend ignorance hereof, We command that the contents of this charter shall be notified by publication or an advertisement, where and in such manner as is proper; for We have found it necessary for the service of this country.

Given under Our great seal, and the signature and seal of Our recorder, at the Hague, on the third day of the month of June, in the year sixteen hundred and twenty-one.

Was countersigned,

J. MAGNUS, Sec.

Underneath was written,

The Ordinance of the High and Mighty Lords the States General.

It was subscribed,

C. AERSSEN,

And had a seal pendent, of red wax, and a string of white silk.

B.

An Agreement between the Managers and Principal Adventurers of the West India Company, made with the approbation of the High and Mighty Lords the States General.

THE States General of the United Netherlands, to all to whom these presents shall be shown, greeting: Know ye, that whereas it has been made to appear to us by certain deputies of the Incorporated West India Company, of the chamber of Amsterdam, that they have been engaged in several ways, as well in the meeting of managers, as also frequently with their committees, to the end that, in time, good order and government may be made and established among them, to the satisfaction of the good members; that they may the better and with more profit speedily apply themselves to this work, and get subsequent matters into a proper channel; beseeching our approbation, that they, by the form of an amplification of their charter, or otherwise by framing an order of the aforesaid particular chamber of Amsterdam, or in such manner as we in council shall think proper, and have presented several things to us for that purpose, and that we, as before, should resolve thereupon: we have thought fit to send a copy thereof to the respective chambers of the West India Company, that they should maturely examine it, confer with the Principal Adventurers and Deputies, and to send some deputies of the principal adventurers to us, fully empowered and authorized for this purpose, and whatever else may serve to promote so necessary a business, to meet in mutual conference, and so to agree practicably and finally, with our approbation. And that a suitable number of deputies of the respective chambers, the directors, and principal adventurers may meet for that purpose, and superintend the following,—the induction and debates of our committees in their different conferences, communications, and deliberations; and finally, that the managers, directors, and principal adventurers, without prejudice to the provinces and respective cities, for promoting the West India business, have mutually agreed upon the following articles:

I. That no alteration, extension, or interpretation of the charter or its dependencies, shall be desired by the managers nor principal adventurers, or any others, except by a previous meeting and communication, and the approbation of a majority of the managers and principal adventurers who shall be present in that meeting.

II. That in all meetings in which the managers and principal adventurers shall be engaged in business together, or the principal adventurers alone and without the managers, all nominations, deputations, and elections shall be made with one name at once, by putting tickets into the hands of the president, or in some other secret manner.

III. That the company shall take up no money on interest or deposite, but with the advice and consent of the major part of the managers and principal adventurers: nevertheless, the respective chambers may, in case of necessity, for one voyage only, each take up the twentieth part of the capital of their chamber, and the said chamber shall not take up any more before that is paid off.

IV. That all accounts, mentioned in the 15th article, shall be drawn out in the style of business, by the committee to be nominated by the principal adventurers, and admitted under oath in the time mentioned in the said 15th article, which committee shall report thereon only in gross to the other principal adventurers. And the said committee shall be bound by an oath not to divulge, but to keep every thing secret which the managers must keep secret. They shall, moreover, be under the prohibition made by the 31st article of the charter for the managers, respecting buying and selling during the time of two years.

V. That the said committee shall have, and exercise, for the principal adventurers, the right given and granted by article 27 to the agents: And, moreover, to examine the books, invoices, and other documents, at their pleasure, and inspect merchandise and letters concerning business.

VI. That the first two vacant places of the managers at Amsterdam, the two first of Zealand, and the first in the chamber of the Maeze, shall successively be supplied and filled up by the principal adventurers of the respective chambers absolutely by plurality of voices, the elected being bound by the same oath with the other managers, and having administration as the other directors, and shall be obliged to communicate to the principal adventurers what concerns them, to preserve their right in the said meetings of the managers, according to the situation of affairs, to call them together, and shall be specially bound to and revokable by the aforesaid principal adventurers, the rest of the directors remaining successively eligible by the respective chambers according to the charter, or so as is already ordained, or shall be hereafter ordained in their respective provinces: And that by provision, two of the principal adventurers of each chamber of Amsterdam and Zealand respectively, and one of the chamber of the Maeze, shall be a committee, besides that mentioned in the foregoing article, to take care of their aforesaid right in the mean time, until one or two places shall be vacant.

VII. When the Nineteen shall meet together, the principal adventurer of the chamber of Amsterdam shall choose one of the two managers or provisional committee aforesaid, that he may be one of the eight managers in the said meeting for the chamber of Amsterdam. In like manner the principal adventurers of Zealand shall choose one of the aforesaid two managers or provisional committee, by them absolutely appointed, to be one of four managers for their chamber in the meeting of Nineteen. And the aforesaid principal adventurers, as well of the chamber of Amsterdam as of Zealand, shall each choose one of the sworn committee, mentioned in articles 4 and 5, to assist each of the aforesaid deputies, in the aforesaid meeting of Nineteen, nevertheless, without that, those who are met shall have a separate vote. And that the other chambers may know the cause of such meeting, those who are met of the chamber of Amsterdam shall communicate it to the principal adventurers of North Holland, and the city and country; and those who are met of the chamber of Zealand shall advise those of the Maeze of the business of the aforesaid meeting, as far as it may be communicated.

VIII. That hereafter no person shall be chosen a manager who is in the service of the East India Company: in like manner a father and son, or brothers, of the whole or half blood, shall not be chosen managers in one chamber. And the managers shall receive no commissions until they give up their service in the other company.

IX. Whereas it is necessary for the satisfaction of every one, that the time of subscribing to this company shall be prolonged, therefore the aforesaid subscription is prolonged,—for inhabitants, to the last of August, and for foreigners, to the last of October next, both new style, and it shall be made known by the advertisements: after that, no person shall be admitted, but every chamber shall be obliged to close its capital the first day after the last of October, and eight days thereafter to send a copy to each other: provided, that the outfit which is got ready shall continue for the use of the company, and that those who have furnished money for others, or shall yet furnish it, shall receive interest therefor at the discretion of the Nineteen.

X. And concerning the general account mentioned in article 16 in the charter, and the changing of a third part of the directors in article 14, to maintain good order and a general equality in all the chambers, it is found necessary that the said general account be made, (six years from the date of the charter beginning the third of June, 1621, new style,) according to the custom of trade, in public with the advice of the aforesaid committee of the principal adventurers of the respective chambers, and so on successively every six years to make a like general account: but the remainder of the accounts shall be deliberated upon, in order, by the meeting of the Nineteen, to the end that the directors who go off may depart with clear accounts if it be practicable. And the first change of a third part of the directors shall be made six years after the third of June, this year, 1623, and so on successively every two years, agreeable to the charter.

XI. And that this company may be under good government to the greatest profit and satisfaction of all the participants, we have ordained that the same government shall consist of five chambers of directors,—one within Amsterdam, who shall have the administration of four-ninth parts; one chamber in Zealand, for two-ninth parts; one chamber in the Maeze, for one-ninth part; one chamber in the north quarter, for one-ninth part; and the fifth chamber in Vreezelandt, together with city and country, (Stadt ende Landen,) also one-ninth part, upon condition entered in the register of our resolution and the acts passed: and the provinces in which there shall be no chamber, shall be accommodated with so many directors, divided among the respective chambers, as they shall furnish one hundred guilders to the company.

And, XII. If any thing should happen from which lawsuits may arise to the disadvantage of the company, the directors shall do all in their power to settle the matter amicably, (if possible;) if not, to communicate it to the principal adventurers, that they may act therein with common advice, in such manner as shall be found most to the advantage of the company.

We having examined and considered the aforesaid articles, and being desirous to promote unity and concord between the directors and principal adventurers, and the advancement of the West India Company, have, with the advice of the Prince of Orange, thought fit to agree to, and approve of, and do hereby agree to, and approve thereof, and direct that the same shall be punctually attended to and observed by the directors, members, and every person concerned therein, in the same manner as if they were inserted in the charter; because we find them proper for the service of the West India Company.

Given under Our great seal, the rubric and signature of Our recorder, at the Hague, the one and twentieth of June, Sixteen hundred and twenty-three.

It was countersigned,

N. van Bouckhorst, Vt.

Underneath was written,

The ordinance of the High and Mighty Lords the States General.

(Subscribed) C. Aerssen.

It had a seal in red wax, pendent by a white silk string.

C.

Names of the Lords Directors who have served the Company from the beginning to the end of the year 1636.

[De Laet, Jaerlyck Verhael.]

In the Amsterdam Chamber.

De Heeren—Jacob Gerritsz. Hoing, Burgomaster,
Jonas Witsz., Burgomaster,
Jan Gysbertsz. de Vries, Schepen,
Jacob Pietersz. Hoog-Camer,
Albaert Coenraets Burgh, Schepen,
Adriaen Krom-hout,
Reynier Reael,
Cornelis Bicker,
Joris Adriaensz,
Hendrick Hamel,
Pieter Beltens,
Elias Pels,
Guilliam Bartilotti,
Samuel Godyn,
Hendrik Broen,
Gommer Spranger,
Samuel Blommaert,
Hans van der Merckt,
Rombout Jacobsz.
Eduard Becker,
Guillaum van Everwyn, on behalf of Gelderlandt,
Matheus Joyen, on behalf of Haerlem,
Willem van Moerberghen, Schepen, } on behalf of Leyden,
Joannes de Laet, } on behalf of Leyden,
Johan Uyttewael, } on behalf of the Province of Utrecht,
Oliver Uyttenhove, } on behalf of the Province of Utrecht,
Johan van Hemart, on behalf of Deventer,
Kiliaen van Rensselaer, } Principal partner director.
Pieter Ranst, } Principal partner director.
Simon van der Does, Schepen,
Marcus van Valckenburgh,
Carel Looten, Principal partner director.
Michiel Pauw, Lord of Achtienhoven,
Jaques de la Myne,
Jehan Gras,
Abraham Oyens,
Warner Ernst van Bassen, Schepen,
Pieter Evertz Hulft,
Willem Bruyn,
Dirck Cornelisz. van Swanenburgh, on behalf of Utrecht,
Johan van Haring-houck,
Nicolaes van Sitterich,
Matthias van Ceulen, Principal partner director.
Toussain Blanche,
Abraham Spiers,
Jaques Beurse,
Marcus de Vogelaar,
Daniel van Lieberghen,
Jacob Reepe-maker,
Jehan Raye, Principal partner director,
Gysbert van Hemart, on behalf of Deventer,
Pieter Jansz. Blaeuwen-haen, on behalf of Deventer,
Matheus de Pauw, on behalf of Utrecht,
Pieter Varleth, on behalf of Utrecht,
Cornelis van Wyckersloot, "
Dirck van Helsdingh, "
Jacob de Key, on behalf of Haerlem,
Mr. Jacob van Broeckhoven, on behalf of Leyden,

Mr. Jehan Panhuysen, on behalf of Leyden,
Johan Wentolt Bartels, on behalf of Gelderlandt,
Eduard Man,
Ferdinando Schuylenburgh,
Frederick de Vries,
Johan Bartringh,
Johan van Gheel,
Abraham de Visscher.

On behalf of the Zealand Chamber.

De Heeren—Joos van der Hooghen, Burgomaster, Mr. Symon Schotte, } on behalf of Middelburg.
Rogier Cobbert, on behalf of Vlissinghen,
Antonio Godyn, Pieter Beurdt, } on behalf of Middelburgh.
Adriaen de Ketelaer, on behalf of Vlissinghen,
Abraham Droogh-broodt, on behalf of Middelburgh,
Adriaen Velters, on behalf of Ter-Veere,
Pieter Muenic, Galeyn ten Haeff, } on behalf of Middelburgh,
Willem Snellen, on behalf of Vissinghen,
Jeremias Waelens, on behalf of Thoolen,
Pieter Boudaen Courten, on behalf of Middelburgh,
Mr. Job Porrenaer, on behalf of Vlissinghen,
Pieter van Essen, Jan Velinx, } Principal partner director on behalf of Middelburgh,
Christoffel Barents, on behalf of Ter-Verre,
Mr. Symon van Beaumont,
Jean van der Poorten,
Woulter Teunemans,
Jan de Moor,
Abraham van Pere,
Bouwen Melssen Schot,
Jehan van der Merckt,
Cornelis Coornne,
Cornelis Claesz Elfsdyck,
Pieter van der Velde,
Jehan Gysselingh,
Abraham Bisschop,
Pieter Joosten Duyvelaer,
Steven Becker,
Pieter Alleman,
Abraham Schooten,
Nicolaes Velinx,
Cornelis Lampsens,
Hendrik Liens,
Pauwels Jansz. Serooskercke,
Jan Louys,
Nicolaes Swancke,
David Taetse.

On behalf of the Maeze Chamber,

At Dordrecht.

De Heeren—Cornelis van Terensteyn,
Mr. Jacob de Witte,
Michiel Pompé,
Cornelis Nicolay,
Wynandt Jansz. Rutgers,
Dirck van der Hasghe,
Johan van der Mast,
Arendt Martenz,
Roeloff Francken,
Cornelis van Beveren,

At Delft.

De Heeren—Philips Doublet,
Hendrik van Milligem,
Jacob Hoghenhoeck,
Adriaen van der Goes,
Adriaen Pietersons,
Mr. Johan de Voocht,

Geerard van Fockenstaert,
Pieter Antheunisz. van den Heuvel,
Mr. Wm. Schade,
Arendt Jacobsz. van der Graeff.

At Rotterdam.

De Heeren—Corns. Claesz. van Driel,
Jacob Velthuysen,
Dirck Pietersz. van Veen,
Henrick Nobel,
Johan Robberts,
Hendrik van Eck,
Thomas Varver,
Adriaen van der Dusse,
Sarich Hairwyck.

On behalf of the North Quarter Chamber.

De Heeren—Jr. Floris van Teyhughen, Burgomaster,
Gerrit Jansz. van der Nieuwburgh, Burgomaster,
Pieter Willemsz. Kessel,
} on behalf of Alcmaer.

Olfert Barentz,
Jr. Johan van Foreest,
Claes Willemsz. Crap, Burgomaster,
Fredrick Broeker,
} on behalf of Hoorn.

Gerrit Jacobsz. Trompet, Burgomaster,
Cornelis Pietersz. Lantman, Burgomaster,
Jacob Menten,
Pieter Hardebol,
} on behalf of Enkhuyzen.

Boudewyn Heynsz.
Jacob Pieter Mienses,
} on behalf of Edam.

Claes Symonsz. Dolphyn, on behalf of Monnickendam,

Willem Dircksz. Everhardt, Burgomaster,
Pieter Vanninghs, Burgomaster,
} on behalf of Medenblick.

Martin Boudewynsz., Burgomaster of Edam,
Cornelis Mathysz. Schaghen, Burgomaster of Medenblick,
Claes Jacobsz. Roch, of Hoorn,
Jan Jansz. Sus, of Hoorn,
Meyndert Thomasz., of Enkhuysen,
Adriaen Cornelisz. Schaghen, of Alkmaer.
Jacob Volckertz, of Enkhuysen,
Cornelis Sweerssz, of Enkhuysen,
Pieter Huygh, of Enkhuysen,
Pieter Claesz. Teenghs, of Edam,
Jan van Neck, Burgomaster at Hoorn,
Symon Maertsz. Lievens, Burgomaster at Medenblick,
Dirck Codde van der Burgh, at Enkhuysen,
Pieter Pauw, of Alcmaer,
Pieter Dircksz. Ben, Burgomaster at Hoorn,
Dr. Johan Gerritsz. Juel, of Hoorn,
Mr. Allert de Groot, of Hoorn,
Mr. Pauwels Swanenburgh, of Alcmaer,
Claes Adriaensz. Clock, of Hoorn,
Pieter Claesz. Bosch-Schieter, Burgomaster of Edam,
Dirck Willemsz. Everhart, of Medenblick,
Sasker Cornelisz. Schaghen, of Medenblick,
Jacob Schaghen Hooghlandt,
Dirck Jacobsz. Haghen, of Monnickendam.

On behalf of the Chamber of Stadt en Landen.

De Heeren—Jochim Altingh, Burgomaster,
Jr. Johan Seckinghe,
Jr. Onno Tamminga,
Jr. Remt Rengers,
Hugo van Nyeveen, Burgomaster,
Jr. Albert Conders,
Pieter Isebrants, Councillor,
Jr. Sygert Syghers,

Jr. Edzard Jacob Clandt,
Jr. Diderich Scharff,
Bartoldt Wickeringhe, Councillor,
Jr. Christoffer van Eussum,
Hillebrandt Gruys, Councillor,
Albert Wyfrink, Councillor,
Joost van Cleve, Councillor,
Nicolaus Mulerius, Professor,
Heer Willem van Vyrssen,
Heer Barent Jansz.,
Hendrick Schonenburgh, Councillor
Hendrick van Royen,
Jr. Rempt Jensema,
Jr. Johan Horenken,
Jr. Barent Conders,
Heer Folckert Folckertsz.
Bernhard Julsingh, Burgomaster,
Jr. Lambert van Starkenburgh,
Heer Tobias Iddekingha,
Pieter Eyssinghe, Burgomaster,
Edzard Rengers, Councillor,
Jr. Evert Leeuwe.

D.

Capt. Mason's Letter to [Mr. Secretary Coke?] relative to the Dutch in New Netherland, 2d April, 1632.

[London Documents, vol. I.]

Right Honorable—In ye yeare of or Lord God 1621, or thereabouts, certaine Hollanders were upon the coast of New England, tradeing wth ye Indians, betwixt Cape Codd and Bay de la Warre, in 40 degrees of northerly latitude, being a parte of that country which was granted to Sir Walter Rawleigh by Queene Elizabeth, in anno 1584, and afterwards to diverse of their subjects, under ye title of Virginia; which countrey was divided by agreement of ye Virginia Company, and the Northeast parte thereof confirmed afterward by King James, in anno 1606, to ye President and Counsell for ye plantations there, which have beene settled in Virginia on ye one hand to the westwards, now about fortie yeares, and in New England on the other hand, to ye eastward, above 25 yeares since. The sayd Hollanders as interlopers fell into ye middle betwixt the sayd plantations, and at their returne of their voyage aforesayd, published a mapp in ye Low Countries of ye sayd sea coaste comp'hended betwixt Virginia and Cape Codd, undr ye tytle of New Netherlands, giveing ye name of the Prince of Aurange to the countrie and river of Manahata, where ye Dutch are now planted, (which sayd countrey was many yeares before discovered by the Englishmen in their voyages to Virginia,) and giveing other Dutch names to other places to ye eastward of ye sayd Manahata River, as farr as Cape Codd, all wch had beene formerly discovered and traded unto diverse tymes by sev'all Englishmen, as may be proved. And Sr Samuell Argall, Knt wth many English planters were p'pareing to goe and sitt downe in his lott of land upon ye sayd Manahata River, at the same tyme when the Dutch intruded, wch caused a demurre in their p'ceeding until King James, upon complaint of my lord of Arundell wh Sr Ferdinando Gorges, Knt and ye Sr Samuell Argall, (form'ly Gov. of Virginia,) and Capt. John Mason, of ye sayd Dutch intruders in ano 1621, had, by his Maties order a lre* to ye sayd Lord of Dorchester, then ambassador at ye Hague, questioned the States of ye Low Countries for that matter. Which ye Lords ye States by answer, (as I take it,) of their ambassador Sir Nowell Carronne, did disclayme, disavowing any such act that was done by their people, wth their authority, wch my Lord Arundell and, I thinke, ye Lord Baltimore, (their Secretary of State,) doe remember, and Sr Ferdinando Gorges and Captaine Mason can witnesse the same. Neverthelesse ye yeare following, wch (as I take it) was 1622, the sayd Dutch, under a pretended authority from ye West India Company of Holland, maintayned as they sayd by commission from ye sayd Prince of Aurange. did returne to ye foresayd river of Manahata and made plantation there, fortifying themselves there in two severall places, and have built shipps there, whereof one was sent into Holland of 600 tunnes or thereabouts. And albeit they were warned by ye

* Those lres of ye Lords doe beare date the 15 of December, 1621.

English plantation at New Plymouth to forbeare trade, and not to make any settlement in those partes, letting them know that they were the territories of ye King of England, yett nev'theless with proude and contumacious answers, (saying they had commission to fight against such as should disturbe their settlement,) they did persist to plant and trade, vilefying o^r nation to the Indians, and extolling their owne people and countrye of Holland, and have made sundry good returnes of commodities from thence into Holland. especially this yeare they have returned (as it is reported) 15,000 beaver skynnes, besides other commodities.

Yor Hors humble servant,

(Signed) JHON MASON.

April 2, 1632.

Sir Ferdinando Gorges to Capt. Mason, about an expedition on the Dutch. 6 *April*, 1632.

[Lond. Doc. i., 50-52.]

SIR—On Thursday night I received yours of the 30th March, by wch I understand howe you have p'ceeded against those of the Dutch plantacon. I am glade the business is before the Lords. I hope they will not bee over hasty in concluding a business of that nature, considering howe much it concerns both the honor of the kinge and State to make good the interest they have therein. You shal bee assured I will not p'tract any time of my comeing upp, butt I must acquaint you with an unhappy accident that befell me the same day I received yours. For haveing bene with my Lord Pawlett, and divers others of my private friends att a horse race, I took a fall from my horse, and am now in soe much extremitie of paine, as I am not able to move or stir but as I am helped by maine strength of my s'vauntes; notwithstanding, by God's favor, I hope to bee wth you in very shorte time, what shifte soever I make to travell. I am sorry to heere you are soe poorely seconded in a mattor soe just and hon^{ble}. I conceive you may have from Mr. Shirly a coppy of that wch came to my hands from those of New Plymouth, wth more p'ticulars than came to mee. Itt may please you that hee may bee spoken wth about it. I doubt not but att my cominge I shall bee able to give both his Ma^{ty} and the Lords sufficient satisfacion for to fortefie the justifyinge, (not the stay of the shippe onely,) but to prosecute their displanting from thence. And that wch is now to bee desired is that wee may bee heard to speake before ought bee done for the shipps dispatch. I hope you will make some shifte to sende away the horses I sent you before the receipte of Mr. Eyres' to the contrary, for I knowe they wilbee of more service and worth then any you will serve yourselves wth all att the islands: besides heere is noe shipping that goes from hence till towards the winter quarter; but what you doe betweene you shall please mee, though I desire extreamly they may goe att this present, thoughe it were wholly on my owne accompte for their transportation wth the horses. Lett this suffice I pray you for this present, for that my paine will suffer mee to say noe more att this time, save only I beseech you to remember my humble service to my Lord Marshall, and to lett his honor knowe the misfortune that retaynes me from attending his Lopp: soe soone as my harte desires, and soe much you may bee pleased to lett my Lord of Warwick knowe in like manner, wth the remembrance of my service to his Lopp: beseeching him not to be slacke wherein you knowe his helpe may further the best wee shall gaine thereby wilbee the knowledge of what may bee expected from him hereafter; and soe I commit you to God, and rest

Your assured loving friend,
(Signed) FERD: GORGES.

BRISTOLL, the 6th April, 1632.

E.

Report and Advice on the condition of New Netherland, drawn up from documents and papers placed by commission of the Assembly of the XIX., dated 15*th Dec.*, 1644, *in the hands of the General Chamber of Accounts, to examine the same, make a digest thereof, and to advise the Assembly how the decay there can be prevented, the population increased, agriculture advanced, and that country wholly improved for the benefit of the company.*

New Netherland, situate in America between English Virginia and New England, extending from the South River, lying in 38½ degrees, to Cape Malabar, in the latitude of 41½ degrees, was first frequented by the inhabitants of this country in the year 1598, and especially by those of the Greenland company, but without making any fixed settlements, only as a shelter in the winter. For which purpose they erected there two little forts on the South and North Rivers against the incursions of the Indians. A charter was afterwards, on the 11th October, 1614, granted by their High Mightinesses to Gerrit Jacobsz. Wittsen, ancient burgomaster of the city of Amsterdam, Jonas Wittsz., Symon Morrissen, Lambert van Tweenhuysen, Wessel Schenck, and associates, all inhabitants of these countries, to trade exclusively to the newly-discovered lands, now called New Netherland, situate in America, between New France and Virginia; to sail thereto exclusively for the term of three years, without any other persons being allowed to sail out of this country to, or frequent that place during that time, on pain of confiscation of ships and goods, and a fine of fifty thousand Netherlands ducats.

In the years 1622 and 1623, the West India Company took possession, by virtue of their charter, of the said country, and conveyed thither in their ship, the New Netherlands, divers colonists under the directorship of Cornelis Jacobsz. Mey and Adriaen Jorisz. Thienpoint. Which directors built, in the year 1624, Fort Orange on the North River, and Fort Nassau on the South River, and after that, in 1626, Fort Amsterdam on the Manhattes, in all of which garrisons were continually maintained by the company, and trade prosecuted in those several districts with yachts, sloops, and other craft. In the year 1629, the Freedoms and Exemptions conceded by the Noble Assembly of the Nineteen, were published with the approbation of their High Mightinesses. Divers Patroons and colonists resorted thither thereupon, and endeavored to advance agriculture and population. For further security, the Fort Good Hope was also erected, in 1633, on the Fresh River. But population did not experience any special increase until the year 1639, when the fur-trade with the Indians, which theretofore was reserved to the company, was thrown free and open to everybody; at which time the inhabitants there resident not only spread themselves far and wide, but new colonists came thither from Fatherland, and the neighboring English, as well from Virginia as from New England, removed under us. So that in place of seven bouweries, full thirty were planted, and full one hundred more expected in a short time from the plantations which were taken up. There was every appearance, in addition, that in two or three years' time provisions could be furnished for ten thousand men.

Although the hope was now entertained, that by such means the conquered province would come to a flourishing state, it nevertheless appeared that the abuse of the free trade was the cause of the said ruin. Firstly, the colonists thereby, with a view, each to push forward his own advantage, separated themselves from one another, and settled far in the interior of the country, the better to drive trade with the Indians, whom they thenceforward sought to allure to their houses with excessive familiarity and treating; whereby they brought themselves into contempt among the Indians, who, not having been always treated alike, made this the cause of enmity. Secondly, in consequence of their proximity to the Indians, whose lands lay unfenced, the cattle belonging to our people, straying without herdsmen, seriously damaged the corn or maize of the savages. This occasioned much complaint, and no redress following, they revenged themselves, killing the cattle and even the horses. Thirdly, not only the colonists, but also the free-traders proceeding from this country in consequence of the large profits, traded away with the Maquaas, arms for full four hundred men, such as muskets, powder and lead, which, having been refused to the other tribes, when demanded, augmented the hatred and the enmity among the latter. Fourthly, it happened that the Director, a few years after, imposed a contribution of maize on the Indians, whereby these were totally estranged from us.

Hence arose various threats and injurious rencontres, which finally broke out into acts of hostility, so that first the Raritan Indians attempted to make way with one of our sloops, and afterwards killed some hogs on Staten Island; whereupon the Director dispatched eighty soldiers thither to avenge this, who burned their corn and killed three or four of their people. Both sides then desisted from further proceedings.

It further happened that a Wechquaeskeeck savage murdered, about the year 1640, an old man with an axe, in his own house, for which, having received no satisfaction from the tribe, the resolution was taken afterwards, in the year 1642, by Twelve Men chosen from the commonalty, to revenge the murder by open war; but nothing was done at the time in consequence of missing the enemy, who, observing what was designed against them, sued for peace.

Some time afterwards the Hackingsack Indians designedly shot with an arrow a Dutchman sitting on the roof of a house, which he was covering. The commonalty were very much troubled at this, dreading the occurrence of more such acts. And while satisfaction was being sought by the Director for this, without success, God seemed to have taken vengeance on the Wechquaeskeecks, through the Mohecan Indians, who, overtaking them, slaughtered full seventy of them, and led many women and children away prisoners. This obliged the remainder to fly to our people to the Manhattans, where they were received into the houses, and fed by the Director during fourteen days. Shortly after this they were seized with another fright. They fled with the Hackingsax, full a thousand strong in the neighborhood of the fort, and over the river of Pavonia. Some of the Twelve Men having noticed this, the Director, at the request of three of these, namely, of Jan Jansz. Damen, Abraham Planck, and Maryn Adriaensz., who signed in the name of all their board, authorized an attack on the above-mentioned Indians, in the course of the night between the 27th and the 28th of February, 1643, by a party of soldiers and burghers, who, with cruel tyranny, slew eighty of them, and took thirty prisoners. And although the commonalty protested against the Director and the aforesaid three persons on account of these hasty and severe proceedings, as having taken place without their knowledge or consent, they were, notwithstanding, obliged to declare open war against full eleven tribes of Indians, who rose up in arms on that account. The consequence was, that about one thousand of these, and many soldiers and colonists belonging to us, were killed. All the bouweries almost were moreover destroyed, so that only three remained on the Manhattes, and two on Staten Island, and the greater part of the cattle was destroyed. Whatever remained of these were obliged to be kept in a very small enclosure, except in Rensselaer's colonie, situate on the North River, in the neighborhood of Fort Orange, which experienced no trouble, and enjoyed peace, because they continued to sell fire-arms and powder to the Indians, even during the war against us.

The company thus experienced the greatest loss and destruction, both by the consumption of their ammunition, and ready money expended in the purchasing this at a dear rate, as well as by reinforcing the garrison by the enlisting of as many Englishmen as could be hired in that country, fifty of whom the colonists solemnly engaged to pay, but the payment not having followed, it remained as a charge on the company. Those indebted to the company were hereby finally reduced to such a state, that they had no means to pay their debts.

To remedy this great decay, various suggestions were proposed by the Director and Commonalty:

Firstly, that to restore peace and quiet throughout the country, the Indians, who waged war against us, should, by force of arms, be utterly destroyed and exterminated. The Director demanded for that purpose, one hundred and fifty soldiers, armed with arquebuses and coats of mail, and provided with sufficient munitions of war, as he estimated the numbers of the Indians, our enemies, not to be above three hundred strong. The Commonalty, maintaining their force to be some thousands strong, considered their extermination impossible, and were of opinion that it would be wiser to establish universal quiet by a general peace. Of this they have but little hope, so long as the present administration remains there, because the Indians will no way be pacified, as they themselves declare to some of ours, until the Director be removed; for their daily cry everywhere is—Wouter, Wouter,—meaning Wouter van Twiller.

Secondly, in order to prevent future wars, the colonists should be settled in a proper situation, near to each other, so being brought everywhere into villages and towns, they would be in better circumstances, in time of need, for self-defence. Thus being separated from the Indians, the cattle would not cause any injury to the crops of the Indians, whereby, heretofore, trouble has frequently arisen; and too great familiarity with the savages avoided, none of these being employed in domestic service.

Thirdly, for better defence against enemies, and to ensure respect from neighbors, that it would be advisable to construct, of stone, Fort Amsterdam, which is now in such a state of decay, that men, without using the gate, pass over the walls. This, according to the estimate of the Director, would cost but from twenty to twenty-five thousand guilders.

Fourthly, that the boundaries between the English and our nation, should be arranged by the crown of England and this state, so that all difficulties with the former people may be prevented. Whereas the Fresh River has been usurped by them since the year 1633, notwithstanding the company had previously taken possession of the whole thereof, and on the 8th June, anno 1633, when no Englishmen had ever been on, or in the neighborhood of that river, had purchased twenty miles of territory from the Indians, and erected Fort Good Hope thereupon, and maintained possession of it with our people. After which, namely, on the 16th September, the English first came from New Plymouth and Mathuses Bay before the said fort, and declared that they would erect a house three miles above the same. The commissary residing there, opposed this so long as he could, but was forced to permit the same, according to instructions, under protest. In the mean time, sundry letters, protests, and summons, passed on both sides between their governor and our director. It finally came to pass, that they arrived on the above-mentioned river in the years 1635 and 1636, with numbers of families and cattle, establishing themselves there, far and near, even on the land situate around and by our fort, and belonging to us. Which land they have divided among themselves, endeavoring to prescribe laws to us, because they having built a house or two at the mouth of the river, pretended thereby to have the key thereof.

Fifthly, that it would be advisable for the benefit of that country all around, to facilitate emigration to New Netherland, as has been done heretofore for a long time, or at least to credit the emigrants for a time, in order to allure colonists thither, and afterwards to introduce a considerable number of farm-servants and negroes into the country, through whose labor agriculture would be so much promoted, that a large quantity of provisions could be transported thence to Brazil.

Sixthly, that a rendezvous for vessels of war should also be established in New Netherland, which is better adapted than the island of Curaçoa, in consequence of the abundance of provisions and building-timber there ; besides, that men can proceed thence safer and quicker to all the points in the West Indies, and discover the designs of the enemy.

Seventhly, that it would be profitable for the company to keep a well-furnished store and cellar there, from which the inhabitants around could be accommodated at a certain reasonable price, for money or produce, which will otherwise be overvalued and exhausted through private traders. But as private individuals have been permitted to carry on trade, let their imported wares be fixed at a certain price.

Finally, it is proposed by them, that the council be composed of four to five persons, in order to maintain justice and the authority of the company, together with the respect of neighbors.

From all which 'tis to be seen into what confusion and ruin New Netherland is now fallen, such being caused by the rash undertaking of so unnecessary a war, without the knowledge, much less the order of the Nineteen, and against the will of the Commonalty there—besides what excessive expense is now required from the company both for succor and redress. There does not seem that any apparent profit can be expected from there for some years. On the contrary, it is found by the company's books in the Department at Amsterdam, that in place of being a source of profit, this district of New Netherland has cost the company from the year 1626 to the year 1644 inclusive, over 550,000 guilders, deducting the returns which have been received from there. It would, therefore, be worthy of consideration if it would not be better for the company to rid themselves, by the abandonment of New Netherland, of such heavy expenses altogether, than by retaining it, to continue them.

But inasmuch as the company has promised, in its conceded Freedoms, to take all colonists, as well freemen as servants, under its protection, and to aid in defending them against all internal wars; and as the improvement of matters by good management here, and better direction there, is not beyond hope, so that this place may be maintained in the first instance with small profit, or at least without loss, it is therefore our opinion, under favor, that the company cannot decently or consistently abandon it.

In order to introduce such regulation and improvement, we submit to the consideration of the Noble Assembly the following points:—

Firstly, The establishment of the boundaries with the English should speedily and first of all be agreed upon, for it is found that they, in consequence of their great population, usurp daily more of our territory. This being first settled, it should be conditioned, that the English who find themselves in our district, or should come in there, should be subject to our government, and not be acknowledged otherwise than as original subjects.

Secondly, The country should be brought, in every respect, into peace and quietness; and the advice of the present Director utterly to exterminate all enemies by force, by no means be adopted, not only because such is impracticable and unchristian, but it would be injurious to the company, necessitating, as it would, so heavy an expenditure on so uncertain an event, and so little appearance of profit. It would not be impolitic, therefore, to adopt the advice of the Commonalty, and to endeavor by all means to appease and satisfy the Indians, and to order hither the Director and council, who are responsible for that bloody exploit of the 28th February, 1643, to justify and vindicate their administration before the Noble Assembly of the Nineteen. In place of whom a person should be sent back as Director, sufficiently qualified to promote the interests of the company and the prosperity of the commonalty on the one hand, and to maintain on the other good correspondence with the neighboring people, especially with the Indians.

Thirdly, It would be advisable to carry into effect and to execute the proposition of the Director previously alluded to—that the colonists should settle on some of the best adapted places with a certain number of householders, in the manner of towns, villages, and hamlets, as the English are in the habit of doing; they thereby will live more secure, according to the intention of the company in the granting of the printed freedoms and the amplification thereof.

Fourthly, It shall be necessary, first of all, to hasten the repairs of the fort, and we are of opinion that this shall be done in a proper manner, and at the least expense, with good clay, and firm sods. The soldiers should be urged thereto by some presents, and obliged to keep it for the future in continual repair. The Director should be strictly commanded to take good care of this.

Fifthly, We consider, under favor, that for the security of the aforesaid fort, and as elsewhere required, the persons specified in the annexed list should be sufficient, on such allowances, as there, moreover, drawn out—adding thereto that the colonists and their servants should be bound, under certain penalties, to provide themselves with good fire-arms and other weapons for self-defence; and to secure themselves in time of need, independent of the garrison, against a general attack, without the Director, colonists, or whosoever it might be, being permitted to hire any soldiers, be they few or many, at the company's expense.

Sixthly, A council should be established there, consisting of three persons; namely, the Director as president; the Second and the Fiscaal as councillors adjunct. Through which council all cases arising relating to the police, justice, dignity, and rights of the company should be treated and administered. With the understanding, nevertheless, that the Commander should take the place of the Fiscaal in criminal matters, with the addition moreover of two capable persons from the commonalty. Further, as by the 28th article of the Freedoms, the respective colonies were allowed to delegate one or two persons to inform at least, once a year, the Director and council of the state and condition of their colonie, so are we of opinion that the said delegates should moreover assemble every six months, at the summons of the Director and council, for mutual good understanding and the common advancement of the welfare of the inhabitants ; besides to assist in advising the same upon all affairs relating to the welfare of their colonies, the preservation of peace with the Indians and neighboring people, the maintenance of the Freedom and privileges, and the redress of all abuses, besides the maintenance of the statutes and the laws ; bearing in mind, always, that throughout the whole of that land the Amsterdam measure, ell, and weight shall be used.

Seventhly, It must be especially attended to that the population and cultivation of the country should be strengthened. It would be serviceable thereto to facilitate, as much as possible, the emigration of the colonists and freemen who intend to proceed thither to settle there, and to cause them to establish themselves, first of all, on the island of Manhattans; allowing them as much land as they were able to cultivate, whether in planting of tobacco, for which that island being very fertile is considered well adapted; or of grain or other crops, from which they may expect to derive the largest profit.

And for the advancement of the reclaiming of the country, it would be wise to allow, at the request of the Patroons, colonists, and other farmers, the introduction from Brazil there, of as many negroes as they would be willing to pay for at a fair price ; which negroes would do their masters more service, and at less cost, than farm-servants, which must be hired here with a great deal of money and much promises to be sent thither.

Eighthly, To increase the population still more, we would advise, that it would be best to reserve the Indian trade exclusively to the Patroons, colonists, and free farmers residing there, without permiting any licensed traders to trade in any manner with the said Indians ; but to be satisfied to exchange their cargoes with the free inhabitants for peltries, tobacco, wheat, and other produce of the country. But it should be absolutely forbidden, that either the freemen should sell to the Indians, or the licensed traders to the freemen, any arms or munitions of war, on pain of a heavy punishment to be inflicted therefor, lest the Indians, being strengthened thereby, may hereafter be encouraged to do us more injury than they can now, in their impotency, inflict. But it shall be obligatory on the freemen to be provided, each with a good musket and side-arms for self-defence, as already mentioned in the 5th point. An inspection thereof shall be had by the Director every six months.

And in order to encourage the good people of New Netherland the more, the Noble Assembly of the Nineteen should, under favor, consider if it would not be advantageous and beneficial to the conquered province, to allow the Patroons and colonists, there resident, to export their produce to the Brazils, under proper recognitions and tolls, as there are there flour, oatmeal, peas, beans, pipe-staves, planks, square timber, and other wood fit for ship and house-building. Also to encourage the fisheries there around, that they and no other persons should be permitted to salt and preserve the fish and caviare which can be caught there, to sell the same at the Reciff, [Pernambuco ;] and that it should also be allowed, that the New Netherlanders should take salt on the Brazil coast around Siara, or in the West Indies, for the purpose of salting wet and dry fish ; and to erect salt-pans in New Netherland to refine the same, and to render it fit to use as fine salt with fish and meat. And, arriving at Brazil, that they shall be bound to deliver all into the company's store, and on payment of the proper duties and tolls, whether in money or specie, to dispose of the same without exporting any money thence, but to take as a return cargo, staves, sugar, confectionary, ginger, tobacco, cotton, and other country produce, with proper entries thereof, both as to quantity and quality ; and therewith to sail straight to New Netherland, without touching at any port, while on the way, to barter or to sell any part thereof, under any pretext whatsoever. Wherefore they should receive on the part of the company a supercargo, to make a report of the whole to the company, and to return in the next ship from New Netherland to the Brazil. And as all further smuggling must be prevented, the skippers must be obligated (on pain of loss of ship and goods) after being visited at the Reciff,* to touch at Paraiba, to be there visited again on the part of the company.

Which trade being thus adjusted, it shall not be necessary for the company to be burdened with any equipages, or purchases of cargoes, and thereby be relieved from numerous servants required therefor. The garrison being established to board themselves, they will be amply provided therein, and with other necessaries, by the freemen and inhabitants there.

But in order to furnish the expenses which the company have to defray for the support of that garrison and other servants, it will be necessary that the receipts of the recognitions, tolls, and other duties, as well on the exported as on the imported goods, already established and hereafter to be imposed, should be sharply attended to ; wherefrom we think that the expenses to be met by the company can be amply received, with the hope that the population increasing, greater and more ample profits can be derived therefrom.

* Nearly south of Pernambuco city, between the river Bibiribe and the sea, a small tongue of land extended, on which stood a village named Reciffe : there all goods were shipped and unshipped. De Laet, Verhael van West Indien, 191.

F.

Patent of Mespath, or Newtown, L. I.

[Translated from Book of Patents GG., p. 49.]

We, Willem Kieft, Director-general, and council of New Netherland, for and in behalf of the High and Mighty Lords, the Lords States General of the United Netherland Provinces, his Highness the Prince of Orange, as well as the Most Noble Lords the Lords Directors of the General Privileged West India Company, To all those who shall see these Letters, MAKE KNOWN, that We have given and granted, as by these Presents We do give and grant, unto Francis Doughty and associates, their heirs and assigns, in real, actual, and perpetual possession, all and every that certain parcel of land situate on Long Island, in this Province, with the pastures and whatever else it includes, containing in superficies six thousand six hundred and sixty-six Dutch acres, or thereabouts, comprehended within four right lines, each two thousand Dutch perches long, the first whereof extends from the east angle of Hans Hanssony's (Jan Janssen's) meadow, dividing, according to the creek, the marsh into two unequal parts, unto the plantation of Richard Britnal, and thence proceeds towards the northeast, passing through the middle of the fresh marsh to the rivulet surrounding the south part of the lands of Henry the Farmer, [Henrici Agricolæ,] and following the same even to its mouth : the other line, taking its origin from thence, bends towards the southeast according to the main bank, going along the same unto the other creek, [fluviolum,] following the course of which from its mouth until it attains the eastern extremity of the said marsh, (from whence the aforesaid creek arises,) thence turns again towards the southeast, until it has gained the length of two thousand Dutch perches ; the third line taking its rise from the end of the latter, tends towards the west, of an equal length with the others ; finally, the fourth running from the last-mentioned point towards the northwest, terminates at the above-mentioned eastern angle of Hans Hanssony's meadow, at which angle a large stone is erected for the greater certainty of the boundaries ;

With power to establish, in the aforesaid tract, a town or towns ; to erect a church or churches ; to exercise the Reformed Christian Religion and church discipline, which they profess ; also, to administer, of right, high, low, and middle jurisdiction ; to decide civil suits not exceeding fifty Dutch florins ; to impose definitively and without appeal in criminal matters, fines to an equal amount ; to pronounce the first sentence in other civil and criminal actions of greater moment, and to execute the same, subject, however, to such execution being deferred, should an appeal be made to the supreme court of New Netherland : Finally, to exercise all rights belonging to the aforesaid jurisdiction, with power, moreover, to nominate some of theirs, and to present them to the Director of New Netherland, that a sufficient number may be chosen from them for political and juridical government : together with the right of hunting, fowling, fishing, and of trading, according to the immunities granted, and to be granted, to the colonists of this province, without any exception :—

Wherefore the aforesaid F. Doughty and his associates, their heirs and assigns, shall be obligated, so long as they are in possession of the above-mentioned lands, to acknowledge the aforesaid lords for their sovereign Lords and Patroons; to pay, after the lapse of ten years, the tenth part of the produce of the land, whether cultivated with the plough, hoe, or otherwise, orchards and kitchen-gardens, not exceeding one Dutch acre, excepted. Finally, to use no other standard than that of Holland; and so as to avoid confusion, to use Dutch weights, the Dutch ell and all other Dutch measures.

All which we promise, under the foregoing conditions inviolably to preserve, and bind our successors to the faithful observance of the same, by virtue of the commission and supreme authority granted to us by the Most Mighty Prince of Orange, Governor of the United Belgic Provinces. In testimony whereof, we have subscribed these presents with our own hand, and caused them to be countersigned by the Secretary of New Netherland, and the seal of New Netherland to be affixed thereto. Given at Fort Amsterdam, on the island Manhattans, in New Netherland, in the year 1642, the 28th of March.

WILLEM KIEFT.

By order of the Director and Council,

CORNELIS VAN TIENHOVEN, Secretary.

Ff.

The Rev. Mr. Doughty.

[From Van der Donck's Vertoogh van N. Nederlandt.]

"THIS minister, FRANCISCUS DOUGHTY, in the time of the first troubles in England, came, in order to escape from them, to New England, and found himself out of the frying-pan in the fire. In order to be able to enjoy freedom of conscience, according to the Dutch Reformation, which he certainly missed in New England, he betook himself under the protection of the Dutch; and an absolute patent, with privileges for a colonie, was granted and conferred on him by the Director. He had reinforced himself now in one year with some families, but in consequence of the breaking out of the war, they were all driven from their lands, with loss of some people, and the destruction of much cattle, losing for the most part all their houses and whatever they possessed. After they had remained awhile, and consumed more than they could collect, they came to the Manhattans, where all the refugees resorted at the time, and Master Doughty was minister there. After the flames of war were spent, and peace was concluded, though in such a way that nobody trusted much to it, some people returned to their lands. The Director perceived clearly that this man would have liked, were every thing well settled, to have gone back also to his land. But inasmuch as the peace was doubtful, and Master Doughty had nothing wherewith to make a commencement, he was not in a hurry. Nevertheless, he proceeded thither, some time after, and dwelt there half a year. But he left it again at Thanksgiving. In tne expectation that some others would make a village there, a suit was entered against the clergyman, and managed so that the place was confiscated. Master Doughty finding himself aggrieved, appealed from the sentence. The Director answered, that no appeal lay from his judgment, but that it must be absolute, and condemned the minister thereupon to imprisonment, in which he must remain for 24 hours, and then pay 25 guilders. Such an act we have always considered one of oppression, and looked upon it as a mark of sovereign power.

" . . . . At first, while Director Kieft was still here, the English preacher requested, as he had lived and done duty a long time without suitable support, and as his land was now confiscated, to be allowed to proceed to the Islands [West Indies] or to the Netherlands; but he always received unfavorable answers, and he was threatened with this and that. Finally he was permitted to depart, on condition that he promised, under his hand, neither to mention nor to complain, in whatever place he should go to, of what Director Kieft or Stuyvesant had done to him here in New Netherland. This the man himself has declared. The Honorable Dincklagen and Commander Looper, who then lived together, say likewise that it is true."

[From Van Tienhoven's "Cort bericht," being a reply to Van der Donck's "Vertoogh."]

"François Doughty, Adriaen van der Donck's father-in-law, an English clergyman, was granted a colonie at Mespacht, not for himself alone, as Patroon, but for him and his co-associates, by whom he was empowered, and who then resided in Rhode Island, at Cohannock and other places, of whom a Mr. Smith was one of the principal. For the said preacher had, of his own, scarcely means enough to build a hut, let alone to people a colonie at his own expense, but was to be employed as minister by his associates, who were to prepare a Bouwery in said colonie for him, in return for which he should perform the duties of preacher, and support himself on the produce of the Bouwerie.

"François Doughty, coming to the Manhattans to live, during the war, was engaged as preacher by the English in and around the Manhattans, who were bound to maintain him, without either the Director or Company being subject to any charge therefor. And the English giving him nothing for his support, two collections were taken up among the Dutch and English, whereon he lived at the Manhattans.

"The said Colonie of Mespacht was never confiscated. That is proved by the owners who still dwell there, who had an equal interest in the colonie with Doughty. But as Doughty would prevent its settlement, and permit no one to plant in the colonie unless those who would pay him a certain sum of money down for every morgen of land, and then moreover, a certain sum annually in shape of quitrent, and sought, also, to make a domain thereof in opposition to the co-interested of the colonie, Mr. Smith having especially complained, it was finally concluded by the Director and Council that the copartners should enter on their property, reserving to Doughty the bouwery and lands which he had in possession, so that he should suffer no loss or damage thereby. That I could also prove, were it not that the documents are in New Netherland and not here. . . . .

"The English preacher, François Doughty, has never been in the company's service. Wherefore the latter was never indebted to him, but the English congregation must pay him, as it can be proved in New Netherland. The company hath assisted the said preacher from time to time with goods and necessary maintenance, amounting to about fl.1,100, ($440,) as the colony's books can testify, whereof he hath never paid any part."

G.

Payment and Expenditure which Kiliaen van Rensselaer has advanced and paid, in his life-time, as Patroon of the Colonie called Rensselaerswyck, situate on the North River of New Netherland, for the support of said Colonie, together with what has been expended and paid after his decease in behalf of said Colonie.

[From the Rensselaerswyck MSS.]

[NOTE.—The Merchants' books in Holland are kept in guilders, stivers, and pennies.]

Date	Item	Amount	Total
1630.			
Jan. 10.	Paid to Wolfert Gerrittsen for Rutger Hendricksen van Soest, Superintendent of a brewery, in advance of what he shall earn, 20 Rix dollars,	fl. 50.00	
	Paid in further advance, by Wolfert Gerrittsen, to Rutger aforesaid,	5.00	
	To Rutger Heindricksen aforesaid for a present,	5.00	*f.* 60.00
14.	Paid to Brant Peelen, from Nieukerck, second farm servant, [Bouw-knecht,] with the promise that he shall be appointed superintendent on the second farm, in advance, 6 Rix dollars,	*f.* 15.00	
	To the same as a present,	10.00	25.00
	To Wolfert Gerrittsen, overseer of farms, (opperboûmeester,) for the following items; for one month's wages, to be deducted,		20.00
	For one month's wages in hand, for which he shall account, or to be otherwise deducted,		20.00
	For 12 ewes with lamb and one ram,	fl. 78.00	
	For payment of his expenses and trouble,	9.00	
	For 16 bushels of oats,	12.00	
	For 150 double cakes of pressed rape-seed,	7.10	
	For lint-seed fl. 1, Hemp-seed fl. 2, Rope fl. 4,	7.00	
	For 2 large bed sacks to contain hay,	5.00	
	For a basket and other small matters,	1.10	120.00
15.	For 2 handsome guns for my servants who shall be sent out for my use,		fl. 37.10
	To Seger Heindricksen from Soest, Shepherd and Ploughman, at fl. 25 yearly, on account, 6 Rix dollars,		15.00
Feb. 8.	To Gillis van Schendel, for one map on parchment, and four ditto on paper, of the islands and other tillage grounds, (bouwlanden) situate in my Colonie, to be sent thither for their convenience, 6 Rix dollars,		15.00

Feb. 19. To Wolfert Gerrittsen, for his disbursements:—
For the sheep, ... fl. 3.00
For veterinary surgeon, ... 6.00
For 10 halters and one sheep-shears, . 4.00
——— 13.00

Mar. 11. Paid, by Wouter van Twiller, to Simon Dircksen Pos, for expenses on the sheep, ... 4 18

To Jacob Janssen, "lansman," for expenses at Texel:—
For purchase of two sheep at Texel, and some hay, fl. 14.00
For the keep (staengelt) of 13 sheep (whereof one died of the mange) for 41 days, and carriage of said sheep, together 13 stivers per day, ... 26.13
To Claes Arissen, for hay and carriage, . . . 6.00
——— 46.13

17. Paid at Middelburg for 2 Zealand ploughs for Wolfert Gerrittsen, and for oats and draff for the sheep, which he bought also in Zealand, ... 22.00

May 17. To Roelof Jansen of Masterlandt, assistant Bouwmeester, who shall serve with his family, according to contract, yearly fl. 180, from which is to be deducted, as having been paid, 40 Rix dollars, ... 100.00

To Claes Claessen of ———, farm-servant to Roelof Jansen, to be deducted from his yearly wages, ... 10.00

To Jacob Govertsen, 8 rix dol. to be dedücted from his yearly salary, 15.00

June 3. To Jacob Schimmel, for 2 guns for Roelof Jansen and his people, which they are to restore, ... 28.00

July 4. Paid to Jacques Spierinck, auger-maker, (boor-maker,) for axes, adzes, borers, augers, sledges, &c., delivered to Roelof Jansen, to be taken along with him, ... 37.15.6

Dec. 7. To Johan Monfoort, for so much bought of him for me in New Netherland, by Wolfert Gerrittsen, viz. 4 ewe milk-sheep and 4 lambs, in all, ... 33.00

12. Paid to Philip Jansen of Harlem, for eight sheets of ruled paper, a writing-book and pen, to make drawings around Fort Orange, 1.13

To John Theisen, trumpeter, to be deducted from the hire of Rutger Heindricksen of Soest, ... 10.00

1631.

June 24. Paid to Maryn Adriaensen van der Veere, who proceeds thither with his people to plant tobacco, according to contract made with him, for the half of 4 guns, 8 axes, 4 adzes, 12 spades, amounting to fl. 74.10, . fl. 37.05
For one half of fl.143.04 to Jasper Ferlyn and Johan Tiers, for guard money, (wachtgelt,) and paid in hand, . 71.12
——— 108.17

26. To Maryn Adriaensen, as per receipt, to be repaid in tobacco, the sum of, ... 100.00

To Maryn Adriaensen aforesaid, repaid the half of fl. 12, which he paid to Cornelis Maasen van Buren Maasen, to be deducted from his hire, ... 6.00

Date	Item		Total
June 30.	For remaining day's wages to Jasper Ferlyn and Cornelis Maasen, who embark on board together, ...		2.00
July 5.	Paid to the following millwrights and sawyers, according to contract made with them:—		
	To Andries Carstensen, master millwright, . .	fl. 40.00	
	To Laurens Laurensen of Copenhagen, . . .	27.10	
	To Barent Thomissen of He gensout, . . .	25.00	
		———	92.10
	To Heindrick op de Camp, for two small millstones for a small grist-mill, ...		20.05
9.	To Lubbert Tamessen, for one iron trap of 155 lbs. at 6 stiv:—fl. 46.10, and twelve stiv. boat freight, ...		47.02
	Pieter Jansen Smit, for one iron trap, 36 lbs. at 6 stiv:—fl. 10.16, besides 4 [erasure] fl. 14 and 8 stiv. freight, ...		25.04
	To Laurens Laurensen, paid for sledges, ...		9.00
	To Coenraedt Notelman, sheriff (schout) of New Netherland, to present to the Skipper of the (ship) Eendracht,	fl. 5.00	
	Besides 12 Rix dollars to be disbursed, on arriving there, for my people, ...	30.00	
		———	35.00
Aug. 5.	To Mr. Schepen Bicker, for the purchase and expense of five Cow calves at Texel, according to account, holden by Coenradt Notelman, ...	fl. 69.12	
	For purchase and expense of 3 calves from Jacob Classen, and had by myself, ...	32.00	
	For freight of three calves, from here to Texel, .	2.10	
		———	104.02
	To Copartner Samuel Bloemmaert, for so much delivered by, and made good to him, 2,222 lbs. of wheat and rye meal, at 4 stivers, ...	fl. 88.00	
	10 bags obtained therefor by him, at 16 stiv., . .	8.00	
		———	96.00
	To Jacques Spierinck, auger-maker, for the master millwrights and wood-sawyers, according to account, ...		27.17
Sept. 27.	To Simon Symensen of Hoorn for rope and lines furnished said wood-sawyers and wood-cutters, ...		39.15.10
			1348.02

For interest of disbursements, according to contract, at one penny for 16, or 6 per cent.

Principal		Interest	Total
fl. 297.10	paid, anno 1630, from 10th to 15th Jan.	fl. 29.05	
101.11	in February and March following, .	9.00	
125.	in May following, ...	10.00	
65. 5.6	in July and June, ...	4.10	
43.	in December, ...	2.10	
218.10	in June, 1631, ...	3. 0	
229. 1	in July, 1631, ...	3. 0	
267.14.10	in August last	0. 0	
———		———	61.5
1348 2			
	Sommarium,		1409.7

Memorandum of what has been received and had by Kiliaen van Rensselaer, as Patroon of the colonie of Rensselaerswyck, on behalf of the same, together with what has come in on behalf of the Colonie after his decease :—

Date	Item	Amount
1631.		
Sept. 29.	From myself for so much which I must bring in for my two-fifth parts of the first estimate	fl. 563.14.8
" "	Received from Samuel Blommaert, in liquidation of his one-fifth part,	281.17.8
Nov.	Received from François Boudewyns for the one-fifth part of	
1632.	Johannes [De Laet] aforesaid,	281.17.8
Feb. 20.	Received in liquidation of Samuel Godyn for one-fifth part as aforesaid,	281.17.8
		fl. 1409.07

[*Cetera desunt.*]

H.

Names of Settlers in Rensselaerswyck from 1630 *to* 1646

Compiled from the books of Monthly Wages and other MSS.]

1630.

Wolfert Gerritsen, superintendent of farms.

Rutger Hendricksen van Soest, superintendent of the brewery.

Seger Hendricksen van Soest, shepherd and ploughman.

Brandt Peelen van Nieukerke, schepen; had two daughters, Lisbet and Gerritje The latter married Goosen Gerritsen van Schaick. The father died in 1644. He is mentioned by the Rev. Mr. Megapolensis in his tract on the Maquaa Indians, and by Van der Donck in his Beschryvinge van N. N., as having raised wheat off one field in Rensselaerswyck eleven years in succession. The land was ploughed twelve times in that period; twice the first and once every succeeding year, when the stubble was ploughed and the wheat sown and harrowed under. Van der Donck adds:—"There are many thousand morgens of as good land there as that of which we have spoken." Several descendants of this individual reside in Albany county, where they go by the name of Brandt.

Simon Dircksen Pos, was one of Minuet's council in 1624; died in 1649.

Jan Tyssen, trumpeter, Fort Orange.

Andries Carstenssen, millwright.

Laurens Laurenssen, } sawyers.
Barent Tomassen, }

Arendt van Curler; a sketch of this gentleman has been already given, p. 322

Jacob Jansen Stol, succeeded Hendrick Albertzsen as ferry-master at Beverwyck.

Martin Gerrittsen van Bergen, married Neeltje Meynderts; his oldest son was Gerrit; his second, Myndert van Bergen. In the year 1668, he had a lease of Castle Island, called after him, Martin Gerritsen's Island, and in 1690 he lived south of that island, on the west side of the river. He had property in Katskill, Coxsackie, and Albany, of which place he was magistrate for a long time

Claes Arissen.

Roeloff Jansen van Maesterlandt, wife and family; came out as farmer to the Patroon, at $72 a year. The Rev. Ev. Bogardus, of New Amsterdam, married his widow.

Claes Claessen, his servant.

Jacob Govertsen.

Jacques Spierinck.

Raynert Harmensen.

Bastiaen Jansen Krol, Fort Orange.

Albert Andriessen Bradt, "de Noorman," married Annetje Barents, by whom he had eight children, viz. Barent; Eva, (who m. Roeloff Swartwout;) Storm; Engeltje, (who m. Teunis Slingerland, of Onisquathaw;) Gisseltje, (who m. Jan van Eechelen;) Andries, Jan, and Dirck. The tradition is, that one of the above children was born on ship-board, on the passage out, in the midst of a heavy storm, in consequence of which he was called "Storm van der Zee." Barent Albertsen succeeded his father, in 1672, as lessee of the water privileges on the Normans Kill, for which he was to pay $150 a year; and Slingerland succeeded, in 1677, as lessee of the farm which his father had occupied until then on the above stream. Albert de Noorman died 7th June, 1686, and Swartwout, mentioning the occurrence, says:—he was "een van de oudste en eerste inwoonders der colonie Rensselaerswyck." He was one of the oldest and earliest of the inhabitants of Rensselaerswyck. At the time of his decease, he was proprietor of some lots and houses on the island of Manhattans. It was after this man that the creek south of Albany was called the Noormans Kill. Many of his descendants are still met with in and around the latter city.

1631.

Maryn Adriaensen van Veere. This was the freebooter who afterwards played so prominent a figure in Kieft's time.

Thomas Witsent.

Gerrit Teunissen de Reus, schepen, had a well-stocked farm in Greenbush

Cornelis Teunissen van Westbroek.

Cornelis Teunissen van Breukelen, Raedts persoon; the descendants of this man now call themselves van Brackelen.

Johan Tiers.

Jasper Ferlyn.

Gerrit Willems Oosterum.

Cornelis Maessen van Buren Maassen (in Gelderland) and Catalyntje Martensen, his wife, came out in the ship Rensselaerswyck. In the passage out was born their first child, Hendrick; had besides him, four other children, viz. Martin, Maas, Steyntje, and Tobias, all of whom were living in the colonie in 1662. Steyntje married, 1663, Dirck Wessels, "free merchant here." The father had a farm at Papskenea. He and his wife died in 1648, and were both buried on the same day! (Beyde op eenen dagh zyn begraaven. MS.)

Cornelis Teunissen Bos, bouwknecht to Cornelis Maassen, was commissary at Fort Orange previous to 1662.

1634.

Jan Labbadie, carpenter, native of France, was subsequently commissary to the Patroon, and after that held a like office at Fort Orange, under the company. He married the widow of Mr. Harman van der Bogaert. He came out previous to this year, and was part owner of the Garce.

Robert Hendricksen.

Lubert Gysbertsen, wheelwright.

Jacob Albertzen Planck, officier, or sheriff.

Hendrick Cornelissen.

Adriaen Gerritsen.

Jan Jacobsen.

Joris Houten, Fort Orange.

Jan Jansen Dam, or Damen; married Adriaentje Cuvel. He removed subsequently to New Amsterdam, where he was elected one of the Eight Men; amassed considerable wealth, and was one of the owners of the privateer La Garce. In

1649–50 he went to Holland with C. van Tienhoven, to defend Stuyvesant against the complaints of Van der Donck and others, and died on his return, 18th June, 1651. He does not seem to have had any children. He had three brothers, Cornelis Jansen Cuyper; Cornelis Jansen Damen; and Willem Jansen Damen; and two sisters, Neiltje and Hendrickje. He adopted the son of the last-named sister—Jan Cornelis Buys—who assumed his name, having been left 600 Car. guilders. Jan Damen, at his death, willed 400 Car. guilders to the poor of Bunick, province of Utrecht. The inventory of his personal property fills ten folio pages in the records.

1635.

Jan Terssen van Franiker.
Jan Cornelissen, Carpenter.
Juriaen Bylvelt.
Johannes Verbeeck; Raedt Persoon, 1658, 1661.

1636.

Barent Pieterse Koyemans, alias Barent the Miller, entered the service of the first Patroon, at 30 guilders a year. Three brothers accompanied him to Rensselaerswyck in 1636: viz. David, Jacob, and Arent, who was a lad. It is presumed that they came originally from Utrecht. Barent worked in the Patroon's grist-mill until 1645, in the fall of which year he took charge, with Jan Gerritsen, his partner, (who came out with him,) of the Patroon's saw-mills, being allowed 150 gl. each a year for board, and 3 stivers a cut for every plank they sawed. He remained in this employment until 1647, having cut between three and four thousand boards in that time. Previous to 1650, he lived a little south of the 5th or Patroon's creek, and in 1655 took a nineteen years' lease of a farm of maize-land at 24 gl. per annum. In 1657 he rented, in company with Cornelis Theunis. van Breukelen, for three years, the Upper Mills, (as the mills on the Patroon's creek were called, in contradistinction to those on the Norman's kill,) which he leased on his own account in 1660 for 13 years. This lease expired in 1673, about which time he purchased, by consent of the Commissioners at Albany, from the Katskill Indians, a large tract of land, some twelve or fifteen miles south of that city, on the west side of the river. The place had been known, for many years previous, as offering peculiar advantages for the erection of saw-mills, Cryn Cornelissen and Hans Jansen having erected saw-mills on the creek immediately north of Beeren Island as early as 1651. Coeymans had, no doubt, these advantages in view when he made his purchase, which began at a point on the shore called Sieskasin, opposite the middle of Jan Ryersen's island called by the Indians Sapanakock, and ran south to the mouth of Pieter Bronck's kill, as Coxsackie creek was then called. Following up this creek to its head, the line then went west until it struck the head of the waters falling into the Hudson, all the land on which belonged to the Katskill Indians, the waters flowing west to the Schoharie creek being the property of the Mohawks. The line then went northerly to the bounds of Rensselaerswyck, and thence returned to the Hudson River. A patent was obtained for this tract, twelve miles deep and some eight or ten front, from Gov. Lovelace, on 7th April, 1673. But falling as it did within the original bounds of Van Rensselaer's colonie, Coeymans purchased out the

Patroon's claims, 22d Oct., 1706, agreeing to pay a quit-rent of nine shillings a year, and he finally obtained letters patent from Queen Anne, confirming the whole to him and his heirs forever, 6th Aug., 1714. This purchase now constitutes the ancient town of Coeymans, in the county of Albany,—Barent Pietersen had five children—Andreas, Samuel, Peter, Ariantje, and Jannitje. Andreas moved to the Raritans, New Jersey, where he purchased a considerable tract of land, and where some of the Coeymans still reside. Peter married twice: by his first wife he had Mayica, who married Andreas Witbeck; and Elizabeth, the wife of Jacob van Allen. By his second wife, Charlotte Amelia Drawyer, he had Gerritje, who married John Barclay, mayor of Albany; Anne Margaret, who married Peter Ten Eyck, and Charlotte A., who married John Bronck. Mrs. Abraham Verplanck of Coeymans is grand-daughter to this Mrs. Bronck All the descendants of Barent Coeymans, after the first generation in a direct line, were females. Owing to this singular circumstance, the family name is now extinct in this State.

Pieter Cornelissen van Munnichendam, millwright.

Dirck Jansen van Edam.

Arent Andriessen van Frederickstad.

Mauritz Janssen, } van Broeckhuysen.
Michel Jansen, }

This Michel brought out his wife and two children. Van Tienhoven says he came out as a "boereknecht," or servant. He amassed a fortune in a few years, in the fur-trade, but not being able to agree with the head men of the colonie, he removed, in 1646, to the island of Manhattans. He purchased Evertsen Bout's farm in Pavonia, with some stock, for 8,000 gl., and was appointed one of the delegates to Holland in 1649, against the colonial administration, but owing to the unsettled state of his private affairs he could not accept that appointment. It was in a room in this man's house, in New Amsterdam, that Van der Donck wrote his celebrated "Vertoogh," or Remonstrance against the maladministration of affairs in New Netherland.

Jacob Jansen van Amsterdam.

Simon Walings van der Belt; was killed at Pavonia, in 1648, by some savages from the south.

Gysbert Claessen van Amsterdam.

Cristen Cristyssen Noorman van Vlecburg and wife.

Tys Barentsen Schoonmaker van Edam.

Hans Zevenhuyzen.

Adriaen Hubertsen.

Rynier Tymanssen van Edam.

Tomas Jansen van Bunick.

Cornelis Tomassen, smith, and wife.

Arent Steveniersen, wife and two children; he married, anno 1637, the widow of Cornelis Tomassen, by whom he had two other children.

Johan Latyn van Verduym.

Claes Jansen van Nykerk.

Rutger Jacobsen van Schoenderwoerdt; married in New Amsterdam, anno 1646, Tryntje Jansen van Briestede, (who died at her son's in Rosendal, in 1711.) By her he had two daughters and one son. Margaret, one of the daughters, married, in 1667, Jan Jansen Bleecker, who came from Meppel, province of Overyssel, to America, in 1658, and was the ancestor of the present highly respectable Bleecker family in this State. Rutger Jacobsen was a magistrate in Rensselaerswyck as early as 1648, and continued to fill that office as late as 1662, and perhaps later. He owned a vessel on the river in 1649, in which year he rented, in partnership with Goosen Gerrittsen, the Patroon's brewery, at 450 gl. a year, paying in addition one guilder for every ton of beer which they brewed. This duty amounted in the first year to 330 gl., and in the following season they worked up 1,500 schepels of malt. On the 2d June, 1656, he laid the corner-stone of the "new church," in Beverwyck, and we find him subsequently part proprietor of Pachonakelick, called by the Dutch Mohican's or Long Island, below Bethlehem. He had the character of an upright citizen, and to his credit it must be added, he rose by his honest industry from small beginnings.

Ryckert Rutgersen; was engaged, when he first came out, at 120 gl. per annum for a term of 6 years. In 1648 he took a 6 years' lease of Bethlehem Island, at 300 gl. per annum, besides the tenths. He received three horses, and two or three cows on halves, and the Patroon was to build him a barn and dwelling-house, he cutting and drawing the timber, and boarding the carpenters. He was exempt from rent and tithes for the first year. In 1652 he surrendered his lease to Jan Ryersen, after whom this island has since been named.

N. B. The Settlers of 1636 came out in the ship Rensselaerswyck, having sailed from Holland on the 1st October of that year.

1637.

Jan Michaelsen van Edam, tailor, and his boy.

Pieter Nicolaussen van Nordinge.

Teunis Cornelissen van Vechten, succeeded Michel Jansen on his farm in 1646, and lived in 1648 at the south end of Greenbush.

Burger Joris, smith.

Jan Ryersen; the island situate opposite the junction of the towns of Bethlehem and Coeymans, on the Hudson, was called Jan Ryersen's island, in consequence of this man having lived there in 1652.

Abraham Stevensen, surnamed Croaet, a boy.

Cornelis Teunissen van Merkerk.

Goosen Gerritsen van Schaick; married, 1st, Gerritje Brants, daughter of Brant Peelen; 2d, in July, 1657, Annetje Lievens. He was a brewer in the colonie in 1649, in which year he accepted, after a good deal of solicitation, the office of magistrate, or Gerechts persoon. Was afterwards one of the part owners of Nachtenack, the Indian name for the site of the present village of Waterford, Saratoga county.

Willem Juriaensen Bakker, was banished from the colonie in 1650, at the age of seventy years, in consequence of his repeated misdeeds.*

* As the minute in the Gerechts rolle, or court register, of the sentence pronounced against this public disturber will afford some idea of the strictness of the police in those days, we are tempted to translate it. It is in this wise:—"Their worships, the Commissioners and Council of the colonie of Rensselaerswyck, having duly considered and weighed the demand of the Honorable Director, as prosecutor against Willem Juriaensen Bakker, and finding that he was already banished out the colonie by their Worshipful Court, on the 4th February, 1644: and afterwards because that he attempted on the Lord's highway with a knife to stab the person of Antonie de Hooges, then commis to the Noble Patroon, whereby he, in as much as in him lay, did commit a murder, for which he, on the 28th August, 1647, was banished from the colonie; and he having by petition prayed for a respite, which was granted to him, he pledged all his goods, and also subjected himself to the banishment of his person, should he happen to insult any person within or without the court, or to do any thing that should be displeasing, or worthy of punishment. Therefore, the Honorable Prosecutor, recapitulating the same, has set forth, to wit, that he, the Delinquent, hath so fright

1638.

Jan Dircksen van Amersfoort.
Wybrant Pietersen.
Willem Meynten.
Martin Hendricksen van Hamelwaard.
Adriaen Berghoorn.
Hendrick Fredricksen.
Gerrit Hendricksen.
Cornelis Leendertsen.
Francis Allertsen, cooper.
Roeloff Cornelissen van Houten
Volckert Jansen.
Jacob Jansen Nostrandt.

Christoffel Davits; lived in 1650 on a farm at Dominie's Hoeck, now called Van Wie's Point.

Claes Jansen Ruyter.
Jacob Flodder, his man.

Gysbert Adriaensen van Bunick; came out in the Key of Calmar.

Teunis Dircksen van Vechten; came out, with wife, child, and two servants, in the "Arms of Norway," and had a farm, in 1648, at Greenbush, north of that occupied by Teunis Cornelissen van Vechten. He is referred to in 1663 as "an old inhabitant here."

1639.

Jacob Adriaensen van Utrecht.
Ryer Stoffelsen.

Cryn Cornelissen; obtained a license in 1651 to erect a sawmill in company with Hans Jansen van Rotterdam, on what is now Coeyman's Creek.

Adam Roelantsen van Hamelwaard; previously a schoolmaster in New Amsterdam.

Sander Leendertsen Glen; married Catalyn Doncassen. He was one of the Indian traders at Beverswyck, and finally moved to Scotia, near Schenectada, of which tract he obtained a patent from Gov. Nicolls, in 1665. Reference is made probably to this gentleman by the French in their account of the burning of Schenectada, anno 1690, in the following terms:—"At daybreak some men were sent to the

ened and shocked a certain woman, [Saertje Cornelis, wife of Thomas Sanderssen Smith,] that according to her complaint, she hath miscarried; Secondly, that he hath unjustly censured some honorable people, among others some of the Worshipful Court here, asserting, as relates to the agreement between him and Jan van Hoesem, that they had written a falsehood; Thirdly, having been quietly spoken to about the purchase of two beasts, he, entering the house, called out that he had a knife in his sleeve, and that, if he were meddled with, he should pay the Honorable Prosecutor with it. Besides, being summoned on account of these enormities, he did openly insult the Honorable Prosecutor here, saying, 'I must bury you; I am summoned before the court; I must hang.' Moreover have we been assured by trustworthy persons, that he hath said to certain females who were proceeding to partake of the Lord's Supper, 'Is it a bit of bread you want? Come to my house and I'll give you a whole loaf;' and divers other things. [On being asked his age, 'to the contempt of the court, he said he was about twenty-one, though it is known to us that he is at least seventy years of age.'] WHEREFORE, he being a blasphemer, a street-scold, a murderer as far as his intentions are concerned, a defamer, a contemner of law and justice, and a disturber of the public peace, their Worships of the court aforesaid have adjudged and sentenced, as they do hereby sentence and adjudge, that the aforesaid sentence of banishment shall stand fast, and he, Willem Juriaensen, is hereby banished out the district and jurisdiction of this colonie, from now henceforth and forever, to leave by the first vessel, and never more to return, on pain of corporal punishment: all with costs of court. Thus sentenced, &c., in College, this 18th July, 1650, to the knowledge of me,

"A. DE HOOGES, Secretary.

"27th July, 1650. Resolved, that Willem Juriaensen shall be conveyed on board of Rutger Jacobsen, and then released, Rutger Jacobsen promising to give him a passage in his yacht to the Manhattans."

dwelling of Mr. Sander, who was Major of the place at the other side of the river. He was not willing to surrender, and began to put himself on the defensive, with his servants and some Indians. But as it was resolved not to do him any harm, in consequence of the good treatment which the French had formerly experienced at his hands, M. d'Iberville and the great Agniez proceeded thither alone, promised him quarter for himself, his people and property, whereupon he laid down his arms on parole."

Pieter Jacobsen and wife.
Johan Poog.
Gilles Barentsen.
Claes Jansen van Breda.
Cornelis Spierinck
Claes Tyssen.

1640.

Nys Jacobsen.
Jannitje Teunissen.
Jan Teunissen, carpenter.

Teunis Jacobsen van Schoenderwordt, brother to Rutger Jacobsen; had 90 gl. a year salary for the first three years, and 100 for the next three. He became a trader in 1651.

Andries Hubertsen Constapel van der Blaes; married Annetje Juriaensen; owned a tile kiln in Beverswyck, and died in 1662.

Andries de Vos, brother-in-law to Barent Pieterse Coeymans; was Gerechts persoon, or magistrate, in 1648.

Adriaen Teunissen van der Belt.
Jan Creynen.
Jan Jansen van Rotterdam; was killed in the Indian war, 1644.
Jacob Jansen van Campen.
Cornelis Kryne van Houtten.
Jan Cornelissen van Houtten.
Claes Gerritsen.

1641.

Adriaen van der Donck, officier, or Sheriff.

Cornelis Antonissen van Slyck, alias Broer Cornelissen, was the first patentee of Katskill, anno 1646. Van Slyck's Island, opposite Schenectada, was so called after one of his sons, Jacques, to whom it was granted, 13th Nov., 1662, by Director Stuyvesant.

Claes Gysbertsen.
Joris Borrelingen, Engelsman.
Jacob Wolfertsen.
Claes Jansen van Ruth.
Teunis de Metselaer.
Cornelis Cornelissen van Schoonderwoerdt, alias "Vosje."

1642.

Dominie Johannes Megapolensis, Jun.,

Matheld Willemsen, his wife,

Hellegond, Dirck, Jan, and Samuel, their children. Samuel M., the last named son, was sent to Harvard College in 1657; spent three years there, and then proceeded to the University of Leyden, where he was licensed, in 1662, as a minister, and obtained the degree of M. D. On his return, he became Collegiate pastor of the church at New Amsterdam, and was appointed by Gov. Stuyvesant one of the commissioners to negotiate with the British the articles relating to the capitulation of the Province. Rev. Dr. De Witt.

Abraham Staes, surgeon.

Evert Pels van Steltyn, brewer, and wife; lived at the Mill Creek, Greenbush.

Cornelis Lambertsen van Doorn. Joachim Kuttelhuys van Cremyn

Johan Helms van Baasle.

Juriaen Bestval van Luyderdorp, (near Leyden.)

Claes Jansen van Waalwyck. Paulus Jansen van Gertruydenburgh.

Hans Vos van Baden, court messenger; was sheriff's constable in New Amsterdam in 1661.

Lucas Smith van Ickemsburgh; left the colonie in the spring of 1646, with the character of "een eerlyk ende vroom Jongman"—an honorable and virtuous young man.

Cornelis Crynnesen.

Cornelis Hendricksen van Es, Gerechts persoon or magistrate. His daughter, Elizabeth, married one Banckers. "Cryn Cornelissen declares that, in the spring of 1643, while conveying some of the guests, on the ice, to the wedding of Van Es's daughter, a mare belonging to him, (Cryn,) and a stud belonging to Van der Donck, were drowned in the neighborhood of Black, or Horse's point—(omtrent de Swarte, ofte Paerde Hoeck)—for which he understands Van der Donck received 150 guilders ($60) from the wedding party." MS.

Cornelis Gerritsen van Schoonderwoerdt.

Wm. Fredericksen van Leyden, free carpenter.

Antonie de Hooges, commis, afterwards Secretary of the Colonie. His daughter, and only child, says Bensen, "married Herman Rutgers, the ancestor of the respectable family of the name among us." De Hooges died 1658. The well-known promontory in the Highlands was called Anthony's Nose, after him.

Johan Holmes.

Juriaen —— van Sleswyck.

Johan Corstiaenssen, mariner.

Hendrick Albertsen; second time of his coming out. He was the first ferrymaster in Beverwyck; died in 1648 or 1649.

Gertrude Dries van Driesbergen, his wife. Hendrick Dries, her brother.

Albert Jansen, van Amsterdam. Jan Jansen Flodder, carpenter.

Geertje Mannix, widow, and two children. Pieter Wyncoop, commis.

Nicolaus Koorn, sergeant or wachtmeester; succeeded Van der Donck as Sheriff.

Adriaen Cornelissen van Bersingeren. Arendt Teunissen van Luyten.

Cornelis Segers van Voorhoudt; succeeded Van der Donck on the farm called Weelysburg, on Castle island; married Bregje Jacobsen, by whom he had six children; Cornelis, Claes, Seger, Jannitje, Neltje, and Lysbeth. The last named married François Boon, without her parents' consent, and was disinherited, having been left by will only £1 Flemish. Seger married Jannitje Teunissen van Vechten, and was killed, anno 1662, by Andries Hubertsen in a brawl. Many of the Segers family are still residents of the county of Albany.

Jacob Aertsen Wagenaar.

Jan Creyne van Houtten.

Jan Dircksen, Engelsman, van Amersfoort.

Herry de Backer. "I have known a gunner, named Harry de Backer, who killed at one shot from his gun, eleven gray geese out of a large flock." Van der Donck.

Adriaen Willemsen; banished for theft in 1644.

1643, 1644, 1645.

Pieter Hertgers van Vee, was one of the commissaries of the court at Fort Orange in 1654; died in Holland, 1670.

Abraham Clock.

Jan Barentsen Wemp, removed subsequently to Schenectada, where he became proprietor of some land. His widow married Sweer Teunissen van Velde

Richard Brigham.

Lambert van Valckenburg.

Jacob Jansen Schermerhorn, married Jannitje, daughter of Cornelis Segers. He was a prominent trader in Beverwyck in 1648, when he was arrested, by Stuyvesant, on a charge of selling fire-arms and ammunition to the Indians. His books and papers were seized, and himself removed a prisoner to Fort Amsterdam, where he was sentenced to banishment for five years, and the confiscation of all his property. By the interference of some leading citizens the first part of the sentence was struck out, but his property was totally lost. These proceedings against Schermerhorn formed, subsequently, a ground of complaint against Stuyvesant to the States General.

Claes Teunnissen, alias "Uylenspiegel."

Gysbert Cornelissen van Wesepe; called also Gysbert op de Berg, from the fact of his having lived on a farm called the "Hooge Berg," situate on the east side of the river, a little below Albany, which he rented in 1649 at 300 gl. a year. This farm still retains its original Dutch name, and is now owned by Joachim Staats, Esq.

1646.

Jan Jansen van Bremen; lived in Bethlehem, and moved, anno 1650, to Katskill.

Harman Mynderts van der Bogaert, arrived in New Netherland, anno 1631, as surgeon of the company's ship the Eendracht; he continued in the company's service to 1633, after which he resided in New Amsterdam until appointed commissary to Fort Orange. He was highly respected, though from all accounts he appears to have been of an irascible temper. An instance is mentioned of his having attempted, in the excitement of a high quarrel, when both appear to have been in a violent passion, to throw the Director-general out of a boat in which they were sailing on the river; he was, it is added, with difficulty prevented from accomplishing his purpose. He occasionally wrote his name Harmanus à Boghardij. He came, I believe, to a violent death in 1649. Carl van Brugge succeeded him as commissary at Fort Orange

Jan van Hoosem.

Hendrick Westercamp.

Jacob Herrick.

Jan Andriessen van Dublin, leased a bouwerie in 1649, described as lying "north of Stoney point, being the north half of the Flatt."

Tomas Higgens.

Jan Willemsen Scuth.

Wolf Nyssen; executed.

Willem Leendertsen, brass-founder.

Pieter Bronck; built a tavern in Beverwyck, in 1651, which was then the third at that place; afterwards lived at Coxsackie, the creek at which place was called by the Dutch, Peter Bronck's kill.

Tomas Kenningh.

Jacob Jansen van Stoutenburgh.

Jan de Neger; Scherprechter, or hangman to the colonie.

56

I.

Legal Custom against the abuse of outstanding accounts in the Colonie of Rensselaerswyck.

[From the Rensselaerswyck MSS.]

N. B. No latitude to be given to the consciences or discretion of the Boors, but the law to be stringently enforced.

Here follows the Act.

1643, *Sept.—Lawful custom against the abuses of outstanding accounts, as well for Principal Masters of Bouweries as for others.*

For the redress of the abuses and faults in the Colonie of Rensselaerswyck, the instruction given by the Lord Patroon, anticipating many things which have fallen into decay, and among these principally the falling off in liquidated accounts, must be specially observed in form and manner in the drawing up of said accounts.

Whereupon it comes to be considered, who they are who are bound or not, to make up these accounts.

That the farmers and inhabitants of the colonie should think that the Commissary of the Lord Patroon should be obliged to make them out for them, is wrong. For he is by no means in the employ of private individuals, but in that of the Patroon. His duty, therefore, is only to take up, provisionally, in the name of the Patroon, all accounts in the colony, and to supervise these: thereunto adding his advice and opinion, and afterwards to send them over to the Lord Patroon, for his approval, examination, or rejection.

Although he is accountable specially to the Patroon, so is he so far accountable to the inhabitants, that he must deliver to them the accounts of such property as is under his administration, whether store goods or others, which they receive from him. But as regards the accounts of property under the management and direction of the Bouwmeesters, (farmers,) and all others who have administration of any property, belonging in whole or in part to the Patroon or the Company, such must not be made out by him, but must be handed in by them to him.

For as it is just that each one should vindicate his own acts, so another cannot know what is without his knowledge ; what in this regard is right or wrong. Wherefore it necessarily follows then, as is customary throughout the whole world:—

That all farmers or others who hold any of the Patroon's property, must make out their own accounts, and deliver them to the Patroon or his commissary to examine them. Should they say that they are not qualified for this, then they ought not to have accepted or undertaken it, much less allow it to run on for several years, lest otherwise the impossibility, the inconvenience, or the loss to result therefrom, may fall on them, and they remain bound, notwithstanding, to render the account.

It is not an impossibility, but a perverse covetousness to defraud the Patroon, and then to sit on a cross-road ;* intending that every thing that they, in this matter, can conceal from him, shall remain concealed, and that he shall know nothing thereof.

That it has also been feasible for them, and is always so, shall appear. But that they design something else thereby, that shall also quickly come to light.

Under the cloak of this simplicity, lurk the following foul deeds:

I. That they become trustees of goods under their administration and direction, of which they must render reckoning, without giving in an account.

II. That they may make out their outlays and expenses according to their own pleasure.

III. That they may include in the expenses of the bouwerie, their own personal expenses which they incur for clothing, furniture, and unlawful drink.

IV. That they can embezzle as much wheat and other produce as they please.

All which the Patroon disclaiming, as inconsistent with right and conscience, so it is a failure, not only in the manner of the accounts, but they thereby alter their contracts and their promises.

They have given promises to him in accordance to the first article of the conditions of Gerrit de Reus, deceased, whereunto all contracts refer, until the arrival of the farmers from Breda, which agreement of the late Gerrit de Reus, as regards the preemption of the grain, they knew well, strictly, and [paper is here destroyed] to plead, as there were copies thereof in the country, to which copies, as well as to the original remaining with him, he, the Patroon, [paper here also destroyed] is appealing. And it will be found in the beginning thereof, that they are bound under oath, on pain of losing their wages and effects, that neither they, nor their people, shall trade in any forbidden peltries of otters or beavers, nor obtain any such in presents or otherwise, without his, the Patroon's, express consent.

So that all such as have done so, have forfeited their effects, unless they have subsequently obtained the consent of the Lord Patroon, proving which to him, he shall approve thereof, provided they fulfil the conditions on which he granted it to them :

Namely, half the profits each time they trade and barter. They must, therefore, render upright account and declaration of what they have gained thereupon, and account for his half. As they now say that they cannot render such account, so he, the Patroon, insists, according to their contract, on the confiscation of their effects ; giving them the choice to take one or the other, and that, moreover, from year to year, and this is the first.

Coming now to the remaining points of their own contracts which they invert :

Brant Peelen and Cornelis van Breuckel are for themselves personally bound to render an account for the goods brought by the Key of Calmar and the Arms of Norway, among which were divers goods which they traded for beavers, whereof Arendt van Curler writes, that not twelve pelts have come into his hands. They remain, besides, bound and accountable as security for Arendt van Curler, whom the Patroon sent over only as assistant, and they promoted as commissary under their bond, as appears by their own hand.

Further, they invert all these following points. According to their contract, they are bound to defray, out of the common produce and profits :

I. The wages of their servants and boys.

* En daermede op eenen kruys wech te zetten.

II. Next, the food.

III. Next, their own expenses, as regards the board in the bouwerie, according to their contract; but in no way for drink, but simply for wages and diet; obliging them, as far as drink is concerned, to make shift, like other Boors, with milk, with ordinary beer; in the harvest, with extraordinary good beer, and for the remainder, whatever the river affords.

IV. That they have undertaken to pay, out of the general produce, all wear of wagons, ploughs; in fine, all damages and losses.

Of all which the most of them are in arrear, leaving not only the wages of the servants to fall on the Patroon, who with trouble hath obtained these for them, but they take, also, on account, without paying any money, such cargoes as the commissary, Arendt van Curler, delivers to them.

From which it appears clearly, that over and above all their debauches in wine and strong drink, every one would fain claim, and hath much to demand by way of deduction. And though the Patroon hath advanced their outfit, furnished them with dwellings, cattle, wagons, and ploughs, for the first time; necessaries of food and shoes, linens and woollens, as the manifests sent by him can prove, still, instead of the returns of his necessaries and profits from the bouweries, he hath large sums to pay which he never intended. Forbidding his commissary to make any deductions to masters or servants, inasmuch as the masters should have first made out and completed the accounts of their servants, (knechts,) and that from year to year and afterwards, the masters should draw up their own accounts in the following manner, charging him, the commissary, not to move his hand, another time, to give any account except of what he hath issued. But to demand, in the name of the Patroon, [paper worn away.] All outstanding accounts shall be made up in said [colonie] by the farmers and other residents.

Firstly, those who settle on half profit and loss, shall afterwards make up their accounts:

I. And give in, every year, uprightly, the whole amount of grain and other produce obtained that year from the bouwerie; and those who neglect to do so, shall incur fine and damages.

II. Item, what they received from the swine which they sold; from milk, butter, and other sources.

III. Item, what grain they delivered to freemen in the colonie and sold.

Herefrom must be deducted, and by them be paid, according to their contract:

I. The wages of the farm-servants, with the 16 fl. yearly for the Patroon.

II. The food for themselves and people.

III. The wear of wagons, ploughs, repairs of houses, barns, palisades, (fences,) and other such things.

This being deducted, make out an account of what then remains; exhibiting to the Patroon, or his commissary, his lawful half which falls to him, deducting beforehand his future tenths.

What now regards the lawful half of the remainder, the future farmer must subtract from that the following:—

I. What he had for himself each year for cloths and house furniture;

II. What he yearly had from the Patroon's store for himself and his servants, which he shall stop in return;

III. What he and his people yearly consumed in wine and strong drink, whereof the Patroon is not bound, according to contract, to pay his half; the Patroon understanding peremptorily, that all the wines which are drunk in the colonie, and paid for in grain, or other common effects, shall not be deducted from the general stock, much less from his share, but from his who hath consumed them, whether man or woman, master or man, having promised no one such (drink,) much less such a flood as many have used.

And as regards the increase of the cattle, each farmer shall pertinently give in an account of what have yearly died; what have been added, and what have been disposed of; and the Patroon understands the price of the pre-emption of the cows is to be estimated by those which calve in their third year, and not in the second, as the valuation on the part of the company, as regards the pre-emption, is understood of cattle which calve in their third year. So that those calving in their second year, gradually pining away, and producing poor stock, are to be entered only on the half, or whatever else is most proper.*

And whereas the farmers commonly have recourse to perverse means, and enter on crooked courses, as for example:—When corn becomes less in quantity (scarce) and more in demand, then many of them have sent a great deal away, and sold it higher than the pre-emption price, or delivered it on their own authority to the company's servants, without receiving special payment therefor, or special bills of exchange, or an assignment to be received in hand, but so delivered it up in gross. Therefore the Patroon resolves, as is just, that [MS. here destroyed] such wheat as is delivered, in this manner, to the company, is not considered as fulfilling [erasement;] all the effect thereof [will come] on his purse. Warning, to this end, the farmers that, from the beginning until this time, being now in the thir [teenth] year, 1,500 guilders in money have only once been received, in all that time; the remainder has been expended in goods and provisions delivered to the farmers, and the people of the colonie have entered down the same in parcels of two to three thousand guilders, without naming man or horse. Which accounts must first be rightly analyzed, as to who have carried away those parcels, or not; making no exceptions and taking no excuses from one or the other: "I have not had this; I have not had that;" every one being willing, by assertion, to clear himself; and inasmuch as some will be more in debt than others, so must it be first cleared up, or adjusted, whence those moneys are to be received. For what the one hath delivered, and the other hath received, that must be found out by those who had (the goods) and not by the Patroon. Nor can any money be charged to the Patroon which has not been received at his counter. Particularly not, if such has, without his consent, been delivered or sent to the company, who have accepted that on the general account of the colonie, as it appears; and such farmers had done better to have immediately proposed their payment there.

And whereas grain is now somewhat less in demand, and will apparently be somewhat lower in price, so the Patroon hereby again warns the farmers who have running accounts, that they shall not hand in their statements (haere leverancie) in gross, but separately:—

I. The tenths;

II. What is for the servants' wages, and what for the yearly expenditure;

* Sulx dat die op haer tweedejaer kalvende, allengskens ve kleynen, en kleynen aert voortbrengende, maer op de helfte, ofte wat meer behooren genomen te worden.

III. The thirds or halves coming to the Patroon.

Which is done that their just income may every year be correctly known, and they may not come to any loss.

The number of muds [four bushels] shall be handed in to the Patroon's commissary, demanding of him, if he, in the name of the Patroon, accepted or refused the pre-emption right, whereupon the commissary shall have to regulate himself according to the order of the Patroon, and according to the expected prices and sales, which he may be able to obtain for it in cash, goods, or peltries, without credit. On the contrary, should he refuse the right of pre-emption, the farmers are at liberty to do their best by it; and this is the legal choice of the pre-emption. But that the farmers should wish to crowd up the commissary and overload him with produce, when it is low in value, and when at a higher price, sell the same, as many have done—that is in no wise the intention of the Patroon. Warning all farmers to watch over their people therefore, and not to deliver any mixed grain; that is to say, whereof the tenths, the thirds, or halves, according to contract, are not separated or paid.

Coming now to the conclusion:—The Patroon declares that he will not accept any accounts which include several years; but that every farmer, or whoever he be, shall deliver in to him yearly account of the year's profits, as well for them as for him.

That also all commission accounts (leverancien) whereof they have not received special payment, or which have not come into the Patroon's counter, must run [original destroyed] in the general account until all out—[original destroyed] are separated.

That none of the inhabitants hath or can have any free or private goods, except such as have rendered their yearly and proper accounts.

And as they possibly may complain of this; the Patroon hath much greater cause to complain, who has not received any accounts from them in all this time. That they should call on the Patroon's commissary is wrong. It has already been stated, that he is not in their service, but in the Patroon's employ; that he is not bound to make out theirs, but the Patroon's accounts; and that every person, be he who he may, as well the Patroon's commissary as all other contractors, farmers, yearly or daily servants, each shall make out his own account. The commissary is specially enjoined to account to the Patroon; and all others, none excepted, shall account to the commissary for his examination first, and afterwards for the approbation of the Patroon.

Should they imagine that all their secret practices of covetousness will, through length of time, be forgotten, they will cheat themselves. They take one course towards the west to escape. The Patroon will take a course from the east, with the rising of the sun, to expose their deception.

The Patroon proposes to wrong no man in the world, much less the least of his inhabitants; but as he will injure no man, so will he by no man be hoodwinked or wronged. Every man, whose conscience is not asleep or seared, will well understand what that means.

And all persons, farmers or servants, are warned, if they come over with any accounts which they extorted from the commissary through ignorance, or by persuasion, or threats, to pass in review the preceding points, ere they go to law with the Patroon.

In the mean time, the Patroon is heartily desirous that all who have obtained their goods, how great soever in quantity, without prejudice to him, shall be fully content, and wishes every luck and prosperity with them. Through carelessness, neither the commissary, nor any one else has, in five or more years, sent him any accounts. The Patroon has first to claim of those who have not, according to their pledged faith, rendered any accounts to the commissary, that every one in the colonie is bound to render such to him, and their neglect shall tend not to accuse, but to excuse the commissary. Notwithstanding, what he was bound to do, and must, and ought, and can do for the goods sent to him, thereof he shall not be excused by the Patroon.

These things then being so, You are required to direct the work so that, for the future, I may precisely know, every year, what profit each bouwerie affords me.

As I have once delivered to them dwellings and cattle, then must they find out means to pay, without diminution, the tenths, the servants' wages, and the Patroon's half and third; what necessaries they have had, must they pay of themselves; and God grant that good order and honest yearly accounts may once more be maintained there. Actum this 16th Sept., 1643, in Amsterdam, and signed with his own hand.

Was subscribed, KILIAEN VAN RENSSELAER,
Patroon of the Colonie of Rensselaerswyck.

Then follows, as on the other side:

There has been sent to me here, from the Manhattans, an extract of the contract of Gerrit de Reus, deceased, whereof several articles are left out. Let Arendt examine among the papers, if he have not a complete contract by him. Otherwise I have it here in the original, which I shall send over if necessary. Then I think that Arendt has it. Vale.

Undersigned, K V. R.

J.

Conditions freely assented to and accepted by Kiliaen van Rensselaer, in his quality as Patroon of his Colonie named Rensselaerswyck, and by Dr. Johannes Megapolensis, minister of the Holy Gospel to the Congregation at Schoorel and Berge, under the venerable Classis of Alkmaar, in the presence of Mr. Adam Bessels, copartner in the said Colonie, and the Rev. Jacobus Laurentius and Petrus Wittewrongel, both Ministers of Amsterdam, as preacher to administer and promote Divine Service in the aforesaid Colonie for the term of six successive years, according to previous demission from his said Classis.

[From the Rensselaerswyck MSS.]

Firstly, Dr. Johannes Megapolensis, 39 years old, with his wife, Machtelt Willemsen, aged 42 years, besides his children, Hellegond, Dirrick, Jan, and Samuel, aged 14, 12, 10, and 8 years, shall furnish and provide themselves as well with clothing, furniture, and other utensils, and these put up in such small and compact parcels, as can be properly stowed away in the ship.

In the mean time, as his six years and his salary shall commence so soon as he shall set foot in the aforesaid colonie, the Patroon, in addition to free board for them all in the ship, until they reach the colonie, shall over and above make him a present, for future service, at once, of three hundred guilders, without deduction.

And in case it happen, which the Lord God in His mercy forbid, that he and his family come to fall in the hands of the Dunkirkers, the Patroon promises to use all diligence to procure his ransom; to forward him afterwards on his voyage, according as occasion shall again offer, and to cause to be paid him, during his detention, for the support of himself and family, forty guilders per month; and also so much here monthly, after he shall have received his liberty and orders, and shall have conveyed him hither, until he embarks.

On his arrival, by God's help, in the colonie, the Patroon shall cause to be shown to him where he and his shall lodge at first, until a fit dwelling shall be erected for him. So soon as he shall reach the colonie, his hereafter-mentioned salary shall commence, and his board and wages cease, and the Patroon be discharged therefrom.

Which salary, in order that he and his family shall be able honorably to maintain themselves, and not be necessitated to have recourse to any other means, whether tilling the land, commerce, rearing of cattle, or such like; but by the diligent performance of his duties for the edifying improvement of the inhabitants and Indians, without being indebted to any person, which he also acknowledges to observe; wherefore the Patroon promises to cause to be paid to him for the first three years' salary, meat, drink, and whatever else he may claim in that regard, one thousand, or ten hundred guilders yearly, one half here in this country, the remaining half in proper account there, according as he requires it, in provisions, clothing, and such like, at the ordinary and accustomed prices, and a further yearly addition of thirty schepels of wheat—I say thirty schepels—and two firkins of butter, or, in place thereof, sixty guilders in money's worth. Should the Patroon be satisfied with his service, he shall give him yearly, the three following years, an increase of two hundred guilders.

In case of decease within the aforesaid six years, at which time the salary shall cease, the Patroon shall pay to his widow, besides the supplement of the half year in which he shall have entered, a yearly sum of one hundred guilders, until the expiration of the aforesaid six years. He shall, besides, befriend and serve the Patroon, in all things wherein he can do so without interfering with or impeding his duties. The aforesaid Johannes Megapolensis having also promised to comport himself in the said colonie as a loyal subject and inhabitant thereof, the abovenamed Patroon, on his side, also promises for him and his successors, to perform and execute what is hereinbefore set forth, and to furnish him with due acte and commission sealed with the seal of the Patroon and the Colonie: and in acknowledgment of the truth, without fraud, guile, or deceit, has this writing been signed by both sides. In Amsterdam, this 6th of March, 1642.

KILIAEN VAN RENSSELAER,
JOHANNES MEGAPOLENSIS.

Call of the Rev. Joannes Megapolensis.

WHEREAS, by the state of the navigation in East and West Indies, a door is opened through the special Providence of God, also in New Netherland for the preaching of the Gospel of Jesus Christ for the salvation of men, as good fruits have been already witnessed there through God's mercy; and whereas the Brethren of the Classis of Amsterdam have been notified that Mr. Kiliaen van Rensselaer hath within the said limits in the North River as Patroon, or Lord, founded a colonie, named Rensselaerswyck, and would fain have the same provided with a good, honest, and pure preacher; therefore they have observed and fixed their eyes on the Reverend, Pious, and Well-learned Dr. JOANNES MEGAPOLENSIS, junior, a faithful servant of the Gospel of the Lord, in the Congregation of Schorel and Berg, under the Classis of Alkmaar, whom ye have also called, after they had spoken with the said Lord, Mr. Kiliaen van Rensselaer, in the same manner as they, with his Honor's approbation, do hereby call him to be sent to New Netherland, there to preach God's Word in the said colonie, to administer the Holy Sacraments of Baptism and the Lord's Supper; to set an example to the Congregation, in a Christianlike manner, by public precept; to ordain elders and deacons according to the form of the Holy Apostle Paul, 1 Tim. c. iii., v. 1; moreover to keep and govern, with the advice and assistance of the same, God's Congregation in good discipline and order, all according to God's Holy Word, and in conformity with the government, confession, and catechism of the Netherland Churches and the Synodal acts of Dordrecht, subscribed by him, to this end, with his own hand, and promised in the presence of God, at his ordination, requesting hereby all and every who shall see and read these, to respect our worthy Brother as a lawfully called Minister, and him to esteem by reason of his office, so that he may perform the duty of the Gospel to the advancement of God's Holy Name and the conversion of many poor blind men.

May the ALMIGHTY GOD, who hath called him to this ministry, and instilled this good zeal in his heart, to proclaim Christ to Christians and heathens in such distant lands, strengthen him, more and more, in this his undertaking; enrich him with all sorts of Spiritual gifts; and bless overflowingly his faithful labors; and when the Chief Shepherd, CHRIST JESUS, shall appear, present him with the imperishable Crown of Eternal Glory. Amen.

Thus given in our Classical Assembly at Amsterdam, this 22d day of March, 1642 Signed in the name and on behalf of the whole body,

WILHELMUS SOMERUS, Loco Præsidis,
ZLOAHAR SWALMIUS, Scriba Classis,
Jonas Abeels, as Elder.

Examined and approved by the Directors of the West India Company, Chamber of Amsterdam, 6th June, 1642.

(Signed,) CHARLES LOOTEN,
ELIAS DE RAET.

Agreement between Kiliaen van Rensselaer and the Directors of the West India Company, relative to the approval of the call of the Rev. Mr. Megapolensis.

WHEREAS, differences have occurred between the Directors of the Amsterdam Chamber of the West India Company and Kiliaen van Rensselaer, Patroon of his Colonie named Rensselaerswyck, in New Netherland, as to the approval of the Acte of Commission granted by the Classis of Amsterdam to Dominie Joannes Megapolensis to be invested with the office of preacher in the aforesaid colonie of Rensselaerswyck in New Netherland, and as the ship wherein the said minister must depart lies ready to sail, so that periculum in mora est of injuring the said voyage—Therefore, the aforesaid Kiliaen van Rensselaer consents that the said Directors shall affix their approbation to the aforesaid Acte of Commission, under express protest that he Rensselaer, shall not be prejudiced in his right, but the parties on either side shall remain unprejudiced in their present rights. In witness whereof, the Directors and Kiliaen van Rensselaer have granted and signed this present Acte at Amsterdam, this 6th June, xvi hundred two and forty.

Signed respectively,

CHARLES LOOTEN,
ELIAS DE RAET.

K.

Memorandum for Dominie Johannes Megapolensis, this 3d June, 1642, proceeding to the Colonie by the ship De Houttuyn, skipper Adriaen Dircksen Houttuyn.

[From the Rensselaerswyck MSS.]

His Reverence will be pleased to take charge of my people and property, which are at present conveyed over in God's name, in the ship De Houttuyn. The persons going over will be these :—

De. Johannes Megapolensis,
Matheld Willemsen, his wife,
Hellegond, Dirrick, John, and Samuel, his children,
Abraham Staes, surgeon,
his servant,
Evert Pels, beer-brewer,
his wife,
his man,
Cornelis Lamberssen, van Doorn, Utrecht, farm servant,
Jochim Kettelhuer, van Cremyn,
Johan Helms, van Barltt, N. Brabant,
Johan Carsterssen, van Barltt, N. Brabant,
Jeuriach Bestvaell, van Luydendorp,
Claes Jansen, van Waalwyck, N. Brabant,
Paulus Jansen, van Geertruydenburg, do.
Hans Vos van Baden.
Juriaen van Sleswyck, N. Brabant,
Hendrick Albertsen van Wuden, 29 years old,
Gertrude Dries, his wife, 23 years old, } From Driesburg.
Hendrick Dries, her brother, 21 years, } From Driesburg.

It is to be remembered that this Hendrick Albertz, for his three; Abraham Staes, for his two; Evert Pels, for his three, must pay the skipper Adriaen Dircksen for their board, in the same manner as all the other freemen. But the farm-servants are to come at my expense.

N. B The book-keeper in the colonie shall usually observe that the expense of the board of the freemen must be charged to their account, as Director Kieft sometimes places it under one head, altogether to the charge of the Patroon.

He shall take care that these persons embark on ship-board, and having arrived, by God's help, at the Manhattans, where the Noble Director Kieft resides, obtain that they, and my goods, be forwarded to the colonie by the first opportunity, and provided with food at my expense, and according to my cordial salutations to the Honorable Director Kieft, which shall be followed.

On the arrival of these persons at the colonie, they shall present themselves first to the Commissary Arendt van Curler, to be by him registered, and allotted their work, by and with the advice of the officer Adriaen van der Donck, who, if so be he should have occasion for the services of the two Bredaelse young men, may keep them by him. Otherwise they are there on my account for closer examination. Whereas the husbandmen, with much unreasonableness, refuse to pay sixteen guilders yearly for each laborer for my expended cost and risk; in order that the said farm-servants, nay some of them, be provided by the commissary with food and lodgings, the wages which they earn shall be put to my account, provided that the husbandmen and others for whom they shall work shall secure their day's wages to me at such rate as they pay others, or according to discretion and number of persons; for by so doing I remain master thereof to use them where it is most necessary in tillage and other of the husbandmen's work, at intervals in planting tobacco, sawing wood, at the grist-mills, and so forth, where it shall be most requisite—principally in winter in assisting the husbendmen to thresh, and whatever else is necessary—but above all things, as there are but few carpenters, some of these fellows who are the most expert shall be employed at proper time and seasons to fell trees, and, as far as they can, to cut them up and draw them, so as to lighten the labor of the carpenters; and Hans Vos, from Baden, who has been a gamekeeper, (wildschut,) may be employed at the proper time in killing game to supply food, and at other times in cutting wood. As he also says he can be useful to farmers, having also a good knowledge thereof, then every thing must be considered for my profit. As I perceive that each one seeks his own, and not my advantage, and this matter thus progressing, so I must expect also that my people shall be employed in what is most profitable to me; and I consent that some of them may be hired to the farmers who shall be found most trustworthy, provided they bind themselves to pay sixteen guilders yearly. Those who dispute this just arrangement will do themselves the greatest injury, and render me unwilling to send them laborers, De. Megapolensis having seen what trouble, expense, and importuning I have had therewith.

I have paid Mauritz Jansen, from Brockhuysen, [North Brabant,] who hath returned from that country before his time, 50 guilders, that he might repay the same there with ordinary advances. I have presented him the freedom of trading in peltries to the same extent as Abraham Staes, at the rate of 20 stiv. the hide; he will give but 15 stiv. He will, perhaps, seek to trade indirectly. Should such happen, proceedings will be instituted against him, according to the conditions which he hath concluded with me, his bounden time expiring in April, 1643, and that for servitude, unless he consents to accept the conditions of the Bouwerye as these lie. He must do one of two things, either agree to my conditions as they are, without dispute, or complete the time for which he is bound, having no choice but to accept one of the two.

Herry Albertzen, who hath equally come home before his time, has allowed me one guilder per hide for recognition, according to contract made with him. Then concerning the amount of tobacco over the tenths, (which he hath consented to,) I have not been able to agree with him. He has been treating with me for the place of ferryman, fixing his dwelling by the Beavers Creek, in order to convey the people to the church neighborhood, [Kerckebuyrte,] and back again from thence. As the church, the minister's house, that of the officer, and, moreover, of all the trades-people, [ambachten,] must henceforward be established there, as Abraham Staes and Evert Pels, the brewer, have undertaken, I am entirely willing, and consent that, with the exception of the farmers and tobacco-planters, who must reside at their farms and plantations, no other tradesman, henceforward and after the expiration of their service, shall establish themselves elsewhere than in the church vicinage, in the order and according to the plan of building sent herewith; for every one residing where he thinks fit, separated far from others, would be, unfortunately, in danger of their lives, in the same manner as sorrowful experience has taught, around the

Manhattans, of all which the commissary, Arendt van Curler, shall give notice to all persons, being called together, so that they may regulate themselves accordingly.

Jan Jansen Flodder, carpenter, has been at me for permission to build in the colonie. I am willing to accept him at day's wages, at the price agreed upon by the freemen there. As he demanded much more, I have not consented to engage him at day's wages, but agreed, if so be he should undertake any work, that I was content that for such and such, he might trade at such a price, it never being my intention to advance the fixed rate of wages according to their pleasure, as it has the appearance here of being pro forma to induce them to trade with me, and afterwards to do what pleased them.

All the other people whose time is expired and who remain in the colonie, whether married or unmarried, or who shall come from without, shall be obliged to take the oath [erasure] like the other freemen [one line defaced or worn away.] Whereas carpenters are somewhat scarce at present, the superintendent of the laborers must proceed with prudence. I had rather have patience than be put under contribution by the people. There are many masters and but few servants. The carpenter who went out with Anthony de Hooges, should be allowed some of these who are going over to act as wood-trimmers [hout bereyders] to assist him. They will endeavor to elude, [colludeeren,] but we must strive to amuse, and as it has already been said, rather to have patience, than to consent to unreasonable wages. The dwellings which have been contracted for, by the advice of the Heer officer, Van der Donck, are much higher than men pay here. As Andries de Vos, however, is bound by his contract, it is well to observe, that should private individuals pay more than my fixed price, that would not affect me. They are bound to serve the Patroon for their contracted wages, in preference to all others. Then it seems that they know how to discover the rates of private persons—for the Patroon fixes the market. In fine, suffer somewhat patiently, and write to me rather than give such advanced wages, contrary to the contract agreed upon.

For whatever purpose the stone and tile-kiln were very necessary, it would not cost much more, and the work would be much more lasting.

Further, 'tis needful to unload all my goods which are now sent out, in the best condition, and again to ship them for above. If my people have not sent a craft, let them know your arrival by an express by land, or, what is much better, by a small-boat by water, requesting from his Excellency, Director Kieft, with my respects, his Excellency's advice, to do every thing for my best advantage, and as the Noble Director Kieft hath heretofore had with my people and goods much trouble, I send herewith as a present and as an acknowledgment of thankfulness, as follows:

1° A saddle with all its furniture, in canvass, addressed by superscription to Director Kieft, which should have arrived with the last ship, but came back, and goes herewith marked No. 24, with the mark of the colonie and packed in the oosterse chest, No. 22, to be presented to the Director Kieft in my name; a gold and silver mounted sword, with one gold [one line here destroyed by the wear of the paper;] a pair of gold and silver plated spurs; a pair of boots with spur leathers. And should any sacks be necessary for the forwarding of the malt, let those be taken which are sewed only loose, in order to be again ripped and sold for canvass, and let a note be made of all.

The goods which are sent over at present by this ship, are packed as follows and marked as in the margin.

4 ✝ R W

Nos. 1, 2, 3, 4, are 4 large barrels containing two lasts, 11 muds of malt for brewing, for Evert Pels, on condition of reimbursing me according to contract;
Nos. 5, 6, 7, 8, are 4 cases with divers goods;
No. 9, one barrel with nails;
No. 10, one case with lead and shot;
No. 11, one hogshead of vinegar;
Nos. 12, 13, 14, 15, 16, 17, 18, 19, are eight cases of duffels;
No. 20, one case with shoes and 7 hides of sole leather;
4000 tiles, 30,000 hard bricks [klinckertsteen] to receive stone from the company;
20 boxes of iron rods, 1000 lbs.;
10 boxes of iron rods, 500 lbs.;
20 bars of beer cask [bierkant] iron hoops, abt. 735 lbs.;
10 bars of very thin iron, about 223 lbs.;
8 caldrons of smiths' coal [smeecoolen.]
No. 21, one case with ploughshares; No. 22, an oosterse-chest, with books and other articles, according to invoice; No. 23, one case with 3 duffels for Van der Donck; No. 24, the saddle; No. 25, No. 26, are two telletgens with vines and madder.

Follows NB. 25

[*Cetera desunt.*]

Catalogue of Books which are sent for the Library in Rensselaerswyck, to be forwarded there.

[Referred to at the end of the preceding Document.]

In Folio.

1. Biblia Græca,
2. Concordantia Bibliorum,
3. Opera Calvini, 8 tom.
4. Opera Ursinii,
5. Polyanthea Langii et Gruteri: tom. 2.
6. Titus Livius,
7. Cursus Philosoph. Roderici de Arriag.
8. Theatrum Terræ Sanctæ Christiani Andrichonii.

In Quarto.

1. Adriani Metii Primum Mobile,
2. Adriani Metii Arithmet.,
3. Theologia Naturalis Alstedii,
4. Manuale Concionum, Did. Alvares,
6 Animadversiones in 4 Evang. Lud: de Dieu,
6. Thesaurus Œconomiæ, J. Casi,
7. Petri Rami Arithm. et Geom.,
8. Distinct. Philos. et Theolog. Castanei,
9. Theologia didactica Alstedii.

Remarks on the above, by Dr. T. Romeyn Beck.

Folio.

No remarks necessary on 1, 2, and 3.

4. Ursinius, (probably Zachary,) the friend of Melancthon and of Sir Philip Sidney. Born in Silesia, in 1534; died, 1583. [Chalmers' General Biographical Dictionary.]

5. John Gruter, (in Latin, Janus Gruterus,) born at Antwerp, 1560; died, 1627. He edited the Polyanthea of Langius. [Biographie Universelle.]

6.

7. Arriaga, (Roderic de.) A learned Jesuit, native of Castile. Born, 1592; died, 1667. Chancellor of the University of Prague; published, in 1632, a Course of Philosophy, in one volume. Folio. [Ibid.]

8. Christian, Andrichonius, a geographer of considerable reputation, born at Delft, in Holland, 1533; died, 1585. The work for which he is best known is Terræ Sanctæ Theatrum et Biblicarum Historiarum, or History of the Holy Land, illustrated by maps. It passed through a number of editions in folio, from 1590 to 1682 [Watt's Bibliotheca Britannica.

Quarto.

1, 2. Adrian Metius, an able Dutch Geometrician, born at Alkmar, in 1571; died, 1635. His "Treatise on Arithmetic" was published in 1611, in quarto. "Primum Mobile astronomice, sciographice, Geometrice, et hydrographice novi methodo explicatum." Amsterdam: Quarto: 1631. [Biographie Universelle.]

3, 9. Alstedius, born at Herborn, county of Nassau, where he became Professor of Philosophy and Theology. He then went as professor to Weissenburg, in Transylvania, where he died in 1638. He was a member of the Synod of Dort. A most indefatigable writer. [Ibid.] Alstedius "Theologia Naturalis" was published in 1615 and in 1662 in quarto. [Biographical Dictionary of the Society for the diffusion of Useful Knowledge, vol. 2.]

4. Didacus (Diego) Alvarez. There were two of this name. One a Spanish Dominican, Archbishop of Trasii, died in 1635; the other a Spanish Jesuit, died 1617 I cannot find the above work among the list of their writings.

5. Lewis de Dieu; Protestant Professor in the Walloon College at Flushing. Born, 1590; died, 1642. His work entitled "Animadversiones in quatuor Evangelia," was published at Leyden, in quarto, in 1631. [Biog. Universelle.]

6. Case, John, M. D., an eminent Physician and Philosopher of Oxford; born at Woodstock, Eng.; died, 1600. He published a number of works, among which is Thesaurus Œconomiæ, seu Commentarius in Œconomia Aristotelis; Oxon. 1597, 1598; Hanov. 1598; 8vo. There is a monument to his memory in St. John's College. [Watt; also Biog. Dict.]

7. Peter Ramus, a celebrated French Mathematician, born 1515; died, 1572. Published "Arithmetica, Græca et Latina," at Paris, quarto, 1555; "Geometria," at Basle, quarto, 1596. [Watt.]

8. Henry Lewis Castaneus published a work entitled "Celebriorum distinctionum tum Philosophicorum et Theologicorum Synopsis." [Watt.]

L.

Van Curler's Letter to the Patroon.

[From the Rensselaerswyck MSS.]

Laus Deo! At the Manhattans, this 16th June, 1643.

Most honorable, wise, powerful, and right discreet Lord, my Lord Patroon—

With submissive salutation shall this serve to greet your Honor and your Honor's beloved Lady, who is dear to you, with wished-for good fortune, prosperity, and steady happiness. On the 4th of this instant, I received your Honor's favor, and seen and read its contents, whereunto this shall serve for answer.

Firstly, touching the serious discontent which your Honor feels towards me, because the accounts and books have not been sent to you, I have not much to oppose. But therein I have not been wholly culpable. For the accounts and books which might be brought to me, I can quickly make clear and ready. But there are boors from whom I can get no returns; and Van der Doncq has not once spoken to them thereof, according to his instructions, nor done any thing about them so long as he has been in this colonie. I have had, once before this, returns from some boors. Neither head nor tail could be made out of them. For they state every thing they expended, but nothing of what they had received; and, moreover, enter in the account, to this one, so much—to that one, so much; without once specifying for what that same was given. Every thing they have laid out on account of the Lord Patroon, they well know how to specify for what that was expended. But what has been laid out for their own private use, that they know nothing about, and yet can manage to remember what appertains to the account of the Noble Patroon, and to book that. To this I say, that I will never allow this; but that they shall deliver to me a clean, clear, just account, to send the same over to the Noble Patroon, for his Honor's approbation; and so soon as an answer shall be received, shall these then be passed, if his Honor so order. Whereupon the farmers reply: We shall then furnish you an account, as you told us that without it being sent to Patria it is good for nothing. In fine, this also has been neglected. But, please God, so soon as the next [ship] comes, the accounts shall be sent to you. So far as I am myself concerned, I hope that his Honor will not be so displeased as he has been. For I consider myself bound to make good to the Patroon whatever shall fall short in the accounts, or shall be stolen. But, so truly help me God Almighty, I am not conscious, willingly or knowingly, so long as I have been in your Honor's service, to have defrauded your Lordship, or to have sought, in any manner, mine own profit, or seek to enrich myself, as others truly do, who, in justice to the Noble Patroon, should observe who wrong him. I shall tell your Honor no tales, but I shall send over by the next ship sufficient proofs thereof.

As to what your Honor would know, what the construction of the boors' houses will cost, it is impossible for me to acquaint you. I have never had any account thereof, as I have told your Honor before. What regards the cost of my own building, I hope that shall not be wanting. I have kept every note of it. Further, I shall furnish, at the same time, an account of what my house-keeping comes to. The Lord shall find therein a few items of what I have presented, or given away, as I have sometimes given some presents to the principal chiefs of the Indians, in order that they should maintain good correspondence with each other.

As your Honor does not know how your account stands with the company, this will serve to inform you that I have never settled with M. Kieft, nor ever attempted it, because he charged the freight and customs [convoyen] so high, that I have invariably referred that to the Lord Patroon. Kieft hath frequently demanded of me to liquidate the account, but I have always deferred it, because I fear imprudently to burn myself with this account; for all the charges, freights, and board, which he brought in his account, are directly contrary to the granted freedoms. And your Honor supposes that I here deduct all the freights, customs, [convoyen,] and duties, wholly from the wheat; the Lord hath always been pleased to excuse me from so doing. For I have never entertained such a thought as to liquidate the account with Kieft. Now that I understand your Honor's intention, I shall never deliver another handful of wheat to the company, unless they either pay me on delivery, [ofte ten sy datse my contant betallen,] or unless I receive other orders from your Honor. However, I have delivered very little grain, except last year, only twelve lasts, and then not a single grain was once on my order. But, heretofore, the boors have always delivered the grain to the company on their own authority. There is no knowing, sometimes, where all the grain that is raised in the colonie remains, or is consumed But I shall send the Lord, by the first opportunity, an extract of an account which I have, through friendship, received out of the A. Croll's book, whereby the Lord shall see and find what has been consumed by the boors, and all paid in wheat, whereof your Honor has been wholly wronged [gefrusteert] and deprived. But so soon as the accounts of the bouweries are made up, and your Honor hath this extract, your Honor then can see who intends best by the Lord Patroon.

What the Lord, my master, commands me to receive in good regard the counsel of Dominie Megapolensis; and therein to follow his Reverence's advice—I have never failed so to do, but have always communicated to him whatever occurred here, to have his opinion thereupon ere I concluded to undertake any thing, and have always thankfully received his reverence's counsel. Further, I shall use my utmost diligence to collect the rest and to post all the debits and credits, [schulden en wederschulden,] Beavers and Seawan. I shall then, without fail, send you all by the next opportunity. As to what appertains to the duffels, I have, in all I received, not perceived any damage worth mentioning, but got them in good condition.

Your honor further orders me in his letter to have some of the studs gelded. This I did last spring to the number of twelve, and two more recently, being fourteen in all. God be thanked they all fared well, without any of them having been injured or killed, though there were some eight or nine years olds among them. There are nine more in the colonie, besides one yearling, to wit:—two ready for use (om te springen) in the five bouweries on the east bank; Andries de Vos and Van Nes have together one for their use; and Brandt and Van der Doncq together, one for theirs; Broer Cornelissen, ditto: on the Great Flatt are four; whereof two of the most delicate will be cut next harvest. Doubtless the Patroon shall have a much greater increase every year than he has had hitherto. For the studs heretofore followed the mares so anxiously that the latter could not be touched, and now they go so tame that it is curious to remark. And, before this, we were obliged, according to the age of the studs, to go look for the horses to the half day, and they came safely home. Teunis Dircksen is here from the master gelder. I have paid him one great pound for each stud he operated on. I have sent the residents all the full number of horses and cows, according to their contract. I have full twenty draft horses, at present, on the Flatt (op de Vlachte) besides the milch cows, but they are all young cattle.

Further, touching the letter sent to your Honor by the Mahicanders, your Honor will please not to be surprised; for I came, by great luck, four or five days after the return of the sloop from above, and overtook it there by reason of contrary winds; and received a day or two after the return of this, the resolution of Pieter Cornelissen and Broer Cornelissen. So that I got on board the sloop, and there hastily wrote a short letter to your Honor, because I thought it was necessary to advise you.

Your Honor further writes that you understand that I had placed Labbatie on the Great Flatt, and promised him twenty guilders per month, and your honor asks what farm work can he do. Those who wrote that to your honor lie like rogues. For I never thought of it; but my intention was that Labbatie should pass the winter on the Flatt to trade, as good trade is drove there from above during the winter, but never has there been any talk of monthly wages. For so long as Labbatie has been out of his bounden time, he has never asked or demanded any increase of wages, but always said that he should leave that to the discretion of the Lord Patroon. But I shrewdly suspect that this report was sent to his Honor by Van der Doncq, whom this undertaken work hath sorely troubled, because he can make nothing by it; and still daily doth he, in my absence, go about finding fault that men expect to make great profit for the masters, but that it will miss. But I have nothing to say. The work is but begun. Yet I hope, please God, to have next harvest as much corn in the ground as the best bouwerie in the colonie. I have, at present, about ten to twelve morgens of oats planted, and had there not been so many hidden stumps in the land, I should have had much more sown. But there is not much fallow. From this year there will be still more rye. But generally the first year is the slimmest. I trust firmly that all the bouweries have not had so much to clear as this Flatt alone. It was all hidden stumps and roots, which were not perceived until the plough struck right on them. Your honor further writes that you do not want any bouwerie for yourself.

I shall therefore keep together an exact account of all the expenses which have been incurred thereon. I shall, then, request of your honor, as I have already done, to be preferred before all others for the same Flatt, and I shall then, according to opportunity, contract with your honor therefor, and willingly meet all expenses. I am assured that there is no bouwerie in the colonie which shall have been less expensive than this; which shall sooner repay the outlay, and that by grain alone, without counting the increase of cattle. I hope, with God's blessing on the grain, that this bouwerie, in two years, will be free of all expense. I have last spring built on this Flatt a farm house, thirty feet covered with tiles, for the residence of the carpenters and laborers.

I had, moreover, contracted with Jan Cornelissen, carpenter, for a large farmhouse; and he had promised to begin it in mid April, which he has not yet done. From May to this date, I believe that he has not worked fourteen days, but has been drunk all the time. I have demanded frequently of him, if he would not go on with the work, and he has always asked for delay; but he will not begin, because I have made a favorable bargain with him. He must build for 700 guilders a house 120 feet long by 28 feet wide; 40 feet is deducted for a dwelling. There remain 80 feet for the farm-house. The dwelling part to be floored above and below; a cellar 20 feet long by 28 feet wide; a half-jutting chamber (een hang-kamer) for the servants' sleeping room; a small room (een kooi) in the farm-house for the farm laborers; an enclosed stable for the studs, and further to make a horse and cow stable, and what else appertains thereto, and that subject to the inspection of persons conversant with such sort of work, and who understand carpentry. The other carpenters will not build it for 1,000 guilders; so that he is not very anxious for the job. I made the contract with him when he was sober in the presence of Dom. Johannes, and Mr. Abraham and Anthony de Hooges, and committed it to writing on the instant. So that I shall be obliged to have that house erected by others under protest; for the time cannot admit of further delay. It must be covered in against the winter, for the cattle must, above all things, have their stabling. I placed all the reed for the house, last harvest, on a pile of lumber, on the spot where the dwelling is to stand.

As regards the tobacco of Albert Andriessen and his brother, I know not otherwise than that your Honor will get the crop, as it was planted in the time of his contract. Your Honor further orders that I should pay this money to Albert here in merchantable goods. All that will go well. But still remains the question or difference between us, which is this:—whereas Albert hath, before this, opposed the placards, and moreover, heretofore, hath scolded the Lord Patroon and the whole council, so that he was condemned in a heavy fine, I shall therefore deduct this fine from the amount to be paid for the delivered tobacco. The fine for which he is indebted according to law, for opposition to the placard and scandalous scolding, amounts to 312 fl. We should long ago have levied this sum by execution, but I have all along waited patiently for the delivered tobacco.

As for the answer which your Honor sent to the pretensions of Andreas Hudde, I shall give an extract thereof to the Heer Kieft, and speak to himself about it.

As for the Church, it is not yet contracted for, nor even begun. I had written last year to your Honor, that I had a building almost ready, namely, the covenanted work, which would have been for Dom. Megapolensis; and this house was not agreeable to the taste of Dom. Johannes; in other respects it was altogether suitable for him, so that I have laid it aside. That which I intend to build this summer in the pine grove, [in het Greynen Bosch,] will be 34 feet long by 19 feet wide. It will be large enough, for the first three or four years, to preach in, and can afterwards always serve for the residence of the sexton, or for a school. I hope your Honor will not take this ill, as it happened through good intention.

Regarding the diamond [het crystal] near Michel Janssen's house, of which your Honor writes that I should send over some more specimens thereof, I have spoken about it to Michel Jansen, and to several others, to engage them to bury it. But they will not do so, apparently because they fear for the labor, and it will terminate badly.

The Lord Patroon is very much surprised that so little care has been taken of the vines which his Honor sent. I planted them in the garden, but they were killed by the frost, like the others brought to the country. I believe, in my opinion, that they did not suffer in the least from the high water.

As regards the formulary which your Honor sent, it shall, for the future, be followed as well for horses as for cows. I should have been pleased that your Honor had sent it before, in order to afford your Honor greater content. Your Honor is, moreover, surprised that Albert Andriesz. hath such privilege ; that a better inventory is not taken of his stock of cattle. The messenger says that he will not allow any preemption, and what is more, will not give you any part of the cattle, although he purchased the cows while your Honor's contract with the mill company was still in existence.

I shall send by Willem Turck as many peltries as I can bring in. Your Honor is surprised that all my letters mention haste ; this, in short, shall serve as an explanation. The ships are sometimes 14 days, and even more, at the Manhattans, before we receive any tidings or intelligence thereof, and then, receiving letters, the sloops remain only five, six, or seven days, so the letters must then be got ready in a hurry. The Lord says that this ought to be done beforehand, which might easily be, if we had not to answer the Lord's letters. For we could well advise the Lord in one of the affairs of the colonie. For the future, whatever will be pleasing to the Patroon, shall be done, for in all things I am subject to obey his order in as much as it lies in my power.

In regard to your Honor's instructions to inquire what price wheat commands in Virginia, I cannot very well undertake that. But so far as I hear and understand, it goes off well there, but it should be sent there ground into meal. If your Honor should be of opinion to send the ship thither, she should be well provided with strong distilled waters, which are much in demand there, together with duffels and wide linen. Tobacco can be had at 2 to 3 advance on the price in Holland. All the corn which will be delivered to me, I shall retain provisionally by me till further advice, should your Honor be pleased to send a ship. Henceforward I will not give a grain more of corn to the company.

As to the boors selling the wheat for 8 to 9 florins the mud, [four bushels,] that is true ; but I cannot say who they are. I believe that 4 to 5 lasts have been thus sold since last spring, and Van der Doncq hath not once been willing to look to it, nor to prevent such a fraud. Your Honor further writes me that I shall speak to Van der Donck and Peter Cornelissen to second me. They will not endeavor to advance the business of their own office, nor do they much try. How can they, then, aid me ? And they are the dogs which bite me, and still daily seek to render me suspected, which Van der Doncq endeavored enough to do and hath already done, as I can infer from the Lord's writings. But what he has perpetrated and still commits, will be made manifest in its own time. I shall not, thereupon, talk any further now. Dom. Megapolensis was well aware of his acts.

Your Honor further states, that Van der Donck complains of the impertinence of Labbatie. These shall serve thereupon. Van der Doncq is very covetous and monopolizing ; during my absence at the Manhattans, this Van der Doncq came, different times, and arrogantly spoke to Labbatie, that he should give him duffels ; sometimes Seewan, and more such goods. Thereupon Labbatie answered that he had no orders to give out any goods—wherefore had he not asked them of me before, when I was at home ; or that he must wait until I should return, and such like things, much more than I can detail. So then hatred became so deeply rooted, that they pursued each other with swords, in like manner as he had done to De Hooges, scolding him as an informer, and moreover struck him ; and thus he acts also towards me, blaming me as well to your Honor, as to the colonists, in order to render me suspected. And he imagines, by reason of his ambition, that men will permit him to do what he pleases ; and that through ignorance, much must be overlooked for the sake of the consequences.

As to what the Lord writes, that what concerns the delivery of the cattle, proceeded out of the head of Broer Cornelissen. That he will not deliver up the same, nor pay for them immediately, is true. He hath frequently spoken thereof in my presence, and moreover, hath also endeavored to stir up others thereto.

What regards the resolution to send Willem Juriaensen Bakker out of the colonie, I have had a very long time ample reason therefor. But no one would second me. Then he hath publicly abused the lord and master as a dishonorable man, whereupon he was condemned in a civil fine. This was well. Furthermore, the residents who had driven their trade there with the Indians to the great loss of the noble Lord, continued this same Willem Juriaensen, and almost destroyed and ruined the whole trade.

As to what the Lord writes that I should not so strictly regulate myself according to the price of the peltries, and that I must exert myself, as well with authority as with censure, to keep strange traders out, this will serve:—

The trade heretofore has always been at six fathoms of seawan. Last year the residents as well as the colonists gave 7 to 7½ fathoms. I also gave the same. So soon as they saw that I and the company's commissary gave so much, they immediately gave 9, and since this spring 10 fathoms. So at last, the trade ran so high, that we of the colonie, and the commissary at the Fort resolved, with one another, to publish a placard as well for the colonists as the residents and company's servants, that they should not presume, on pain of heavy fine and confiscation of their goods, to trade with the Indians for furs at more than 9 fathoms of white wampum, or 4½ fathoms of black; and that none, on pain of confiscation aforesaid, should go into the bush to trade; and the order was that the officer should prevent it. And he hath not even once attended to this; nor even now will he do so. When he was told that he should look to the frauds and abuses, in order to prevent the same as much as possible, he gave for answer: that he would not consent to be the worst man—to others, that he would not make himself suspected by the colonists, as his years, as officer, were few. And it happened, last year, that we concluded together on a placard that no residents should presume to come, with their boats, within the limits of the colonie, on confiscation of the same. Thereupon there were great complaints on the part of the colonists, and they gave in remonstrances as to where they should receive goods and necessaries. Whereupon the council promised the colonists, that if there were any to be had at the Manhattans or elsewhere, that I should procure them, on condition for this promise, that they would in return pay immediately for the wares which they might get from me, and that I should have nothing to do with the transfer of accounts, but to pay me, acting thus as merchant, (so doende koopman,) right off. They were all satisfied, and promised to adhere to it, and to assist me. We further resolved, on the next court day, to issue another placard for the further strengthening of the first; namely, that no inhabitants of the colonie should presume to buy any goods from the residents. So it happened that a few days after a sloop arrived with some goods. Immediately a party of colonists came to me and said—"This and that are come; no body must make any purchases there; you gave us the promise." To this I replied:—"What I promised, I shall perform and accomplish." I inquired if they had any beavers wherewith to buy these goods and wares. They answered, "No! You must purchase them, and debit us with them in the account;" which I was wholly unwilling to do. So that each one went and bought what he wished, as well duffels as otherwise. Dom. Megapolensis and I then sent for Van der Doncq, and told him to go quietly with his servant, Hans Vos, and search the several houses. Now he came to visit Reyer Stoffelzen's house. There he gossiped without once making a search, and then went to Willem Juriaensen's in the same manner, and so forth. He further went to Dirck Jansen's mill, where he was told there were three pieces of duffels, and he removed one of them. He further went to the house of Cornelis van Merckerck. There he chatted without once making a search. In like manner he proceeded to Broer Cornelissen's, where he did not search once, but only asked, "How are ye all here?" looked in, and returned back, while he well knew that there were duffels there. Leaving there, he went home. In the same way he went to Claes Janssen van Nyckerck's house, who, he also well knew, had duffels. He said—"Claes, I shall come here to-morrow to make a search. Have you any duffels? Put them away in your cellar, which I shall not search." Claes himself told me this out of his own mouth, and promised to give me an affidavit of it, which I shall send your Honor by the next ship.

Moreover, I had contracted last harvest for the building of a house for Dom. Megapolensis, which should be ready precisely at Christmas. They let the time pass neglected and go by till November. Then I said that I should not allow it to be built; there was hail, snow, rain, and wind every day, and expecting that the house would cause great expense in meat and drink, and the work not be advanced, I broke the contract, because they did not perform their promise.

Maryn Adriaensen was, at this time, among us, who offered to sell me a house of oak wood, all ready—cross casings, door casings, all of oak. So the Dominie having consulted with us both, and concluded that Maryn's house would be a much better bargain than the other, so that I purchased the house from him for 350 guilders. Van der Doncq coming to hear this, got into company, in the mean time, with the carpenters and several others, and there told them that we had issued placards forbidding the colonists to trade with the residents, and whoever this interested should mutiny—that whoever had first concocted this had not only concocted the placards, and that I likewise sought to steal the bread out of the mouths of the colonists. Whereupon some of them were surprised that the officer should so persuade the people. Some, with others, forthwith conspired together to protest against me, and to draw a circle under the protest, within which to place their names, so that it should not be known who had first signed it. This protest having been drawn up, some were for driving me out of the colonie as a rogue; others wished to take my life. But nothing resulted from these threats. Herein Van der Doncq said he would honestly, and to our satisfaction, assist me and the council. But when need pressed him, (maer als den noot aende man gingh,) he then withdrew from me and the council to second them, whereof I shall send your Honor affidavits of two persons who told me so with their own lips. So that your Honor can form, at once, an opinion of the matter in itself, and what sort of officer you have here, who causes so much injury to a whole colonie. He intends, next year, to return home. He has been to Katskill with some colonists to examine that place, and your Honor may be assured he intends to look for partners to plant a colonie there. Borger Jorissen, who has heretofore been in the Lord's colonie, will live there also. He hath let his bouwerie to Brant Peelen for 200 guilders a year, on which Brant Peelen intends to settle his brother-in-law. This shall not be with my consent.

Concerning the bark, about the building which the Patroon had written, so that I might employ it in the colonie to advantage, which was my intention and meaning, but I was dissuaded therefrom. It should be well adapted in breadth to convey cattle, and that about to be built would have been too crank. I have purchased another for 1100 guilders, which is a very tidy bark, provided with new sails, with anchor and cable ; can carry at sea, 7 lasts ; inland, 8 lasts. It has been this spring to the north, and there traded a good deal of seawan, [wampum.] 'Tis now at the South River to trade. I have spoken to Cornelis Leendertzen and Mauritz Janssen van Broeckhuysen, who returned from that quarter over two days ago, and they told me that it would be a good speculation, for neither the company nor the Swedes had any cargoes there, and there were still there 7 to 800 beavers, which lay there expecting seawan and other goods, with all which was well provided our bark, which Cornelis Leendertsen spoke in the mouth of the river. So that I hope good profit will result there. So soon as she returns, I will, if I can accomplish it, send her with wheat to Virginia, to see if that can be traded there for tobacco. Inquiry shall be then made what merchandise is admitted there, and shall then advise your Honor thereof.

As the Heer Master orders that the day of accounts shall not be changed, his Honor's letter shall be attended to. The Heer Patroon is very much surprised that no mention has been made in the inventory of sheep and swine. This will inform him that the farmers have frequently been spoken to. They say that the swine stray into the woods. We do not know ourselves how many pigs we have. We were obliged to give a number to other freemen, which were forwarded on payment ; but your Honor must know that many mishaps have occurred to these. As to the sheep, to count which Mauritz Janssen was appointed, they were correctly counted ; but the year after, they died off like mice. A part of them were destroyed by the wolves. There are at present in the colonie, young and old, about 15 to 16 sheep.

Further, may it please the Lord to understand, that three islands lie between Broer Cornelissen and the Flatt, [de Vlachte,] one of which, right opposite the Flatt, is about 20 to 25 morgens in extent, which have not been yet purchased from the owners. I shall allow that island opposite the Flatt, and a portion of fallow, to be ploughed, in order to be sowed next harvest with wheat ; for on the Flatt I have only 16 to 17 morgens which I can have under the plough this year. Because there is so much to regulate, and I do not wish to have the time of the servants wasted, I have begun on the aforesaid island. By regularity, every thing can be done at a proper season ; as men have more leisure at present than at any other time, so please God, there will be fully 30 morgens sown next fall with winter grain. I shall therefore be obliged to purchase the said islands from the Indians, though they will ill bear to part with them. For we are bound now and hereafter [schier of morgen] to give the Indians no provocation to rebel.

I have been on horseback with Labbatie and Jacob Janssen van Amsterdam, last year, to the Mohawk country, where three Frenchmen were prisoners ; one of whom was a Jesuit, a very learned scholar, who was very cruelly treated, his finger and thumb being cut off. I carried presents there, and requested that we should preserve good neighborship, and that no injury should be done, either to the colonists or to their cattle, which all the Indians at the three castles have thankfully accepted. We were entertained right well in every friendly manner there. We were obliged to halt a quarter of an hour before each castle, until the Indians there saluted us with divers musket-shots. There was also great joy among them because I had come there. Indians were immediately ordered to go out to shoot, who brought us in excellent turkeys. I then thoroughly visited all their castles, and invited all the chiefs of all the three castles to assemble together, and proposed to them to release the French prisoners. But there was no appearance of this, which they refused with good reason. Said they, "We shall manifest toward you every friendship that is in our power, but on this subject we will be silent. Besides, you well know how they treat our people who fall into their hands. Had we delayed to reach there three or four days longer, they would have been burnt." I presented them, for the ransom of the Frenchmen, about 600 guilders in goods, to which all the colonie will contribute. But they would not accept them. But we persuaded them so far, that they promised not to kill them, and to convey them back to their country. The French captives ran screaming after us, and besought us that we would do all in our power to release them out of the hands of the barbarians. But there was no likelihood at all of this. On my return, they gave me an escort of 10 to 12 armed men, who conducted us back home. Within half a day's journey from the colonie, lies the most beautiful land on the Mohawk River that eye ever saw ; full a day's journey long, and mostly contiguous the one to the other. But it is impossible to reach there in a boat, on account of the strength of the stream which runs there, and on the other hand, of the shallowness of the water ; but I think that it could be reached with wagons. Two of these Frenchmen, of whom the Jesuit was one, have been to my house last May. They said they hoped that means could be found now to procure their release. So soon as the Indians return from hunting, I shall endeavor to obtain their freedom. I shall send your Honor, by the first opportunity, the journal of my journey.

I have purchased at the mill-kill from Jan Michaelsen, a house, and a large oblong building, which he bought from Sander Leendertsen, for 600 gl., according to his receipt. But I shall pay for it mostly through his account. As a passable barn stands thereon, a good bouwerie can be made there. In the same way, as there is a good barn by the house of Cornelis Teunissen on the Fifth kill, where also a good bouwerie can be established.

Cornelis Teunissen goes also over. He hath given in his account, both debit and credit. There is to his credit, an item of 20 pieces of timber [balken] which come on account of the yacht. They were sold again at the Manhattans for 100 guilders. There is also a parcel of 100 pieces of timber, which I delivered to the company for 2 sloops' freight. Each sloop's voyage lasted six weeks, which should have greatly swelled the freight.

Of the 30m. stone which your honor sent out last year per the Houttuyn, I have not received above 10 thousand, as I'm told by my skipper Louwerns and others. The skipper of the Houttuyn retained them for ballast. Your honor will be pleased not to send any more stone, for we can purchase them cheaper at the north than those cost which your honor sent, and they are as large again. The four thousand tiles which your honor sent are not worth the freight ; for they crumble all away like sand. I have not had from these more than 10 to 12 hundred good tiles. The rest are good for nothing. The broker who purchased the tiles for your honor hath grossly cheated you.

I am, at present, betrothed to the widow of the late M. Jonas Bronck. May the good God vouchsafe to bless me in my undertaking, and please to grant that it might conduce to His honor, to our mutual salvation. Amen.

I expect to send the Heer (Lord) by the next opportunity the accounts ; and I intend, if his honor please to consent, to go over (to Holland) next year, as soon as I shall have received his honor's answer, to request of his honor a favorable lease of a bouwerie, there to fix my residence in the colonie for a good number of years, if the Lord spare my life. If your honor should please to permit me to return home, as I hope, I request, with all submission, that the noble Lord will please to grant my future wife leave to reside until my return in his honor's house, by Anthonie de Hooges. I trust that the noble Lord will not receive damage thereby, for she is a good housekeeper, as I hope the noble Lord shall learn from others. I should not altogether wish to take her over and hither with me; for we are subject to divers dangers from the sea. Otherwise, I hope to make my journey to Patria as short as possible.

Neither I nor the company have scarcely had any trade this year. I believe the residents have conveyed fully 3 to 4,000 furs from above. So great a trade has never been driven, as this year, and it would be very profitable if your honor could bring about, with a higher hand, that the residents should not come to the colonie to trade Otherwise your honor will never derive any profit.

Herewith ending, I beg to advise the noble Lord, if I have used any boldness, to be pleased to take it in the best part. Happiness to your honor, and your honor's beloved wife and children, and that God may preserve you in His grace, is mine, and my future partner's greeting.

Your Honor's dutiful and obliged servant,

ARENDT VAN CURLER.

M.

Insinuation, Protest, and Presentment, on behalf of the Pat-oon of the Colonie of Rensselaerswyck.

[From the Rensselaerswyck MSS.]

I, Nicholas Coorn, Wacht-meester over Rensselaers-Steyn, and on behalf of the noble Lord Kiliaen van Rensselaer, under the High Jurisdiction of the High and Mighty Lords States General of the United Netherlands, and the Privileged West India Company, Hereditary Commander of the Colonies on this North River of New Netherland, and as Vice Commander thereof in his place, let you

know that you shall not presume to abuse this river to the injury of the acquired right of the aforesaid Lord, in his quality as Patroon of the Colonie of Rensselaerswyck, the first and oldest on this river.

Which right he hath obtained on the 19th November, 1629, pursuant to his freedoms and exemptions from the Assembly of the XIX. of the Privileged West India Company, by the fifth article of which it was promised that care would be taken that the first occupiers (being he the Patroon) should not be prejudiced in the right which they obtained.

Which by the High and Mighty Lords States General aforesaid was further confirmed and enlarged by their High Mightinesses' sealed letters, dated fifth Feb. 1641, which were granted to him and to his heirs for ever.

And, whereas he declares to be greatly prejudiced;

Firstly, Inasmuch as you frequent this river without his knowledge, and have come thus far against his will;

Secondly, Endeavoring afterwards to withdraw from him and allure to yourself the tribes round about, who for many years have been accustomed to trade either at Fort Orange with the Company's Commis, or with his Commis in particular; and if possible to divert them away to his injury, and to show these tribes other secret trading places, greatly to the prejudice of the West India Company and of him the Patroon;

Thirdly, That you have destroyed the trade in furs by advancing and raising the price thereof on the Company's commis at Fort Orange, as well as on his, the Patroon's commis; that you are satisfied if you get merely some booty from it, not caring afterwards whether or not the trade be so ruined that the Patroon will thereby be unable to meet the expenses of his colonie, the same being greatly prejudicial to him, the Patroon.

Fourthly, That you sought to debauch and pervert his own inhabitants and subjects against their lord and master, furnishing them, among other things, with wine and strong drink, and selling this to them at an usurious and high price, against his will; causing yourself to be paid in peltries, which they, contrary to his orders and their own promise, trade for, or in wheat, which they purloin from their lord; whereof they have given no account; whereof the lawful tenths were not legally drawn; whereof he, the Patroon, hath not even received his third part or half according to contract; and whereof he hath not refused the right of pre-ëmption, obliging the Patroon, whom his people hath assisted with little or no advances, considering his outlay, to enter these on his books, while you pass away with that, yea, with his share, whereby he is rendered unable to provide his people with all they require, because you so exhaust them and impoverish his colonie, which is highly prejudicial to him the Patroon.

All which not being bound to suffer from any private individuals, he doth warn you entirely to refrain therefrom. Protesting in the name aforesaid, should you presume, in defiance of law, to endeavor, contrary to this protest, to pass by force, that I am directed to prevent you. Nevertheless, with power under this presentment, to trade with his commis, but in no wise with the Indians or his particular subjects, as is further to be seen and read in the admonition and instruction given by him, the Patroon, to Pieter Wyncoop, as commis, and Arendt van Curler, as commissary-general, and that in conformity to the restrictions of the Reglement therein contained.

And to declare to you, should you use force, that you will be guilty of,

Firstly, Crime against the High and Mighty Lords States General.

Secondly, Crime against the West India Company, and their Governor.

Thirdly, Crime against him, the Patroon, and his command, under whose jurisdiction you at present are residing in his despite and against his will, obliging us to necessary resistance.

Wherefore, I, in the name aforesaid, shall await what you will answer, do, or permit, to regulate myself accordingly, still fully admonishing you that you can have no Acte (except from the High and Mighty Lords the States General, themselves) which can deprive him of this his right, and that in case of loss you will have to indemnify him the Patroon.

Which aforesaid Acte passed by the aforesaid Lord Patroon and Commander, he hereby approves with the signature by his own hand, and by the sealing with the seal of him the Patroon, and of the Colonie of Rensselaerswyck, this 8th of September, 1643. In Amsterdam,

Was subscribed,

KILIAEN VAN RENSSELAER.

N.

Statement of the Assets belonging to the first Patroon at his death.

[From the Rensselaerswyck MSS.]

COPIA.

DEBIT. *Balance of the Estate hereinabove more fully described.* CREDIT.

DEBIT.		CREDIT.	
To Moneys in deposite, folio 7 and 8, amount to	fl. 192,360	By Real Estate hereinbefore (folio 1) amounting, according to valuation thereof	fl. 154,761
To Current debts to be paid (96) amount to	103,156	By purchase of Pearls, (folio 2, 3 and 4,) amounting to	189,925
	295,516	By debts to be received, (folio 6)	58,824
To so much this Estate is in advance	107,994		
	fl. 403,510		fl. 403,510

From the opposite side the surviving widow must draw her advanced marriage portion, amounting to		fl. 18,000
And for her jointure by marriage contract		6,000
After the death of the deceased is paid for interest of the moneys in deposite		29,668
And for the agio of the bank money, as all the moneys in deposite were to be paid in banco, and when the goods per cassa were sold		5,091
And with the equipage of the ship The Arms of Rensselaerswyck is carried		5,912
For the sold jewels of the surviving widow, wherefrom cash has come into the common estate:—		
1 Diamond ring	fl. 800	
Bracelets	2,000	
1 Collar that is not to be found		
		2,800
		fl. 67,471

After the death of the late Van Rensselaer, and sale of his property and payment of debts, there was still found in his Corpse house remaining	fl. 107,994
Deduct the items at the opposite side from the surplus of his Estate	67,471
Remains for Father's Estate	fl. 40,523
	[Equal to $16,207.]

N. B. Which aforesaid Father's property must be divided into ten parts, to wit:—For one child by the first marriage, and eight by the second, whom their father has left, whereof two deceased have made their mother their heiress; and then still a child's share for mother herself, make altogether ten parts.

N. B. This is independent of our share in the Colonie, which is besides.

This above stated account or balance is made up by Johan van Wely, as Executor and Administrator of the Estate (Sterfhuys) of Father Kiliaen van Rensselaer, deceased.

O.

Van Curler's Account of the Quarrel between himself and Van der Donck.

[From the Rensselaerswyck MS.]

WHEREAS, I have great reason to presume that Adriaen van der Donck, in my absence and when I am away, may seek, by backbiting, to blame me, (for I know well his disposition, Mel in ore, Fel in corde,) and in other ways to impute lies; so have I thought well to note the following by way of memorandum, in order that the time, the recollection, and the trutn may not be obscured.

It happened then at the house of our worthy pastor Dominie Megapolensis, that Van der Donck was in treaty with Michael Jansen about hiring him his bouwerio for so long as his lease was concerned, for which purpose they had come together at the aforesaid place. And as I had also come there, I mentioned to him that before he gave it up, it was to be remarked, that he must resign it on the conditions of De Vos and Van Es, which he denied, maintaining that after-writing broke not a contract. But this afterwards appeared otherwise, which is too long here to detail. Secondly, as Michael would first insist, as was right, that he should have nothing to do with former questions and losses, but every thing must be given to him clear, so Van der Donck and I fell to talk over the late burning of his house. He maintained firmly that the loss of the house should fall on the Patroon, as he undertook to prove out of books. I, on the contrary, said, no; and that I should prove it from his contract, which excluded all law, and contained a special condition as it happened, as I afterwards showed him. Many other reasons were given, not worth recapitulating. No particular question grew out of them, so they may be passed over as irrelevant.

Out of the foregoing words then we fell into a quarrel, and one word borrowing another, I stated to him some things which he had reported of me behind my back, whereupon, in the presence of some honorable people, he gave me, who told him so, the lie. Here came the wolf out of the sheep's clothing! Here hypocrisy removed the mask from her own face! Here he showed that he undoubtedly, long before this time, had fed his ingratitude in his breast, which is also apparent from the censure which he had reported of me. I always had done him good. The day after that misfortune had happened him—namely, the 18th January, 1646—I sent him a ton of meat. I had beside brought him and his wife to my house, and let them share whatever I had, good or bad, to the date 23d February aforesaid. I say this not through boasting; only to show his mask. To come to the point:—

Having given me the lie, for my blood was warm, I took occasion to tell him immediately, that he should quit my house, being unwilling to sit at the table with such a man; and therefore, besides, that if he did not remove his chest to some place by Wednesday the 21st, (this conversation passed on the 19th of Feb.,) I should put it out of doors. But he had it removed.

He remained another day. But as I had sworn that he should not eat six meals in my house, he was present at mealtimes only once. Pretending much sorrow, he then came to me and would have an account of all that he was indebted to me. To which I answered—that his cunning was well known to me—that he intended one thing or the other with it, as I had fully considered. But, I said, that he required this for a bad purpose. For the Lord the Patroon had charged him to render an account to the commissary, and he wished me first to render him an account. But that I should keep my finger well out of his mouth.

I gave him, at the same time, these reasons why I had told him to quit:—

I. To avoid trouble.

II. That my stock of provisions was nearly exhausted.

III. On account of my freedom. For I sometimes had something to write or to say which I was not willing that all men should know.

That I had fixed a day for his leaving.

Because I had already told him twice that he should depart, but that as yet I had seen no preparations for so doing.

That I was so particular as to the day because I had sworn, for which he had already given me cause.

That I now had noted these things so closely, and no man should think it strange if their craft and practices were known.

And hereupon, forthwith, he proceeded from my house to Mr. Harmanus [Van der Bogaerd,] in the fort, and crept there into a cottage, or hut, into which no one would scarce be willing to enter. Forsooth, 'twill be seen at once how I am turned out! When one misfortune overtakes me, then it is that I am smote upon the head! Miserere mei!

This is plausible. But when we view it right, it is not altogether so. For I have presented, and still present him with a suitable house, wherein Officier Coorn resided, into which he can move. But he must do something in the way of penance. That he had rather inhabit a hut under the wings of the company, than live in a decent house in the colonie, hath apparently its object. God knows that. Practica est multiplex.

In troubled waters, 'tis said, there is good fishing. So it happened on the occasion above narrated. For the following persons warm themselves by the coals of the burning fire.

[The MS. terminates abruptly here.]

Minute referring Van der Donck's claims to Holland.

[From the Rensselaerswyck MSS.]

Whereas I have seen the credit which Adriaen van der Donck pretends to claim, according to his account, from the Lord Patroon; and, again, his debit set off against the same;

So his credit is found to amount to	fl. 6097.17
And his debit to	3039. 1
Amount claimed by him,	fl. 3058.16

But as the house has been burnt, and some other things which increase a large portion of his credit, and which in my opinion ought, according to his contract, be charged to him ; also, as some items belong to his debit, such as sixteen guilders per annum for each servant, [knecht,] together with the pay for their board on coming over.

On the other hand, Van der Donck thinks that he was to be held free from loss and expenses ; it is therefore resolved to let the matter rest so, and to transmit it as it is to the Honorable Masters, so that their advice might be learned thereupon.

Actum, Rensselaerswyck,
28th April, anno 1646.

Adriaen van der Donck.

Note of Hand to the Deacons of the Church of Rensselaerswyck, Anno 1647.

I, the undersigned, Anthonie de Hooges, have, on the part of the Noble Patroon of the Colonie Rensselaerswyck, borrowed from the Diaconie of the aforesaid place, for the term of one year, to be repaid in cash, at the option of the lenders, with ten per cent. interest per annum, the sum of three hundred guilders in seawan, whereof one hundred and twenty is in ordinary seawan, promising thankfully to produce at the aforesaid time, in stated specie aforesaid, to the Diaconie of the aforesaid place. In testimony whereof, have I subscribed this Acte with mine own hand. Actum R. Wyck, 9th May, 1647.

P.

Tenths of those who still reside with the Patroon on the common domain.

[From the Rensselaerswyck MSS.]

NAMES OF SETTLERS.	Year.	Wheat. Schepels.	Oats. Schepels.	Rye. Schepels.	Barley. Schepels.	Buck-wheat. Schepels.	Peas. Schepels.
Michel Janssen.	1645	20	20				2
Teunis Dircksen van Vechten.	1642	32	48				
	1643		18				
	1644	22	44				
	1645	16	54				2
	1646	24	25				
	1647	30	30				
Cornelis Maessen.	1644	12	30	8			1
	1645	17	22	4			2
	1646	10	16		12	2	3
Simon Walinghen.	1644	24	26				
	1645	10	20				1
	1646	16	10				
Cryn Cornelissen.	1645	12	30				
	1646	16	24				
Cornelissens Clerk.	1646	36	24				

The tenths of Broer Cornelissen for 1645 are not ascertained.

Composition for Tenths and Thirds for those who hold under that contract

NAMES OF SETTLERS.	Year.	Wheat. Schepels.	Oats. Schepels.	Rye. Schepels.	Barley. Schepels.	Buck-wheat. Schepels.	Peas. Schepels.
Adriaen van der Donck.	1643		28				
	1644	112					
	1645	145	55				12
Cornelis Segers.	1644	276	320				
	1645	100	150		50		1
	1646	60			66		
Cornelis van Es.	1642		60				
	1643	30	64				
	1644	120					
	1645	70	55			35	5
	1646	fl. 140	in grain				
Andries de Vos.	1642		100				
	1643	30	6				
	1644	188					
	1645	105	95			35	2
	1646	45	50			20	2
Rutger Jacobsen, [tenths.]	1645	9	20				1
	1646	16	35				
Willem Fredericksen.	1645		8				
Adriaen Hybertzen.	1646		6				
Christoffel Davits.	1646	fl. 30 for tobacco and oats.					

N. B. Willem Fredericksen quit his bouwerie after a year, because it did not suit him. The bouwerie heretofore occupied by A. Van der Donck, has, by purchase of whatever belonged to him, and of his lease, been transferred to Cornelis Segers. So this year [1646] it brings little or no rent because no seed of any account has been sown there.

Q.

Two ancient Leases for Land in the Colonie of Rensseiaerswyck.

[From the Rensselaerswyck MSS.]

In the name of the Lord, Amen.

This day, 7th September, anno 1646, the presiding officers of the Colonie Rensselaerswyck on one side, and Thomas Chamber on the other, have agreed and consented about a certain parcel of land, lying right opposite the Bouwerie, called the Flatt, [de Vlachte,] on the east bank of the river, between the two kills, which land he, Thomas aforesaid, shall occupy as a bouwerie for the term of five successive years, commencing the 15th November, anno 1647, on the following conditions:

Thomas Chamber shall build free of all cost and charges, and without claiming a doit in return from the Lord Patroon, at his own expense, a farm-house, sixty feet long, twenty feet wide in the clear, the projection and all in proportion, as occasion may require, all faithful and firm work, without further specifying the same; but in all its parts and members similar to the barn of Poentje. A dwelling-house apart and separate from the barn, thirty-two feet long, eighteen feet wide, with a projection [uytlaetingh] on one side, the posts above the beams projecting two feet and a half, honest work, without specification, and without any expense to the Patroon as aforesaid. Further, the haggards, palisades, and in fine, every thing free of charge to the Patroon.

On condition of receiving in hand two mares and two studs, and moreover, two milch cows, the increase being on halves; but herein he shall enjoy the privilege of the bouweries which shall be leased on the arrival of the Director; the risk is also half and half, except such as the Indians may kill, which shall be at the sole risk of the Patroon, on sufficient proof being brought thereof. In case any opportunity shall offer to erect a mill near the aforesaid bouwerie, the said Thomas shall be preferred before all others, on the same conditions as others, or as shall then be agreed upon. From the summer sowing of the year 1647, shall he give tenths, and therewith be quit. The last seed which he shall plant in the bouwerie he is at liberty to thrash without payment.

The tenths of the lease years remain, as on the other bouweries. The risk of the houses and barns and fences remain at the charge of Thomas Chamber. The said Thomas shall preserve the said house and barns above and around, and within, in firm and fast repair, without allowing any damage to befall them, and the land all around as far as is necessary, enclose with fences not over two years old, delivering up and transporting the same to the Lord Patroon, or his resident agent here, free of cost and charges, at the expiration of his lease. And the said houses, barns, and fences, shall be the Patroon's rent for the aforesaid five years.

In case it should happen, which God forbid, that war should break out between us and the Indians, and Thomas be obliged to fly from the bouwerie, the time that he shall be absent shall be allowed him, and his time begin again from the date of his return.

And whereas Thomas Chambers demands assurance that these conditions shall be ratified by the Lords Masters without diminution, addition, or annulment, therefore do we, in the name of the Lords aforesaid, promise and guaranty to the said Thomas, that there shall be no failure or neglect in whatever is mentioned and agreed upon here, but, on the contrary, all shall be maintained even as if our Lords aforesaid them selves drew them up.

Thomas Chambers shall yearly pay, as an acknowledgment, five and twenty pounds of butter during his lease. He shall make use of his pasture above and below his bouwerie without let or hinderance.

Their worships, the presiding officers aforesaid, agree that he, Thomas, at the expiration of the above five successive years, shall cultivate the said bouwerie still three further years, provided he pay in addition to the tenths, five hundred guilders yearly, from the produce of the said bouwerie, at a valuation according to the rate that grain shall sell for at that time; and in addition to the aforesaid horses, one mare and one stud shall be delivered to him, according to agreement.

To all which the said Thomas Chambers hath agreed under his signature, in the same manner as their worships the presiding officers have promised that on their part there shall be no failure in the performance of these conditions, and punctually to observe the same under confiscation of all his goods, having and to have, present and future, how much soever they may be, under the obligation of renouncing, according to law, all [other] lords, courts, judges, and rulers. Promising, moreover, to be in all obedience subject to all his (the Patroon's) magistrates; to be true and faithful to them as occasion may demand, as a good subject is bound to be.

In acknowledgment hereof hath Thomas Chamber signed this with his own hand. Actum Rensselaerswyck, as above dated.

THOMAS CHAMBERS.

In presence of me the Secretary, in the name of their honors the Board aforesaid,

ANTONIO DE HOOGES.

We, guardians and tutors of Jean van Rensselaer, Patroon of the colonie called Rensselaerswyck, situate on the North River, in New Netherland, &c., have leased and farmed unto Arent van Curler, who hereby also acknowledges to have leased and farmed from us, under the following stated conditions, restrictions, and stipulations, the Bouwery named the Flatte, (de Vlachte,) and the hereafter mentioned appurtenances, for the term of six successive years, the farm lease beginning and terminating on the first of September, and that of the house on the first of May, one thousand six hundred eight and forty.

I. Firstly, the Patroon retains for himself the tenths of all grain, fruits, and products which shall be raised off this bouwery.

II. This bouwery contains about . . . . morgens of farmland, of which the lessee shall be bound yearly to cultivate . . . . morgens, and may, in addition, clear as much land as he shall be able to till with his people, without subletting or farming the same during the continuance of the lease, with the understanding that the lessee shall take the crops standing in the field, on the commencement hereof, such as they are paying the Patroon therefor according to the valuation of impartial persons, the Patroon agreeing on the other side, to take the crops which shall be standing on the expiration of this lease, at a valuation.

III. The lessee shall be entitled to so much pasture as he shall require for his cattle without paying any extra rent further than only one guilder for every swine that ranges in the woods.

IV. And for the cultivation of the said bouwerie there shall be delivered to him for his use six cows, two heifers, [veers pincken,] six mares, and two studs or oxen from among those on this bouwery, and that on halves, to wit:—one half the produce shall be for the Patroon, and the other half for the lessee, it being well understood that the lessee is bound to restore the given number according to the choice of the Patroon, and to divide the remainder, half and half, without the lessee pretending to have any claim for their maintenance or payment, or for the above-mentioned restitution.

V. And it is specially conditioned that the lessee shall not have power to keep on this bouwery any other cattle of private individuals, nor to lend, alienate, or give away during the continuance of the lease of this bouwery, any of the received stock, without our special consent, and he shall duly convey and ride all the manure on and over the land.

VI. For the use of which bouwery and occupancy of the house, the lessee shall pay yearly to the Patroon the sum of five hundred guilders, ($200,) but for the first year a deduction of one hundred and fifty guilders ($60) shall be made in regard that he convey his laborers thither at his own expense—which payment shall be made, the first half in November, and the other half in February, in merchantable beaver-hides, at four guilders ($1 60) the pound, or in grain at the current rate as the same is sold in the colonie, or in ready current money.

VII. The lessee shall be holden to keep the houses and buildings on the bouwerye in good repair, and to preserve and maintain the bouwerye in good order at his own expense, provided the house shall be first delivered to him wind and weather-tight, and at the expiration of the lease, he shall deliver it up in the same state.

VIII. It is well understood that the lessee is holden, over and above the aforesaid rent, during the winter season, to cut in the forest for the Patroon, ten pieces of oak or fir-wood, which shall be pointed out to him, and bring the same to the shore; also, every year, to give three days' service with his wagon and horses, to the Patroon or his guardians; also, each year, to cut, split, and bring to the waterside, two fathoms of hickory or other firewood; further, to deliver yearly to the Director as quit-rent, one-half mud [two bushels] of wheat, five and twenty pounds of butter, and two pair of fowls.

IX. The lessee shall not lodge any strange traders in his house, nor bring nor receive their goods on pain of forfeiting all the conditions granted to him, and to be ejected as a perfidious man.

X. And in case any question should arise between the lessee and others, the same shall be submitted to the commissaries there, without any appeal or further complaint being allowed.

XI. The lessee submits himself, moreover, as a faithful subject, to all regulations, orders, and conditions made by the Patroon and read before him, regarding dwelling together, and to all the statutes and ordinances to be hereafter made.

XII. The lessee promising, on the passing of the aforesaid lease, to comport himself faithfully in the said quality, and to fully follow the same; not to defraud the Patroon in the least nor in the most, directly nor indirectly, all under mortgage of his person and goods, moveable and immoveable, having and to have, submitting the whole thereof, and the adjudication thereof, to the constraint of all laws and judges.

XIII. Finally have the guardians and lessors reserved, in case the aforesaid bouwerye should be leased by the commissaries there, before the arrival of the lessee there, that this lease shall be null, and the aforesaid Curler being shewn another bouwerye, the commissaries there shall in that case agree with him thereupon, wherewith Curler is satisfied and agreed.

In witness whereof is this by each party subscribed, in Amsterdam this 30th September, 1647. Jehan van Weely, W. van Twiller, Arendt van Curler, in presence of me as witness, F. van de Ven, Not. Pub. residing in Amsterdam.

R.

Prices of imported articles and domestic produce in the Colonie of Rensselaerswyck from 1630 *to* 1646.

[Compiled from the account books of the Colonie.]

N. B. 20 stivers make one florin of 40 cents, and 2½ florins, one dollar.

Imports.

	fl. st.
Kersey, red, blue, or white, per ell,	2.00
Cloth, " "	2 to 5.00
Canvass, " "	15
Osnabruck linen, " "	9
Duffels, " "	3.00
Linen breeches, ...	1.10
A trimmed shirt, or chemise, .	3.10
A blanket, or coverlet, .	7 to 8.00
A linen gown, [roke,] . . .	1.10
Shoes, per pair, . .	2 to 4.00
Children's do., ...	1. 4
Stockings, per pair, . . .	18
A skein of silk, . . .	5
A hat, ...	10.00
A peajacket, ...	4.10
Sugar, per lb., . .	15
Yarn, " . .	2.00
Cotton yarn, " . .	1.10
Net yarn, " . .	12
Shoemakers' yarn, " . .	1.10
A gun, ...	11 to 17.10
A musket and cartouch box, .	19.00
An axe, or hatchet, . . .	1½ to 2.00
A cheese, ...	2 to 5.00
A grindstone, ...	1.00
A scythe, ...	2.10
A spade, ...	1½ to 2.10
A winnowing fan, . . .	4.10
A plough and iron-work, . .	28.16
A wooden yoke, ...	1.05
A ploughshare, ...	25.00
Sheep's bell, copper, . . .	1.06

	fl. st.
A chisel, ...	1.00
An iron hammer, . . .	14
A seine	6.00
A hoop net, ...	7.10
A lanthorn, ...	15
A kettle, ...	3 to 6.00
A wooden ladle, . .	1.10
An English knife, . .	1 to 2.10
Knives per doz., ...	4.16
Silk buttons per doz., . . .	6
Gunpowder, per lb., .	1.00
Lead, " .	3
Cheese, " .	3
Soap, " .	6
Prunes, " .	2
Steel, " .	1
Nails, [100 to the lb.,] " .	8
Large pins, per 1000, . .	18
Sole-leather per lb., . . .	1.02
Upper-leather " . .	1.10
Spanish wine, per can or pot, .	1.00
Vinegar, " " . .	10
Spruce beer [1637] " " . .	18
Oil, " " . .	1.12
Train oil, " " . .	16
Brandy, " " . .	1.05
Malt per schepel, [3 pecks,] .	3.00
A ton of white salt, . . .	7.13
Half barrel of salt, . . .	2.12
A small barrel of salt meat,	33.00
An iron anvil, ...	100.00
Smiths' coals per chaldron, . .	19.10

	fl. st.			fl. st.
101 bars of flat iron, . . .	485.00	Cloves,	per oz.,	10
1 Blacksmith's bellows, . .	47.00	Mace,	" "	16
Nutmegs, per oz., . . .	10	Pepper,	" "	2
Ginger, " " . . .	2	A glass tumbler, ...		1.00

Domestic Produce.

Wheat, [1635]	per schepel,	2.10	Butter, per lb., ...	8
Indian corn, [1637]	" " .	2.00	Small beer, per ton, . . .	6.00
Barley,	" " .	2.10	Strong beer " " . .	18 to 20.00
Oats,	" " .	1.00	Wampum, per ell, . . .	2.17
Bread corn,	" " .	2.10	Palisades, per 1000, .	15.00
Rye,	" " .	2.00	Plank, each, . . .	1.10 to 1.16
Turnips,	" " .	15	Day laborers' wages, [1637] per diem, ...	1 to 1.10
Indian corn, [1643]	" " .	1.10	Carpenters' do., do.	2.00
Malt,	" " .	2.10	Reed, per 100 bundles, . .	1.00
An ox, [1637] . .		80 to 140.00	Yellow brick, per 1000, . .	15.00
A horse, ...		80.00	300 Carrots, ...	2.00
A pig, . .		12, 26, 30, to 45.00	A wagon, ...	30.00
A she-goat, [1642] . . .		36.00	A barn, plough, and harrow, were valued, in 1643, by the council of Rensselaerswyck, at .	825.00
Beaver each, . . .		6 to 7.00	or	$330.00
A beaver coat, ...		25.00		
Use of a stud for a year, . .		30.00		
Use of a mare " " . .		40.00		
A pair of fowls, ...		2.00		

1646.

		fl. st.		fl.
Wheat,	per schepel,	2.10	A gun, ...	35
Oats,	" "	1.00	A mare and stud, . . .	330
Peas,	" "	3.10	Use of a stud for 1 year, .	30
Rye,	" "	2.00	Use of a cow, ...	20
Indian corn,	" "	1.05	A horse, ...	160
Little beans, (boontje,)	"	2.10	A cow, ...	50 to 120
Buckwheat,	" "	1.10	A yearling bull-calf, . . .	8
Barley,	" "	2.05	A pig, ...	25 to 26
Wild beans,	" "	1.10	A tun of small beer, . . .	6
Butter,	per pound,	.08	A barrel of strong beer, . .	18
Pork,	" "	9st to 10	An anchor of vinegar, . .	21
Old iron,	" "	2	Mackerel, per 100, . . .	14
New iron,	" "	3½	A mare 3 to 6 years old, . .	120
Tobacco,	" "	1.	" 2 " " . .	70
Hops,	" "	.17	A stud, 2 " " . .	60
Plank, per 100,	" "	100.	A cow, 3 to 6 " " . .	80
Sawing do,	per piece,	.03	Freight of the Yacht Rensselaerswyck, per day, . . .	5
Beaver,		6 to 7.00		

S.

PAPERS RELATING TO THE COLONIE OF ZWANENDAL.

[From a Notarial copy, which is among papers of the late Proprietaries of Pennsylvania.]

Extract from the Register of Resolutions agreed to at the Assembly of the Lords Directors of the Old West India Company, at the Chamber at Amsterdam.

Tuesday the 19th June, 1629.

The Heer Samuel Godyn having heretofore given notice here that he intended to plant a colonie in N. Netherland, and that he also to that end had engaged two persons to proceed thither to examine into the situation of those quarters, declares that he, now in quality of Patroon, has undertaken to occupy the Bay of the South River, on the conditions concluded in the last Assembly of the XIX., as he hath likewise advised the Director Pieter Minuet, and charged him to register the same there.

Another Extract, or Authentic Copy, from a bundle of papers relating to New Netherland, beginning 7th Feb., 1635, *and ending* 2*d June*, 1653.

WHEREAS, Directors of the General West India Company were commissioned on the 22d August, 1634, by the Assembly of the XIX., to treat and transact with all the Patroons and colonists in New Netherland, for the purchase of the Patroonships, Colonies, dignities, houses, buildings, lands, merchandises, and all the rights, effects, appendages, and dependencies thereof, which they were in possession of there, Therefore the aforesaid commissioners, having reported, have, with the approbation of the Chamber at Amsterdam, dated 27th November, 1634, agreed and concluded with Samuel Bloemmaert, Kiliaen van Rensselaer, Jacques de la Miue, Hendrick Hamel, Nicolaus van Setterich, Johan van Harinckhouck, and the heirs of Samuel Godyn, deceased, each for their contingent, and they further representing Johan de Laet, (endehaer vorden sterk maeckende voor J. de L.,) that they conjointly, and each for himself in particular, for the behoof of the aforesaid company, shall surrender, as they do hereby, their two colonies, named SWAENENDAEL, in New Netherland, together with the jurisdictions, dignities, lands, rights, appendages, and dependencies thereunto belonging, which they there, by virtue of their two distinct sealed patents obtained before the Council of New Netherland, resident on the island Manhattes, dated the 15th July, 1630, and 3d June, 1631, in pursuance of letters of conveyance passed by Queskakous and Ensanckes, Sickonesyns, and inhabitants of their villages, and the other by Sawotbouc, Wiewyt, Pemhacky, and others appearing on the aforesaid date, both situate on the South River, as well on the south hook of the Bay, as on the east side of the said river, with all such houses, buildings, outhouses, as they or their servants may have purchased, erected, or brought there, none excepted to trade with there, together with their own free goods, without reserving therein any right of action, placing such property from now henceforward in full possession of the aforesaid company, according to the aforesaid original letters, which they do hereby deliver over, consenting at all times to grant to the aforesaid Company, before the Director and Council of New Netherland, when required, further conveyance, acknowledgment, and discharge, and to give therefor suitable authority, without their being bound for any further indemnity.

Likewise, they promise and deliver over, besides these, to the said company, all charters, maps, and papers, concerning the aforesaid colonies and affairs of New Netherland, as far as it remains with them, and moreover to let them remain to the company as their free property, without claiming thereunto any right, action, or pretension. And that for the sum of fifteen thousand, six hundred guilders to be paid—one third part six months after the aforesaid 27th November, 1634, to wit, on the 27th May, anno 1635, and fifteen months after that, to wit, on the 27th August, 1636, the second third part, and fifteen months afterwards, to wit, the 27th November, 1637, the last third part.

For which sum, the company shall deliver to each participant (partner) of the said colonie, according to their quota and rata, by the said comparants surrendered, its particular (special) obligation, without the one being for all that holden to wait on the other for his money.

It being well understood that they conjointly, for the good of the company, shall take care that no man, henceforward, shall claim any thing on account of the aforesaid colonie under penalty according to law, as they hereby agree to.

It shall be lawful to the sellers, or any of them, for the sum to which their obligation amounts—to wit, each according to estimation, for the sum of nineteen hundred and fifty guilders, to purchase, or cause to be purchased, goods from the company, in conformity to the Octroy or amplification thereof, and to deduct in whole or in part, at the rate of 6 per cent. per annum, from the time the bill is due according to the bargain to be made by them, or from the day that they shall notify the discount to the day of payment.

And all claims and accounts which the aforesaid sellers and the company, on account of the aforesaid Colonies, or other transactions in New Netherland, both as to receipts and expenses, with other outstanding odd accounts, without pretending any other claims or actions in the world, shall be included in this sale, and shall hereby remain discharged, and stand erased on the books.

Only that the aforesaid sellers or their assigns shall, moreover, be free and exempt from the duties on the cargo of timber which the ship West Friesland, whereof Jan Symonz is skipper, shall bring back on this voyage.

And that the lawsuit between the Patroons of Swaenendael and the company, depending before the court of Amsterdam, is not included in this transaction, and the parties on both sides, so far as concerns that, remain wholly free to pursue their right as they shall think proper.

And the aforesaid contracting parties shall observe, and allow each other peaceably and freely to enjoy the effect of this contract, under bond of law, namely, that those of the company shall pledge only the effects and goods of the company, moveable and immoveable, present and future, and the aforesaid sellers, their persons and goods a manner aforesaid, all without fraud or guile. In testimony whereof, two instruments only being made, are signed by the respective parties, in Amsterdam, this 7th February, 1635. Was subscribed, Albert Kounraetsburgh, Daniel van Libergen, Jean Raye, F. de Vries, Marcus van Valckenburgh, S. Bloemmaert, Henrick Hamel, N. van Setterich, J. van Harinckhouck ; Hendrick Crip, for the heirs of Samuel Godyn ; Jacques de la Miue, Kiliaen van Rensselaer, for his part in the Colonie of Swaenendael aforesaid, and no more

INDEX

[WHERE THE SUBJECT REFERRED TO IN THIS INDEX IS NOT FOUND IN THE TEXT, IT WILL BE MET IN THE NOTES.]

A.

Achter Cul, attack on, 286.
Achterveldt, where situate, 172.
Agriculture, Indian, 51.
Ages of the Rev. Mr. Megapolensis, his wife and children, when they came to N. Netherland, 448.
Agreement between the Rev. Mr. Megapolensis and the first Patroon, 448 ; between Kiliaen van Rensselaer and the Directors of the West India Company relative to the approval of the Rev. J. Megapolensis as minister at Rensselaerswyck, 450.
Ahasimus, 126.
Albany, The Half Moon, in the neighborhood of, 39 ; the ship William ascends near, 145.
America, Jean and Sebastian Cabot sail along the coast of, 26.
American seas, the first Dutch ships in the, 26.
Amersfoort, New, first settlement of, 173
Amsterdam Fort, erected, 104; cost of 171.
Amusements among the Indians, 65.
Amusing anecdote of an Indian, 53.
Anchor bay, where situate, 73.
Animals of New Netherland, 46.
Aquehonga-Manacknong, 48.
Archipelagoes, situation of the, 73 ; purchased by the Dutch, 215.
Ardent spirits manufactured in N. Netherland, 228.
Argal, Captain, visits the Manhattans, 69.
Armenveruis, 156.
Arms of Rensselaerswyck, The, sails for New Netherland, 340 ; is confiscated, 342 ; returns to Holland, 343.
Assembly of the XIX., composition of the, 90.
Awiehaken, 274.
Azores, The, discovered, 26.

B.

Bancroft, Mr., his error as to the source of popular freedom in New Netherland, 393.
Banishment, sentences of, pronounced by the Court of Rensselaerswyck, 320, 439.
Barentzoon, Willem, his voyage to the north, 28.
Baxter, George, appointed English Secretary, 259.
Bays, Anchor and Sloop, 73.
Beer, ordinance prohibiting an individual brewing, 389.
Beeren island, Indian name of, 122 ; fortified, 341.
Beets, his proposal to the States of Holland, 27.
Bergen, 389.
Bermuda, the Dutch send some Indians as a present to the Governor of, 313.
Betencour discovers the Azores, 26.
Bethlehem, 390.
Beversreede, fort, 156.
Beverswyck, 326 ; number of houses in, in 1646, 390.
Biographical sketch of the Rev. Peter Plancius, 94; of the Rev. Hugh Peters, 234.
Birds of New Netherland, 46.
Blanck, Juriaen, 142.
Blessing, the bark, arrives at the Manhattans, 151.
Bloemmaert and Godyn purchase land, 121, 125 ; sell their colonie to the West India Company, 365.
Blue Cock, The, arrives with troops at New Netherland, 310.
Block, Adriaen, sails for the Manhattans, 72 ; name of his ship, ib. ; builds the Restless, ib. ; his discoveries, 73.
Bogaerdt, Joost de, commander, 366

Bogardus, Rev. E., minister at Manhattans, 142 ; quarrels with Van Twiller, 167 ; complaints against him, 173 ; remonstrates against the war, 266 ; quarrels with Kieft, 362 ; indicted, 364.
Books, catalogue of, sent to Rensselaerswyck, 454.
Bout, Jan Evertz., superintendent in Pavonia, 167 ; elected one of the Eight Men, 285.
Bradford, Gov. of New Plymouth, 106 ; letters of De Razier to, 107 ; writes to Director Minuit, 108.
Bradt, Albert Andriessen, 433
Brandy, first introduction of, among the Indians, 38 ; manufactured on Staten Island, 228.
Brazil, Dutch expelled from several provinces in, 309.
Bressani, Father, taken prisoner by the Indians, 336 ; is ransomed by the Dutch, 337.
Breukelen, why so called, 101 ; incorporated, 383.
Brewers, The, resist the payment of the excise, 311.
Bronck, Jonas, residence of, 250.
Brown, Rev. Richard, separates from the Established church, 82.
Burials among the Indians, 61.

C.

Cabot, Jean and Sebastian, follow Columbus, 26.
Call of the Rev. Johannes Megapolensis, 449.
Canada, Dutch visit The River of, 32.
———, dates of some of the early patents for Seigneuries in, 120.
Canarsee Indians, location of the, 49.
Canoes, Indian, 54.
Carleton, Sir Dudley, remonstrates against the Dutch, 96 ; his letter to the States General, 97 ; Walloons apply to him for leave to settle in Virginia, 100.
Castle island, dimensions of the fort on, 76 ; the fort on destroyed, 78.
Castleton Indians entertain Hudson, 37.
Castle Rensselaer, 342.
Catalogue of books for the Colonie of Rensselaerswyck, 454.
Causes estranging the Indians from the Dutch, 223.
Charges against the Dutch for betraying the Puritans, falsehood of the, exposed, 86.
Charles I., Dutch ambassadors visit, 132.
Charles II., Rev. N. van Rensselaer's prophecy relating to, 122.
Charles V. grants an island in America, 26.
Charter to the Dutch West India Company, 89, 90, 399 ; its provisions compared with those granted by other European powers, 91 ; to Patroons, 112 ; legality thereof admitted, 159 : of 1640, 219.
Children of manumitted slaves not free, 385.
Church at Rensselaerswyck, erection of a, 330 ; promissory note to the deacons of, 471.
Church, site of the first in N. Amsterdam, 155 ; measures taken to build a new, in Fort Amsterdam, 259 ; inscription on the front of, 262.
Civil list, estimate of a, for N. N., 351.
Coeymans, Barent Pieterse, some account of him, 435.
Cogswell, Robert, protest against, 231.
Cole, Lenaert, assistant secretary, 103, 124.
Colen-donck, situation and boundarie of the colonie of, 383.
Collision with the Haverstraw Indians 40 ; between Dutch and English nea Fort Orange, 145.
Colman, John, killed, 36.
Colonies, charter to plant, in N. N., 112.
Commissions to attack Indians, 267 268.
Connecticut, The River, discovered, 73 land on purchased, 150 ; Fort Good Hope erected on, 151 ; English take possession of, 154 ; troubles between the Dutch and the English on the, 209.
Consent of the Patroon of Rensselaerswyck that the Directors of the West India Company should approve of the Rev. Mr. Megapolensis, 450.
Consistory, the first in N. N., 260.
Contract for building a church at New Amsterdam, 262 ; for a horse mill, 388 ; between Mr. Van Rensselaer and the Rev. Mr. Megapolensis, 448.
Country produce, prices of, at Rensselaerswyck, 478.
Coorn, Nicolaus, 343 ; fires at the Hope, 344 ; protests against Van der Huyghens and appointed fiscal of Rensselaerswyck, 345.
Corchaug Indians, location of the, 50.
Corssen, Arent, commissary at Fort Nassau, 142 ; purchases land on the Schuylkill, 156 ; is drowned, 359.
Corstiaenssen, Henrick, second voyage to the Manhattans, 72 ; erects a fort there, 77.

Coster, Willem Cornelisz., murdered, 283.
Council—names of Peter Minuit's council, 101; of Wouter van Twiller's, 142; of Director Kieft's, 180.
Court-day established at New Amster dam, 184.
Creation, Indians' ideas of the, 64.
Croton River, Indian name of the, 278.

D.

Dam Jan Jansen, one of the Twelve Men, 242; one of the first consistory, 260; signs a letter demanding the attack of the Indians, 265; elected one of the Eight Men, 284; expelled the board, 285. [See "Names of Settlers in Rensselaerswyck," 434.]
Deacons of the Church at Rensselaerswyck, note of hand to the, 471.
Debit and credit account of the estate of Kiliaen van Rensselaer at his death, 468.
Deed of sale of the Colonie of Zwanendael to the West India Company, 479.
De Forest family, some particulars of the, 186.
De Hooges, Antonie, 322.
De Laet, freedoms and conditions submitted by Johannes, 192.
Delaware, Hudson anchors in the great bay of the, 34; subdivision of the Indian tribes on the, 49; first settlement of Europeans on the, 100; the Dutch plant a colonie at the mouth of the, 129; the Swedes settle on the, 189; the English attempt a settlement on the, 231.
De Razier, Isaac, 103; visits New Plymouth, 108; disgraced, 130.
De Vries, Capt. David P., one of the South River Company, 128; arrives at Zwanendal, 129; returns to the Delaware and finds the colonie destroyed, 139; makes peace with the Indians, ib.; quarrels with Van Twiller, 147; his opinion of the company's servants at Fort Amsterdam, 148.
Dimensions of the first church in Rensselaerswyck, 330.
Director General of N. N., his powers, 244.
Dismissal of the Rev. Mr. Megapolensis by the Classis of Amsterdam, 449.
Doughty, Rev. Francis, removes to Long Island, 257; appeals from a decision rendered by Kieft, and is fined and imprisoned, 394; further particulars about him, 427, 428.
Droit Belgique, what, 90.
Dutch, The, begin to trade with New England, 105; settlements in 1630, condition of the, 128; ambassadors, reply of the Lords Commissioners, to the, 134; drive the English from the North River, 146; and from the South River, 253.
Dutchman's Island, 174.
Duyckingh, Evert, wounded at Fort Hope, 214.
Dwellings of the Indians, 53.

E.

East India Company, The, incorporated, 30.
East River, The, called the Hellegat, 72.
Eaton, Gov., his answer to Kieft, 376.
Education, neglected state of, 396.
Election of magistrates authorized in the fifteenth century, 392.
Eelkens, Jacob Jacobz., commander of the fort on Castle Island, 76; supercargo of the William, 143; difficulties with, 144; attempts to trade with the Indians, 145; is obliged to leave the Hudson River, 146.
Eendracht, The ship, seized at Plymouth, 131; Dutch ambassadors demand her release, 133; released, 136.
Eghquaous, 48, 104.
Eight Men, The, elected, 284; their proceedings, 285, 288; write to Holland, 289; object to the excise, 306; complain against Kieft, 312.
English, jealous of the Dutch, 95; encroachments of the, on N. N., 168; tear down Dutch arms, 170; attempt a settlement on the South River, 170, 231; expelled therefrom, 253; residents at N. Amsterdam, names of the, 208; settle New Haven, ib.; assault the Dutch at Fort Hope, 209, 232; begin to settle on Long Island, 210; continue to quarrel with the Dutch, 213; tear down the Dutch arms at Oyster Bay, 216; brought prisoners to Fort Amsterdam, 217; send agents to England, 234; their instructions, 235, and proposals to the W. I. Co., 236; their complaints against the Dutch, 251; send deputies to New Amsterdam, 254.
English colonies form a confederation, 279.
——— corps formed in N. Amsterdam, 286.

English of New Haven build a trading-house near the North River, 375.
——— commissioners write to Kieft, 378.
——— complaints of the, against the Dutch, like those of the wolf against the lamb, 379.
——— commissioners' reply to Kieft, 380.
Esopus, a Dutch fort built there, 390.
Estate of Kiliaen van Rensselaer, debit and credit account of the, at his death, 468.
Estimate of a civil list for N. N., 351.
Europeans, first settlement of, on the Delaware, 100.
Evertsen family, the, 181.
Expenditure for the first settlement of Rensselaerswyck in 1630, account of the, 249.
Exports of N. N., value of in 1632, 1633, 157.

F.

Fairs established at New Amsterdam, 239.
Farrett, Mr., agent to Lord Stirling, arrives at New Amsterdam, 215; sells land on Long Island, 217.
First English ship sails up the Hudson River, 143.
Fishes of New Netherland, 46.
Five Nations, tribes composing the, 79.
Flatlands, first settlement of, 173.
Food among the Indians, 52.
Foreign countries, company of, 29.
Fort Amsterdam built, 104; officers at, 142; dimensions of, 171.
Fort Good Hope erected, 151.
Freedoms and exemptions proposed by De Laet, 192; by the Patroons, 197; disapproved, 199: of 1640, 218.
Free traders, Form of a protest against, by the Patroon of Rensselaerswyck, 466.
Fresh Water River, The, discovered, 73.
Fruits of New Netherland, 45.
Fuyck, The, 326.

G.

Gambling among the Indians, 65.
Gardiner's Island settled, 211.
General Peace, terms of the treaty of, between the Dutch and the Indians, 356.
Glen Sander Leendertsen, 438.
Gorges', Sir Ferdinando, letter to Capt. Mason about an expedition against the Dutch, 416.
Godyn and Bloemmaert, lands in N. N. purchased by, 121, 125.
Godyn, Samuel, notice of his intention to plant a colonie at the Bay of the South River, 479.
Government among the Indians, 56.
Government, municipal, forms of, 390.
Governor Island, Indian name of, 174.
Gravenzande, first settlement of, 258; attacked by Indians, 287; incorporated, 358.
Greenbush, Indian name for, 330.
Greenwich submits to the Dutch, 252.
Gustavus Adolphus incorporates a Swedish West India Company, 188.

H.

Hackingsacks, location of the, 48.
Half Moon, the, 33.
——— returns to Holland, 42.
Heemskirk, Jacob, sails to the north, 28; conquers a Spanish fleet, 67.
Heemstede, battle at, 299; town of planted, 317.
Hellegat, the river, 44; why so called, 72.
Hendricksen, Capt. Cornelis, lays a report of his voyage before States General, 77; substance of his report, 78.
Heyn, Admiral Pieter Pietersen, 111.
Hindlopen, Cape, why so called, 73.
Hobokan-hacking, 125; why so called, 126.
Holland, number of Manors in, entitled to municipal rights, 392.
Hollandaer, Peter, arrives at the Delaware, 365.
Holmes, Lieut., sails to the Connecticut, 153; builds a house there, 154; his reply to the Dutch protest, ib.
Holmes, Geo., and associates taken prisoners by the Dutch, 170.
Hopkins, Gov., difficulties with him, 213.
Horsimus, 126.
Horse mill in Rensselaerswyck, 388.
Houses round Forts Amsterdam and Orange, description of the, 388.
Houten, Hans Jorissen, commissary at Fort Orange, 142.

Houtman, Cornelis, his proposal, 29.
Hudde, Andries, appointed surveyor, 259 ; sent as commissary to the South River, 371 ; differences with the Swedish governor there, 372 ; purchases land from the Indians, 373 ; complains of the Swedes, 375.
Hudson, Henry, his voyages to the north, 32 ; sails in the Half Moon, 33 ; visits Penobscot Bay and the Delaware, 34 ; enters the North River, 35 ; detains some Indians as hostages, 36 ; lands near Castleton, 37 ; furnishes brandy to the Indians, 38 ; leaves the North River and arrives at Dartmouth, 41 ; his death, 42.
Hunting among the Indians, 51.
Hutchinson, Mrs. Anne, murdered by the Indians, 287 ; her daughter ransomed by the Dutch, 357.

I.

Immortality of the soul, opinion among the Indians on the, 63.
Imports, value of, in 1634, 167.
Imported goods, prices of, at Rensselaerswyck, 477.
Incorporation of the W. I. Company, 89.
Indians, first introduction of ardent spirits among the, 38 ; collision with the Haverstraw, 40 ; tribes of N. Netherland enumerated, 46 ; of Long Island, 49 ; physical appearance of the, 50 ; agriculture and hunting among the, 51 ; food, clothing, and ornaments of the, 52 ; their dwellings, 53 ; women, villages, canoes of the, 54 ; marriages among the, 55 ; slavery unknown to the, ib. ; laws, form of government, and authority of the chiefs among the, 56 ; manner of waging war, 57 ; their mode of treating prisoners, 58 ; their ideas of money, and mode of interment, 61 ; ideas of a Supreme Being, 62 ; superstitions of the, 63 ; amusements and games among the, 65 ; the island of Manhattans purchased from the, 104 ; take possession of Fort Nassau, 139 ; peace with the South River, 139 ; grant a deed for a tract of land on the Connecticut, 150 ; Dutch levy tribute on the, 223 ; attack a Dutch boat on the Raritan, 226 ; general peace with the, 355, 356.

J.

Jacobsen Rutger, 436.
Jan Ryersen's island, Indian name of, 435
Jogues, Father, a prisoner among the Mohawks, 334 ; escapes and sails for Holland, 336.

K.

Katskill, the Half Moon anchors in front of, 37 ; Van der Donck proposes to plant a colonie at, 338 ; Van Rensselaer lays claims to, 339 ; granted to Van Slyck, 381 ; the patent for, 382.
Kieft, Willem, Director-general, 174 ; arrives at New Amsterdam, 180 ; his council, ib. ; public affairs under, 181 ; issues divers proclamations, 183 ; sends to Curaçoa for negroes, 185 ; purchases land on Long Island, ib. ; regulates the inspection of tobacco, 186 ; protests against Peter Minuit, 191 ; purchases additional lands on L. Island, 210, 213 ; protests against the English at Greenwich, 218 ; levies tribute on the Indians, 223 ; calls on the Dutch settlers to provide themselves with arms, 225 ; sends a military force against the Raritans, 226, 239 ; protests against Cogswell, 231 ; calls the commonalty together, 241 ; sends an expedition against the Wechquaesqueecks, 249 ; abolishes the board of Twelve Men, 249 ; orders a non-intercourse with Hartford, 252 ; dispatches two vessels against the English on the Delaware, 253 ; erects a new church, 262 ; demands the surrender of the murderer of Van Vorst, 264 ; resolves to attack the Indians, 266 ; proclaims a general fast, 272 ; attempt on his life, 273 ; concludes a peace with the Indians, 276, 277, 302, 303 ; addresses letters to the N. E. colonies, 279, 281 ; calls the commonalty together to choose select men, 283 ; arms the citizens, 286 ; sends Messrs. Underhill and Allerton to New Haven, 289 ; calls together the Eight Men, 306 ; establishes an excise, 307 ; forces the brewers to pay that impost, 311 ; complaints against him, 312 ; his letter in behalf of a Jesuit priest, 337 ; concludes a treaty with the Mo-

hawks, 355; makes a general peace with the Indians, 356; explores for minerals, 358; quarrels with Dominie Bogardus, 362; reconciled, 365; protests against those of New Haven, 376; his letter to the New England colonies, 378; protests against them, 379; writes to Holland, 381; accusations brought against him, 384; recalled, ib.; denies the right of appeal to Holland, 394; his unpopularity, 395; applies church funds to his own use, ib.

Kievits hoeck purchased, 149.

Kip, Hendrick, advises to depose Director Kieft, 272; refuses to assist at the making of peace, ib.

Kling, Mounce, arrives at the Delaware, 366.

Koorn, Nicolaus, [see "Coorn."]

L.

La Garce, privateer, sent against the Spaniards, 296; captures two Spanish prizes, 305.

La Montagne, Johannes, arrives in New Netherland, and is appointed one of the council, 180; begins a plantation on Manhattans, 185; its name, 186; opposes the attack on the Indians, 266; prevents Kieft being assassinated, 273; commands a party against the Indians on Staten Island, 297; also, against those of Schouts' bay, 299.

Lampo, Jan, schout-fiscaal of N. Netherland, 103, 124; sails for Holland, 130.

Laws among the Indians, 56.

Leases of lands in Rensselaerswyck in the years 1646 and 1647, 473.

Legal custom in the Colonie of Rensselaerswyck, 442.

Letter from Arendt van Curler to the Patroon of Rensselaerswyck, 456.

Long Island, Indian tribes on, 49; Indian name of, 73; granted to the Earl of Stirling, 210; English begin to settle on, ib.

Lupold, Ulrich, appointed schout fiscaal, 173; removed from office, 211; appointed commissary of wares, ib.; found guilty of malversation, 228.

Lynn, freedoms granted to several Englishmen from, 237.

M.

Magistrates, towns in N. Netherland entitled to elect their, 392.

Manhattans, location of the, 47; why so called, ib.; by whom originally so named, 48; Hendrick Corstiaensen's establishment on the, 69; visited by Capt. Argal, ib.; Block sails to the, 72; Corstiaensen's second voyage to the, ib.; purchased by the Dutch, 104.

Manittous, what, 62.

Map of Rensselaerswyck, price paid for drawing a, in 1630, 429.

Marriages among the Indians, 55.

Marrakkawick Indians, the, plundered, 270; reject the friendly advances of the Dutch, 271.

Marsapeague Indians, 49.

Maryn Adriaensen attempts to assassinate Kieft, 272; banished to Holland, 274.

Mason, Capt., complains of the Dutch, 131; his letter, 415.

Mattinecocks, territory of the,49; strength of the, in 1650, 50.

Mauritius, the river, 100.

Mayn Mayano attacks some Christians, and is killed, 297.

Medicine men, 64.

Megapolensis, Rev. J., appointed minister of Rensselaerswyck, 328, 439; allowance to, 329; agreement between him and the first Patroon, 448; his call, 449; instructions to him, 451.

Melyn, Cornelis, Patroon of Staten Island, 238.

Members of the United New Netherland Company, names of the, 74.

Memorandum for the Rev. Mr. Megapolensis, 451.

Merekoke Indians, 49.

Mespath, original patent for planting, 425.

Mey, Capt. Cornelis Jacobs., sails to New Netherland, 72; his discoveries, 73; returns to Holland and petitions for exclusive right of trade, 86; his third voyage to New Netherland, 99.

Military force, the first in N. N., 142.

Minquas, The, 49.

Minsi tribes, their location, 48.

Minuit, Peter, first Director General of New Netherland, 100; names of his council, 101, 124; purchases the island of Manhattans and erects Fort Amsterdam, 104; opens a trade with

New Plymouth, 105; recalled, 130; visits London, 131; proceeds to Sweden, 188; sails for the Delaware, 189; establishes a colony there, 190.
Minute referring Adriaen van der Donck's claims to Holland, 470.
Moenimines' castle, where situate, 123.
Mohawks, location of the, 47; treaty of peace with the, 355.
Mohegans, their locality, 47; the Dutch conclude a treaty of peace with them, 355.
Mohicans Island, Indian name of, 437.
Moloch, Anthony, sails to the Cape de Verde, 27.
Momma, Maria, Van Twiller's wife, 142.
Monopoly of the Indian trade abolished, 200; consequences thereof, 222.
Moody, Lady, removes to L. I., 258; attacked by the Indians, 287.
Moucheron, Balthazar, opposes Hudson's views, 32.
Mountains, the Great River of the, 44.
Municipal government, origin of free, 391.

N.

Nahicans, The, where located, 73.
Names of the members of the United N. N. Company, 74; of Wouter van Twiller's council, 142; of the English who took the oath of allegiance to the Dutch, 208; of the Twelve Men, 242; of those who assisted at the election of the Eight Men, 284; of the directors of the West India Company, 411; of the first settlers in Rensselaerswyck, 433.
Naraticongs, The, where located, 49.
Naragansett Bay, the Dutch name for, 73; a Dutch ship stranded in, 105.
Nassau, Bay of, 73.
Nassau, Fort, erected, 100; abandoned, 139.
Naugattuck, 376.
Navesinck, the Highlands of, 35.
Nederhorst, a new colonie planted by de Heer, 238.
Negro, value of a, 385.
New Albion, boundaries of, 281.
New Amsterdam, irregularities in, 171; condition of, 1638, 182; population, in and around, 386; its condition, 1646, 395.
New countries, privileges granted to the discoverers of, 70.
New England, population of in 1648, 386; not the source of popular privileges in New Netherland, 393.
New Gottenburg, 369.
New Haven settled, 208; refuses to assist the Dutch, 289; builds a trading-post near the North River, 375.
New Holland, 34.
New Netherland, first visit of the Dutch to, 29; the Great North River of, 35; latitude of, 43, 74; boundaries of, 43; rivers of, 44; soil, trees, fruits, and plants of, 45; birds, water-fowls, animals, fishes, reptiles, and Indians of, 46; Cornelis Mey sails to, 72; grant in favor of the United Company of, 74; first time this country called, ib.; the Scheld sails to, 81; the Puritans express a desire to move to, 83; erected into a province, 99; first Christian child born in, 101; trade of, in 1624 and 1625, 103; in 1626, 104; in 1627, 110; in 1632, 139; the States General declare it must not be lost by force or intrigue, 179; condition of, in 1638, 175; a source of great loss to the West India Company, 350; condition of at the close of Kieft's administration, 384; population and revenue of, 386; indebted to Holland for whatever municipal freedoms its towns possessed, 393.
New Plymouth, the Dutch correspond with, 105; open a trade to, 108; the Dutch complain of the English at, 109.
New project, a, proposed, 197.
New Sweden, 189; first governor of, 190; second governor of, 365; boundaries of, 366; third governor of, 367.
Newtown, original patent of, 425.
Nineteen, Assembly of the, how composed, 90.
Nissquagues, territory of the, 50.
Normans Kill, Indian name of the, 78; why called the, ib.
Notelman, Conraed, schout-fiscaal, 142; his character, 148; is superseded, ib.

O.

Ogden, John and Richard, contract to build a church in New Amsterdam, 262.
Olden-barneveldt, birthplace of, 173.
Orange, Fort, situation of, 100; buildings erected there, 156.
Orange, date of the erection of Fort, 390.
Orange Tree, the Dutch ship, detained at Plymouth, 103.

P.

Paauw, Michel, lands purchased for, 125; name of his colonie, 126; sells his claims to the West India Company, 199.
Pacham urges the Indians to rise on the Dutch, 282.
Pachamis, location of the, 47.
Page, Abraham, 208.
Pagganck, 174.
Papsskenea purchased, 124.
Patent for Katskill, 382.
Patentees of Vlissingen, names of, 357.
Patents, comparison between the Dutch, English, and French, 91.
Patrick, Capt. Daniel, submits to the Dutch, 252; killed, 298.
Patroons, charter to the, 112; the, receive the congratulations of the Directors of the W. I. Co., 128; patents of, registered, ib.; provisions of the charter to, questioned, 129; difficulties with the, 137, 147; further differences between them and the company, 158; referred to the States General, 159; their demands, 160; how disposed of, 163; effects of their charter on the settlement of New Netherland, 178; they propose a new project, 197; legal privileges of, 320.
Paugussett River, 376.
Pavonia, colonie of, 126; sold to the West India Co., 199.
Peace, Indian mode of concluding, 60.
Pennoyer, Robt., 273.
Pennawitz, lands belonging to, purchased, 215; his speech to the Dutch, 275.
Penobscot Bay visited by Hudson, 34.
Pequods, trouble with the, 157.
Peters, Rev. Hugh, agent to England, 234; biographical sketch of him, ib.; his instructions, 235.
Petuquapaen, 218.
Plancius, Rev. Peter, sketch of his life, 94.
Planck, Jacob Albertzen, sheriff of Rensselaerswyck, 322.
Plants of New Netherland, 46.
Plato fleet, capture of the, 111.
Ployden, Sir Edmund, claims part of N. N., 281.
Plymouth Company remonstrate against the Dutch, 95.
Poulawz, Michel, 142.
PREFACE, 5.
Prices in New Netherland in 1637, 174; in 1640, 227; in 1643, 289; in Rensselaerswyck from 1630 to 1646, 477.
Prince Hendrick's River, 100.
Prince Maurice's River, 76.
Printz John, Governor of New Sweden, 367; his instructions, 368; establishes his residence at New Gottenburg, 369; orders a Dutch ship to leave the Delaware, 372; protest against Hudde, 373; haughty demeanor towards the Dutch, 374.
Privy Council, the, instruct Sir Dudley Carleton to remonstrate against the Dutch, 96.
Proclamation opening the Indian trade, 201; effects of the, 222; against the Twelve Men, 249.
Protest, form of, against free traders in Rensselaerswyck, 466.
Provost, David, resists an English guard, 378.
Public execution at New Amsterdam, scene at a, 230.
Public officers under Kieft, 181.
Puritans, original rise of, 82; intimate their wish to move to New Netherland, 83; their application laid before the States General and Prince of Orange, 84; refused, 85; land at Cape Cod, 86.
Puritans, charge against the Dutch for betraying the, examined, 86.
Pyncheon, Mr., erects a trading post on the Connecticut, 170.

Q.

Quarrel between two English skippers at the Manhattans, 146; between Adriaen van der Donck and Arendt van Curler, statement of the, by the latter, 469.
Quotenis, 174.

R.

Raritan Indians, the, visit the Half Moon, 35; their location, 48; trouble with the, 157; the Dutch attack the, 226; Staten Island attacked by the, 239.
Regulations for the soldiers on guard, 294.
Rekenkamer, report of the, 349;
Religion, Indian ideas on the subject of, 62.
Remarks on the Catalogue of Books sent to Rensselaerswyck, 455.
Rensselaers Stein, 342.

Rensselaerswyck, Colonie of, 126 ; company formed for the settlement of, 126 ; nature of the association, 127 ; first magistrates of, 322 ; first minister in, 328 ; first church in, 330 ; expenses incurred for its support in 1630, 429 ; name of settlers in 1630–1646, 433.
Report on the condition of New Netherland, 1644, 349, 418.
Reptiles of New Netherland, 46.
Restless, The, built, 72.
Rio Montanies, or North River, latitude of the, 44.
Riviere van den Vorst Mauritius, 76.
Robinson, Rev. John, head of the English Congregation at Leyden, 82 ; intimates a desire to move to N. Netherland, 83.
Rockaway Indians, location of the, 49.
Roelantzen, Adam, schoolmaster, 143.
Ross, supercargo, killed, 227.
Roy, Jacob Jacobz., wounded in firing a salute, 354.
Rutgers, Ryckert, 437.
Ryp, Jan Cornelissen, accompanies Heemskirk, 28.

S.

Salaries of public officers, 1638, 181.
Sandy Hook, latitude of, 35.
Sannahagog purchased, 122.
Say, Lord, his letter against the Dutch, 255.
Saybrook, Dutch name for, 149.
School-house, funds subscribed for the erection of a, misapplied, 396.
Schout Fiscaal, his duties, 102.
Schuylkill, the, discovered, 77 ; lands on the, purchased, 156.
Seawan, what, 60.
Seawanhacky, 73.
Secataugs, territory of the, 50.
Settlements in N. Netherland, extent of, 389.
Settlers in Rensselaerswyck from 1630 to 1646, names of the, 433.
Sheep, number of, in Rensselaerswyck, 463.
Shenecock Indians, where located, 50.
Slavery unknown among the Indians, 55.
Slaves, their condition under the Dutch, 384 ; terms on which some of them received their liberty, 385.
Sloop Bay, where situate, 173.
Smith, Claes Cornelissen, murdered, 241.
Southhampton, provisions of the treaty of, extended to the ships of the Dutch, 109.
Southampton planted, 217.
Southold planted, 217.
South River, latitude of the, 44 ; opinions entertained by the Dutch of the, 369 ; Samuel Godyn's notice of his intention to plant a colonie at the bay of the, 479.
Spain, termination of the truce with, 85
St. Martin, island of, attacked, 359
Staes, (or Staats,) Dr. Abraham. embarks for N. N., 329, 439.
Staple right, what, 155.
Staten Island, Indian name for, 48 ; purchased, 104 ; erected into a colonie, 238 ; attacked by the Indians, 286 ; expedition against the Indians of, 297
States General, Sir Dudley Carleton s letter to the, 97 ; memorial of the W. I. Co. to the, 133 ; order an inquiry into the condition of New Netherland, 348.
Stevensen, Oloff, commissary, 211.
Stirling, Earl of, obtains a grant of Long Island, 210.
Strickland's Plain, battle of, 301.
STUYVESANT, PETRUS, Director of Curaçoa, wounded, 359 ; returns to Holland and is appointed Director-general of N. N., 360 ; his departure postponed, 361.
Superstitions among the Indians, 63.
Swedes settle on the Delaware, 189 ; propose removing to the Manhattans, 365 ; abandon that design, 366 ; monopolize the trade of the South River, 369 ; tear down the Dutch arms, 373.
Swedish vessel seized in Holland, 370 ; released, 371.

T.

Tankitekes, location of the, 47.
Tavern, a, erected in New Amsterdam, 259.
Tawalsontha, 78, 100.
Tawassgunshee, Dutch erect a fort on, 78.
Techaacho, 100.
Tenths of Rensselaerswyck, 472.
Thanksgiving, a day of general, proclaimed, 357.
Throgmorton, Mr., settles at Westchester, 258.
Tienpont, Adriaen Jorisz. proceeds to New Netherland, 99.
Tinnicum, where situate, 369.

Tobacco, an ordinance regulating inspection of, 186; inspectors of appointed, 187.
Towns and villages in N. Netherland, privileges of, 392.
Trees of New Netherland, 45.
Trade of New Netherland in 1631, 139; in 1632, 139; with the Indians opened, 200; changes proposed in the, 360; reconsidered, 361.
Truce between Spain and Holland, 67.
Twelve Men, election of the, 242; their advice, 243, 244; board of the, abolished, 249.

U.

Underhill, Capt. John, engaged to lead the Dutch forces, 289; attacks Indians at Heemstede, 299; ordered to Stanford, 300; conquers the Indians on Strickland's plain, 301.
United English colonies, confederation of the, 279.
United Provinces, the Seven, take up arms, 27,
Usselincx, Wm., proposes erection of a Dutch West India Company, 30; submits a plan for the establishment of a Swedish West India Co., 188.

V.

Van Beyeren, Annetje, 298.
Van Cortlandt family, some particulars of the, 212.
Van Couwenhoven, Jacob, 142.
Van Curler, Arendt, biographical sketch of, 322; colonists conspire against him, 333; visits the Mohawks, 334; endeavors to obtain the release of some Christians, 335; his letter to the Patroon of Rensselaerswyck, giving an account of the affairs of the colonie in 1643, 456.
Van Curler, Jacob, 142; purchases land on the Connecticut, 150; serves a protest on Holmes, 154; commences a plantation in Flattlands, 172.
Van der Bogaert, Harman Meynderts, 441.
Van der Donck, Adriaen, appointed sheriff of Rensselaerswyck, 327; differences between him and the other functionaries of that colonie, 333; attempts to found a colonie at Katskill, 338; quarrels with Van Curler, 345; removes to the Manhattans, 346; obtains a patent for Colen-donck, 382; his account referred to Holland, 470.
Van der Huyghens, Cornelis, appointed schout-fiscaal of New Netherland, 211; censured by Kieft, 295; protests against Wyncoop, 342; against the erection of the fort on Beeren Island, 344.
Van Dinclage, Lubbertus, schout-fiscaal, 148; opposes Van Twiller, and dismissed from office, 173; appointed provisionally Director of New Netherland, 348; that appointment cancelled, 360.
Van Dyck, Hendrick, sent against the Wechquaesqueecks, 249; wounded, 287.
Van Elslandt, Claes, 142; appointed tobacco inspector, 187.
Van Es, Cornelis Hendricksen, 440.
Van Hardenberg, Arnoldus, appeals from a decision of the Director-general, 394; sentence pronounced, in consequence, against him, 395.
Van Remund, Jan, secretary to New Netherland, 103, 124.
Van Rensselaer, Kiliaen, Patroon, 122, 124; forms a copartnership for the settlement of his colonie, 126; and of the South River, 128; his privileges as Patroon, 320; his instructions to Van der Donck, 327; for the establishment of a village, 330; forbids Van der Donck purchasing lands at Katskill, 338; fortifies Beeren island, 341; claims staple right, 343; his death, 345; expenses incurred by him in 1630, for the settling of Rensselaerswyck, 429; ordinance issued by him describing his rights, 442.
Van Rensselaer, Rev. Nicolaus, prophesies the restoration of King Charles II., 122.
Van Schaick, Goosie Gerritts, 437.
Van Tienhoven, Cornelis, 142; sent to purchase the Norwalk islands, 215; proceeds to Scout's bay, 216; sent against the Raritans, 226; his description of Wechquaesqueeck, 240; advises the extermination of the savages, 265; sent to reconnoitre the position of the Indians at Pavonia, 266, 267; unfeminine conduct of his mother-in-law, 269.
Van Twiller, Wouter, appointed Director-general of New Netherland, 141; his council, 142; difficulties with the captain and factor of the English ship, the William, 143; with De Vries, 147;

purchases a tract of land on the Connecticut, 150; receives letters from Boston, 151; his reply, 152; protests against Holmes, 154; writes to Holland for troops, 155; builds sundry forts, ib.; purchases land on the Schuylkill, 156; quarrels with Bogardus, 167; concludes a peace with the Raritans, ib.; appropriates large portions of the public domain, 172; opposed by Van Dinclage, 173; recalled, 174.
Van Slyck, Cornelis A., obtains a patent for Katskill, 381.
Van Vorst, Gerrit, murdered, 263.
Van Weely, Anna, account of her death, 123.
Verplanck family, some particulars of the, 185; Abraham V. obtains land on South River, 373.
Verrazzano, Jean de, enters the bay of New York, 26.
Villages, Indian, 54.
Virginia, a representative government, when accorded to, 93.
Vlissingen, town of, incorporated, 358

W.

Wahlebocht, the, 101.
Walloons apply for leave to settle in Virginia, 100; remove to New Netherland, 101.
Walvisch island, 347.
Wappings, the, 49; murder Willem C. Coster, 283.
Wampum, what, 60; proclamation regulating the value of, 230.
War, Indian mode of waging, 58; between the Dutch and Indians, 270, 286.
Waranancongyns, location of the, 47.
Waraonckins, where situated, 47.
Water fowls of New Netherland, 46.
Wechquaesqueecks, location of the, 47, 240; murder of one of their tribe, 105; expedition against them, 249; peace with the, 250; attacked by the Mohawks, 264; fly to the Dutch, 265; massacred by orders of Kieft, 267, 268; party of troops sent against them, 298.
Weelysburg, Van der Donck takes a lease of, 327.
Westchester, Dutch name for, 258.
West India Company, A, proposed in Holland, 30; proposal approved, 31; incorporated, 89; provisions of the charter to the, 90; memorial to the States General of the, 133; reply of the English to the, 134; available force of the, in 1633, 157; their memorial relative to the William, 164; a new, established in Sweden, 188; address to the States General by the, 304; complaints against Kieft sent to the, 312; evil effects of its policy on the prosperity of New Netherland, 387; charter to the, 399; agreement between the partners of the, 408; names of the Directors of the, in 1636, 411.
West Indies, Dutch vessels sent to the, 29.
William, the ship, visits the River Mauritius, 143; sails to Fort Orange, 145; forced to leave the Hudson River, 146; owners of the, their complaints, 164; reply of West India Co. thereto, 165.
Whales ascend the North River, 346.
Wind mills, 388.
Winslow, Gov., imprisoned by Laud, 170.
Winthrop, Gov., Van Twiller's letter to, 152; answers to Kieft, 280.
Winthrop, John, erects a fort at Kievitts Hoeck, 169.
Women, Indian, 54.
Wyncoop, Pieter, supercargo, 342.

Y.

Yonkers, situation of, 383.

Z.

Zwanendal, The colonie of, 126; company formed for the settlement of, 128; settlers arrive at, 129; destroyed, 137; purchased by the West India Company, 365; old papers relating to, 479.

www.ingramcontent.com/pod-product-compliance
Lightning Source LLC
LaVergne TN
LVHW020915110826
845150LV00004B/681

* 9 7 8 1 4 2 5 5 5 5 7 1 9 *